D0131682

The Gendered Society Reader

Canadian edition

Edited by

Michael S. Kimmel | Amy Aronson | Amy Kaler

OXFORD

UNIVERSITY PRESS

OXFORD
UNIVERSITY PRESS

8 Sampson Mews, Suite 204, Don Mills, Ontario M3C 0H5
www.oupcanada.com

Oxford University Press is a department of the University of Oxford.
It furthers the University's objective of excellence in research, scholarship,
and education by publishing worldwide in

Oxford New York

Auckland Cape Town Dar es Salaam Hong Kong Karachi
Kuala Lumpur Madrid Melbourne Mexico City Nairobi
New Delhi Shanghai Taipei Toronto

With offices in

Argentina Austria Brazil Chile Czech Republic France Greece
Guatemala Hungary Italy Japan Poland Portugal Singapore
South Korea Switzerland Thailand Turkey Ukraine Vietnam

Oxford is a trade mark of Oxford University Press
in the UK and in certain other countries

Published in Canada
by Oxford University Press

Copyright © Oxford University Press Canada 2008

The moral rights of the author have been asserted.

Database right Oxford University Press (maker)

First published 2008

Copyright © 2004 Oxford University Press, Inc.

Oxford University Press Inc., 198 Madison Avenue, New York, N.Y. 10016-4314, USA

All rights reserved. No part of this publication may be reproduced,
stored in a retrieval system, or transmitted, in any form or by any means,
without the prior permission in writing of Oxford University Press,
or as expressly permitted by law, or under terms agreed with the appropriate
reprographics rights organization. Enquiries concerning reproduction
outside the scope of the above should be sent to the Rights Department,
Oxford University Press, at the address above.

Every effort has been made to determine and contact copyright owners. In the case of any omissions,
the publisher will be pleased to make suitable acknowledgement in future editions.

You must not circulate this book in any other binding or cover
and you must impose this same condition on any acquirer.

Library and Archives Canada Cataloguing in Publication

The gendered society reader / edited by Michael S. Kimmel, Amy Aronson, and Amy Kaler. — Canadian ed.

Complements the text: The gendered society.
Includes bibliographical references.
ISBN 978-0-19-542166-8

1. Sex role—Textbooks.   2. Sex differences (Psychology)—Textbooks.
3. Gender identity—Textbooks.   4. Sex discrimination—Textbooks.   5. Equality—Textbooks.
I. Kimmel, Michael S.   II. Aronson, Amy   III. Kaler, Amy, 1966–   IV. Kimmel, Michael S. Gendered Society

HQ1075.G4672 2007   305.3   C2007-900981-6

6 7 8 – 12 11 10

Cover Design: Brett J. Miller

Cover image: Photodisc / First Light

Printed in Canada.

Mixed Sources
Product group from well-managed
forests, and other controlled sources
www.fsc.org Cert no. SW-COC-002358
© 1996 Forest Stewardship Council
FSC

Contents

Preface to the Canadian Edition   x

Introduction   xii

PART I   **Anatomy and Destiny: Biological Arguments About Gender Difference**   **1**

Chapter 1   Psychological Sex Differences Through Sexual Selection   2
            David M. Buss

Chapter 2   Believing is Seeing: Biology as Ideology   7
            Judith Lorber

Chapter 3   Testosterone Rules   17
            Robert M. Sapolsky

            Questions for Critical Thought   22

PART II   **Cultural Constructions of Gender**   **23**

Chapter 4   Rape-Prone versus Rape-Free Campus Cultures   24
            Peggy Sanday

Chapter 5   Listening to the Voices of *Hijab*   34
            Tabassum F. Ruby

Chapter 6   Coming of Age and Coming-Out Ceremonies Across Cultures   45
            Gilbert Herdt

Chapter 7   'The Pecker Detectors are Back': Regulation of the Family Form in Ontario
            Welfare Policy   60
            Margaret Hillyard Little and Ian Morrison

Chapter 8   Sk8er Girls: Skateboarders, Girlhood, and Feminism in Motion   71
                Shauna Pomerantz, Dawn H. Currie, and Deirdre M. Kelly

                Questions for Critical Thought   79

PART III   The Social Construction of Gender Relations   80

Chapter 9   Boundaries, Negotiation, and Consciousness: Reconceptualizing Gender
                Relations   81
                Judith M. Gerson and Kathy Peiss

Chapter 10   Doing Gender   91
                Candace West and Don H. Zimmerman

Chapter 11   Coming Out and Crossing Over: Identity Formation and Proclamation in
                a Transgender Community   106
                Patricia Gagné, Richard Tewksbury, and Deanna McGaughey

Chapter 12   'It's Part of the Game': Physicality and the Production of Gender in Women's
                Hockey   121
                Nancy Theberge

                Questions for Critical Thought   130

PART IV   The Gendered Family   131

Chapter 13   The Transformation of Family Life   132
                Lillian Rubin

Chapter 14   Shift Work, Childcare, and Domestic Work: Divisions of Labour in Canadian
                Paper Mill Communities   143
                Valerie Preston, Damaris Rose, Glen Norcliffe, and John Holmes

Chapter 15   No Longer 'One of the Boys': Negotiations with Motherhood, as Prospect or
                Reality, among Women in Engineering   157
                Gillian Ranson

Chapter 16   Can Women's Social Networks Migrate?   167
                Janet W. Salaf and Arent Greve

Chapter 17   Household Labour and the Routine Production of Gender   178
              Scott Coltrane

              Questions for Critical Thought   196

PART V   The Gendered Classroom   **197**

Chapter 18   Gender Equity in the Classroom: The Unfinished Agenda   198
              Myra Sadker, David Sadker, Lynn Fox, and Melinda Salata

Chapter 19   Warrior Narratives in the Kindergarten Classroom: Renegotiating the Social
              Contract?   203
              Ellen Jordan and Angela Cowan

Chapter 20   What Do You Call an Indian Woman with a Law Degree: Nine Aboriginal
              Women at the University of Saskatchewan College of Law Speak Out   217
              Tracey Lindberg

Chapter 21   Micro Inequities and Everyday Inequalities: 'Race', Gender, Sexuality, and
              Class in Medical School   227
              Brenda Beagan

Chapter 22   Women's Perspective as a Radical Critique of Sociology   240
              Dorothy E. Smith

              Questions for Critical Thought   247

PART VI   The Gendered Workplace   **248**

Chapter 23   Bringing the Men Back In: Sex Differentiation and the Devaluation of
              Women's Work   249
              Barbara F. Reskin

Chapter 24   Hierarchies, Jobs, Bodies: A Theory of Gendered Organizations   260
              Joan Acker

Chapter 25   Cautious Caregivers: Gender Stereotypes and the Sexualization of Men
              Nurses' Touch   272
              Joan A. Evans

Chapter 26   Privilege and Oppression: The Configuration of Race, Gender, and Class in
              Southern Ontario Auto Plants, 1939 to 1949   280
              Pamela Sugiman

Chapter 27   Domestic Distinctions: Constructing Difference among Paid Domestic
              Workers in Toronto   289
              Bernadette Stiell and Kim England

              Questions for Critical Thought   301

PART VII   The Gendered Body   302

Chapter 28   The Body and the Reproduction of Femininity   303
              Susan Bordo

Chapter 29   Mass Media and Gender Identity in High Performance Canadian Figure Skating   318
              Karen McGarry

Chapter 30   Contours of Everyday Life: Women's Reflections on Embodiment and Health
              Over Time   321
              Pamela Wakewich

Chapter 31   The Five Sexes: Why Male and Female Are Not Enough   329
              Anne Fausto-Sterling

              Questions for Critical Thought   335

PART VIII   Gendered Intimacies   336

Chapter 32   The Feminization of Love   337
              Francesca M. Cancian

Chapter 33   Dating and Romantic Relationships among Gay, Lesbian, and Bisexual Youths   347
              Ritch C. Savin-Williams

Chapter 34   Losing It: Similarities and Differences in First Intercourse Experiences of Men
              and Women   358
              Lily Tsui and Elena Nicoladis

Chapter 35   'It just happens': Negotiating Casual Heterosexual Sex   370
              Melanie Beres

Chapter 36   The Bedroom and The State: Women's Struggle to Limit Their Fertility   382
Angus McLaren and Arlene Tigar McLaren

Questions for Critical Thought   391

PART IX   The Gender of Violence   392

Chapter 37   Moral Panic and the Nasty Girl   393
Christie Barron and Dany Lacombe

Chapter 38   War, Wimps, and Women: Talking Gender and Thinking War   402
Carol Cohn

Chapter 39   Genderbashing: Sexuality, Gender, and the Regulation of the Public Space   412
Viviane K. Namaste

Chapter 40   The Myth of Sexual Symmetry in Marital Violence   422
Russell P. Dobash, R. Emerson Dobash, Margo Wilson, and Martin Daly

Chapter 41   The White Ribbon Campaign: Involving Men and Boys in Ending Global
Violence Against Women   436
Michael Kaufman

Questions for Critical Thought   445

Acknowledgements   446

Preface to the Canadian Edition

Editing the Canadian version of *The Gendered Society Reader* has been a pleasure and a challenge. The pleasure lay in the chance to read widely and to familiarize myself with the liveliness and curiosity that characterizes the best gender research in Canada today. The challenge lay in the difficulty of making choices among the wide array of materials—for every text chosen for inclusion, many others could not be chosen, and in addition, one of the articles from the American edition needed to be deleted. The challenge also lay in moving into a textual space already delineated by Michael Kimmel, one of the most prominent international figures in gender studies. My changes to this book will inevitably alter this space in directions of my own choosing, and I hope that I've been able to do justice to Dr Kimmel's original vision for *The Gendered Society Reader*. In particular, I hope I've been able to retain his sense of gender as something that saturates the social world, differentiating the experiences of men and women and manifesting itself in actions, relationships, ideas, and dreams. At the same time, as Dr Kimmel himself has said, gender is not destiny—we can transform gender in our everyday lives and in our institutions, and produce a better, more humane world for everyone, male and female alike.

In editing the Canadian version, I chose texts based on several criteria. The most obvious criterion was that they had to be Canadian—dealing with the lives and experiences of Canadians, and ideally also written by a Canadian author. I focused on the nationality of the texts not because I wanted to fill some arbitrary quota for 'Canadian content' but because I wanted to enable students to take a critical, analytical look at the country in which their own gendered subjectivities are being formed. I wanted to avoid the problem my own students often complain about—the tendency to universalize American experiences; to treat the United States as the norm for the entire world. This desire on my part is consistent with the broader feminist imperative to question all universalizing tendencies, and to attempt to decentre the centres of power, including academic power, in our writing, thinking, and teaching. There is no question that Canada and the United States are similar in many ways when it comes to the workings of gender, but it's important not to take this similarity for granted, and to look for gender at work in the social world around us, rather than just gazing across the border to the south.

Along the same lines, I have prioritized qualitative accounts of lived experience over heavily quantitative texts. I don't think that qualitative research is somehow 'better' or 'truer' than quantitative studies, but I do think that qualitative work offers undergraduates a way to at least partially get inside the life-worlds of gendered subjects, including those who are gendered differently than the students themselves. Qualitative work also enables readers to get a sense of the complex intersections of gender and other social categories, such as race, socioeconomic class, sexuality, and bodily status, all which shape the experience of being gendered in subtle but very powerful ways.

I was graced with an excellent team at Oxford University Press Canada—many thanks to Lisa Meschino, Roberta Osborne, and Jessica Coffey for all their work on behalf of this book. I'd also like to acknowledge the students in my Sociology of Gender classes at the University of Alberta, from whom I am slowly learning what teaching gender can be at its best. I hope this book intrigues, entertains, and possibly enlightens all the future students and professors who will make use of it.

Introduction

Michael S. Kimmel

Every day there's another story about how women and men are different. They say we come from different planets—women from Venus, men from Mars. They say we have different brain chemistries, different brain organization, and different hormones. Different bodies and different selves. They say we have different ways of knowing, that we listen to different moral voices, and that we have different ways of speaking and hearing each other.

You would think we were different species. In his best-selling book, the pop psychologist John Gray informs us that not only do women and men communicate differently, 'but they think, feel, perceive, react, respond, love, need, and appreciate differently' (Gray, 1995: 5). It's a miracle of cosmic proportions that we ever understand one another!

Yet here we all are, together, in the same classes, eating in the same dining halls, walking on the same campus, reading the same books, being subject to the same criteria for grading. We live in the same houses, eat the same meals, read the same newspapers, and watch the same TV shows. What gives?

One thing that seems to be happening is that we are increasingly aware of the centrality of gender in our lives. In the past three decades, the pioneering work of feminist scholars, both in traditional disciplines and in women's studies, has made us increasingly aware of the centrality of gender in shaping social life. We now know that gender is one of the central organizing principles around which social life revolves.

This wasn't always the case. Three decades ago, social scientists would have only listed social class and race as the master statuses that defined and proscribed social life. If you wanted to study gender in the 1960s in social science, for example, you would have found one course to meet your needs—'Marriage and the Family'—which was sort of the 'Ladies Auxiliary' of the Social Sciences. There were no courses on gender. But today, gender has joined race and class in our understanding of the foundations of an individual's identity. Gender, we now know, is one of the axes around which social life is organized, and through which we understand our own experiences.

While much of our cultural preoccupation seems to be about the differences between women and men, there are two near-universal phenomena that define the experiences of women and men in virtually every culture we have ever known. First: *Why is it that virtually every single society differentiates people on the basis of gender?* Why are women and men perceived as different in every known society? What are the differences that are perceived? Why is gender at least one—if not the central—basis for the division of labour? And, second: *Why is it that virtually every known society is also based on male domination?* Why does virtually every society divide social, political, and economic resources unequally between the genders? Why is a gendered division of labour also an unequal division of labour? Why are women's tasks and men's tasks valued differently?

Of course, there are dramatic differences among societies regarding the type of gender differences, the levels of gender inequality, and the amount of violence (implied or real) that is necessary to maintain both systems of difference and domination. But the basic facts remain: *virtually every society known to us is founded upon assumptions of gender difference and the politics of gender inequality.*

Most of the arguments about gender difference begin, as will this book, with biology. Women and men *are* biologically different, after all. Our reproductive anatomies are different, as are our reproductive destinies. Our brain structures differ, our brain chemistries differ. Our musculature is different. We have different levels of different hormones circulating through our different bodies. Surely, these add up to fundamental, intractable, and universal differences, and these differences provide the foundation for male domination, don't they?

In these models, biological 'sex'—by which we mean the chromosomal, chemical, anatomical apparatuses that make us either male or female—leads inevitably to 'gender', by which we mean the cultural and social meanings, experiences, and institutional structures that are defined as appropriate for those males and females. 'Sex' is male and female; 'gender' refers to cultural definitions of masculinity and femininity—the meanings of maleness or femaleness.

Biological models of sex difference occupy the 'nature' side of the age-old question about whether it is nature or nurture that determines our personalities. Of course, most sensible people recognize that both nature *and* nurture are necessary for gender development. Our biological sex provides the raw material for our development—and all that evolution, different chromosomes, and hormones have to have some effect on who we are and who we become.

But biological sex varies very little, and yet the cultural definitions of gender vary enormously. And it has been the task of the social and behavioural sciences to explore the variations in definitions of gender. Launched originally as

critiques of biological universalism, the social and behavioural sciences—anthropology, history, psychology, sociology—have all had an important role to play in our understanding of gender.

What they suggest is that what it means to be a man or a woman will vary in four significant ways. First, the meanings of gender vary from one society to another. What it means to be a man or a woman among aboriginal peoples in the Australian outback or in the Yukon territories is probably very different from what it means to be a man or a woman in Norway or Ireland. It has been the task of anthropologists to specify some of those differences, to explore the different meanings that gender has in different cultures. Some cultures, like our own, encourage men to be stoic and to prove their masculinity, and men in other cultures seem even more preoccupied with demonstrating sexual prowess than North American men seem to be. Other cultures prescribe a more relaxed definition of masculinity, based on civic participation, emotional responsiveness, and the collective provision for the community's needs. Some cultures encourage women to be decisive and competitive; others insist that women are naturally passive, helpless, and dependent.

Second, the meanings of masculinity and femininity vary within any one culture over time. What it meant to be a man or a woman in seventeenth-century France is probably very different from what it might mean today. My own research has suggested that the meanings of manhood have changed dramatically from the founding of America in 1776 to the present (see Kimmel, 1996). (Although for reasons of space I do not include any historical material in this volume, inquiries into the changing definitions of gender have become an area of increasing visibility.)

Third, the meaning of masculinity and femininity will change as any individual person grows. Following Freudian ideas that individuals face different developmental tasks as they grow and develop, psychologists have examined the ways in which the meanings of masculinity and femininity change over the course of a person's life. The issues confronting a man about proving himself, feeling successful, and the social institutions in which he will attempt to enact those experiences will change, as will the meanings of femininity for prepubescent women, women in child-bearing years, and post-menopausal women, or for women entering the labour market or those retiring from it.

Finally, the meanings of gender will vary *among* different groups of women and men within any particular culture at any particular time. Simply put, not all American men and women are the same. Our experiences are also structured by class, race, ethnicity, age, sexuality, and region of the country. Each of these axes modifies the others. Just because we make gender visible doesn't mean that we make these other organizing principles of social life invisible. Imagine, for example, an older, black, gay man in Chicago and a young, white, heterosexual farm boy in Iowa. Wouldn't they have different definitions of masculinity? Or imagine a 22-year-old heterosexual, poor, Asian American woman in San Francisco and a wealthy, white, Irish Catholic, lesbian in Boston. Wouldn't their ideas about what it means to be a woman be somewhat different? The interplanetary theory of gender differences collapses all such differences, and focuses *only* on gender. One of the important elements of a sociological approach is to explore the differences *among* men and *among* women, since, as it turns out, these are often more decisive than the differences between women and men.

If gender varies across cultures, over historical time, among men and women within any one culture, and over the life course, that means we really cannot speak of masculinity or femininity as though they were constant, universal essences, common to all women and to all men. Rather, gender is an ever-changing fluid assemblage of meanings and behaviours. In that sense, we must speak of *masculinities* and *femininities*, in recognition of the different definitions of masculinity and femininity that we construct. By pluralizing the terms, we acknowledge that masculinity and femininity mean different things to different groups of people at different times.

At the same time, we can't forget that all masculinities and femininities are not created equal. American men and women must also contend with a dominant definition, a culturally preferred version that is held up as the model against which we are expected to measure ourselves. We thus come to know what it means to be a man or a woman in our culture by setting our definitions in opposition to a set of 'others'—racial minorities, sexual minorities. For men, the classic 'other' is of course, women. If often feels imperative that men make it clear—eternally, compulsively, decidedly—that they are not 'like' women.

For both women and men, this is the 'hegemonic' definition—the one that is held up as the model for all of us. The hegemonic definition of masculinity is 'constructed in relation to various subordinated masculinities as well as in relation to women', writes sociologist R.W. Connell (1987: 183). The sociologist Erving Goffman once described this hegemonic definition of masculinity like this:

> In an important sense there is only one complete unblushing male in America: a young, married, white, urban, northern, heterosexual, Protestant, father, of college education, fully employed, of good complexion, weight, and height, and a recent record in sports. . . . Any male who fails to qualify in any one of these ways is likely to view himself—during moments at least—as unworthy, incomplete, and inferior (Goffman, 1963: 128).

Women also must contend with such an exaggerated ideal of femininity. Connell calls it 'emphasized femininity'. Emphasized femininity is organized around compliance with gender inequality, and is 'oriented to accommodating the interests and desires of men'. One sees emphasized femininity in 'the display of sociability rather than technical competence, fragility in mating scenes, compliance with men's desire for titillation and ego-stroking in office relationships, acceptance of marriage and child care as a response to labor-market discrimination against women' (Connell, 1987: 183, 188, 187). Emphasized femininity exaggerates gender difference as a strategy of 'adaptation to men's power' stressing empathy and nurturance; 'real' womanhood is described as 'fascinating' and women are advised that they can wrap men around their fingers by knowing and playing by 'the rules'.

The articles in the first three sections of this book recapitulate these disciplinary concerns and also present the development of the sociological argument chronologically. Following Darwin and others, biological evidence was employed in the nineteenth century to assert the primacy of sex differences, and the section on biological differences presents some evidence of distinct and categorical biological differences, and a couple of critiques of that research from a neurobiologist and a psychologist respectively. Cross-cultural research by anthropologists offered a way to critique the claims of biological inevitability and universality lodged in those biological arguments. The selections in this section demonstrate how anthropologists have observed those cross-cultural differences and have used such specific cultural rituals as initiation ceremonies or the prevalence of rape in a culture to assess different definitions of gender.

It falls to the sociologist to explore the variations among different groups of women and men, and also to specify the ways in which some versions of masculinity or femininity are held up as the hegemonic models against which all others are arrayed and measured. Sociologists are concerned less with the specification of sex roles, and more with the understanding of *gender relations*—the social and political dynamics that shape our conceptions of 'appropriate' sex roles. Thus, sociologists are interested not only in gendered individuals—the ways in which we acquire our gendered identities—but also in gendered institutions—the ways in which those gendered individuals interact with one another in the institutions of our lives that shape, reproduce, and reconstitute gender.

In that sense, sociologists return us to the original framing questions—the near-universality of assumptions about gender difference and the near-universality of male domination over women. Sociologists argue that male domination is reproduced not only by socializing women and men differently, but also by placing them in organizations and institutions in which specifically gendered norms and values predominate and by which both women and men are then evaluated and judged. Gendered individuals do not inhabit gender-neutral social situations; both individual and institution bear the mark of gender.

The three central, institutional sections of this book explore how the fundamental institutions of family, education, and the workplace express and normalize gender difference, and, in so doing, reproduce relations of inequality between women and men. In each of these arenas, the debates about gender difference and inequality have been intense—from the questions about the division of household labour, divorce, day care, coeducation or single-sex schooling, comparable worth, sexual harassment, workplace discrimination, and a variety of other critical policy debates. The articles in these sections will enable the reader to make better sense of these debates and understand the ways in which gender is performed and elaborated within social institutions.

Finally, we turn to our intimate lives, our bodies, and our experiences of friendship, love, and sex. Here differences between women and men do emerge. Men and women have different ways of loving, of caring, and of having sex. And it turns out that this is true whether the women and men are heterosexual or homosexual—that is, gay men and heterosexual men are more similar to each other than they are different; and, equally, lesbians and heterosexual women have more in common than either does with men. On the other hand, the differences between women and men seem to have as much to do with the shifting definitions of love and intimacy, and the social arenas in which we express (or suppress) our emotions, as they do with the differences in our personalities. And there is significant evidence that the gender gap in love and sex and friendship is shrinking as women claim greater degrees of sexual agency and men find their emotional lives (with lovers, children, and friends) impoverished by adherence to hegemonic definitions of masculinity. Men and women do express some differences in our intimate lives, but these differences are hardly of interplanetary cosmic significance. It appears that women and men are not from different planets— not opposite sexes, but neighbouring sexes. And we are moving closer and closer to each other.

This may be the most startling finding that runs through many of these articles. What we find consistently is that the differences between women and men do not account for very much of the different experiences that men and women have. Differences *between* women and men are not nearly as great as the differences *among* women or *among* men—differences based on class, race, ethnicity, sexuality, age, and other variables. Women and men enter the workplace for similar reasons, though what they find there often reproduces the differences that 'predicted' they would have different motivations. Boys and girls are far more similar to each other in the classroom, from elementary school through college, although everything in the school—from their textbooks, their teachers, their experiences in the playground, the social expectations of their aptitudes and abilities—pushes them to move farther and farther apart.

The most startling conclusion that one reaches from examining the evidence on gender difference is that women and men are not from different planets at all. In the end, we're all Earthlings!

References

Connell, R.W. 1987. *Gender and Power*. Stanford, CA: Stanford University Press.

Goffman, E. 1963. *Stigma*. Englewood Cliffs, NJ: Prentice-Hall.

Gray, J. 1995. *Men Are from Mars, Women Are from Venus*. New York: Harper Collins.

Kimmel, M. 1996. *Manhood in America: A Cultural History*. New York: The Free Press.

PART I

Anatomy and Destiny: Biological Arguments About Gender Difference

A natomy, many of us believe, is destiny; our constitution of our bodies determines our social and psychological disposition. Biological sex decides our gendered experiences. Sex is temperament. Biological explanations offer perhaps the tidiest and most coherent explanations for both gender difference and gender inequality. The observable differences between males and females derive from different anatomical organization, which makes us different as men and women, and those anatomical differences are the origin of gender inequality. These differences, as one biologist put it, are 'innate, biologically determined, and relatively resistant to change through the influences of culture'.

Biologists rely on three different sets of evidence. Evolutionists, such as sociobiologists and evolutionary psychologists, argue that sex differences derive from the differences in our reproductive anatomies—which compel different reproductive 'strategies'. Because females must invest much energy and time in ensuring the survival of one baby, their 'natural' evolutionary instinct is toward high sexual selectivity and monogamy; females are naturally modest and monogamous. Males, by contrast, are naturally promiscuous, since their reproductive success depends upon fertilizing as many eggs as possible without emotional constraint. Males that are reproductively unsuccessful by seduction, biologists tell us, may resort to rape as a way to ensure their reproductive material is successfully transmitted to their offspring.

A second source of evidence of biological difference comes from some differences in brain function and brain chemistry. In the late nineteenth century, studies showed definitively that men's brains were heavier, or more complex, than women's, and thus that women ought not to seek higher education or vote. (Similar studies also 'proved' that the brains of white people were heavier and more complex than those of black people.) Today, such studies are largely discredited, but we still may read about how males and females use different halves of their brains, or that they use them differently, or that the two halves are differently connected.

Finally, some biologists rely on the ways in which the hormonal differences that produce secondary sex characteristics determine the dramatically divergent paths that males and females take from puberty onwards. Testosterone causes aggression, and since males have far more testosterone than females, male aggression—and social, political, and economic dominance—is explained.

To the social scientist, though, this evidence obscures as much as it reveals, telling us more about our own cultural needs to find these differences than the differences themselves. Biological explanations collapse all other sources of difference—race, ethnicity, and age—into one single dichotomous variable that exaggerates the differences between women and men, and also minimizes the similarities between them. 'Believing is seeing,' notes sociologist Judith Lorber in the title of her essay, and seeing these differences as decisive is often used as a justification for gender inequality.

The readings in this section offer a cross-section of those biological arguments. David M. Buss summarizes the evidence from evolutionary psychology that different reproductive strategies determine different psychological dispositions. Neurobiologist Robert Sapolsky suggests that the research on hormonal differences do not make a convincing case, while Judith Lorber challenges the assumptions of biological research, arguing that biology's inherent conservatism—justifying existing inequalities by reference to observed differences and ignoring observed similarities—is more than bad politics: it's also bad science.

CHAPTER 1

Psychological Sex Differences Through Sexual Selection

David M. Buss

Evolutionary psychology predicts that males and females will be the same or similar in all those domains in which the sexes have faced the same or similar adaptive problems. Both sexes have sweat glands because both sexes have faced the adaptive problem of thermal regulation. Both sexes have similar (although not identical) taste preferences for fat, sugar, salt, and particular amino acids because both sexes have faced similar (although not identical) food consumption problems. Both sexes grow calluses when they experience repeated rubbing on their skin because both sexes have faced the adaptive problem of physical damage from environmental friction.

In other domains, men and women have faced substantially different adaptive problems throughout human evolutionary history. In the physical realm, for example, women have faced the problem of childbirth; men have not. Women, therefore, have evolved particular adaptations that are absent in men, such as a cervix that dilates to 10 centimetres just prior to giving birth, mechanisms for producing labour contractions, and the release of oxytocin in the bloodstream during childbirth.

Men and women have also faced different information-processing problems in some adaptive domains. Because fertilization occurs internally within the woman, for example, men have faced the adaptive problem of uncertain paternity in putative offspring. Men who failed to solve this problem risked investing resources in children who were not their own. All people descend from a long line of ancestral men whose adaptations (i.e., psychological mechanisms) led them to behave in ways that increased their likelihood of paternity and decreased the odds of investing in children who were putatively theirs but whose genetic fathers were other men. This does not imply, of course, that men were or are consciously aware of the adaptive problem of compromised paternity.

Women faced the problem of securing a reliable or replenishable supply of resources to carry them through pregnancy and lactation, especially when food resources were scarce (e.g., during droughts or harsh winters). All people are descendants of a long and unbroken line of women who successfully solved this adaptive challenge—for example, by preferring mates who showed the ability to accrue resources and the willingness to provide them for particular women. Those women who failed to solve this problem failed to survive, imperiled the survival chances of their children, and hence failed to continue their lineage.

Evolutionary psychologists predict that the sexes will differ in precisely those domains in which women and men have faced different sorts of adaptive problems. To an evolutionary psychologist, the likelihood that the sexes are psychologically identical in domains in which they have recurrently confronted different adaptive problems over the long expanse of human evolutionary history is essentially zero. The key question, therefore, is not whether men and women differ psychologically. Rather, the key questions about sex differences, from an evolutionary psychological perspective, are (1) In what domains have women and men faced different adaptive problems; (2) What are the sex-differentiated psychological mechanisms of women and men that have evolved in response to these sex-differentiated adaptive problems; and (3) Which social, cultural, and contextual inputs moderate the magnitude of expressed sex differences?

Sexual Selection Defines the Primary Domains in which the Sexes Have Faced Different Adaptive Challenges

Although many who are not biologists equate evolution with natural selection or survival selection, Darwin (1871) sculpted what he believed to be a second theory of evolution—the theory of sexual selection. Sexual selection is the causal process of the evolution of characteristics on the basis of reproductive advantage, as opposed to survival advantage. Sexual selection occurs in two forms. First, members of one sex can successfully outcompete members of their own sex in a process of intrasexual competition. Whatever characteristics lead to success in these same-sex competitions—be they greater size, strength, cunning, or social skills—can evolve or increase in frequency by virtue of the reproductive advantage accrued by the winners through increased access to more numerous or more desirable mates.

Second, members of one sex can evolve preferences for desirable qualities in potential mates through the process of intersexual selection. If members of one sex exhibit some consensus about which qualities are desirable in the other sex, then members of the other sex who possess the desirable qualities will gain a preferential mating advantage. Hence, the desirable qualities—be they morphological features such as antlers or plumage or psychological features such as a lower threshold for risk-taking to acquire resources—can evolve by virtue of the reproductive advantage attained by those who are preferentially chosen for possessing the desirable qualities. Among humans, both causal processes—preferential mate choice and same-sex competition for access to mates—are prevalent between both sexes, and probably have been throughout human evolutionary history.

Hypotheses about Psychological Sex Differences Follow from Sexual Asymmetries in Mate Selection and Intrasexual Competition

Although a detailed analysis of psychological sex differences is well beyond the scope of this article, a few of the most obvious differences in adaptive problems include the following.

PATERNITY UNCERTAINTY

Because fertilization occurs internally within women, men are always less than 100 per cent certain (again, no conscious awareness implied) that their putative children are genetically their own. Some cultures have phrases to describe this, such as 'Mama's baby, papa's maybe.' Women are always 100 per cent certain that the children they bear are their own.

IDENTIFYING REPRODUCTIVELY VALUABLE WOMEN

Because women's ovulation is concealed and there is no evidence that men can detect when women ovulate, ancestral men had the difficult adaptive challenge of identifying which women were more fertile. Although ancestral women would also have faced the problem of identifying fertile men, the

problem is considerably less severe both because most men remain fertile throughout their life span, whereas fertility is steeply age graded among women, and because women invest more heavily in offspring, making them the more 'valuable' sex and more intensely competed for by men seeking sexual access. Thus, there is rarely a shortage of men willing to contribute the sperm necessary for fertilization, whereas from a man's perspective, there is a pervasive shortage of fertile women.

GAINING SEXUAL ACCESS TO WOMEN

Because of the large asymmetry between men and women in their minimum obligatory parental investment—nine months gestation for women versus an act of sex for men—the direct reproductive benefits of gaining sexual access to a variety of mates would have been much higher for men than for women throughout human evolutionary history. Therefore, in social contexts that allowed some short-term mating or polygynous mating, men who succeeded in gaining sexual access to a variety of women—other things being equal—would have experienced greater reproductive success than men who failed to gain such access.

IDENTIFYING MEN WHO ARE ABLE TO INVEST

Because of the tremendous burdens of a nine-month pregnancy and subsequent lactation, women who selected men who were able to invest resources in them and their offspring would have been at a tremendous advantage in survival and reproductive currencies compared to women who were indifferent to the investment capabilities of the men with whom they chose to mate.

IDENTIFYING MEN WHO ARE WILLING TO INVEST

Having resources is not enough. Copulating with a man who had resources but who displayed a hasty post-copulatory departure would have been detrimental to the woman, particularly if she became pregnant and faced raising a child without the aid and protection of an investing father. A man with excellent resource-accruing capacities might channel resources to another woman or pursue short-term sexual opportunities with a variety of women. A woman who had the ability to detect a man's willingness to invest in her and her children would have an adaptive advantage compared to women who were oblivious to a man's willingness or unwillingness to invest.

These are just a few of the adaptive problems that women and men have confronted differently or to differing degrees. Other examples of sex-linked adaptive problems include those of coalitional warfare, coalitional defense, hunting, gathering, combating sex-linked forms of reputational damage, embodying sex-linked prestige criteria, and attracting mates by fulfilling the differing desires of the other sex—domains that all have consequences for mating but are sufficiently wide-ranging to span a great deal of social psychology. It is in these domains that evolutionary psychologists anticipate the most pronounced sex differences—differences in solutions to sex-linked adaptive problems in the form of evolved psychological mechanisms.

Psychological Sex Differences are Well Documented Empirically in the Domains Predicted by Theories Anchored in Sexual Selection

When Maccoby and Jacklin (1974) published their classic book on the psychology of sex differences, knowledge was spotty and methods for summarizing the literature were largely subjective and interpretive. Since that time, there has been a veritable explosion of empirical findings, along with quantitative meta-analytic procedures for evaluating them. Although new domains of sex differences continue to surface, such as the recently documented female advantage in spatial location memory, the outlines of where researchers find large, medium, small, and no sex differences are starting to emerge more clearly.

A few selected findings illustrate the heuristic power of evolutionary psychology. Cohen (1977) used the widely adopted d statistic as the index of magnitude of effect to propose a rule of thumb for evaluating effect sizes: 0.20 = 'small', 0.50 = 'medium', and 0.80 = 'large'. In *Sex, Power, Conflict: Feminist and Evolutionary Persepctives* (Buss and Malamuth, 1996), J.S Hyde has pointed out that sex differences in the intellectual and cognitive ability domains tend to be small. Women's verbal skills tend to be slightly higher than men's ($d = -0.11$). Sex differences in math also tend to be small ($d = 0.15$). Most tests of general cognitive ability, in short, reveal small sex differences.

The primary exception to the general trend of small sex differences in the cognitive abilities domain occurs with spatial rotation. This ability is essential for successful hunting, in which the trajectory and velocity of a spear must anticipate correctly the trajectory of an animal as each moves with different speeds through space and time. For spatial rotation ability, $d = 0.73$. Other sorts of skills involved in hunting also show large magnitudes of sex differences, such as throwing velocity ($d = 2.18$), throwing distance ($d = 1.98$), and throwing accuracy ($d = 0.96$; Ashmore, 1990). Skilled hunters, as good providers, are known to be sexually attractive to women in current and traditional tribal societies.

Large sex differences appear reliably for precisely the aspects of sexuality and mating predicted by evolutionary theories of sexual strategies. Oliver and Hyde (1993), for example, documented a large sex difference in attitudes toward casual sex ($d = 0.81$). Similar sex differences have been found with other measures of men's desire for casual sex partners, a psychological solution to the problem of seeking sexual access to a variety of partners. For example, men state that they would ideally like to have more than 18 sex partners in their lifetimes, whereas women state that they would desire only 4 or 5. In another study that has been replicated twice, 75 per cent of the men but 0 per cent of the women approached by an attractive stranger of the opposite sex consented to a request for sex.

Women tend to be more exacting than men, as predicted, in their standards for a short-term mate ($d = 0.79$). Women tend to place greater value on good financial prospects in a mate—a finding confirmed in a study of 10,047 individuals residing in 37 cultures located on six continents and five islands from around the world (Buss, 1989). More so than men, women especially disdain qualities in a potential mate that signal an inability to accrue resources, such as lack of ambition ($d = 1.38$) and lack of education ($d = 1.06$). Women desire physical protection abilities more than men, both in short-term mating ($d = 0.94$) and in long-term mating ($d = 0.66$).

Men and women also differ in the weighting given to cues that trigger sexual jealousy. Buss, Larsen, Westen, and Semmelroth (1992) presented men and women with the following dilemma: 'What would upset or distress you more: (a) imagining your partner forming a deep emotional attachment to someone else or (b) imagining your partner enjoying passionate sexual intercourse with that other person' (252). Men expressed greater distress about sexual than emotional infidelity, whereas women showed the opposite pattern. The difference between the sexes in which scenario was more distressing was 43 per cent ($d = 0.98$). These sex differences have been replicated by different investigators with physiological recording devices and have been replicated in other cultures.

These sex differences are precisely those predicted by evolutionary psychological theories based on sexual selection. They represent only a sampling from a larger body of supporting evidence. The sexes also differ substantially in a wide variety of other ways that are predicted by sexual selection theory, such as in thresholds for physical risk-taking, in frequency of perpetrating homicides, in thresholds for inferring sexual intent in others, in perceptions of the magnitude of upset that people experience as the victims of sexual

aggression, and in the frequency of committing violent crimes of all sorts. As noted by Donald Brown (1991), 'it will be irresponsible to continue shunting these [findings] aside, fraud to deny that they exist' (156). Evolutionary psychology sheds light on why these differences exist.

Conclusions

Strong sex differences occur reliably in domains closely linked with sex and mating, precisely as predicted by psychological theories based on sexual selection. Within these domains, the psychological sex differences are patterned in a manner that maps precisely onto the adaptive problems men and women have faced over human evolutionary history. Indeed, in most cases, the evolutionary hypotheses about sex differences were generated a decade or more before the empirical tests were conducted and the sex differences discovered. These models thus have heuristic and predictive power.

The evolutionary psychology perspective also offers several insights into the broader discourse on sex differences. First, neither women nor men can be considered 'superior' or 'inferior' to the other, any more than a bird's wings can be considered superior or inferior to a fish's fins or a kangaroo's legs. Each sex possesses mechanisms designed to deal with its own adaptive challenges—some similar and some different—and so notions of superiority or inferiority are logically incoherent from the vantage point of evolutionary psychology. The meta-theory of evolutionary psychology is descriptive, not prescriptive—it carries no values in its teeth.

Second, contrary to common misconceptions about evolutionary psychology, finding that sex differences originated through a causal process of sexual selection does not imply that the differences are unchangeable or intractable. On the contrary, understanding their origins provides a powerful heuristic to the contexts in which the sex differences are most likely to be manifested (e.g., in the context of mate competition) and hence provides a guide to effective loci for intervention if change is judged to be desirable.

Third, although some worry that inquiries into the existence and evolutionary origins of sex differences will lead to justification for the status quo, it is hard to believe that attempts to change the status quo can be very effective if they are undertaken in ignorance of sex differences that actually exist. Knowledge is power, and attempts to intervene in the absence of knowledge may resemble a surgeon operating blindfolded—there may be more bloodshed than healing.

The perspective of evolutionary psychology jettisons the outmoded dualistic thinking inherent in much current discourse by eliminating the false dichotomy between biological and social. It offers a truly interactionist position that specifies the particular features of social context that are especially critical for processing by our evolved psychological mechanisms. No other theory of sex differences has been capable of predicting and explaining the large number of precise, detailed, patterned sex differences discovered by research guided by evolutionary psychology. Evolutionary psychology possesses the heuristic power to guide investigators to the particular domains in which the most pronounced sex differences, as well as similarities, will be found. People grappling with the existence and implications of psychological sex differences cannot afford to ignore their most likely evolutionary origins through sexual selection.

References

Brown, D. 1991. *Human Universals*. Philadelphia: Temple University Press.

Buss, D.M. 1989. 'Sex Differences in Human Mate Preferences: Evolutionary Hypotheses Tested in 37 Cultures', *Behavioral and Brain Sciences* 12: 1–49.

Buss, D.M., R. Larsen, D. Westen, and J. Semmelroth. 1992. 'Sex Differences in Jealousy: Evolution, Physiology, and Psychology', *Psychological Science* 3: 251–5.

Cohen, J. 1977. *Statistical Power Analysis for the Behavioral Sciences*. San Diego, CA: Academic Press.

Darwin, C. 1871. *The Descent of Man and Selection in Relation to Sex*. London: Murray.

Hyde, J.S. 1996. 'Where Are the Gender Differences? Where are the Gender Similarities?', in D.M. Buss and Malamuth, eds, *Sex, Power, Conflict: Feminist and Evolutionary Perspectives*. New York: Oxford University Press.

Maccoby, E.E., and C.N. Jacklin. 1974. *The Psychology of Sex Differences*. Stanford, CA: Stanford University Press.

Oliver, M.B., and J.S. Hyde. 1993. 'Gender Differences in Sexuality: A Meta-analysis', *Psychological Bulletin* 114: 29–51.

CHAPTER 2

Believing is Seeing: Biology as Ideology

Judith Lorber

Until the eighteenth century, Western philosophers and scientists thought that there was one sex and that women's internal genitalia were the inverse of men's external genitalia: the womb and vagina were the penis and scrotum turned inside out (Laqueur, 1990). Current Western thinking sees women and men as so different physically as to sometimes seem to be two species. The bodies, which have been mapped inside and out for hundreds of years, have not changed. What have changed are the justifications for gender inequality. When the social position of all human beings was believed to be set by natural law or was considered God-given, biology was irrelevant; women and men of different classes all had their assigned places. When scientists began to question the divine basis of social order and replaced faith with empirical knowledge, what they saw was that women were very different from men in that they had wombs and menstruated. Such anatomical differences destined them for an entirely different social life from men.

In actuality, the basic bodily material is the same for females and males, and except for procreative hormones and organs, female and male human beings have similar bodies (Naftolin and Butz, 1981). Furthermore, as has been known since the middle of the nineteenth century, male and female genitalia develop from the same fetal tissue, and so infants can be born with ambiguous genitalia (Money and Ehrhardt, 1972). When they are, biology is used quite arbitrarily in sex assignment. Suzanne Kessler (1990) interviewed six medical specialists in pediatric intersexuality and found that whether an infant with XY chromosomes and anomalous genitalia was categorized as a boy or a girl depended on the size of the penis—if a penis was very small, the child was categorized as a girl, and sex-change surgery was used to make an artificial vagina. In the late nineteenth century, the presence or absence of ovaries was the determining criterion of gender assignment for hermaphrodites because a woman who could not procreate was not a complete woman (Kessler, 1990: 20).

Yet in Western societies, we see two discrete sexes and two distinguishable genders because our society is built on two classes of people, 'women' and 'men'. Once the gender category is given, the attributes of the person are also gendered: Whatever a 'woman' is must be 'female'; whatever a 'man' is must be 'male'. Analyzing

the social processes that construct the categories we call 'female and male', 'women and men', and 'homosexual and heterosexual' uncovers the ideology and power differentials congealed in these categories (Foucault, 1978). This article will use two familiar areas of social life—sports and technological competence—to show how myriad physiological differences are transformed into similar-appearing, gendered social bodies. My perspective goes beyond accepted feminist views that gender is a cultural overlay that modifies physiological sex differences. That perspective assumes either that there are two fairly similar sexes distorted by social practices into two genders with purposefully different characteristics or that there are two sexes whose essential differences are rendered unequal by social practices. I am arguing that bodies differ in many ways physiologically, but they are completely transformed by social practices to fit into the salient categories of a society, the most pervasive of which are 'female' and 'male' and 'women' and 'men'.

Neither sex nor gender are pure categories. Combinations of incongruous genes, genitalia, and hormonal input are ignored in sex categorization, just as combinations of incongruous physiology, identity, sexuality, appearance, and behaviour are ignored in the social construction of gender statuses. Menstruation, lactation, and gestation do not demarcate women from men. Only some women are pregnant and then only some of the time; some women do not have a uterus or ovaries. Some women have stopped menstruating temporarily, others have reached menopause, and some have had hysterectomies. Some women breast-feed some of the time, but some men lactate (Jaggar, 1983: 165 fn). Menstruation, lactation, and gestation are individual experiences of womanhood (Levesque-Lopman, 1988), but not determinants of the social category 'woman', or even 'female'. Similarly, 'men are not always sperm-producers, and in fact, not all sperm producers are men. A male-to-female transsexual, prior to surgery, can be socially a woman, though still potentially (or actually) capable of spermatogenesis' (Kessler and McKenna, [1978] 1985: 2).

When gender assignment is contested in sports, where the categories of competitors are rigidly divided into women and men, chromosomes are now used to determine in which category the athlete is to compete. However, an anomaly common enough to be found in several women at every major international sports competition are XY chromosomes that have not produced male anatomy or physiology because of a genetic defect. Because these women are women in every way significant to the sports competition, the prestigious International Amateur Athletic Federation has urged that sex be determined by simple genital inspection (Kolata, 1992). Transsexuals would pass this test, but it took a lawsuit for Renée Richards, a male-to-female transsexual, to be able to play tournament tennis as a woman, despite his male sex chromosomes (Richards, 1983). Oddly, neither basis for gender categorization—chromosomes nor genitalia—has anything to do with sports prowess (Birrell and Cole, 1990).

In the Olympics, in cases of chromosomal ambiguity, women must undergo 'a battery of gynecological and physical exams to see if she is "female enough" to compete. Men are not tested' (Carlson, 1991: 26). The purpose is not to categorize women and men accurately, but to make sure men don't enter women's competitions, where, it is felt, they will have the advantage of size and strength. This practice sounds fair only because it is assumed that all men are similar in size and strength and different from all women. Yet in Olympic boxing and wrestling matches, men are matched within weight classes. Some women might similarly successfully compete with some men in many sports. Women did not run in marathons until about twenty years ago. In twenty years of marathon competition, women have reduced their finish times by more than 90 minutes; they might catch up with men's running times in races of other lengths within the next 50 years because they are increasing their fastest

speeds more rapidly than are men (Fausto-Sterling, 1985: 213–18).

The reliance on only two sex and gender categories in the biological and social sciences is as epistemologically spurious as the reliance on chromosomal or genital tests to group athletes. Most research designs do not investigate whether physical skills or physical abilities are really more or less common in women and men (Epstein, 1988). They start out with two social categories ('women', 'men'), assume they are biologically different ('female', 'male'), look for similarities among them and differences between them, and attribute what they have found for the social categories to sex differences (Gelman, Collman, and Maccoby, 1986).

These designs rarely question the categorization of their subjects into two and only two groups, even though they often find more significant within-group differences than between-group differences (Hyde, 1990). The social construction perspective on sex and gender suggests that instead of starting with the two presumed dichotomies in each category—female, male; woman, man—it might be more useful in gender studies to group patterns of behaviour and only then look for identifying markers of the people likely to enact such behaviours.

What Sports Illustrate

Competitive sports have become, for boys and men, as players and as spectators, a way of constructing a masculine identity, a legitimated outlet for violence and aggression, and an avenue for upward mobility (Dunning, 1986; Kemper, 1990, 167–206; Messner, 1992). For men in Western societies, physical competence is an important marker of masculinity (Fine, 1987; Majors, 1990; Glassner, 1992). In professional and collegiate sports, physiological differences are invoked to justify women's secondary status, despite the clear evidence that gender status overrides physiological capabilities. Assumptions about women's physiology have influenced rules of competition;

subsequent sports performances then validate how women and men are treated in sports competitions.

Gymnastic equipment is geared to slim, wiry, prepubescent girls and not to mature women; conversely, men's gymnastic equipment is tailored for muscular, mature men, not slim, wiry, prepubescent boys. Boys could compete with girls, but are not allowed to; women gymnasts are left out entirely. Girl gymnasts are just that—little girls who will be disqualified as soon as they grow up (Vecsey, 1990). Men gymnasts have men's status. In women's basketball, the size of the ball and rules for handling the ball change the style of play to 'a slower, less intense, and less exciting modification of the "regular" or men's game' (Watson, 1987: 441). In the 1992 Winter Olympics, men figure skaters were required to complete three triple jumps in their required program; women figure skaters were forbidden to do more than one. These rules penalized artistic men skaters and athletic women skaters (Janofsky, 1992). For the most part, Western sports are built on physically trained men's bodies:

> Speed, size, and strength seem to be the essence of sports. Women *are* naturally inferior at 'sports' so conceived.
>
> But if women had been the historically dominant sex, our concept of sport would no doubt have evolved differently. Competitions emphasizing flexibility, balance, strength, timing, and small size might dominate Sunday afternoon television and offer salaries in six figures (English, 1982: 266, emphasis in original).

Organized sports are big businesses and, thus, who has access and at what level is a distributive or equity issue. The overall status of women and men athletes is an economic, political, and ideological issue that has less to do with individual physiological capabilities than with their cultural and social meaning and who defines and profits from them (Messner and Sabo, 1990; Slatton and

Birrell, 1984). Twenty years after the passage of Title IX of the US Civil Rights Act, which forbade gender inequality in any school receiving federal funds, the goal for collegiate sports in the next five years is 60 per cent men, 40 per cent women in sports participation, scholarships, and funding (Moran, 1992).

How access and distribution of rewards (prestigious and financial) are justified is an ideological, even moral, issue (Birrell, 1988: 473–6, Hargreaves, 1982). One way is that men athletes are glorified and women athletes ignored in the mass media. Messner and his colleagues found that in 1989, in TV sports news in the United States, men's sports got 92 per cent of the coverage and women's sports 5 per cent, with the rest mixed or gender-neutral (Messner, Duncan, and Jensen, 1993). In 1990, in four of the top-selling newspapers in the United States, stories on men's sports outnumbered those on women's sports 23-to-1. Messner and his colleagues also found an implicit hierarchy in naming, with women athletes most likely to be called by first names, followed by black men athletes, and only white men athletes routinely referred to by their last names. Similarly, women's collegiate sports teams are named or marked in ways that symbolically feminize and trivialize them—the men's team is called Tigers, the women's Kittens (Eitzen and Baca Zinn, 1989).

Assumptions about men's and women's bodies and their capacities are crafted in ways that make unequal access and distribution of rewards acceptable (Hudson, 1978; Messner, 1988). Media images of modern men athletes glorify their strength and power, even their violence (Hargreaves, 1986). Media images of modern women athletes tend to focus on feminine beauty and grace (so they are not really athletes) or on their thin, small, wiry, androgenous bodies (so they are not really women). In coverage of the Olympics,

> loving and detailed attention is paid to pixie-like gymnasts; special and extended coverage

is given to graceful and dazzling figure skaters; the camera painstakingly records the fluid movements of swimmers and divers. And then, in a blinding flash of fragmented images, viewers see a few minutes of volleyball, basketball, speed skating, track and field, and alpine skiing, as television gives its nod to the mere existence of these events (Boutilier and SanGiovanni, 1983: 190).

Extraordinary feats by women athletes who were presented as mature adults might force sports organizers and audiences to rethink their stereo-types of women's capabilities, the way elves, mer-maids, and ice queens do not. Sports, therefore, construct men's bodies to be powerful and women's bodies to be sexual. As Connell (1987: 85) says,

> The meanings in the bodily sense of masculinity concern, above all else, the superiority of men to women, and the exaltation of hegemonic masculinity over other groups of men which is essential for the domination of women.

In the late 1970s, as women entered more and more athletic competitions, supposedly good scientific studies showed that women who exercised intensely would cease menstruating because they would not have enough body fat to sustain ovulation (Brozan, 1978). When one set of researchers did a year-long study that compared 66 women—21 who were training for a marathon, 22 who ran more than an hour a week, and 23 who did less than an hour of aerobic exercise a week—they discovered that only 20 per cent of the women in any of these groups had 'normal' menstrual cycles every month (Prior et al., 1990). The dangers of intensive training for women's fertility therefore were exaggerated as women began to compete successfully in arenas formerly closed to them.

Given the association of sports with mascu-linity in the United States, women athletes have to manage a contradictory status. One study of women college basketball players found that although they 'did athlete' on the court, 'pushing, shoving, fouling, hard running, fast breaks, defense, obscenities and sweat' (Watson, 1987: 441), they 'did woman' off the court, using the locker room as their staging area:

> While it typically took fifteen minutes to prepare for the game, it took approximately fifteen minutes after the game to shower and remove the sweat of an athlete, and it took another thirty minutes to dress, apply make-up and style hair. It did not seem to matter whether the players were going out into the public or getting on a van for a long ride home. Average dressing time and rituals did not change (Watson, 1987: 443).

Another way women manage these status dilem-mas is to redefine the activity or its result as feminine or womanly (Mangan and Park, 1987). Thus women bodybuilders claim 'flex appeal is sex appeal' (Duff and Hong, 1984: 378).

Such a redefinition of women's physical-ity affirms the ideological subtext of sports that physical strength is men's prerogative and justifies men's physical and sexual domination of women (Hargreaves, 1986; Messner, 1992; Olson, 1990; Theberge, 1987; Willis, 1982). When women demonstrate physical strength, they are labelled unfeminine:

> It's threatening to one's takeability, one's repeability, one's femininity, to be strong and physically self-possessed. To be able to resist rape, not to communicate rapeability with one's body, to hold one's body for uses and meanings other than that can transform what *being a woman means* (MacKinnon, 1987: 122, emphasis in original).

Resistance to that transformation, ironically, was evident in the policies of American women phys-ical education professionals throughout most of the twentieth century. They minimized exertion, maximized a feminine appearance and manner, and left organized sports competition to men (Birrell, 1988; Mangan and Park, 1987).

Dirty Little Secrets

As sports construct gendered bodies, technology constructs gendered skills. Meta-analyses of studies of gender differences in spatial and mathematical ability have found that men have a large advantage in ability to mentally rotate an image, a moderate advantage in a visual perception of horizontality and verticality and in mathematical performance, and a small advantage in ability to pick a figure out of a field (Hyde, 1990). It could be argued that these advantages explain why, within the short space of time that computers have become ubiquitous in offices, schools, and homes, work on them and with them has become gendered: men create, program, and market computers, make war and produce science and art with them; women microwire them in computer factories and enter data in computerized offices; boys play games, socialize, and commit crimes with computers; girls are rarely seen in computer clubs, camps, and classrooms. But women were hired as computer programmers in the 1940s because

> the work seemed to resemble simple clerical tasks. In fact, however, programming demanded complex skills in abstract logic, mathematics, electrical circuitry, and machinery, all of which . . . women used to perform in their work. Once programming was recognized as 'intellectually demanding', it became attractive to men (Donato, 1990: 170).

A woman mathematician and pioneer in data processing, Grace M. Hopper, was famous for her work on programming language (Perry and Greber, 1990: 86). By the 1960s, programming was split into more and less skilled specialties, and the entry of women into the computer field

in the 1970s and 1980s was confined to the lower-paid specialties. At each stage, employers invoked women's and men's purportedly natural capabilities for the jobs for which they were hired (Cockburn, 1983, 1985; Zimmerman, 1983; Hartmann, Kraut, and Tilly, 1986; Hartmann, 1987; Wright et al., 1987; Donato, 1990; Kramer and Lehman, 1990).

It is the taken-for-grantedness of such everyday gendered behaviour that gives credence to the belief that the widespread differences in what women and men do must come from biology. To take one ordinarily unremarked scenario: In modern societies, if a man and woman who are a couple are in a car together, he is much more likely to take the wheel than she is, even if she is the more competent driver. Molly Haskell calls this taken-for-granted phenomenon 'the dirty little secret of marriage: the husband-lousy-driver syndrome' (1989: 26). Men drive cars whether they are good drivers or not because men and machines are a 'natural' combination (Scharff, 1991). But the ability to drive gives one mobility; it is a form of social power.

In the early days of the automobile, feminists co-opted the symbolism of mobility as emancipation: 'Donning goggles and dusters, wielding tire irons and tool kits, taking the wheel, they announced their intention to move beyond the bounds of women's place' (Scharff, 1991: 68). Driving enabled them to campaign for women's suffrage in parts of the United States not served by public transportation, and they effectively used motorcades and speaking from cars as campaign tactics (Scharff, 1991). Sandra Gilbert also notes that during the First World War, women's ability to drive was physically, mentally, and even sensually liberating:

> For nurses and ambulance drivers, women doctors and women messengers, the phenomenon of modern battle was very different from that experienced by entrenched combatants. Finally given a chance to take the wheel, these

post-Victorian girls raced motorcars along foreign roads like adventurers exploring new lands, while their brothers dug deeper into the mud of France. . . . Retrieving the wounded and the dead from deadly positions, these once-decorous daughters had at last been allowed to prove their valor, and they swooped over the wastelands of the war with the energetic love of Wagnerian Valkyries, their mobility alone transporting countless immobilized heroes to safe havens (1983: 438–9).

Not incidentally, women in the United States and England got the vote for their war efforts in the First World War.

Social Bodies and the Bathroom Problem

People of the same racial ethnic group and social class are roughly the same size and shape—but there are many varieties of bodies. People have different genitalia, different secondary sex characteristics, different contributions to procreation, different orgasmic experiences, different patterns of illness and aging. Each of us experiences our bodies differently, and these experiences change as we grow, age, sicken, and die. The bodies of pregnant and non-pregnant women, short and tall people, those with intact and functioning limbs and those whose bodies are physically challenged are all different. But the salient categories of a society group these attributes in ways that ride roughshod over individual experiences and more meaningful clusters of people.

I am not saying that physical differences between male and female bodies don't exist, but that these differences are socially meaningless until social practices transform them into social facts. West Point Military Academy's curriculum is designed to produce leaders, and physical competence is used as a significant measure of leadership ability (Yoder, 1989). When women were accepted as West Point cadets, it became clear that the tests

of physical competence, such as rapidly scaling an eight-foot wall, had been constructed for male physiques—pulling oneself up and over using upper-body strength. Rather than devise tests of physical competence for women, West Point provided boosters that mostly women used—but that lost them test points—in the case of the wall, a platform. Finally, the women themselves figured out how to use their bodies successfully. Janice Yoder describes this situation:

> I was observing this obstacle one day, when a woman approached the wall in the old prescribed way, got her fingertips grip, and did an unusual thing: she walked her dangling legs up the wall until she was in a position where both her hands and feet were atop the wall. She then simply pulled up her sagging bottom and went over. She solved the problem by capitalizing on one of women's physical assets: lower-body strength (1989: 530).

In short, if West Point is going to measure leadership capability by physical strength, women's pelvises will do just as well as men's shoulders.

The social transformation of female and male physiology into a condition of inequality is well illustrated by the bathroom problem. Most buildings that have gender-segregated bathrooms have an equal number for women and for men. Where there are crowds, there are always long lines in front of women's bathrooms but rarely in front of men's bathrooms. The cultural, physiological, and demographic combinations of clothing, frequency of urination, menstruation, and childcare add up to generally greater bathroom use by women than men. Thus, although an equal number of bathrooms seems fair, equity would mean more women's bathrooms or allowing women to use men's bathrooms for a certain amount of time (Molotch, 1988).

The bathroom problem is the outcome of the way gendered bodies are differentially evaluated in Western cultures: men's social bodies are the measure of what is 'human'. Gray's *Anatomy*, in use for 100 years, well into the twentieth century, presented the human body as male. The female body was shown only where it differed from the male (Laqueur, 1990). Denise Riley says that if we envisage women's bodies, men's bodies, and human bodies 'as a triangle of identifications, then it is rarely an equilateral triangle in which both sexes are pitched at matching distances from the apex of the human' (1988: 197). Catharine MacKinnon also contends that in Western society, universal 'humanness' is male because

> virtually every quality that distinguishes men from women is already affirmatively compensated in this society. Men's physiology defines most sports, their needs define auto and health insurance coverage, their socially defined biographies define workplace expectations and successful career patterns, their perspectives and concerns define quality in scholarship, their experiences and obsessions define merit, their objectification of life defines art, their military service defines citizenship, their presence defines family, their inability to get along with each other—their wars and rulerships—define history, their image defines god, and their genitals define sex. For each of their differences from women, what amounts to an affirmative action plan is in effect, otherwise known as the structure and values of American society (1987: 36).

The Paradox of Human Nature

Gendered people do not emerge from physiology or hormones but from the exigencies of the social order, mostly, from the need for a reliable division of the work of food production and the social (not physical) reproduction of new members. The moral imperatives of religion and cultural representations reinforce the boundary lines among genders and ensure that what is demanded, what is permitted, and what is tabooed for the people

in each gender is well-known and followed by most. Political power, control of scarce resources, and, if necessary, violence uphold the gendered social order in the face of resistance and rebellion. Most people, however, voluntarily go along with their society's prescriptions for those of their gender status because the norms and expectations get built into their sense of worth and identity as a certain kind of human being and because they believe their society's way is the natural way. These beliefs emerge from the imagery that pervades the way we think, the way we see and hear and speak, the way we fantasize, and the way we feel. There is no core or bedrock human nature below these endlessly looping processes of the social production of sex and gender, self and other, identity and psyche, each of which is a 'complex cultural construction' (Butler, 1990: 36). The paradox of 'human nature' is that it is always a manifestation of cultural meanings, social relationships, and power politics—'not biology, but culture, becomes destiny' (Butler, 1990: 8).

Feminist inquiry has long questioned the conventional categories of social science, but much of the current work in feminist sociology has not gone beyond adding the universal category 'women' to the universal category 'men'. Our current debates over the global assumptions of only two categories and the insistence that they must be nuanced to include race and class are steps in the direction I would like to see feminist research go, but race and class are also global categories (Spelman, 1988; Collins, 1990). Deconstructing sex, sexuality, and gender reveals many possible categories embedded in the social experiences and social practices of what Dorothy Smith calls the 'everyday/everynight world' (1990). These emergent categories group some people together for comparison with other people without prior assumptions about who is like whom. Categories can be broken up and people regrouped differently into new categories for comparison. This process of discovering categories from similarities and differences in people's behaviour or responses can be more meaningful for feminist research than discovering similarities and differences between 'females' and 'males' or 'women' and 'men' because the social construction of the conventional sex and gender categories already assumes differences between them and similarities among them. When we rely only on the conventional categories of sex and gender, we end up finding what we looked for—we see what we believe, whether it is that 'females' and 'males' are essentially different or that 'women' and 'men' are essentially the same.

References

Birrell, S.J. 1988. 'Discourses on the Gender/Sport Relationship: From Women in Sport to Gender Relations', in K. Pandolf, ed., *Exercise and Sport Science Reviews*, Vol. 16. New York: Macmillan.

Birrell, S.J., and S.L. Cole. 1990. 'Double Fault: Renee Richards and the Construction and Naturalization of Difference', *Sociology of Sport Journal* 7: 1–21.

Boutilier, M.A., and L. SanGiovanni. 1983. *The Sporting Woman*. Champaign, IL: Human Kinetics.

Brozan, N. 1978. 'Training Linked to Disruption of Female Reproductive Cycle', *New York Times*, 17 April.

Butler, J. 1990. *Gender Trouble: Feminism and the Subversion of Identity*. New York and London: Routledge & Kegan Paul.

Carlson, A. 1991. 'When is a Woman Not a Woman?', *Women's Sport and Fitness* (March): 24–9.

Cockburn, C. 1983. *Brothers: Male Dominance and Technological Change*. London: Pluto.

———. 1985. *Machinery of Dominance: Women, Men, and Technical Know-How*. London: Pluto.

Collins, P.H. 1990. *Black Feminist Thought: Knowledge, Consciousness, and the Politics of Empowerment*. Boston: Unwin Hyman.

Connell, R.W. 1987. *Gender and Power*. Stanford, CA: Stanford University Press.

Donato, K.M. 1990. 'Programming for Change? The Growing Demand for Women Systems Analysts', in B.F. Reskin and P.A Roos, eds, *Job Queues, Gender Queues: Explaining Women's Inroads into Male Occupations*. Philadelphia: Temple University Press.

Duff, R.W., and L.K. Hong. 1984. 'Self-images of Women Bodybuilders', *Sociology of Sport Journal* 2: 374–80.

Dunning, E. 1986. 'Sport as a Male Preserve: Notes on the Social Sources of Masculine Identity and Its Transformations', *Theory, Culture, and Society* 3: 79–90.

Eitzen, D.S., and M.B. Zinn. 1989. 'The Deathleticization of Women: The Naming and Gender Marking of Collegiate Sport Teams', *Sociology of Sport Journal* 6: 362–70.

English, J. 1982. 'Sex Equality in Sports', in M. Vetterling-Braggin, ed., *Femininity, Masculinity, and Androgyny*. Boston: Littlefield, Adams.

Epstein, C.F. 1988. *Deceptive Distinctions: Sex, Gender, and the Social Order*. New Haven, CT: Yale University Press.

Fausto-Sterling, A. 1985. *Myths of Gender: Biological Theories about Women and Men*. New York: Basic Books.

Fine, G.A. 1987. *With the Boys: Little League Baseball and Preadolescent Culture*. Chicago: University of Chicago Press.

Foucault, M. 1978. *The History of Sexuality: An Introduction*. R. Hurley, trans. New York: Pantheon.

Gelman, S.A., P. Collman, and E.E. Maccoby. 1986. 'Inferring Properties from Categories versus Inferring Categories from Properties: The Case of Gender', *Child Development* 57: 396–404.

Gilbert, S.M. 1983. 'Soldier's Heart: Literary Men, Literary Women, and the Great War', *Signs: Journal of Women in Culture and Society* 8: 422–50.

Glassner, B. 1992. 'Men and Muscles', in M.S. Kimmel and M.A. Messner, eds, *Men's Lives*. New York: Macmillan.

Hargreaves, J.A., ed. 1982. *Sport, Culture, and Ideology*. London: Routledge & Kegan Paul.

———. 1986. 'Where's the Virtue? Where's the Grace? A Discussion of the Social Production of Gender Relations In and Through Sport', *Theory, Culture, and Society* 3: 109–21.

————, ed. 1987. *Computer Chips and Paper Clips: Technology and Women's Employment*, Vol. 2. Washington, DC: National Academy Press.

Hargreaves, J.A., R.E. Kraut, and L.A. Tilly, eds. 1986. *Computer Chips and Paper Clips: Technology and Women's Employment*, Vol. 1. Washington, DC: National Academy Press.

Haskell, M. 1989. 'Hers: He Drives Me Crazy', *New York Times Magazine* (24 September): 26, 28.

Hudson, J. 1978. 'Physical Parameters Used for Female Exclusion from Law Enforcement and Athletics', in C.A. Oglesby, ed., *Women and Sport: From Myth to Reality*. Philadelphia: Lea and Febiger.

Hyde, J.S. 1990. 'Meta-analysis and the Psychology of Gender Differences', *Signs: Journal of Women in Culture and Society* 16: 55–73.

Jaggar, A.M. 1983. *Feminist Politics and Human Nature*. Totowa, NJ: Rowman & Allanheld.

Janofsky, M. 1992. 'Yamaguchi Has the Delicate and Golden Touch', *New York Times*, 22 February.

Kemper, T.D. 1990. *Social Structure and Testosterone: Explorations of the Sociobiosocial Chain*. New Brunswick, NJ: Rutgers University Press.

Kessler, S.J. 1990. 'The Medical Construction of Gender: Case Management of Intersexed Infants', *Signs: Journal of Women in Culture and Society* 16: 3–26.

Kessler, S.J., and W. McKenna. [1978] 1985. *Gender: An Ethnomethodological Approach*. Chicago: University of Chicago Press.

Kolata, G. 1992. 'Track Federation Urges End to Gene Test for Femaleness', *New York Times*, 12 February.

Kramer, P.E., and S. Lehman. 1990. 'Mismeasuring Women: A Critique of Research on Computer Ability and Avoidance', *Signs: Journal of Women in Culture and Society* 16: 158–72.

Laqueur, T. 1990. *Making Sex: Body and Gender from the Greeks to Freud*. Cambridge, MA: Harvard University Press.

Levesque-Lopman, L. 1988. *Claiming Reality: Phenomenology and Women's Experience*. Totowa, NJ: Rowman & Littlefield.

MacKinnon, C. 1987. *Feminism Unmodified*. Cambridge, MA: Harvard University Press.

Majors, R. 1990. 'Cool Pose: Black Masculinity in Sports', in M.A. Messner and D.F. Sabo, eds, *Sport, Men, and the Gender Order: Critical Feminist Perspectives*. Champaign, IL: Human Kinetics.

Mangan, J.A., and R.J. Park. 1987. *From Fair Sex to Feminism: Sport and the Socialization of Women in the Industrial and Post-industrial Eras*. London: Frank Cass.

Messner, M.A. 1988. 'Sports and Male Domination: The Female Athlete as Contested Ideological Terrain', *Sociology of Sport Journal* 5: 197–211.

————. 1992. *Power at Play: Sports and the Problem of Masculinity*. Boston: Beacon Press.

Messner, M.A., M.C. Duncan, and K. Jensen. 1993. 'Separating the Men from the Girls: The Gendered Language of Television Sports', *Gender & Society* 7: 121–37.

Messner, M.A., and D.F. Sabo, eds. 1990. *Sport, Men, and the Gender Order: Critical Feminist Perspectives*. Champaign, IL: Human Kinetics.

Molotch, H. 1988. 'The Restroom and Equal Opportunity', *Sociological Forum* 3: 128–32.

Money, J., and A.A. Ehrhardt. 1972. *Man & Woman, Boy & Girl*. Baltimore, MD: Johns Hopkins University Press.

Moran, M. 1992. 'Title IX: A 20-year Search for Equity', *New York Times* (Sports Section), 21–23 June.

Naftolin, F., and E. Butz, eds. 1981. 'Sexual Dimorphism', *Science* 211: 1263–324.

Olson, W. 1990. 'Beyond Title IX: Toward an Agenda for Women and Sports in the 1990s', *Yale Journal of Law and Feminism* 3: 105–51.

Perry, R., and L. Greber. 1990. 'Women and Computers: An Introduction', *Signs: Journal of Women in Culture and Society* 16: 74–101.

Prior, J.C., Y.M. Yigna, M.T. Shechter, and A.E. Burgess. 1990. 'Spinal Bone Loss and Ovulatory Disturbances', *New England Journal of Medicine* 323: 1221–7.

Richards, R., with J. Ames. 1983. *Second Serve*. New York: Stein and Day.

Riley, D. 1988. *Am I That Name? Feminism and the Category of Women in History*. Minneapolis: University of Minnesota Press.

Scharff, V. 1991. *Taking the Wheel: Women and the Coming of the Motor Age*. New York: Free Press.

Slatton, B., and S. Birrel. 1984. 'The Politics of Women's Sport', *Arena Review* 8 (July).

Smith, D.E. 1990. *The Conceptual Practices of Power: A Feminist Sociology of Knowledge*. Toronto: University of Toronto Press.

Spelman, E. 1988. *Inessential Woman: Problems of Exclusion in Feminist Thought*. Boston: Beacon Press.

Theberge, N. 1987. 'Sport and Women's Empowerment', *Women Studies International Forum* 10: 387–93.

Vecsey, G. 1990. 'Cathy Rigby, unlike Peter, Did Grow Up', *New York Times* (Sports Section), 19 December.

Watson, T. 1987. 'Women Athletes and Athletic Women: The Dilemmas and Contradictions of Managing Incongruent Identities', *Sociological Inquiry* 57: 431–6.

Willis, P. 1982. 'Women in Sport in Ideology', in J.A. Hargreaves, ed., *Sport, Culture, and Ideology*. London: Routledge & Kegan Paul.

Wright, B.D., M.M. Ferree, G.O. Mellow, L.H. Lewis, M-L.D. Samper, R. Asher, and K. Claspell, eds. 1987. *Women, Work, and Technology: Transformations*. Ann Arbor, MI: University of Michigan Press.

Yoder, J.D. 1989. 'Women at West Point: Lessons for Token Women in Male-dominated Occupations', in J. Freeman, ed., *Women: A Feminist Perspective*, 4th ed. Palo Alto, CA: Mayfield.

Zimmerman, J., ed. 1983. *The Technological Woman: Interfacing with Tomorrow*. New York: Praeger.

CHAPTER 3

Testosterone Rules

Robert M. Sapolsky

Face it, we all do it—we all believe in stereotypes about minorities. These stereotypes are typically pejorative and false, but every now and then they have a core of truth. I know, because I belong to a minority that lives up to its reputation. I have a genetic abnormality generally considered to be associated with high rates of certain socially abhorrent behaviours: I am male. Thanks to an array of genes that produce some hormone-synthesizing enzymes, my testes churn out a corrosive chemical and dump the stuff into my bloodstream, and this probably has behavioural consequences. We males account for less than 50 per cent of the population, yet we generate a huge proportion of the violence. Whether it is something as primal as having an ax fight in a rain forest clearing or as detached as using computer-guided aircraft to strafe a village, something as condemned as assaulting a cripple or as glorified as killing someone wearing the wrong uniform, if it is violent, we males excel at it.

Why should this be? We all think we know the answer: something to do with those genes being expressed down in the testes. A dozen millennia ago or so, an adventurous soul managed to lop off a surly bull's testicles, thus inventing behavioural endocrinology. It is unclear from the historical records whether the experiment resulted in grants and tenure, but it certainly generated an influential finding: that the testes do something or other to make males aggressive pains in the ass.

That something or other is synthesizing the infamous corrosive chemical, testosterone (or rather, a family of related androgen hormones that I'll call testosterone for the sake of simplicity, hoping the androgen specialists won't take it the wrong way). Testosterone bulks up muscle cells—including those in the larynx, giving rise to operatic basses. It makes hair sprout here and there, undermines the health of blood vessels, alters biochemical events in the liver too dizzying to contemplate, and has a profound impact, no doubt, on the workings of cells in big toes. And it seeps into the brain, where it influences behaviour in a way highly relevant to understanding aggression.

Genes are the hand behind the scene, directing testosterone's actions. They specify whether steroidal building blocks are turned into testosterone or estrogen, how much of each, and how quickly. They regulate how fast the liver breaks down circulating testosterone, thereby determining how long an androgenic signal remains in the bloodstream. They direct the synthesis of testosterone receptors—specialized proteins that catch hold of testosterone and allow it to have its characteristic effects on target cells. And genes specify how many such receptors the body has, and how sensitive they are. Insofar as testosterone alters brain function and produces aggression, and genes regulate how much testosterone is made and how effectively it works, this should be the archetypal case for studying how genes can control our behaviour. Instead, however, it's the archetypal case for learning how little genes actually do so.

Some pretty obvious evidence links testosterone with aggression. Males tend to have higher testosterone levels in their circulation than do females, and to be more aggressive. Times of life when males are swimming in testosterone—for example, after reaching puberty—correspond to when aggression peaks. Among many species, testes are mothballed most of the year, kicking into action and pouring out testosterone only during a very circumscribed mating season—precisely the time when male–male aggression soars.

Impressive though they seem, these data are only correlative—testosterone found on the scene repeatedly with no alibi when some aggression has occurred. The proof comes with the knife, the performance of what is euphemistically known as a subtraction experiment. Remove the source of testosterone in species after species, and levels of aggression typically plummet. Reinstate normal testosterone levels afterward with injections of synthetic testosterone, and aggression returns.

The subtraction and replacement paradigm represents pretty damning proof that this hormone, with its synthesis and efficacy under genetic control, is involved in aggression. 'Normal testosterone levels appear to be a prerequisite for normative levels of aggressive behaviour' is the sort of catchy, hum-able phrase the textbooks would use. That probably explains why you shouldn't mess with a bull moose during rutting season. But it's not why a lot of people want to understand this sliver of science. Does the action of testosterone tell us anything about individual differences in levels of aggression, anything about why some males—some human males—are exceptionally violent? Among an array of males, are the highest testosterone levels found in the most aggressive individuals?

Generate some extreme differences and that is precisely what you see. Castrate some of the well-paid study subjects, inject others with enough testosterone to quadruple the normal human levels, and the high-testosterone males are overwhelmingly likely to be the more aggressive ones. Obviously, extreme conditions don't tell us much about the real world, but studies of the normative variability in testosterone—in other words, seeing what everyone's natural levels are like without manipulating anything—also suggest that high levels of testosterone and high levels of aggression tend to go together. This would seem to seal the case that interindividual differences in levels of aggression among normal individuals are probably driven by differences in levels of testosterone. But that conclusion turns out to be wrong.

Here's why. Suppose you note a correlation between levels of aggression and levels of testosterone among normal males. It could be because (a) testosterone elevates aggression; (b) aggression elevates testosterone secretion; or (c) neither causes the other. There's a huge bias to assume option a, while b is the answer. Study after study has shown that if you examine testosterone levels when males are first placed together in the social group, testosterone levels predict nothing about who is going to be aggressive. The subsequent behavioural differences drive the hormonal changes, rather than the other way around.

Because of a strong bias among certain scientists, it has taken forever to convince them of this point. Suppose you're studying what behaviour and hormones have to do with each other. How do you study the behavioural part? You get yourself a notebook, a stopwatch, and a pair of binoculars. How do you measure the hormones and analyze the genes that regulate them? You need some gazillion-dollar machines; you muck around with radiation and chemicals, wear a lab coat, and maybe even goggles—the whole nine yards. Which toys would you rather get for Christmas? Which facet of science are you going to believe in more? The higher the technology, then the more scientific the discipline. Hormones seem to many to be more substantive than behaviour, so when a correlation occurs, it must be because hormones regulate behaviour, not the other way around.

This is a classic case of what is often called physics envy, a disease that causes behavioural biologists to fear their discipline lacks the rigour of physiology, physiologists to wish for the techniques of biochemists, biochemists to covet the clarity of the answers revealed by molecular geneticists, all the way down until you get to the physicists who confer only with God. Recently, a zoologist friend had obtained blood samples from the carnivores he studies and wanted some hormones in the samples tested in my lab. Although inexperienced with the technique, he offered to help in any way possible. I felt hesitant asking him to do anything tedious, but since he had offered, I tentatively said, 'Well, if you don't mind some unspeakable drudgery, you could number about a thousand assay vials.' And this scientist, whose superb work has graced the most prestigious science journals in the world, cheerfully answered, 'That's okay. How often do I get to do real science, working with test tubes?'

Difficult though scientists with physics envy find it to believe, interindividual differences in testosterone levels don't predict subsequent differences in aggressive behaviour among individuals. Similarly, fluctuations in testosterone levels within one individual over time don't predict subsequent changes in the levels of aggression in that one individual—get a hiccup in testosterone secretion one afternoon and that's not when the guy goes postal.

Look at our confusing state: normal levels of testosterone are a prerequisite for normal levels of aggression. Yet if one male's genetic makeup predisposes him to higher levels of testosterone than the next guy, he isn't necessarily going to be more aggressive. Like clockwork, that statement makes the students suddenly start coming to office hours in a panic, asking whether they missed something in their lecture notes.

Yes, it's going to be on the final, and it's one of the more subtle points in endocrinology—what's referred to as a hormone having a 'permissive effect'. Remove someone's testes and, as noted, the frequency of aggressive behaviour is likely to plummet. Reinstate pre-castration levels of testosterone by injecting the hormone, and pre-castration levels of aggression typically return. Fair enough. Now, this time, castrate an individual and restore testosterone levels to only 20 per cent of normal. Amazingly, normal pre-castration levels of aggression come back. Castrate and now introduce twice the testosterone levels from before castration, and the same level of aggressive behaviour returns. You need some testosterone around for normal aggressive behaviour. Zero levels after castration, and down it usually goes; quadruple levels (the sort of range generated in weight lifters abusing anabolic steroids), and aggression typically increases. But anywhere from roughly 20 per cent of normal to twice normal and it's all the same. The brain can't distinguish among this wide range of basically normal values.

If you knew a great deal about the genetic makeup of a bunch of males, enough to understand how much testosterone they secreted into their bloodstream, you still couldn't predict levels of aggression among those individuals. Nevertheless, the subtraction and reinstatement data seem to indicate that, in a broad sort of way, testosterone causes aggressive behaviour. But that turns out not to be true either, and the implications of this are lost on most people the first 30 times they hear about it. Those implications are important, however—so important that it's worth saying 31 times.

Round up some male monkeys. Put them in a group together and give them plenty of time to sort out where they stand with each other—grudges, affiliative friendships. Give them enough time to form a dominance hierarchy, the sort of linear ranking in which number 3, for example, can pass his day throwing around his weight with numbers 4 and 5, ripping off their monkey chow, forcing them to relinquish the best spots to sit in, but numbers 1 and 2 still expect and receive from him the most obsequious brown-nosing.

Hierarchy in place, it's time to do your experiment. Take that third-ranking monkey and give him some testosterone. None of this within-the-normal-range stuff. Inject a ton of it, way higher than what you normally see in rhesus monkeys, give him enough testosterone to grow antlers and a beard on every neuron in his brain. And, no surprise, when you check the behavioural data, he will probably be participating in more aggressive interactions than before.

So even though small fluctuations in the levels of the hormone don't seem to matter much, testosterone still causes aggression, right? Wrong. Check out number 3 more closely. Is he raining aggressive terror on everyone in the group, frothing with indiscriminate violence? Not at all. He's still judiciously kow-towing to numbers 1 and 2 but has become a total bastard to numbers 4 and 5. Testosterone isn't causing aggression, it's exaggerating the aggression that's already there.

Another example, just to show we're serious. There's a part of your brain that probably has lots to do with aggression, a region called the amygdala. Sitting near it is the Grand Central Station of emotion-related activity in your brain, the

hypothalamus. The amygdala communicates with the hypothalamus by way of a cable of neuronal connections called the stria terminalis. (No more jargon, I promise.) The amygdala influences aggression via that pathway, sending bursts of electrical excitation that ripple down the stria terminalis to the hypothalamus and put it in a pissy mood.

Once again, do your hormonal intervention: flood the area with testosterone. You can inject the hormone into the bloodstream, where it eventually makes its way to the amygdala. You can surgically microinject the stuff directly into the area. In a few years, you may even be able to construct animals with extra copies of the genes that direct testosterone synthesis, producing extra hormone that way. Six of one, half a dozen of the other. The key thing is what doesn't happen next. Does testosterone make waves of electrical excitation surge down the stria terminalis? Does it turn on that pathway? Not at all. If and only if the amygdala is already sending an excited volley down the stria terminalis, testosterone increases the rate of such activity by shortening the resting time between bouts. It's not turning on the pathway, it's increasing the volume of signalling if it is already turned on. It's not causing aggression, it's exaggerating the pre-existing pattern of it, exaggerating the response to environmental triggers of aggression.

In every generation, it is the duty of behavioural biologists to try to teach this critical point, one that seems a maddening cliché once you get it. You take that hoary old dichotomy between nature and nurture, between intrinsic factors and extrinsic ones, between genes and environment, and regardless of which behaviour and underlying biology you're studying, the dichotomy is a sham. No genes. No environment. Just the interaction between the two.

Do you want to know how important environment and experience are in understanding testosterone and aggression? Look back at how the effects of castration are discussed earlier. There were statements like 'Remove the source of testosterone in species after species and levels of aggression typically plummet.' Not 'Remove the source . . . and aggression always goes to zero.' On the average it declines, but rarely to zero, and not at all in some individuals. And the more social experience an individual had being aggressive prior to castration, the more likely that behaviour persists sans cojones. In the right context, social conditioning can more than make up for the complete absence of the hormone.

A case in point: the spotted hyena. These animals are fast becoming the darlings of endocrinologists, sociobiologists, gynecologists, and tabloid writers because of their wild sex reversal system. Females are more muscular and more aggressive than males, and are socially dominant to them; rare traits in the mammalian world. And get this: females secrete more of certain testosterone-related hormones than the males do, producing muscles, aggression, and masculinized private parts that make it supremely difficult to tell the sex of a hyena. So high androgen levels would seem, again, to cause aggression and social dominance. But that's not the whole answer.

High in the hills above the University of California at Berkeley is the world's largest colony of spotted hyenas, massive bone-crunching beasts who fight each other for the chance to have their ears scratched by Laurence Frank, the zoologist who brought them over as infants from Kenya. Various scientists are studying their sex reversal system. The female hyenas are bigger and more muscular than the males and have the same weirdo genitals and elevated androgen levels as their female cousins back in the savanna. Everything is just as it is in the wild—except the social system. As those hyenas grew up, there was a very significant delay in the time it took for the females to begin socially dominating the males, even though the females were stoked on androgens. They had to grow up without the established social system to learn from.

When people first realize that genes have a great deal to do with behaviour—even subtle, complex,

human behaviour—they are often struck with an initial evangelical enthusiasm, placing a convert's faith in the genetic components of the story. This enthusiasm is typically reductive—because of physics envy, because reductionism is so impressive, because it would be so nice if there were a single gene (or hormone or neurotransmitter or part of the brain) responsible for everything. But even if you completely understood how genes regulate all the important physical factors involved in aggression—testosterone synthesis and secretion, the brain's testosterone receptors, the amygdala neurons and their levels of transmitters, the favourite colour of the hypothalamus—you still wouldn't be able to predict levels of aggression accurately in a group of normal individuals.

This is no mere academic subject. We are a fine species with some potential, yet we are racked by sickening amounts of violence. Unless we are hermits, we feel the threat of it, often every day, and should our leaders push the button, we will all be lost in a final global violence. But as we try to understand this feature of our sociality, it is critical to remember the limits of the biology. Knowing the genome, the complete DNA sequence, of some suburban teenager is never going to tell us why that kid, in his after-school chess club, has developed a particularly aggressive style with his bishops. And it certainly isn't going to tell us much about the teenager in some inner city hellhole who has taken to mugging people. 'Testosterone equals aggression' is inadequate for those who would offer a simple biological solution to the violent male. And 'testosterone equals aggression' is certainly inadequate for those who would offer the simple excuse that boys will be boys. Violence is more complex than a single hormone, and it is supremely rare that any of our behaviours can be reduced to genetic destiny. This is science for the bleeding-heart liberal: the genetics of behaviour is usually meaningless outside the context of the social factors and environment in which it occurs.

QUESTIONS FOR CRITICAL THOUGHT

1. Imagine waking up tomorrow and reading in the newspaper that a team of scientists has proven conclusively, emphatically, and beyond all doubt that all gender differences are based in biology and that men and women are biologically 'programmed' to behave as they do. How might this change the way you think about your life?

2. Sapolsky argues that attributing male aggression to testosterone is a misleading oversimplification of a complex set of biological processes. Do you know of any other biological processes that have been subject to similar oversimplification?

3. Why has so much time, money, and effort been invested in trying to determine whether gender differences are attributable to biology? Why has this particular research area been so active and so controversial?

4. What do you think about Buss's argument that physical asymmetries between the sexes in reproductive capacities have produced major differences in gendered behaviour?

5. Do you believe that the differences between males and females have been exaggerated, as Lorber does? Or do you believe that these differences have not been sufficiently appreciated? Or are you not sure?

PART II

Cultural Constructions of Gender

B iological evidence offers some explanation for the ubiquity of gender difference and gender inequality, but social scientific evidence modifies both the universality and the inevitability implicit in biological claims. Cross-cultural research suggests that gender and sexuality are far more changeable and variable than biological models would have predicted. If biological sex alone produced observed sex differences, Margaret Mead asked in the 1920s and 1930s, why did it produce such *different* definitions of masculinity and femininity in different cultures? In her path-breaking study, *Sex and Temperament in Three Primitive Societies*, Mead began an anthropological tradition of exploring and often celebrating the dramatically rich and varied cultural constructions of gender.

Anthropologists are likely to locate the origins of gender difference and gender inequality in a sex-based division of labour—the ways in which the basic provision and distribution of goods and resources are organized, and whether these goods and resources are material or more symbolic. They have found that when women's and men's spheres are most distinctly divided—where women and men do different things in different places—women's status tends to be lower than when men and women share both work and workplaces.

Peggy Reeves Sanday takes up this theme as she explores the ways in which gender inequality serves as a predictor for the likelihood that a culture will have either high or low rape rates. By locating the origins of rape in male domination—dramatic separation of spheres, gender inequality, low levels of male participation in child care—Sanday effectively lays to rest the facile biological argument that rape is the evolutionary sexual strategy of male 'failures' in reproduction.

Tabassum Ruby's work complicates the assumption that the cultural architecture separating women from men automatically means the devaluation of women. In her investigation of the *hijab*—the veil worn by some devout Muslim women—she demonstrates that what may superficially appear to be a symbol of separation is actually endowed with multiple meanings by the women who adopt it.

The veil is clearly a powerful symbol of gender, and is one of a class of symbols and rituals that mark out individuals as members of a particular gender. Many anthropologists have explored the function of various cultural rituals and representations in creating the symbolic justification for gender differences, including gender inequalities. For example, Gilbert Herdt describes a variety of 'coming out' processes in a variety of cultures, thus demonstrating (1) the connections between sexual identity and gender identity, and (2) the dramatic variation among those identities.

Gender differences and inequalities are also maintained in less visible forms than the symbols and rituals described above. Many institutions of everyday life prescribe and police 'appropriate' gendered behaviour, either overtly or subtly. Such gender policing may not be an explicit function of those institutions, but is nonetheless implicit in the way that the institutions operate. Margaret Hillyard Little and Ian Morrison provide a subtle and powerful look at the ways in which institutions make gender through their examination of the operations of Ontario's family welfare policy. Although welfare policies are meant to provide support for people in need, Hillyard Little and Morrison show that these policies also reinforce a particular form of gendered relations in which women are expected to depend financially on male partners.

Since Mead's day, one of the most important new insights from cultural anthropology has been that 'cultures' are not homogenous, monolithic entities that permit only one way of being masculine or one way of being feminine. Subcultures—constellations of people and practices that coexist with dominant or 'mainstream' culture—provide alternative ways to negotiate masculinity and femininity, as Dawn Currie and Deirdre Kelly find as they look at the lives of girls who participate in Vancouver's skateboard subculture. The world of skateboarding has its own norms of femininity, but the 'Park Gang' skater girls contest these expectations, and fight to participate in this subculture on their own terms.

CHAPTER 4

Rape-Prone versus Rape-Free Campus Cultures

Peggy Reeves Sanday

In *Fraternity Gang Rape* (Sanday, 1990) I describe the discourse, rituals, sexual ideology, and practices that make some fraternity environments rape-prone. The reaction of fraternity brothers to the book was decidedly mixed. Individuals in some chapters were motivated to rethink their initiation ritual and party behaviour. In sarcastic opinion pieces written for campus newspapers other people dismissed the book on the grounds that I was 'out to get' fraternities. As recently as December 1995, a young man wrote a letter to the editor of *The Washington Post* criticizing me for allegedly connecting hate speech and sexual crimes on college campuses with 'single-sex organizations'. Having set me up as the avenging witch, this young man then blames me for perpetuating the problem. My '[a]cross-the-board generalizations,' he claimed 'only make it more difficult for supportive men to become involved and stay active in the fight against these attacks.'

It is one of the tragedies of today's ideological warfare that this writer finds such an easy excuse to exempt himself from participating in the struggle to end violence against women. To make matters worse, his rationalization for opting out is based on a trumped-up charge. In the Introduction to my book, I carefully note that I am dealing with only 'a few of the many fraternities at U. and on several other campuses'. I state the case very clearly:

> The sexual aggression evident in these particular cases does not mean that sexual aggression is restricted to fraternities or that all fraternities indulge in sexual aggression. Sexist attitudes and the phallo-centric mentality associated with 'pulling train' have a long history in Western society. For example, venting homoerotic desire in the gang rape of women who are treated as male property is the subject of several biblical stories. Susan Brownmiller describes instances of gang rape by men in war and in street gangs. Male bonding that rejects women and commodifies sex is evident in many other social contexts outside of universities. Thus, it would be wrong to place blame solely on fraternities. However, it is a fact also that most of the reported incidents of 'pulling train' on campus have been associated with fraternities (Sanday, 1990: 19).

As an anthropologist interested in the particulars of sexual ideologies cross-culturally, I am very wary of generalizations of any sort. In 1975 I was very disturbed to read Susan Brownmiller's claim in the opening chapter of *Against Our Will* (1975) that rape is 'a conscious process of intimidation by which all men keep all women in a state of fear' (15). This statement was inconsistent with the compelling argument she presents in subsequent chapters that rape is culturally constructed and my own subsequent research on the sociocultural context of rape cross-culturally, which provided evidence of rape-free as well as rape-prone societies.

In this chapter, I will briefly summarize what we know about rape-prone fraternity cultures and contrast this information with what a rape-free context might look like. Since the available data are sparse my goal here is mostly programmatic, namely to encourage studies of intra-campus and cross-campus variation in the rates and correlates of sexual assault.

Rape-Prone Campus Environments

The concept of rape-free versus rape-prone comes from my study of 95 band and tribal societies in which I concluded that 47 per cent were rape-free and 18 per cent were rape-prone (Sanday, 1981). For this study I defined a rape-prone society as one in which the incidence of rape is reported by observers to be high, or rape is excused as a ceremonial expression of masculinity, or rape is an act by which men are allowed to punish or threaten women. I defined a rape-free society as one in which the act of rape is either infrequent or does not occur. I used the term 'rape-free' not to suggest that rape was entirely absent in a given society but as a label to indicate that sexual aggression is socially disapproved and punished severely. Thus, while there may be some men in all societies who might be potential rapists, there is abundant evidence from many societies that sexual aggression is rarely expressed.

Rape in tribal societies is part of a cultural configuration that includes interpersonal violence, male dominance, and sexual separation. Peallo-centrism is a dominant psycho-sexual symbol in these societies and men 'use the penis to dominate their women' as Yolanda and Robert Murphy say about the Mundurucu (Sanday, 1981: 25). Rape-prone behaviour is associated with environmental insecurity and females are turned into objects to be controlled as men struggle to retain or to gain control of their environment. Behaviours and atti-tudes prevail that separate the sexes and force men into a posture of proving their manhood. Sexual violence is one of the ways in which men remind themselves that they are superior. As such, rape is part of a broader struggle for control in the face of difficult circumstances. Where men are in harmony with their environment, rape is usually absent.

In *Fraternity Gang Rape* I suggest that rape-prone attitudes and behaviour on American cam-puses are adopted by insecure young men who bond through homophobia and 'getting sex'. The homoeroticism of their bonding leads them to display their masculinity through heterosexist dis-plays of sexual performance. The phallus becomes the dominant symbol of discourse. A fraternity brother described to me the way in which he felt accepted by the brothers while he was a pledge.

> We . . . liked to share ridiculously exaggerated sexual boasting, such as our mythical 'Sixteen Kilometre Flesh-Weapon'. . . . By including me in this perpetual, hysterical banter and sharing laughter with me, they showed their affection for me. I felt happy, confident, and loved. This really helped my feelings of loneli-ness and my fear of being sexually unappeal-ing. We managed to give ourselves a satisfying substitute for sexual relations. We acted out all of the sexual tensions between us as brothers on a verbal level. Women, women everywhere, feminists, homosexuality, etc., all provided the material for the jokes (Sanday, 1990: 140–1).

Getting their information about women and sex from pornography, some brothers don't see anything wrong with forcing a woman, especially if she's drunk. After the 1983 case of alleged gang rape I describe in the book, one of the partici-pants—a virgin at the time—told a news reporter:

> We have this Select TV in the house, and there's soft porn on every midnight. All the guys watch it and talk about it and stuff, and [gang banging] didn't seem that odd because it's something that you see and hear about all the time. I've heard stories from other frater-nities about group sex and trains and stuff like that. It was just like, you know, so this is what I've heard about, this is what it's like. . . . (Sanday, 1990: 34).

Watching their buddies have sex is another favour-ite activity in rape-prone campus environments. A woman is targeted at a party and brothers are informed; they then hide out on the roof outside the window, or secret themselves in a closet, or look through holes in the wall. Since the goal is to supply a live pornography show for their buddies, the perpetrators in these cases may easily overlook a woman's ability to consent. They certainly don't seek her consent to being watched. It is assumed that if she came to the house to party she is pre-pared for anything that might happen, especially if she gets drunk. On some campuses I have been told that this practice is called 'beaching' or 'whaling'.

Taking advantage of a drunk woman is widely accepted. As a group of brothers said in a taped conversation in which they discussed the young woman in the 1983 case:

> 'She was drugged.'
> 'She drugged herself.'
> 'Yeah, she was responsible for her condition, and that just leaves her wide open . . . so to speak.'
> [laughter] (Sanday, 1990: 119)

In a 1990 talk show—on which I appeared with the victim of gang rape—a young man from a local university called up and admitted that the goal of all parties at his fraternity was 'To get 'em drunk and go for it.' In 1991, I read an article entitled 'Men, Alcohol, and Manipulation', in a campus newspaper from still another university. The author reported hearing several members of a fraternity talking with the bartender about an upcoming social event as follows:

Brother 1:   Hey, don't forget—make the women's drinks really strong.

Bartender: Yeah, I won't forget. Just like usual.

Brother 2:   We need to get them good and drunk.

Bartender: Don't worry, we'll take care of it.

Brother 3:   That'll loosen up some of those inhibitions.

This is the kind of discourse I would classify as rape-prone.

Getting a woman drunk to have sex in a show staged for one's buddies is tragically evident in the testimony heard in the St Johns' sex case tried in Queens, New York, in 1991–2. This case involved six members of the St Johns University lacrosse team who were indicted for acts ranging from unlawful imprisonment and sexual abuse to sodomy. A seventh defendant pleaded guilty and agreed to testify for immunity (see Sanday, 1996, for a description of the case and the subsequent trial). From the testimony in the case and interviews with the complainant and members of the prosecution team, I reconstructed the following scenario.

A young, naive woman student, whom I call Angela (pseudonym), accepted a ride home from school from a male friend, Michael. On the way, he stopped at the house he shares with members of the St Johns lacrosse team to get gas money and invited her inside. At first she refused to go in but upon his insistence accepted the invitation. Inside she met his roommates. Left alone in the third floor bedroom, she accepted a drink from Michael:

The drink tasted terrible. It was bitter and stung her throat. When she asked what was in it, Michael said he put a little vodka in it. When she explained that she never drank, because drinking made her sick, Michael didn't listen. Then she tried to tell him that she hadn't eaten anything since lunch, but this did not move him. 'Vodka is a before dinner drink,' he explained, insisting that she drink it.

Finally, she gave into his pressure and downed the contents of the first cup in a few gulps because of the bitter taste. When she finished, Michael went over to the refrigerator and brought back a large container, which he said was orange soda with vodka. He placed the container on the floor beside her feet. When Michael poured another cup, she told him, 'But Michael, I couldn't finish the first one. I don't think I will be able to finish another.' Michael said again: 'It's only vodka. It can't do anything to you, Angela.' He also said, 'You know, Angela, in college everyone does something, something wild they can look back on.'

'Something wild?' Angela asked quizzically.

'Something wild,' Michael said again. 'Something you can look back on and talk about later in life.' With the beer can that he was holding in his hand but never drank from, he hit her cup and said, 'Here's to college life.' Later, Angela blamed herself for accepting the drinks from Michael. She was caught between wanting to please the host and wanting to assert her own needs. She had tried to please him by finishing the first drink. Now, she drank the second.

Then, he poured a third drink. When she balked at drinking this one, he started getting upset and annoyed. He told her it was a special drink, made just for her. He accused her of making him waste it. He started pushing the drink up to her mouth. He put his hands over the cup and pushed it to her lips. He said, 'Oh Angela, don't make me waste it. It's only vodka. A little vodka can't do anything to you.'

By now, Angela felt dizzy and her hands were shaking. She felt lost, unable to move. She had spent a lifetime doing what she was told to avoid being punished. Here was Michael upset with her because she didn't want the drink he had made for her. She thought to herself, 'If he wants me to drink it, I'll drink it for him.' After she drank most of the third cup, Michael went to put the container back. Her head was spinning and she began to feel really sick, like she was going to vomit. She tried to tell Michael that she was sick, but he didn't seem interested in how she was feeling.

Michael sat next to her and massaged her shoulder. She would never forget his pseudo-seductive voice. She hardly knew him, and here he was talking to her like he really cared for her. It was so obviously a put-on, she was shocked by the insincerity. He kept telling her, 'You need to relax. You are too tense. If you relax, you will feel better.' She tried to get up but she was too weak and she fell back down (Sanday, 1996: 11–12).

Testimony in the case revealed that after Angela passed out from Michael's drinks, three house members stood on the landing and watched as Michael engaged in oral sodomy. After Michael left the house, these three took their turns while visitors invited over from another lacrosse team house watched. At the trial these visitors testified that they left the room when Angela woke up and started screaming. One of the lead prosecutors speculated that they left because they realized only then that she was not consenting. They did not understand that the law applies to using drugs and alcohol as it does to using force.

Cross-Campus Variation in Rape and Sexual Coercion

In his paper, Boeringer reports that 55.7 per cent of the males in his study at a large southeastern university obtained sex by verbal harassment (i.e., 'threatening to end a relationship unless the victim consents to sex, falsely professing love, or telling the victim lies to render her more sexually receptive', the variable labelled Coercion). One-quarter of the males in Boeringer's study reported using drugs or alcohol to obtain sex (Drugs/Alcohol) and 8.6 per cent of the sample reported at least one use of force or threatened force to obtain sex (Rape).

Schwartz and Nogrady found a much lower incidence of sexual coercion and assault at their research site, a large mid-western university. These authors (private communication) reported that 18.1 per cent of the 116 males in their sample reported some form of unwanted sex: sex by pressure (6.9 per cent); forced sex play/attempted rape (5.2 per cent); or completed rape (6.0 per cent). Of the 177 women interviewed 58.6 per cent reported some form of unwanted sex; sex by pressure (24.1 per cent); forced sex play/attempted rape (14.4 per cent); and completed rape (20.1 per cent).

The effect of fraternities is quite different on the two campuses. Boeringer found that fraternity men reported a higher overall use of coercion short of physical force to obtain sex. According to Boeringer, 'fraternity members engage in significantly greater levels of sexual assault through drugging or intoxicating women to render them incapable of consent or refusal' (9). Fraternity members are also more likely than independents to use 'nonassaultative sexual coercion', or verbal pressure. 'While not criminal in nature,' Boeringer points out, 'these verbally coercive tactics are nonetheless disturbing in that they suggest a more adversarial view of sexuality in which one should use deceit and guile to "win favors" from a woman' (10). From his study, Boeringer concludes that 'fraternity members are disproportionately involved in some forms of campus sexual aggression.' Like the prosecutor in the St John's case mentioned above, he suggests that in all likelihood the process of 'working a yes out' which I describe (Sanday, 1990: 113) is viewed by fraternity members as a 'safer path to gaining sexual access to a reluctant, non-consenting woman than use of physical force' (12).

Schwartz and Nogrady found no effect of fraternity membership. The most important predictor of sexual victimization in their study involves alcohol. It is not drinking per se that they found important, but whether or not a male perceives that his friends approve of getting a woman drunk for the purpose of having sex (the Approve variable). Also important is whether a male reports that he has friends that actually engage in this behaviour (the Get Drunk variable). The drinking variable that is the most influential in predicting a man's reported sexual assault is the intensity of his drinking, that is, the number of drinks he consumes when he goes out drinking (Drinks). Thus, the authors conclude that 'the level of the perceived male peer support system for exploiting women through alcohol, plus the amount of alcohol actually consumed by men when they drink, are the primary predictors of whether they will report themselves as sexual victimizers of women.'

The differences reported by Boeringer and Schwartz and Nogrady suggest not only that fraternities vary with respect to rape-prone behaviours but also that campuses vary with respect to overall rates of sexual assault. The latter result suggests that we need to look at cross-campus variation as well as at intra-campus variation. There are several problems that need to be addressed before either intra-campus or cross-campus variation can be established. First, in studying intra-campus variation we must be careful in reaching conclusions about the effect of such factors as drinking intensity or fraternity membership because the dependent variable is frequently lifetime prevalence rates rather than incidence in the past year.

Regarding cross-campus variation, there is the problem of comparability of studies. Boeringer (private communication), for example, measures prevalence rates in his study, while Schwartz and Nogrady (private communication) measure

incidence. Since incidence rates are always lower, we cannot conclude that the campuses studied by these authors are much different. Additionally, as noted by Schwartz and Nogrady as well as by Koss (1993), victimization rates from one study to another may not be comparable because of different methodologies, definitions, questions, and sampling procedures.

Nevertheless, some trends can be noticed. The available evidence against variation is seen in the fact that Koss's 15 per cent completed rape prevalence rate in the national study of 32 campuses is replicated by other studies of college students on particular campuses. Koss and Cook (1993: 109) note, for example, that estimates of completed rape frequency in the 12 per cent range have been reported for two campuses and estimates 'as high or higher than 12 per cent for unwanted intercourse have been reported in more than 10 additional studies lacking representative sampling methods'. According to these authors 'there are no studies that have reported substantially lower or higher rates of rape among college students.'

Evidence for variation comes from Koss's analysis of the relationship of prevalence rates to the institutional parameters used to design the sample (Koss, 1988). She found that rates varied by region and by governance of the institution. Rates were twice as high at private colleges and major universities (14 per cent and 17 per cent respectively) than they were at religiously affiliated institutions (7 per cent).

Ethnicity of the respondent (but, interestingly not the respondent's family income) was also associated with prevalence rates. More white women (16 per cent) reported victimization than did Hispanic (12 per cent), black (10 per cent), or Asian women (7 per cent). These figures were almost reversed for men. Rape was reported by 4 per cent of white men, 10 per cent of black men, 7 per cent of Hispanic men, and 2 per cent of Asian men. Prevalence rates reported by men also differed by region of the country. More men in the Southeast region (6 per cent) admitted to raping compared with men in the Plains states (3 per cent) and those in the West (2 per cent) (Koss, 1988).

Intriguing evidence for cross-campus variation in rape rates and related variables comes from Koss's national study of 32 campuses. Using Koss's data I looked at prevalence and incidence rates for each of 30 campuses in her study (2 campuses were excluded because of the amount of missing information). The results show a wide discrepancy when campuses are compared. For example the campus percentages of males admitting that they have used alcohol or force to obtain sex (Koss's 1988 11 rape variables) range from 0–10 per cent. Campus percentages of males who admit to perpetrating unwanted sex in the past year (as opposed to since the age of 14) range from 6–22 per cent. The latter percentages are higher because I computed them using all the sexual experience questions (excluding the two authority questions). Since the latter percentages are based on a question that measures incidence ('How many times in the past school year?') the results provide a measure of an dependent variable that can be compared with drinking intensity.

The Koss survey includes two questions that might be taken as measures of drinking intensity. Both questions are asked in such a fashion as to measure drinking intensity in the past year. One asks 'How often do you drink to the point of intoxication or drunkenness?'; the other asks 'On a typical drinking occasion, how much do you usually drink?' The campus percentages of males checking the most extreme categories of the first question (1–2 or more times a week) ranges from 1–24 per cent. The campus percentages of males checking the most extreme categories of the second question (more than 5 or 6 cans of beer or other alcoholic beverages) ranges from 6–71 per cent. Since all studies—Schwartz, Boeringer, Koss, and Gaines (1993)—are unanimous on the effect of drinking this information, perhaps more than any other, is suggestive of variation in the rape-prone nature of campus environments.

The Concept of a Rape-Free Society

Assuming that we could identify campuses on which both males and females reported a low incidence of rape and/or unwanted sex, the next question would be whether there is a significant difference in the sexual culture on these campuses compared to the more rape-prone campuses. My cross-cultural research which demonstrated differences in the character of heterosexual interaction in rape-free as opposed to rape-prone societies would suggest that the answer to this question is yes. The outstanding feature of rape-free societies is the ceremonial importance of women and the respect accorded to the contribution women make to social continuity, a respect which places men and women in relatively balanced power spheres. Rape-free societies are characterized by sexual equality and the notion that the sexes are complementary. Although the sexes may not perform the same duties or have the same rights or privileges, each is indispensable to the activities of the other.

Since 1981 when this research was published, I have spent approximately 24 months (extended over a period of 14 years) doing ethnographic research among the Minangkabau, a rape-free Indonesian society. I chose the Minangkabau because of social factors that conformed with my profile of rape-free societies. The Minangkabau are the largest and most modern matrilineal society in the world today. Women play an undisputed role in Minangkabau symbol system and daily life, especially in the villages. Among the most populous of the ethnic groups of Indonesia, the Minangkabau are not an isolated tribal society in some far off corner of the world. Banks, universities, and modern governmental buildings are found in two of the major cities of West Sumatra, the traditional homeland of the Minangkabau people. At the major universities, it is not uncommon to find Minangkabau PhD's trained in the United States. People own cars and travel by bus throughout the province. Most children go to local schools and, increasingly, many attend college.

The challenge facing me when I went to West Sumatra was first to find out whether the incidence of rape was low and, if so, to crack the cultural code that made it so. In the early years there was ample evidence from police reports and from interviews conducted all over the province that this was a rape-free society. Ethnographic research conducted in several villages provided confirmation. This research demonstrated that women are the mainstays of village life. The all-important family rice fields are inherited through the female line. Husbands live in their wives' houses. It is believed that this is the way it should be, because otherwise in the event of a divorce women and children would be left destitute. The main reason given for the matrilineal inheritance of property is that since women bear the infant and raise the child it is in keeping with the laws of nature to give women control of the ancestral property so that they will have the wherewithal to house and nurture the young.

Missing from the Minangkabau conception of sexuality is any show of interest in sex for the sake of sex alone. Sex is neither a commodity nor a notch in the male belt in this society. A man's sense of himself is not predicated by his sexual functioning. Although aggression is present, it is not linked to sex nor is it deemed a manly trait. The Minangkabau have yet to discover sex as a commodity or turn it into a fetish.

There is a cultural category for rape, which is defined as 'forced sex' and is punishable by law. Rape is conceived as something that happens in the wild, which places men who rape beyond the pale of society. In answer to my questions regarding the relative absence of rape among them compared to the United States, Minangkabau informants replied that rape was impossible in their society because custom, law, and religion forbade it and punished it severely. In the years that I worked in West Sumatra, I heard of only two cases of rape in the village where I lived. One case involved a group of males who ganged up on a young, retarded woman. In this case the leader

of the group hanged himself the next day out of fear of avenging villagers. The rest of the assailants went to jail. The second case involved a local woman and a Japanese soldier during the Japanese occupation of the Second World War and after. To this day people remember the case and talk about the horror of the Japanese occupation.

In the past few years, Indonesia's entrance into the global economy has been accompanied by an amazing shift in the eroticization of popular culture seen on TV. In 1995 the signs that this culture was filtering into Minangkabau villages were very evident. To the extent that commodification and eroticization breaks down the cultural supports for its matrilineal social system, the Minangkabau sexual culture will also change. Indeed, today in the provincial capital some argue that the Minangkabau are not rape-free.

During my last field trip in 1995, I heard of many more reports of rape in the provincial capital. In the early 1990s, for example, there was a widely publicized acquaintance gang rape of a young woman by a group of boys. Interviewing court officers in the capital, I was told that this was the only case of its kind. Compared with similar cases in the United States, such as the St Johns case, the outcome was still very different. While the St Johns defendants were either acquitted or got probation after pleading guilty, all the defendants in the Sumatran case were convicted and sent to jail. But, one may well ask whether the criminal justice system will continue to convict defendants as tolerance for sexual coercion begins to permeate popular beliefs.

Rape-Free Campus Cultures

A rape-free campus is relatively easy to imagine, but equally hard to find. Based on anecdotal information one candidate comes to mind. On this campus everyone—administrators, faculty, and students—are on a first-name basis, which makes the atmosphere more egalitarian than most campuses. Decision-making is by consensus and interpersonal interaction is guided by an ethic of respect for the individual. Those who are disrespectful of others are ostracized as campus life is motivated by a strong sense of community and the common good. No one group (such as fraternities, males, or athletes) dominates the social scene. Sexual assault is a serious offense treated with suspension or expulsion. Homophobic, racist, and sexist attitudes are virtually nonexistent. Individuals bond together in groups drawn together by mutual interests, not to turn against others. Interviews suggest that the incidence of unwanted sex on this campus is low, however this must be corroborated by a campus-wide survey.

For information on a rape-free fraternity culture I turn to a description offered by a student who wrote a mini-ethnography on his fraternity for a class project. Another brother in the same fraternity corroborated his description after reading the ethnography and adding additional information. In the following, the fraternity is referred to by the pseudonym QRS. With their permission, the fraternity brothers are identified by name.

Noel Morrison and Josh Marcus recognize that fraternities on their campus (called U.) 'propagate sexist attitudes and provide a breeding ground for insecure acts of sexism, racism, and homophobia'. According to Noel, U.'s fraternities 'tend to be self-segregating entities which seek to maintain the inferior social position of women and minority students through exclusion' and social intolerance. QRS, however, consciously fights against this norm.

QRS is one of the oldest fraternities at U., going back at least 100 years. It was like all other fraternities at U. until 1977 when it was almost forced to disband due to insufficient numbers. At that time, a group of nine first-year males pledged as a group knowing that their numbers would give them control of house decisions. They exercised this control by rewriting the house constitution and initiation rituals. Today the brothers are proud to say that they are 'not a real fraternity'. Interestingly, although both Joel and Noel treasure their lives in QRS (because of the fun, companionship

of respected friends, and community the house offers), both feel that fraternities should be abolished.

Partly as a defense mechanism and partly to underscore their difference, QRS brothers stigmatize members of other fraternities as 'jarheads'. The word 'jarhead' is used to refer to the 'loud, obnoxious, sexist, racist, homophobic' members of U.'s fraternities. Most of the brothers in QRS do not participate in the campus inter-fraternity council and prefer to see themselves as 'a group of friends', rather than as a fraternity, and their house as 'a place to have concerts'. Parties are always open to anyone and are either free to everyone or everyone pays, contrary to parties at other houses in which men pay and women are admitted for free.

At QRS heavy drinking is not a requisite for membership and is not a part of initiation. There are no drinking games and binge drinking does not occur. While some brothers drink to get drunk more than once a week, most don't. At parties there are always brothers who watch out for women or house members who have had too much to drink. Josh stressed that 'it is clearly not acceptable for someone to take advantage of a drunk woman, because that's rape.' There is no talk in the house about getting a girl drunk to have sex, he says. Members are very aware that where there is heavy drinking someone can be taken advantage of. If a female passes out or is very drunk she is watched or escorted home. Both Josh and Noel remember an incident during a party in the fraternity next door, in which several members of QRS came to the aid of a young woman whose shirt was above her waist and who had passed out on their porch, left there perhaps by friends from the party who had deserted her. Their intervention may have saved her life. When they were unable to get her to talk, they took her to the emergency room of a nearby hospital only to learn that she was in a coma and her heart had stopped. Fortunately, they were in time and she responded to treatment.

Women are not seen as sex objects in the house, but as friends. Unlike other fraternities at U., there is no distinction drawn between 'girlfriends' and friends and there are no 'party girls'. Noel says that when he was rushing he would often hear women referred to as 'sluts' in other fraternities. However, at QRS this is unheard of. According to Josh, a brother who acted 'inappropriately' with a woman would be severely reprimanded, perhaps even expelled from the fraternity. The brothers are not afraid of strong women. There are women's studies students who are regulars at the house, along with outspoken feminists and activists. Noel quotes one of them:

> I guess there're a few brothers who make sexist jokes, but I don't know how seriously people take them. I remember last year in the middle of midterms I was studying late at night and was feeling sick and tired, and in a span of about five minutes, four people offered their beds to me, not as a sexual thing at all, but just because they cared.

One QRS brother started the Men's Association for Change and Openness (MAChO) and is an active participant in U's student peer-counselling group for sexual health. One brother displays a 'Refuse and Resist' sticker on his door, proclaiming, 'Date rape: cut it out or cut it off.' In a 1993 pamphlet advertising QRS as the site of the National Anarchist gathering, the brothers wrote 'Although QRS is a frat, it is generally a friendly place, along with being a safe haven for women.'

Most interesting about QRS is its acceptance of homosexuality and bisexuality. Homophobia does not become the basis for males to prove their virility to one another. Because of its openness about sex and acceptance of homosexuality, QRS has earned the reputation on campus of being 'the gay frat' or 'faggot house'. Josh comments on this reputation and what it means to him:

> QRS's attitudes about homosexuality are complex, but fundamentally tolerant and respectful. Some brothers revel in rumours that

we are the 'gay frat'. It is rumored that a few years ago a few of the brothers were involved sexually, and one of our most involved alumni is homosexual.

Although most fraternities have had or have a few homosexual brothers, this honest acceptance of homosexuality is unusual. QRS brothers are proud of being called the 'gay frat'. Evidence of this is the humorous statement in the letters given prospective pledges offering bids, which ends with the phrase 'we are all gay'.

Conclusion

The first step in the struggle against 'hidden rape', which began in the late sixties with consciousness raising groups (see Sanday, 1996: Chapter 8), was to recognize the problem and speak out against it. The next step was to change outmoded rape laws and assess the causes and frequency of sexual violence against women. Mary Koss's national survey of 1985 demonstrated that one in four women will experience rape or attempted rape in her lifetime. Since the eighties many other surveys have replicated her findings. The search for causes has been the subject of numerous studies, including those represented in this volume.

The next step is to go beyond the causes and study solutions. One approach would be to find naturally occurring rape-free environments on today's college campuses. QRS is one example. No rape-free campuses have been identified by research, yet I have heard descriptions from students that lead me to believe that such campuses exist. Identifying such campuses and seeking out environments like QRS is the next step for research. In this paper I have identified the kinds of problems such research must address. First, it is necessary to obtain incidence as well as prevalence data. Secondly, we need more subtle measures of the kinds of sociocultural correlates that have been discussed in this paper: drinking intensity; using pornography to learn about sex rather than talking with one's partner; bragging about sexual conquests; setting women up to display one's masculinity to other men; hetero-sexism; homophobia; and using pornography as a guide to female sexuality. Finally, we need to develop a consensus on the criteria for labelling a campus either rape-free or rape-prone. If at least one in five women on a given campus say they have experienced unwanted sex in the last year, I would label the campus rape-prone. However, others may want to propose different criteria. Once a consensus is reached, the movement to make our campuses safe for women might include identifying rape-free and rape-prone campuses.

Note

This article has benefitted from the comments of Mary P. Koss. I am also grateful to Koss for supplying me with the data on her 1986 study of 32 campuses. Martin D. Schwartz and Scot B. Boerginer graciously supplied me with additional data from their studies and answered my many questions. Noel Morrison played an important role by giving me permission to summarize his description of his fraternity. John Marcus, a brother in the same fraternity, was also helpful in corroborating Noel's observations and supplying a few of his own.

References

Brownmiller, S. 1975. *Against Our Will: Men, Women, and Rape*. New York: Simon and Schuster.

Koss, M.P. 1988. 'Hidden Rape: Sexual Aggression and Victimization in a National Sample of Students in Higher Education', in A.W. Burgess, ed., *Rape and Sexual Assault II*, pp. 3–25. New York: Garland.

———. 1993. 'Rape: Scope, Impact, Interventions, and Public Policy Responses', *American Psychologist* (October): 1062–9.

Koss, M.P., and J.A. Gaines. 1993. 'The Prediction of Sexual Aggression by Alcohol Use, Athletic Participation, and Fraternity Affiliation', *Journal of Interpersonal Violence* 8: 94–108.

Koss, M.P., and S.L. Cook. 1993. 'Facing the Facts: Date and Acquaintance Rape are Significant Problems for Women', in R.J. Gelles and D.R. Loseke, eds, *Current Controversies on Family Violence*, pp. 104–19. Newbury Park, CA: Sage.

Sanday, P.R. 1981. 'The Socio-cultural Context of Rape: A Cross-Cultural Study', *Journal of Social Issues* 37: 5–27.

———. 1990. *Fraternity Gang Rape: Sex, Brotherhood and Privilege on Campus*. New York: New York University Press.

———. 1996. *A Woman Scorned: Acquaintance Rape on Trial*. New York: Doubleday.

CHAPTER 5

Listening to the Voices of *Hijab*

Tabassum F. Ruby

With the increasing number of *muhajibah*[1] around the globe, the issue of the *hijab* has become a topic of debate among Muslim and non-Muslim scholars. Researchers such as Nasser (1999) have pointed out that the 'new *hijab* phenomenon' initially began two decades ago in countries such as Egypt, and Muslim women around the globe have since embraced the practice. In Canada, the *hijab* is often seen as a symbol of Muslim women's oppression and a restriction to their mobility, particularly in the media.[2] Many Muslim women, however, claim that the *hijab* empowers them in numerous ways: making their identities[3] distinct; taking control of their bodies; and giving them a sense of belonging to a wider Muslim world. Thus, the discussion on the *hijab* is contentious, revealing the complexity of the issue.

The intricacy of the issue of *hijab*, nonetheless, is not limited to whether the *hijab* oppresses a Muslim woman or liberates her. Most often the Muslim community and the dominant culture recognize the *hijab* as clothing that is used to cover the female body (i.e., a headscarf and/or long coat). This research, however, indicates that immigrant Muslim women[4] perceive the *hijab* in a variety of ways and associate it with diverse meanings that range from covering of the head to modest behaviour. As a result, the participants often negotiate their places in the larger community as well as in the Muslim community, because they feel pressure whether wearing or not wearing the *hijab*.

Methodology and Sampling

There is a small population of immigrant Muslim women in Saskatoon (the geographical location of my research), and most of them know each other. I have personal contact with many of these Muslim women, and through the use of the 'snowball technique', I was able to identify participants. The 'snowball' or 'chain' method occurs when 'sampling identifies cases of interest from people who know other people with relevant cases' (Bradshaw and Straford, 2000: 44). In recruiting the sample, the Islamic Association of Saskatchewan played a particularly important role. Along with Friday prayers, weekly gatherings in the mosque facilitated meetings with diverse groups of women and provided opportunities to talk with them about my research project.[5]

Using focus groups, I interviewed 14 women who came from 12 different countries. I conducted three interview sessions and divided my participants into two groups of five based on whether or not they wore a headscarf. I conducted one interview session with participants who did not wear a headscarf and one with those who did. Each interview session was 90 minutes long. My third group consisted of a mix of participants, some of whom wore the headscarf and some who did not. The session with the mixed group, which had four participants, lasted 110 minutes. With the participants' permission, the interviews were audiotaped.

In order to protect the anonymity of my participants, personal details such as place of birth, age, and occupation cannot be fully described here, but general characteristics are as follows. The participants' countries of origin include Afghanistan, Bangladesh, Brunei, Burma, Egypt, Guyana, India, Iran, Jordan, Kuwait, Pakistan, and Turkey. The women's ages range from just under 20 to 60. The participants' occupations vary from physician to accountant, writer to insurance officer, and students. Their immigrant experiences range from arrival in Canada within the last few years to immigration more than two decades ago. Some informants have lived in other cities such as Toronto and Edmonton; others have resided in Saskatoon since they emigrated. Six participants did not wear the *hijab*, and eight were *muhajibah*. As the overall number of participants is quite small, the results of this study may best serve as a 'case study'.

Before illustrating the participants' views about the *hijab,* I would like to outline some of the basic concepts of the *hijab* in the Muslim context, because many participants referred to them. The Qur'anic verses that are traditionally cited to describe women's dress code are as follows:

> And say to the believing women that they should lower their gaze and guard their modesty, that they should not display their beauty and ornaments except what (must ordinarily) appear thereof; that they should draw their veils over their bosoms and not

display their beauty . . . And that they should not strike their feet in order to draw attention to their hidden ornaments (24:31).

O Prophet! Tell thy wives and daughters, and the believing women, that they should cast their outer garments over their persons (when abroad): this is most convenient, that they should be known (as such) and not molested. And God is oft forgiving, most merciful (33:59).

The scholars' explanation that women should cover their bodies is not only based on the interpretation of the cited verses, but also on *hadith*[6] literature. However, many *hadiths* that are often cited as justification for women's covering have been challenged, with researchers arguing that these *hadiths* are not authentic[7] (*sahih*'). Ibe-al-Jawzi (d. 1201), as cited in Roald (2001), argues that women should stay at home and, if they need to go out, should wear the *hijab* because they can cause *fitnah* (temptation).[8] Ibe-al-Jawzi bases his argument on a *hadith* that reads: the Prophet says that 'the best mosque for woman is her home.' Contrary to Ibe-al-Jawzi, however, Al-Ghazzali (1989) argues that there are many *hadiths* that provide evidence that women used to pray at the mosque during the Prophet's time and that those *hadiths* are stronger than the one cited (Roald, 2001).

Khaled (2001) argues that the debate on the *hijab* among classical and contemporary scholars is fundamentally rooted in the previously mentioned idea of *fitnah*[9] (temptation). He states that the Qur'an uses the word *fitnah* for non-sexual temptations, such as 'money and severe trials and tribulations' (Khaled, 2001: 233). Nonetheless, scholars often associate the notion of *fitnah* with women's sexuality, which is signalled, in part, by an uncovered appearance in public. Khaled writes that women are prohibited from attending mosques or driving cars, and that 'every item and colour of clothing is analyzed under the doctrine of *fitnah*' (Khaled, 2001: 235). He argues, however, that these restrictions are misplaced, and that

fitnah reflects men's fantasies of uncontrollable lust, which they have associated with women's sexuality.

Khaled further argues that the injunction that women need to cover their bodies to avoid bringing on *fitnah* is not in harmony with Islam's message; the Qur'an does not use the word to imply women's temptation, and does not view women's bodies as *fitnah*. Moreover, Islam requires lowering of the gaze and guarding modesty for both men and women; thus, a covered female body will not lead to a modest society (the essence of the *hijab*) until men behave in a similar manner.

What is the *Hijab*? The Discussion among the Participants

That is a question that I ask myself (Almas).[10]

The extent to which Muslim women should cover their bodies is not only a controversial issue among scholars, but also emerged as a contentious matter among the participants in this study, where the meanings of the *hijab* are interpreted in a variety of ways. The *hijab* in the form of physical garments signifies headscarves (as worn by some of the women interviewed), but also modest clothing that does not include the covering of the head. Equally important, the *hijab* in this research also refers to modest behaviour.

Some participants indicated that although the Qur'an requires head covering, 'the instructions are not clear, and people have diverse views about the *hijab*.' Scholars such as Asad (1980) have pointed out that there are sound reasons for not stating precise rules regarding the covering of women's bodies. He argues that human circumstances vary over time, and that the verses are moral guidelines that could be observed against the ever-changing background of time and social environment. Similarly, Dilshad', one of the participants, recognized the purpose of the vague regulations of Islam, and stated that the religion accommodates people's cultural differences. She remarked:

Islam defines certain [rules] very strictly, because you have to follow them throughout your life. Even till the end of the world . . . these rules will remain the same. But some things are [a] little flexible, because you have to adjust with time, culture, and country.

The idea of the *hijab* with reference to head-scarves or covering of the body, however, is only one element of the *hijab*. Most participants reported that physical articles such as clothing would not serve the purpose of the *hijab* unless women *believe* in the practice. Islam requires lowering the gaze, avoiding seeing what is forbidden, and not inviting the male gaze. For these reasons, many participants mentioned that whether a woman wears a headscarf or not, modest behaviour is a fundamental aspect of the *hijab*. Raheelah, for example, remarked that the *hijab* is not limited to head covering; conducting life unpretentiously is also significant in fulfilling the requirements of the *hijab*. 'To me,' she stated, 'the *hijab* is not just covering of your head . . . it is your life, your portrayal of yourself as a person. As long as you dress decently, and you do not draw attention to yourself, that to me is the *hijab*.' Raheelah does not wear a headscarf, but her concept of the *hijab* dictates modesty of dress, such as not wearing miniskirts or tight dresses that could be seen as bringing attention to oneself. She also believes that moral behaviour is part of the *hijab*. This indicates that she sees the *hijab* not as a material garment, but as an ethical belief. Raheelah then, while not wearing the headscarf, feels that she is maintaining the boundaries of the *hijab*.

Why or Why Not Wear the *Hijab*?

It keeps the society pure in many, many ways (Dilshad').

Following the discussion of the concept of the *hijab,* some participants mentioned the rationale of the Qur'an in requiring the *hijab*. For example,

Farza'nah' argues that the *hijab*[11] sets a boundary between men and women that helps them avoid premarital relationships, which are not permissible in Islam. She commented that a woman's beauty needs to be concealed, because beauty brings a 'lot of other things . . . freedom, the kind that we see here'. Farza'nah' identifies the *hijab* as a means of minimizing easy interaction between men and women, which in turn promotes chastity. However, according to Farza'nah's views, chastity is not restricted to women's behaviour, but it is extended to society, where women's modesty grants chaste society.

Contrary to Farza'nah's opinion, Dilshad' did not think that women's bodies should be covered simply because they are eye-catching. She believes that the *hijab* is a tool that diminishes sexual appeal and, as a result, promotes a virtuous public domain. She stated that women need to wear the *hijab* because 'it keeps the society pure in many, many ways'. Despite the seeming differences about the attractiveness of women's bodies, both Farza'nah' and Dilshad' linked the *hijab* with women's sexuality. Underlying their views is a concept of women's bodies as either tempting (their beauty will seduce men) or polluting (their immodest behaviour can corrupt society). The status of women's bodies, in turn, is seen as a sign of the moral status of the nation, because women are perceived as the cultural carriers of their society (Yuval-Davis, 1994). Thus, a chaste, moral, or pure society is dependent upon the condition of women's bodies according to Farza'nah' and Dilshad'.

Farza'nah's and Dilshad's reasoning also indicates that because they see women's bodies as *fitna,* their views contradict the Qur'an as discussed earlier. In verse 33:59, already mentioned, the Qur'an states that women should cover themselves so as not to be 'molested'. The context of the verse indicates that at the time this verse was revealed, men treated slave women very disrespectfully, and there were incidents in Medina[12] when the men assaulted Muslim women. The offenders' excuse was that they did not know that these were Muslim women. In order to protect Muslim women, it was stated that they should dress modestly so that they could be recognized. Implied in the Qur'an is the idea that men are the aggressors and women the victims, whereas according to these participants, women are the actors and men the victims (Roald, 2001). Thus, as Roald (2001) points out, many Muslims have turned the Qur'anic view around to suggest that women are responsible for a corrupted and unchaste society.

While some women wear the *hijab* because they feel responsible for a moral society, others wear it because it offers them respect, dignity, and protection. Almas, for example, is just under 20 and away from her country of origin, as well as her family, for the first time. She reported that because she is living by herself, the *hijab* has become a security measure, that men are respectful towards *muhajibah* and do not treat them like sexual objects. She remarked that 'to me now it's like protection . . . I wear the *hijab* and people do not treat you the way they treat other girls here. They are more respectful.' Although she had difficulty explaining why men respect *muhajibah,* for Almas the *hijab,* as it desexualizes her body, is a device for earning respect and ensuring her safety from potential male viewers. Many studies, such as Read and Bartkowski (2000) have found that many women wear the *hijab* because they think men will respect them. These researchers did not discuss why men respect *muhajibah,* and it was difficult for me to speculate about the reason(s). Nonetheless, Almas's remarks indicate that she feels that the *hijab* gives her the status of a respectable person, which shows that the *hijab* has a significant impact on its wearer regarding her social relationships and her perception of her 'self'.

Since people often recognize the *hijab*[13] as a religious sign that offers its wearers respect and dignity, many Muslims look negatively upon women who do not wear it, and non-wearers often feel community pressure to conform.

Despite the dominant view that the *hijab* is a symbol of religious commitment, non-wearers of headscarves[14] argue that a woman not wearing a headscarf still could be a dedicated *muslimah.*[15] Bilqis', for instance, remarked:

> Within the Muslim community, if you are not wearing the *hijab,* then you know you are not Muslim or you are not Muslim enough, when . . . it's a totally personal choice, you know. My relationship as a Muslim and my spiritual development is between me and God, and that's it.

The participants who did not wear headscarves perceived the *hijab* as a cultural dress code rather than as a religious symbol. These women indicated that wearing the *hijab* is a new cultural phenomenon locally and globally, and that it does not have a religious connotation. Ati'yah, for example, remarked, 'I think it's more like a culture that is the way they are raised there ["back home"]. . . . I do not think it is taken as a religion when they started.' According to Ati'yah, women are taught traditionally to cover their bodies with the *hijab,* and they do not wear it because of religious requirement.

Although non-wearers of the headscarves ascribed different reasons for wearing the *hijab* from those who did wear it, both group categories felt that the *hijab* was a way of demonstrating the difference between Muslim and Western values. Mali'hah, for instance, commented that morality is declining in Canadian society, and wearing the *hijab* shows people that its wearers do not subscribe to immoral values; also, she added, *muhajibah* are afraid, because they do not have control over these undesired values.

The *Hijab* as an Identity Symbol

> In the global context, if I see a woman in the *hijab* I know she is a Muslim and it creates a

sense of community in that respect, which is a nice feeling, I think (Bilqis').

The reasons for wearing it can be diverse, but the *hijab* has become a very powerful, pervasive symbol of Muslim women's identity, particularly in the West. Ibrahim (1999) states that it is a growing feeling on the part of Muslim women that they no longer wish to identify with the West, and that reaffirmation of their identities as Muslims requires the kind of visible sign that the adoption of traditional clothing implies. For these women, the issue is not that they *have* to dress traditionally, but that they *choose* to embrace the *hijab* as a marker of their Muslim identities.

Similarly, many participants who wear the *hijab*[16] claimed that it was a mark of their Muslim identities, ensuring that people immediately recognize them as Muslim women. Sima, for example, who wears a headscarf, commented that her distinct clothing symbolizes Muslim identities, and that the *hijab* makes her visible in a non-Muslim society. Being visible as a Muslim, however, also means encountering the negative stereotypes that are linked with Muslims, and Sima is aware of that. She remarked:

> Nothing else tells them that I am a Muslim, just my *hijab*. And . . . if they have the idea, oh, Muslims are terrorists, they might look at me like [that], and if they have the idea that, oh, Muslims are good people, they might look at me [with] respect. But still it gives me . . . identity.

Nasser (1999: 409) writes that adoption of the *hijab* 'conveys a public message/statement, both about the wearer and about the relationship between the wearer and potential viewers'. Accordingly, Sima's response shows that she recognizes her *hijab* as a public statement. However, whether she would be identified as a 'terrorist' or a 'good' person in Canada is a secondary consideration for

her. The significant element to her is that she will be known as a Muslim in a non-Muslim country. Sima thus uses her *hijab* as a tool for declaring her Muslim identities.

The concept of the *hijab* is not limited to personal identity; it has also become the symbol of the Muslim *ummah*, or community. An immigrant Muslim woman's attempt to identify herself as a Muslim by wearing a headscarf is an acknowledgement of general support for the attitudes, values, and beliefs of Islam and her culture that links her to the broader community of believers (Daly, 1999; Read and Bartkowski, 2000). Some participants in this study also saw the *hijab* as representative of the Muslim community, and argued that the *hijab* helped them to stay away from un-Islamic practices. Farza'nah' stated that the practice of the *hijab* defined boundaries for her, and that she would not do anything that could portray the religion negatively:

> The *hijab* limits me from doing certain things. When I have the *hijab* on . . . as a Muslim woman, I consider myself basically representative of the whole Muslim community. So, I do not go to bars with my *hijab* on. I do not go to strip clubs with my *hijab* on because I know [that] by wearing the *hijab,* I am not representing only myself . . . it's the whole Muslim community, basically.

The *hijab* not only links the wearers with a larger community, but it is also a symbol of rites of passage. In Iran, reported Pervin', when a young woman begins to wear the *hijab*, the family celebrates it. It is a 'memorable' event and 'part of the life of a girl as a graduation party'. According to Sima,[17] it signifies that a young woman is now a responsible person, and family and friends rejoice in her honour. In this cultural context, the *hijab* appears as a sign of adulthood and offers the wearer prestige and appreciation from friends and family members.

The participants in this study who have maintained the practice of wearing headscarves in Canada indicated that they are stricter in the use of their *hijab* in Canada than are those 'back home'. Shaffir (1978) states that usually people become more loyal to their traditions and customs if their identities are threatened by the larger society:

A feature common to groups that perceive the outside world as a threat is the belief that they must resist the assimilative influence of the larger society . . . [This helps the] group members to feel more committed and increases their awareness of their separate identity (Shaffir, 1978: 41).

Confirming Shaffir's observations, a number of informants in this study reported that they have embraced the *hijab* in Canada more enthusiastically than have people in their country of origin. Pervin', for instance, stated, 'I find that our *hijab* here is better than people are wearing in Iran . . . and I think the reason is [that] . . . somehow we need more to do this here than there.' The *hijab* helps Pervin' keep her distinct identities in a non-Muslim country, and it appears as a sign of resistance to the assimilative influence of the larger society.

In comparing the practice of wearing the *hijab* in Canada to its usage 'back home', the wearers of headscarves are crafting their Muslim identities not only in relation to the dominant values of their residing country, but also to the values of their country of origin. Many informants held a static view of their places of birth, and on their occasional visits they were surprised that the societies had changed. They argued that there is now a tendency 'back home' for women to dress in tight clothes and not to wear 'proper' *hijab*. The contrast of two different places allows these informants to notice differences in the *hijab,* and 'improper' *hijab* emerges as a symbol of the loss of Islamic values. Thus, the *hijab* for these participants stands as a guardian of Muslim standards,

and they thought that 'back home' people were careless in not maintaining it.

The *Hijab*, Body, and Gaze

The study of dress as situated practice requires moving between, on the one hand, the discursive and representational aspects of dress, and the way the body/dress is caught up in relations of power, and on the other, the embodied experience of dress and the use of dress as a means by which individuals orientate themselves to the social world (Entwistle, 2000: 39).

Many prominent scholars, such as El Saadawi (1980) and Mernissi (1987, 1991) have situated the practice of *veiling* as an act of controlling women both physically and psychologically. These writers argue that *veiling* represents, and is a result of, oppressive social hierarchies and male domination (Read and Bartkowski, 2000; Roald, 2001); therefore, it should be condemned. Mernissi (1991), for instance, states 'all debates on democracy get tied up in the woman question and that piece of cloth [the *hijab*] that opponents of human rights today claim to be the very essence of Muslim identity' (188). Mernissi views the *hijab* as a hindrance to accessing human rights and, consequently, inherently oppressive. Equally important, she denies the lived experiences of many of those women who recognize the *hijab* as a positive experience that empowers them and grants them Muslim identities.

For the wearers of the headscarves in this study, the *hijab* is a tool that confers power and, contrary to the above writers' opinions, helps many of them to take control of their bodies. Many of the participants seem to be utilizing the *hijab* to set boundaries between themselves and the outside world. Di'ba, for example, commented that she likes keeping her curtains closed when she has the lights on, because otherwise people walking down the street can see her. One of Di'ba's friends, however, finds her precautions odd, and argues that Islam is not that strict, that she can relax without the *hijab* while she is in her home. For Di'ba, putting a barrier between herself and potential viewers is not due to Islamic restrictions; rather, she wants to create a space where she feels free from the male gaze. Di'ba reported her friend's reaction:

> What's the big deal? Like, you are in your house . . . Allah is not going to punish you for what you are doing in your own house, you know. And I am, like, but it is not about being punished . . . I do not know how Allah is going to view this, but I do not want people, like [some] guy, [looking in]. . . that's the thing.

Secor (2002) writes that veiling, as a form of dress, is a spatial practice embedded in relations of power and resistance. Accordingly, extending the idea of the *hijab* from headscarf to the creation of 'safe' space, Di'ba uses her curtains to assert power and resistance, her freedom from the undesired gaze.

The notion that the *hijab* liberates women from the male gaze and helps them to be in charge of their own bodies is a very prominent claim by those Muslim women who wear it. They argue that the *hijab* is not a mark of oppression; rather, it is a sign of liberation that protects them from a sexist society. The *hijab* allows Muslim women physical mobility because they feel free from the male gaze. Consequently, they move in the public sphere more comfortably (Hoodfar, 1993; Odeh, 1993; Khan, 1995). Noreen's story of being released from the gaze by wearing the *hijab* is particularly significant, because she suffered heavily from the 'inspecting gaze'. Noreen was 18 years old when she got married and came to Canada. When her husband did not let her wear the *hijab*, she reports, 'it got [her] into real trouble.' She and her husband ran a store where she often worked there by herself. After being harassed in her workplace by some non-Muslim men, her husband consented to allowing her to wear the *hijab*.

From the conversation in other parts of my interview with Noreen about her experience of harassment, she was not only the victim of harassment, but her response to the harassers was also inspected by her husband. The behaviour of Noreen's spouse indicates that he blamed the victim, as if Noreen were responsible for the harassment. The *hijab*, however, elevated her position from the 'observed' to the 'observer', as she felt free from the male gaze. This granted Noreen the protection that otherwise might not have been possible for her.

Contrary to the opinions of those women who perceive the *hijab* as protection, the non-wearers of the headscarves argued that the *hijab* is not an appropriate dress in Canada. These participants stated that while the basic purpose of the *hijab* is not to draw attention to oneself, in Canada, where it is not customary dress, people often scrutinize women who wear the *hijab*. Citing the example of her daughters who wear the *hijab*, Ati'yah reported that whenever she goes out with her daughters, she notices that people stare at them, which 'is the opposite of what the *hijab* is supposed to be'. Ati'yah's observation indicates that the *hijab* is a marker of difference in Canada, as people find it 'strange'. Equally important, since it draws attention to the wearer, Ati'yah sees it as contrary to the teachings of the Qur'an.

While some women in this study retain their distinct Muslim identities by wearing the *hijab*, Ati'yah, in order to be more anonymous in mainstream society, did not wear the *hijab*. Both wearers and non-wearers are crafting their identities and negotiating a place as Muslim women immigrants in a Western society.

As noted earlier, the sample of this study is very small and the results cannot be generalized to the larger population of Muslim women in Saskatoon. Nonetheless, the results indicate that the reasons for wearing or not wearing the *hijab* are varied and complex, and cannot be reduced simply to religious or cultural reasons.

Western Perception of the *Hijab*

Veiling—to *Western eyes*, the most visible marker of the differentness and inferiority of Islamic societies—became the symbol now of both the oppression of women (or, in the language of the day, Islam's degradation of women) and the backwardness of Islam, and it became the open target of colonial attack and the spearhead of the assault on Muslim societies (Ahmed, 1992: 152).

The formation of identities is not only restricted to the ways in which we relate and present ourselves to others; it also depends on how others perceive us. One avenue for understanding the ways in which a society views different people or cultures is to study media representations, because the media often play a powerful role in suggesting and shaping national and personal identities. Studies such as Bullock and Jafri (2000), Jafri (1998), and Kutty (1997) show that mainstream North American media have consistently portrayed an image of 'the Muslim woman' as an oppressed and passive *hijab* wearer. Bullock and Jafri (2000) argue that Muslim women are presented by the media as 'others', members of a religion that does not promote 'Canadian' values but, rather, anti-Canadian values such as indiscriminate violence and gender oppression.

In mainstream society, the negative stereotypes of Muslim women have become more visible since the attacks in New York on 11 September 2001, and the *hijab* has become a sign of a 'terrorist' woman. There are a number of incidents in Canada where *muhajibah* were harassed after September 11,[18] and some participants mentioned that they also had encountered racist harassment. Pervin', for instance, who has also experienced racism in Canada, reported that someone has since called her a 'terrorist', and she inferred that it was because she wore the *hijab*. 'Some guy said "Terrorist", because I wear the *hijab*', she remarked. 'Some people stare at me. They think that if you

have the *hijab*, you are a "terrorist" . . . really, some of them think so.' Pervin's experience reveals the powerful and negative stereotypes that have linked the *hijab*—the sign of Muslim identity—with terrorism, resulting in verbal, racial, and ethnic assaults like the one cited above. These racist incidents demonstrate that Muslim women (and men) are often seen as 'other' in Canadian society and, despite claims that it is a multicultural country, many Muslims face difficulties living in Canada.

The participants not only mentioned the negative stereotype of the *hijab,* but they also recognized that many Western-style clothes could be construed as oppressive. Bilqis', for example, remarked that many North American women wear short dresses and expose their bodies, but this is not perceived as an act of oppression in Canada, whereas covering the body is interpreted as a sign of subjugation. She commented:

> Western women, when they see a Muslim woman in the *hijab*, they think, ah, oppression. But you know, ten-inch heels and a miniskirt is not seen as oppressive. To me it is more oppressive than a putting a scarf on your head.

Wolf (1991) has demonstrated that the 'beauty myth' has often resulted in the objectification of women, and the expenditure of large amounts of money to achieve the ideal body. Wolf (1991: 13) writes that there is no justification for the beauty myth: 'What it is doing to women today is a result of nothing more exalted than the need of today's power structure, economy, and culture to mount a counteroffensive against women.' Similarly, Bilqis' argues that the Western style of wearing scanty outfits is a form of women's oppression.

Conclusion

This article discussed the concept of the *hijab* and its meanings to immigrant Muslim women. Wearing the *hijab* in the last two decades has become a popular phenomenon, locally and globally; however, to what extent Muslim women need to cover is a debatable question among scholars as well as among the participants. The idea of the *hijab* ranges from wearing headscarves to demonstrating modest behaviour, depending on one's understanding of religious precepts. The participants described the *hijab* in a variety of ways; some linked it with the moral Muslim society and others thought that it was a sign of opposing immoral values. For those informants who wear the *hijab*, it is a religious obligation. The non-wearers of the headscarves view it as a cultural symbol. The *hijab* as a mark of identity is a persistent theme and the *muhajibah* use the *hijab* to assert agency, which in turn confers status and dignity to its wearers. At the same time, however, the *hijab* disempowers non-wearers because the Muslim community does not perceive them as 'good' *muslimah*.

While the *hijab* holds multiple meanings for Muslim women, mainstream North American society's perception of the *hijab* is usually negative, and the practice is often is presented in the Canadian media without proper cultural and historical reference. Unlike the participants' views, the depiction of the *hijab* in Canada suggests that there is only one form of the *hijab*, that is, as a symbol of the oppression of Muslim women.

Canadian attitudes towards the *hijab* suggest that Westerners 'know the Orient better than the Orient can know itself' (Khan, 1995: 149).

In some situations the *hijab* may indeed be imposed on Muslim women, but in this study many of the participants chose to wear it. Living in Canada, where the connotation of the *hijab* is often negative, has a strong impact on those immigrant Muslim women who wear it, as they consequently face negative stereotypes of Muslim women such as being labelled 'terrorists'. In spite of these racist acts, the *muhajibah* wear the *hijab* as a sign of their Muslim identities and in opposition to 'immodest' Western values. Those who do not identify with the visible marker recognize that the *hijab* is not an acceptable dress code in Canada. In fact, their refusal to wear the *hijab* could be read as a symbol of assimilation, but in not drawing attention to themselves and by wearing modest clothes (without the headscarf) these women, nonetheless, maintain the practice of the *hijab*. Thus, the non-wearers of the headscarves may not confront the racism that wearing the *hijab* can prompt; however, they usually encounter criticism within the Muslim community. The *hijab*, therefore, in the form of Muslim woman's clothing, emerges as a device to negotiate spaces within the Muslim community, as well as in the dominant western culture.

Notes

1. A woman who wears a *hijab*, such as a head-scarf, is called *muhajibah*.
2. Media is defined here as any form of written text (i.e., books, magazines, journal articles, reports or articles in newspapers) and audio or visual productions (i.e., radio, television shows, and documentary films).
3. The use of the word 'identities' in plural form is more appropriate here because a person's identity is multi-faceted. For instance, a Muslim woman living in Saskatoon is not only viewed as a woman, but also as a woman of colour, an immigrant, and a member of an ethnic, as well as a religious, group.
4. The term refers here to any Muslim woman born outside Canada, but currently is residing in Canada with any kind of official documents, such as a Canadian passport or student visa.
5. Please note that men's and women's gatherings are held separately in the mosque.
6. A collection of the Prophet's sayings and actions is called *hadiths*.
7. There is a science of knowledge that studies the authenticity of *hadiths*.

8. I will discuss this issue below. The idea of *fitnah* is also found in the Judeo-Christian veiling tradition, where it was thought that an uncovered female head aroused sexual desire in men (Bronner, 1993; D'Angelo, 1995).

9. Please note that he discusses the *hadith* literature in reference to the *fitnah*, and argues that they are not authentic *hadiths*.

10. Please note that all participants have been given pseudonyms.

11. The *hijab* here signifies a headscarf.

12. Geographical location where the Prophet was residing.

13. Here the *hijab* is identified by the form of headscarf and/or long coat.

14. I used the word headscarf here to make a distinction between those whose concept of the *hijab* includes the physical article, such as a headscarf, and those who view the *hijab* as modest clothing (without the head covering) and modest behaviour.

15. *Muslimah* is the feminine for a Muslim woman.

16. The *hijab* here particularly refers to the material article; nonetheless, modest behaviour is not excluded.

17. As stated earlier, please note that as I conducted focus groups, the participants talked among themselves and commented on each other's views.

18. See for instance, *The Globe and Mail* (15 October 2001), and Jain (2001).

References

Al-Ghazzali, M. 1989. *as-sunna an-anbawiya bayna ahl al-fiqh wa ahl al-hadith*. Cairo: Dar ash-Shuruq.

Asad, M., trans. 1980. *The Message of The Qur'an*. Gibraltar: Dar Al-Andalus.

Bradshaw, M., and E. Straford. 2000. 'Qualitative Research Design and Rigour', in Iain Hay, ed., *Qualitative Research Methods in Human Geography*, pp. 37–49. South Melbourne: Oxford University Press.

Bronner, L.L. 1993. 'From Veil to Wig: Jewish Women's Hair Covering', *Judaism* 42, 4: 465–77.

Bullock, K., and J. Jafri. 2000. 'Media (Mis)Representations: Muslim Women in the Canadian Nation', *Canadian Woman Studies* 20, 2 (Summer): 35–40.

Daly, C.M. 1999. 'The Paarda' Expression of Hejaab among Afghan Women in a non-Muslim community', in L. Arthur, ed., *Religion, Dress and the Body*, pp. 147–61. Oxford: Berg.

D'Angelo, R.M. 1995. 'Veils, Virgins, and the Tongues of Men and Angels: Women's Heads in Early Christianity', in H. Eilberg-Schwartz and W. Doniger, eds, *Off With Her Head! The Denial of Women's Identity in Myth, Religion, and Culture*, pp. 131–64. Berkeley, CA: University of California Press.

El Saadawi, N. 1980. *The Hidden Face of Eve: Women in the Arab World*, Hetata, trans. London: ZED Press.

Entwistle, J. 2000. *The Fashioned Body: Fashion, Dress, and Modern Social Theory*. Cambridge: Polity Press; Malden, MA: Blackwell.

Hoodfar, H. 1993. 'The Veil in Their Minds and on our Heads: The Persistence of Colonial Images of Muslim Women', *Resources for Feminist Research* 22, 3/4: 5–18.

Ibrahim, B.S. 1999. *Women in Islam: Hijab*. Aalim: Islamic Research Foundation (IRF).

Jafri, G.J. 1998. 'The Portrayal of Muslim Women in Canadian Mainstream Media: A Community-based Analysis'. Online Afghan Women's Organization. Project report. Available at http://www.fmw.org/political_activities.htm.

Khaled, A. 2001. *Speaking in God's Name: Islamic Law, Authority and Women*. Oxford: Oneworld.

Khan, S. 1995. 'The Veil as a Site of Struggle: The Hejab in Quebec', *Canadian Woman Studies* 15, 2/3: 146–52.

Kutty, S. 1997. 'Speaking for Her: The Representation of the Muslim Woman in Popular Culture'. Canadian Muslim Civil Liberties Association. Pamphlet.

Mernissi, F. 1987. *Beyond the Veil: Male-Female Dynamics in Modern Muslim Society*. London: Al Sagi Books.

———. 1991. *Women and Islam: A Historical and Theological Enquiry*, M.J. Lakeland, trans. Oxford: B. Blackwell. Basil.

Nasser, M. 1999. 'The New Veiling Phenomenon—Is It an Anorexic Equivalent? A Polemic', *Journal of Community & Applied Social Psychology* 9: 407–12.

Odeh, L.A. 1993. 'Post-colonial Feminism and the Veil: Thinking the Difference', *Feminist Review* 43 (Spring): 26–37.

Read, G., and P.J. Bartkowski. 2000. 'To Veil or Not to Veil? A Case Study of Identity Negotiation among Muslim Women in Austin, Texas', *Gender and Society* 14, 3 (June): 395–417.

Roald, S.A. 2001. *Women in Islam: The Western Experience*. London: Routledge.

Shaffir, W. 1978. 'Canada: Witnessing as Identity Consolidation: The Case of the Lubavitcher Chassidim', in H. Mol, ed., *Identity and Religion: International, Cross-cultural Approaches*, pp. 39–57. Beverly Hills, CA: Sage Publications.

Wolf, N. 1991. *The Beauty Myth*. Toronto: Vintage Books.

Yusuf, A.A., trans. 1946. *The Holy Qur'an*. Durban: Islamic Propagation Center International.

Yuval-Davis, N. 1994. 'Identity Politics and Women's Ethnicity', in V. Moghadam, ed., *Identity Politics and Women: Cultural Reassertions and Feminism in International Perspective*, pp. 408–24. Boulder, CO: Westview Press.

CHAPTER 6

Coming of Age and Coming Out Ceremonies Across Cultures

Gilbert Herdt

Coming of age and being socialized into the sexual lifeways of the culture through ceremonies and initiation rites are common in many cultures of the world. These traditions help to incorporate the individual—previously a child, possibly outside of the moral rules and sexual roles of the adult group—into the public institutions and practices that bring full citizenship. Coming of age or 'puberty' ceremonies around the world are commonly assumed to introduce the young person to sexual life as a heterosexual. In both traditional and modern societies, ritual plays a role in the emergence of sexuality and the support of desires and relationships expected in later life.

Yet not all of this is seamless continuity, and in the study of homosexuality across cultures we must be aware of the gaps and barriers that exist between what is experienced in childhood or adolescence, and the roles and customs in adulthood that may negate or oppose these experiences.

Ruth Benedict (1938) stresses how development in a society may create cultural discontinuities in this sexual and gender cycle of identities and roles, necessitating rituals. She hints that homosexuality in particular may cause discontinuity of this kind, and the life stories of many gays and lesbians in western society reveal this problem. But in all societies, there is an issue of connecting childhood with adulthood, with the transition from sexual or biological immaturity to sexual maturity. In short, these transitions may create a 'life crisis' that requires a social solution—and this is the aim of initiation ceremonies and rites of transition. Rituals may provide for the individual the necessary means to achieve difficult changes in sexual and gender status. Particularly in deeply emotional rituals, the energy of the person can be fully invested or bonded to the newfound group. This may create incredible attachments of the kind we have observed among the ancient Greeks, the feudal Japanese, and the Sambia of New Guinea, wherein the younger boy is erotically involved or partnered with an older male. In the conditions of a warrior society, homoerotic partnerships are particularly powerful when they are geared to the survival of the group.

The transition out of presumptive heterosexuality and secrecy and into the active process of self-identifying as gay or lesbian in the western tradition bears close comparison with these rites of passage. In the process of 'coming out'—the current western concept of ritual passage—as gay or lesbian, a person undergoes emotional changes and a transformation in sexuality and gender that are remarkable and perhaps equal in their social drama to the initiation rites of small societies in New Guinea and Africa. Thus, the collective aspirations and desires of the adolescent or child going through the ritual to belong, participate in, and make commitments to communities of his or her own kind take on a new and broader scope.

Coming out is an implicit rite of passage for people who are in a crisis of identity that finds them 'betwixt and between' being presumed to be heterosexual and living a totally secret and hidden life as a homosexual. Not until they enter into the gay or lesbian lifeway or the sexual culture of the gay and lesbian community will they begin to learn and be socialized into the rules, knowledge, and social roles and relationships of the new cultures. For many people, this experience is liberating; it is a highly charged, emotional, and dramatic process that changes them into adult gays or lesbians in all areas of their lives—with biological families, with coworkers, with friends or schoolmates, and with a sexual and romantic partner of the same gender, possibly for the rest of their lives.

This transformation in the self and in social relations brings much that is new and sometimes frightening. The rituals open up an alternative moral system. Why people who desire the same gender require a ritual when others in our society do not is painfully clear. Ritual is necessary because of the negative images, stigma, and

intense social contamination that continue to exist in the stereotypes and anti-homosexual laws of our society. To be homosexual is to be discredited as a full person in society; it is to have a spoiled identity—as a homosexual in society or as a frightened closet homosexual who may be disliked by openly gay and lesbian friends. But perhaps of greatest importance are the repression and social censorship involved: to have one's desires suppressed, to even experience the inner or 'true' self as a secret.

It is hard to break through this taboo alone or without the support of a community because doing so exposes the person to all sorts of risk, requires considerable personal resources, and precipitates an emotional vulnerability that, for many, is very difficult to bear. But that is not all. For some people in our society, homosexuality is a danger and a source of pollution. Once the person's homosexuality is revealed, the stigma can also spread to the family, bringing the pollution of shame and dishonour to father and mother, clan and community. This is the old mask of the evil of homosexuality, and this is what we have found in a study of these matters in Chicago (Herdt and Boxer, 1996).

It is very typical to see an intense and negative reaction of family members to the declaration of same-sex desires by adolescents, even in the twenty-first century. Society changes slowly and its myths change even more slowly. For many people, homosexuality is an evil, as frightening to the imagination as the monsters of bad Hollywood movies. Many people find it extremely difficult to deal with homosexuality and may exert strong pressures on their young to hide and suppress their feelings. Consequently, young people may feel that by declaring their same-sex desires, they will betray their families or the traditions of their sexual culture and its lifeways, which privilege marriage and the carrying on of the family name. And the younger person who desires the same gender may be afraid to come out for fear of dishonouring his or her ethnic community in the same way. To prevent these reactions, many people hide their basic feelings and all of their desires from their friends and families.

Here is where we may learn a lesson from other cultures. The mechanism of ritual helps to teach about the trials and ordeals of passages in other times and places, which in itself is a comfort because it signals something basic in the human condition. To come out is to openly challenge sexual chauvinism, homophobia, and bias—refusing to continue the stigma and pollution of the past and opening new support and positive role models where before there were none. Through examples from New Guinea, the Mojave, and the Chicago gay and lesbian group, I examine these ideas in the following pages.

Many cultures around the world celebrate coming of age with a variety of events and rituals that introduce the person to sexual life. Indeed, initiation can be an introduction to sexual development and erotic life (Hart, 1963). In Aboriginal Australia and New Guinea wherever the pre-colonial secret societies of the region flourished, the nature of all sexual interaction was generally withheld from pre-pubertal boys and girls until initiation. It often began their sense of sexual being, even if they had not achieved sexual puberty, since maturation often occurred late in these societies. Many of the Pacific societies actually disapproved of childhood sexual play, for this was felt to disrupt marriage and social regulation of premarital social relations. The Sambia are no different, having delayed sexual education until the initiation of boys and girls in different secret contexts for each. The stories of Sambia boys are clear in associating the awakening of their sexuality in late childhood with their initiation rites and fellatio debut with adolescent bachelor partners. The definition of social reality was thus opened up to same-gender sexuality.

Sambia Boys' Ritual Initiation

The Sambia are a tribe numbering more than 2,000 people in the Eastern Highlands of Papua New Guinea. Most elements of culture and social organization are constructed around the nagging destructive presence of warfare in the area. Descent is patrilineal and residence is patrilocal to maximize the cohesion of the local group as a warriorhood. Hamlets are composed of tiny exogamous patriclans that facilitate marriage within the group and exchange with other hamlets, again based on the local politics of warfare. Traditionally, all marriage was arranged; courtship is unknown, and social relationships between the sexes are not only ritually polarized but also often hostile. Like other Highlands societies of New Guinea, these groups are associated with a men's secret society that ideologically disparages women as dangerous creatures who can pollute men and deplete them of their masculine substance. The means of creating and maintaining the village-based secret society is primarily through the ritual initiation of boys beginning at ages seven through ten and continuing until their arranged and consummated marriages, many years later. The warriorhood is guaranteed by collective ritual initiations connecting neighboring hamlets. Within a hamlet, this warriorhood is locally identified with the men's clubhouse, wherein all initiated bachelors reside. Married men frequent the clubhouse constantly; and on occasion (during fight times, rituals, or their wives' menstrual periods) they sleep there. An account of Sambia culture and society has been published elsewhere and need not be repeated here (Herdt, 1981).

Sambia sexual culture, which operates on the basis of a strongly essentializing model of sexual development, also incorporates many ideas of social support and cultural creation of the sexual; these ideas derive from the role of ritual and supporting structures of gendered ontologies throughout the life course of men and women. Sexual development, according to the cultural ideals of the Sambia life plan, is fundamentally distinct for men and women. Biological femaleness is considered 'naturally' competent and innately complete; maleness, in contrast, is considered more problematic since males are believed incapable of achieving adult reproductive manliness without ritual treatment. Girls are born with female genitalia, a birth canal, a womb, and, behind that, a functional menstrual-blood organ, or *tingu*. Feminine behaviours such as gardening and mothering are thought to be by-products of women's natural *tingu* functioning. As the *tingu* and womb become engorged with blood, puberty and menarche occur; the menses regularly follow, and they are linked with women's child-bearing capacities. According to the canonical male view, all women then need is a penis (i.e., semen) in facilitating adult procreation by bestowing breast milk (transformed from semen), which prepares a woman for nursing her newborn. According to the women's point of view, however, women are biologically competent and can produce their own breast milk—a point of conflict between the two gendered ontologies. This gives rise to a notion that women have a greater internal resilience and health than males and an almost inexhaustible sexual appetite. By comparison, males are not competent biologically until they achieve manhood, and thus they require constant interventions of ritual to facilitate maturation.

The Sambia believe that boys will not 'naturally' achieve adult competence without the interventions of ritual, an idea that may seem strange but is actually common throughout New Guinea, even in societies that do not practice boy-inseminating rites (Herdt, 1993). Among the Sambia, the practice of age-structured homoerotic relations is a transition into adulthood. The insemination of boys ideally ends when a man marries and fathers a child. In fact, the vast majority of males—more than 90 per cent—terminate their sexual relations with boys at that time. Almost all the men do so because of the taboos and, to a lesser degree, because they have 'matured' to a new level of having exclusive sexual access to one or more wives, with genital sexual pleasure being conceived of as a greater privilege.

The sexual culture of the Sambia men instills definite and customary lifeways that involves a formula for the life course. Once initiated (before age ten), the boys undergo ordeals to have their 'female' traces (left over from birth and from living with their mothers) removed; these ordeals involve painful rites, such as nose-bleedings, that are intended to promote masculinity and aggression. The boys are then in a ritually 'clean' state that enables the treatment of their bodies and minds in new ways. These boys are regarded as 'pure' sexual virgins, which is important for their insemination. The men believe that the boys are unspoiled because they have not been exposed to the sexual pollution of women, which the men greatly fear. It is thus through oral intercourse that the men receive a special kind of pleasure, unfettered by pollution, and the boys are thought to acquire semen for growth, becoming strong and fertile. All the younger males are thus inseminated by older bachelors, who were once themselves semen recipients.

The younger initiates are semen recipients until their third-stage 'puberty' ceremony, around age fifteen. Afterward, they become semen donors to the younger boys. According to the men's sacred lore and the dogmas of their secret society, the bachelors are 'married' to the younger recipient males—as symbolized by secret ritual flutes, made of bamboo and believed to be empowered by female spirits that are said to be hostile to women. During this time, the older adolescents are 'bisexuals' who may inseminate their wives orally, in addition to the secret insemination of the boys. Eventually these youths have marriages arranged for them. After they become new fathers, they in turn stop sexual relations with boys. The men's family duties would be compromised by boy relations, the Sambia men say.

The growth of males is believed to be slower and more difficult than that of females. Men say that boys lack an endogenous means for creating manliness. Males do possess a *tingu* (menstrual blood) organ, but it is believed to be 'dry' and nonfunctional. They reiterate that a mother's womb, menstrual blood, and vaginal fluids—all containing pollution—impede masculine growth for the boy until he is separated by initiation from mother and the women's world. Males also possess a semen organ (*keriku-keriku*), but unlike the female menstrual blood organ, it is intrinsically small, hard, and empty, containing no semen of its own. Although semen is believed to be the spark of human life and, moreover, the sole precipitant of biological maleness (strong bones and muscles and, later, male secondary-sex traits: a flat abdomen, a hairy body, a mature glans penis), the Sambia hold that the human body cannot naturally produce semen; it must be externally introduced. The purpose of ritual insemination through fellatio is to fill up the *keriku-keriku* (which then stores semen for adult use) and thereby masculinize the boy's body as well as his phallus. Biological maleness is therefore distinct from the mere possession of male genitalia, and only repeated inseminations begun at an early age and regularly continued for years confer the reproductive competence that culminates in sexual development and manliness.

There are four functions of semen exchange: (1) the cultural purpose of 'growing' boys through insemination, which is thought to substitute for mother's milk; (2) the 'masculinizing' of boys' bodies, again through insemination, but also through ritual ordeals meant to prepare them for warrior life; (3) the provision of 'sexual play' or pleasure for the older youths, who have no other sexual outlet prior to marriage; and (4) the transmission of semen and soul substance from one generation of clansmen to the next, which is vital for spiritual and ritual power to achieve its rightful ends (Herdt, 1984). These elements of institutionalized boy-inseminating practices are the object of the most vital and secret ritual teachings in first-stage initiation, which occurs before puberty. The novices are expected to be orally inseminated during the rituals and to continue the practice on a regular basis for years to come. The semen transactions are, however,

rigidly structured homoerotically: Novices may act only as fellators in private sexual interactions with older bachelors, who are typically seen as dominant and in control of the same-sex contacts. The adolescent youth is the erotically active party during fellatio, for his erection and ejaculation are necessary for intercourse, and a boy's oral insemination is the socially prescribed outcome of the encounter. Boys must never reverse roles with the older partners or take younger partners before the proper ritual initiations. The violation of such rules is a moral wrong that is sanctioned by a variety of punishments. Boy-inseminating, then, is a matter of sexual relations between unrelated kin and must be seen in the same light as the semen exchanges of delayed sister exchange marriage: Hamlets of potential enemies exchange women and participate in semen exchange of boys, which is necessary for the production of children and the maturation of new warriors.

Ritual initiation for boys is conducted every three or four years for a whole group of boys as an age-set from neighbouring villages. This event lasts several months and consists of many ordeals and transitions, some of them frightening and unpleasant, but overall welcomed as the entry into honourable masculinity and access to social power. It culminates in the boys' entry into the men's clubhouse, which is forbidden to women and children. The boys change their identities and roles and live on their own away from their parents until they are grown up and married. The men's house thus becomes their permanent dormitory and secret place of gender segregation.

Sambia girls do not experience initiation until many years later, when they undergo a formal marriage ceremony. Based on what is known, it seems doubtful that the girls undergo a sexual period of same-gender relations like those of the boys, but I cannot be sure because I was not permitted to enter the menstrual hut, where the initiations of girls were conducted. Males begin their ritual careers and the change in their sexual lives early because the transformation expected of the boys is so great. Girls live on with their parents until they are married and achieve their first menstruation, which occurs very late, age nineteen on average for the Sambia and their neighbours. A secret initiation is performed for the girls in the menstrual hut. Only then can they begin to have sexual relations with their husbands and live with them in a new house built by husband and wife.

The first-stage initiation ceremonies begin the events of life crisis and change in identities for the boys. They are young. After a period of time they are removed to the forest, where the most critical rituals begin to introduce them to the secrets of the men's house and the secret society of the men's warriorhood. The key events involve blood-letting rituals and penis-and-flute rites, which we study here from observations of the initiation conducted in 1975 (Herdt, 1982). Here the boys experience the revelation of sexuality and the basic elements of their transition into age-structured homoerotic relations.

On the first morning of the secret rituals in the forest, the boys have fierce and painful nose-bleeding rituals performed on them. This is believed to remove the pollution of their mothers and the women's world that is identified with the boys' bodies. But it is also a testing ground to see how brave they are and the degree to which their fathers, older brothers, and the war leaders of the village can rely on the boys not to run and hide in times of war. Afterward, the boys are prepared by their ritual guardian, who is referred to as their 'mother's brother', a kind of 'male mother', for the main secret teaching that is to follow. They are dressed in the finest warrior decorations, which they have earned the right to wear through the initiation ordeals. And this begins their preparation for the rites of insemination that will follow. Now that their insides have been 'cleansed' to receive the magical gift of manhood—semen— they are taken into the sacred chamber of a forest setting, and there they see for the first time the magical flutes, believed to be animated by the

female spirit of the flute, which protects the men and the secrecy of the clubhouse and is thought to be hostile to women.

The key ceremony here is the penis-and-flutes ritual. It focuses on a secret teaching about boy insemination and is regarded by the men and boys alike as the most dramatic and awesome of all Sambia rituals. It begins with the older bachelors, the youths with whom the boys will engage in sexual relations later, who enter the chamber dressed up as the 'female spirits of the flutes'. The flute players appear, and in their presence, to the accompaniment of the wailing flutes, some powerful secrets of the men's cult are revealed. The setting is awesome: a great crowd waiting in silence as the mysterious sounds are first revealed; boys obediently lining up for threatening review by elders; and boys being told that secret fellatio exists and being taught how to engage in it. Throughout the ritual boys hear at close range the flute sounds associated since childhood with collective masculine power and mystery and pride. The flutes are unequivocally treated as phallic—as symbols of the penis and the power of men to openly flaunt their sexuality. The intent of the flutes' revelation is threatening to the boys as they begin to guess its meaning.

I have observed this flute ceremony during two different initiations, and although my western experience differs greatly from that of Sambia, one thing was intuitively striking to me: the men were revealing the *homoerotic meanings* of the sexual culture. This includes a great preoccupation with the penis and with semen but also with the mouth of the boy and penile erection, sexual impulses, homoerotic activities in particular, and the commencement of sexuality in its broadest sense for the boys. If there is a homoerotic core to the secret society of the Sambia, then this is surely where it begins. These revelations come as boys are enjoined to become fellators, made the sharers of ritual secrets, and threatened with death if they tell women or children what they have learned. They have to keep the secret forever.

Over the course of many years I collected the stories of the boys' experiences as they went through these rituals. The boys' comments indicated that they perceived several different social values bound up with the expression of homoerotic instruction in the flute ceremony. A good place to begin is with childhood training regarding shame about one's genitals. Here is Kambo, a boy who was initiated, talking about his own experience: 'I thought—not good that they [elders] are lying or just playing a trick. That's [the penis] not for eating. . . . When I was a child our fathers said, 'This [penis] is not for handling; if you hold it you'll become lazy.' And because of that [at first in the cult house] I felt—it's not for sucking.' Childhood experience is a contributing source of shame about fellatio: children are taught to avoid handling their own genitals. In a wider sense Kambo's remark pertains to the taboo on masturbation, the sexual naïveté of children, and the boys' prior lack of knowledge about their fathers' homosexual activities.

Another key ritual story concerns the nutritive and 'growth' values of semen. A primary source of this idea is men's ritual equation of semen with mother's breast milk, as noted before. The initiates take up this idea quickly in their own subjective orientations toward fellatio. (Pandanus nuts, like coconut, are regarded as another equivalent of semen.) The following remark by Moondi is a typical example of such semen identifications in the teachings of the flute ceremony: 'The "juice" of the pandanus nuts, . . . it's the same as the "water" of a man, the same as a man's "juice" [semen]. And I like to eat a lot of it [because it can give me more water], . . . for the milk of women is also the same as the milk of men. Milk [breast milk] is for when she carries a child—it belongs to the infant who drinks it.' The association between semen and the infant's breast food is also explicit in this observation by Gaimbako, a second-stage initiate: 'Semen is the same kind as that [breast milk] of women. . . . It's the very same kind as theirs, . . . the same as pandanus nuts too. . . . But when milk [semen]

falls into my mouth [during fellatio], I think it's the milk of women.' So the boys are taught beliefs that are highly motivating in support of same-gender sexual relations.

But the ritual also creates in boys a new awareness about their subordination to the older men. Kambo related this thought as his immediate response to the penis teaching of the flute ceremony: 'I was afraid of penis. It's the same as mine—why should I eat it? It's the same kind; [our penises are] only one kind. We're men, not *different* kinds.' This supposition is fundamental and implied in many boys' understandings. Kambo felt that males are of one kind, that is, 'one sex', as distinct from females. This implies tacit recognition of the sameness of men, which ironically suggests that they should be not sexually involved but in competition for the other gender. Remember, too, the coercive character of the setting: the men's attempt to have boys suck the flutes is laden with overt hostility, much stronger than the latent hostility expressed in lewd homosexual jokes made during the preceding body decoration. The boys are placed in a sexually subordinate position, a fact that is symbolically communicated in the idiom that the novices are 'married' to the flutes. (Novices suck the small flute, which resembles the mature glans penis, the men say.) The men thus place the boys in an invidious state of subordination during which the boys may sense that they are being treated too much like women. Sometimes this makes them panic and creates fear and shame. In time, however, a different feeling about the practice sets in.

Nearly all the novices perform their first act of fellatio during the days of initiation, and their story helps us to understand what happens later in their masculine development. Let me cite several responses of Moondi to this highly emotional act:

I was wondering what they [elders] were going to do to us. And . . . I felt afraid. What will they do to us next? But they put the bamboo in and out of the mouth; and I wondered, what are they doing? Then, when they tried out our mouths, I began to understand . . . that they were talking about the penis. Oh, that little bamboo is the penis of the men. . . . My whole body was afraid, completely afraid, . . . and I was heavy, I wanted to cry.

At that point my thoughts went back to how I used to think it was the *aatmwogwambu* [flute spirit], but then I knew that the men did it [made the sounds]. And . . . I felt a little better, for before [I thought that] the aatmwogwambu would get me. But now I saw that they [the men] did it.

They told us the penis story. . . . Then I thought a lot, as my thoughts raced quickly. I was afraid—not good that the men 'shoot' me [penetrate my mouth] and break my neck. Aye! Why should they put that [penis] inside our mouths! It's not a good thing. They all hide it [the penis] inside their grass skirts, and it's got lots of hair too!

'You must listen well,' the elders said. 'You all won't grow by yourselves; if you sleep with the men you'll become a *strong* man.' They said that; I was afraid. . . . And then they told us clearly: semen is inside—and when you hold a man's penis, you must put it inside your mouth—he can give you semen. . . . It's the same as your mother's breast milk.

'This is no lie!' the men said. 'You can't go tell the children, your sisters.' . . . And then later I tried it [fellatio], and I thought: Oh, they told us about *aamoonaalyi* [breast milk; Moondi means semen]—it [semen] is in there.

Despite great social pressures, some boys evince a low interest in the practice from the start, and they seldom participate in fellatio. Some novices feverishly join in. Those are the extremes. The great majority of Sambia boys regularly engage in fellatio for years as constrained by taboo. Homoerotic activities are a touchy subject among males for many reasons. These activities begin with ceremony, it is true, but their occurrence and meaning fan out to embrace a whole secret way of life. What matters is that the boys become sharers of this hidden tradition; and we should expect them to acquire powerful feelings about bachelors, fellatio, semen, and the whole male sexual culture.

One story must stand for many in the way that the Sambia boys grow into this sexual lifeway. One day, while I was talking idly with Kambo, he mentioned singing to himself as he walked in the forest. I asked him what he sang about; and from this innocuous departure point, he said this: 'When I think of men's name songs then I sing them: that of a bachelor who is sweet on me; a man of another line or my own line. When I sing the song of a creek in the forest I am happy about that place. . . . Or some man who sleeps with me—when he goes elsewhere, I sing his song. I think of that man who gave me a lot of semen; later, I must sleep with him. I feel like this: he gave me a lot of water [semen]. . . . Later, I will have a lot of water like him.'

Here we see established in Kambo's thought the male emphasis on 'accumulating semen' and the powerful homoerotic relationships that accompany it. Even a simple activity like singing can create a mood of subjective association with past fellatio and same-gender relationships with the older males. Kambo's last sentence contains a wish: that he will acquire abundant manliness, like that of the friend of whom he sings.

No issue in recent reviews has inspired more debate than the basic question of whether—or to what extent—sexual feelings and erotic desires are motives or consequences of these cultural practices. Does the Sambia boy desire sexual intercourse with the older male? Is the older male sexually attracted to the boy? Indeed, what does 'erotic' or 'sexual' mean in this context, and is 'desire' the proper concept with which to gauge the ontology? Or do other factors, such as power or kinship, produce the sexual attraction and excitement (conscious or unconscious) necessary to produce arousal and uphold the tradition (Herdt, 1991)?

Although Sambia culture requires that men eventually change their focus to marriage and give up boy-inseminating, some of the men continue to practice age-structured relations because they find them so pleasurable. A small number of individual men enjoy inseminating boys too much to give up the practice. They develop favourites among the boys and even resort to payment of meat when they find it difficult to obtain a boy who will service them. In our culture these men would probably be called homosexuals because of their preference for the boys, their desires, and their need to mask their activities within the secret domain of ritual. But such an identity of homosexual or gay does not exist for the Sambia, and we must be careful not to project these meanings onto them, for that would be ethnocentric. We can, however, see how they live and what it means to have such an experience—in the absence of the sexual identity system of western culture.

One of these men, Kalutwo, has been interviewed by me over a long period of time, and his sexual and social history reveals a pattern of broken, childless marriages and an exclusive attraction to boys. As he got older, he would have to 'pay' the boys with gifts to engage in sex, but when he was younger, some of the boys were known to be fond of him as well (Herdt and Stoller, 1990). Several other males are different from Kalutwo in liking boys but also liking women and being successfully married with children. They would be called bisexual in our society. They seem to enjoy sexual pleasure with women and take pride in making babies through their wives, yet they continue illicitly to enjoy oral sex with boys. But Kalutwo disliked women sexually and generally preferred the closeness, sexual intimacy, and emotional security of young men and boys. As he got older, it was increasingly difficult for him to obtain boys as sexual partners, and this seemed to make him feel depressed. Moreover, as he got older, he was increasingly at odds with his male peers socially and stood out from the crowd, having no wife or children, as expected of customary adult manhood. Some people made fun of him behind his back; so did some of the boys. In a society that had a homosexual role, Kalutwo might have found more social support or comfort and perhaps might have been able to make a different transition into middle age. But his village still accepts him, and he has not been turned away or destroyed—as might have occurred in another time had he lived in a western country.

Perhaps in these cases we begin to understand the culture of male camaraderie and emotional intimacy that created such deeply felt desire for same-gender relations in ancient Greece and Japan, in which sexual pleasures and social intimacies with the same gender were as prized as those of intercourse and family life with women. No difficulty was posed to society or to self-esteem so long as these men met their social and sexual obligations and were honorable in their relations with younger males. We know from the anthropological reports from New Guinea that such individuals existed elsewhere as well, and among the Malekula and Marind-anim tribes, for example, adult married men would continue such relations with boys even after reaching the age of being grandfathers in the group, for this was expected.

Mojave Two-Spirit Initiation

My reading of the gender-transformed role among American Indians has shown the importance of two spirits in Native American society for the broader understanding of alternative sexualities. What I have not established thus far is the development of the role in the life of the individual. Among the Mojave Indians, a special ceremony in late childhood marked a transition into the third-gender role that allowed for homoerotic relations so long as they were between people in different gender roles. The two spirit was the product of a long cultural history that involved myth and ceremonial initiation. The ceremonies were sacred and of such importance that their official charter was established in the origin myths of the tribe, known from time immemorial. The meanings of this transition deserve to be highlighted as another variation on coming of age ceremonies in nonwestern cultures.

The Mojave child was only about ten years old when he participated in the ceremony for determining whether a change to two spirit would occur. Perhaps this seems young for a coming of age ceremony; but it might be that the very degree of change and the special nature of the desires to become a man-woman required a childhood transition. In the Mojave case, it was said that a Mojave boy could act 'strangely' at the time, turning away from male tasks and refusing the toys of his own sex. The parents would view this as a sign of personal and gender change. Recall that mothers had dreams that their sons would grow up to become two spirits. No doubt this spiritual sign helped to lend religious support for the ceremony. At any rate these signs of gender change were said by the Mojave to express the 'true' intentions of the child to change into a man-woman. Nahwera, a Mojave elder, stated: 'When there is a desire in a child's heart to become a transvestite that child will act different. It will let people become aware of that desire' (Devereux, 1937: 503). Clearly, the child was beginning to act on desires that transgressed his role and required an adjustment, through ritual, to a new kind of being and social status in the culture.

Arrangements for the ceremony were made by the parents. The boy was reported to have been 'surprised' by being offered 'female apparel', whereon the relatives waited nervously to see his response. Devereux reported that this was considered both an initiation and an ultimate test of the child's true desires. 'If he submitted to it, he was considered a genuine homosexual. . . . If the boy acted in the expected fashion during the ceremony he was considered an initiated homosexual, if not, the gathering scattered, much to the relief of the boy's family' (Devereux, 1937: 508). The story suggests that the parents in general may have been ambivalent about this change and may not have

wanted it. Nevertheless, true to Mojave culture, they accepted the actions of the boy and supported his decision to become a two-spirit person. The Mojave thus allowed a special combination of a child's ontological being and the support of the family to find its symbolic expression in a ready-made institutionalized cultural practice. It only awaited the right individual and circumstances for the two-spirit person to emerge in each community in each generation.

Both the Sambia example of age-structured relations and the Mojave illustration of gender-transformed homosexuality reveal transitions in late childhood up to age ten. What is magical about age ten? It may be that certain critical developmental changes begin to occur around this time—desires and attractions that indicate the first real sexuality and growing sense of becoming a sexual person. In fact, our study in Chicago revealed that nine and one-half years for boys and ten years for girls were the average age when they were first attracted to the same gender (Herdt and Boxer, 1996).

Coming Out—Gay and Lesbian Teens in America

Ours is a culture that defines male and female as absolutely different and then goes to great lengths to deny having done so. American culture reckons 'heterosexual' and 'homosexual' as fundamentally distinctive kinds of 'human nature' but then struggles to find a place for both. Although such gender dimorphism is common in the thinking of nonwestern peoples, the latter idea is rare in, even absent from, many cultures—including our own cultural ancestors, the ancient Greeks. The Greeks described people's sexual behaviours but not their being as homosexual or heterosexual. As we have seen, the Greeks did not place people in categories of sexuality or create sexual classifications that erased all other cultural and personality traits. In our society today this kind of thinking is common and permeates the great symbolic types that define personal being and social action in most spheres of our lives. For many heterosexuals, their worldview and life course goals remain focused on the greatest ritual of reproduction: the church-ordained marriage. And this leads to parenting and family formation. Many think of this ritual process as 'good' in all of its aspects. Others see same-gender desire as an attack on that reproductive and moral order, a kind of crisis of gender and sexuality that requires the assertion of a mythical 'family values', descended from nineteenth-century ideals, that are seldom relevant to heterosexuals today, let alone to gays and lesbians.

Coming out is another form of ritual that intensifies change in a young person's sexual identity development and social being. It gives public expression to desires long felt to be basic to the person's sexual nature but formerly hidden because of social taboos and homophobia. The process leads to many events that reach a peak in the person's young adult years, especially in the development of gay or lesbian selves, roles, and social relations. Coming out continues to unfold across the entire course of life: there is never really an end to the process for the simple reason that as gay or lesbian people age and their social situations change, they continue to express in new, relevant ways what it means to be gay or lesbian. Such a social and existential crisis of identity—acted out on the stage of the lesbian and gay community—links the social drama of American youths' experiences with those of tribal initiations, such as those of the Sambia and Mojave, played out in the traditional communities. Of course, these two kinds of drama are different and should not be confused, but they share the issues of handling same-gender desires in cultural context.

Two different processes are involved. First is the secretive act of 'passing' as heterosexual, involving the lone individual in largely hidden social networks and secret social spaces. In many towns and cities, especially unsophisticated and traditionally conservative areas of the country, the possibilities are only now emerging for gay/lesbian

identification and social action. Second is the coming out in adolescence or young adulthood.

Initially the gay or lesbian grows up with the assumption of being heterosexual. As an awareness of same-gender desires emerges, a feeling of having to hide these desires and pretend otherwise, of acting straight, leads to many moments of secrecy. Later, however, sexual and social experiences may yield a divergent awareness and a desire to be open. What follows is a process of coming out—typically begun in urban centres, sometimes in high school, sometimes later, after the young person has left home for college, work, or the service—that leads to self-identification as gay or lesbian. Through these ritual steps of disclosure all kinds of new socialization and opportunities emerge, including entrance into the gay and lesbian community.

Being and doing gay life are provisioned by the rituals of coming out, and they open significant questions for thinking about youths in search of positive same-gender roles. American teenagers may seem less exotic to the gay or lesbian reader; but they are more of an oddity to the heterosexual adult community as they come out. To many in our own society, these youths look 'queer' and 'strange' and 'diseased', attitudes that reflect historical stereotypes and cultural homophobia.

The growing visibility of the lesbian and gay movement in the United States has made it increasingly possible for people to disclose their desires and 'come out' at younger ages. Over the past quarter century, the evidence suggests that the average age of the declaration of same-gender desires has gotten earlier—a lot earlier, as much as ten years earlier than it was in the 1970s—and is for the first time in history a matter of adolescent development. It is not a matter for everyone, of course, but increasingly for those who become aware and are lucky to have the opportunities to begin a new life. In our study of gay and lesbian self-identified youths in Chicago, we found that the average age for boys and girls' 'coming out' was sixteen. But we also found that the earliest awareness of same-gender attraction begins at about age ten, which suggests that the desires are a part of the deeper being of the gay or lesbian person.

Gay and lesbian teenagers are growing up with all of the usual problems of our society, including the political, economic, and social troubles of our country, as well as the sexual and social awakening that typifies the adolescent experience. I have already noted how American society and western cultures in general have changed in the direction of more positive regard for gays. This does not mean, however, that the hatred and homophobia of the past are gone or that the secrecy and fear of passing have faded away. People still fear, and rightly so, the effects of coming out on their lives and safety, their well-being and jobs, their social standing and community prestige. These youths are opting to come out as openly lesbian or gay earlier in the life course than ever before in our society. Yet they experience the troubles of feeling themselves attracted to the same gender, with its taboos and sorrows of stigma and shame, not knowing what to do about it. Fortunately, the gay and lesbian culture provides new contexts of support; these youths have institutions and media that talk about it; they learn from adult role models that they can live relatively happy and rewarding lives with their desires.

We can study how one group of adolescents in Chicago has struggled with these issues while preparing for socialization and coming out in the context of the lesbian and gay community. The study of gay, lesbian, and bisexual youths in Chicago was located in the largest gay social services agency of the city, Horizons Community Services. Horizons was created in the early 1970s out of the gay liberation movement, and by 1979 it had founded a gay and lesbian youth group, one of the first in the United States. The agency is based in the gay neighbourhood of the city, and it depends on volunteers and the goodwill and interest of friends of the agency. In recent years the youths have lead the Gay and Lesbian Pride

Day Parade in Chicago and have become a symbol of social and political progress in gay culture in the city.

The Horizons study was organized around the youth group, for ages thirteen to twenty, but the average age of the youths interviewed in depth was about eighteen. We interviewed a total of 202 male and female youths of all backgrounds from the suburbs and inner city, white and black and brown. Many people of colour and of diverse ethnic subcultures in Chicago have experienced racism and many forms of homophobia, and these have effectively barred their coming out. The group tries to find a place for all of these diverse adolescents; no one is turned away. Group meetings are coordinated by lesbian and gay adults, esteemed role models of the teens. They facilitate a discussion of a variety of topics, particularly in matters of the coming out process, such as fears and homophobic problems at school or home, and issues of special interest to the teens. The youth group has an active social life as well, hosting parties and organizing social events, such as the annual alternative gay and lesbian prom, held on the weekend of high school proms in Chicago, for the youth members.

Protecting teens from the risk of infection from AIDS is another key goal of Horizons' sponsorship of the youth group. AIDS has become an increasingly important element of the youth group discussions. 'Safe sex' is promoted through educational material and special public speakers. In general, the socialization rituals of the group prepare the youths for their new status in the gay and lesbian community, and the rituals culminate in marching in the Gay and Lesbian Pride Day Parade every June.

The lesbian or gay youth is in the throes of moving through the symbolic 'death' of the heterosexual identity and role and into the 'rebirth' of their social being as gay. As a life crisis and a passage between the past and future, the person is betwixt and between normal social states, that is, between the heterosexual worlds of parents and the cultural system of gay and lesbian adults. To the anthropologist, the youths are symbolically exiting what was once called 'homosexuality' and entering what is now called 'gay and lesbian'. To the psychologist, their transition is from dependence and internalized homophobia to a more open and mature competence and pride in the sexual/gender domains of their lives. The transformative power contained in the rituals of coming out as facilitated by Horizons helps in the newfound development of the person. But it also helps in the lives of everyone touched by a youth who is coming out. As long as this process is blocked or resisted, the pull back into passing as heterosexual is very tempting.

Back in the 1960s, coming out was a secret incorporation into the closet 'homosexual' community. Studies at the time showed that the more visible contexts of engaging in same-sex contacts might lead to de facto coming out, but these were generally marginal and dangerous places, such as public toilets, where victimization and violence could occur. To come out in secret bars, the military, toilets, or bus depots did not create a positive identification with the category of gay/lesbian. There was generally no identity that positively accorded with gay or lesbian self-esteem as we think of it today. Thus, we can understand how many people found it revolutionary to fight back against homophobia and begin to march openly in parades in the 1970s. Nevertheless, the change was uneven and difficult.

People who continue to pass as straight when they desire people of the same gender and may in fact have sexual relations with them present a perplexing issue—not only for lesbians and gay men but also for society as a whole. This kind of person, through secrecy and passing, serves as a negative role model of what not to be. Alas, there are many movie stars, celebrities, and sports heroes who live closeted lives of this kind—until they are discovered or 'outed' by someone. Many youths are frightened or intimidated when they discover adults they know and love, such as teachers, uncles, family friends, or pastors, who pass as heterosexual but have been discovered to desire the same gender. Adolescents can be angered to discover that a media person they admire has two lives, one publicly heterosexual and one privately homosexual. This is a cultural survival of the nineteenth-century system of closet homosexuality, with its hide-and-seek games to escape the very real dangers of homophobia. In contrast, positive role models provided by the largely white middle-class adult advisers at Horizons are the crucial source for learning how to enter the gay and lesbian community.

Cultural homophobia in high school is a powerful force against coming out. Learning to hide one's desires is crucial for the survival of some youths, especially at home and at school, the two greatest institutions that perpetuate homophobia in the United States. Our informants tell us that standard slurs to put people down in the schools remain intact. To be slurred as a 'dyke' or a 'faggot' is a real blow to social esteem. But 'queer' is the most troubling epithet of all. To be targeted as a 'queer' in high school is enormously troubling for the youths, somehow more alienating and isolating, an accusation not just of doing something 'different' but of being something 'unnatural'. One seventeen-year-old eleventh grade boy remarked to us that he was secretive at school. 'I'm hidden mostly—cause of the ways they'll treat you. Okay, there are lots of gangs. . . . They find out you're [what they call] a faggot and they beat on you and stuff. If they ask me I say it's none of their business.' The role of secrecy, passing, and hiding continues the homophobia. Ironically, as Michelle Fine (1988: 36) notes in her study of black adolescent girls in New York City high schools, it was the gay and lesbian organization in the school that was the most open and safe environment in which young African-American girls could access their own feelings. They could, with the support of the lesbian and gay teenage group, start to become the agents of their *own* desires. Our study has shown that in Chicago most lesbian or gay youths have experienced harassment in school; and when this is combined with harassment and problems at home, it signals a serious mental health risk, especially for suicide. And the risk of suicide before lesbian or gay youths come to find the support of the Horizons group is very great.

The ritual of coming out means giving up the secrecy of the closet. This is a positive step toward mental health, for life in the closet involves not only a lot of hiding but also a good deal of magical thinking, which may be detrimental to the person's well-being. By magical thinking, I mean mainly contagious beliefs about homosexuality such as the common folk ideas of our culture that stereotype homosexuality as a disease that spreads, as well as the historical images of homosexuality as a mental illness or a crime against nature. These magical beliefs support homophobia and warn about the dangers of going to a gay community organization, whispering how the adolescent might turn into a monster or sex find or be raped or murdered or sold into slavery.

Another common contagious fear is the belief that by merely contacting other gays, the adolescent's 'sin or disease' will spread to the self and will then unwittingly spread to others, such as friends and siblings. One of the common magical beliefs of many adults and parents is that the youth has merely to avoid other gay and lesbians in order to 'go straight'. This is surely another cultural 'leftover' from the dark myth of homosexuality as evil. If the adolescent will only associate with straights, the parent feels, this strange period of 'confusion' will pass, and he or she will become heterosexual like everyone else. Such silly stereotypes are strongly associated with the false notion that all gay or lesbian teens are simply 'confused', which was promoted by psychologists in the prior generation. This belief is based on the cultural myth that same-sex desires are 'adolescent' desires of a transient nature that may be acquired or learned but can go away; and if the self ignores them, the desire for the opposite sex will grow in their place. Magical fears of contracting AIDS is a new and

most powerful deterrent to coming out among some youths. Many youths fear their initial social contact with anyone gay because they think they might contagiously contract AIDS by being gay or lesbian or by interacting socially with gays.

The gender difference in the experience of coming out as a male or a female highlights the cultural pressures that are still exerted on teens to conform to the norm of heterosexuality in our society. Girls typically have more heterosexual experience in their histories, with two-thirds of the girls having had significant heterosexual contact before they came to Horizons. Since the age of our sample was about eighteen, it is easy to see that relatively early on, between the ages of thirteen and seventeen, girls were being inducted into sexual relations with boys. We face here the problem of what is socially necessary and what is preferred. Only one-third of the boys had had heterosexual experience, and fully two-fifths of them had had no sexual experience with girls. Note also that for many of the boys, their sexual contacts with girls were their lesbian-identified friends at the Horizons youth group. The boys tended to achieve sexual experiences earlier than the girls, by age sixteen, at which point the differences in development had evened out. Both genders were beginning to live openly lesbian or gay lives.

Clearly, powerful gender role pressures are exerted on girls to conform to the wishes of parents, siblings, peers, and boyfriends. Some of this, to use a phrase by Nancy Chodorow (1992) about heterosexuality as a compromise formation, results in a compromise of their desires, even of their personal integrity, in the development of their sexual and self-concept. But as we know from the work of Michele Fine (1992), who studied adolescent sexuality among African-American girls in the New York City schools, females were not able to explore and express their desires until they located a safe space that enabled them to think out loud. In fact, they could not become the agents of their own desires until they had located the gay and lesbian youth group in the high school!

There, some of them had to admit, contrary to their stereotypes, they found the gay youths more accepting and open of variations than any of their peers or the adults. The lesson here is that when a cultural space is created, people can explore their own desires and better achieve their own identities and sociosexual goals in life.

We have found that four powerful magical beliefs exist in the implicit learning of homophobia and self-hatred among gay and lesbian youths. First is the idea that homosexuals are crazy and heterosexuals are sane. Unlearning this idea involves giving up the assumption of heterosexual normalcy in favour of positive attitudes and role models. Second is the idea that the problem with same-gender desires is in the self, not in society. Unlearning this belief means recognizing cultural homophobia and discovering that the problem with hatred lies not in the self but in society. Third is the magical belief that to have same-gender desires means giving up gendered roles as they were previously known and acting as a gender-transformed person, a boy acting or dressing as a girl, a girl living as a boy, or either living as an androgyne. There is nothing wrong with these transformations. What we have seen in the cross-cultural study, however, is that there are a variety of ways to organize same-gender desires. The old ways of gender inversion from the nineteenth century are only one of these. Unlearning gender reversal means accepting one's own gendered desires and enactments of roles, whatever these are, rather than living up to social standards—either in the gay or straight community.

Fourth is the belief that if one is going to be gay, there are necessary goals, rules, roles, and political and social beliefs that must be performed or expressed. This idea goes against the grain of American expressive individualism, in which we feel that each one of us is unique and entitled to 'know thyself' as the means of social fulfillment. The key is that there is not one perfect way to be gay; there are many divergent ways. Nor is there any single event, or magic pill, that will enable the

process of coming out. It is a lifelong process, as long as it takes to live and find a fulfilling social and spiritual lifeway in our culture.

Lesbian and gay youths have shown that coming out is a powerful means of confronting the unjust, false, wrongful social faces and values of prejudice in our culture. Before being out, youths are asking, 'What can we be?' or 'How can we fit into this society?' Emerging from the secrecy, these youths are making new claims on society to live up to its own standards of justice. The rituals of coming out are a way of unlearning and creating new learning about living with same-gender desires and creating a positive set of relationships around them. Surely the lesson of the gay movement is that hiding desires and passing as something other than what one is are no less injurious to the normal heart and the healthy mind of gay youths than was, say, passing as a Christian if one was a Jew in Nazi Germany or passing as white in the old South or in South Africa under apartheid.

Lesbian and gay youths are challenging society in ways that are no less revolutionary than discriminations based on skin color, gender, or religion. A new of kind of social and political activism has arisen; it goes beyond AIDS/HIV, but builds on the grief and anger that the entire generation feels about the impact of the pandemic on gay and lesbian culture. Some call this new generation queer. But others prefer lesbian or gay or bisexual or transgendered. Perhaps the word is less important than the commitment to building a rich and meaningful social world in which all people, including lesbians and gays, have a place to live and plan for the future.

We have seen in this chapter how a new generation of lesbian- and gay-identified youths has utilized transition rituals to find a place in the gay and lesbian community. It was the activism and social progress of the lesbian and gay culture that made this huge transformation possible. The emergence of a community enabled the support of youth groups and other institutions for the creation of a new positive role model and self-concept. Youths are beginning to take up new status rights and duties, having a new set of cultural ideas to create the moral voice of being gay, bisexual, lesbian, or queer. The rituals, such as the annual Gay and Lesbian Pride Day Parade, make these newly created traditions a lived reality; they codify and socialize gay and lesbian ideals, knowledge, and social roles, bonding past and future in a timeless present that will enable these youths to find a place in a better society.

References

Benedict, R. 1938. 'Continuities and Discontinuities in Cultural Conditioning', *Psychiatry* 1: 161–7.

Chodorow, N.J. 1992. 'Heterosexuality as a Compromise Formation: Reflections on the Psychoanalytic Theory of Sexual Development', *Psychoanalysis and Contemporary Thought* 15: 267–304.

Devereux, G. 1937. 'Institutionalized Homosexuality Among the Mohave Indians', *Human Biology* 9: 498–527.

Fine, M. 1988. 'Sexuality, Schooling, and Adolescent Females: The Missing Discourse of Desire', *Harvard Education Review* 58: 29–53.

Hart, C.W.M. 1963. 'Contrasts Between Prepubertal and Postpubertal Education', in G. Spindler, ed., *Education and Culture*, pp. 400–25. New York: Holt, Rinehart and Winston.

Herdt, G. 1981. *Guardians of the Flutes: Idioms of Masculinity*. New York: McGraw-Hill.

———. 1982. 'Fetish and Fantasy in Sambia Initiation', in G. Herdt, ed., *Rituals of Manhood*, pp. 44–98. Berkeley and Los Angeles: University of California Press.

———. 1984. 'Semen Transactions in Sambia Culture', in G. Herdt, ed., *Ritualized Homosexuality in Melanesia*, pp. 167–210. Berkeley and Los Angeles: University of California Press.

———. 1991. 'Representations of Homosexuality in Traditional Societies: An Essay on Cultural Ontology and Historical Comparison, Part II', *Journal of the History of Sexuality* 2: 603–32.

———. 1993. 'Introduction', in G. Herdt, ed., *Ritualized Homosexuality in Melanesia*, pp. vii–xliv. Berkeley and Los Angeles: University of California Press.

Herdt, G., and A. Boxer. 1996. *Children of Horizons: How Gay and Lesbian Youth Are Forging a New Way Out of the Closet*. Boston: Beacon Press.

Herdt, G., and R.J. Stoller. 1990. *Intimate Communications: Erotics and the Study of Culture*. New York: Columbia University Press.

CHAPTER 7

'The Pecker Detectors are Back': Regulation of the Family Form in Ontario Welfare Policy

Margaret Hillyard Little and Ian Morrison

In 1940 Gladys Walker, a single mother, had her Mothers' Allowance cheque cancelled after the welfare worker made several surprise visits to her home. The welfare worker wrote:

I was mystified by a 'boy friend' who was in the house when I called and stayed right through the time I was there and had many suggestions as to why the allowance should be granted. I didn't like his manner at all—he was decidedly too much at home. I asked Mrs Walker if he boarded there—'No, just a close friend.' Mrs Walker seemed most anxious to secure the allowance at once as she needed some new clothes for a special occasion. I thought the close friend would likely be there for life when the occasion occurred ('Letter to Investigator', 1940).

The occasion that was on the welfare worker's mind was probably marriage.

In the fall of 1995 Bonnie Nye, whose boyfriend was in jail, moved to Prescott, Ontario. She was desperate for a place to live and could not find one within her welfare budget. In October, on her boyfriend's suggestion, she moved in with his best friend, Jerome Arthurs. She filled out a spouse-in-the-house questionnaire and provided other evidence that she and Jerome were co-residents and not a couple. In December she waited and waited for the welfare cheque to arrive but it never did. Instead, she discovered that she had been cut off welfare because a neighbour had made an anonymous phone call to the welfare office and said that Bonnie's co-resident was actually her boyfriend and that they were living common-law ('Affidavit of Bonnie Nye', 1995).[1]

These are two very different eras in the administration of Ontario Mothers' Allowance (OMA).[2] Yet, in both cases, these single mothers lost their welfare cheques because it was assumed that they had an intimate relationship with a man. How do we understand the state's need to police the social and sexual lives of single mothers? To what extent has this policy changed over time in its regulation of single mothers' relationships? This paper will attempt to explain how the state determines who is and who is not worthy of Mothers' Allowance based on a mother's associations with men—and how this regulation has been contested by those subject to it. Following a brief historical examination of the policy's determination of moral worthiness, we will pay particular attention to a 1995

change to the definition of 'spouse' in the social assistance system that has meant a return to the practice of intense surveillance of poor mothers' relationships and contacts with men. Those who police these relationships have been nicknamed the 'Pecker Detectors'.[3]

In the eyes of low-income single mothers, the Pecker Detectors are back and with a vengeance. The 1995 changes had a dramatic effect on how the social assistance system constructs the experience of poverty for low-income mothers. Its immediate impact was to disqualify from assistance thousands of women who had been receiving assistance as 'single' mothers prior to October 1995. For others, the new rule has intensified the scrutiny of their personal lives. It sharply restricts their financial and social autonomy by forcing them to apply for public assistance as members of 'couples' with men who are not their spouses for any other legal purposes, regardless of their own understanding of the nature of their relationships and regardless of their wishes to remain financially independent of these men.

Viewing Social Assistance Through the Lens of Moral Regulation

The history of how the welfare system has treated the definition of 'family' and poor women's relationships with men clearly reflects the entanglement of the issues of economic need and moral worthiness. Throughout the history of this policy the state has always been concerned about how to provide aid to single mothers and yet ensure that the policy did not promote this 'deviant family form'. Moral worthiness has always been a concern for the provision of any kind of social assistance, but the moral test has always been gendered. Poor relief for the destitute employable man has always depended upon demonstrated willingness to work at any available job (Struthers, 1994). Poor relief for destitute mothers depended upon compliance with standards of behaviour judged in relation to women's (idealized) role in the traditional heterosexual nuclear family. This family model assumed that the man was the sole breadwinner with an economically dependent wife and children. Assistance was provided to women with children outside such relationships only where they conformed adequately to this family model especially, in respect to sexual behaviour. Historically, the granting of sexual access by a single mother to a man disentitled her to further state assistance.

The History of the 'Man in the House' Rule

Ontario Mothers' Allowance was the first formal state organized social assistance programme in Ontario, established in 1920 to provide government aid to single mothers who could prove themselves to be both morally deserving and in economic need. Through this income assistance programme the provincial state became more intimately involved in the lives and homes of needy single mothers and their children. As a result the state was able to help shape the definitions of women, motherhood, and family. These women entered a unique relationship with the state. In order to become clients of the state these mothers had to prove themselves deserving. This notion of deservedness was broad, encompassing almost all aspects of a mother's life including her associations with men.

Initially, the Ontario Mothers' Allowance Act stated that a mother had to be a 'fit and proper person' in order to receive the monthly allowance cheque (OMA Act, 1920). This permitted state workers to intrude and to examine almost every aspect of a low-income single mother's life. For the first few decades this involved detailed inquiry into a variety of moral issues—cleanliness, sobriety, governance of children, and chastity being most important. By the 1950s the range of moral scrutiny had been largely narrowed to financial honesty and sexual conduct. Under this standard, any implication of sexual 'misbehaviour' could disentitle a recipient.

In 1968 the OMA was repealed and provision of assistance to sole support mothers was incorporated into the new Family Benefits Act (FBA). With this change the formal commitment to explicit moral standards was dropped. Reference to being a 'fit and proper' person was removed; however, the programme still only provided benefits to women considered 'single' by the state. The Family Benefits program required that a mother be 'living as a single person', defined (somewhat tautologically) as not 'living together [with another person] as husband and wife'.[4] Although this definition apparently narrowed the scope of the rule to people actually residing together in a 'marriage like' relationship, historical evidence indicates that there was little change in the actual practices of scrutiny of sexual behaviour.

Policing this requirement—commonly referred to as the 'man in the house' rule—had a dual nature. The first concern was to discover whether a man was 'in the house' at all. If so, the welfare system sought to discover the nature of the relationship between the woman and the male resident (although as we shall see, these two concerns often merge in practice). The administration of this rule was oppressive and intrusive. One former recipient turned community activist and advocate summarized experiences of the rule thus:

> This notorious rule was the basis for widespread surveillance of poor women, intrusive investigations into every aspect of their private lives and arbitrary and capricious administration. It was frequently abused, as women would be cut off simply because it was claimed that they had a boyfriend, even where the supposed boyfriend did not live with the recipient ('Affidavit of Nancy Vander Plaats', 1995).

Histories of OMA have catalogued the extraordinary lengths to which welfare investigators would go in their efforts to determine whether a man was present overnight in a recipient's residence (Little, 1998). This zeal to uncover implications of sexual contact suggests that the more overt moralization of the 'fit and proper person' standard continued into welfare administration long after its formal repeal. OMA recipients interviewed by Margaret Little in the 1980s and 1990s certainly understood the rule this way. Some recipients at least (especially in smaller communities) were so worried about the rule that they would avoid contact with men altogether rather than run the risk of arousing the suspicion of neighbours and other 'good citizens' whose reports often triggered investigations and threats of cancellation of benefits.

By the late 1960s and early 1970s, however, the 'man in the house' rule became more openly contested. Resistance to the rule emerged as welfare recipients, including OMA recipients, increasingly developed a public political presence and voice. More importantly, the definition of spouse became a legal issue that was frequently contested in the Ontario courts. The creation of a social assistance appeals system (established as a condition of funding under the 1967 Canada Assistance Plan), the establishment and growth of legal aid programmes providing assistance in 'welfare law' and the development of feminist legal analysis which began to reconceptualize the 'man in the house' administration as issues of systemic discrimination all contributed to this process. People who lost benefits because of the 'man in the house' rule were able to, and increasingly did, challenge these decisions in legal proceedings.

The political problems of the spouse in the house rule were only one part of a crisis in the welfare system that deepened throughout the 1990s. The explosive growth in welfare caseloads and widespread insecurity of the recession of the early 1990s gave rise to a massive backlash against the welfare system and welfare recipients, a backlash exploited fully by the Harris Conservatives in the 1995 Ontario election campaign. Resentment of single mothers was an important part of this backlash. The Tory promise to 'crack down' on a welfare system perceived as being out of control

was an important contributing factor to their June 1995 electoral victory (Morrison, 1997, 1998). Changes were announced August 1995, only two months after election, to take effect in October. Significantly, the changes were announced as part of an 'anti-fraud' initiative (MCSS, 1995a), continuing the demonization of welfare recipients that had proved such a successful political strategy in the election.

The 1995 changes have now been entrenched in new Ontario social assistance legislation, the Ontario Works Act.[5] Under the new definition, if a man 'resides in the same dwelling place'[6] as a woman, he will be considered her spouse in three circumstances. First, if they declare themselves to be spouses (clause [a]). Second, if he has a legal support obligation to her or any of her children arising from contract, court order or by statute (clauses [b] and [c]), for example, if he is the father of one or more of her children. Third, even if neither of these situations exists, he may still be found to be spouse under clause (d) of the definition if he is:

> (d) subject to subsection (3), a person of the opposite sex to the applicant or recipient who is residing in the same dwelling place as the applicant or recipient if the social and familial aspects of the relationship between the person and the applicant or recipient amount to cohabitation and,
>
>> (i) the person is providing financial support to the applicant or recipient,
>>
>> (ii) the applicant or recipient is providing financial support to the person, or
>>
>> (iii) the person and the applicant or recipient have a mutual agreement or arrangement regarding their financial affairs.

Who is a Spouse?

From 1987 to 1995, the definition of spouse for people who were not married or did not have children together was easy to administer. The presence of a co-resident of either sex was taken into account in determining a recipient's allowance,[7] but the nature of the relationship was ignored for three years.[8] The 1995 amendment purported to replace this 'arbitrary' line with what the government has called a 'functional' definition. But in the absence of marriage, what is a couple? The state faces an increasingly intractable dilemma here. The ideological force of 'family' particularly the traditional—that is, the heterosexual nuclear family—remains powerful, but has been problematized and complicated by awareness and varying degrees of acceptance of diversity within the umbrella of 'family'.

The welfare system now operates in a profoundly different social context than that which existed through most of the history of Mothers' Allowance. Historically, most women became single mothers as widows and remained so permanently. Today, both the cause and the duration of episodes of single motherhood have dramatically changed. The breakdown of marriage or a common-law relationship now accounts for almost 60 per cent of all single motherhood. A smaller but increasing percentage of single mother families are formed by women giving birth without a male partner at the time of conception, who decide to raise the child alone. Single motherhood tends now to be a temporary rather than a permanent condition, as it was in earlier times. Most single mothers will eventually form part of a new heterosexual family unit (Little, 1998) and a growing number will do so more than once.[9] Over 90 per cent of women who are single at the time of giving birth later form a heterosexual partnership, most within three or four years (Marcil-Gratton, 1993). The relationships that single mothers come from or enter into may or may not ever involve marriage. Unmarried cohabitation has become increasingly common as a prelude to or a substitute for marriage. The percentage of self-identified couples who cohabit rather than marry increased from 5.6 per cent in 1981 to 9.9 per cent in 1991 (Statistics Canada,

1996); close to a third of all adults have cohabited at least once (Canadian Social Trends, 1991). Younger adults are far more likely to cohabit than older adults, although cohabitation is increasingly common at all age groups (Canadian Social Trends, 1991). Well over half of all couples under age 24 are living 'common law'.

The economic role of women in families has also changed dramatically. Most mothers now have paid employment of some kind outside the home. Almost all modest and low-income families need this income to maintain their living standards.

On the surface, the 'man in the house' rule has now entirely abandoned any overt concern with sexual morality per se (although we argue below that this is not really so). At a more fundamental level, though, the moral underpinnings of the rule remain the same: the 'normal' economic unit of society, at least for the purposes of state aid and poor relief, is the family. And not just any family, but the heterosexual nuclear family, the 'married couple' and their children. For welfare purposes, couples (unlike any other people who live together such as friends, siblings, other relatives) are conclusively deemed to operate as an economic unit. The welfare system assumes for this grouping alone that all income and assets of each partner are fully shared and equally available to each other.[10] Providing state support to a poor mother who is, or appears to be, living as part of a couple is to privilege her in relation to women who live with 'husbands'. The concern with welfare as a moral hazard for the behaviour of women has changed little from the first days of Mothers' Allowance.

The 'man in the house' rule no longer assumes that female dependency in male–female relationships is normal and no longer expressly demands chastity in behaviour, but the fundamental principle remains much the same. State aid will not be given to single mothers and their children if she appears to have granted sexual access to a man in a relationship which the state—not the woman—decides is spousal. The welfare system still assigns women to 'couple' relationships based on an expressly heterosexual (and implicitly sexual) model. Women seeking benefits for themselves and their children lose the autonomy to define the conditions of their relationships with men that all other women in society can exercise.

What does the new definition mean in practice? Before we turn to look at the systemic impact of the 1995 changes and the ongoing consequences for low income mothers, it will be useful to look at how the spousal definition is actually applied. To understand what it means in the lives of those affected, it is necessary to look at how the welfare system deals with the presence—or the alleged presence—of an opposite sex co-resident in the home of a woman claiming sole-support parent benefits.

Who Does the Laundry? The 'Spouse in the House' Questionnaire

Opposite sex co-residents are deemed to be spouses unless they can satisfy a welfare worker that they are not. The main tool for making this assessment is an exhaustive questionnaire that involves some 80 questions, covering almost every imaginable aspect of the recipient's living situation. The economic relationship between a single mother and a male boarder is particularly scrutinized. Training material for welfare workers suggest that all arrangements in which common expenses are shared will be considered a spousal relationship under the new rule. Caseworkers are explicitly directed to assess whether such items as televisions, cars, furniture, or telephones are used jointly by co-residents, and to take such sharing as evidence of financial interdependence (MCSS, 1998). It is interesting to note that other financial criteria in regards to this policy are quite explicit. The act clearly states how much a single mother can earn, the amount of assets she can have, and how much her car can be worth. Yet, when it comes to financial arrangements within a household the criteria are quite vague. There is no stated

dollar figure or percentage of household expenses that can be shared without repercussions.

Social and familial interdependence is also assessed through this questionnaire. Some of the questions asked in this regard include the following:

14. Do you and your co-resident have common friends?

15b. Do other people invite the two of you over together?

18. Do you and your co-resident spend spare time at home together?

22a. Do you and your co-resident attend holiday celebrations together (e.g., Christmas, Thanksgiving dinners, birthdays)? Does (s)he buy holiday presents?

24a. How do you and your co-resident divide the household chores (e.g., mowing the lawn, shovelling snow, raking leaves, repairs, laundry, housework)?

24b. Does your co-resident ever do your laundry (or the children's)?

27. Who takes care of you and your co-resident when either of you are ill?

There are also numerous questions to determine the relationship between the co-resident and the single mother's children. They include:

30a. Do you ask your co-resident for advice regarding the children?

32. Does your co-resident impose discipline or corrective action on your children?

35a. Does your co-resident attend your children's birthday parties?

Community members are engaged both directly and indirectly in the assessment of the nature of the relationship. The opinions of landlords, neighbours, teachers, policy, charity workers, and ex-husbands are often considered by workers in deciding how to characterize a relationship with a co-resident. These opinions are also implicitly mirrored in the questionnaire, in which applicants or recipients are asked:

13.   Do people think of you as a couple?
16.   Are you known as a couple by public agencies or service (e.g., Children's Aid Society, the police, bank, school, doctors, recreational activities)?

These questions clearly encourage a single mother to be concerned about how all those around her interpret her relationships, while reflecting the continued role of the community in the moral scrutiny of those seeking welfare assistance.

The Impact of the 1995 Rate Changes

The 1995 changes had an impact far beyond the government's expectations. After the rule changes, welfare authorities began systematic file reviews of the thousands of recipients recorded as having opposite sex co-residents. The government had estimated that 3,820 single parents would lose eligibility as a result of the changed definition ('Affidavit of Mary Kardos Burton', 1995). Six months later, by April 1996, over 10,000 recipients from the social assistance caseload had been deemed ineligible under the new definition, 89 per cent of whom were women ('Affidavit of Kevin Costante', 1995).

Women cut off under the rule often faced difficult personal choices. A recipient could stay eligible if she moved or asked the man to leave, often a difficult decision both emotionally and financially—especially as the terminations coincided with a 21.6 per cent cut in social assistance allowances, which left most recipients financially desperate (Morrison, 1996). Or, she could appeal the decision and be reinstated pending the appeal, but this option only existed for people who understood the appeals process and were capable of negotiating it.[11] Six months after the rule change, only about 800 of those cut off had been reinstated. Another 2,341 of those terminated had applied for welfare as a couple. Some did

so under severe protest but feeling that for financial or emotional reasons—or both—they had no choice.[12] By doing so, a woman in this position became dependent upon the conduct of a man with no legal responsibility to her or her children. Welfare offices issue only one cheque to a household and it is still usually assumed in practice that the head of household is the man (although the legal definition is gender neutral) ('Affidavit of Nancy Vander Plaats', 1995).[13] In fact, the inertia of this assumption is so strong that a man may be designated 'head of household' even where he is a recovering alcoholic and drug abuser—directly contrary to official welfare policy.[14] Sometimes, applying for welfare as a couple was not legally possible because the man was ineligible under the complicated rules of the welfare system and this made the whole 'family' ineligible. The great majority of those cut off during this initial period, almost 7,000 in total, remained off assistance. What happened to them is unknown.

Back to the Future: Living in the Shadow of the Man in the House Rule

The 1995 amendments along with the Harris government's changes to welfare administration mean a new era in policing the lives of recipients. Much of the energy of the welfare system is devoted not to determining the nature of the relationship between a recipient and her roommate, but to finding out whether a man is there at all. Historically, these surveillance practices were the main focus of complaints about the intrusive and oppressive nature of the rule. These concerns diminished during the period 1987 to 1995 although they did not disappear.[15] With the 1995 changes and the increasing emphasis of the system on 'fraud' detection, investigations to determine the presence of a man in the house have once again become an important presence in recipients' lives.

Investigations of an alleged man in the house can be triggered many ways: random home visits by welfare workers, suspicious computer cross-referencing, observations recounted to the welfare office by neighbours, family members, employers, landlords or other 'concerned citizens', retaliatory denunciations by former spouses or boyfriends seeking revenge through harassment, etc. Both the initial reports and the investigations often involve the participation of community members, who are sought out by welfare investigators for questioning. Community surveillance and anonymous reporting of welfare recipients is actively encouraged by the Ontario government. The 1995 'anti fraud' initiatives included a highly publicized welfare 'snitch line' with a 1-800 number. While there are no data available on the use of this Ontario fraud line a similar province-wide telephone service in Manitoba revealed that the majority of the callers complained about single mothers and their associations with men (Little, 1996). Of the cases reported to the snitch line where action was taken, by far the largest category (42 per cent) was 'spouse not declared'. It is also important to note that the vast majority of calls to the snitch line either were not even investigated or revealed no fraud or error upon investigation (MCSS, 1997).

Conclusion

The 1995 amendments have had an enormous impact on the lives of poor single mothers. Single mothers have experienced a new heightened level of moral scrutiny and surveillance. While single mothers on welfare have always experienced intrusive moral investigation into their lives, this scrutiny waned somewhat during the 1970s and early 1980s. Today, the administration of this amendment, alone, signifies a renewed and intensive level of investigation into the moral behaviour of single mothers. This scrutiny is not merely carried out by welfare administrators. Numerous community members are also highly involved in the determination of the spousal status of single mothers on welfare. And, in fact, the government has taken measures to encourage the community to be

more involved in this determination. Indeed, this amendment ensures a role for both government and community versions of the 'Pecker Detector'.

All of this suggests that low-income single mothers have become a target for moral scrutiny and blame in the 1990s. This not only impacts single mothers on welfare but it affects all women. Condemning single mothers to abject poverty and moral scrutiny deters other women from leaving unhappy or abusive relationships. Therefore this policy amendment impedes the ability of all women to become full and equal citizens in Ontario society.

Epilogue

Shortly after it was enacted, a legal challenge to the 1995 amendments was commenced in Ontario on behalf of four women who lost sole-support parent benefits as a result of the changes. Much of the material on which this paper is based is drawn from the evidence and testimony led by both sides in that case. In August 1998 a panel of the Ontario Social Assistance Review Board ruled that clause (d) of the definition as enacted in 1995 was inconsistent with the Canadian Charter of Rights and Freedoms. The board held that the definition violated the right to equality protected under section 15 of the Charter, because it discriminated against sole-support parents on social assistance vis-à-vis all other sole-support parents in Ontario; the board held further that the rule violated rights to privacy and personal autonomy under section 7 of the Charter. The board ordered benefits reinstated to the four appellants.

Response to the ruling was, predictably, polarized along lines that are familiar to all students of the rule's history. One newspaper columnist accused the Social Assistance Review Board of 'social engineering' and demanded that the government appeal the decision as a 'moral imperative' for the sake of children, claiming that the rule placed children at risk in unstable (unmarried) relationships and discourages partners from marrying (Blizzard, 1998). Anti-poverty activists and community legal workers, on the other hand, saw the ruling as a victory for single mothers and hoped that the decision would permit low-income women more freedom in their living arrangements and personal lives.

This is far from the final word on the spouse in the house rule. The Ontario government filed an appeal to the SARB decision almost immediately. There are several levels of possible appeal remaining, including the eventual possibility of an appeal to the Supreme Court of Canada. How far the case will actually be appealed—and what will happen if the courts ultimately affirm the board's decision—cannot be predicted at this point. In the meantime, the new definition remains in effect and the spouse in the house rule continues to regulate the lives of low-income women.[16] What can be safely predicted is that the issue will remain contentious—and the behaviour and life choices of low-income women will continue to be scrutinized and moralized. As long as the state chooses to distinguish between 'single' mothers and 'couples' in providing support to women with children, a line must be drawn between the groups. Where this line should be drawn, however, and the important consequences that flow from this choice, remains an inescapable dilemma of social assistance policy in a social order that refuses to value women's caregiving work in and of itself.

Notes

1. In *Re Sandra Elizabeth Falkiner et al. and Ontario*, Ontario Court of Justice (Divisional Court), File #310-95, (hereafter, 'Falkiner Record'). The Falkiner case involves a legal challenge to the 1995 regulation changes, based on the Canadian Charter of Rights and Freedom. The case is still under appeal at the time of writing. Much of the information in this paper is taken from the many volumes of evidence filed by both sides in this case.

2. Mothers' Allowance was the original name of this programme. As discussed below, the Ontario Mothers' Allowance Act was repealed in 1968 and the programme name has changed twice since then; however, the name 'Mothers' Allowance' is still in common popular usage.

3. Brenda Thompson made the nickname infamous in her book, *A Survival Guide for Single Mothers on Welfare in Nova Scotia* (Halifax: Dalhousie Public Interest Research Group, 1990). Some Ontario low-income mothers interviewed by Margaret Little have used the same term.

4. From 1968 to 1998 social assistance in Ontario was delivered through two programmes, General Welfare Assistance, a provincially mandated but municipally delivered system aimed primarily at 'employable' people in need, and Family Benefits, a provincially delivered programme whose clients were primarily sole-support parents and people with disabilities. The definition of 'single person' was the same in both programmes. It is clear, however, that concern over the issue of singleness remained primarily bound up in the moral anxieties created by the existence of the single mother family, and that actual investigative attention was overwhelmingly although never exclusively directed at women.

5. For a brief discussion of how the Ontario Works Act treats sole-support parents and the weakening of women's moral claims to state assistance based on their caregiving work as mothers, see Morrison, 1998, 'Ontario Works'. For a review of how this moral claim eroded over time even before the Ontario Works programme, see Pat Evans, 'Single Mothers and Ontario's Welfare Policy: Restructuring the Debate', *Women and Canadian Public Policy*, Janine Brodie, ed. (Toronto: Harcourt Brace, 1996).

6. This wording was substituted for an earlier phrase, 'living with', to circumvent decisions that had occasionally held that a woman was not 'living with' a man who would otherwise be a spouse, if the relationship was violent and she was unable to leave, or if there was clearly no conjugal aspect to the relationship.

7. It is not commonly understood that whenever another adult was present in the residence of a social assistance recipient, a deduction was

made from the allowance. Welfare regulations simply assumed that the co-resident was paying a prescribed portion of the rent (whether or not this was actually the case).

8. Disputes could and did arise at the end of three years as to whether the co-resident was a 'spouse'; however, these were relatively infrequent. In most cases, after three years the nature of the relationship and the evidence as to the nature of the relationship was fairly clear. A more common dispute during this period was whether an admitted 'spouse', a husband or the father of the recipient's children, had returned to the home.

9. According to a study based on the 1990 General Social Survey, the number of children who have experienced multiple changes in family composition (including periods of living with a lone parent) is rising. Growing numbers by age cohort will have experienced two or even three successive two-adult families, usually with intervening periods in a single-parent family. See Nicole Marcil-Gratton's article, 'Growing Up with a Single Parent, A Transitional Experience? Some Demographic Measurements', *Single Parent Families: Perspectives on Research and Policy*, Joe Hudson and Burt Galaway, eds. (Toronto: Thompson Educational Publishing, 1993), 73–90.

10. Under welfare regulations, the income and assets of all members of the 'benefit unit' (i.e., family) are lumped together to determine eligibility: Ontario Regulation 134/98 (Ontario Works) s. 38, s. 48.

11. Access to legal assistance and legal information are unequally distributed across Ontario. Despite the existence of legal aid, some parts of the province have no community legal clinics and many people are not aware of them when they do exist. About three quarters of all appellants to the Social Assistance Review Board are not assisted by a lawyer or oterh legal representative.

12. The impossible dilemma facing many recipients in this situation is well illustrated in the evidence given by the appellants in the Falkiner Charter challenge. Both in correspondence and in oral testimony the recipients repeated time and again, often with mounting frustration, their

refusal to characterize their relationships within a rigid dichotomy of single/couple in the face of government insistence that they do so. Two of the four appellants did in fact apply for welfare after being terminated, in financial desperation.

13. One recent large-scale survey of Ontario social assistance recipients found that in about 85 per cent of all couples, the man was treated as the household despite the ostensible gender neutrality of the definition: Michael Orenstein, *A Profile of Social Assistance Recipients in Ontario* (Toronto: York University Institute for Social Research, 1995) at 10. The single cheque practice has also been strongly criticized by the Ontario Ombudsman, but to no effect: Legislative Assembly of Ontario, Standing Committee on the Ombudsman, *Hansard*, 4 December 1996, B-53 to B-63.

14. MCSS policies for implementation of the regulation changes stated emphatically that the 'head of household' designation should not be given to a man with 'a recent or current problem, i.e., drinking or gambling, that may result in misuse of the allowance': Ontario, MCSS, 1995b, 'Residing with a Spouse: New Rules for Determining Spousal Status (FBA and GWA) Effective 1 October 1995' (29 September 1995). Nevertheless, when one of appellants in the Falkiner case applied, under protest, for general welfare assistance with her co-resident, a recovering alcholic and drug user, he was designated head of household and sent the welfare cheque for a family of six: 'Affidavit of Deborah Sears', Falkiner Record.

15. From 1987 to 1995 allegations of an unreported spouse in the house usually arose with respect to men who were spouses under clauses (b) or (c) of the definition, that is, an ex-husband or the father of a recipient's child(ren). Also, under the three-year rule women were still obliged to report the presence of a co-resident, as this still affected the calculation of an allowance.

16. A decision by an administrative tribunal such as the Social Assistance Review Board does not change the law. Only a ruling by a court will have that effect. Moreover, when the Ontario Works Act came into force in the summer of 1998, the Social Assistance Review Board was

replaced by a new appeals body called the Social Benefits Tribunal. Unlike the SARB, the SBT does not have the power to rule on constitutional questions—a jurisdiction specifically excluded by the new legislation. In theory, women affected by the rule under the new legislation could start new court applications to challenge the application of the new definition. In practice, the burden of bringing such an application is so enormous that no one has done so and it is not likely that this will happen while an appeal is outstanding.

References

'Affidavit of Bonnie Nye'. 1995. *Re Sandra Elizabeth Falkiner et al. and Ontario*, Ontario Court of Justice (Divisional Court), File #310-95.

'Affidavit of Deborah Sears'. 1995. *Re Sandra Elizabeth Falkiner et al. and Ontario*, Ontario Court of Justice (Divisional Court), File #310-95.

'Affidavit of Kevin Costante'. 1995. *Re Sandra Elizabeth Falkiner et al. and Ontario*, Ontario Court of Justice (Divisional Court), File #310-95.

'Affidavit of Mary Kardos Burton'. 1995. *Re Sandra Elizabeth Falkiner et al. and Ontario*, Ontario Court of Justice (Divisional Court), File #310-95.

'Affidavit of Nancy Vander Plaats'. 1995. *Re Sandra Elizabeth Falkiner et al. and Ontario*, Ontario Court of Justice (Divisional Court), File #310-95.

Blizzard, C. 1998. 'Turning Back the Welfare Clock', *Toronto Sun*, 15 September.

'Common Law: A Growing Alternative'. 1991. *Canadian Social Trends* 18 (Winter).

Evans, P. 1996. 'Single Mothers and Ontario's Welfare Policy: Restructuring the Debate', in J. Brodie, ed., *Women and Canadian Public Policy*. Toronto: Harcourt Brace.

Legislative Assembly of Ontario, Standing Committee on the Ombudsman, *Hansard*, 4 December 1996, B-53 to B-63.

'Letter from Investigator to Local Mothers' Allowance Board, 27 August 1940'. 1940. D.B. Weldon Library, Western Regional Collection, London, Ontario, Mothers' Allowance Case Files, London, Ontario.

Little, M. 1996. 'He Said, She Said: The Role of Gossip in Determining Eligibility for Ontario Mothers' Allowance'. Paper presented to the Canadian Historical Association, Brock University, St Catharines, 31 May.

———. 1998. *'No Car, No Radio, No Liquor Permit': The Moral Regulation of Single Mothers in Ontario, 1920–1997*. Don Mills, ON: Oxford University Press.

Marcil-Gratton, N. 1993. 'Growing Up with a Single Parent, A Transitional Experience? Some Demographic Measurements', in J. Hudson and B. Galaway, eds, *Single Parent Families: Perspectives on Research and Policy*, pp. 73–90. Toronto: Thompson Educational Publishing.

MCSS. 1995. 'Government Combats Fraud and Tightens Welfare Rules', *News Release 95-83* (23 August).

———. 1995. 'Residing with a Spouse: New Rules for Determining Spousal Status (FBA and GWA) effective 1 October 1995'. 28 September.

———. 1998. *Ontario Works Policy Directives* (1 June).

Morrison, I. 1996. *Ontario's Welfare Rate Cuts: An Anniversary Report I*. Toronto: Ontario Social Safety Network. October.

———. 1997. 'Rights and the Right: Ending Social Citizenship in Tory Ontario', in D. Ralph, A. Régimbald, and N. St-Armand, eds, *Open for Business, Closed to People: Mike Harris's Ontario*. Halifax: Fernwood.

———. 1998. 'Ontario Works: A Preliminary Assessment', *Journal of Law and Social Policy* 13: 28–30.

'Ontario Mothers' Allowance Act'. 1920. Statutes of Onatrio.

Orenstein, M. 1995. *A Profile of Social Assistance Recipients in Ontario*. Toronto: York University Institute for Social Research.

Re Sandra Elizabeth Falkiner et al. and Ontario. 1995. Ontario Court of Justice (Divisional Court), File #310-95.

Statistics Canada. 1996. *Families in Canada*. Catalogue No. 96-307 E, Chart 2.1.

Struthers, J. 1994. *The Limits of Affluence: Welfare in Ontario, 1920–1970*. Toronto: University of Toronto Press.

Thompson, B. *A Survival Guide for Single Mothers on Welfare in Nova Scotia*. Halifax: Dalhousie Public Interest Research Group.

CHAPTER 8

Sk8ter Girls: Skateboarders, Girlhood, and Feminism in Motion

Shauna Pomerantz, Dawn H. Currie, and Deirdre M. Kelly

Labelled 'postfeminist' by some of the academic and popular press, teenage girls have often been accused of letting feminism down (Douglas, 1994; Pipher, 1994; Summers, 1994; Abraham, 1997; Curthoys, 1997; Gamer, 1997; Bellafante, 1998; Rapping, 2000; Preston, 2001).[1] Younger generations are frequently charged with enjoying all the freedoms won for them by the women's movement without engaging in the struggle themselves. Teenage girls are repeatedly labelled postfeminist as a way of suggesting that they are not carrying on the traditions of the women's movement and have in some sense failed second wave feminism in its legacy of collective political action and social change.

In the wake of postfeminist discourses, we wonder if today's girls really have let feminism down or if they have simply been ignored. There is little emphasis on the lives of 'regular' girls and their practical experiences of the social world. Where are the 'everyday' girls who do 'everyday' things? When we talk to girls about everyday things, we may begin to hear all the ways in which girls are quietly but powerfully changing the face of girlhood through localized and specific gender struggles.

In her study of bedroom culture in the new millennium, Anita Harris (2001) suggests that girls have developed 'new forms of political expression' (128) that take place in new spaces. Harris explores how girls 'express their politics when the prevailing view is that they have no politics to speak of at all' (139). Focusing on 'gurl' websites, alternative music spheres, and underground zines, she demonstrates 'that young women are passionately engaged in social change agendas, but that these occur in marginal, virtual or underground places' (139). It is here, at the margins of space and place, where girls may be 'doing' feminism. Furthermore, girls may be pushing feminism in exciting and diverse directions away from the usual possibilities that currently receive postfeminist attention. What follows is one such example that was an 'incidental' find in a larger study on alternative girlhoods.[2] While interviewing girls within the frame of new subjectivities, we happened upon a group of eight (girl) skateboarders, whom we call the 'Park Gang'. Becoming girl skateboarders meant that the Park Gang had to challenge the skater boys who dominated the park. They also consciously stood in resistance to what Connell (1987) calls 'emphasized femininity.'[3]

Emphasized femininity is a kind of traditional femininity based on subordination to men and boys. In order to resist emphasized femininity, the Park Gang engaged in a transgressively feminine bodily comportment that is not common for girls. As becoming a girl skater in today's North American context often necessitates engaging in these discursive and embodied struggles, the subject position of 'skater girl' is a social category that holds the possibility for a feminist politics. Subject positions contribute to subjectivity or how we understand ourselves in relation to the world.

Subjectivity 'is produced in a whole range of discursive practices—economic, social, and political—the meanings of which are a constant site of struggle over power' (Weedon, 1987: 21). By occupying the subject position of skater, the Park Gang worked towards a subjectivity that indicated a feminist politics through resistance to the male-dominated space of the park and the emphasized femininity of the girls who hung around the skater boys. By 'doing' skateboarding, the Park Gang worked to resist the traditional femininity modelled by other girls at the park—the girls 'who just watched'. Thus, skateboarding became a subject position fraught with gendered struggles that highlighted the discursive and embodied construction of girlhood.

Legitimation at the Skate Park: Skateboarding as a Discursive Resignification of Girlhood

> Most skaters are young teenage boys who think they are kings and the world sits below them. Trying to tell them that women should be able to skate without being harassed may be an impossible task, but it must be done (Jigsaw Youth, 2002).

Skate parks are generally awash in a grey, graffiti-ridden concrete that is the necessary landscape for practicing tricks. Vancouver has several good places for skateboarding, but most are burdened with a reputation for drugs and vandalism. The largest indoor park in the city was recently shut down for its high level of drug trafficking and defacement of property. Underground skaters who detest anything remotely mainstream avoid the parks, confining their practice to the streets, the parking lots of local establishments, and the (now monitored by security) area surrounding the art gallery downtown. For those skaters who do not mind mainstream skateboarding, the parks are the best place to practice, learn tricks, and participate in skate culture. But no matter which skate park

or street location you choose to frequent, one thing is abundantly clear—there are very few girl skateboarders.

As Sandy, a self-proclaimed skateboarding 'coach' for her friends announced in no uncertain terms, 'Like, a lot of girls don't skateboard!'[4] Skateboarding is not a common activity for girls and finding a girl on a skateboard is rare. Despite the recent media frenzy around teen pop singer Avril Lavigne, who has been dubbed a 'skate punk' for her style and loose connections to skateboarding, girls are often relegated to the sidelines while the boys 'do their thing'. Further evidence can be found by visiting skate parks, where girls hang off the railing as watchers, fans, and girlfriends. Evidence of this can also be found on numerous Internet skater zines dedicated to girls.[5] One girl skater writes, 'Every time I venture out to skate, either alone or with friends, I am in some way harassed, threatened, or opposition to my skating is voiced in some manner' (Jigsaw Youth, 2002). And there is this testimonial of frustration by Morgan:

> Once upon a time, I was a lonely girl skater in a big city. I went to the indoor park a few times a week, but there were never any other girls there and the guys seemed to want little to do with the girl in the corner teaching herself kickturns. As much as I loved skating, it was necessary to give myself a serious pep talk to get motivated to go back to the park each day (Frontside Betty, 2002).

These accounts of life at the skate park indicate the gendered nature of skater culture, where girls have to work much harder and overcome many more obstacles than boys to gain legitimate skater status. The subordination and delegitimation of girls to boys is a common theme in youth sub-cultures. Paul Willis (1981) represents girls in working class 'lad' culture as sexual objects for the more powerful boys. In Dick Hebdige's (1979) analysis of punk culture, girls are represented as accoutrement and secondary figures. McRobbie and Garber (1997 [1976]) first pointed out that youth cultural studies theorists saw girls as backdrop characters in male dominated subcultures, whose lives revolved around finding a boyfriend, looking attractive, and being promiscuous. But in their own analysis of girls in male subcultures, they concluded that traditional sex roles were also dominant in biker culture, mod culture, and hippy culture. Girls were given very little status and almost no legitimation. In skater culture, girls are assigned a similar kind of derogatory positioning. Yet despite the sexism of the skate park and of skateboarding in general, there are still some girls who choose to take up the label of 'skater.'

The members of the Park Gang were 14 and 15 years old at the time of the study—born in the decade defined by a backlash against second wave feminism (Faludi, 1991). They all lived in an area of Vancouver known for its family orientation, professional demographic, and urban chic. Four were Canadian-born Chinese girls, two were white, one was a Canadian-born Latina, and one was half First Nations, half white. This racial mix is representative of the city of Vancouver itself, which is ethnically and racially highly diverse. With the exception of one girl, who attended a Catholic school, the girls all attended a large urban high school known for its Asian population and academic achievement. Skateboarding was a passion for four of the girls; two of the girls called themselves 'coaches' in the sense that they skated but preferred to 'just help'; and two of the girls were skaters by association, meaning that they were involved in skate culture, music, and style—like all of the Park Gang—but without the desire to actually skate.[6] They all hung out at a skate park that would be considered amateurish compared to the larger and more daunting parks downtown. This particular park was connected to a community centre in an affluent neighbourhood. It was relatively clean and safe.

Members of the Park Gang were relatively new skaters when we met them. They came to the sport through older brothers or boys at school. Grover noted that she got started because a friend did not want to learn alone:

> There are not too many girl skateboarders so it is kind of better—she felt more comfortable if there was, like, you know, another person that, you know, could be with her. And so she asked if I wanted to try it, so I said sure, and, um, her brothers started teaching us and I found it was something that, it was a lot of fun, so I just stayed with it, so I'm still learning.

When more of the Park Gang decided to try skateboarding, they ventured into the skate park with their boards for the first time, hoping to gain acceptance and practice. But the park proved to be a location of struggle that was dominated by skater boys, who put the girls under surveillance. The skater boys were always asking members of the Park Gang to show them what they could do and Zoey spoke of the constant questioning of the girls' abilities. They often asked her, 'Why don't you skate *more*?' She admitted that, 'sometimes we don't want to skate around them 'cause, like, they do really good stuff and we're just kind of learning.'

The Park Gang quickly realized that being the only girl skaters at the park singled them out for some harassment. To the skater boys who dominated the park and acted as its gatekeepers, the park was their space—a space that left very little room for girls, unless they were occupying the traditionally feminine subject positions of watcher, fan, or girlfriend. Gracie theorized that girls skate less than boys due to this kind of territorial attitude: 'some [girls] are kind of, like, scared, because, um, of what people might think of them.' When asked what she meant, Gracie noted that the lack of girls who skated at the park might make the boys question girls' right to belong. Onyx added that the skater boys viewed the Park Gang as 'invading their space'. Grover felt that the Park Gang threatened the skater boys 'just because, you know, girls are doing their sport.' She went on to explain the attitudes of some of the boys at the park.

> Sometimes, they'll be kind of, like, rude, like, I don't know if it's on purpose, but they just, you know, have this kind of attitude . . . I guess they think they're so good and one of them or two of them—I'm not sure if all of them are, like, sponsored by skateboarding companies—so they always feel, like, you know, they're kind of superior and so, you know, we're only a year younger, so it's kind of, like, we're obviously not as good as them, but they kind of forget that they had to start somewhere too, so, and it would be harder for us because we're girls.

The territory of the park became a contested space. The boys saw it as theirs. The girls wanted access. Grover, Gracie, and Onyx understood that the boys were threatened by their presence, but wished the boys could appreciate how hard it was for girls to get started. They wanted the boys to see them as equals who deserved the same kind of camaraderie that they gave each other. But instead, the boys saw them as interlopers with little legitimate claim to the space. Some of the boys accused some of the Park Gang of being 'posers'. Often, girls who try to gain skater status are seen as posers. A poser wears the right clothes, such as wide sneakers with fat laces, brand-name pants and hoodies, and, of course, carries a skateboard. But posers do not really skate. Although boys can be posers too, girls who attempt access to the label 'skater' are singled out for this derogatory title. It is assumed that girls hang around the skate park as a way to meet skater boys, to flirt.

When this accusation was levelled at some of the Park Gang, they immediately took action to prove the skater boys wrong. Zoey recounted the story.

> There's this one time where a couple of the guys thought we were just—they said it out loud that we're just there for the guys and

we're like, 'No!' And they're like, 'But you're here all the time, like almost every day, skateboarding, and so are we.' So we did this whole thing where we didn't come there for quite awhile just to show them; and then we came back and they stopped bugging us about it.

The girls involved in the park boycott practiced at an elementary school for two weeks and went to the park only when they knew the boys would not be around. When asked what they had gained by boycotting the park, Zoey responded, 'That we're not there just for the guys and we're not there to watch them and be around them.' Suddenly, the girls received more respect and experienced less harassment from the skater boys. Zoey noted a distinct change in their attitude. 'I guess to some level, they treated us like an equal to them, kind of.' Instead of placing the girls under surveillance, the skater boys watched the Park Gang in order to see 'how they were doing'. They suddenly became curious about the girls' progress. When asked if they thought they had successfully changed the opinions of the skater boys, Zoey enthusiastically replied, 'Well yes!'

Before the boycott, the skater girls were thought of in a very specific way: as posers, flirts, or interlopers. But through the boycott, the girls believed they altered how the boys thought of them and, more significantly, how they thought of themselves. In their efforts to change the meaning of 'skater', the Park Gang acknowledged how they had been subordinated at the park and successfully resignified the commonly accepted process of belonging. They carved out a space for girls where none used to exist. In this way, the Park Gang legitimated the subject position of 'skater' for girls at the park and expanded the possibilities for subjectivity within girlhood. As Pete pointed out, 'lots of girls have actually started [skating] because my group started and then they kind of feel in power. I think they kind of feel empowered that they can start now, that it's okay for girls to skate.' This discursive resignification of girlhood through the skater label enacted a feminist politics that worked to reshape gender categories in a male-dominated locale. As a result of their purposeful positioning as skaters, the Park Gang also worked towards an embodied resignification of girlhood that challenged not just the skater boys, but the traditional femininity of other girls at the park.

Kickflipping Femininity: Skateboarding as an Embodied Resignification of Girlhood

First of all don't play dumb. If you are going to skate, skate!!! Who cares what the guys think. And please don't hang out at the skate park with your skateboard just to pick up guys. Cause it ain't working! Just be yourself and you will go a lot farther (Whitney, 2001).

The skate park was a hangout for all different kinds of youth, many of whom did not skate, but instead chose to sit on the benches, picnic tables, and steps that surrounded the concrete area designated for skaters. It was a place where girls and boys could gather to socialize. Some of the girls were well known as the 'popular' girls at school. They had boyfriends, money to spend on 'the right' clothes, and a nickname ascribed to them by the Park Gang based on the fact that they often wore buns in their hair—'Bun Girls'. The Park Gang saw Bun Girls as representative of a certain kind of girl that they did not respect. Pete explained that the Bun Girls were annoying people who lived by an image 'that kind of pisses me off'. When asked to explain, Pete painted this picture: 'Skinny, the whole thing, the whole skinniness, having, being skinny, thin, pretty, makeup, umm, lots of money, shoes, be spoiled and then kind of living their life for a guy. That kind of annoys me too!' She went on to say: 'I notice that they [Bun Girls], like, all dress, like, they have, they have to have some sort of motivation to dress up like that and I think it's to be popular, to kind of, um,

get guys. And so, I don't like that. I think it's just totally wrong to live your life like that!'

The Park Gang continuously described the Bun Girls as trendy, boy crazy, and clueless. Their 'ditzy' reputation stemmed from the fact that they spent much of their energy worrying about clothes, looks, and boyfriends. Bun Girls wore tight, low-cut tank tops and tight, low-cut jeans from expensive, brand-name stores. Their appearance was coiffed, polished, and en vogue. The Bun Girls had a power that was based on bodily display, sexiness, and a perceived maturity or sophistication. While some of the skater boys responded to the Bun Girls' sexuality, the Park Gang generally tried to resist enacting this kind of power, seeing it as 'fake' and built around a passive bid for attention from the boys.[7] Gracie noted that Bun Girls often played 'dumb' and 'tough' when they did not mean it at all. Sandy explained this fake attitude: 'Yeah, like, [the Bun Girls are like] 'Oh, I don't care about that!' when really they would care or they're just hiding it. Like, as if people are putting up, like, a façade!'

Members of the Park Gang often actively worked to resist Bun Girl femininity. Instead of caring about what others thought of them, the Park Gang saw themselves as individuals with unique personalities who took pride in being different, fun, and alternative. A Bun Girl was seen to be a carbon copy without any sort of defining characteristics, except, as Grover put it 'caring what other people think'. For members of the Park Gang, this kind of self-conscious behaviour was all too typical and gave girls a bad name. Zoey put it like this: 'Yeah, because, you know, the whole thing, like, where a lot of girls want to be sexy? That is totally the opposite of us. We don't. We don't and we kind of don't really like those kind of girls that do, because it's for popularity and stuff like that.'

The Bun Girls were 'watchers' at the park who used their inability to skate as a way to meet skater boys. As Zoey described them: 'They're [Bun Girls] always, like, they get on the board and ask for, like, the guys to hold their hand and pull them and they start screaming, you know, acting weird.' When asked what members of the Park Gang did when they saw the Bun Girls acting this way, Zoey replied, 'We just roll our eyes and walk away.' Bun Girl femininity was giggly, ditzy, and purposefully subordinate to boys. It was based on physical appearance, money, clothing, and inactivity. Creating a distance between the Bun Girls and themselves was as important to the Park Gang as gaining the respect of the skater boys. By purposefully juxtaposing themselves to the Bun Girls, members of the Park Gang demonstrated an embodied resistance to a dominant form of femininity that they saw as detrimental to girlhood itself. For example, in order to differentiate themselves from Bun Girl femininity, the Park Gang dressed casually and comfortably. They avoided wearing makeup and did not engage in sexual display through style. They also worked to speak their minds and did not pretend to be 'ditzy' or in need of skater boy assistance on their boards. But the real distinction between Bun Girl femininity and the embodied resistance of the Park Gang was the difference between 'watcher' and 'doer' at the skate park. As 'doers', or girls who actually skated, the Park Gang engaged in the embodied resignification of Bun Girl femininity through a distinct bodily comportment.

Skateboarding is a sport that demands physicality and bravery. To skate is to know how to fall and how to attempt many complicated and risky tricks. Even the most basic trick, the ollie, where a skater jumps in the air with her board attached to her feet and then lands smoothly on it again, runs the risk of injury. Ollies, kickflips, grinding, and carving are all skater tricks that must be performed fearlessly and with the full knowledge that falling is likely (especially for the Park Gang, who were new to tricks and only just attempting them for the first time). This kind of physical audacity is not generally associated with being a girl. As Iris Marion Young (1989) suggests, typical motility and spatiality for girls can be timid, uncertain,

and hesitant, as girls are not brought up to have the same kind of confidence and freedom in their movements as boys. Young sees femininity as based on a particular bodily comportment that is restrictive of big movement and risk-taking. Girls are not often seen to be capable of achieving physical acts that require strength and power or handling the pain that such physical acts can incur. Willingly inviting pain is seen to be boys' territory. Boys are ascribed the kind of confidence and craziness needed to carry skater tricks through to completion. Girls are not. Members of the Park Gang were aware of this gendered notion of motility and bodily comportment. When asked why girls did not skate as much as boys, Onyx noted that girls might see skateboarding as 'a guy thing to do. It is our thing to sit around and chit chat and gossip and stuff and watch them skateboard.' Grover added, 'Yeah, and some girls are kind of, like, scared.' But Onyx retorted that she and her friends did not 'think like that. We wanted to try it.' Emily, too, reasoned that girls 'don't want to continuously fall', and realized that skater boys are much less worried: 'Like, guys there, they fall and they keep falling, but it's amazing, but they always get back up and, like, try the same thing again. It's quite amazing.'

By 'doing' skateboarding, members of the Park Gang engaged in a transgressive bodily comportment for girls. They were willing to straddle their boards with a wide stance; dangle their arms freely by their sides; and spread eagle for balance. They knowingly made spectacles out of themselves, courting the gaze of the skater boys and the Bun Girls. While some members of the Park Gang were not keen to 'wipe out', others, like Zoey, lovingly recounted their experiences of falling: 'like, the first time I wiped out, I was just, like, "Whoa!" I fell really hard. I was, like, "Aahh!" kind of. And then I just wanted to do it again, because it was like, "Wow!"' The adrenaline rush some of the Park Gang felt came from knowing they were engaged in an activity that most girls (and boys) did not have the guts to try. As Amanda suggested, most boys at the park were more 'risk taking' than girls. 'They don't care if they, like, get bruises and stuff. They'll be, like, "Yeah! Cuts!" And then girls will be, like, "Oh no!"' But some members of the Park Gang willingly accepted the risks involved in skateboarding as a way of setting themselves apart from Bun Girl femininity. Not only could they become skaters who challenged the skater boys at the park, but the Park Gang also realized that they could challenge forms of femininity with which they disagreed. The Park Gang's purposeful positioning as skaters once again worked to push the boundaries of girlhood in productive directions.

Acknowledgements

We would like to thank the Social Sciences and Humanities Research Council of Canada for providing support for this research.

Notes

1. Susan Bolotin (1982) originally introduced the term 'postfeminist' in the *New York Times Magazine*. Her article, entitled *Voices from the Post-Feminist Generation,* was a firsthand look at young women and their disinterest in feminism. Susan Faludi (1991) characterizes the emergence of postfeminism in the media as an example of feminist backlash that gives young women the 'false impression that equality has been achieved and encourages young women to pursue their individual freedoms at the expense of a collective female identity' (13). Similarly, Budgeon and Currie (1995: 184) see the postfeminist discourse in the media as an endorsement of a 'women-centred individualism' that 'assumes rather than questions equal opportunity for women'.

2. The larger study, entitled *Girl Power,* was a three-year research project carried out in Vancouver, Canada from 2000–2003. Shauna Pomerantz conducted the skater girl interviews over this period, interviewing each girl twice in various pairings. Pairings for the first set of interviews were not always the same for the second set.

3. For a detailed discussion of 'emphasized femininity' and its relation to skater girlhood, see Kelly, Pomerantz, and Currie (in press).

4. All names are pseudonyms chosen by the girls in the study.

5. Examples of online skater girl zines include: frontsidebetty.com, withitgirl.com, sk8rgirl.com, girlskateboarding.com, girlsskatebetter.com, and gurlzonboards.com.

6. Although skate culture has been continuously redefined since its original incarnation in 1970s Californian surf culture, many elements remain the same today—a dedication to punk rock (now splintered into pop punk, old school punk, hardcore, and Goth), a love of baggy clothes, a close connection to marijuana and 'partying', and a slacker reputation (think 'Bart Simpson'). In contemporary North American society, skateboarding has been taken up by mainstream marketing machines, such as Nike and Adidas and sold back to its constituents as a skater image, composed of expensive sneakers, brand name clothes, and flashy accoutrement. While the Park Gang liked pop punk bands, such as Linkin Park, Sum 41, and Green Day, they did not buy expensive skater clothes from the numerous skate shops in Vancouver's trendiest neighbourhoods, opting instead for an alternative second-hand look. Grover, for instance, wore men's dress shirts and black gloves with the fingers cut off. The Park Gang also did not smoke marijuana or 'party' and considered themselves to be 'good' girls who listened to their parents. They saw skate culture as 'fun', 'crazy', and 'alternative', but had no wish to be lumped in with other skaters, who broke the law, drank, did drugs, or slacked off in school.

7. It should be noted, though, that Onyx—a very pretty member of the Park Gang—was aware of the attention she garnered through her looks and was just beginning to notice the power she held.

References

Abraham, Y. 1997. 'Lipstick Liberation', *Worcester Phoenix*, 30 May–6 June. Available at http://www.worcesterphoenix.com/archive/features/97/05/30LIPSTICK% 5LIBERATION.html (renewed 24 September 2004).

Bellafante, G. 1998. 'Feminism: It's All About Me!', *Time* [online], 29 March 2000. Available at http://www.time.com/time/magazine/1998/dom/980629/cover2.html.

Bolotin, S. 1982. 'Voices from the Poor Feminist Generation', *New York Times Magazine* (13 October): 28–31.

Budgeon, S., and D.H. Currie. 1995. 'From Feminism to Postfeminism: Women's Liberation in Fashion Magazines', *Women's Studies International Forum* 18, 2: 173–86.

Connell, R.W. 1987. *Gender and Power*. Stanford, CT: Stanford University Press.

Curthoys, J. 1997. *Feminist Amnesia: The Wake of Women's Liberation*. London: Routledge.

Douglas, S.J. 1994. *Where the Girls Are: Growing Up Female with the Mass Media*. New York: Times Books.

Faludi, S. 1991. *Backlash: The Undeclared War against American Women*. New York: Crown Publishers.

Frontside Betty. 2002. 'About Frontside Betty'. Available at http://www.frontsidebetty.com/about/index.html (accessed 23 March 2002).

Garner, H. 1997. *The First Stone*. Sydney: Picador.

Harris, A. 2001. 'Revisiting Bedroom Culture: New Spaces for Young Women's Politics', *Hectate* 27, 1: 128–39.

Hebdige, D. 1979. *Subculture: The Meaning of Style*. London: Methuen.

Jigsaw Youth. 2002. 'Women in Skateboarding'. Available at http://gurlpages.com/unitedgirlfront/skate.html.

McRobbie, A., and J. Garber. 1997 [1976]. 'Girls and Subcultures', in K. Gelder and S. Thornton, eds, *The Subcultures Reader*, pp. 112–20. London: Routledge.

Pipher, M. 1994. *Reviving Ophelia: Saving the Selves of Adolescent Girls*. New York: Putnam.

Preston, C.B. 2001. 'Baby Spice: Lost Between Feminine and Feminist', *Journal of Gender, Social Policy & the Law* 9, 3: 541–619.

Rapping, E. 2000. 'You've Come Which Way, Baby? The Road that Leads from June Cleaver to Ally McBeal Looks A Lot Like a U-turn', *Womens Review of Books* 17, 10/11: 20–3.

Stacey, J. 1990. 'Sexism By a Subtler Name? Post-structural Conditions and Postfeminist Consciousness in Silicon Valley', in K.V. Hansen, and I.J. Philipson, eds, *Women, Class, and the Feminist Imagination: A Socialist Feminist Reader*, pp. 338–56. Philadelphia, PA: Temple University Press.

Summers, A. 1994. 'The Future of Feminism—A Letter to the Next Generation', *Damned Whores and God's Police*. Harmondsworth: Penguin.

Weedon, C. 1987. *Feminist Practice and Poststructuralist Theory*. Oxford, UK: Blackwell.

Whitney, A. 2001. 'Guys vs. Girls'. Available at http://www.realskate.com/girlsvsguys.htm (accessed 16 June 2002).

Willis, P.E. 1981. *Learning to Labor: How Working Class Kids Get Working Class Jobs*. New York: Columbia University Press.

Young, I.M. 1989. 'Throwing Like a Girl: A Phenomenology of Feminine Body Comportment, Motility, and Spatiality', in J. Allen and I.M. Young, eds, *The Thinking Muse: Feminism and Modern French Philosophy*, pp. 51–70. Bloomington: Indiana University Press.

QUESTIONS FOR CRITICAL THOUGHT

1. Hillyard and Morrison look at the welfare system in Ontario as a set of institutions that operate on assumptions about gender, particularly about the gendered relationships between men and women. What institutions have you encountered that operate on assumptions about gender and about what constitutes acceptable behaviour for each gender?

2. Are you involved in, or familiar with, any youth subcultures, like the skateboarders described in 'S8kter Girls'? If so, how is gender enacted in these subcultures?

3. Do you live in a 'rape-prone' culture?

4. How convincing is the assertion that cultural norms prescribing separation between men and women are linked to inequality between men and women? Is it possible for genders to be 'separate but equal'?

5. Ruby describes the *hijab* as an article of clothing that has a wide variety of meanings for the women who wear it. Can you think of other examples of clothing, or of other items, that also carry multiple gendered meanings?

PART III

The Social Construction of Gender Relations

A s is probably clear after reading the last section, gender does not exist in isolation from the activities of everyday life. Sociologists claim that gender is interactively produced—that it is manifested in the ways that we behave with others, whether or not we share a gender identity with them. By looking at gender relations, as well as cultural constructions of gender, we can see how inequalities and differences are embedded in the ways that we do gender as we shape our behaviour to conform, or to refuse to conform, to the presence and expectations of others.

You may be familiar with the concepts of 'gender roles' from psychology classes. Within a sociological approach to gender, these 'roles' should be understood as sets of improvisations on some basic underlying themes of gender, not as fixed scripts that must be acted out as written. In our relations with others—and in the everyday interactions that make up these relations—we 'perform' gender in millions of different ways.

 Our performances, however, often also serve to solidify power differentials and male domination. In their essay, Judith Gerson and Kathy Peiss provide a conceptual mapping of the field of gender relations based on asymmetries of power and inequality between women and men. Using the terms *boundaries*, *negotiation*, and *consciousness*, they re-navigate the study of gender toward a model that explains both difference and domination, as well as establishing the foundations for resistance. Taking a different approach toward a similar end, Candace West and Don Zimmerman make it clear that gender is not a property of the individual—something that one *has*—but rather is a process that one *does* in everyday interaction with others.

West and Zimmerman's enormously influential work on 'doing gender' has inspired a raft of sociologists to examine how gender is 'done' in different settings by different people. Patricia Gagné, Richard Tewksbury, and Deanna McGaughey examine the experiences of a group of people who are particularly conscious of the effort and strategy that goes into doing gender successfully: people who are transgendered, who believe that their psychosocial gender is not consistent with their biological sex and their physical appearance. The experiences of transgendered people as they negotiate new gendered identities for themselves make it clear that for both men and women that gender is constructed through thousands of daily actions, interactions, preferences, and responses to the world around us.

In a twist on the 'doing gender' approach to analyzing daily life, the women hockey players interviewed by Nancy Theberge insist that they do not, in fact, 'do gender' when they are on the ice, and that they are not creating a feminized version of hockey. As Theberge points out, since hockey is one of the 'flag carrier' sports of Canadian masculinity, women's insistence that they are not 'doing gender' is crucial for supporters of women's hockey to claim that the women's games are just as good, and almost the same, as the men's. This acceptance of men's hockey as the 'gold standard' for hockey in general, she argues, weakens the potential for women's hockey teams to pose a real challenge to male dominance in the world of team sports.

CHAPTER 9

Boundaries, Negotiation, and Consciousness: Reconceptualizing Gender Relations

Judith M. Gerson and Kathy Peiss

Over the last 15 years, research on sex and gender has examined the role of women in the past and present, recovered neglected human experiences, and transformed social analysis. A key contribution of this work—one that directly confronts traditional interpretations of women—is that gender is a primary social category that cannot be subsumed under such analytical categories as class and caste. Conceptualizing gender, however, remains a problem. Questions of how gender systems operate, their cultural construction, and their relation to individual and social interactions are often implicit in the analysis of women's experience. As a result, calls for greater definitional and theoretical clarity have been issued and scholars in this field have increasingly asserted the need to understand gender as a system of social relations.

This formulation of gender asserts that gender is defined by socially constructed relationships between women and men, among women, and among men in social groups. Gender is not a rigid or reified analytic category imposed on human experience, but a fluid one whose meaning emerges in specific social contexts as it is created and recreated through human actions. Analysis of gender relations necessarily goes beyond comparisons of the status and power of the sexes, involving examination of the dynamic, reciprocal, and interdependent interactions between and among women and men. In these relationships—those, for example, which construct the sexual division of labour and the social organization of sexuality and reproduction—women and men constitute distinct social groups.

While the problems of conceptualization remain significant, scholars have identified and elaborated several major constructs central to an analysis of gender as a system of social relations: (1) separate spheres; (2) domination of women; and (3) sex-related consciousness. The first, separate spheres, has allowed scholars to examine the different material and ideological worlds in which women and men work, live, and think. The literature on domination explains the forms and processes of physical intimidation, economic exploitation, and ideological control to which women are subjected. Lastly, women's consciousness, as well as feminist consciousness, has been analyzed as rooted in women's distinctive experiences as a social category.

Our aim in this paper is to recast these basic constructs in several ways, by reconsidering gender relations in terms of boundaries, processes of negotiation and domination, and gender consciousness as an interactive and multidimensional process. The concept of boundaries describes the complex structures—physical, social, ideological, and psychological—that establish the differences and commonalities between women and men, among women, and among men, shaping and constraining the behaviour and attitudes of each gender group. The reciprocal processes of negotiation and domination elucidate the ways in which women and men act to support and challenge the existing system of gender relations. Domination describes the systems of male control and coercion, while negotiation addresses the processes by which men and women bargain for privileges and resources. Each group has some assets that enable cooperation with or resistance to existing social arrangements, although clearly these resources and the consequent power are unequal. Finally, although women's consciousness is grounded conceptually in shared female experiences, it is also an interactive and multidimensional process, developing dialectically in the social relations of the sexes,

and involving different forms of awareness among individuals and social groups. We argue that thinking about gender in this way provides a set of more sensitive and complex analytical tools for understanding women's experiences.

Boundaries

The development of the idea of separate spheres in the social science literature has stressed the assignment of women to the domestic realm, men to the public one, the physical separation between both spheres, and the social prestige attached to the public domain. Research on sex and gender has been influenced profoundly by the description of this basic structural division between the sexes, the apparent universality of the concept, and its explanatory power in the analysis of women's experience. Concurrently, the concept of separate spheres has been criticized for its tendency to reify the division of social experience into public/male and private/female worlds, and to overlook the interactions between them.

The use of the 'separate spheres' formulation becomes increasingly problematic in the analysis of contemporary society. Unlike nineteenth century social life with its rigid social, physical, and ideological separation of the sexes, North American society today is marked by the blurring of the public and private spheres, as women have entered the workforce in larger numbers, and men seemingly have become more involved in family life. At the same time, considerable social and cultural distance remains. Women's positions in the marketplace are neither secure nor taken for granted, while men's household roles are often marginal and limited. The dichotomy of separate spheres tends to simplify and reduce social life to two discrete physical environments without capturing the complexity of social and cultural divisions. Moreover, the concept has been used in a relatively static way, as a descriptive tool to chronicle and compare women's and men's activities. Only rarely have scholars gone beyond this approach to analyze the interactions between women and men (and among them) as they are influenced by and in turn shape these spheres.

We need a conceptualization that will allow us to express a basic commonality in the division(s) between the sexes and also to encompass definitions of changing patterns of social relations. Refocusing the analysis of gender divisions by using the concept of boundaries has several distinct advantages. First, it overcomes the problem of universality in the 'separate spheres' formulation. Boundary is a more generic term that simultaneously allows us to see specific commonalities and discern actual differences in historical and current patterns of gender-based experiences. Second, the concept of boundaries allays the problem of bifurcating gender relations through the assignment of women and men to separate spheres. There are many more boundaries marking people's lives than the public–private dichotomy suggests. There are boundaries dividing women and men in leisure and work activities, as well as in face-to-face interactions. There are also smaller boundaries within larger ones. In the workplace, for example, gender difference may be maintained by an overall segmentation of the labour force by sex, denoted by the allocation of social space and privileges (e.g., typing pools versus executive offices, different dining facilities, etc.) and reinforced by limitations on interpersonal behaviour (e.g., unidirectional patterns of touch and naming). Finally, the concept of boundaries also suggests permeability, whereas the image of spheres connotes comparatively autonomous environments. Boundaries mark the social territories of gender relations, signalling who ought to be admitted or excluded. There are codes and rules to guide and regulate traffic, with instructions on which boundaries may be transversed and under what conditions. As a consequence, boundaries are an important place to observe gender relations; these intersections reveal the normal, acceptable behaviours and attitudes as well as deviant, inappropriate ones. At the same

time, boundaries highlight the dynamic quality of the structures of gender relations, as they influence and are shaped by social interactions.

Describing the nature of boundaries and analyzing their congruence or lack of congruence will reveal a complex picture of gender arrangements. This approach should be particularly useful in comparative studies across time and in different cultures. In some periods and places, boundaries are mutually reinforcing or complementary, while in other instances they come into conflict. Within the American middle class in the nineteenth century, for example, the growing physical boundary between home and workplace was reinforced by a hegemonic ideological boundary, the cult of domesticity, as well as smaller social and cultural distinctions. While some women crossed these boundaries and entered the public arena of education and voluntary association, most did so within the dynamics of their assignment to the home, rationalizing their activities as an extension of women's mission to protect and uplift the family. A somewhat similar ideological boundary marked the 1950s, in the set of ideas and images Betty Friedan (1963) labelled the 'feminine mystique'. Unlike the nineteenth century, however, other boundaries operated at cross-purposes. Physical boundaries between home and workplace become less salient in the mid-twentieth century as middle-class women entered the labour force in large numbers. Moreover, the ideology of companionate marriage cut across the feminine mystique with its assertion of mutuality, togetherness, and male involvement in family life. Examination of the different relationships between boundaries may provide descriptive categories for viewing gender relations over time and in different settings.

The analysis of boundaries—their congruence and contradictions—may be useful in assessing stability and change in a system of gender relations. The above example suggests that mutually reinforcing boundaries will be indicators of relatively stable gender relations, while those that are contradictory may promote or reflect social change. An analysis of such change raises two important questions: How are boundaries reconstituted as existing boundaries are challenged and lose importance? What boundaries become or remain significant in defining gender difference and asymmetry as macro-level divisions become less distinct over time?

The boundaries between home and work provide examples of such changes. How is women's place redefined when family/work divisions become less rigid and women are no longer anomalies as wage-earners? One consequence is that boundaries *within* the workplace (e.g., occupational segregation) and interactional, micro-level boundaries assume increased significance in defining the subordinate position of women. Occupational segregation sets up divisions within the labour force that reduce women to secondary status. With low-paying, low-status jobs and their continued assignment to the home, women retain their primary definition as housewives. For women entering non-traditional occupations, other boundaries maintain women's marginal and subordinate place. Micro-level phenomena—the persistence of informal group behaviour among men (e.g., after-work socializing, the uses of male humour, modes of corporate attire)—act to define insiders and outsiders, and thus maintain gender-based distinctions.

A similar definition of boundaries may be seen in the current debate over men's growing role in the household. Men's household labour appears to have increased somewhat in recent years, while ideological support for it (e.g., public discussion of paternity leaves) has grown. At the same time, women and men continue to define male household activity as secondary and marginal, taking the form of 'helping out'. The bulk of housework, child-drearing and care-taking remains women's work.

In both these examples, boundaries shift in small but important ways, indicating a change in gender relations and the ways individual women

and men may experience them. At the same time, challenges to the stability of patriarchal social arrangements may be met by concessions, which in effect readjust the boundaries but allow the overall system of male dominance to persist.

Since gender involves the accentuation of human difference into dichotomous categories of femininity and masculinity, the social divisions between women and men constitute the primary boundary of gender relations. On the micro level of analysis, what happens at the boundaries between sexes is frequently evidence of exaggerated gender-specific behaviour, as compared with same-sex behaviour. Perhaps the most common example of this phenomenon is heterosexual dating behaviour, with women and men often playing out traditional stereotypical feminine and masculine roles. On a broader level of analysis, the primacy of the heterosocial boundary is assured by the sexual division of labour and the enforcement of compulsory heterosexuality, both of which assert women's difference from men, their subordinate position, and their dependency.

The concept of boundaries should help delineate the interaction between homosocial and heterosocial relationships, and their role in the construction of gender. Recent research has identified the significance of female friendships, networks, and cultures in providing women with varying degrees of autonomy, support, and influence. Similarly, scholars have documented the same-sex bonding in the realms of business, sports, and the military, which supply men with resources, skills, solidarity, and power. Such homosocial relations are influenced by the boundaries between the sexes, and in turn shape these same boundaries. Among nineteenth century middle-class women, for example, friendships centered on the home, kinship, and ritualistic events; these constituted a separate 'female world', which owed its emergence to the rigid structural differentiation between male/public and female/private domains. At the same time, the dynamics of female solidarity led some women into political agitation and reform activities, crossing and subverting this primary boundary. On the other hand, homosocial bonds among men may operate to strengthen the boundaries between the sexes, as they have in the world of sports. Women may pursue individual athletic activities that conflict least with social definitions of femininity, but they do not participate in team sports characterized by masculine rituals. Such rituals not only affirm male dominance through the exclusion of women, but they also promote group bonding, teamwork, and skills at negotiation and conflict resolution, qualities which help build and reinforce men's power in other realms of life.

At the same time, there are boundaries within same-sex groups that influence and, in turn, are shaped by the division between women and men. For example, the historical barriers between prostitutes and 'respectable' married women have reinforced the double standard by strengthening male sexual privilege while dividing women on the basis of sexual morality. In contemporary society, aging is a boundary separating younger and older women according to standards of physical attractiveness and youth, standards not applied to men. This in turn reinforces competition among women for men, thus buttressing the institutional heterosexuality that constructs the primary male–female division and women's subordination.

Boundaries between the sexes and within each sex, in their respective spatial, social, and psychological dimensions, delineate the structure of gender relations at a given time and place. However, to explain how and why boundaries change, we must uncover the ways in which individuals make and reshape their social worlds. Thus, the interpretation of gender relations must involve a theory of social process and consciousness. First we examine the social interactions between individuals and groups that establish, maintain, and potentially subvert boundaries; these are the processes of negotiation and domination.

Processes of Negotiation and Domination

A major contribution of scholarship on gender has been the analysis of *domination* in explaining the subordinate position of women. In numerous studies of sex and gender, researchers have documented the ways in which men as a group have power over women as a group. Theorists have raised fundamental questions about the sources of domination and have proposed strategies for changing extant power relations. Analyses of social life in the past and present reveal the extent of male control through physical coercion, reproductive policies, the institution of heterosexuality, economic exploitation, and ideology.

Although this analysis is essential for understanding the dynamics of gender arrangements, it nevertheless has an inherent conceptual shortcoming. Regardless of the theoretical orientation, the assumption is made that women are the passive victims of a system of power or domination. While women are not responsible for their own oppression and exploitation, at the same time they are not fully passive either. We need to explore the various ways women participate in setting up, maintaining, and altering the system of gender relations. This statement does not presume that women somehow ask for the sexism they experience. Rather we are suggesting that there is more than one process going on, perhaps simultaneously. Domination explains the ways women are oppressed and either accommodate or resist, while negotiation describes the ways women and men bargain for privileges and resources. Given the considerable scholarship about domination, we focus our discussion on the process of negotiation, recognizing that the two processes are interdependent and exist concurrently.

The concept of negotiation suggests human agency. Both women and men are active participants, sometimes asking or inviting—sometimes demanding—that resources be shared or real located. Implicit in this formulation is the recognition that both women and men have some resources they initially control. In addition, this conceptualization suggests that both parties to a negotiation must somehow agree in order for it to take effect. Not only must there be mutuality in consent, but the process of negotiation is reciprocal. Though men seem to do most of the inviting, women also have done the asking and made demands. Furthermore, the heterosocial negotiations that occur usually involve crossing a boundary, however small. The negotiations that do take place may act to either maintain or change structural boundaries.

The entry of women into the office as clerical workers provides one such example of gender negotiation. Margery Davies (1982) has shown that women were allowed into the office only after the invention of the typewriter and its popular acceptance as a tool for low-paid, unskilled labour. In other words, women were 'invited' into the office as clerical workers, crossing a boundary that years earlier they could not have trespassed. Office work for women appeared to be a real asset to them since other opportunities for wage earning were limited. Women may choose to participate because they perceive possibilities for economic gains or status enhancement. While we can speak of individual women being invited into the office by individual male bosses, it is important to remember that the processes of invitation and negotiation operate on the level of social groups.

Women also have the resources to negotiate with men for access to privileges and opportunities. Micaela di Leonardo (1984) has demonstrated that women do the kin work—the labour involved in sustaining and nurturing ties and affiliations among family kin. Her sample, a group of Italian American families living in California, showed a pattern in which women had greater knowledge about kin, had stronger familial ties, and did more of the planning of kin gatherings than did the men. These women derived not only responsibilities and obligations from these duties,

but prerogatives and power as well. As a result, women had control over a set of kin-based resources and permitted men access to those resources only if and when the women so desired.

While these examples demonstrate that women and men actively participate in negotiations, they also suggest a fundamental asymmetry in the process of negotiation that is integrally tied to the process of domination. Women's dependency is ensured through domination in many forms, including exploitation in the system of wage labour, structured through occupational segregation. Given their low economic status, most women are in some way ultimately dependent on men's work, a dependency reinforced by the ideology and material conditions of compulsory heterosexuality. Given their relative lack of structural power, women have fewer resources with which to negotiate, experience fewer situations in which they can set up negotiations, and derive fewer advantages from their negotiations.

What then is the effect of these negotiations on the system of gender relations? On the one hand, they may permit the system to continue in 'dynamic stasis', with reciprocal negotiations between women and men reifying structural boundaries in daily life. The traditional act of marriage exemplifies this form of negotiation, being a 'free' exchange of obligations and responsibilities that reinforce heterosexuality and the sexual division of labour. However, an alternative consequence might be an adjustment in the boundaries, either proceeded, accompanied, or followed by an alteration in consciousness. Men inviting women to cross a boundary or vice versa will not necessarily lead to lasting structural change. Indeed, ample evidence suggests that boundaries may be transversed and consciousness reconstructed in such a way that a changed status for women is largely cosmetic or minimal. When women were invited into the office, for example, a change in consciousness occurred (i.e., it was then considered proper for women to be secretaries), but the boundaries merely shifted to incorporate the precise change without seriously disrupting the dominant system of gender relations. One could even argue that the system was strengthened, since the ideological and material conditions of secretarial work reinforced women's role in the family.

A similar pattern emerges for women in traditionally male occupations. Women are now 'invited' to enter the corporation, but the consequences of the negotiation are contradictory: by insisting that women be 'male' in their job performance (i.e., have managerial ability) while retaining their 'femaleness', the rules ensure that women will remain outsiders. The popular literature on dress for success and assertiveness training exemplifies forms of negotiation that may lead to a change in some women's behaviours and consciousness, but not to lasting changes in the structure of opportunity, achievement, and power for all women.

At the same time, changes in consciousness and shifts in boundaries arising from negotiations, however small, may have real and direct consequences in people's lives, even if they do not result in a major change in women's status or in the system of gender relations. To understand the creation and impact of those changes, it is necessary to explore the realm of consciousness. At the most general of levels, consciousness may be depicted in a reciprocal and dynamic relation to social structure. The structural location of a person or group in a social system (i.e., boundaries) as well as individual or collective acts (i.e., social processes), both shape and are shaped by social consciousness.

Consciousness

Traditionally, when researchers have studied gender consciousness they have focused their efforts essentially on one of two questions. Either they have investigated the conditions and consequences of feminist consciousness or they have considered the foundations and components of female consciousness. Studies of feminist consciousness have concentrated on the social and historical context which gives rise to an active awareness and visible consequences of that awareness. For example, DuBois (1978) has chronicled the relationship between the anti-slavery movement and the subsequent movement for women's suffrage; Eisenstein (1983) has traced the growth of feminist consciousness in women's groups. Studies such as these generally situate feminist consciousness in an active social movement, associating consciousness with those people participating in the movement and conversely attributing a lack of feminist consciousness to those outside it. One of the tendencies of this research, therefore, is to understand feminist consciousness as an either/or phenomenon—either you have it or you do not.

Scholars working on the content of female consciousness have proposed a similar formulation. They understand female consciousness as the outcome of women's unique set of experiences. Whether as the primary caretakers of children or more generally because of their social roles that are distinct from men's, women apprehend the world in ways that are unique to them. This female consciousness replicates the same dichotomy apparent in the treatment of feminist consciousness. Women share a common culture, ostensibly autonomous from the male world, from which they derive their consciousness. Comparable to the problem with feminist consciousness, female consciousness is understood as a dichotomous, discrete variable.

One shortcoming of these formulations is that the possible varieties of feminist and female consciousness often remain unexplored. We know very little about the actual forms of nascent consciousness and which factors help explain the means by which that consciousness develops or recedes. Moreover, if gender relations shape women's experience then it is necessary to consider both the interaction of women and men as social groups as well as the dynamics within 'women's culture' if we are to apprehend the formation of female and feminist consciousness. We propose that viewing forms of gender consciousness along a continuum produces a more useful conception of consciousness, while examining gender-based interactions allows us to explain how these forms of consciousness develop and change.

Our analysis of consciousness distinguishes among three types—gender awareness, female/male consciousness, feminist/anti-feminist consciousness—that represent three points along a continuum. The first, gender awareness, is central to the development of the subsequent two forms—female/male and feminist/anti-feminist consciousness. Social scientists studying child development and socialization consistently report that very young children understand that they are either a girl or a boy and that this understanding has actual consequences for what they may or may not do. This form of consciousness, which we label gender awareness, is the most basic type. In this culture gender awareness is virtually universal past infancy, although it is neither infantile nor restricted to youngsters; it is present in parallel or reciprocal forms among both females and males. Gender awareness permeates most facets of everyday life in either real or symbolic ways. People continue to believe in a dimorphic world, even though the research on sex differences has shown that no quality or trait is associated exclusively with one sex or the other, except primary sex characteristics. Women are still thought of as weak or dependent, although we routinely encounter women who 'objectively' are strong and independent. In fact gender attribution is so strong that it frequently distorts the empirical phenomenon.

Gender awareness involves a non-critical description of the existing system of gender relations, whereby people accept the current social definitions of gender as natural and inevitable. Gender awareness, then, means that people may associate or correlate certain phenomena with one gender group or another, but there is

no evaluation of the ultimate significance or meaning of these attributions. For example, while a person's awareness of gender might indicate that women, in contrast to men, tend to be more sensitive and nurturing, this awareness would not enable her or him to discern the causes or effects of these traits. This form of gender consciousness ultimately involves a statement about the status quo, a remark concerning the way things are for males and females. Moreover, as gender awareness is characterized by a basic acceptance of gender arrangements, any lingering or residual dissatisfaction with the status quo is individualized as a personal trouble. Being overly sensitive is seen as a personal female shortcoming; there is no social context for this problem. Similarly, a woman's failure to gain a job in the skilled trades is perceived as a result of her personal shortcomings, not an outcome of sexist hiring practices. Small dissatisfactions with gender arrangements may arise, but they do not result in a questioning of that system or one's place within it.

The second form of gender consciousness female or male consciousness is based on is gender awareness but it goes beyond the descriptive attributions to a recognition of the rights and obligations associated with being female or male. These privileges and responsibilities are socially constructed and specific to a particular culture at a given point in time. The gender-linked traits, which are descriptive of women and men at the level of gender awareness, come to be vested with a sense of reciprocal rights and responsibilities at the level of female or male consciousness.

Kaplan (1982) defines female consciousness as acceptance of a society's gender system. Female consciousness 'emerges from the division of labor by sex, which assigns women the responsibility of preserving life. But, accepting this task, women with female consciousness demand the rights that their obligations entail' (Kaplan, 1982: 545). While we agree with Kaplan, we want to offer two refinements. First, our understanding of boundaries tells us that the sexual division of labour represents a sum total of several more discrete boundaries. Thus, our model suggests that the source of this form of consciousness is more accurately depicted as a person's specific location in a system of gender arrangements. Second, we want to emphasize a notion implicit in Kaplan's definition. By demanding rights, the conceptualization of female consciousness connotes the idea that this consciousness is dynamic and malleable. Female consciousness is the outcome of processes of negotiation and domination, and their reciprocal interaction, as well as the result of women's structural location. Moreover, female consciousness influences processes of negotiation and domination, and ultimately, the boundaries shaping gender relations.

Recent research suggests the general dimensions of female consciousness: First, women are concerned with immediate material reality. The sexual division of labour situates women in the position of child bearers who are responsible for sustaining life. As such, women are obligated and feel responsible for meeting the survival needs of their families. Women, therefore, behave in accordance with normative expectations and act to further support those expectations. Concerns for the necessities of everyday life take numerous forms. Women concerned about food, shelter, and well-being, for example, have organized and protested when state regulations made it difficult, if not impossible, for them to feed their families.

At a more general level, responsibility for everyday life has meant that women are more apt to apprehend phenomena concretely rather than abstractly. In part because of their heightened responsibility for others, women act as mediators. Gilligan (1982: 147) discusses women's complex negotiation between the ethic of self sacrifice and the sense of moral responsibility: 'Thus morality, rather than being opposed to integrity or to an ideal of agreement, is aligned with "the kind of integrity" that comes from "making decisions after working through everything you think is involved and important in the situation", and taking

responsibility for choice.' Finally, the constraints women experience in their daily lives lead to a consciousness of female inferiority. In comparison with men, women learn intellectual, moral, emotional, and physical inferiority. This generalized sense of inferiority leads women to believe that they are incomplete and inadequate without a man—father, husband, etc. Moreover, because of their perceived inabilities and the existence of real threats, women learn fear and have an ingrained sense of curfew and exclusion.

As Kaplan (1982) clearly documents in her research, female consciousness has both a progressive, revolutionary potential as well as a conservative, reactionary one. When women act to protest or disrupt the existing social order because they cannot satisfactorily fulfill their obligations, they challenge existing powers. The eventual outcome of such protests depends on a larger social context, but at a minimum underscores the value women place on maintaining social life (Kaplan, 1982). We would want to know what the relationship is between clearly demarcated boundaries of gender and the development of female consciousness.

An understanding of female consciousness and more broadly, gender relations, must entail an analysis of male consciousness. Is it identical to or even comparable to female consciousness? Given the differences in structural locations and social processes between women and men, male consciousness appears to be profoundly distinct from female consciousness. Male consciousness is characterized by the value placed on individual autonomy, a sense of entitlement, and a relative superiority to women. Men's moral judgments are guided by abstract principles rather than the concrete dimensions of everyday life. Recently Ehrenreich (1983) has chronicled some of the changes in male consciousness over the last thirty years. Her analysis is instructive but raises additional questions central to our concerns here. For example, what is the effect of relative power, and differences in the type or form of power, on consciousness? In what way is consciousness heightened or diminished by such power? Further research into the relationship between female and male consciousness, and its consequences for the system of gender relations is needed.

Finally, female/male consciousness must be distinguished from consciousness that is explicitly feminist or antifeminist/masculinist. To paraphrase Marx, we need to understand the formation of a gender *for* itself. Feminist and antifeminist consciousness involves a highly articulated challenge to or defense of the system of gender relations in the form of ideology, as well as a shared group identity and a growing politicization resulting in a social movement. Recent research extensively explores this issue, documenting the origins, organizational development, and ideology of the first and second waves of feminism. It also has examined the circumstances in which feminist consciousness reinforced or conflicted with other forms of consciousness based on class, race, ethnicity, or sexual preference. In investigating the circumstances in which women define their interests as gender-based, it is necessary to examine the areas of female assertion and power, and the ways women move from female to feminist consciousness. At the same time, the formation of feminist consciousness must be seen in relation to antifeminist ideology and activity. The rise of feminism occurs in a dialectical context, in which the feminist challenge to the existing system of gender arrangements evokes an organized response, which in turn influences the nature of feminist consciousness and practice. This process has become particularly apparent in the New Right's movement against feminist demands for legal equality, economic justice, and reproductive rights; it may also be seen in earlier historical periods such as the organized opposition to suffrage in the late nineteenth century. The dynamics of gender-conscious groups, particularly in the last one hundred years, have forcefully shaped gender relations, contributing to the changing definition of boundaries and rules for negotiation and domination.

Conclusions

In this paper we have argued that gender relations can be fruitfully understood by recasting our conceptual framework. These redefinitions should focus our attention on several issues that have consequences for future research on sex and gender.

From a definitional perspective, the conception of gender as a set of socially constructed relationships produced and reproduced through people's actions is central. Such a view highlights social interaction rather than more unidirectional processes of socialization, adaptation, and/or oppression. This emphasis suggests that we appreciate women as the active creators of their own destines within certain constraints, rather than as passive victims or objects. At the same time, this suggests that feminist scholars must avoid analyzing men as one-dimensional, omnipotent oppressors. Male behaviour and consciousness emerge from a complex interaction with women as they at times initiate and control, while at other times, cooperate or resist the action of women. Clearly researchers need to examine men in the context of gender relations more precisely and extensively than they have at the present time.

This conceptualization also urges us to examine stasis and change in a more consistent and comprehensive fashion, thereby avoiding the mistake of studying change as an either/or phenomenon. We want to identify the mechanisms perpetuating existing gender arrangements and those that tend to elicit change. Changes in gender relations occur along the three dimensions of boundaries, negotiation/domination, and consciousness; change in any one variable elicits change in the other two. For example, there cannot be a boundary shift unless it is preceded, accompanied, or followed by changes in negotiation/domination and consciousness. The sequencing of such changes, both in terms of patterns and timing, needs further study. In addition to these questions we also need to look at the magnitude of change. Large versus small-scale change in gender arrangements must be evaluated in terms of the number and proportion of groups affected, their centrality and susceptibility to change, and the degree and suddenness of change. We are also interested in the durability of change. Which kinds of changes are resistant to countervailing forces, and which seem to be more tentative, temporary, or makeshift? How are changes in gender relations challenged or co-opted? With the nature of change specified, we will be able to compare more precisely systems of gender relations across historical time and across cultures.

Grounding our research in these dimensions will also facilitate comparisons of systems of gender relations with other systems of domination. Such comparative work is important because it yields a greater understanding of the dynamics of domination. We can distinguish the forms of oppression that are unique to gender from those that are common to all systems of oppression.

Recently, scholars have pointed to the concepts of gender, gender relations, and sex/gender systems as potentially integrating the wide-ranging empirical research on women. Toward this end, our approach has been to redefine three concrete categories for the analysis of gender. These categories offer both a conceptual framework and a research strategy that recommend greater specificity and comparability in examining gender relations. We hope that this framework will encourage researchers to clarify and extend their analyses of gender relations along both empirical and theoretical dimensions.

References

Bernard, J. 1981. *The Female World*. New York: Free Press.

Davies, M. 1982. *Women's Place Is at the Typewriter. Office Work and Office Workers 1870–1930*. Philadelphia: Temple University Press.

di Leonardo, M. 1984. *The Varieties of Ethnic Experience: Kinship, Class and Gender Among Italian Americans in Northern California*. Ithaca, NY: Cornell University Press.

DuBois, E.C. 1978. *Feminism and Suffrage: The Emergence of an Independent Women's Movement in America 1848–1869*. Ithaca, NY: Cornell University Press.

Ehrenreich, B. 1983. *The Hearts of Men: American Dreams and the Flight from Commitment*. Garden City, NY: Anchor/Doubleday.

Eisenstein, H. 1983. *Contemporary Feminist Thought*. Boston: G.K. Hall & Co.

Friedan, B. 1963. *The Feminine Mystique*. New York: Dell.

Gilligan, C. 1982. *In a Different Voice: Psychological Theory and Women's Development*. Cambridge: Harvard University Press.

Kaplan, T. 1982. 'Female Consciousness and Collective Action: The Case of Barcelona, 1910–1918', *Signs* 7: 545–66.

CHAPTER 10

Doing Gender

Candace West and Don H. Zimmerman

In the beginning, there was sex and there was gender. Those of us who taught courses in the area in the late 1960s and early 1970s were careful to distinguish one from the other. Sex, we told students, was what was ascribed by biology: anatomy, hormones, and physiology. Gender, we said, was an achieved status: that which is constructed through psychological, cultural, and social means. To introduce the difference between the two, we drew on singular case studies of hermaphrodites and anthropological investigations of 'strange and exotic tribes'.

Inevitably (and understandably), in the ensuing weeks of each term, our students became confused. Sex hardly seemed a 'given' in the context of research that illustrated the sometimes ambiguous and often conflicting criteria for its ascription. And gender seemed much less an 'achievement' in the context of the anthropological, psychological, and social imperatives we studied—the division of labour, the formation of gender identities, and the social subordination of women by men. Moreover, the received doctrine of gender socialization theories conveyed the strong message that while gender may be 'achieved', by about age five it was certainly fixed, unvarying, and static—much like sex.

Since about 1975, the confusion has intensified and spread far beyond our individual classrooms. For one thing, we learned that the relationship between biological and cultural processes was far more complex—and reflexive—than we previously had supposed. For another, we discovered that certain structural arrangements, for example, between work and family, actually produce or enable some capacities, such as to mother, that we formerly associated with biology. In the midst of all this, the notion of gender as a recurring achievement somehow fell by the wayside.

Our purpose in this article is to propose an ethnomethodologically-informed, and therefore distinctively sociological, understanding of gender as a routine, methodical, and recurring accomplishment. We contend that the 'doing' of gender is undertaken by women and men whose competence as members of society is hostage to its production. Doing gender involves a complex of socially guided perceptual, interactional, and micropolitical activities that cast particular pursuits as expressions of masculine and feminine 'natures'.

When we view gender as an accomplishment, an achieved property of situated conduct, our attention shifts from matters internal to the individual and focuses on interactional and, ultimately, institutional arenas. In one sense, of course, it is individuals who 'do' gender. But it is a situated doing, carried out in the virtual or real presence of others who are presumed to be oriented to its production. Rather than as a property of individuals, we conceive of gender as an emergent feature of social situations: both as an outcome of and a rationale for various social arrangements and as a means of legitimating one of the most fundamental divisions of society.

To advance our argument, we undertake a critical examination of what sociologists have meant by *gender*, including its treatment as a role enactment in the conventional sense and as a 'display' in Goffman's (1976) terminology. Both *gender role* and *gender display* focus on behavioural aspects of being a woman or a man (as opposed, for example, to biological differences between the two). However, we contend that the notion of gender as a role obscures the work that is involved in producing gender in everyday activities, while the notion of gender as a display relegates it to the periphery of interaction. We argue instead that participants in interaction organize their various and manifold activities to reflect or express gender, and they are disposed to perceive the behaviour of others in a similar light.

To elaborate our proposal, we suggest at the outset that important but often overlooked distinctions be observed among *sex*, *sex category*, and *gender*. *Sex* is a determination made through the application of socially agreed upon biological criteria for classifying persons as females or males. The criteria for classification can be genitalia at birth or chromosomal typing before birth, and they do not necessarily agree with one another. Placement in a *sex category* is achieved through application of the sex criteria, but in everyday life, categorization is established and sustained by the socially required identificatory displays that proclaim one's membership in one or the other category. In this sense, one's sex category presumes one's sex and stands as proxy for it in many situations, but sex and sex category can vary independently; that is, it is possible to claim membership in a sex category even when the sex criteria are lacking. *Gender*, in contrast, is the activity of managing situated conduct in light of normative conceptions of attitudes and activities appropriate for one's sex category. Gender activities emerge from and bolster claims to membership in a sex category.

We contend that recognition of the analytical independence of sex, sex category, and gender is essential for understanding the relationships among these elements and the interactional work involved in 'being' a gendered person in society. While our primary aim is theoretical, there will be occasion to discuss fruitful directions for empirical research following from the formulation of gender that we propose.

We begin with an assessment of the received meaning of gender, particularly in relation to the roots of this notion in presumed biological differences between women and men.

Perspectives on Sex and Gender

In Western societies, the accepted cultural perspective on gender views women and men as naturally and unequivocally defined categories of being with distinctive psychological and behavioural propensities that can be predicted from their reproductive functions. Competent adult members of these societies see differences between the two as fundamental and enduring—differences seemingly supported by the division of labour into women's and men's work and an often elaborate differentiation of feminine and masculine attitudes and behaviours that are prominent features of social organization. Things are the way they are by virtue of the fact that men are men and women are women—a division perceived to be natural and rooted in biology, producing in turn profound psychological, behavioural, and social consequences. The structural arrangements of a society are presumed to be responsive to these differences.

Analyses of sex and gender in the social sciences, though less likely to accept uncritically the naive biological determinism of the view just presented, often retain a conception of sex-linked behaviours and traits as essential properties of individuals. The 'sex differences approach' is more commonly attributed to psychologists than to sociologists, but the survey researcher who determines the 'gender' of respondents on the basis of the sound of their voices over the telephone is also making trait-oriented assumptions. Reducing gender to a fixed set of psychological traits or to a unitary 'variable' precludes serious consideration of the ways it is used to structure distinct domains of social experience.

Taking a different tack, role theory has attended to the social construction of gender categories, called 'sex roles' or, more recently, 'gender roles' and has analyzed how these are learned and enacted. Beginning with Linton (1936) and continuing through the works of Parsons (Parsons, 1951; Parsons and Bales, 1955) and Komarovsky (1946, 1950), role theory has emphasized the social and dynamic aspect of role construction and enactment. But at the level of face-to-face interaction, the application of role theory to gender poses problems of its own. Roles are *situated* identities—assumed and relinquished as the situation demands—rather than *master identities*, such as the sex category, that cut across situations. Unlike most roles, such as 'nurse', 'doctor', and 'patient', or 'professor' and 'student', gender has no specific site or organizational context.

Moreover, many roles are already gender marked, so that special qualifiers— such as 'female doctor' or 'male nurse'—must be added to exceptions to the rule. Thorne (1980) observes that conceptualizing gender as a role makes it difficult to assess its influence on other roles and reduces its explanatory usefulness in discussions of power and inequality. Drawing on Rubin (1975), Thorne calls for a reconceptualization of women and men as distinct social groups, constituted in 'concrete, historically changing—and generally unequal—social relationships' (Thorne, 1980: 11).

We argue that gender is not a set of traits, nor a variable, nor a role, but the product of social doings of some sort. What then is the social doing of gender? It is more than the continuous creation of the meaning of gender through human actions. We claim that gender itself is constituted through interaction. To develop the implications of our claim, we turn to Goffman's (1976) account of 'gender display'. Our object here is to explore how gender might be exhibited or portrayed through interaction, and thus be seen as 'natural', while it is being produced as a socially organized achievement.

Gender Display

Goffman contends that when human beings interact with others in their environment, they assume that each possesses an 'essential nature'—a nature that can be discerned through the 'natural signs given off or expressed by them' (1976: 75). Femininity and masculinity are regarded as 'prototypes of essential expression—something that can be conveyed fleetingly in any social situation and yet something that strikes at the most basic characterization of the individual' (1976: 75). The means through which we provide such expressions are 'perfunctory, conventionalized acts' (1976: 69), which convey to others our regard for them, indicate our alignment in an encounter, and tentatively establish the terms of contact for that social situation. But they are also regarded as expressive behaviour, testimony to our 'essential natures'.

Goffman (1976) sees *displays* as highly conventionalized behaviours structured as two-part exchanges of the statement–reply type, in which the presence or absence of symmetry can establish deference or dominance. These rituals are viewed as distinct from but articulated with more consequential activities, such as performing tasks or

engaging in discourse. Hence, we have what he terms the 'scheduling' of displays at junctures in activities, such as the beginning or end, to avoid interfering with the activities themselves. Goffman formulates *gender display* as follows:

> If gender be defined as the culturally established correlates of sex (whether in consequence of biology or learning), then gender display refers to conventionalized portrayals of these correlates (1976: 69).

These gendered expressions might reveal clues to the underlying, fundamental dimensions of the female and male, but they are, in Goffman's view, optional performances. Masculine courtesies may or may not be offered and, if offered, may or may not be declined (1976: 71). Moreover, human beings 'themselves employ the term "expression", and conduct themselves to fit their own notions of expressivity' (1976: 75). Gender depictions are less a consequence of our 'essential sexual natures' than interactional portrayals of what we would like to convey about sexual natures, using conventionalized gestures. Our human nature gives us the ability to learn to produce and recognize masculine and feminine gender displays—'a capacity [we] have by virtue of being persons, not males and females' (1976: 76).

Upon first inspection, it would appear that Goffman's formulation offers an engaging sociological corrective to existing formulations of gender. In his view, gender is a socially scripted dramatization of the culture's *idealization* of feminine and masculine natures, played for an audience that is well schooled in the presentational idiom. To continue the metaphor, there are scheduled performances presented in special locations, and like plays, they constitute introductions to or time out from more serious activities.

There are fundamental equivocations in this perspective. By segregating gender display from the serious business of interaction, Goffman obscures the effects of gender on a wide range of human activities. Gender is not merely something that happens in the nooks and crannies of interaction, fitted in here and there and not interfering with the serious business of life. While it is plausible to contend that gender displays—construed as conventionalized expressions—are optional, it does not seem plausible to say that we have the option of being seen by others as female or male.

It is necessary to move beyond the notion of gender display to consider what is involved in doing gender as an ongoing activity embedded in everyday interaction. Toward this end, we return to the distinctions among sex, sex category, and gender introduced earlier.

Sex, Sex Category, and Gender

Garfinkel's (1967) case study of Agnes, a transsexual raised as a boy who adopted a female identity at age 17 and underwent a sex reassignment operation several years later, demonstrates how gender is created through interaction and at the same time structures interaction. Agnes, whom Garfinkel characterized as a 'practical methodologist', developed a number of procedures for passing as a 'normal, natural female' both prior to and after her surgery. She had the practical task of managing the fact that she possessed male genitalia and that she lacked the social resources a girl's biography would presumably provide in everyday interaction. In short, she needed to display herself as a woman, simultaneously learning what it was to be a woman. Of necessity, this full-time pursuit took place at a time when most people's gender would be well-accredited and routinized. Agnes had to consciously contrive what the vast majority of women do without thinking. She was not 'faking' what 'real' women do naturally. She was obliged to analyze and figure out how to act within socially structured circumstances and conceptions of femininity that women born with appropriate biological credentials come to take for granted early on. As in the case of others who

must 'pass', such as transvestites, Kabuki actors, or Dustin Hoffman's 'Tootsie', Agnes's case makes visible what culture has made invisible—the accomplishment of gender.

Garfinkel's (1967) discussion of Agnes does not explicitly separate three analytically distinct, although empirically overlapping, concepts—sex, sex category, and gender.

SEX

Agnes did not possess the socially agreed upon biological criteria for classification as a member of the female sex. Still, Agnes regarded herself as a female, albeit a female with a penis, which a woman ought not to possess. The penis, she insisted, was a 'mistake' in need of remedy (Garfinkel, 1967). Like other competent members of our culture, Agnes honoured the notion that there are 'essential' biological criteria that unequivocally distinguish females from males. However, if we move away from the commonsense viewpoint, we discover that the reliability of these criteria is not beyond question. Moreover, other cultures have acknowledged the existence of 'cross-genders' and the possibility of more than two sexes.

More central to our argument is Kessler and McKenna's (1978) point that genitalia are conventionally hidden from public inspection in everyday life; yet we continue through our social rounds to 'observe' a world of two naturally, normally sexed persons. It is the *presumption* that essential criteria exist and would or should be there if looked for that provides the basis for sex categorization. Drawing on Garfinkel, Kessler and McKenna argue that 'female' and 'male' are cultural events—products of what they term the 'gender attribution process'—rather than some collection of traits, behaviours, or even physical attributes. Illustratively they cite the child who, viewing a picture of someone clad in a suit and a tie, contends, 'It's a man, because he has a pee-pee' (Kessler and McKenna, 1978: 154). Translation: 'He must have a pee-pee [an essential characteristic] because I see the *insignia* of a suit and tie.'

Neither initial sex assignment (pronouncement at birth as a female or male) nor the actual existence of essential criteria for that assignment (possession of a clitoris and vagina or penis and testicles) has much—if anything—to do with the identification of sex category in everyday life. There, Kessler and McKenna note, we operate with a moral certainty of a world of two sexes. We do not think, 'Most persons with penises are men, but some may not be' or 'Most persons who dress as men have penises.' Rather, we take it for granted that sex and sex category are congruent—that knowing the latter, we can deduce the rest.

SEX CATEGORIZATION

Agnes's claim to the categorical status of female, which she sustained by appropriate identificatory displays and other characteristics, could be *discredited* before her transsexual operation if her possession of a penis became known and after by her surgically constructed genitalia. In this regard, Agnes had to be continually alert to actual or potential threats to the security of her sex category. Her problem was not so much about living up to some prototype of essential femininity but preserving her categorization as female. This task was made easy for her by a very powerful resource, namely, the process of commonsense categorization in everyday life.

The categorization of members of society into indigenous categories such as 'girl' or 'boy', or 'woman' or 'man', operates in a distinctively social way. The act of categorization does not involve a positive test, in the sense of a well-defined set of criteria that must be explicitly satisfied prior to making an identification. Rather, the application of membership categories relies on an 'if–can' test in everyday interaction. This test stipulates that if people *can be seen* as members of relevant categories, *then categorize them that way*. That is, use the category that seems appropriate, except in the presence of discrepant information or obvious features that would rule out its use. This procedure is quite in keeping with the attitude of everyday life,

which has us take appearances at face value unless we have special reason to doubt. It should be added that it is precisely when we have special reason to doubt that the issue of applying rigorous criteria arises, but it is rare, outside legal or bureaucratic contexts, to encounter insistence on positive tests.

Agnes's initial resource was the predisposition of those she encountered to take her appearance (her figure, clothing, hair style, and so on), as the undoubted appearance of a normal female. Her further resource was our cultural perspective on the properties of 'natural, normally sexed persons'. Garfinkel (1967) notes that in everyday life, we live in a world of two—and only two—sexes. This arrangement has a moral status, in that we include ourselves and others in it as 'essentially, originally, in the first place, always have been, always will be, once and for all, in the final analysis, either "male" or "female"' (Garfinkel, 1967: 122). Consider the following case:

This issue reminds me of a visit I made to a computer store a couple of years ago. The person who answered my questions was truly a *salesperson*. I could not categorize him/her as a woman or a man. What did I look for? (1) Facial hair: She/he was smooth skinned, but some men have little or no facial hair. (This varies by race; Native Americans and Blacks often have none.) (2) Breasts: She/he was wearing a loose shirt that hung from his/her shoulders. And, as many women who suffered through a 1950s' adolescence know to their shame, women are often flat-chested. (3) Shoulders: His/hers were small and round for a man, broad for a woman. (4) Hands: Long and slender fingers, knuckles a bit large for a woman, small for a man. (5) Voice: Middle range, unexpressive for a woman, not at all the exaggerated tones some gay males affect. (6) His/her treatment of me: Gave off no signs that would let me know if I were of the same or different sex as this person. There were not even any signs that he/she knew his/her sex would be difficult to categorize and I wondered about that even as I did my best to hide these questions so I would not embarrass him/her while we talked of computer paper. I left still not knowing the sex of my salesperson, and was disturbed by that unanswered question (child of my culture that I am) (Diane Margolis, personal communication).

What can this case tell us about situations such as Agnes's or the process of sex categorization in general? First, we infer from this description that the computer salesperson's identificatory display was ambiguous, since she or he was not dressed or adorned in an unequivocally female or male fashion. It is when such a display *fails* to provide grounds for categorization that factors such as facial hair or tone of voice are assessed to determine membership in a sex category. Second, beyond the fact that this incident could be recalled after 'a couple of years', the customer was not only 'disturbed' by the ambiguity of the salesperson's category but also assumed that to acknowledge this ambiguity would be embarrassing to the salesclerk. Not only do we want to know the sex category of those around us (to see it at a glance, perhaps), but we also presume that others are displaying it for us, in as decisive a fashion as they can.

GENDER

Agnes attempted to be '120 per cent female' (Garfinkel, 1967: 129), that is, unquestionably in all ways and at all times feminine. She thought she could protect herself from disclosure before and after surgical intervention by comporting herself in a feminine manner, but she also could have given herself away by overdoing her performance. Sex categorization and the accomplishment of gender are not the same. Agnes's categorization could be secure or suspect, but did not depend on whether or not she lived up to some ideal conception of femininity. Women can be seen as unfeminine, but that does not make them 'unfemale'. Agnes faced an ongoing task of being a woman—something

beyond style of dress (an identificatory display) or allowing men to light her cigarette (a gender display). Her problem was to produce configurations of behaviour that would be seen by others as normative gender behaviour.

Agnes's strategy of 'secret apprenticeship', through which she learned expected feminine decorum by carefully attending to her fiancé's criticisms of other women, was one means of masking incompetencies and simultaneously acquiring the needed skills (Garfinkel, 1967). It was through her fiancé that Agnes learned that sunbathing on the lawn in front of her apartment was 'offensive' (because it put her on display to other men). She also learned from his critiques of other women that she should not insist on having things her way and that she should not offer her opinions or claim equality with men (Garfinkel, 1967: 147–8). (Like other women in our society, Agnes learned something about power in the course of her 'education'.)

Popular culture abounds with books and magazines that compile idealized depictions of relations between women and men. Those focused on the etiquette of dating or prevailing standards of feminine comportment are meant to be of practical help in these matters. However, the use of any such source *as a manual of procedure* requires the assumption that doing gender merely involves making use of discrete, well-defined bundles of behaviour that can simply be plugged into interactional situations to produce recognizable enactments of masculinity and femininity. The man 'does' being masculine by, for example, taking the woman's arm to guide her across a street, and she 'does' being feminine by consenting to be guided and not initiating such behaviour with a man.

Agnes could perhaps have used such sources as manuals, but, we contend, doing gender is not so easily regimented. Such sources may list and describe the sorts of behaviours that mark or display gender, but they are necessarily incomplete. And to be successful, marking or displaying gender must be finely fitted to situations and modified or transformed as the occasion demands. Doing gender consists of managing such occasions so that, whatever the particulars, the outcome is seen and seeable in context as gender-appropriate or, as the case may be, gender-*in*appropriate, that is, *accountable*.

Gender and Accountability

As Heritage (1984: 136–7) notes, members of society regularly engage in 'descriptive account-ings of states of affairs to one another', and such accounts are both serious and consequential. These descriptions name, characterize, formulate, explain, excuse, excoriate, or merely take notice of some circumstance or activity and thus place it within some social framework (locating it relative to other activities, like and unlike).

Such descriptions are themselves accountable, and societal members orient to the fact that their activities are subject to comment. Actions are often designed with an eye to their accountability, that is, how they might look and how they might be characterized. The notion of accountability also encompasses those actions undertaken so that they are specifically unremarkable and thus not worthy of more than a passing remark, because they are seen to be in accord with culturally approved standards.

Heritage observes that the process of rendering something accountable is interactional in character:

[This] permits actors to design their actions in relation to their circumstances so as to permit others, by methodically taking account of cir-cumstances, to recognize the action for what it is (1984: 179).

The key word here is *circumstances*. One circum-stance that attends virtually all actions is the sex category of the actor. As Garfinkel comments:

[T]he work and socially structured occasions of sexual passing were obstinately unyielding

to [Agnes's] attempts to routinize the grounds of daily activities. This obstinacy points to the *omnirelevance* of sexual status to affairs of daily life as an invariant but unnoticed background in the texture of relevances that compose the changing actual scenes of everyday life (1967: 118, emphasis added).

If sex category is omnirelevant (or even approaches being so), then a person engaged in virtually any activity may be held accountable for performance of that activity as a *woman* or a *man*, and their incumbency in one or the other sex category can be used to legitimate or discredit their other activities. Accordingly, virtually any activity can be assessed as to its womanly or manly nature. And note, to 'do' gender is not always to live up to nor-mative conceptions of femininity or masculinity; it is to engage in behaviour *at the risk of gender assess-ment*. While it is individuals who do gender, the enterprise is fundamentally interactional and insti-tutional in character, for accountability is a feature of social relationships and its idiom is drawn from the institutional arena in which those relation-ships are enacted. If this be the case, can we ever *not* do gender? Insofar as a society is partitioned by 'essential' differences between women and men and placement in a sex category is both rel-evant and enforced, doing gender is unavoidable.

Resources for Doing Gender

Doing gender means creating differences between girls and boys and women and men, differences that are not natural, essential, or biological. Once the differences have been constructed, they are used to reinforce the 'essentialness' of gender. In a delightful account of the 'arrangement between the sexes', Goffman (1977) observes the creation of a variety of institutionalized frameworks through which our 'natural, normal sexedness' can be enacted. The physical features of social setting provide one obvious resource for the expression of our 'essential' differences. For example, the sex segregation of North American public bathrooms distinguishes 'ladies' from 'gentlemen' in matters held to be fundamentally biological, even though both 'are somewhat similar in the question of waste products and their elimination' (Goffman, 1977: 315). These settings are furnished with dimorphic equipment (such as urinals for men or elaborate grooming facilities for women), even though both sexes may achieve the same ends through the same means (and apparently do so in the privacy of their own homes). To be stressed here is the fact that:

> The *functioning* of sex-differentiated organs is involved, but there is nothing in this functioning that biologically recommends segregation; that arrangement is a totally cultural matter . . . toilet segregation is presented as a natural consequence of the difference between the sex-classes when in fact it is a means of honoring, if not producing, this difference (Goffman, 1977: 316).

Standardized social occasions also provide stages for evocations of the 'essential female and male natures'. Goffman cites organized sports as one such institutionalized framework for the expression of manliness. There, those qualities that ought 'properly' to be associated with masculinity, such as endurance, strength, and competitive spirit, are celebrated by all parties concerned—participants, who may be seen to demonstrate such traits, and spectators, who applaud their demonstrations from the safety of the sidelines (1977: 322).

Assortative mating practices among heterosexual couples afford still further means to create and maintain differences between women and men. For example, even though size, strength, and age tend to be normally distributed among females and males (with considerable overlap between them), selective pairing ensures couples in which boys and men are visibly bigger, stronger, and older (if not 'wiser') than the girls and women with whom

they are paired. So, should situations emerge in which greater size, strength, or experience is called for, boys and men will be ever ready to display it and girls and women, to appreciate its display.

Gender may be routinely fashioned in a variety of situations that seem conventionally expressive to begin with, such as those that present 'helpless' women next to heavy objects or flat tires. But, as Goffman notes, heavy, messy, and precarious concerns can be constructed from *any* social situation, 'even though by standards set in other settings, this may involve something that is light, clean, and safe' (Goffman, 1977: 324). Given these resources, it is clear that any interactional situation sets the stage for depictions of 'essential' sexual natures. In sum, these situations 'do not so much allow for the expression of natural differences as for the production of that difference itself' (Goffman, 1977: 324).

Many situations are not clearly sex categorized to begin with, nor is what transpires within them obviously gender relevant. Yet any social encounter can be pressed into service in the interests of doing gender. Thus, Fishman's (1978) research on casual conversations found an asymmetrical 'division of labour' in talk between heterosexual intimates. Women had to ask more questions, fill more silences, and use more attention-getting beginnings in order to be heard. Her conclusions are particularly pertinent here:

> Since interactional work is related to what constitutes being a woman, with what a woman is, the idea that it is work is obscured. The work is not seen as what women do, but as part of what they are (Fishman, 1978: 405).

We would argue that it is precisely such labour that helps to constitute the essential nature of women as women in interactional contexts.

Individuals have many social identities that may be donned or shed, muted or made more salient, depending on the situation. One may be a friend, spouse, professional, citizen, and many other things to many different people—or, to the same person at different times. But we are always women or men—unless we shift into another sex category. What this means is that our identificatory displays will provide an ever-available resource for doing gender under an infinitely diverse set of circumstances.

Some occasions are organized to routinely display and celebrate behaviours that are conventionally linked to one or the other sex category. On such occasions, everyone knows his or her place in the interactional scheme of things. If an individual identified as a member of one sex category engages in behaviour usually associated with the other category, this routinization is challenged. Hughes (1945: 356) provides an illustration of such a dilemma:

> [A] young woman . . . became part of that virile profession, engineering. The designer of an airplane is expected to go up on the maiden flight of the first plane built according to the design. He [sic] then gives a dinner to the engineers and workmen who worked on the new plane. The dinner is naturally a stag party. The young woman in question designed a plane. Her co-workers urged her not to take the risk—for which, presumably, men only are fit—of the maiden voyage. They were, in effect, asking her to be a lady instead of an engineer. She chose to be an engineer. She then gave the party and paid for it like a man. After food and the first round of toasts, she left like a lady.

On this occasion, parties reached an accommodation that allowed a woman to engage in presumptively masculine behaviours. However, we note that in the end, this compromise permitted demonstration of her 'essential' femininity, through accountably 'ladylike' behaviour.

Hughes (1945: 357) suggests that such contradictions may be countered by managing interactions on a very narrow basis, for example, 'keeping the relationship formal and specific'. But the heart of the matter is that even—perhaps, especially—if the relationship is a formal one, gender is still something one is accountable for. Thus a woman physician (notice the special qualifier in her case) may be accorded respect for her skill and even addressed by an appropriate title. Nonetheless, she is subject to evaluation in terms of normative conceptions of appropriate attitudes and activities for her sex category and under pressure to prove that she is an 'essentially' feminine being, despite appearances to the contrary. Her sex category is used to discredit her participation in important clinical activities, while her involvement in medicine is used to discredit her commitment to her responsibilities as a wife and mother. Simultaneously, her exclusion from the physician colleague community is maintained and her accountability *as a woman* is ensured.

In this context, 'role conflict' can be viewed as a dynamic aspect of our current 'arrangement between the sexes' (Goffman, 1977), an arrangement that provides for occasions on which persons of a particular sex category can 'see' quite clearly that they are out of place and that if they were not there, their current troubles would not exist. What is at stake is, from the standpoint of interaction, the management of our 'essential' natures, and from the standpoint of the individual, the continuing accomplishment of gender. If, as we have argued, sex category is omnirelevant, then any occasion, conflicted or not, offers the resources for doing gender.

We have sought to show that sex category and gender are managed properties of conduct that are contrived with respect to the fact that others will judge and respond to us in particular ways. We have claimed that a person's gender is not simply an aspect of what one is, but, more fundamentally, it is something that one does, and *does* recurrently, in interaction with others.

What are the consequences of this theoretical formulation? If, for example, individuals strive to achieve gender in encounters with others, how does a culture instill the need to achieve it? What is the relationship between the production of gender at the level of interaction and such institutional arrangements as the division of labour in society? And, perhaps most important, how does doing gender contribute to the subordination of women by men?

Research Agendas

To bring the social production of gender under empirical scrutiny, we might begin at the beginning, with a reconsideration of the process through which societal members acquire the requisite categorical apparatus and other skills to become gendered human beings.

RECRUITMENT TO GENDER IDENTITIES

The conventional approach to the process of becoming girls and boys has been sex-role socialization. In recent years, recurring problems arising from this approach have been linked to inadequacies inherent in role theory *per se*—its emphasis on 'consensus, stability and continuity' (Stacey and Thorne, 1985: 307), its a historical and depoliticizing focus (Thorne, 1980: 9; Stacey and Thorne, 1985: 307), and the fact that its 'social' dimension relies on 'a general assumption that people choose to maintain existing customs' (Connell, 1985: 263).

In contrast, Cahill (1982, 1986a, 1986b) analyzes the experiences of preschool children using a social model of recruitment into normally gendered identities. Cahill argues that categorization practices are fundamental to learning and displaying feminine and masculine behaviour. Initially, he observes, children are primarily concerned with distinguishing between themselves and others on the basis of social competence. Categorically, their concern resolves itself into the opposition of 'girl/boy' classification versus 'baby' classification (the latter designating children whose social behaviour is problematic and who must be closely supervised). It is children's concern with being seen as socially competent that evokes their initial claims to gender identities:

> During the exploratory stage of children's socialization . . . they learn that only two social identities are routinely available to them, the identity of 'baby', or, depending on the configuration of their external genitalia, either 'big boy' or 'big girl'. Moreover, others subtly inform them that the identity of 'baby' is a discrediting one. When, for example, children engage in disapproved behavior, they are often told 'You're a baby' or 'Be a big boy.' In effect, these typical verbal responses to young children's behavior convey to them that they must behaviorally choose between the discrediting identity of 'baby' and their anatomically determined sex identity (Cahill, 1986a: 175).

Subsequently, little boys appropriate the gender ideal of 'efficaciousness', that is, being able to affect the physical and social environment through the exercise of physical strength or appropriate skills. In contrast, little girls learn to value 'appearance', that is, managing themselves as ornamental objects. Both classes of children learn that the recognition and use of sex categorization in interaction are not optional, but mandatory.

Being a 'girl' or a 'boy' then, is not only being more competent than a 'baby', but also being competently female or male, that is, learning to produce behavioural displays of one's 'essential' female or male identity. In this respect, the task of four- to five-year-old children is very similar to Agnes's:

> For example, the following interaction occurred on a preschool playground. A 55-month-old boy (D) was attempting to unfasten the clasp of a necklace when a preschool aide walked over to him.
>
> A: Do you want to put that on?
> D: No. It's for girls.
> A: You don't have to be a girl to wear things

around your neck. Kings wear things around their neck. You could pretend that you're a king.

D: I'm not a king. I'm a boy (Cahill, 1986a: 176).

As Cahill notes in this example, although D may have been unclear as to the sex status of a king's identity, he was obviously aware that necklaces are used to announce the identity 'girl'. Having claimed the identity 'boy' and having developed a behavioural commitment to it, he was leery of any display that might furnish grounds for questioning his claim.

In this way, new members of society come to be involved in a *self-regulating process* as they begin to monitor their own and others' conduct with regard to its gender implications. The 'recruitment' process involves not only the appropriation of gender ideals (by the valuation of those ideals as proper ways of being and behaving) but also *gender identities* that are important to individuals and that they strive to maintain. Thus gender differences, or the sociocultural shaping of 'essential female and male natures', achieve the status of objective facts. They are rendered normal, natural features of persons and provide the tacit rationale for differing fates of women and men within the social order.

Additional studies of children's play activities as routine occasions for the expression of gender-appropriate behaviour can yield new insights into how our 'essential natures' are constructed. In particular, the transition from what Cahill (1986a) terms 'apprentice participation' in the sex-segregated worlds that are common among elementary school children to 'bona fide participation' in the heterosocial world so frightening to adolescents is likely to be a keystone in our understanding of the recruitment process.

GENDER AND THE DIVISION OF LABOUR

Whenever people face issues of *allocation*—who is to do what, get what, plan or execute action, direct or be directed, incumbency in significant social categories such as 'female' and 'male' seems to become pointedly relevant. How such issues are resolved conditions the exhibition, dramatization, or celebration of one's 'essential nature' as a woman or man.

Berk (1985) offers elegant demonstration of this point in her investigation of the allocation of household labour and the attitudes of married couples toward the division of household tasks. Berk found little variation in either the actual distribution of tasks or perceptions of equity in regard to that distribution. Wives, even when employed outside the home, do the vast majority of household and childcare tasks. Moreover, both wives and husbands tend to perceive this as a 'fair' arrangement. Noting the failure of conventional sociological and economic theories to explain this seeming contradiction, Berk contends that something more complex is involved than rational arrangements for the production of household goods and services:

> Hardly a question simply of who has more time, or whose time is worth more, who has more skill or more power, it is clear that a complicated relationship between the structure of work imperatives and the structure of normative expectations attached to work as *gendered* determines the ultimate allocation of members' time to work and home (Berk, 1985: 195–6).

She notes, for example, that the most important factor influencing wives' contribution of labour is the total amount of work demanded or expected by the household; such demands had no bearing on husbands' contributions. Wives reported various rationales (their own and their husbands') that justified their level of contribution and, as a general matter, underscored the presumption that wives are essentially responsible for household production.

Berk contends that it is difficult to see how people 'could rationally establish the arrangements that they do solely for the production of household goods and services' (1985: 201)—much less, how people could consider them 'fair'. She argues that our current arrangements for the domestic division of labour support *two* production processes: household goods and services (meals, clean children, and so on) and, at the same time, gender. As she puts it:

> Simultaneously, members 'do' gender, as they 'do' housework and child care, and what [has] been called the division of labor provides for the joint production of household labor and gender; it is the mechanism by which both the material and symbolic products of the household are realized (1985: 201).

It is not simply that household labour is designated as 'women's work', but that for a woman to engage in it and a man not to engage in it is to draw on and exhibit the 'essential nature' of each. What is produced and reproduced is not merely the activity and artifact of domestic life, but the material embodiment of wifely and husbandly roles, and derivatively, of womanly and manly conduct. What are also frequently produced and reproduced are the dominant and subordinate statuses of the sex categories.

How does gender get done in work settings outside the home, where dominance and subordination are themes of overarching importance? Hochschild's (1983) analysis of the work of flight attendants offers some promising insights. She found that the occupation of flight attendant consisted of something altogether different for women than for men:

> As the company's main shock absorbers against 'mishandled' passengers, their own feelings are more frequently subjected to rough treatment. In addition, a day's exposure to people who resist authority in a woman is a different experience than it is for a man. . . . In this respect, it is a disadvantage to be a woman. And in this case, they are not simply women

in the biological sense. They are also a highly visible distillation of middle-class American notions of femininity. They symbolize Woman. Insofar as the category 'female' is mentally associated with having less status and authority, female flight attendants are more readily classified as 'really' females than other females are (1983: 175).

In performing what Hochschild terms the 'emotional labor' necessary to maintain airline profits, women flight attendants simultaneously produce enactments of their 'essential' femininity.

SEX AND SEXUALITY

What is the relationship between doing gender and a culture's prescription of 'obligatory heterosexuality'? As Frye (1983: 22) observes, the monitoring of sexual feelings in relation to other appropriately sexed persons requires the ready recognition of such persons 'before one can allow one's heart to beat or one's blood to flow in erotic enjoyment of that person'. The appearance of heterosexuality is produced through emphatic and unambiguous indicators of one's sex, layered on in ever more conclusive fashion (Frye, 1983: 24). Thus, lesbians and gay men concerned with passing as heterosexuals can rely on these indicators for camouflage; in contrast, those who would avoid the assumption of heterosexuality may foster ambiguous indicators of their categorical status through their dress, behaviours, and style. But 'ambiguous' sex indicators are sex indicators nonetheless. If one wishes to be recognized as a lesbian (or heterosexual woman), one must first establish a categorical status as female. Even as popular images portray lesbians as 'females who are not feminine' (Frye, 1983: 129), the accountability of persons for their 'normal, natural sexedness' is preserved.

Nor is accountability threatened by the existence of 'sex-change operations'—presumably, the most radical challenge to our cultural perspective on sex and gender. Although no one coerces transsexuals into hormone therapy, electrolysis, or surgery, the alternatives available to them are undeniably constrained:

> When the transsexual experts maintain that they use transsexual procedures only with people who ask for them, and who prove that they can 'pass', they obscure the social reality. Given patriarchy's prescription that one must be *either* masculine or feminine, free choice is conditioned (Raymond, 1979: 135, emphasis added).

The physical reconstruction of sex criteria pays ultimate tribute to the 'essentialness' of our sexual natures—as women *or* as men.

Gender, Power, and Social Change

Let us return to the question: Can we avoid doing gender? Earlier, we proposed that insofar as sex category is used as a fundamental criterion for differentiation, doing gender is unavoidable. It is unavoidable because of the social consequences of sex category membership: the allocation of power and resources not only in the domestic, economic, and political domains but also in the broad arena of interpersonal relations. In virtually any situation, one's sex category can be relevant, and one's performance as an incumbent of that category (i.e., gender) can be subjected to evaluation. Maintaining such pervasive and faithful assignment of lifetime status requires legitimation.

But doing gender also renders the social arrangements based on sex category accountable as normal and natural, that is, legitimate ways of organizing social life. Differences between women and men that are created by this process can then be portrayed as fundamental and enduring dispositions. In this light, the institutional arrangements of a society can be seen as responsive to the differences—the social order being merely an accommodation to the natural order. Thus if, in doing gender, men are also doing dominance and

women are doing deference, the resultant social order, which supposedly reflects 'natural differences', is a powerful reinforcer and legitimator of hierarchical arrangements. Frye observes:

> For efficient subordination, what's wanted is that the structure not appear to be a cultural artifact kept in place by human decision or custom, but that it appear *natural*—that it appear to be quite a direct consequence of facts about the beast which are beyond the scope of human manipulation. . . . That we are trained to behave so differently as women and men, and to behave so differently toward women and men, itself contributes mightily to the appearance of extreme dimorphism, but also, the *ways* we act as women and men, and the *ways* we act toward women and men, mold our bodies and our minds to the shape of subordination and dominance. We do become what we practice being (Frye, 1983: 34).

If we do gender appropriately, we simultaneously sustain, reproduce, and render legitimate the institutional arrangements that are based on sex category. If we fail to do gender appropriately, we as individuals—not the institutional arrangements—may be called to account (for our character, motives, and predispositions).

Social movements such as feminism can provide the ideology and impetus to question existing arrangements, and the social support for individuals to explore alternatives to them. Legislative changes, such as those proposed by the Equal Rights Amendment, can also weaken the accountability of conduct to sex category, thereby affording the possibility of more widespread loosening of accountability in general. To be sure, equality under the law does not guarantee equality in other arenas. As Lorber (1986: 577) points out, assurance of 'scrupulous equality of categories of people considered essentially different needs constant monitoring.' What such proposed changes can do is provide the warrant for asking why, if we wish to treat women and men as equals, there needs to be two sex categories at all.

The sex category/gender relationship links the institutional and interactional levels, a coupling that legitimates social arrangements based on sex category and reproduces their asymmetry in face-to-face interaction. Doing gender furnishes the interactional scaffolding of social structure, along with a built-in mechanism of social control. In appreciating the institutional forces that maintain distinctions between women and men, we must not lose sight of the interactional validation of those distinctions that confers upon them their sense of 'naturalness' and 'rightness'.

Social change, then, must be pursued both at the institutional and cultural level of sex category and at the interactional level of gender. Such a conclusion is hardly novel. Nevertheless, we suggest that it is important to recognize that the analytical distinction between institutional and interactional spheres does not pose an either/or choice when it comes to the question of effecting social change. Reconceptualizing gender not as a simple property of individuals but as an integral dynamic of social orders implies a new perspective on the entire network of gender relations:

> [T]he social subordination of women, and the cultural practices which help sustain it; the politics of sexual object choice, and particularly the oppression of homosexual people; the sexual division of labor, the formation of character and motive, so far as they are organized as femininity and masculinity; the role of the body in social relations, especially the politics of childbirth; and the nature of strategies of sexual liberation movements (Connell, 1985: 261).

Gender is a powerful ideological device, which produces, reproduces, and legitimates the choices and limits that are predicated on sex category. An understanding of how gender is produced in social situations will afford clarification of the interactional scaffolding of social structure and the social control processes that sustain it.

References

Berk, S.F. 1985. *The Gender Factory: The Apportionment of Work in American Households*. New York: Plenum.

Cahill, S.E. 1982. 'Becoming Boys and Girls'. PhD dissertation, Department of Sociology, University of California, Santa Barbara.

———. 1986a. 'Childhood Socialization as Recruitment Process: Some Lessons from the Study of Gender Development', in P. Adler and P. Adler, eds, *Sociological Studies of Child Development*, pp. 163–86. Greenwich, CT: JAI Press.

———. 1986b. 'Language Practices and Self-Definition: The Case of Gender Identity Acquisition', *The Sociological Quarterly* 27: 295–311.

Connell, R.W. 1985. 'Theorizing Gender', *Sociology* 19: 260–72. Fishman, P. 1978. 'Interaction: The Work Women Do', *Social Problems* 25: 397–406.

Frye, M. 1983. *The Politics of Reality: Essays in Feminist Theory*. Trumansburg, NY: The Crossing Press.

Garfinkel, H. 1967. *Studies in Ethnomethodology*. Englewood Cliffs, NJ: Prentice-Hall. Goffman, E. 1976. 'Gender Display', *Studies in the Anthropology of Visual Communication* 3: 69–77.

———. 1977. 'The Arrangement Between the Sexes', *Theory and Society* 4: 301–31. Heritage, J. 1984. *Garfinkel and Ethnomethodology*. Cambridge, UK: Polity Press.

Hochschild, A.R. 1983. *The Managed Heart. Commercialization of Human Feeling*. Berkeley: University of California Press.

Hughes, E.C. 1945. 'Dilemmas and Contradictions of Status', *American Journal of Sociology* 50: 353–59.

Kessler, S.J., and W. McKenna. 1978. *Gender: An Ethnomethodological Approach*. New York: Wiley.

Komarovsky, M. 1946. 'Cultural Contradictions and Sex Roles', *American Journal of Sociology* 52: 184–9.

———. 1950. 'Functional Analysis of Sex Roles', *American Sociological Review* 15: 508–16.

Linton, R. 1936. *The Study of Man*. New York: Appleton-Century.

Lorber, J. 1986. 'Dismantling Noah's Ark', *Sex Roles* 14: 567–80.

Parsons, T. 1951. *The Social System*. New York: Free Press.

Parsons, T., and R.F. Bales. 1955. *Family, Socialization and Interaction Process*. New York: Free Press.

Raymond, J.G. 1979. *The Transsexual Empire*. Boston: Beacon.

Rossi, A. 1984. 'Gender and Parenthood', *American Sociological Review* 49: 1–19.

Rubin, G. 1975. 'The Traffic in Women: Notes on the "Political Economy" of Sex', in R. Reiter, ed., *Toward an Anthropology of Women*, pp. 157–210. New York: Monthly Review Press.

Stacey, J., and B. Thorne. 1985. 'The Missing Feminist Revolution in Sociology', *Social Problems* 32: 301–16.

Thorne, B. 1980. 'Gender . . . How Is It Best Conceptualized?' Unpublished manuscript.

CHAPTER 11

Coming Out and Crossing Over: Identity Formation and Proclamation in a Transgender Community

Patricia Gagné, Richard Tewksbury, and Deanna McGaughey

Much of the social scientific focus on transgendered individuals has derived from an interest in understanding 'deviation' from the 'normal' and 'natural' two-sex system (see Herdt, 1994). With the exception of Weinberg, Williams, and Pryor's (1994) research on transsexual bisexuals and treatises written by transgendered individuals (Morris 1974; Bornstein 1994; Rothblatt, 1995), the literature on transgenderism has focused primarily on issues of sex and gender. Within this literature, there has been little examination of sexuality (but see Herdt, 1994) and a virtual absence of research on the coming-out experiences of transgendered individuals.

In this article, we examine the coming-out experiences of a non-random sample of individuals who were members of the transgender community at the time we solicited volunteers for our project. Transgenderism refers to 'the lives and experiences of diverse groups of people who live outside normative sex/gender relations' (Namaste,

1994: 228). Persons who enact alternative gender presentations or who have internalized alternative gender identities are referred to as 'transgenderists' (Tewksbury and Gagné, 1996). When looking at the experiences of transgenderists, identity management concerns are at least as complex as those of bisexuals, gay men, and lesbians, if not more so. While there are some similarities between the coming-out processes of transgenderists and gay men, lesbians, and bisexuals, there are also salient differences. First, since around the end of the nineteenth century, homosexuality has been defined as an identity (D'Emilio, 1983; Foucault, [1978] 1990). As that identity and the communities and institutions built around it have become more visible, lesbians and gay men, and more recently bisexuals, have had opportunities to find similar others. Thus, feelings of 'difference' are more easily identified, labelled, and accepted than they were before homosexuality defined 'who' the person was. While gay men, lesbians,

and bisexuals have challenged the medical definition of homosexuality as a mental illness, they
have, for the most part, adhered to the notion that
sexuality is an important component in defining
who the person is (D'Emilio, 1983; Adam, 1995).
Challenges to this trend are only now emerging
within queer communities and queer theory
(Epstein, 1994; Namaste, 1994; Seidman, 1994,
1996; Stein and Plummer, 1994).

Although barriers to self-awareness and acceptance are declining, transgenderists continue to
grapple with many of the issues that confronted
sexual minorities in the United States prior to
the 1970s. Most masculine-to-feminine transgenderists conform to traditional beliefs about
sex and gender, whereas a minority attempt to
step outside the gender binary by defining themselves in non-gendered or multiply gendered
ways (Raymond, 1994). For example, within
the transgender community, the declassification
of transsexualism as a psychiatric diagnosis has
been hotly debated, with those seeking to challenge medical definitions arguing that it should be
removed from the *Diagnostic and Statistical Manual
of Mental Disorders* (DSM-IV) and those still seeking
access to hormones and sex reassignment surgery
(SRS) arguing that being diagnosed transsexual is
the only way they may become the women they
truly are. In other words, they must 'confess' their
transsexualism in ways that adhere to medical
models in order to proceed from one sex to the
other. Similarly, most transsexuals adhere to
beliefs that their desires to live as women were the
result of biological 'mistakes' that left them as feminine persons in male bodies (Stoller, 1971; Pauly,
1990). Rather than choosing to live as feminine
males, they opt to cross over to full-time womanhood. Similarly, most cross-dressers look on their
sartorial transitions as opportunities to express
their feminine selves (Talamini, 1981; Woodhouse, 1989). They deem feminine behaviour in
masculine attire to be highly inappropriate.

While transgenderism is an issue of sex
and gender, it does entail aspects of sexual

reorientation. Thus, sexually active transgenderists
must recognize, tolerate, and learn to accept an
alternative gender identity; develop a repertoire
of coping strategies to manage public presentations of gender; and, in some cases, manage the
actual transformation of permanent identity and
anatomy. Whether gender transformations are
temporary or permanent, the sense that one really
is the sex associated with the gender portrayed
involves a reexamination of sexual identity. For
example, some anatomically male transsexuals
and cross-dressers, in the process of establishing a
feminine self, engage in sexual activity with other
anatomical male persons. While the observers may
morphologically define the experience as *homosexual* or *same sexed*, the social women experiencing
the interaction tend to define it as *heterosexual*.
Such activity is highly valued as a way of exploring femininity. For transgenderists, the discovery
of a sexual identity, or a sense of who the individual is as a sexual person, frequently occurs within
a sex/gender system. That does not address sexual
issues among those whose sex and gender do not
fit within the binary system. Furthermore, those
who do have SRS must sexually 'come out' to
themselves and others by reexamining their sexual
preferences and orientations. As gender and/or
sex changes, the subjective arid social meanings
of sexual interactions are also transformed. While
gay men, lesbians, and bisexuals must come out
sexually, their experiences are not confounded by
alterations in gender and genital makeup.

Research on the coming-out processes and
experiences of transgenderists provides an opportunity to examine the management of the transformation of three aspects of socially normative
expectations, rather than just one. Whereas lesbians, gay men, and bisexuals are able to carefully
control information dissemination, transgenderists
must manage both their actual and virtual social
identities (Goffman, 1963) on three dimensions.
Lesbians, gay men, and bisexuals can selectively
come out, whereas transgenderists, because of
changes in gender or biological appearance, are

often forced out of the closet, creating awkward—or even dangerous—situations. Transgenderists provide an opportunity to examine the private and public dimensions of achieving a new gender through interaction with others and the emergence and management of alternative sex, gender, and sexual identities.

Method

We completed 65 semi-structured, in-depth, tape-recorded interviews with masculine-to-feminine individuals from several points along the transgender spectrum (see Tewksbury and Gagné, 1996). *Transgenderism* is an umbrella term that encompasses a variety of identities—including transsexual; fetish and non-fetishistic cross-dresser; drag queen, and other terms—as devised by individuals who live outside the dominant gender system. In this study, we have categorized individuals on the basis of the identity they proclaimed to us. All volunteers in our sample were members of the transgender communities through which we recruited volunteers for our study. The majority in our sample had refined their self-identifications in the process of coming out.

Included in our sample are individuals who self-identify as pre ($n = 27$), post ($n = 10$), and nonoperative ($n = 4$) transsexual. Transsexuals are people who believe themselves to be female and who wish to, or do, live full-time as women. Preoperative transsexuals are those who desire to have, but have not yet had, SRS. Postoperative transsexuals are those who have had SRS. Nonoperative transsexuals are those who live full-time or nearly full-time as women but who do not wish to have SRS. Some have availed themselves of other medical and cosmetic procedures—including female hormones, breast implants, and electrolysis, whereas others alter their gender presentations without bodily alteration. During childhood (before age 10), about one-third ($n = 16$) felt a strong desire to become a girl or believed themselves to be female. The remainder began to recognize a desire to be female during adolescence ($n = 15$) or adulthood ($n = 10$). They self-identified as heterosexual, bisexual, lesbian, and asexual. Although our sample included many male individuals who had had sexual relationships or encounters with other male persons, no one in our sample self-identified as gay at the time of the interview or at any time during their lives.

A small number of persons ($n = 5$) who cross-dressed and had no desire for SRS referred to themselves in more politically oriented terms. While there are subtle differences in politics, all five of these people have used transgenderism to challenge binary assumptions about sex, gender, and sexuality. Their intent is not to 'pass' as women but to challenge the idea that gender is a 'natural' expression of sex and sexuality. This group of five includes one 'radical transgenderist'—an anatomical, heterosexual male person with a masculine gender identity, who uses cross-dressing as a means to express feminine aspects of self and to challenge traditional binary conceptualizations of sex, gender, and sexuality. It also includes one 'ambigenderist', an individual who lives alternatively as a man and a woman, and who believes that categories of sexual orientation do not exist and that sexuality is a spectrum. Depending on how he or she feels, he or she frequently went out 'in between'—as neither a man nor a woman (with long hair, makeup, high heels, tight pants, and a two-day growth of beard). In addition, this group includes three people who self-identified as a 'third gender'. These three individuals believed that all people have both masculine and feminine attributes. Their desire was to develop and be able to publicly present both aspects of self and to live as a combination of both genders. Like the ambigenderist, they resisted categorizing themselves according to sexual identity. In our discussions of the transgendered people in our sample, we have self-consciously adhered to the self-identifications used by our volunteers, with the exception of the final group of five. For purposes of clarity, we refer to this group as gender radicals. We have taken the liberty of doing this because all of them emphasized their desire to eliminate the existing system of gender, rather than just their own gender.

Our research was conducted over a one-year period, spanning 1994 and 1995. Early in the research process, we made a conscious decision to include all full-time or nearly full-time transgenderists who volunteered. We solicited volunteers through 14 transgender support groups, transgender online services, and by responding to personal ads in a national transgender publication. People in every region of the contiguous 48 states volunteered for interviews, making our research national in scope. Participants resided in large urban areas, small towns, suburbs, and rural areas. Our sample includes 4 African Americans, 2 Asians, 1 Hispanic, and 58 Caucasians. Participants ranged in age from 24–68 years, with a mean age of 44. Occupationally, they were diverse with jobs ranging from doctors, airline pilots, computer systems analysts, engineers, college professors, schoolteachers, enlisted members of the military, police officers, welders, mechanics, food service and clerical workers, and janitors. Although our sample was occupationally diverse, the majority was well educated and had long employment histories in the skilled trades and professions. Most members of our sample were either employed or voluntarily unemployed (i.e., retired or student) at the time we talked with them. Nonetheless, one postoperative and eight preoperative transsexuals were unemployed, and the majority of those who lived full-time as the gender into which they were not assigned at birth were vastly underemployed.[1]

Respondents were guided through several areas of inquiry, including their earliest transgender experiences or feelings; being discovered crossdressed; acquiring girls' or women's clothing, makeup, and wigs; learning about and refining a feminine appearance or persona; participating in transgender support groups or online communities; finding therapists and surgeons and experiences with the medical community; identifying and labelling emotions, feelings, behaviours, and identity; telling others; transformations or stability in sexual fantasy, behaviour, and identity; and political and gender attitudes. Interviews ranged from 45 minutes to eight hours in length, averaging about three hours.

Early Transgendered Experiences

Examination of the earliest recollections that transgendered individuals have of feeling that either their sex or gender was 'wrong' or did not 'fit' for them are useful in providing insight into the earliest manifestations that become alternative identities. Many recollections of childhood may, in fact, be reconstructed biographies. Nonetheless, these are materials from which individuals mold current identities and, therefore are valid and significant.[2] This is the process in which the collective creation of biographical stories brings phenomenologically real 'true selves' into being (Mason-Schrock, 1996).

Gender constancy—a sense that a person's gender is a permanent aspect of self—is acquired between the ages of three and five years (Kohlberg, 1966; Kohlberg and Ulian, 1974). In our sample, 16 transsexuals recalled wanting to be girls or knowing that they really were girls during early childhood. For all but one of the remainder, feelings of being or wanting to be a woman emerged during adolescence or adulthood. Among crossdressers, all reported knowing they were boys in early childhood and throughout adolescence, but four said they remembered wishing they could be girls during early childhood, and two reported knowing they were male but wishing they could become female during adolescence. Fetishistic cross-dressers and gender radicals did not report feeling they were or wanting to become women. Feminine behaviours and feelings of being or wanting to be girls created confusion for young children and adolescents, particularly when they received messages that they could not be or act that way.

For transsexuals and cross-dressers, one way of making sense of the incongruity between sex and gender was to explore whether a feminine boy might actually be able to become a girl. For example, one cross-dresser explained that at about the age of five, 'I remember . . . asking my mother out in the backyard, "Am I always going to be a boy? Could I change and be a girl someday?"' Such questions are undoubtedly common among young children. For most children, clothing and other expressions of gender are signifiers of maleness or femaleness. Cross-dressers explained that they were satisfied with explanations that they could not change their anatomy and become female but that they continued to want to temporarily 'become' girls by wearing feminine clothing, makeup, and wigs. As adults, all but four cross-dressers (who were exploring the possibility they might be transsexual) reported knowing they were male and being happy with their sex and gender identity. Throughout their lives, they were able to conceal their transgenderism much more easily than were transsexuals, who felt compelled to act and be feminine at all times.

Among transsexuals, confusion over gender, desires to be female, or feelings of being female were commonly reported in childhood and over the life course. Many of the transsexuals in our sample thought they really were girls (in the dominant cultural sense) until they began to receive messages to the contrary. For example, one postoperative transsexual explained her earliest understanding of gender and the way in which it started to be corrected. She said,

> I was probably three or four years old. . . . I remember playing with paper dolls and Barbie dolls and stuff with my sisters and wearing their clothes. I didn't even know I wasn't a girl until [at school] I was told it was time to line up for a restroom break.

Differentiating themselves from girls did not come easily for these 16 transsexuals. Socializing messages might be gentle and subtle, as the ones above, or more laden with overt hostility and anger. For example, another preoperative transsexual explained,

> I can remember begging my mother to let me wear her clothes. . . . I kicked and screamed. . . . Another time she was ironing and I wanted my own ironing board and iron and be just like mommy. This time she got really angry and I guess I was becoming aware of the fact that I wasn't ever going to be a little girl, that it was socially unacceptable . . . because she said, 'You want to be a little girl? Well, we'll put you in a little dress and tie your hair up in ribbons.' . . . She became aggressive about it and at that point I understood that it was socially unacceptable.

In early childhood, cross-dressing and cross-gender behaviour appear to have been tolerated. However, as children advanced beyond the 'toddler' stage, they were pressured by adults and other children to recognize and adhere to traditional conceptualizations of gender and conform to masculine stereotypes. Pressures to conform to the gender binary were often based on homophobic assumptions about gender 'deviants'. For example, a nonoperative transsexual said,

> Around the time I was 9 or 10 years old, there was one boy in the neighborhood . . . [who] was never allowed to spend the night at my house. . . . All he would tell me is, 'My dad won't let me.' One afternoon I approached his dad about it. . . . This man turned an incredible red-purple color and shaking and pointing a finger in my face [said], 'Because you're a fucking queer!' I didn't know what those words meant, but it was clear from his body language that whatever those words were tied to was not OK.

The pressure to adhere to the masculine stereotype was strong, and many in our sample tried to conform. Cross-dressers hid their dressing, segmenting it off from the rest of their lives. Among transsexuals, such segmentation of the feminine aspect of self was more difficult. The majority felt more comfortable playing with girls, participating in 'girls' activities, and expressing and presenting themselves in more feminine ways. For those whose transgender feelings and behaviours began in early childhood, pressures to 'fit' into the masculine stereotype and 'act' like boys created confusion about identity, an internalized sense of deviance, and frequently strong self-loathing. For example, a preoperative transsexual said, 'I didn't know it was transsexual. I just didn't feel like a male. Everyone was telling me I was and I felt I had to act that way . . . I felt it was something very, very wrong.'

After an initial period of confusion about sex and gender, most children recognized that cross-dressing and feminine behaviour were deviant and, therefore, they tried to repress it and keep it secret. This suggests that as children begin to understand the binary gender system, they become ashamed of feminine or transgendered feelings, learn to hide their behaviours, and become confused about who they are and how they fit into the world. Many in our sample talked about becoming addicted to alcohol or drugs later in life, in an effort to numb the emotional pain they experienced and to repress the 'true self', which did not fit and, therefore, needed to be repressed. Throughout adolescence and adulthood, most went through periods of 'purging', when they would stop engaging in transgendered behaviour and throw out feminine clothing, makeup, and wigs. Despite the stigma attached to transgenderism, however, the need to 'be themselves' was strong. Even as they tried to stop, and as their feminine attributes were criticized and sanctioned, they found it impossible to stop and learned to become more and more secretive. For example, a preoperative transsexual explained,

> I was being beat up, called sissy. . . . I didn't feel normal. I felt like, 'Why are you doing this?

This isn't right. You're a boy.' But I couldn't stop. The curiosity kept drawing me to it and I kept doing it. I felt guilty and I always thought after I . . . took the clothes off, 'I'm not going to do this anymore. This is silly.' A few days later . . . I was back doing it again.

Coming Out to One's Self

For many transgendered individuals, coming to terms with identity is driven by three factors: (1) events that inform them that to feel as they do is 'wrong' (2) finding that there are names for their feelings, and (3) learning that there are others who have had similar experiences. The search for authenticity is a motivating factor in the desire to resolve identity (Gecas, 1991). Because of the centrality of community in the formation and legitimation of identity (see Taylor and Whittier, 1992), the efforts of transgenderists to find and express a 'true self' are mitigated by their contacts with the transgendered world, just as they are affected by the dominant culture. To 'confess' gender (or transgenderism), one must communicate in an established idiom or risk the desired authenticity. While new identities are emergent, they are created within the constraints of current understandings. Furthermore, because of dominant beliefs that incongruity between assumed sex and presented gender is indicative of homosexuality, and that such is deviant, as transgenderists mix or replace masculinity with femininity on either a temporary or permanent basis, they frequently wonder what this implies about their sexuality.

When individuals fail to adhere to the gender binary, they are often told they are wrong or bad, so they tend to initially think of themselves as sick or deviant. Until they find similar others who have rejected stigma, self-blame and the internalization of deviance are common. As the transgenderists in our sample became aware that there were others in the world like them, they experienced a sense of self-recognition, and most quickly aligned themselves with new potential identities. The refinement and adoption of relatively stable identities occurred within the possibilities offered by the transgender subculture, which has been heavily influenced by medical models of transgenderism.

Most transsexuals and a minority of the cross-dressers in our sample reported being labelled 'sissies' by parents, siblings, and schoolmates. Those labelled 'sissy' or 'girl-like' experienced extreme stigmatization, isolation, and at times abuse. Derogative comments from family members seemed to affect the self-esteem and self-concept more than insults from peers or other non-relatives. One nonoperative transsexual married to a woman recounted how her parents and friends pressured her to be more masculine. She said,

> The kids in the neighborhood that I wanted to be friends with . . . were the girls. . . . I wanted my own doll and remember the boys in the neighborhood seemed to have a real problem with that. . . . In that same time period, my dad came into my bedroom one night and he took all the dolls out of my bed. He said I could keep the animals but the dolls had to go because, 'You're a little boy and little boys don't sleep with dolls.'

Even with such social sanctions the feelings persisted. Among transsexuals and a minority of cross-dressers, to be doing what girls were doing felt comfortable and natural. For many, playing with boys was stressful, anxiety provoking, and often induced feelings of failure and low self-esteem. Consequently, many transgenderists found ways to separate themselves from those who reinforced the feeling of difference and deviance, staying to themselves as much as possible.

Just as children tried to conceal transgenderism or conform to the expectations of family and other socializing agents, adults were likely to engage in similar coping strategies until they began to accept themselves as transgenderists. Transsexuals tended to react to negative messages by being hypermasculine. As adults, many in our sample went into physically strenuous or high-risk occupations where they could prove their masculinity. [One participant] said, 'I would avoid doing anything that someone might see as being a remotely feminine kind of thing. I wouldn't even help my ex-[wife] plant a flower garden.' Out of our entire sample, 18 had served in the military. Most said they hoped the experience would make men out of them. Although an extreme example of this sentiment, another preoperative transsexual explained,

> I knew there was something wrong with me and I wanted to do whatever I could to make a real man out of myself. So I joined the army. Voluntarily went to Vietnam. Voluntarily carried a machine gun in the jungle. I was a paratrooper. I was a Green Beret. I did everything I could do in that three-year period to make a man out of myself.

Cross-dressers were less likely to react in hypermasculine ways, primarily because they kept their feminine side hidden.

Throughout childhood, adolescence, and early to mid adulthood most transgenderists in our study experienced shame and confusion for not being 'right'. They lived in a social region for which there was no idiom. Because they were sanctioned for feminine attributes and behaviour, they learned that there was no place for feminine boys or men in society. Feeling more comfortable with girls, they began to understand gender and sex within the social options presented to them. The socially constructed aspects of reality were so strong that believing they were born with the wrong genitals seemed more plausible than violating the gender binary. Even in adulthood, transsexuals frequently made efforts to conceal their genitals, even from themselves, by tucking them between the legs or taping them up. While relatively uncommon in our sample (during adulthood, $n = 2$), when transsexuals were unaware of available medical options or were unable to afford SRS, they attempted self-castration. These efforts indicate the degree to which gender is signified by genitalia.

It was common in our sample for transgenderists to experience sexual attractions to other men, to have sexual fantasies about men, or both. At the same time, they experienced social sanctions and pressures to conform to dominant conceptualizations of gender. While they worried they might be gay, they began to experience and explore sexuality within the binary system and its ancillary compulsory heterosexuality (Rich, 1989). As a 36-year-old bisexual cross-dresser explained, 'You're getting all kinds of messages that men are men and women are women. Sissy boys and fags. The adolescent years are really, really hard on homosexuals and anything not mainstream sexually.' Within our sample, adolescent male persons and adult men in the early stages of identity formation were frequently confused about the implications feminine behaviour had on their sexuality. As men, they knew sex with male individuals was unacceptable; but as women, it was a source of validation. Most reacted by repressing attractions to men, at least until they began to go out in public as women, when sexual interactions with men were indicative of passage into social womanhood.

None of the people in our sample adopted a gay identity, even temporarily, although sexual experimentation with male persons was a common aspect of the coming-out experience. Because of an understanding that transgenderism, homosexuality, and femininity were wrong, all but two transgenderists made efforts to conceal, to purge, to deny, and to cure themselves in order to avoid acceptance of their transgenderism.

Most commonly, the triggering event for acceptance of an identity came when, either accidentally or intentionally, the individual encountered others who served as symbols for available identities. However, role models who challenged binary conceptualizations of gender were largely unavailable because 'there is no place for a person who is neither a woman or a man' (Lorber, 1994: 96), finding role models and formulating an identity outside the gender binary is virtually impossible. Thus, alternative identities were restricted to those available within the gender binary, usually found among those who had crossed *from* one gender *to* the only other one known to be legitimately available.

Learning of the availability of transsexualism and seeing such women on television and reading about them in newspapers and magazines provided opportunities to know that there were alternative identities available. One newly postoperative transsexual looked back on her late teens as generally unhappy and confusing but says that she made a major discovery about both herself and society when

> I was in high school and I started to hear about Renee Richards. I graduated high school in '72, so she was just coming out when I was just starting high school. At that time, I still thought that I was alone in the world. . . . When I started to hear about Renee Richards, then I said, 'Maybe there is somebody else, but this is the only other person that knows where I'm coming from.'

Finding others who felt as they did helped to alleviate, but not remove, the sense of isolation experienced by transgendered individuals. Nonetheless, through such initial exposures, many individuals learned that there were alternatives to living in confusion and shame, if one was willing to transform (either temporarily or permanently) to the other gender. Simply learning that SRS was possible led some to reconfigure their identities and reassess their place in the world.

In today's information age, online computer services appear to be emerging as a primary location for finding both virtual and real mentors. It was common for transgenderists who deciphered and accepted their identities in the 1990s to have done so with the assistance of online bulletin boards and personal conversations with already-identifying transgenderists. Here, in the privacy of one's home or work area, contacts could be made that allowed both experimentation with identities and informational inquiries that did not jeopardize existing identities or social, occupational, and familial relationships. In addition, online services allowed individuals to access information beyond that concerning the strictly erotic aspects of cross-dressing. For some transgenderists, this was a critical factor, as tabloid media and sensationalist reports have created a common misperception of cross-dressing as primarily an erotic activity. A self-identified radical transgenderist credits his subscription to one online service with helping him understand that cross-dressing need not be sexually charged. He said, 'It wasn't until I got a hold of [online service] that I got exposed to aspects other than the erotic aspects, which are all over the place.'

For some, the occasion of encountering both real and reported transgenderists served only to raise more issues to be resolved. For example, one cross-dresser recalled finding fetishistic cross-dressers and transexuals in cyberspace. He related, 'Although there were similarities, there were also some grave differences, primarily in the fact that I felt more romantic interest. I didn't feel I was a heterosexual female trapped in a male body. I liked my male body.' Still, finding others even tangentially similar provided a forum in which to discover options and explore alternative identities. Thus, while we 'do' gender in interaction with others, it appears that the emergence of transgender identity and alternatives to the gender binary are dependent on others who will recognize one as an authentic social actor (West and Zimmerman, 1987).

Coming Out to Others

Accepting an identity for one's self was one thing; proclaiming and working to get others to accept it was quite different. Going public with a transgendered identity could be an intimidating experience, to say the least. The degree to which transgenderists were intimidated about revealing their transgenderism may be heard in the words of a 10-month, postoperative transsexual, who said,

> For somebody who's been a freak, a hippie, and a marijuana dealer, . . . and a flamboyant dresser, and somebody who refuses to get a conventional job and all this, somebody who's not been afraid of public opinion, it's, I think, notable that the gender area of my life and the social expectations were the one area I was afraid of public opinion.

Intimidation came from two fronts: (1) fears about how one would be treated by others and (2) anxieties about how others would cope with what was certainly seen by many as 'non-traditional' behaviour. Fear of the responses one will receive is to be expected. With the close cultural association drawn between transgenderism and homosexuality (Altman, 1982; Talamini, 1982; Bullough and Bullough, 1993), fears of violent and isolating homophobic reactions seem warranted.[3] In addition, as people become involved in significant relationships with others, many expressed concerns about how the news that they were transgendered would affect those close to them. These concerns typically centered on one's family, both nuclear and extended.

According to the accounts of those who have proclaimed their transgender identities to significant others, the fears about negative reactions were largely exaggerated, but not altogether unwarranted. Less than one-fourth of all persons interviewed for this project reported that their first experience of coming out to someone else lead to a negative reaction. This was related to several factors. First, transgenderists had exaggerated fears about the reactions of most significant others. Second, most individuals were actually successful at controlling knowledge of their transgenderism. They consciously selected individuals to come out to those who were, in fact, sympathetic to the alternative identity. Who would be accepting was ascertained through discussions of various potentially volatile issues. In that way, transgenderists learned if there was a need for caution or preparatory education of the recipient. Those who received negative reactions to their proclamations were least likely to have gathered information or to have laid the necessary groundwork. Instead, they simply announced the new identity. For example, a preoperative transsexual decided to tell an 18-year-old daughter, who did not even know that her father had been cross-dressing, when the daughter moved back home. She said,

> After a week or two there, it seemed inappropriate not to tell my daughter. The girl lives in the house. For crying out loud, she's 18 years old. So I told her and I didn't really build up to it or anything. . . . She was always in the bathroom, doing hair and makeup and stuff. I stopped in to chat. I suppose it was like a bomb or something like that. 'By the way . . . I'm going to have a sex change.' She turned into an ice cube.

Although the experience of telling one's first 'other' was not necessarily a negative experience, fears remained, and careful, often painful, decisions were made regarding with whom to share an emergent identity. Interestingly, two factors stand out about these early disclosures. First, they were usually done only out of a sense of responsibility, when someone was perceived as 'needing to know'. Second, the individuals with whom this information was shared were almost always female, most often a significant other. This was true among all groups of transgenderists in our sample.

While some elected to share with their mothers, there was a characteristic tendency for most to report that it was extremely difficult to share their new identity with their parents. For some, this was more easily accomplished when the interaction with one's parents was not face-to-face or when the situation could be escaped quickly. Despite the urge to deliver the news and run, those who came out to others face-to-face, who had provided (or offered to provide) information about transgenderism, and gave others time and space to cope with the information were most likely to receive tolerant, accepting, or supportive reactions. Still, much of the reaction to being told was dependent on the values of the recipient of the news, as well as the relationship itself. For example, a two-year postoperative transsexual who had been living with her male partner prior to having surgery recalled telling her mother about her decision to have SRS. She said, 'I told her, "Mom, I'm transsexual and I'm going to have SRS." My mom's response was, "Oh, thank God! I can deal with this." She thought I was going to tell her [my partner] and I were HIV positive.'

The arena where transgenderists (usually transsexuals) were least likely to receive positive reactions was at work. Although there were a few people who were permitted to transition on the job, it was more common for transsexuals to be fired, demoted, pressured to quit, and harassed by other workers. Some found employment in unskilled, low-wage jobs, such as janitors or in fast-food restaurants; others worked for temporary agencies. A few in our sample went back to college, transitioning as students. The loss of identity and the structure of one's daily routine that comes with a career was more difficult for transsexuals to cope with than the actual loss of income. After accepting a severance package in exchange for her silence about her job termination, one postoperative transsexual wrote to the first author, 'I have spent my entire life becoming the best [job title] I could be. Today I sold myself for 50 pieces of silver.' Frequently, the loss of professional identity and income came at the same time that relationships with old friends and family members were being risked and sometimes lost.

Early excursions into the public domain were commonly as frightening as coming out to significant others or on the job. While going out and passing in public may be thought to be different from coming out, it is important to recognize that for the majority of transgenderists, the goal is to be perceived and accepted as a woman, not a transgenderist. Telling others about their transgenderism is done primarily to lay the groundwork for greater expression, acceptance, and legitimation of a feminine identity, and this was accomplished in public and in private interactions. Although there was variation between going out in public or telling a significant other first, every person in our sample felt a need to expand their spheres of interaction with others. While control over access to information about the transgendered identity remained important, this became less salient as the need to interact with others publicly increased. Because of the fear of the danger inherent in negative public reactions, most transgenderists carefully planned and carried out their initial public excursions in limited-access locations.

When transgenderists began to go out in public, they did so because of a need to receive reactions from others to legitimate identity. While some have undoubtedly been driven back into the closet by their initial forays into public places, in our sample, such excursions served to increase commitment to the emergent identity. Selection of safe places for public ventures meant that transgenderists looked for locations where they could make quick and easy entrances and exits and where they are unlikely to encounter disapproving others. Transgenderists most commonly reported that their first ventures were to gay community events or locations, simply driving in their cars, or going to known meeting places for transgenderists. The most common site for first ventures was gay bars. Here, among other marginalized community members, individuals could try out their new identities. Despite a strong desire to avoid being perceived as homosexual, gay bars were defined as safe havens (Levine, Shaiova, and Mihailovic, 1975). For example, a preoperative transsexual, who had been living as a woman full-time for seven months, related that 'while I was working on coming out full-time, I needed a safe place to go while I practiced. The bar was it. I know the drag queens might not like that. It was still a safe place for me though.'

Typically, successful ventures provided the impetus and courage for transgenderists to move forward and present themselves face-to-face with others; however, these steps were taken slowly and carefully. Movement was usually into either a gay bar or a gathering of other transgenderists. For example, a preoperative transsexual who is fully out only to one family member and acquaintances in the transgender community, explained her first time out in public as follows:

About 10 years ago. . . . I was out very late one night, got in my car, drove downtown to the north side of the city which is known for its gays, lesbians, and an occasional transvestite. Walked to what I thought was a bar where transvestites hung out and sat down, had a couple of drinks, couple cigarettes. . . . I did things like get dressed and drove around. I'd go for a short walk around the block or something. I didn't think I was good enough yet to go out in daylight and try to pull it off as a woman.

In gay bars and neighbourhoods, transgenderists were most likely to be interpreted as marginal members of the queer subculture. Such settings provide a place where one who is 'neither woman nor man' (Lorber, 1994: 96) is most likely to find a social place that does not disturb the social order.

For others, the impetus to appear in public for the first time surfaced when opportunities arose to meet other transgenderists in the context of a support group. Support groups were one location where the most important identity tests occurred, when the individual encountered other transgenderists. As they entered such groups, transgenderists commonly reported a feeling of total acceptance and freedom to be themselves, often for the first time in their lives. If these supposedly similar others were willing to accept the individual, and the individual felt safe in the group, this communicated that she or he truly was transgendered. The value of support groups, online services, organizations, and publications becomes most clear in this context.

Support groups can be very important in facilitating identity exploration and the arrival at a 'final' identity, but they could also induce anxiety, confusion, and fright in individual transgenderists. While they may have already confronted their 'difference' in their own minds and with others in their lives, to come face-to-face with 'the real thing' could be intimidating. For those who were courageous enough to take such steps, support groups almost always functioned as they were intended: they provided support for a stigmatized identity. Nonetheless, such acceptance was provided within a narrow range of social options that were based on acceptance of a binary system of sex and gender. Transsexualism was commonly explained by biological theories, and those who had completed the transition process gave insight on how to gain access to medical procedures to those in earlier stages. Among cross-dressers, 'dressing' was encouraged as an acceptable way for men to express the feminine self. All transgenderists were encouraged to perfect their ability to pass during informal interactions and copious seminars on style, makeup, feminine body language, and the feminine voice and diction.

Resolution of Identity

After a lifetime of being stigmatized and feeling as if they did not fit, the transgenderists in our sample engaged in a long process of identity exploration. The majority in our sample explained that they had arrived at a 'true' identity, with which they felt they could 'be themselves'. Only a minority of men who cross-dressed but were exploring

transsexualism had not yet resolved their identities. In their efforts to resolve and establish an identity that was comfortable, the individuals in our sample shared diverse goals and visions for themselves and the community. Transsexuals sought to 'completely' transform and live convincingly as their true (female) selves. Cross-dressers sought only to have opportunities to temporarily vary their public identity presentations, express their femininity, and be recognized and treated as women. Only the gender radicals in our sample wished to live and be recognized as transgendered. Significant differences appeared among specific transgender identities. Among most transsexuals and cross-dressers, there was an overwhelming desire that femininity and treatment as a woman were achieved. For a minority, as experience and confidence were gained, passing was a desirable, but no longer essential, aspect of going out in public. These people tended to recognize that physical stature, including height and musculature, made it difficult, if not impossible, for them to pass. Among gender radicals, concerns with presenting a convincing appearance as a woman were secondary, if at all important for them, the goal was to challenge dominant conceptualizations of gender and create new possibilities.

Among transsexuals, because of the internalized identity as women, it was most common to find an aspiration to be seen and identified by others as real women. When discussing this feeling, transsexuals expressed a need to 'pass' in their daily interactions. This desire was paramount for such individuals and taken as a symbolic testament of final arrival at their desired self and socially constructed identity. One divorced, preoperative transsexual summarized this sentiment well when she commented, '[Passing] to me is the most important aspect of the whole thing. If you can't do that, I don't see the point of living this way.' Enduring the internal and social struggles encountered in the process of recognizing and accepting a new identity and introducing oneself to the outside world was valued only if there could be a non-stigmatizing, 'normal' resolution to the process. Transsexuals did not wish to challenge the gender binary, although most perceived their transitions as very radical actions. Rather, their goal was to 'become' the women they 'truly are' and to pass from being their masculine selves into full womanhood. Often, after learning to pass and completing the transformation process, transsexuals dropped out of the transgender community and assumed their place as women in society.

Within the transgender community, a desire to pass and blend into society sometimes introduced tensions and additional levels of hierarchy and structure. Those who sought to pass, and believed they had the ability to do so, sometimes believed that varying statuses of achievement (passing ability) were important. Some passable transgenderists, therefore, viewed those who could not pass as liabilities. One transsexual showed her aptitude for clear expression when she explained her withdrawal from a local support group because, 'I didn't feel the group gave me anything. I was too far ahead of them. . . . We're still friends, but I won't walk down the street with them.'

Although most transgenderists were concerned with passing as well as possible, there is an emergent group within the community that seeks a free expression of gender, outside of the binary system. For example, the ambigenderist in our sample explained that she had moved beyond such concerns, focusing on her own welfare and identity, not the perceptions of others.

> At one time, [passing] was important. I don't care anymore. A lot of times I'll go out in a dress . . . no makeup on. I'm not trying to pass and I know I'm not going to pass. I am who I am. . . . It is political, everything's political. A social statement about who I am and I'm going to express myself.

For both those who were and were not seeking to pass when in public, the most common, overwhelming desire was to simply be accepted. This was difficult unless they could find ways to fit within the binary and symbolically communicate identity within the idiomatic system of gender expression. To 'blend in' to society as a woman was something most transgenderists, especially transsexuals, saw as an ultimate goal. The ultimate resolution was an identity that was not wrapped in the language of transgenderism. To be known as simply just another person was desirable.

Despite one's own aspirations for individual identity and ability to blend socially, there was a sense of community among the vast majority of transgenderists that facilitated a desire to work with others and to contribute to the developmental processes of other community members.

This attempt to contribute to the development of others in the community came in both implicit and explicit forms. For some, this could be accomplished simply by being visible to other community members. More often, such forms of encouragement and assistance were much more direct and overt. For example, a gender radical, who is an active member of a local support group, editor of a local transgender community newsletter, and who conducts research on the structure of the transgender community, merged the implicit and explicit. This person explained,

> I feel the best thing I can do to create change is just to thrive, to be myself, to present myself in a way that I am comfortable with. The hell with everything else. We need to be more open. We need to be more proud of who we are as opposed to being more ashamed. I think our movement could be much stronger. . . . I want people to start questioning things even though they may look at me oddly. People always say that I am sick or insane. Maybe one person may start to look at things differently. If other people start seeing that, we can act normally in the open with people knowing about you and that they don't have to be frightened.

Conclusion

Gender is so pervasive that it is taken for granted and often completely over-looked, until the norms of gender presentation, interaction, or organization are inadvertently violated or deliberately challenged (Lorber, 1994). Gender receives constant surveillance and is continually policed through social interactions that socialize new and existing members of society and sanction those who violate the rules (see Gagné and Tewksbury, 1996). At the organizational level, individuals are categorized and assigned meaning and roles on the basis of gender. This is based on the erroneous assumption that gender will be congruent with sex. In organizational settings, sleeping arrangements are often based on sex/gender (as in dormitory arrangements) and bathrooms and locker rooms are segregated by sex/gender (see Rothblatt, 1995). Where individuals' gender does not 'match' their sex, there is little organizational space in which they can exist. At the institutional level (in the military, economic, religious, legal, political, and medical realms), individuals' roles, rights, and responsibilities are determined by gender, under the assumption that gender is indicative of sex (or sexuality) and that labour must continue to be divided on that basis. In everyday life gender is achieved and reinforced through interactions, where its idiom is derived from, and either legitimated or stigmatized by, the very superstructure and infrastructure in which it exists (West and Fenstermaker, 1995).

Individuals who attempt to challenge the binary conceptualization of sex and gender, by living androgynously between genders, are likely to be ridiculed and stigmatized (see Gagné and Tewksbury, 1996). Those who attempt to live outside of the sex/gender binary, for example, by publicly confessing that they are male persons with (or who would like to have) breasts or vaginas, are also likely to be ostracized. Those who are willingly or unwittingly unconvincing in their gender presentations and interactions are subject to greater levels of emotional and physical abuse than are those who are able to pass. It is those who are publicly perceived as 'not women/not men' who pose the greatest challenge to the binary system. Nonetheless, the goal of most is to be perceived as a woman and treated like a lady. Those who pass are perceived as women, and any challenge they might have posed to the gender system goes unnoticed.

As we have shown, the recognition, exploration, establishment, and final resolution of an identity outside cultural understandings is a difficult, complex, and for some, impossible process. Despite the policing of gender that was experienced by the transgenderists in our sample, the need to express a 'true self' was an overwhelming urge that could not be denied. Although many tried to hide their femininity through hypermasculine activity or self-isolation, and most tried to deny transgendered feelings and urges, all eventually found the urge to 'be themselves' overwhelmingly undeniable. Among our sample, others' reactions to them playing with girls, engaging in 'girls' activities, cross-dressing, wearing makeup, and other expressions of a feminine self caused confusion, anxiety, and a deep sense of shame. Only when they discovered that there were others like them were they able to begin to make sense of what they were experiencing and who they were. Entering into a community of supportive others allowed for an exploration and resolution of identity. Our data suggest that gender is not a natural and inevitable outgrowth of sex. Those who are not comfortable expressing gender that is congruent with genital configuration experience an overwhelming urge to express gender in alternative ways. Nonetheless, the vast majority stay within the gender binary as masculine men and feminine women. The tendency to stay within the binary gender system is so strong that as Hausman (1993) has asserted, gender determines sex, rather than the reverse. Given the limited range of identities available to them, it is interesting, but not surprising, that the overwhelming

majority of transgendered individuals adhere to traditional conceptualizations of sex and gender.

Notes

1. We recognize that there is a transgender community within the impoverished class, but we were unable to solicit volunteers from that segment of the population through the routes we used.

2. This view, however, is disputed by others who believe that retrospective biography construction is actually a search for ways 'to fashion this information into a story that leads inexorably to

the identity' that is being constructed (Mason-Schrock, 1996: 176–7).

3. A substantial minority of our sample talked about experiencing intimidation, harassment, and violence in public places. It was not uncommon for those learning to 'pass' to be called 'faggot' or other homophobic epithets. One very tall, muscular cross-dresser told us about having her wig pulled off and being physically assaulted.

References

Adam, B. 1995. *The Rise of a Gay and Lesbian Movement*, rev. ed. New York: Twayne.

Altman, D. 1982. *The Homosexualization of America*. Boston: Beacon.

Bornstein, K. 1994. *Gender Outlaw. On Men, Women, and the Rest of Us*. New York: Random House.

Bullough, V.L., and B. Bullough. 1993. *Cross Dressing, Sex, and Gender*. Philadelphia: University of Pennsylvania Press.

D'Emilio, J. 1983. *Sexual Politics, Sexual Communities: The Making of a Homosexual Minority in the United States, 1940–1970*. Chicago: University of Chicago Press.

Epstein, S. 1994. 'A Queer Encounter: Sociology and the Study of Sexuality', *Sociological Theory* 12: 188–202.

Foucault, M. [1978] 1990. *The History of Sexuality: An Introduction*. Vol. 1, R. Hurley, trans. New York: Vintage.

Gagné, P., and R. Tewksbury. 1996. 'No "Man's" Land: Transgenderism and the Stigma of the Feminine Man', in M. Texler Segal and V. Demos, eds, *Advances in Gender Research*. Vol. 1. Greenwich, CT: JAI Press.

Gecas, V. 1991. 'The Self-Consent as a Basis for a Theory of Motitvation', in J.A. Howard and P.L. Callero, eds, *The Self–Society Dynamic*. Cambridge, UK: Cambridge University Press.

Goffman, E. 1963. *Stigma: Notes on the Management of a Spoiled Identity*. Englewood Cliffs, NJ: Prentice-Hall.

Hausman, B.L. 1993. 'Demanding Subjectivity: Transsexualism, Medicine and the Technologies of Gender', *Journal of the History of Sexuality* 3: 270–302.

Herdt, G. 1994. 'Introduction: Third Sexes and Third Genders', in G. Herdt, ed., *Third Sex, Third Gender: Beyond Sexual Dimorphism in Culture and History*. New York: Zone Books.

Kohlberg, L. 1966. 'A Cognitive-Developmental Analysis of Children's Sex-role Concepts and Attitudes', in E.E. Maccoby, ed., *The Development of Sex Differences*. Stanford, CA: Stanford University Press.

Kohlberg, L., and D.Z. Ulian. 1974. 'Stages in the Development of Psychosexual Concepts and Attitudes', in R.C. Friedman, R.M. Richard, and R.L. Vande Wiele, eds, *Sex Differences in Behavior*. New York: Wiley.

Laqueur, T. 1990. *Making Sex: Body and Gender from the Greeks to Freud*. Cambridge, MA: Harvard University Press.

Levine, E.M., C.H. Shaiova, and M. Mihailovic. 1975. 'Male to Female: The Role Transformation of Transexuals', *Archives of Sexual Behavior* 5: 173–85.

Lorber, J. 1994. *Paradoxes of Gender*. New Haven, CT: Yale University Press.

Mason-Schrock, D. 1996. 'Transsexuals' Narrative Construction of the "true self"', *Social Psychology Quarterly* 59: 176–92.

Morris, J. 1974. *Conundrum*. Faber & Faber.

Namaste, K. 1994. 'The Politics of Inside/Out: Queer Theory, Poststructuralism, and a Sociological Approach to Sexuality', *Sociological Theory* 12: 220–31.

Pauly, I.B. 1990. 'Gender Identity Disorders: Evaluation and Treatment', *Journal of Sex Education & Therapy* 16: 2–24.

Raymond, J.G. 1994. *The Transsexual Empire: The Making of the She-male*. New York: Teachers College Press.

Rich, A. 1989. 'Compulsory Heterosexuality and Lesbian Existence', in L. Richardson and V. Taylor, eds, *Feminist Frontiers II: Rethinking Sex, Gender, and Society*. New York: Random House.

Rothblatt, M. 1995. *The Apartheid of Sex: A Manifesto on the Freedom of Gender*. New York: Crown.

Seidman, S. 1994. 'Symposium: Queer Theory/Sociology: A Dialogue', *Sociological Theory* 12: 166–77.

———, ed. 1996. *Queer Theory/Sociology*. Cambridge, MA: Blackwell.

Stein, A., and K. Plummer. 1994. 'I can't even think straight': Queer Theory and the Missing Sexual Revolution in Sociology', *Sociological Theory* 12: 1778–87.

Stoller, R.J. 1971. 'The Term "Transvestism"', *Archives of General Psychiatry* 24: 230–7.

Stone, G.P. 1975. 'Appearance and the Self', in D. Brissett and C. Edgley, eds, *Life as Theatre: A Dramaturgical Sourcebook*. Chicago: Aldine.

Talamini, J.T. 1981. 'Transvestim: Expression of a Second Self', *Free Inquiry in Creative Sociology* 9: 72–4.

———. 1982. *Boys Will Be Girls: The Hidden World of the Heterosexual Male Transvestite*. Lanham, MD: University Press of America.

Taylor, V., and N. Whittier. 1992. 'Collective Identity and Social Movement Communities: Lesbian Feminist Mobilization', in A.D. Morris and C. McClurg Mueller, eds, *Frontiers in Social Movement Theory*. New Haven, CT: Yale University Press.

Tewksbury, R., and P. Gagné. 1996. 'Transgenderists: Products of Non-normative Intersections of Sex, Gender, and Sexuality', *Journal of Men's Studies* 5: 105–29.

Weinberg, R.S. 1978. 'On "Doing" and "Being" Gay: Sexual Behavior and Homosexual Male Self-identity', *Journal of Homosexuality* 4: 563–78.

West, C., and D.H. Zimmerman. 1987. 'Doing Gender', *Gender & Society* 1: 125–51.

West, C., and S. Fenstermaker. 1995. 'Doing Difference', *Gender & Society* 9: 8–37.

Woodhouse, A. 1989. *Fantastic Women: Sex, Gender and Transvestism*. New Brunswick, NJ: Rutgers University Press.

CHAPTER 12

'It's Part of the Game': Physicality and the Production of Gender in Women's Hockey

Nancy Theberge

Perhaps as much as any social setting in the contemporary period, the world of sport is seeing considerable change regarding the condition of women and gender relations. To be sure, professional sport remains largely a male preserve in which the majority of opportunities and rewards go to men. In other contexts, including school and university sport and international competitions including most notably the Olympics, opportunities for women are expanding, performances are improving, and public interest in rising. These developments pose a challenge to ideologies of gender and to the historical association between gender, physicality, and power.

A particularly significant challenge to gender ideologies is the increased involvement of women in sports that Bryson (1990: 174) calls 'flag carriers' of masculinity. These are sports that 'quintessentially promote hegemonic masculinity and to which a majority of people are regularly exposed' (Bryson, 1990: 174). Writing from an Australian setting, Bryson cites as examples cricket and football (i.e., soccer). In the North American context, the best examples are football and ice hockey. In these sports, which celebrate force and toughness and involve direct confrontation between competitors, it is 'dominate or lose' (Whitson, 1994: 359).

This article provides an analysis of challenges to hegemonic masculinity posed by women's participation in the 'flag carrier' sport of ice hockey. Data are taken from fieldwork and interviews with players and coaches participating at the highest levels of the sports in Canada. The analysis begins with a discussion of the satisfaction players derive from the physicality of sport. This is followed by a detailed examination of the material and ideological conditions that structure the experience of physicality. A key determinant of the practice of women's hockey is rules that limit—but by no means eliminate—body contact. Debates about the place of contact in women's hockey and its relationship to injury occur within a framework in which men's sport is positioned as the 'real' thing. The conclusion contrasts the transformative potential of sports organized within the dominant model of masculine sport with possibilities presented by activities organized outside the framework of institutionalized sport.

Data and Methodology

Women's hockey is now experiencing a period of growth and development, with the most notable event in this regard being its inclusion in the Olympic program for the 1998 games in Nagano, Japan. The first World Championships were held in 1990, with subsequent events in 1992 and 1994. Canada has won all three of these competitions.

In Canada, the sport is growing; the number of female players registered with the Canadian Hockey Association increased form 8,146 in 1990–1 to 19,050 in 1994–5. These figures do not include girls playing on boys' teams, for which there are no reliable statistics (Etue and Williams, 1996). While school and university programs are expanding, the sport is primarily organized in clubs that are affiliated with provincial associations, which in turn are affiliated with the national governing body, the Canadian Hockey Association.

The analysis presented here is part of a broader study of women's ice hockey in Canada. The primary focus of the research is a team I call the Blades, which plays in a league located in a large Canadian metropolitan area. The league is which the Blades play is generally considered to be the strongest in the country. As an indication of this strength, several players from the Blades and from other teams in its league were members of one or more Canadian national teams that won World Championships in 1990, 1992, and 1994.

The research began when I attended the Annual General Meeting of the Provincial Women's Hockey Association in May 1992, where I met a woman who plays on the Blades and also operates a girls' hockey camp. In July I spent several days at the camp, where I met the Blades coach and told him of my interest in doing research in women's hockey. He was supportive, and in November, shortly after the start of the season, I attended a practice during which the coach introduced me to the team. I then met with the players in the coach's absence, explained my interests, and asked for permission to spend time with the team for the purpose of doing research.

Following this meeting, I began to attend games, practices, and other events such as the annual Christmas party. The fieldwork continued from November 1992 until the completion of the season in April 1993 and through the following season, from October 1993 until April 1994. I had complete access to team activities, including access to the team change room where I spent time with the players before and after games and practices. I also accompanied the team to out-of-town tournaments, including the provincial and national championships. Following each game, practice, or other events, I wrote field notes. The field notes cover a range of issues concerned with the practice and organization of the sport, team activities, and team dynamics.

To provide some perspective on experiences of players from elsewhere in the sport, I interviewed an additional eight players from three provinces, all of whom played at an elite level. I also interviewed 11 coaches from three provinces, all of whom also have experience at the highest levels of women's hockey. These additional interviews, conducted between 1993 and 1995, focused on the practice of the sport and the organization of women's hockey in Canada. All of the interviews were tape-recorded and transcribed.

There is no professional women's hockey in Canada, and the women who are the subject of this research have 'day jobs' or are students. Their involvement in hockey is nonetheless of a very high calibre, and they are committed athletes. For the purpose of the analysis provided here, it is important to note that the data are taken from athletes who participate at the highest level of the sport.

Playing the Game: The Construction of Women's Hockey

The rules of play in men's and women's ice hockey are substantially the same, with one major difference: the rules on women's hockey prohibit intentional body checking—that is, intentional efforts to hit, or 'take out', an opposing player. To be sure, there is still considerable use of the body and body contact in women's hockey, both intentional and unintentional. To watch a game is to see players constantly try to outmaneuver and outmuscle one another. At the same time, women's games are noticeably different from the full contact game played at the higher levels of the men's sport.

Interviews with players and coaches reveal a variety of views about the elimination of body checking from women's hockey. Respondents generally agree this results in a game in which speed, strategy, and playing skills are featured more prominently than in a full-contact game, which emphasizes power and force. Beyond this point of agreement, however, lies greater debate about the construction of women's hockey, with contrasting assessments of the relation of women's and men's hockey.

Until the late 1980s, the rules regarding body contact in women's hockey varied across Canada. The sample of women interviewed for this research includes a number who have played both full contact and the current game, which prohibits body checking. These players see advantages to both versions. While most acknowledge the attraction of the game that favours speed and playmaking, a number of these same players also express a sense of pleasure and accomplishment in playing the full-contact game and in receiving and taking a body check well. In interviews, these women describe body checking as 'part of the game', 'the way it should be', and 'part of the fun'. In this view, body checking is a skill, one among a repertoire of abilities that players can master. The following statement by a player is a representative account:

It's a certain aggressiveness. You're putting your strength against, your technique against. It's still a technique. It's not somebody, to me it's not go and kill that person, they hurt me, I'm going to get them back. It's nothing like that. It's a technique that you've learned and you can complete, and maybe you can complete it better than they can. You can prove your flexibility and your stamina, your stability on the ice.

Other players support the limitations on contact. One woman, who has never played the full-contact game, said:

> I prefer it without. Maybe just because I've always played without. You know the women's game being a bit different from the men's game, it may actually be better without it. I like to think of it as more of a finesse fame. And I don't know if body contact has any part in it, really if it would enhance it in any way. I mean I think maybe the reason for having the body contact in the men's game is possibly just to make it more exciting to watch. I don't know. It's hard to say when you haven't really played that much.

Coaches also express a range of views. Some indicate that the women's game as it is played today is ideal—it is physical, sometimes very physical, and 'just right' in this regard. Some see the inclusion of body checking as the 'wedge' that lead to the unacceptably rough play that characterizes men's hockey. One coach offered the following comments:

> I ask myself sometimes, 'Would body contact be a good thing?' It could be good if they stay within the limits, which seems very hard to do. And if the guys didn't do it, we're not smarter than the guys. . . . Women's hockey, if you were allowed body contact, to me, we'll end up as guys' hockey with slashing and cross checking. In my head, it's hard to believe it won't happen.

Other coaches have reservations about, or actively disagree with, the current formulation. Like some players, these coaches say checking is 'part of the game' and a skill that can be—and should be—taught and used effectively. The argument that body checking is responsible for the violence that plagues the men's game is also disputed. Several respondents noted that women's hockey

already has severe penalties—usually suspension for several games—that limit the incidence of dirty play. So long as these sanctions are in place, it is argued, introducing body checking will not lead to an increased incidence of other, undesirable features of men's hockey.

A number of players recognized the dilemma of playing an alternative version of the sport. The player quoted above on the technique of body checking has extensive experience playing boys' hockey before moving to women's hockey in late adolescence. She commented on the women's game:

> It is a different game and there are different rules. . . . I think a lot of women think it's better. But I prefer the game where you're allowed contact. I grew up playing that game. I just think it's different and why make it different . . . I want to be able to say I play hockey and [people] understand it's the same hockey. But now I have to say I play girls' hockey. It's not the same game as boys' hockey. . . . They're changing the game.

Another player, whose only experience is in women's hockey, offered further commentary. She described her reaction to a seminar she attended during which an official from the Canadian Hockey Association emphasized the uniqueness of the game:

> When you're playing a sport, you don't go out there saying, 'OK, I'm a woman. OK, I have to play like one.' You go out there and you play aggressive, you play your game and that's that, whereas people are trying, I think, to give the image that it's just an all-skill game and it's a woman's game kind of thing. Basically they were saying that you know women don't compare to men. Which is true, when you get to the older ages. I mean there's no NHL calibre women in the game right now and that's fine. Strength factor and everything, I mean people

are going to know that no matter what. But you don't have to go around saying that this is a woman's sport, there's no contact, it's totally skill, and make it sound like it's a nothing sport either. I think that's part of the reason why women's hockey went nowhere for so many years.

A third player, who played women's hockey when body checking was allowed, also expressed cynicism about efforts to de-emphasize the physical aspects and to promote women's hockey on the basis of its difference from the men's game. This player explicitly acknowledged a connection between the rules of play in women's hockey and concerns about its image:

> It doesn't make any sense to me. If they want to say, I don't know, the words feminine, I don't like those types of terms, masculine, feminine, all that crap. If they want to do it [promote women's hockey], that's not the way to do it, for my view. Hitting doesn't make you any more of a boy than non-hitting. I just don't know what they are trying to do.

The relationship between the risk of injury and the place of body checking is one of the contested features of the debate about the construction of women's hockey. Some coaches and players believe that a main reason for eliminating body checking is to reduce the risk of injury. Others dispute this association and believe that eliminating body checking has actually increased the risk of injury.[1] The explanation is that without checking, there is more illegal contact and stick work. One player who said, 'I think I've had more injuries with the no intentional body checking rule in,' explained the effect of the rule on the practice of the game:

> I think because [with no body checking] I'm not expecting some of the hits that I'm getting because some people don't play within the rules. And if they can hit you or hurt you and

hit you and put you into the boards or whatever when you're not expecting it, which usually I don't because I think, no, we play within the rules, they don't want to get a penalty, they don't want to hurt me. You know I'm nice person [she laughs]. So I don't expect it.

Another player offered further explanation:

> I think most of the players at first liked the idea of no checking, no intentional body checking. Some of them I think have come around and said, 'hey, yeah, less stick work.' So okay, say you get frustrated out there and you hit somebody clean and you know it's coming, like if you know it's coming you're not going to get hurt. That's the way I always feel. If . . . there's body checking I know I'm going to get hurt. Fine. I know how to go into the boards a little differently. . . . So with that in mind, yeah, I prefer the body checking, myself. It's the game.

When asked why players seem to see an inevitable trade-off between checking and illegal stick work, she explained:

> Well because you've got to slow them down somehow. You've got to get in front of them somehow and usually if you can't hit them or at least take a piece of them, that's the only thing left. And that's your stick to slow them down. Myself—unless you can outskate them. Well, that's not me.

This player's comments speak to the view that checking is part of the repertoire of a hockey player's skills. When it is not available, players resort to other tactics to accomplish their task. These tactics include illegal and sometimes dangerous practices.

Other players who spoke of the risks of body checking attributed these risks to the fact that players are not taught to receive and take checks.

One player said that when there was body checking:

> It wasn't clean at all. Girls aren't taught how to hit. 'Cause you don't hit all the way up. Then all of a sudden you get to senior A and there's contact. No one knows how to hit; sticks are up, hands are up.

A second player provided a similar analysis. When asked about playing the game when there was body checking, she said:

> Well to be honest with you checking was fine but I believe that the women weren't taught properly how to check. And there was a lot of injuries, like I was pretty scared of a few people out there just because I know, they were going to hit you like this [demonstrates], with their fists up or whatever. If checking had been taught, you know properly at a young age, just like the boys, they learn checking at a young age up, then maybe it wouldn't be so bad. Like you know, to take a hit on the boards is fine. It's just, I don't think women know how to check properly.

Conclusion: Women's Hockey and the Challenge to Masculine Hegemony

This discussion has focused on two aspects of the debate around physicality in women's hockey: the risk of injury and the appeal of a full-contact version of the sport versus one that prohibits body checking but is nonetheless very physical. Debate over these issues occurs within a material and ideological context that conditions the practice of the sport.

Suggestions that a 'problem' with body checking is that girls are not taught this skill complement the observation that eliminating checking improves the game by making it easier to officiate. Both imply that the 'problem' with checking is not the practice, per se, but limitations in the organization of the sport regarding training and skill development of athletes and officials.

Some respondents likened their support for the inclusion of body checking in women's hockey to the professionalization of the sport. When asked about reasons for the prohibition of body checking, a coach and a player both responded, 'these people [we] aren't being paid to play' and 'they [we] have to get up and go to work the next day.' Another coach who endorsed the inclusion of body checking went on to note that it would only be feasible if the game were organized professionally and women could earn a living by their efforts. In effect, he was arguing for a structure that offers material rewards to athletes commensurate with their own investment and commitment.

Gender equality has received increased attention in many sports, including hockey, in recent years (Williams, 1995). Calls for better training of players, coaches, and officials, and improved material conditions, including medical support, are an important aspect of the struggle within women's hockey to gain legitimation. At the same time, this struggle heightens the significance of the debate around the construction of the sport. As women players become bigger, stronger, and more skilled and as the practices of the game becomes more intense and physical, the question 'How should women play hockey?' raises the ideological stakes.

Women's hockey is played in a cultural context in which men's sport is hegemonic. This view that body checking is an integral 'part of the game' is emblematic of hockey as it has historically been conceptualized, practiced, and epitomized by the National Hockey League. Debates about what version of the game is most appealing, and the relation between physicality and the incidence of dirty play, occur in a context in which this version has been positioned as the 'real' game and the model against which others have been compared and evaluated (Theberge, 1995).

The dominance of the 'NHL model' of hockey is under challenge today not only from women's hockey but also from within boys' hockey, about which parents and officials have expressed concern. Targets of criticism in boys' hockey are the style of play, which emphasizes intimidation and domination, and the competitive and elitist system that eliminates boys by early adolescence boys who are unable to perform by these standards. In response to these concerns, some provincial and local hockey associations have implemented programs that prohibit body checking, reduce the emphasis on winning, and stress the enjoyment of participation (Gruneau and Whitson, 1993). Other alternatives to the dominant model are recreational men's leagues that prohibit body checking in the interests of safety and make the game more attractive to participants. As Gruneau and Whitson (1993: 162) note, however, 'NHL-style customs and values remain those ones that really "count" in the subculture of Canadian hockey.'

The dominance of men's hockey provides the background to much of the debate over the construction of the women's game. Against this background, to argue that women's hockey need not be the same as men's is to position the women's game as not only different from but inferior to the 'real' game. Alternatively, to argue women should play the same game as men is to capitulate to the violence and other problems that plague men's hockey. Within the confines of a debate structured by the model of the 'NHL style' of play, the challenge posed by women's hockey to dominant views of how the game should be played is severely diminished.

As noted, some of the players and coaches interviewed for this research dispute the contention that playing by the same rules as men will inevitably lead to the reproduction of the problems in the men's hockey. They argue that women's hockey can be constructed, and the rules enforced, in a way that eliminates the violence and other unacceptable features of the men's game while including full body contact. Some contest the view that body checking increases the rate of injury. These views are significant because they suggest that debate about the construction of the women's game should not be contained by the practices and experiences of men's hockey. These arguments, however, are rarely part of the public discussion of women's hockey.

The prohibition of body checking is central to a strategy to promote women's hockey by emphasizing its differences form the men's game.[2] While the game clearly is different from men's hockey in the absence of body checking, evidence of troubling similarities is provided in the discussion of pain and injury in women's hockey. A growing body of literature examines the violence inflicted on athletic bodies through the routinization of pain and injury in sport. Initial interest is this issue focused on male athletes (Messner, 1990; Curry, 1993; Young 1993; Young, White, and McTeer, 1994). More recent work has extended the discussion to women. Young and White (1995) examined experiences of pain and injury among a sample of elite women athletes who had incurred a variety of injuries, including broken bones, separated shoulders, dislocated knee caps, and herniated disks. These athletes normalized the presence of pain in their lives, through strategies of denial and 'disrespect' or indignation toward painful injuries. Citing comparisons with earlier work they conducted with male athletes, Young and White (1995: 51) identify similarities in the acceptance of physical danger and injury and conclude that 'if difference exists between the way male and female athletes in our projects appear to understand pain and injury, it is only a matter of degree.' In a study of university students, Nixon (1996) found higher pain thresholds among athletes than non-athletes and no significant gender differences in their acceptance of pain.

Injury and pain were routine features of the lives of the hockey players examined here. For these athletes, overcoming injury and pain is a measure of both ability and commitment. Like the athletes Young and White (1995) studied, the hockey players in this study showed little critical awareness of the physical dangers of their sport participation. In interviews, players were asked to comment on the element of risk in women's hockey. Most denied that it was risky, often following this assessment with rationalizations about the presence of danger in everyday life, for example, the possibility of being hit by a car while crossing a street. The increasing evidence that women athletes readily accept violence inflicted on their bodies in competitive sport suggests an incorporation of, rather than resistance to, the dominant model of men's sport.

Testimony provided at the outset of this discussion indicates the satisfaction and sense of accomplishment women hockey players derive from their sport participation. These sentiments are directly tied to the physicality of sport and the possibility for the exercise of skill and force in athletic competition. A number of writers (MacKinnon, 1987; Theberge, 1987; Whitson, 1994) have identified these features as the basis of sport's potential to challenge traditional ideologies of gender and empower women. While women hockey players experience empowerment from their sport participation, the challenge to masculine hegemony posed by the sport is diminished in two key ways.

The transformative possibilities of women's sport are seriously compromised by the uncritical adoption of a 'sport ethic' (Hughes and Coakley, 1991) that celebrates toughness in the face of physical violence. One of the troubling ironies of improved material resources in women's hockey is that players now have greater affinities with a system that normalizes injury and pain.

Ideologically, the challenge to masculine hegemony is weakened by the location of the debate about the practice of women's hockey within a framework that positions men's hockey as the 'real' game. While women's hockey provides clear and compelling refutation of the myth of female frailty, the potential of the sport to challenge traditional ideologies of gender is diminished by its construction as a milder version of the sport that 'really counts'.

The analysis presented here suggests the complexities inherent in women's involvement in 'flag carrier' sports such as ice hockey. Drawing from Connell's (1983) observation that every sport involves a balance between force and skill, Whitson (1994) suggests that the more force is decisive, the more a physically dominating hegemonic masculinity can be celebrated and the more likely it is that the culture of sport will be part of the defense of the existing gender order. Whitson acknowledges that sports such as hockey and football do allow for empowerment in the absence of domination and cites testimony from former NHL player Eric Nesterenko (in Terkel, 1974) on the pleasure of performing the skills required in ice hockey. This pleasure, however, was never allowed to be the central purpose of participation and usually was subordinated by the quest for victory, a quest that demanded an emphasis on force and domination. This quest, Whitson argues, becomes the norm in organized male sport at an early age.

Possibilities for challenge to masculine hegemony do exist within the context of team sports. An example is provided in Birrell and Richter's (1987) account of a women's recreational softball league. The women Birrell and Richter interviewed consciously rejected the view that the dominant model of sport, which many referred to as the 'male model', is the only 'real' version. Informed by this belief, they rejected an excessive emphasis on winning and domination and an ethic of endangerment that values performance over safety. Instead, they actively worked to construct and practice their own vision of sport, which emphasized the pleasure and satisfaction of participation and the development of physical skills in a supportive context.

In an analysis of the historical significance of sport for the politics of gender relations, Messner (1988) argues women's increasing athleticism represents a genuine quest for equality. This quest, however, is marked by contradictions and ambiguities over the socially constructed meanings of sport and gender. Messner concludes that in the contemporary period the women athlete is 'contested ideological terrain'.

The cultural struggle in women's hockey is conditioned by its relation to the dominant male model. Unlike the recreational softball community studied by Birrell and Richter (1987), in which participants consciously challenged the 'male model', the struggle within elite-level women's hockey occurs largely within a value system regulated by this model. While women's hockey provides participants with pleasure and a sense of personal empowerment, it does so in a context that reproduces the problems of institutionalized sport. A more fully transformative vision of hockey would offer empowerment in a setting that rejects violence and the normalization of injury in favour of an ethic of care.

Notes

1. Interviews with women who played full contact hockey during the 1980s reveal that part of the collective memory of the league in which the Blades compete is stories of particular hits and players who had an especially forceful game. While these stories are an important part of the history of the sport, there are no data to test the relationship between playing full-contact hockey and rates of injury. Some believe that to the extent body checking increases injuries, this is 'limited' to serious injuries such as broken bones.

2. The main challenge to the prohibition against body checking comes not domestically but within the International Ice Hockey Federation, in which some countries argue for the inclusion of body checking in international women's hockey. Proponents of the rule change generally are from countries where development lags behind that in Canada and the United States, the dominant countries in the sport. Because the inclusion of body checking is generally agreed to slow the game down and reduce the advantage of superior playing skills, body checking is thought to offer an advantage to weaker teams. (My thanks to Elizabeth Etue for information on this issue.) It should be noted that it is unlikely that Canadian support for prohibiting body checking arises out of a concern for a loss of competitive dominance should the rules be changed. The first World Championships in 1990 were played with body checking. Canada won this tournament, as well as subsequent tournaments in 1992 and 1994 played without body checking.

References

Birrell, S., and D. Richter. 1987. 'Is a Diamond Forever? Feminist Transformations of Sport', *Women's Studies International Forum* 10: 395–409.

Bryson, L. 1990. 'Challenges to Male Hegemony in Sport', in M. Messner and D. Sabo, eds, *Sport, Men and the Gender Order*. Champaign, IL: Human Kinetics.

Connell, R.W. 1983. 'Men's Bodies', in R.W. Connell, ed., *Which Way is Up?* Sydney: Allen & Unwin.

Curry, T. 1993. 'A Little Pain Never Hurt Anyone: Athletic Career Socialization and the Normalization of Sport Injury', *Symbolic Interaction* 16: 273–90.

Etue, E., and M. Williams. 1996. *On the Edge: Women Making Hockey History*. Toronto: Second Story.

Gruneau, R., and D. Whitson. 1993. *Hockey Night in Canada*. Toronto: Garamond.

Hughes, R., and J. Coackley. 1991. 'Positive Deviance among Athletes: The Implications of Overconformity to the Sport Ethic', *Sociology of Sport Journal* 8: 307–25.

MacKinnon, C. 1987. 'Women, Self-possession, and Sport', in C. MacKinnon, ed., *Feminism Unmodified*. Cambridge, MA: Harvard University Press.

Messner, M. 1988. 'Sports as Male Domination: The Female Athlete as Contested Ideological Terrain', *Sociology of Sport Journal* 5: 197–211.

————. 1990. 'When Bodies are Weapons: Masculinity and Violence in Sport', *International Review for the Sociology of Sport* 25: 203–18.

Nixon, H. 1996. 'The Relationship of Friendship Networks, Sports Experiences, and Gender to Expressed Pain Thresholds', *Sociology of Sport Journal* 13: 78–86.

Terkel, S. 1974. *Working*. New York: Avon Books.

Theberge, N. 1987. 'Sport and Women's Empowerment', *Women's Studies International Forum* 10: 387–93.

————. 1995. 'Sport, Caractere Physicque et Differenciation Sexuelle', *Sociologie et Societes* 27: 105–16.

Whitson, D. 1994. 'The Embodiment of Gender: Discipline, Domination, and Empowerment', in S. Birrell and C. Cole, eds, *Women, Sport, and Culture*. Champaign, IL: Human Kinetics.

Williams, M. 1995. 'Women's Hockey: Heating Up the Equity Debate', *Canadian Woman Studies* 15: 78–81.

Young K. 1993. 'Violence, Risk, and Liability in Male Sports Culture', *Sociology of Sport Journal* 10: 373–97.

Young, K., and P. White. 1995. 'Sport, Physical Danger, and Injury: The Experiences of Elite Women Athletes', *Journal of Sport and Social Issues* 19: 45–61.

Young, K., P. White, and W. McTeer. 1994. 'Body Talk: Male Athletes Reflect on Sport, Injury, and Pain', *Sociology of Sport Journal* 11: 175–94.

QUESTIONS FOR CRITICAL THOUGHT

1. Do you 'do gender' (as West and Zimmerman would say) with the people around you? In what circumstances do you find yourself 'doing' masculinity or femininity?

2. If you were to wake up one morning and find that you had turned into a member of the other sex, how would your daily life be different?

3. What is involved for a transgendered person to successfully 'pass' in a society that is based on the assumption that there are two, and only two, genders?

4. The hockey players studied by Theberge discuss whether there is a 'masculine' or a 'feminine' way to play hockey. Do you think there are 'masculine' or 'feminine' ways to carry out some of the activities of everyday life such as dating, raising children, and making friends?

5. Suppose you wanted to 'un-do' gender in your daily interactions. How might you do that?

PART IV

The Gendered Family

T he current debates about the 'crisis' of the family—a traditional arrangement that some fear is collapsing under the weight of contemporary trends ranging from relaxed sexual attitudes, increased divorce, and women's entry into the labour force, to rap music and violence in the media—actually underscores how central the family is to the reproduction of social life and to gender identity. If gender identity were biologically 'natural', we probably wouldn't need such strong family structures to make sure that everything turned out all right.

Though the 'typical' family of the 1950s television sitcom—breadwinner father, housewife mother, and 2.5 happy, well-adjusted children—is the empirical reality for less than 10 per cent of all households, it remains the cultural ideal against which contemporary family styles are measured. And some would like to see us 'return' as closely as possible to that imagined idealized model—perhaps by restricting access to easy divorce or restricting women's entry into the labour force, or by promoting sexual abstinence and delegitimating homosexuality.

Others, though, see the problem differently. Sociologist Lillian Rubin provides a careful portrait of the ways in which different groups of Americans—based on class, race, and ethnicity—are struggling to make family life coherent and meaningful. Valerie Preston and her co-authors examine the ways in which Canadian men and women, in gender-differentiated ways, battle to keep their families happy and secure in the face of challenges from a capitalist economy that requires around-the-clock availability of labour. The disjunctures between the demands of the workplace and the demands (and desires) of home are also evident in Gillian Ranson's account of women engineers who find that motherhood marks a major turning point in their relationship with their high-intensity, high-skill careers. Childbearing and raising children do not fit easily into the professional world—at least not the intensive-mothering form of child-raising that most North Americans have learned to value.

Janet Salaff and Arent Greve glimpse into the lives of immigrant families from China, and show that these mothers and fathers face similar challenges as they attempt to create the kind of environment for their children which they see as the most valuable. The mothers take on the lion's share of the caregiving work, and carry it out within dense female networks of relatives and in-laws that extend across countries and continents, thereby 'globalizing' the traditional feminine work of care.

Family life consists of more than just caring for children, of course. The physical maintenance of the home has also been an arena of contestation between men and women, although this is an arena in which changes are happening. Sociologist Scott Coltrane discusses the relationship between housework, childcare, and the status of women in society: the more housework and childcare women do, the lower their status. As a result, he suggests that sharing housework and childcare is not only a way for husbands and wives to enact more egalitarian relationships, but also a way to ensure that the next generation will maintain egalitarian attitudes.

CHAPTER 13

The Transformation of Family Life

Lillian Rubin

'I know my wife works all day, just like I do,' says Gary Braunswig, a 29-year-old white drill press operator, 'but it's not the same. She doesn't *have* to do it. I mean, she *has* to because we need the money, but it's different. It's not really her job to have to be working; it's mine.' He stops, irritated with himself because he can't find exactly the words he wants, and asks, 'Know what I mean? I'm not saying it right; I mean, it's the man who's supposed to support his family, so I've got to be responsible for that, not her. And that makes one damn big difference.'

'I mean, women complain all the time about how hard they work with the house and the kids and all. I'm not saying it's not hard, but that's her responsibility, just like the finances are mine.'

'But she's now sharing that burden with you, isn't she?' I remark.

'Yeah, and I do my share around the house, only she doesn't see it that way. Maybe if you add

it all up, I don't do as much as she does, but then she doesn't bring in as much money as I do. And she doesn't always have to be looking for overtime to make an extra buck. I got no complaints about that, so how come she's always complaining about me? I mean, she helps me out financially, and I help her out with the kids and stuff. What's wrong with that? It seems pretty equal to me.'

Cast that way, his formulation seems reasonable: They're each responsible for one part of family life; they each help out with the other. But the abstract formula doesn't square with the lived reality. For him, helping her adds relatively little to the burden of household tasks he *must* do each day. A recent study by University of Wisconsin researchers, for example, found that in families where both wife and husband work full-time, the women average over twenty-six hours a week in household labour, while the men do about ten.[1] That's because there's nothing in the family system to force him to accountability or responsibility on a daily basis. He may 'help her out with the kids and stuff' one day and be too busy or preoccupied the next.

But for Gary's wife, Irene, helping him means an extra eight hours every working day. Consequently, she wants something more consistent from him than a helping hand with a particular task when he has the time, desire, or feels guilty enough. 'Sure, he helps me out,' she says, her words tinged with resentment. 'He'll give the kids a bath or help with the dishes. But only when I ask him. He doesn't have to *ask* me to go to work every day, does he? Why should I have to ask him?'

'Why should I have to ask him?'—words that suggest a radically different consciousness from the working-class women I met twenty years ago. Then, they counted their blessings. 'He's a steady worker; he doesn't drink; he doesn't hit me,' they told me by way of explaining why they had 'no right to complain' (Rubin, 1976: 93). True, these words were reminders to themselves that life could be worse, that they shouldn't take these things for granted—reminders that didn't wholly work to obscure their discontent with other aspects of the marriage. But they were nevertheless meaningful statements of value that put a brake on the kinds of demands they felt they could make of their men, whether about the unequal division of household tasks or about the emotional content of their lives together.

Now, the same women who reminded themselves to be thankful two decades ago speak openly about their dissatisfaction with the role divisions in the family. Some husbands, especially the younger ones, greet their wives' demands sympathetically. 'I try to do as much as I can for Sue, and when I can't, I feel bad about it,' says 29-year-old Don Dominguez, a Latino father of three children, who is a construction worker.

Others are more ambivalent. 'I don't know, as long as she's got a job, too, I guess it's right that I should help out in the house. But that doesn't mean I've got to like it,' says 28-year-old Joe Kempinski, a white warehouse worker with two children.

Some men are hostile, insisting that their wives' complaints are unreasonable, unjust, and oppressive. 'I'm damn tired of women griping all the time; it's nothing but nags and complaints,' Ralph Danesen, a 36-year-old white factory worker and the father of three children, says indignantly. 'It's enough! You'd think they're the only ones who've got it hard. What about me? I'm not living in a bed of roses either.

'Christ, what does a guy have to do to keep a wife quiet these days? What does she want? It's not like I don't do anything to help her out, but it's never enough.'

In the past there was a clear understanding about the obligations and entitlements each partner took on when they married. He was obliged to work outside the home; she would take care of life inside. He was entitled to her ministrations, she to his financial support. But this neat division of labour with its clear-cut separation of rights and obligations no longer works. Now, women feel obliged to hold up their share of the family economy—a partnership men welcome. In return, women believe they're entitled to their husband's full participation in domestic labour. And here is the rub. For while men enjoy the fruits of their wives' paid work outside the home, they have been slow to accept the reciprocal responsibilities—that is, to become real partners in the work inside the home.

The women, exhausted from doing two days' work in one, angry at the need to assume obligations without corresponding entitlements, push their men in ways unknown before. The men, battered by economic uncertainty and by the escalating demands of their wives, feel embattled and victimized on two fronts—one outside the home, the other inside. Consequently, when their wives seem not to see the family work they do, when they don't acknowledge and credit it, when they fail to appreciate them, the men feel violated and betrayed. 'You come home and you want to be appreciated a little. But it doesn't work that way, leastwise not here anymore,' complains Gary Braunswig, his angry words at odds with sadness in his eyes. 'There's no peace, I guess that's the real problem; there's no peace anywhere anymore.'

The women often understand what motivates their husbands' sense of victimization and even speak sympathetically about it at times. But to understand and sympathize is not to condone, especially when they feel equally assaulted on both the home and the economic fronts. 'I know I complain a lot, but I really don't ask for that much. I just want him to help out a little more,' explains Ralph Danesen's wife, Helen, a 35-year-old office worker. 'It isn't like I'm asking him to cook the meals or anything like that. I know he can't do that, and I don't expect him to. But every time I try to talk to him, you know, to ask him if I couldn't get a little more help around here, there's a fight.'

One of the ways the men excuse their behaviour toward family work is by insisting that their responsibility as breadwinner burdens them in ways that are alien to their wives. 'The plant's laying off people left and right; it could be me tomorrow. Then what'll we do? Isn't it enough I got to worry about that? I'm the one who's got all the worries; she doesn't. How come that doesn't count?' demands Bob Duckworth, a 29-year-old factory worker.

But, in fact, the women don't take second place to their men in worrying about what will happen to the family if the husband loses his job. True, the burden of finding another one that will pay the bills isn't theirs—not a trivial difference. But the other side of this truth is that women are stuck with the reality that the financial welfare of the family is out of their control, that they're helpless to do anything to prevent its economic collapse or to rectify it should it happen. 'He thinks I've got it easy because it's not my job to support the family,' says Bob's wife, Ruthanne. 'But sometimes I think it's worse for me. I worry all the time that he's going to get laid off, just like he does. But I can't do anything about it. And if I try to talk to him about it, you know, like maybe make a plan in case it happens, he won't even listen. How does he think *that* makes me feel? It's my life, too, and I can't even talk to him about it.'

Not surprisingly, there are generational differences in what fuels the conflict around the division of labour in these families. For the older couples—those who grew up in a different time, whose marriages started with another set of ground rules—the struggle is not simply around how much men do or about whether they take responsibility for the daily tasks of living without being pushed, prodded, and reminded. That's the overt manifestation of the discord, the trigger that starts the fight. But the noise of the explosion when it comes serves to conceal the more fundamental issue underlying the dissension: legitimacy. What does she have a *right* to expect? 'What do I know about doing stuff around the house?' asks Frank Moreno, a 48-year-old foreman in a warehouse. 'I wasn't brought up like that. My pop, he never did one damn thing, and my mother never complained. It was her job; she did it and kept quiet. Besides, I work my ass off every day. Isn't that enough?'

For the younger couples, those under 40, the problem is somewhat different. The men may complain about the expectation that they'll participate more fully in the care and feeding of the family, but talk to them about it quietly and they'll usually admit that it's not really unfair, given that their wives also work outside the home. In these homes, the issue between husband and wife isn't only who does what. That's there, and it's a source of more or less conflict, depending upon what the men actually do and how forceful their wives are in their demands. But in most of these families there's at least a verbal consensus that men *ought* to participate in the tasks of daily life. Which raises the next and perhaps more difficult issue in contest between them: Who feels responsible for getting the tasks done? Who regards them as a duty, and for whom are they an option? On this, tradition rules.

Even in families where husbands now share many of the tasks, their wives still bear full responsibility for the organization of family life. A man may help cook the meal these days, but a woman is most likely to be the one who has planned it. He may take the children to childcare, but she virtually always has had to arrange it. It's she also who is accountable for the emotional life of the family, for monitoring the emotional temperature of its members and making the necessary corrections. It's this need to be responsible for it all that often feels as burdensome as the tasks themselves. 'It's not just doing all the stuff that needs doing,' explains Maria Jankowicz, a white 28-year-old assembler in an electronics factory. 'It's worrying all the time about everything and always having to arrange everything, you know what I mean. It's like I run the whole show. If I don't stay on top of it all, things fall apart because nobody else is going to do it. The kids can't and Nick, well, forget it,' she concludes angrily.

If, regardless of age, life stage, or verbal consensus, women usually still carry the greatest share of the household burdens, why is it important to notice that younger men grant legitimacy to their wives' demands and older men generally do not? Because men who believe their wives have a right to expect their participation tend to suffer guilt and discomfort when they don't live up to those expectations. And no one lives comfortably with guilt. 'I know I don't always help enough, and I feel bad about it, you know, guilty sometimes,' explains Bob Beardsley, a 30-year-old white machine operator, his eyes registering the discomfort he feels as he speaks.

'Does it change anything when you feel guilty?' I ask.

A small smile flits across his face, and he says, 'Sometimes. I try to do a little more, but then I get busy with something and forget that she needs me to help out. My wife says I don't pay attention, that's why I forget. But I don't know. Seems like I've just got my mind on other things.'

It's possible, of course, that the men who speak of guilt and rights are only trying to impress me by mouthing the politically correct words. But even if true, they display a sensitivity to the issue that's missing from the men who don't speak those words. For words are more than just words. They embody ideas; they are the symbols that give meaning to our thoughts; they shape our consciousness. New ideas come to us on the wings of words. It's words that bring those ideas to life, and that allow us to see possibilities unrecognized before we gave them words. Indeed, without words, there is no conscious thought, no possibility for the kind of self-reflection that lights the path of change.[2]

True, there's often a long way between word and deed. But the man who feels guilty when he disappoints his wife's expectations has a different consciousness than the one who doesn't—a difference that usually makes for at least some small change in his behaviour. Although the emergence of this changing male consciousness is visible in all the racial groups in this study, there also are differences among them that are worthy of comment.

Virtually all the men do some work inside the family—tending the children, washing dishes, running the vacuum, and going to the market. And they generally also remain responsible for those tasks that have always been traditionally male—mowing the lawn, shovelling the snow, fixing the car, cleaning the garage, and doing repairs around the house. Among the white families in this study, 16 per cent of the men share the family work relatively equally, almost always those who live in families where they and their wives work different shifts or where the men are unemployed. 'What choice do I have?' asks Don Bartlett, a 30-year-old white handyman who works days while his wife is on the swing shift. 'I'm the only one here, so I do what's got to be done.'

Asian and Latino men of all ages, however, tend to operate more often on the old male model, even when they work different shifts or are unemployed, a finding that puzzled me at first. Why, I wondered, did I find only two Asian men and one Latino who are real partners in the work of the family? Aren't these men subject to the same social and personal pressures others experience?

The answer is both yes and no. The pressures are there but, depending upon where they live, there's more or less support for resisting them. The Latino and Asian men who live in ethnic neighbourhoods—settings where they are embedded in an intergenerational community and where the language and culture of the home country is kept alive by a steady stream of new immigrants—find strong support for clinging to the old ways. Therefore, change comes much more slowly in those families. The men who live outside the ethnic quarter are freer from the mandates and constraints of these often tight-knit communities, therefore are more responsive to the winds of change in the larger society.

These distinctions notwithstanding, it's clear that Asian and Latino men generally participate least in the work of the household and are the least likely to believe they have much responsibility there beyond bringing home a paycheck. 'Taking care of the house and kids is my wife's job, that's all,' says Joe Gomez flatly.

'A Chinese man mopping a floor? I've never seen it yet,' says Amy Lee angrily. Her husband, Dennis, trying to make a joke of the conflict with his wife, says with a smile, 'In Chinese families men don't do floors and windows. I help with the dishes sometimes if she needs me to or,' he laughs, 'if she screams loud enough. The rest, well, it's pretty much her job.'

The commonly held stereotype about black men abandoning women and children, however, doesn't square with the families in this study.

In fact, black men are the most likely to be real participants in the daily life of the family and are more intimately involved in raising their children than any of the others. True, the men's family workload doesn't always match their wives', and the women are articulate in their complaints about this. Nevertheless, compared to their white, Asian, or Latino counterparts, the black families look like models of egalitarianism.

Nearly three-quarters of the men in the African American families in this study do a substantial amount of the cooking, cleaning, and child care, sometimes even more than their wives. All explain it by saying one version or another of: 'I just figure it's my job, too.' Which simply says what is, without explaining how it came to be that way.

To understand that, we have to look at family histories that tell the story of generations of African American women who could find work and men who could not, and to the family culture that grew from this difficult and painful reality. 'My mother worked six days a week cleaning other people's houses, and my father was an ordinary labourer, when he could find work, which wasn't very often,' explains 32-year-old Troy Payne, a black waiter and father of two children. 'So he was home a lot more than she was, and he'd do what he had to do around the house. The kids all had to do their share, too. It seemed only fair, I guess.'

Difficult as the conflict around the division of labour is, it's only one of the many issues that have become flash points in family life since mother went to work. Most important, perhaps, is the question: Who will care for the children? For the lack of decent, affordable facilities for the care of the children creates unbearable problems and tensions for these working-class families.

It's hardly news that childcare is an enormous headache and expense for all two-job families. In many professional middle-class families, where the childcare bill can be $1,500–$2,000 a month, it competes with the mortgage payment as the biggest single monthly expenditure. Problematic as this may be, however, these families are the lucky ones when compared to working-class families, many which don't earn much more than the cost of childcare in these upper middleclass families. Even the families in this study at the highest end of the earnings scale, those who earn $42,000 a year, can't dream of such costly arrangements.

For most working-class families, therefore, childcare often is patched together in ways that leave parents anxious and children in jeopardy. 'Care for the little ones, that's a real big problem,' says Beverly Waldov, a 30-year-old white mother of three children, the youngest two children under three years old, products of a second marriage. 'My oldest girl is nine, so she's not such a problem. I hate the idea of her being a latchkey kid, but what can I do? We don't even have the money to put the little ones in one of those good day-care places, so I don't have any choice with her. She's just *got* to be able to take care of herself after school,' she says, her words a contest between anxiety and hope.

'We have a kind of complicated arrangement for the little kids. Two days a week, my mom takes care of them. We pay her, but at least I don't have to worry when they're with her; I know it's fine. But she works the rest of the time, so the other days we take them to this woman's house. It's the best we can afford, but it's not great because she keeps too many kids, and I know they don't get good attention. Especially the little one; she's just a baby, you know.' She pauses and looks away, anguished. 'She's so clingy when I bring her home; she can't let go of me, like nobody's paid her any mind all day. But it's not like I have a choice. We barely make it now; if I stop working, we'd be in real trouble.'

Even such makeshift solutions don't work for many families. Some speak of being unable to afford day care at all. 'We couldn't pay our bills if we had to pay for somebody to take care of the kids.'

Some say they're unwilling to leave the children in the care of strangers. 'I just don't believe someone else should be raising our kids, that's all.'

Some have tried a variety of childcare arrangements, only to have them fail in a moment of need. 'We tried a whole bunch of things, and maybe they work for a little while,' says Faye Ensey, a black 28-year-old office worker. 'But what happens when your kid gets sick? Or when the baby sitter's kids get sick? I lost two jobs in a row because my kids kept getting sick and I couldn't go to work. Or else I couldn't take my little one to the baby sitter because her kids were sick. They finally fired me for absenteeism. I didn't really blame them, but it felt terrible anyway. It's such a hassle, I sometimes think I'd be glad to just stay home. But we can't afford for me not to work, so we had to figure out something else.'

For such families, that 'something else' is the decision to take jobs on different shifts—a decision made by one-fifth of the families in this study. With one working days and the other on swing or graveyard, one parent is home with the children at all times. 'We were getting along okay before Daryl junior was born, because Shona, my daughter, was getting on. You know, she didn't need somebody with her all the time, so we could both work days,' explains Daryl Adams, a black 30-year-old postal clerk with a 10-year-old daughter and a nine-month-old son. 'I used to work the early shift—seven to three—so I'd get home a little bit after she got here. It worked out okay. But then this here big surprise came along.' He stops, smiles down fondly at his young son and runs his hand over his nearly bald head.

'Now between the two of us working, we don't make enough money to pay for childcare and have anything left over, so this is the only way we can manage. Besides, both of us, Alesha and me, we think it's better for one of us to be here, not just for the baby, for my daughter, too. She's growing up and, you know, I think maybe they need even more watching than when they were younger. She's coming to the time when she could get into all kinds of trouble if we're not here to put the brakes on.'

But the cost such arrangements exact on a marriage can be very high. When I asked these husbands and wives when they have time to talk, more often than not I got a look of annoyance at a question that, on its face, seemed stupid to them. 'Talk? How can we talk when we hardly see each other?' 'Talk? What's that?' 'Talk? Ha, that's a joke.'

Mostly, conversation is limited to the logistics that take place at shift-changing time when children and chores are handed off from one to the other. With children dancing around underfoot, the incoming parent gets a quick summary of the day's or night's events, a list of reminders about things to be done, perhaps about what's cooking in the pot on the stove. 'Sometimes when I'm coming home and it's been a hard day, I think: Wouldn't it be wonderful if I could just sit down with Leon for half an hour and we could have a quiet beer together?' 31-year-old Emma Guerrero, a Latina baker, says wistfully.

But it's not to be. If the arriving spouse gets home early enough, there may be an hour when both are there together. But with the pressures of the workday fresh for one and awaiting the other, and with children clamoring for parental attention, this isn't a promising moment for any serious conversation. 'I usually get home about forty-five minutes or so before my wife has to leave for work,' says Ralph Jo, a 36-year-old Asian repairman whose children, ages three and five, are the product of a second marriage. 'So we try to take a few minutes just to make contact. But it's hard with the kids and all. Most days the whole time gets spent with taking care of business—you know, who did what, what the kids need, what's for supper, what bill collector was hassling her while I was gone—all the damn garbage of living. It makes me nuts.'

Most of the time even this brief hour isn't available. Then the ritual changing of the guard takes only a few minutes—a quick peck on the cheek in greeting, a few words, and it's over. 'It's like we pass each other. He comes in; I go out; that's it.'

Some of the luckier couples work different shifts on the same days, so they're home together on weekends. But even in these families there's so little time for normal family life that there's hardly any room for anyone or anything outside. 'There's so much to do when I get home that there's no time for anything but the chores and the kids,' says Daryl's wife, Alesha Adams. 'I never get to see anybody or do anything else anymore and, even so, I'm always feeling upset and guilty because there's not enough time for them. Daryl leaves a few minutes after I get home, and the rest of the night is like a blur—Shona's homework, getting the kids fed and down for the night, cleaning up, getting everything ready for tomorrow. I don't know; there's always something I'm running around doing. I sometimes feel like—What do you call them?—one of those whirling dervishes, rushing around all the time and never getting everything done.

'Then on the weekends, you sort of want to make things nice for the kids—and for us, too. It's the only time we're here together, like a real family, so we always eat with the kids. And we try to take them someplace nice one of the days, like to the park or something. But sometimes we're too tired, or there're too many other catch-up things you have to do. I don't even get to see my sister anymore. She's been working weekends for the last year or so, and I'm too busy weeknights, so there's no time.

'I don't mean to complain; we're lucky in a lot of ways. We've got two great kids, and we're a pretty good team, Daryl and me. But I worry sometimes. When you live on this kind of schedule, communication's not so good.'

For those whose days off don't match, the problems of sustaining both the couple relationship and family life are magnified enormously. 'The last two years have been hell for us,' says 35-year-old Tina Mulvaney, a white mother of two teenagers. 'My son got into bad company and had some trouble, so Mike and I decided one of us had to be home. But we can't make it without my check, so I can't quit.

'Mike drives a cab and I work in a hospital, so we figured one of us could transfer to nights. We talked it over and decided it would be best if I was here during the day and he was here at night. He controls the kids, especially my son, better than I do. When he lays down the law, they listen.' She interrupts her narrative to reflect on the difficulty of raising children. 'You know, when they were little, I used to think about how much easier it would be when they got older. But now I see it's not true; that's when you really have to begin to worry about them. This is when they need someone to be here all the time to make sure they stay out of trouble.'

She stops again, this time fighting tears, then takes up where she left off. 'So now Mike works days and I work graveyard. I hate it, but it's the only answer; at least this way somebody's here all the time. I get home about 8:30 in the morning. The kids and Mike are gone. It's the best time of the day because it's the only time I have a little quiet here. I clean up the house a little, do the shopping and the laundry and whatever, then I go to sleep for a couple of hours until the kids come home from school.

'Mike gets home at five; we eat; then he takes over for the night, and I go back to sleep for another couple of hours. I try to get up by 9 so we can all have a little time together, but I'm so tired that I don't make it a lot of times. And by 10, he's sleeping because he has to be up by 6 in the morning. So if I don't get up, we hardly see each other at all. Mike's here on weekends, but I'm not. Right now I have Tuesday and Wednesday off. I keep hoping for a Monday–Friday shift, but it's what everybody wants, and I don't have the seniority yet. It's hard, very hard; there's no time to live or anything,' she concludes with a listless sigh.

Even in families where wife and husband work the same shift, there's less time for leisure pursuits and social activities than ever before, not just because both parents work full-time but also because people work longer hours now than they did twenty years ago.[3] Two decades ago, weekends saw occasional family outings, Friday-evening bowling, a Saturday trip to the shopping mall, a Sunday with extended family, once in a while an evening out without the children. In summer, when the children weren't in school, a weeknight might find the family paying a short visit to a friend, a relative, or a neighbour. Now almost everyone I speak with complains that it's hard to find time for even these occasional outings. Instead, most off-work hours are spent trying to catch up with the dozens of family and household tasks that were left undone during the regular work-week. When they aren't doing chores, parents guiltily try to do in two days a week what usually takes seven—that is, to establish a sense of family life for themselves and their children.

'Leisure,' snorts Peter Pittman, a 28-year-old African-American father of two, married six years. 'With both of us working like we do, there's no time for anything. We got two little kids; I commute better than an hour each way to my job. Then we live here for half rent because I take care of the place for the landlord. So if somebody's got a complaint, I've got to take care of it, you know, fix it myself or get the landlord to get somebody out to do it if I can't. Most things I can do myself, but it takes time. I sometimes wonder what this life's all about, because this sure ain't what I call living. We don't go anyplace; we don't do anything; Christ, we hardly have time to go to the toilet. There's always some damn thing that's waiting that you've got to do.'

Clearly, such complaints aren't unique to the working class. The pressures of time, the impoverishment of social life, the anxieties about child care, the fear that children will live in a world of increasing scarcity, the threat of divorce—all these are part of family life today, regardless of class. Nevertheless, there are important differences between those in the higher reaches of the class structure and the families of the working class. The simple fact that middle-class families have more discretionary income is enough to make a big difference in the quality of their social life. For they generally have enough money to pay for a baby sitter once in a while so that parents can have some time to themselves; enough, too, for a family vacation, for tickets to a concert, a play, or a movie. At $7.50 a ticket in a New York or San Francisco movie house, a working-class couple will settle for a $3.00 rental that the whole family can watch together.

Finding time and energy for sex is also a problem, one that's obviously an issue for two-job families of any class. But it's harder to resolve in working-class families because they have so few resources with which to buy some time and privacy for themselves. Ask about their sex lives and you'll be met with an angry, 'What's that?' or a wistful, 'I wish.' When it happens, it is, as one woman put it, 'on the run'—a situation that's particularly unsatisfactory for most women. For them, the pleasure of sex is related to the whole of the interaction—to a sense of intimacy and connection, to at least a few relaxed, loving moments. When they can't have these, they're likely to avoid sex altogether—a situation the men find equally unsatisfactory.

'Sex?' asks Lisa Scranton, a white 29-year-old mother of three who feigns a puzzled frown, as if she doesn't quite know the meaning of the word. 'Oh yeah, that; I remember now,' she says, her lips smiling, her eyes sad. 'At the beginning, when we first got together, it was WOW, real hot, great. But after a while it cools down, doesn't it? Right now, it's down the toilet. I wonder, does it happen to everybody like that?' she asks dejectedly.

'I guess the worst is when you work different shifts like we do and you get to see each other maybe six minutes a day. There's no time for sex. Sometimes we try to steal a few minutes for ourselves but, I don't know, I can't get into it that way. He can. You know how men are; they can do it

any time. Give them two minutes, and they can get off. But it takes me time; I mean, I like to feel close, and you can't do that in three minutes. And there's the kids; they're right here all the time. I don't want to do it if it means being interrupted. Then he gets mad, so sometimes I do. But it's a problem, a real problem.'

The men aren't content with these quick sexual exchanges either. But for them it's generally better than no sex at all, while for the women it's often the other way around. 'You want to talk about sex, huh?' asks Lisa's husband, Chuck, his voice crackling with anger. 'Yeah, I don't mind; it's fine, only I got nothing to talk about. Far as I'm concerned, that's one of the things I found out about marriage. You get married, you give up sex. We hardly ever do it anymore, and when we do, it's like she's doing me a favor.

'Christ, I know the way we've got to do things now isn't great,' he protests, running a hand through his hair agitatedly. 'We don't see each other but a few minutes a day, but I don't see why we can't take five and have a little fun in the sack. Sure, I like it better when we've got more time, too. But for her, if it can't be perfect, she gets all wound and uptight and it's like . . . '. He stops, groping for words, then explodes, 'It's like screwing a cold fish.'

She isn't just a 'cold fish', however. The problems they face are deeper than that. For once such conflicts arise, spontaneity takes flight and sex becomes a problem that needs attention rather than a time out for pleasure and renewal. Between times, therefore, he's busy calculating how much time has passed: 'It's been over two weeks'; nursing his wounds: 'I don't want to have to beg her'; feeling deprived and angry: 'I don't know why I got married.' When they finally do come together, he's disappointed. How could it be otherwise, given the mix of feelings he brings to the bed with him—the frustration and anger, the humiliation of feeling he has to beg her, the wounded sense of manhood.

Meanwhile, she, too, is preoccupied with sex, not with thoughts of pleasure but with figuring out how much time she has before, as she puts it, 'he walks around with his mouth stuck out. I know I'm in real big trouble if we don't do it once a week. So I make sure we do, even if I don't want to.' She doesn't say those words to him, of course. But he knows. And it's precisely this, the knowledge that she's servicing him rather than desiring him that's so hard for him to take.

The sexual arena is one of the most common places to find a 'his and her' marriage—one marriage, two different sex lives.[4] Each partner has a different story to tell; each is convinced that his or her version is the real one. A husband says mournfully, 'I'm lucky if we get to make love once a week.' His wife reports with irritation, 'It's two, sometimes three times a week.' It's impossible to know whose account is closest to the reality. And it's irrelevant. If that's what they were after, they could keep tabs and get it straight. But facts and feelings are often at war in family life. And nowhere does right or wrong, true or false, count for less than in their sexual interactions. It isn't that people arbitrarily distort the truth. They simply report their experience, and it's feeling, not fact, which dominates that experience; feeling, not fact, that is their truth.

But it's also true that, especially for women, the difference in frequency of sexual desire can be a response—sometimes conscious, sometimes not—to other conflicts in the marriage. It isn't that men never withhold sex as a weapon in the family wars, only that they're much more likely than women to be able to split sex from emotion, to feel their anger and still experience sexual desire. For a man, too, a sexual connection with his wife can relieve the pressures and tensions of the day, can make him feel whole again, even if they've barely spoken a word to each other.

For a woman it's different. What happens—or, more likely, what doesn't happen—in the kitchen, the living room, and the laundry room profoundly affects what's possible in the bedroom. When she feels distant, unconnected, angry; when her pressured life leaves her feeling fragmented; when she hasn't had a real conversation with her husband for a couple of days, sex is very far from either her mind or her loins. 'I run around busy all the time, and he just sits there, so by the time we go to bed, I'm too tired,' explains Linda Bloodworth, a white 31-year-old telephone operator.

'Do you think your lack of sexual response has something to do with your anger at your husband's refusal to participate more fully in the household?' I ask.

Her eyes smoldering, her voice tight, she snaps, 'No, I'm just tired, that's all.' Then noticing something in my response, she adds, 'I know what you're thinking; I saw that look. But really, I don't think it's *because* I'm angry; I really am tired. I have to admit, though, that I tell him if he helped more, maybe I wouldn't be so tired all the time. And,' she adds defiantly, 'maybe I wouldn't be.'

Some couples, of course, manage their sexual relationship with greater ease. Often that's because they have less conflict in other areas of living. But whether they accommodate well or poorly, for all two-job families, sex requires a level of attention and concern that leaves most people wanting much of the time. 'It's a problem, and I tell you, it has to be well planned,' explains 34-year-old Dan Stolman, a black construction worker. 'But we manage okay; we make dates or try to slip it in when the baby's asleep and my daughter's out with a friend or something. I don't mean things are great in that department. I'm not always satisfied and neither is Lorraine. But what can you do? We try to do the best we can. Sex isn't all there is to a marriage, you know. We get along really well, so that makes up for a lot.

'What I really miss is that we don't ever make love anymore. I mean, we have sex like I said, but we don't have the kind of time you need to make love. We talk about getting away for an overnight by ourselves once in a while. Lorraine's mother would come watch the kids if we asked her; the problem is we don't have any extra cash to spare right now.'

Time and money—precious commodities in short supply. These are the twin plagues of family life, the missing ingredients that combine to create families that are both frantic and fragile. Yet there's no mystery about what would alleviate the crisis that now threatens to engulf them: A job that pays a living wage, quality childcare facilities at rates people can pay, health care for all, parental leave, flexible work schedules, decent and affordable housing, a shorter work week so that parents and children have time to spend together, and tax breaks for those in need rather than for those in greed, to mention just a few. These are the policies we need to put in place if we're to have any hope of making our families stable and healthy.

What we have, instead, are families in which mother goes to work to relieve financial distress, only to find that time takes its place next to money as a source of strain, tension, and conflict. Time for the children, time for the couple's relationship, time for self, time for social life—none of it easily available for anyone in two-job families, not even for the children, who are hurried along at every step of the way (Elkind, 1981). And money! Never enough, not for the clothes children need, not for the doctor's bill, not for a vacation, not even for the kind of childcare that would allow parents to go to work in peace. But large as these problems loom in the lives of working-class families, difficult as they are to manage, they pale beside those they face when unemployment strikes, especially if it's father who loses his job.

Notes

1. James Sweet, Larry Bumpass, and Vaugn Call, *National Survey of Families and Households* (Madison, WI: Center for Demography and Ecology, University of Wisconsin, 1988). This study featured a probability sample of 5,518 households and included couples with and without children. See also Joseph Pleck, *Working Wives/Working Husbands* (Beverly Hills: Sage Publications, 1985), who summarizes time-budget studies; and Iona Mara-Drita, 'The Effects of Power, Ideology, and Experience on Men's Participation in Housework', unpublished paper (1993), whose analysis of Sweet, Bumpass, and Call's data shows that when housework and employment hours are added together, a woman's work week totals 69 hours, compared to 52 hours for a man.

2. See Daniel Stern, *The Interpersonal World of the Infant* (New York: Basic Books, 1985), who argues that a child's capacity for self-reflection coincides with the development of language

3. For an excellent analysis of the increasing amount of time Americans spend at work and the consequences to family and social life, see Juliet B. Schor, *The Over-worked American* (New York: Basic Books, 1992). See also Carmen Sirianni and Andrea Walsh, 'Through the Prism of Time: Temporal Structures in Postindustrial America', in Alan Wolfe, ed., *America at Century's End* (Berkeley: University of California Press, 1991), for their discussion of the 'time famine'.

4. For the origin of the term 'his and her marriage', see Jessie Bernard, *The Future of Marriage* (New York: Bantam Books, 1973).

References

Elkind, D. 1981. *The Hurried Child*. New York: Addison-Wesley.

Rubin, L.B. 1976. *Worlds of Pain*. New York: Basic Books.

Stern, D. 1985. *The Interpersonal World of the Infant*. New York: Basic Books.

Sweet, J., L. Bumpass, and V. Call. 1988. *National Survey of Families and Households*. Madison, WI: Center for Demography and Ecology, University of Wisconsin.

CHAPTER 14

Shift Work, Childcare, and Domestic Work: Divisions of Labour in Canadian Paper Mill Communities

Valerie Preston, Damaris Rose, Glen Norcliffe, and John Holmes

Introduction

The growing prevalence of non-standard employment in Canadian labour markets—part-time, short-term, temporary, and contract jobs and own account self-employment (Canada, 1994)—is being accompanied by transformations in working hours and work schedules. Increasingly, workers are being asked to work outside the hours of nine to five and during weekends and holidays (Brayfield, 1995). In their analysis of the 1990 General Social Survey, Le Bourdais and Sauriol (1998) found that about half of all Canadian couples with minor children included two wage earners and of these, 49 per cent of men and 37 per cent of women regularly worked evenings, nights, or weekends.

The changing configuration of working hours increasingly challenges our taken-for-granted notions about household life. While some household members may welcome non-standard working hours that allow parents to share childcare and pursue educational, recreational, and other interests (Hanson and Pratt, 1995), for many, shift work is disruptive (Statistics Canada, 1998). Most industrial shift work is still done by men (Simon, 1990), so many women have little choice but to adapt to and cope with the shift schedules of their partners. The continuing wage gap between men and women may also shape women's reactions to shifts.

The effects of shift work vary among households depending upon men's and women's participation in paid work.[1] For two-earner families in which both parents must accommodate the often competing demands of paid employment and unpaid domestic work (Gill, 1986; Luxton, 1986), shifts may pose particular challenges regarding childcare and housework. A few researchers have wondered whether and to what extent traditional gendered divisions of labour and responsibility within the household may be altered when men and women are employed on different shifts (Presser, 1989: 524; Pratt, 1993; Presser, 1994).

Local circumstances mediate the strategies households deploy with regard to coping with shift work. For example, the availability of childcare services and informal childcare may affect women's and men's decisions to enter the paid labour market. The types and hours of employment available to women may also influence the division of domestic labour. The extent to which private dissatisfaction with shift schedules and their disruption of household life results in public action many also vary from place to place (Gibson-Graham, 1996).

This article examines the effects of shift work in one industry, the Canadian newsprint industry,[2] on the division of labour in childcare and domestic work in the households of shift workers employed in three different mills. . . . The analysis begins with a brief review of existing literature, and then explores the general characteristics of the three places and the history of shifts in the newsprint mill in each town are outlined; followed by a detailed comparison of the impacts of shifts on childcare and housework. The article ends with a brief discussion of the main empirical findings and their implications for our understanding of how households deal with the imperatives of contemporary industrial production and the work schedules it entails.

Shift Work and Domestic Life: Existing Literature

. . . The growing number of dual-earner households has generated new questions about how women and men combine paid and unpaid labour in the household when at least one of them works shifts (Luxton, 1986; Wharton, 1994; Brayfield, 1995; Le Bourdais and Sauriol, 1998). Whereas the earlier studies took women's responsibilities for unpaid household-based tasks for granted, this has begun to change. In this context, shift working has received some attention, mainly with respect to childcare. Several studies indicate that shift workers rely more on other family members and relatives for childcare and less on formal daycare services (Presser, 1986; Weiss and Liss, 1988; Lapierre-Adamcyck and Marcil-Gratton, 1995), which is to be expected given the limited range of hours often offered by formal day-care services (Friendly et al., 1989). In the USA, men working non-day shifts are more likely to take on sole responsibility for childcare of preschoolers when their wives are at work than are men working day shifts, according to the 1990 National Child Care Survey (Brayfield, 1995). Several American and Canadian surveys have identified the existence of 'sequential scheduling' in which parents deliberately set out to work different shifts so as to minimize recourse to extra-familial childcare (Morgan, 1981; Lero et al., 1992; Hanson and Pratt, 1995); this had been interpreted as a

strategy for enabling each parent to spend time with the children as well as providing what they see as quality childcare at the least cost.

While the performance of childcare by shift-working men may indicate some blurring of traditional, strictly demarcated gender roles within the home (Pratt, 1993; Presser, 1994), the weight of evidence suggests that greater sharing of childcare between parents is more likely to be an outcome of rather than a reason for fathers taking on shift work (Presser, 1989). Presser (1989) reports that when the 1985 US Current Population Survey asked parents who worked fixed non-day shifts and had children under six years of age why they worked these hours, almost three-quarters of the fathers said it was because 'their employment situation left them with no choice as to their hours' whereas more than half of the mothers said they opted for these hours for childcare or other family reasons.[3] Similar findings are reported in other American and Canadian research (Simon, 1990; Johnson, 1998).

There appears, then, to be very little blurring of 'patriarchy at work' when it comes to industries organized on a shift work basis: the shift work schedule of the male 'breadwinner' essentially determines who does the 'adapting', and how. In general, as an article in a human resources periodical bluntly puts it, 'most shift workers do not have a choice about working shifts, because they usually don't have the seniority to transfer to regular day shifts or the education to find other jobs that would pay as well' (Overman, 1993: 47).[4] Thus, what at first sight appear to be pragmatic 'family strategies' for coping with shift work usually turn out to be primarily adaptations made by the wife and mother to male shift schedules (see Hanson and Pratt, 1995: 137–8).[5] It is she who arranges her employment hours around the schedules of her husband (see O'Connell, 1993, cited in Folk and Yi, 1994: 678–9), and around those of her children, if they are school-aged (Rose, 1993), while maintaining primary responsibility for domestic labour (Wharton, 1994). . . .

Shift Work and Domestic Work in Case Study Communities

In 1993–4 we conducted questionnaire surveys and in-depth interviews with newsprint production workers, who were almost exclusively male, and their spouses/partners living in three different communities across Canada. The information gathered enables us to address some of the gaps in our understanding of how rotating shift schedules shape household strategies with respect to childcare and unpaid domestic work.[6] . . .

The three communities—Corner Brook, Gatineau, and Whitecourt—were selected to include long established mills, a new 'greenfield' mill, and mills located in both metropolitan and non-metropolitan labour markets (Figure 14.1). Corner Brook, on the west coast of Newfoundland and over 500 kilometres along the Trans Canada Highway from the nearest major city, St John's, is physically the most isolated of the three communities. By contrast, Gatineau, on the north shore of the Ottawa River in western Quebec (the Outaouais region), lies on the edge of the central Canadian economic heartland and is well connected by rail and road to markets in both Canada and the northeastern USA. The mills at both Corner Brook and Gatineau date from the 1920s and were originally the nuclei of one-industry towns (Norcliffe and Bates, 1997; Rose and Villemaire, 1997). Today, Corner Brook is a regional service centre with a population of over 32,000 while Gatineau is a sprawling and diffuse municipality of some 92,000 inhabitants on the fringes of Canada's national capital and fourth largest metropolitan region, the Ottawa (Ontario)-Hull (Quebec) agglomeration. The mill at Whitecourt, Albert—located 160 km from Edmonton toward the Alaska Highway—is virtually new; it opened in 1990 in a resource-based community of just under 7,000 inhabitants that already had a sawmill, pulp mill, and oil and gas operations.

Millworkers at Gatineau and Corner Brook are drawn largely from families with local or regional roots and with long traditions of work in the pulp and paper or ancillary industries. By contrast, not only is Whitecourt located in a part of western Canada where many people come from elsewhere, but many of the experienced papermakers hired to work at the 'greenfield' Whitecourt mill had to be recruited from eastern Canadian mills (Preston et al., 1997). Thus, the Whitecourt mill-worker families are much less likely to have locally-based family support networks to draw on for needs such as childcare than those in Gatineau or Corner Brook, and so are likely to depend more on formal childcare services when one or other parent is not available. There may also be variations from place to place in gender role ideologies due to the age of the workforce in each mill. Existing research indicates that younger men and women generally have less traditional gender role ideologies and more egalitarian views about task-sharing (Hochschild, 1989). The Whitecourt mill is one of the few mills in Canada with a relatively young workforce, whereas the majority of workers in Corner Brook and Gatineau are considerably older.

In 1991 in Gatineau the labour force participation rate of women with children at home was 72.7 per cent, whereas the corresponding figures for Corner Brook and Whitecourt were 65 per cent and 72.4 per cent.[7] Among women whose children were of preschool age, 76.5 per cent of those in Gatineau were in the labour force, in Corner Brook 79 per cent, whereas in Whitecourt only 63.9 per cent (Statistics Canada, 1994a, 1994b, 1994c; Table 14.1), indicating that in Whitecourt mothers of young children are more likely not to be in paid employment. Indicative of generational differences among mothers, in both Gatineau and Corner Brook mothers of young children are more likely to participate in the labour market than mothers of older children.

In both Gatineau and Corner Brook, opportunities for semi-skilled male employment at rates anywhere near the high wages paid in the pulp and paper industry were few and far between, since neither is located in a region of traditional

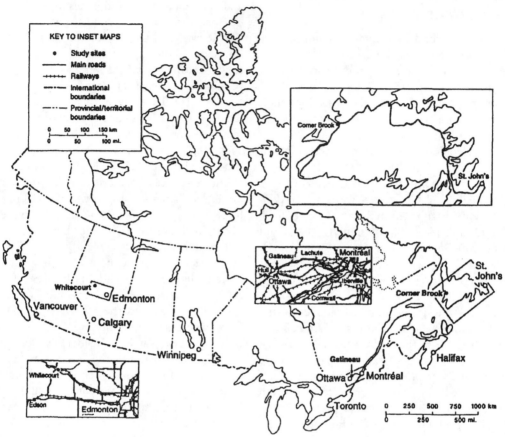

Figure 14.1

manufacturing and jobs were being severely cut throughout the pulp and paper and forestry sectors in both regions in the early 1990s (Rose and Villemaire, 1997; Norcliffe and Bates, 1997). In Whitecourt alternative prospects for male workers were subject to the boom-bust cycles of the oil and gas industries. In all three places, mill-worker families were highly dependent on the paper mill for remunerative male employment, although in Gatineau there was a likelihood of a greater female contribution to household income than in the other two communities.

There are major differences between the three communities in the availability of formal childcare and related services. At the time of our study, Corner Brook had only one day care centre listed in the Yellow Pages, and four other licensed centres (whose operators complained about lack of demand!). Following embedded Newfoundland traditions, extended families still play an important role in childcare during the preschool years and in supervising children at the end of the school day and before their parents return home from work. In contrast, Whitecourt is well supplied with childcare services. Three organized services provide group and in-home licensed care for preschool and school-age children. While shift schedules may reduce the usefulness of the

Table 14.1 Personal characteristics of mill-workers and partners*

	Whitecourt n = 78		Corner Brook n = 73		Gatineau n = 13	
	Number	%	Number	%	Number	%
Number of children at home						
0	40	40.8	11	15.1	3	23.1
1	10	10.2	32	43.8	4	30.8
2	33	33.6	19	26.0	2	15.4
3	12	12.2	8	11.0	1	7.7
4	3	3.1	3	4.1	3	23.1
Year of birth: mill-worker						
1930–9	2	2.1	11	15.1	1	7.7
1940–9	7	7.2	24	32.9	2	15.4
1950–9	49	50.5	29	39.7	8	61.5
1960–9	32	33.0	9	12.3	2	15.4
1970–9	7	8.2	0	0	0	0.0
Year of birth: partner						
1930–9	1	1.4	4	5.5	0	0.0
1940–9	6	8.6	22	30.1	2	15.4
1950–9	28	40.0	31	42.5	8	61.5
1960–9	25	35.7	14	19.2	3	23.1
1970–9	6	8.6	2	2.7	0	0.0
Year of marriage						
1950–9	1	1.4	4	5.5	0	0.0
1960–9	6	8.6	19	27.5	2	15.4
1970–9	22	31.4	23	33.3	2	15.4
1980–9	29	41.4	18	26.1	7	53.8
1990–9	12	17.1	5	7.2	2	15.4
Work status of partner						
Full-time	23	32.9	24	32.9	6	46.1
Part-time	10	14.3	15	20.5	3	23.1
Not in paid work	37	52.9	34	46.6	4	30.8
Highest level of schooling: mill-worker						
Some elementary	0	0.0	1	1.4	0	0.0
Completed elementary	0	0.0	1	1.4	1	7.7
Some high school	9	9.2	8	11.1	4	30.8
Completed high school	22	22.4	31	43.1	3	23.1
Some college	6	6.1	24	33.3	4	30.8
Some university	6	6.1	7	9.7	0	0.0
Completed college	45	45.9	0	0.0	0	0.0
Completed university	10	10.2	0	0.0	1	7.7

Table 14.1 continued

	Whitecourt n = 78		Corner Brook n = 73		Gatineau n = 13	
	Number	%	Number	%	Number	%
Highest level of schooling: partner						
Some elementary	0	0.0	1	1.4	0	0.0
Completed elementary	0	0.0	1	1.4	0	0.0
Some high school	10	14.3	17	23.6	3	23.8
Completed high school	20	28.6	26	36.1	6	46.1
Some college	13	18.6	16	22.2	1	7.7
Some university	5	7.1	11	15.3	0	0.0
Completed college	13	18.6	0	0.0	3	23.8
Completed university	9	12.9	0	0.0	0	0.0
Total family income						
$10,000–$19,999	0	0.0	1	1.4	0	0.0
$20,000–$29,999	0	0.0	3	4.1	0	0.0
$30,000–$39,999	1	1.0	3	4.1	1	7.7
$40,000–$49,999	2	2.0	14	19.2	4	30.8
$50,000–$59,999	11	11.2	22	30.1	2	15.4
$60,000–$69,999	23	23.5	11	15.1	3	23.1
$70,000–$79,999	22	22.4	15	20.5	3	23.1
$80,000–$89,999	21	21.4	2	2.7	0	0.0
$90,000 +	16	16.3	0	0.0	0	0.0

* In each community, the number of responses to each question varies depending upon the applicability of the question and the willingness of respondents to answer. For the purposes of this article, information is drawn only from those interviews and questionnaires completed with households containing a currently employed newsprint shift worker.

group day care facility, which is open from 7:00 AM until 6:00 PM, both in-home childcare services encourage parents to negotiate hours of care with each provider. Other forms of childcare include a cooperative play program organized by parents (mainly mothers) and a cooperative nursery school that operates a half-day program for preschool age children. In the Gatineau case, there were 11 formal day care centres within the city limits at the time of our study, mostly parent-controlled cooperatives receiving a government operating subsidy, although as in Whitecourt, these do not offer 'off-hours'. There were 300 places in licensed family home day care, and before- and after-school programs for children aged 12 and under were available in 15 schools. It should be noted that none of the mills themselves organize programs to help employees with childcare needs.[8] Both Whitecourt and Gatineau also have numerous recreational programs after school, on the weekends, and during holiday periods for school-age children. . . .

Shift Work and Childcare

. . . The decisions that women make concerning labour force participation while their children are young is clearly a fundamental parameter in how workers' shift work at the paper mills shaped the ways families dealt with childcare. These decisions are shaped, in part, by local opportunities for jobs and by the possibilities of arranging childcare through the formal system or through relatives, but also by broader considerations as to the most appropriate ways of dealing with situations where the mill-workers' shift work alters the 'normal' patterns of family life.

Some women opt not to take on paid employment because of their husbands' shifts. For example, Alice (G26), aged 46 at the time of the interview, quit her job at a life insurance company as soon as she had the first of three children, because her husband's shifts would have made arrangements too complicated and disrupted family life. 'To me, it's no life if one's at work, the other one's leaving when one's coming.' Some women who tried initially to keep working found that the limited time family members could spend together led them to re-evaluate the situation:

Francine: 'So we discussed it, and, well, with the salary he was making, we could allow ourselves . . .'

Marcel: 'It was either me or her who had to give up [their job]'. [G09, translation]

So Francine quit and only returned to work (as a part-time day-care educator) when the child was 11.

Another strategy employed by women who had quit formal jobs was informal paid work in their homes. While the husband's job insecurity was often the major reason these women returned to paid work, the shift schedule was their reason for opting for this type of work. Being at home with young children, their own or others', did not necessarily mesh easily with shift schedules; a number of interviewees (male and female) in the different communities mentioned a problem that arose when the mill-worker was doing night shifts:

It was hard, especially, our house is so noisy . . . like in the summer I could go outside in the morning for a while, but in the winter, it was hard on the kids, like shhh! Daddy's sleeping. They wanna yell and scream (Ellen, W039)

Several Whitecourt women noted, nonetheless, that the alteration of two day and two night shifts meant they only had to keep the house quiet on two successive days, which they felt was more manageable than five or seven days as is the case under eight-hour shift systems. One Gatineau woman resolved childcare, financial issues, and noise problems by opening a licensed family home day care centre in the downstairs unit of the duplex owned by the couple (Christine, G25).

Among families where mothers were always employed outside the home while their children were young, we found varied and sometimes complex strategies for dealing with childcare needs. In Corner Brook, some households could rely on extended family members for childcare. Others resorted to a Newfoundland tradition—taking in a teenage girl from a rural area as a nanny. This enabled Carol (who variously worked days and evenings at the mill while raising seven children) and her husband Bill (a butcher in a retail shop) to manage since they had no relatives in the Corner Brook area:

Carol: We had an actual live-in-babysitter for quite a long time. . . . We knew her family, but she came from [an outport] and I guess her living with her family didn't work out too well so actually she needed somewhere to live so we sort of took her in and made a place for her to live and it was helpful to us. She was quite good with the children too . . . she didn't only babysit, she did other chores. . . . Well she was part of the family because actually she lived here, and then she had a little girl of her own. They didn't have anywhere to live. Her daughter still lives with us, she's 27. She calls [us] dad and mum all the time. (CB057)

In the Gatineau case, in contrast, live-in caregiver arrangements were rare. Families who relied heavily on non-family caregivers or day care centres had at times to contend with complex logistical problems. Husbands and wives tried to share drop-off and pick-up of children but the husbands' shift schedules sometimes made this impossible. When Robert (G20) worked the 4 PM–midnight shift and Monique was also working evenings at the credit union in Ottawa she had to drive back and forth across the Ottawa River during her supper break to shuttle the children from the day-time caregiver to their home before the evening caregiver came in; for unlike in White-court where shift workers were relatively much more numerous in the local community, caregivers did not organize their services with shift workers' schedule in mind. Monique (G20) went to see the school day care service every month with the 'little blue book,' the shift schedule diary published a year in advance, to arrange the weeks the children would attend the after-school program and the weeks they would be sent home on the bus from school. However, Nicole's (G21) circuit-board assembly job started at 7 AM, several kilometres away from the school day care service that only opened at 7 AM, so when Georges was on night shift and could not drop off their daughter at day care it was Nicole who had to negotiate a special arrangement with her boss.

Several of the dual-earner families interviewed employed multiple childcare arrangements to make use of father care whenever possible. Nathalie and Simon (G01) were lucky to find a caregiver willing to take and to charge for their preschooler only on the weekdays when Simon had to work or sleep during the day. This arrangement saved them money as well as allowing the father to spend more time with his daughter. Sometimes relatives filled the gaps. For example, Lynn (G15) called on her mother for childcare when Mike was working on day or night shifts, while Mike took charge of day-time childcare the week he worked the 4 PM–midnight shifts. The

work of coordinating childcare is done by the mother. Josee (G24) explained that with Alain's 'little blue book' in one hand, and her irregular shift schedule at a supermarket (given out a month in advance) in the other, she took charge of working out the caregiving arrangements, which included both parents, her mother, their oldest daughter, and a non-family caregiver.

Some Gatineau women tailored their working hours around childcare arrangements so as to minimize the disruptive effects of shifts on their children. Lucie (G12) was committed to her career as an infant nurse, but changed from a rotating shift schedule to working mostly evenings after the first of two children was born, to maximize sequential caregiving with her husband Réjean. Once her first child began school, Lucie made it priority to be there when the child got home; she was able to switch to a part-time schedule involving a mixture of day, evening, and weekend work.

Although some couples spoke of actively wanting to seize the opportunity of the husband's shift work to share childcare, for others, this was essentially just part of a pragmatic coping strategy, a way of life they approached with a certain degree of resignation. In one Corner Brook family [CB016]

I was working 6 days and 2 nights, and Ken stared working shift work. So we didn't see each other a lot anyway, so you just go used to it and when . . . the kids came along you were just so used to it—it was just a part of life. . . . His mother lived just down the street. . . . With our daughter, her mother took care of her when we'd work, so I didn't have any worries. [When Ken was doing 12-hours shifts and off in the day] he babysat, he was Mr Mom. We shared.

To what extent sequential childcare strategies involving father care actually foster emergent changes in gender relations, as suggested by some authors (Hanson and Pratt, 1995), remains a moot point as regards our mill-worker families. In a study of household divisions of labour in a Manitoba mining community, Luxton found that the attitude of husbands tended to be one of 'babysitting' their own children rather than taking on the role of primary caregiver for the time concerned (1986: 29). Our interviews did not systematically probe for parents' attitudes towards or opinions of father care, and the comments we heard are somewhat ambiguous:

Mike: Being on shifts I got to spend a lot of time with Alison, more time than most fathers would probably.

Lynn: More time than me. When you think about it you would be with her all day.

Mike: And that's what I really liked about shifts. I miss that now [he'd recently been laid off from the mill and got a day job in a service industry]. We used to go to McDonald's for breakfast sometimes. She used to love it. She'd say, 'where are we going today daddy?' I'd say, 'All the pit stops. We have to go to Canadian Tire, Jean Coutu, IGA.' I can't do that any more except on the weekend or something. (G15)

Nonetheless, there were indications in a few of the Gatineau interviews that the fact of having (or choosing) to take care of their preschool children some of the time when their wives were at work, had made them more appreciative of the value of 'family time'. While the shift system gave them little room to manoeuvre, some workers had, as a result of these experiences, begun rethinking that value of doing a lot of overtime, for example (Rose and Villemaire, 1997). During the long 1990 Gatineau strike, Mike (G15) loved taking care of his daughter: 'I was with her every day for four months straight and would see her growing up'; he greatly missed this when he went back to work. Some Corner Brook workers were rueful about the effects of the overtime they had worked

under the old shift system: 'the work was pulling you away all the time . . . I never seen the kids growing up' (Fred, CB022).

In Whitecourt, in addition to appropriate local childcare services, some women relied on their social networks to help them cope with the mill's work schedule. Mothers of preschoolers commented that they hired the children of friends to baby sit, while others remarked that people living in the neighbourhood could help them out. Ellen coped with shifts by taking her three preschool-aged children to the cooperative play group, CHIPS, in the winter, and going outside in the summer (W39). Another women was able to drop off her preschooler at the town's day care centre on a casual basis whenever she wanted a break.

However, it is important not to overestimate the women's ability to rely on resources embedded in local social networks. When Whitecourt mothers were asked how they reacted to an unexpected crisis such as a sick child, 65 per cent said they cancelled their plans and stayed at home.[9] Help from neighbours was mentioned second but by only 27 per cent of the women. In only 10 per cent of the households did the fathers stay at home. This was the least frequently mentioned response, mainly because the men's shift drew them away from the household so much. The situation was similar at Gatineau and Corner Brook, but with relatives playing a more important role than friends and neighbours and with the situation exacerbated in families where father often worked on-call. As Nathalie (G01) pointed out, 'it's an environment for MEN [at the mill]', unlike the female-dominated electronics assembly plant where Nicole (G21) could make special arrangements because she was a valued employee. The mill makes no accommodation for occasional childcare need unless there is a major family emergency. Also, as one Whitecourt mother explained, 'the money is too good for him to miss work.' . . .

While there is more sharing of childcare than routine housework between husbands and their wives, few men assume sole responsibility for

Table 14.2 Frequency of wife (W) or husband (H) doing housework

Household task	Gatineau					Whitecourt					Corner Brook				
	W	H	Both	Other	n^*	W	H	Both	Other	n^*	W	H	Both	Other	n^*
Mows lawn	0	10	1	2	13	9	29	14	11	63	1	24	7	5	37
Shovels snow	0	7	5	1	13	4	28	24	11	67	0	19	11	11	41
Minor car repairs	0	9	1	3	13	3	58	1	8	70	0	31	0	0	38
Washes car	1	5	6	0	12	8	25	33	4	70	2	13	10	10	38
Does shopping	4	0	9	0	13	44	2	23	1	70	19	3	16	16	41
Makes grocery list	9	0	4	0	13	55	1	11	3	70	21	1	11	11	35
Does laundry	7	0	6	0	13	52	2	12	4	70	22	1	11	11	41
Vacuums	3	4	6	0	13	48	6	10	6	70	15	1	13	13	41
Puts out garbage	1	3	8	1	13	13	18	26	13	70	1	19	15	15	40
Washes dishes	3	0	8	2	13	28	2	21	19	70	10	1	19	19	41
Cans/freezes produce	5	0	3	1	9	36	1	6	1	44	7	3	8	8	19
Prepares main meal on days . . .	3	1	4	0	8	11	7	10	2	30	4	9	12	12	27
when husband works	10	0	2	1	13	50	1	7	2	60	34	0	1	4	39
when wife works	3	7	2	0	12	21	9	12	4	46	3	10	8	4	25
when both work	4	0	6	3	13	30	1	10	6	47	9	0	8	5	22
when no one works	6	0	7	0	13	30	5	21	5	61	17	2	18	4	41
Gardening	3	2	5	1	11	21	6	27	5	59	7	13	10	1	31

* n refers to husband–wife households with a currently-employed shift worker.

any aspect of their children's care. On the whole, household strategies around childcare and other child-related activities tend to reflect the household nature of gender divisions in mill-worker families in the three communities. The daily responsibilities of taking children to medical and childcare services and watching them after school are assumed mainly by women acting alone, although several of the Gatineau mothers used the 'little blue book' to schedule children's medical appointments for days when their husband could take them. Where men do share responsibility for their children with their wives, their involvement is greatest for recreational and special events and attending parent/teacher meetings at school when shift schedule permit (Table 14.2).

> You know, the 4 days on and the 4 days off, like sometimes, Lyle's home during the week and he can take them for their practices and stuff. The next month, then I know I have to take them to all their practices and he can take

'em to their games on the weekends and stuff. (Susan, W63)

But even here, several interviewees commented that their partners were simply not available to attend school events or take children to sports and other activities:

Yeah, get home at 5:30 and go to the rink from 6 to 8. . . . Anyways, shifts kind of screw that up a little bit. I'd rather be off at 4:30. (Howard, W26)

Shift Work and Housework

A traditional gender division of labour is also apparent in the mill-workers' households when it comes to housework, with few differences among the three communities. Men do far fewer household chores by themselves than women. Tasks are differentiated on the basis of gender. Men are more likely to do outside work and to take care of the car (Table 14.2). Indeed, the only three types of domestic work in which men are more involved than women are mowing the lawn, shovelling snow, and minor car repairs. Four other jobs—washing the cars, washing the dishes, putting out the garbage, and gardening—are shared between both partners. By themselves, women are responsible for grocery shopping, food and meal preparation, and laundry, the routine tasks that must be completed on a daily or regular basis.

The reliance on either or both partners is noteworthy. Few children help with domestic work and there is even less use of commercial services. The frequency with which people other than the mill-worker and his partner do the housework ranges from a high of 27.2 per cent for washing dishes to a low of 1.4 per cent for grocery shopping. Older children are sometimes responsible for washing the dishes, taking out the garbage, and heating dinner. They also help mow lawns and shovel snow. Friends and relatives are more likely to help with minor car repairs.

To minimize disruptions to family time that is limited already by the shift schedule, women often schedule unpaid work to accommodate mill-workers' hours. Among the many strategies that women deploy, rescheduling housework is one of the most frequent. Women try to complete all their housework on days when men are working so that they are available when their partners are off work. Women also limit their housework on days when men need to sleep in preparation for a night shift. Finally, women often take responsibility for organizing family life because their partners are too tired to do these managerial tasks.

Among women who have paid employment, there are diverse arrangements for housework. Some women reported a gradual evolution in the gender division of labour whereby they successfully encouraged their partners to take more responsibility. In Gatineau, Fred's (G26) chronic job insecurity led Alice, who had been out of the workforce for almost 20 years until her youngest child was 12, to take retraining courses and land a demanding federal government position. This motivated Fred to take on much more domestic labour and start calling himself Mr Mom.

Men sometimes make 'pragmatic' adaptations to the shift schedule similar to those adopted by many women. To free time when both partners are not at work for leisure and recreation, some men do housework on their days off. This strategy is typical of households where women work long hours at demanding jobs. For example, Don, whose wife had a full-time job, does all the jobs around the house including cooking meals, baking, and the laundry when he is off work (CB101).

Occasionally, women's paid work encourages an explicit commitment to a more egalitarian division of housework (Suzanne and Denis, G16). As the literature suggests, these women typically have well-paid jobs that provide relatively high incomes, which may give women more power to insist that their partners do housework. The following excerpt from an interview with the only female production worker in Corner Brook exemplifies this relationship (CB57):

Bill: Put it this way, Carol's got a good job and she got good pay so I got no choice but go along with it.

Interviewer: Does Bill cook the dinners?

Bill: Oh yes, I washes and hangs out the clothes. I always did.

Carol: Bill helps with everything . . . he had to when the children were small.

Interviewer: And then when Carol's off, it's Carol's turn?

Bill: We share it between us. I still does it if Carol's home, and if two of us is off on Sunday, I cooks dinner. And when the family all comes they all wants me to cook.

However, it must be emphasized that this relationship was very much the exception among the households that we interviewed.

Discussion and Concluding Remarks

Our study found that the onus of adjustments to shifts fell mostly on women, the partners of mill-works. Women felt constrained in their choices by the demanding regime of their husbands' shift work. They felt obliged to do most of the adapting, for the sake of the family (see Olson and Shopes, 1991). They did not expect their husbands to change their jobs, probably because they recognized that working at the mill was the best-paying job available to these men, who in a number of cases had never finished high school. Although often better educated than their partners, the women still had lower earning potential in most instances. When employed, women's incomes were generally lower than those of mill-workers. This financial reality probably encouraged women to adjust to the shift system rather than resist it. The importance of this income differential is underscored by consistent evidence that mill-workers do more housework and child-care in the minority of cases where their partners do have well-paid employment. These factors may help to explain why, especially in regard to housework, we found few differences between the communities despite variations in female labour force participation, age structures, and levels of overtime being worked. . . .

Some parents took advantage of rotating shifts to maximize their involvement in childcare; however, few mill-workers expressly chose shift work so as to be available to care for young children. 'Father care' was, as Presser (1989) argues, mainly an unintended outcome of these couples' intermittently sequential schedules, rather than a planned strategy. In some dual-earner couples that had tried to use complementary shift schedules to manage their childcare needs, the lack of time to be together as a family led them to seek alternative work schedule. Our findings may be specific to the newsprint industry, in which many workers have little choice but to accept imposed shift schedules since there are few alternative, equally remunerative jobs for workers in the three localities we studied. In a large urban area, such as Ottawa-Hull, with more abundant job opportunities of women, shift work may nonetheless be deployed more often as a household strategy for managing childcare needs.

In answer to our original question about how shift work affects the gender divisions of domestic labour, in the few couples where women had demanding and well-paid jobs that confer greater power within the household, men took responsibility for more childcare and housework. In this sense, our empirical analysis has confirmed previous findings that gender divisions of domestic labour are affected profoundly by women's earnings (Hochschild, 1989; Presser, 1994; Brayfield, 1995; Bernier et al., 1996). However, in the vast majority of households, a traditional division of labour predominates, mainly for pragmatic reasons.

Notes

This article is dedicated to our colleague and friend, Suzanne Mackenzie (1950–98), who reminded us that capital is not hegemonic. The research was funded by the Social Sciences and Humanities Research Council of Canada, research grant no. 410-91-1763. Travel grants from the Quebec–Ontario Universities Exchange Programme facilitated our collaboration in analyzing the data and writing the present article. Some of this material was presented in much earlier form in three separate conference papers at the 1995 Annual Meeting of the Canadian Association of Geographers where we received a number of valuable comments and criticisms.

The version of this paper presented in this volume has been abridged. Please see *Gender, Place, and Culture* (2000, Volume 7, no. 1) for the full text and acknowledgements.

1. The number and ages of children in the household may also be important factors influencing the effect of shift work on family life but the data presented in this article do not permit us to systematically examine this potentially important factor.
2. As a continuous process industry, the production of newsprint must be run as a 24-hour operation and so there is a long history of shift work in the industry. Recently, throughout North American, the trend in newsprint mills has been to move from 8-hour to 12-hour shifts and to increase the use of rotating as opposed to fixed shifts. Competitive pressures and the economies of continuous production provide incentives to maximize capacity utilization by reducing maintenance and holiday downtime to an absolute minimum (Holmes, 1997).
3. In the CPS, the question was not asked of

mothers who worked days while their husbands worked non-days.
4. Compared with older and more senior workers, shift workers who are parents of young children tend to be younger, with little seniority in the workplace. Of all shift workers, the young and less senior are least likely to have much choice about their shift schedules.
5. See Wolf (1991) for a trenchant critique of the notion of household strategy.
6. We also collected data on patterns of leisure and home-improvement projects, but, for reasons of space and coherence, this material is not presented here. The discussion of household labour in the interviews was part of a larger study designed to investigate the diverse ways that households and communities have been shaped by and have shaped the restructuring of the newsprint industry (Mackenzie and Norcliffe, 1997).
7. The difference between the rates for Gatineau and Whitecourt is surprisingly small given what we have said about the differences in labour market structure between the two communities. This may be due to the offsetting effect of differences in age structure between the two communities.
8. A few such schemes do exist for shift workers in the USA and Canada (see Mayfield, 1990; Stam and Sodano, 1991).
9. Women were not asked to specify the nature of the plans that were disrupted by unexpected childcare needs. However, in Whitecourt plans are unlikely to include paid work since more than half the women in Whitecourt and most mothers of preschool age children were not involved in paid work (Table 14.1)

References

Bernier, C., S. LaFlamme, and R. Zhou. 1996. 'Le Travail Domestique: Tendances à la Désexisation et à la Complexification', *Canadian Review of Sociology and Anthropology* 33: 1–21.

Brayfield, A. 1995. 'Juggling Jobs and Kids: The Impact of Employment Schedules on Fathers' Caring for Children', *Journal of Marriage and the Family* 57: 321–32.

Canada, Human Resources Development Canada. 1994. *Report of the Advisory Group on Working Time and the Distribution of Work*. Ottawa: Supply and Services Canada.

Folk, K., and Y. Yi. 1994. 'Piecing Together Child Care with Multiple Arrangements: Crazy Quilt or Preferred Pattern for Employed Parents of Pre-school Children?', *Journal of Marriage and the Family* 56: 66–80.

Friendly, M., G. Cleveland, and T. Willis. 1989. *Flexible Child Care in Canada. A Report on Child Care for Evenings, Overnight and Weekends, Emergencies and Ill Children, and in Rural Areas*. Toronto: University of Toronto, Centre for Urban and Community Studies, Childcare Resource and Research Unit.

Gibson-Graham, J.K. 1996. *The End of Capitalism (As We Knew It): A Feminist Critique of Political Economy*. Cambridge, MA; Oxford: Blackwell.

Gill, A. 1986. 'New Resource Communities: The Challenge of Meeting the Needs of Canada's Modern Frontierspersons', *Environments* 18, 3: 21–34.

Hanson, S., and G. Pratt. 1995. *Gender, Work and Space*. London and New York: Routledge.

Hochschild, A.R. 1989. *The Second Shift: Working Parents and the Revolution at Home*. New York: Avon.

Holmes, J. 1997. 'In Search of Competitive Efficiency: Labour Process Flexibility in Canadian Newsprint Mills', *Canadian Geographer* 41: 7–25.

Johnson, K.L. 1998. *Shiftwork from a Work and Family Perspective*. Research Paper R-98-2E. Hull, QC: Human Resources Development Canada, Strategic Policy, Applied Research Branch.

LaPierre-Adamcyk, E., and N. Marcil-Gratton. 1995. 'Prise en Charge des Enfants: Stratégies Individuelles et Organisation Sociale', *Sociologie et sociétés* 26, 92: 121–42.

Le Bourdais, C., and A. Sauriol. 1998. *La Part des Pères dans la Division du Travail au Sein des Familles Canadiennes*. Études et documents, no. 69. Montreal: Institut national de la recherché scientifique, INRS-Urbanisation.

Lero, D.S., H. Goelman, A.R. Pence, L.M. Brockman, and S. Nuttal. 1992. *Canadian National Child Care Study, Parental Work Patterns and Child Care Needs*. Cat. 89-529E. Ottawa: Statistics Canada & Health and Welfare Canada.

Luxton, M. 1986. 'Two Hands for the Clock: Changing Patterns in the Gendered Division of Labour in the Home', in M. Luxton and H. Rosenberg, eds, *Through the Kitchen Window: The Politics of Home and Family*, pp. 17–36. Toronto: Garamond.

Mackenzie, S., and G. Norcliffe. 1997. 'Restructuring in the Canadian Newsprint Industry', *Canadian Geographer* 41: 2–6.

Mayfield, M.I. 1990. *Work-related Child Care in Canada*. Cat. L38-42/90E. Ottawa: Labour Canada Women's Bureau.

Morgan, J.N. 1981. 'Childcare When Parents are Employed', in M.S. Hill, D.H. Hill, and J.N. Morgan, eds, *Five Thousand American Families: Patterns of Economic Progress, Vol. IX: Analyses of the First Twelve Years of the Panel Study of Income Dynamics*, pp. 441–56. Ann Arbor, MI: University of Michigan, Institute for Social Research, Survey Research Center.

Norcliffe, G., and J. Bates. 1997. 'Implementing Lean Production in an Old Industrial Space: Restructuring at Corner Brook, Newfoundland, 1984–1994', *Canadian Geographer* 41: 41–60.

O'Connell, M. 1993. *Where's Papa? Fathers' Role in Child Care, Population Trends and Public Policy*. Report no. 20. Washington, DC: Population Reference Bureau.

Olson, K., and L. Shopes. 1991. 'Crossing Boundaries, Building Bridges: Doing Oral History among Working Class Women and Men', in S.B. Gluck and D. Patai, eds, *Women's Words: The Feminist Practice of Oral History*, pp. 189–204. New York & London: Routledge.

Overmand, S. 1993. 'Not the Usual 9–5: For Employees and Their Families, Shift Work is a Lifestyle Not Just a Work Schedule', *HR Magazine* 38: 47.

Pratt, G. 1993. 'Reflections on Poststructuralism and Feminist Empirics, Theory and Practice', *Antipode* 25: 51–63.

Presser, H.B. 1986. 'Shift Work among American Women and Childcare', *Journal of Marriage and the Family* 48: 551–63.

———. 1989. 'Can We Make Time for Children? The Economy, Work Schedules and Child Care', *Demography* 26: 523–43.

———. 1994. 'Employment Schedules among Dual-earner Families and the Division of Household

Labour by Gender', *American Sociological Review* 59: 348–64.

Preston, V., J. Holmes, and A. Williams. 1997. 'Working with "Wild Rose 1": Lean Production in a Greenfield Mill', *Canadian Geographer* 41: 88–104.

Rose, D. 1993. 'Local Childcare Strategies in Montreal, Quebec: The Mediations of State Policies, Class and Ethnicity in the Life Courses of Families with Young Children', in C. Katz and J. Monk, eds, *Life Space: Geographies of Women over the Life Course*, pp. 188–207. London and New York: Routledge.

Rose, D., and M. Villeneuve. 1997. 'Reshuffling Paperworkers: Technological Change and Experiences of Reorganization at a Quebec Newsprint Mill', *Canadian Geographer* 41: 61–87.

Stam, J., and A. Sodano. 1991. 'A Productive—and Human—Approach to Shift-work Operations', *National Productivity Review* 10: 465–79.

Statistics Canada. 1994a. *Profile of Census Divisions and Subdivisions in Alberta, Part B, 1991 Census of Canada*. Cat. 95-373. Ottawa: Industry, Science and Technology Canada.

———. 1994b. *Profile of Census Divisions and Subdivisions in Newfoundland, Part B, 1991 Census of Canada*. Cat. 95-302. Ottawa: Industry, Science and Technology Canada.

———. 1994c. *Profile of Census Divisions and Subdivisions in Quebec, Part B, 1991 Census of Canada*. Cat. 95-326. Ottawa: Industry, Science and Technology Canada.

———. 1998. 'Couples Who Do Shift Work', *The Daily*, 9 September: 2.

Weiss, M.G., and M.B. Liss. 1988. 'Night Shift Work: Job and Family Concerns', *Journal of Social Behavior and Personality* 3: 279–86.

Wharton, C.S. 1994. 'Finding Time for the "Second Shift": The Impact of Flexible Work Schedules on Women's Double Days', *Gender and Society* 8: 189–205.

Wolf, D.L. 1991. 'Does Father Know Best? A Feminist Critique of Household Strategy Research', *Research in Rural Sociology and Development* 5: 29–43.

CHAPTER 15

No Longer 'One of the Boys': Negotiations with Motherhood, as Prospect or Reality, among Women in Engineering[1]

Gillian Ranson

Women who train and work as professional engineers in Canada and other industrialized countries are women operating on male turf. Unlike professions such as medicine and law, both of which are much closer to gender parity, engineering remains 'archetypically masculine' (Wajcman, 1991: 145). In spite of nearly two decades of 'women into engineering' campaigns supported by government and industry, the numbers of women entering engineering have been described as 'derisory in most countries' (Faulkner, 2000: 92). The Canadian Council of Professional Engineers (CCPE) notes that, though the proportion of women in Canadian engineering schools increased annually after 1972, in the last few years it has levelled off at about 20 per cent (CCPE, 2003). While hardly derisory, these numbers fall far short of gender parity.

Retention of women in engineering over the long haul is also likely to be a problem given that the growth in numbers of those actually practising the profession is among women in their late 20s and early 30s (CCPE, 1998). These women are also at the age where family formation becomes salient. The arrival of children seems to be one critical point at which women, but not men, leave the profession, move to part-time work, and in many other ways put their careers 'on the back burner' (Ranson, 1998, 2000).

Motherhood, it seems clear, is a significant watershed, and one that policymakers and others concerned about retaining women in engineering should take seriously. But the reasons why it is such a watershed—and hence what needs to be done to compensate for its effects—may be more complicated than the conventional explanations about work and family balance suggest. A more elaborated explanation is that motherhood, as embodied and as material experience, exposes a major fallacy inherent in the liberal discourses of equality and gender neutrality, which establish the terms for women's entry into male-dominated occupations and workplaces in the first place. These terms allow women to enter, not as women, but as conceptual men (Snitow, 1990: 26). This conceptual cover is blown when they become, or think about becoming, mothers. For many women (especially those who themselves internalize the gender neutrality discourse), actual or prospective motherhood compels them to confront identities as 'engineer' and 'mother' that may be 'mutually incongruous' (Jorgenson, 2000: 7) and require complex negotiation and management.

In this paper I examine this more nuanced explanation, and explore its implications for all women in male-dominated occupations and workplaces who face the challenges of being 'travellers in a male world' (Marshall, 1984; Gherardi, 1996).

Women in a Man's World

Recent women entrants to male-dominated occupations have had more legal, and, increasingly,

cultural support for their presence on male turf. But while the terms of their participation have changed somewhat, difficulties persist. A 1992 report by the Canadian Committee on Women in Engineering cited many stories of sexism, systemic discrimination and workplace inequality, and a series of 'common and difficult' barriers faced by women engineers (Canadian Committee on Women in Engineering, 1992: 60).

Why should such barriers persist, especially in a discursive climate of gender equality and 'family-friendly' workplaces? Acker (1990) contends that organizations are not gender-neutral spaces that women may enter on the same footing as men; neither can a 'job' be defined as abstract and gender-neutral, performed by an abstract and disembodied 'worker' who exists only in relation to the job. Acker's widely cited argument is that in the real world of actual workers, the closest approximation to the disembodied worker who exists only for the job is 'the male worker whose life centers on his full-time, life-long job, while his wife or another woman takes care of his personal needs and his children' (Acker, 1990: 149).

Acker's description was, until recently, a good fit for most engineers. Recent initiatives to get women into engineering have usually been predicated on the assumption that 'women must be modified to fit into engineering, not the other way round' (Faulkner, 2000: 93). In ethnographic research on engineering women in a variety of educational and work settings, Eisenhart and Finkel (1998) found that organizational expectations regarding commitment to workplace activities and the worker identity favoured people who were able to put work demands first. At the same time, these expectations were perceived by everyone concerned, women and men alike, as gender-neutral. The researchers came to view gender neutrality as a socially and culturally constructed discourse that 'confers legitimacy on women's professional contribution only when they act like men' and 'makes discussion of women's distinctive issues virtually impossible' (Eisenhart and Finkel, 1998: 181).

Mothers in a Man's World

Motherhood as a barrier to women's career progress in engineering is demonstrated in much research through the 1990s. Studies in the United States (McIlwee and Robinson, 1992), Britain (Devine, 1992; Evetts, 1994, 1996; Corcoran-Nantes and Roberts, 1995; Wajcman, 1998) and Canada (Ranson, 1998, 2000) all point to the challenges for women in combining 'masculine' professional work and motherhood. They may find themselves, as noted earlier, in workplaces in which a discourse of gender neutrality masks clearly masculinist expectations about work performance and career progress. At the same time, they confront cultural expectations about mothers, framed around a dominant ideology of 'intensive mothering' (Hays, 1996; Arendell, 2000) that directly contradicts workplace expectations.

In contrast, the men with whom these women work are not subject to the same expectations regarding their family involvement. These men are much more likely than their women colleagues to have partners who can take on the bulk of family responsibilities (Wajcman, 1998; Ranson, 2000).[2] For most men, the prevailing cultural expectation is that they will be responsible for their family's financial provision, whether or not their contribution is supplemented by working partners, and whether or not they are also involved caregivers (Christiansen and Palkovitz, 2001; Ranson, 2001).

Organizational responses in the form of 'family-friendly' policies and programs would seem to be the way to overcome this under-resourcing. But research evidence suggests they are not helping nearly as much as company rhetoric and popular discourse would suggest. While policies like parental leave or flexible work schedules are generally couched in gender-neutral terms, and are purported to be directed to both women and men, in practice their take-up by men has been minimal (Andrews and Bailyn, 1993; Pleck, 1993; Rapoport and Bailyn, 1996; Hochschild, 1997). This constitutes women as the prime beneficiaries of such policies, and further entrenches the idea that they are special concessions or benefits for women (Jones and Causer, 1995; Lewis, 1997) rather than rights to which all workers are entitled.

Managing Gender

If women's entry to male occupational turf is largely based on liberal assumptions that women are for practical purposes the same as men, it follows that women themselves will need to 'manage gender' in order to fit themselves into existing organizational cultures and structures (Rubin, 1997: 31). Whatever their standing as 'conceptual men', real-life embodied women must negotiate feminine subjectivity as well.[2] This is neatly illustrated by one of Miller's (2004) interviewees, a woman engineer working in the same city as the women in this study:

> When you go to the field, you don't take a purse because you're really rubbing that female helplessness thing in, and you put all your junk—the female hygiene stuff—in your little pockets. Another thing you do when you work downtown is you always wear wide skirts because sometimes you're going to be going to the field in the afternoon. And you can wear high heels to the office but keep a pair of flat loafers there . . . (Miller, 2004: 54).

While some of the women engineers in a 1999 study by Kvande did indeed, as noted above, strive to be 'one of the boys', others drew on other discourses (or, in Kvande's terms, constructed other femininities) that corresponded to a view of themselves as *different from*, not the same as their male colleagues. Kvande found that the women who saw themselves in this way were invariably women with children. Jorgenson, whose research (2000, 2002) focused particularly on the ways women engineers with children managed the potentially contradictory discourses of motherhood and engineering, found similar complexity. Sometimes the women positioned themselves as competent career-oriented professionals, sometimes as caring mothers, but usually with an awareness of the incompatibility of the mother–engineer identities. As one of her interviewees commented, 'I didn't want to try to be the perfect engineer because I knew I wanted a family' (Jorgenson, 2002: 370).

Jorgenson's work summarizes the position outlined at the start of the paper, that women enter engineering work as 'conceptual men', and that motherhood is, in many cases, a 'defining moment', separating mothers from others.

'Conceptual Men', Alternative Subjectivities, and Motherhood in Engineering

WOMEN WITHOUT CHILDREN

Sally, who was 41 and childless, provides a good example of the sort of long-term engineering careers available to competent and highly motivated women able to be single-minded about their professional work. This was not the case for the younger women, who still needed to confront the possibility of motherhood. Among these women, particular understandings both of motherhood and engineering work framed talk that was also significantly shaped by age and family or relationship circumstance.

The experience of Sally—a senior manager in a major oil company—provides a link to the issue of motherhood because she attributed her career success to the fact that—not from choice—she didn't have children. Sally noted that despite her company's public claims to being 'family-friendly', the 'day-to-day business environment' included the perception that to get ahead 'you've got to put in the long hours' and be 'willing to sacrifice'. Asked if she thought more women in the organization would make a difference, she said: 'I think that may be the sort of thing that *keeps* women from making a difference.' She was explicit about the difference it had made to her career: 'Because

I don't have the child connection. . . .I have been able to, if need be, go the extra mile, every time they've asked.'

The single women's responses to the prospect of motherhood were provisional and speculative, since all saw a permanent relationship as a prerequisite. For example, Rosemary, four years post-graduation, commented:

> I'm probably indifferent either way, you know. I think it would depend on my spouse. Like, if I met somebody and they wanted kids, then I would be open to having one, maybe two. And hopefully maybe they would like to adopt children rather than (laughter) . . . I just can't see myself just, just staying home and being mom. . . . So, but if, hey, my previous boyfriend, he was more than happy to be a stay-at-home dad. So that, that's a fit for me as well.

In this way, at the hypothetical level at least, she constructed a family scenario that would allow her to remain 'one of the boys'. This scenario did not challenge the 'intensive' version of mothering that would remove her from the workplace. Instead, Rosemary discursively nominated her hypothetical partner as the full-time caregiver, and gave herself a family role similar to those of her male colleagues. In other words, she positioned herself as a conceptual 'father'.

Like Rosemary, Julia was also 27 and four years past graduation. Though she did not self-identify as 'one of the boys' in the way Rosemary did, she was relishing the hands-on, technical, outdoor nature of her fieldwork job. But she also saw this way of working as contingent:

> [N]ow I don't have the five-year to ten-year plan. I mean, between you and I, I would love to be a stay-at-home mom. . . . But, I'm not married. And I don't have any kids. So *until then*, I'm going to do the best job that I can, and follow my career, and if it happens, it

happens. If it doesn't, it doesn't (emphasis added).

Julia's vision of motherhood included the view that 'if you have children. . . somebody should be at home'—and she was clear that, in her family, unlike Rosemary's, she would be that somebody. She presented this version of mothering as incompatible with engineering work: 'If I could work from home, or if I could work part-time, then that would be my ideal. But in engineering, you don't seem to be able to do that. . . .'

Other single, childless women, with more work experience than Julia, took her story to another level: children needed care that mothers should provide and that they, as mothers, would potentially be willing to provide; in the absence of these family obligations, they were devoting their energies to engineering work; this engineering work was getting to be of a kind and at a level that would not easily accommodate maternal responsibilities. Thus, for example, Sarah—a 34-year-old engineer who had recently been promoted to manage a major energy project for her company—expressed excitement that this project could be 'a stepping stone' to 'a lot more exciting projects'. Asked if she thought she would be able to combine her present job with children and family responsibilities, Sarah said:

> I think I would. I know women that do do that here but they have to have a very understanding spouse that's more flexible. It's very difficult to do this job and have a spouse that's doing exactly the same thing with exactly the same sort of aspirations, I think.

Sarah's immediate qualification of the possibility of a work–family balance in her current job (by positioning herself, like Rosemary, as a father) was qualified still further by her comment later that she 'couldn't go on maternity leave in the next two years' even if she wanted to, and that she had 'sort of accepted the fact that [having children] might

not happen'. Sarah had recognized, in Wajcman's (1996) terms, the 'domestic basis for the managerial career'.

Different versions of the engineering–motherhood balance came from women who were in permanent relationships with men, and who were all anticipating having children sooner or later. These women were in two groups. When interviewed, four were recent graduates, within six years of graduation, and all were in their 20s. Three were a little older and more experienced (all were 34 and had 12 years of engineering experience behind them).

Among the younger four, the ideology of intensive mothering appeared in comments rejecting nannies or daycare as strategies enabling full-time work while having young children. But they also rejected the stay-at-home mother option; all planned to work part-time when their children were young. They all assumed that part-time work would be viable, even when—as in Sheila's case—there was some evidence from a colleague working an 80 per cent schedule that it might be hard to manage. (Sheila commented, 'I honestly think that she's a little bit less organized and that I could probably handle it a little better.') These women also expressed a strong sense of entitlement with respect to what their employer ought to do for them. And they were united in their conviction that their partners—all of whom were also engineers—would share the childcare responsibilities, likely also moving to part-time work to do so. This conviction was striking, given their collective experience of working in resoundingly masculinist workplace cultures where men, for the most part, were able to delegate their family responsibilities, and where male engineers working less than full-time were almost unheard of.

The three older women were characteristic of many women in male-dominated occupations in having deferred childbearing (see Ranson, 1998). All three spoke about their work, and their current workplaces, in terms that clearly indicated career success: a raise or stock options whenever she thought about leaving (Marcie); promotion from a junior position to the same grade as her male colleagues (Helen); a senior management position in a company she had helped to grow (Shelley). All three intended to keep working after having children, and all three, in different ways, planned to make their experience and seniority work for them as they thought about accommodating their jobs to family responsibilities. As Shelley said:

> I've been with the company for a long time and I've always been a very good employee. As a result I'm paid well now, and I have a lot of responsibility and respect [within] the company. And, you know, that's my money to cash in when I need to negotiate a deal. . . . A position of strength to bargain from is always a good thing.

What seems to be the case is that this position of strength is achieved by proof of successful career performance according to male standards—in other words, by women paying their dues as 'conceptual men'. This is not to suggest that these women achieved their success by aligning themselves with men. For example, some of the experience that earned Helen her current job was gained in an overtly sexist work environment that she was 'not ever going to be a part of'. It is also not to suggest that 'male standards' are uniform. For example, most of Shelley's male colleagues and superiors were about her age; she suggested that their relative youth made them less conventional. But in every case, the standards in place were standards established by men. Having met those standards, women felt freer to negotiate as women for changes they needed to accommodate their family responsibilities.

To summarize, the women without children produced a number of different scenarios for the way motherhood might combine with engineering: motherhood viewed as incompatible with engineering, and chosen as its alternative; motherhood refused, delegated, or privatized

to enable the continuation of the engineering career; motherhood and engineering combined by means of modified work arrangements (earned by male-defined career success), and the equal participation of husbands and partners. Of these scenarios, only the first assumed that motherhood and engineering were truly 'mutually incongruous', and this was not a common position. But the 'strong' view of intensive mothering it implied appeared in more diluted form in all the accounts. This in turn shaped how women thought they would need to accommodate their work. Unless (as in Rosemary's case) they planned to become 'fathers', motherhood was seen as putting an end to business as usual.

WOMEN WITH CHILDREN

The choices and accommodations anticipated by the childless women turned out to be a generally accurate summary of the routes the mothers took. As with the mothers in Kvande's study, though, they were generally more likely to position themselves as women, differently situated from their current or former male colleagues.

Five of the women gave up full-time engineering work at or shortly after the arrival of their children. At the time they were interviewed, two were not in paid employment at all, and spoke as if a return to engineering was unlikely. Holly commented: 'As soon as I had a baby, my total perspective changed.' For Jenny, the other stay-at-home mother, her first baby's arrival signalled not so much a change of perspective as the opportunity to retreat gratefully from a world she had never wholeheartedly embraced. Jenny's choice was motherhood over engineering:

> It's not a door that I've closed and I don't have bad memories. Although what I hear about engineering now . . . I think, oh, man, I don't want to get into that any more. I really don't.

The others had had longer and more conventionally successful careers as engineers before having children. All undertook intermittent consulting contracts, but at the time they were interviewed none were working more than a day or so a week. Kate, at home with her first child, (aged nine months at the time of the interview) framed her stay-at-home-mom status as 'a wonderful break' after having worked in engineering for 15 years. The baby was long-awaited. She commented: 'I didn't sort of have huge expectations of it but when we finally did [have] him, I just thought, oh, why wouldn't I just kind of stay and enjoy him?' Kate had worked long enough, and recently enough, that the engineer identity was still strong ('even though I'm not working I'll always be an engineer'). But asked whether she would be an engineer 10 years down the road, she replied, 'Probably not.'

Lisa's work history was similar to Kate's. She had worked full-time for 10 years for one company, then switched to part-time with the birth of her first child. But half-time work with a second child heightened the tension between work and family responsibilities:

I wasn't doing a good job with anything. . . . If it had gone on any longer I would have regretted it and you can't live your life like that. You've just got to do what you know you can.

Like Julia, cited earlier, Lisa had broader aspirations about family and motherhood, to which this decision conformed:

I really wanted to be the one with the babies. I wanted to nurse them, I wanted to raise them. . . . It would have been a sacrifice to not be home with them, to me. I really wanted to do that. It was the life experience I wanted to have.

While for all four women, the commitment to motherhood rather than engineering could be construed as voluntary, for Ellie, the fifth woman in the group, it was not. At the time she was interviewed she was recovering from two very difficult pregnancies, residual physical problems following childbirth, and an extremely demanding second baby. ('I think I literally lost my mind', she commented.) In Rothman's (1994) terms, she was experiencing the 'embodied challenges' to working like a man—challenges she resisted as much as she could. Echoes of the energetic and driven women engineers described by Kate appeared in her talk of working while pregnant and sick, or doing from her hospital bed the work her (female) replacement was supposed to be doing. Ellie spoke optimistically about returning to work: 'I do want to work. I really enjoy working. I never wanted really to be a stay-at-home.' The clear implication was that when she was physically able, she would pick up her working life.

Six of the women with children continued to work full-time, or close to full-time, in engineering jobs. But the conscious downplaying of career goals in order to accommodate family responsibilities expressed by Lisa was evident in the talk of these women as well. It was also reflected in their practices—a shift in the kind of work being done to something perceived to be less stressful (Linda), a refusal of promotion in order to remain in a familiar and manageable work environment (Joanne), a move from permanent employment to consulting as a means to achieve flexibility (Kelly), the use of a pregnancy to signal a shifting of gears after a successful corporate career (Hilary), cutting back to four instead of five days a week (Shauna). These work arrangements were accompanied by talk that linked them to family benefits.

The third group of mothers is those whose careers appeared on the surface to have been less affected by motherhood. Given the way these women were working, and the jobs they were doing, they could be described as mothers in careers more often associated with men. The nine women in this group had all reached senior levels of management and/or technical specialty. But in this group also, the balance of motherhood and career was complicated and fluid. It was also in this group that the most vivid images of 'conceptual men' becoming mothers emerged. Cassie was one example. As a woman who had always been able to work as 'one of the boys', Cassie downplayed issues of gender in the workplace, noting that she had never experienced 'discrimination, or anything like that', and was 'not a supporter of affirmative action-type programs'. She said she thought 'opportunities go to those people who are willing to work for them'. But this perspective was challenged by an unplanned pregnancy at a time when she was making dramatic career progress.

Carla's case is worth noting because it is such a good example of the discursive positioning of the 'professional engineer' and the (very much embodied) mother. When Carla returned to work after her first maternity leave, she tried to breast-feed her baby during her lunch break as a way to continue nursing. She said:

Well, I tried it for two weeks, but then my milk supply was so big, it was just like . . . you know, here I am a professional engineer and my boobs are leaking all over the place and I just couldn't, couldn't do that.

Asked if those around her at work were supportive, she replied, 'Well, I didn't really talk about it with anybody. It was kind of a private thing.' Carla's acknowledgement of the incongruity of 'professional engineers' breast-feeding, and of breast-feeding itself as belonging in the private domain, hinted at the subjective shifts she also negotiated. Carla's career choices were constrained by her family's need for her income. Like many men also, she was the family breadwinner, in a position to delegate family work to her partner. Unlike most men, however, she expressed unease about this arrangement. Her interview was interspersed with comments that clearly indicated what Smith (1987) would call a bifurcated consciousness, divided between a focus on her work (which she enjoyed), and preoccupation with a domestic life over which she had reluctantly surrendered control. 'There are really times that I long to be the stay-at-home parent,' she commented.

For other women, there was a more conscious crossing over from a family focus to a more explicit career orientation. Zoe responded to an appeal by a friend to leave her flexible consulting arrangement and lead a small company; Ingrid's long-time male mentor asked her to return to work part-time two months after her second child was born. Ingrid spoke of having planned not to return to work until the children were in school. But the part-time work quickly turned to full-time, then a partnership. Her account combined expressions of her enjoyment of her job with regrets about its costs.

I think once a woman works, it's hard not to work. It's hard to stay home and not have that challenge. . . . Knowing that other people are advancing, advancing, advancing. . . . The downside is the time. You don't know (if you raised) your kids yourself. I don't consider, myself, that I've raised my kids . . . I consider that they spend more time with their babysitter than they do with me, right? I consider that and now it's more time at school than with me, right? So I consider myself kind of the secondary raiser, kind of in their lives, my husband and I.

But in this group of mothers there were also those whose accounts were much less conflicted. For example, Denise had her first, and only child, at 35. She took 20 weeks of maternity leave, the maximum her company allowed—'and honestly, I was dying to get back to work.' She commented:

It didn't change much in my life. I still worked the same hours. I was still the same person at work as I was before. Just because I have a full-time nanny during the day, I was pretty uninterrupted, having a child, compared to what it could be.

To summarize, the 20 women with children followed fairly closely the paths anticipated by the childless women engineers described earlier with respect to the combination of engineering and motherhood. A very few voluntarily 'chose' motherhood. All the others negotiated a balance between being an engineer and being a mother that was both discursive and practical. For some of these negotiators, the balance was achieved by a conscious gearing down on the work side—but usually only after careers had been established and dues paid. For the others, it was achieved (as just noted) by means of privatizing and delegating family responsibilities in order to maintain career progress.

Conclusion

This study has proceeded from the assumption that motherhood is a watershed for women in engineering, and has explored what was described at the start of the paper as a more nuanced explanation for why this might be the case: that women enter engineering jobs as 'conceptual men', and that problems arise because mothers can't *be* conceptual men.

What it means to work as a 'conceptual man' is not self-evident. In this paper I chose to see women engineers working in this way if they were doing the same kind of work, in the same conditions, for the same hours, and with the same general expectations about quality of performance as their male colleagues. Another part of the definition was that this work was done in workplaces dominated by men—a condition that was more than met in every case. I also tried to distinguish between *working as* a conceptual man, and *aligning oneself*, or *discursively positioning oneself*, with men. On the basis of this definition, all of the women without children were working as conceptual men. Often, though not invariably, they also positioned themselves as 'one of the boys'—though this positioning was seldom sustained and consistent. Nine of the 20 women with children were also working

as conceptual men—though they were much less likely to position themselves with 'the boys'.

In my discussion of these nine, and in comments about the plans of some of the childless women also proposing to delegate to partners or otherwise privatize their family responsibilities, I have suggested that these women were or would become 'fathers'. This proposition is not entirely theoretical. In a separate study (Ranson, 2001) I explored the ways the men with children interviewed for the same engineering project balanced work and family responsibilities. Serious accommodation to family responsibilities generally took two forms: a choice of work (generally office, rather that field-based, with predictable hours); or downshifting from an intensive work focus to a more relaxed pace—usually the choice of men who had achieved considerable career success first. But for all of these men, the balance of work and family still typically involved working days of 8–10 hours, and in almost every case, also involved a partner working part-time or not in paid employment, and available to pick up the slack. Access to this private infrastructure of support characterized almost all the fathers. For those mothers who have access to something similar, the 'father' analogy has some merit.

For the mothers, 'downshifting' to accommodate children went much further: an opting out of engineering, temporarily or permanently, or a reduction in work hours. Fathers never employed these strategies; indeed, men with young families working less than full-time never emerged in the larger study. This is why such strategies come to be identified with women, and why so-called 'family-friendly' organizational policies purporting to help employees balance work and family responsibilities come to be perceived as helping women fit in to men's workplaces. As noted by researchers cited earlier (Jones and Causer, 1995; Lewis, 1997; Rubin, 1997; Liff and Ward, 2001), these policies may become another organizational device for differentiating women from 'the boys'—and mothers from fathers.

Notes

1. The author would like to thank Marilyn Porter and the CRSA reviewers for very helpful comments on an earlier version of the paper. This manuscript was first submitted in September 2003 and accepted in March 2005.
2. In the larger project from which the present study is drawn, only 25 per cent of fathers in engineering jobs had partners who also worked full-time, compared to 92 per cent of the engineering mothers.
3. I am grateful to the anonymous reviewer who urged that this point be made more explicit.

References

Acker, J. 1990. 'Hierarchies, Jobs, Bodies: A Theory of Gendered Organizations', *Gender & Society* 4, 2: 139–58.

Andrews, A., and L. Bailyn. 1993. 'Segmentation and Synergy: Two Models of Linking Work and Family', in J. Hood, ed., *Men, Work and Family*, pp. 262–75. Newbury Park, CA: Sage.

Arendell, T. 2000. 'Conceiving and Investigating Motherhood: The Decade's Scholarship', *Journal of Marriage and Family* 62, 4: 1192–207.

Canadian Committee on Women and Engineering. 1992. *More than Just Numbers*. Fredericton: University of New Brunswick.

Canadian Council of Professional Engineers. 1998. *National Survey of the Canadian Engineering Profession in 1997*. Ottawa: Canadian Council of Professional Engineers.

———. 2003. 'Women in Engineering'. Available at http://www.ccpe.ca/e/prog_women_1.cfm.

Christiansen, S., and R. Palkovitz. 2001. 'Why the "good provider" Role Still Matters: Providing as a Form of Paternal Involvement', *Journal of Family Issues* 22, 1: 84–106.

Corcoran-Nantes, Y. and K. Roberts. 1995. '"We've got one of those": The Peripheral Status of Women in Male-dominated Industries', *Gender, Work and Organization* 2, 1: 21–33.

Devine, F. 1992. 'Gender Segregation in the Engineering and Science Professions: A Case of Continuity and Change', *Work, Employment and Society* 6, 4: 557–75.

Eisenhart, M., and E. Finkel. 1998. *Women's Science*. Chicago, IL: University of Chicago Press.

Evetts, J. 1994. 'Women and Career in Engineering: Continuity and Change in the Organisation', *Work, Employment and Society* 8, 1: 101–12.

———. 1996. *Gender and Career in Science and Engineering*. London: Taylor & Francis Ltd.

Faulkner, W. 2000. 'The Power and the Pleasure? A Research Agenda for "making gender stick" to Engineers', *Science, Technology, & Human Values* 25, 1: 87–119.

Gherardi, S. 1996. 'Gendered Organizational Cultures: Narratives of Women Travellers in a Male World', *Gender, Work and Organization* 3, 4: 187–201.

Hays, S. 1996. *The Cultural Contradictions of Motherhood*. New Haven, CT: Yale University Press.

Hochschild, A. 1997. *The Time Bind*. New York: Metropolitan Books.

Jones, C., and G. Causer. 1995. '"Men don't have families": Equality and Motherhood in Technical Employment', *Gender, Work and Organization* 2, 2: 51–62.

Jorgenson, J. 2000. 'Interpreting the Intersections of Work and Family: Frame Conflicts in Women's Work', *The Electronic Journal of Communication* 10, 3–4.

———. 2002. 'Engineering Selves: Negotiating Gender and Identity in Technical Work', *Management Communication Quarterly* 15, 3: 350–80.

Kvande, E. 1999. '"In the belly of the beast": Constructing Femininities in Engineering Organizations', *European Journal of Women's Studies* 6, 3: 305–28.

Lewis, S. 1997. '"Family-friendly" Employment Policies: A Route to Changing Organizational Culture or Playing About at the Margins?', *Gender, Work and Organization* 4, 1: 13–23.

Liff, S., and K. Ward. 2001. 'Distorted Views Through the Glass Ceiling: The Construction of Women's Understandings of Promotion and Senior Management Positions', *Gender, Work and Organization* 8, 1: 19–36.

Marshall, J. 1984. *Women Managers: Travellers in a Male World*. Chichester: John Wiley and Sons.

McIlwee, J., and J. Robinson. 1992. *Women in Engineering*. Albany, NY: SUNY Press.

Miller, G. 2004. 'Frontier Masculinity in the Oil Industry: The Experience of Women Engineers', *Gender, Work and Organization* 11, 1: 47–73.

Pleck, J. 1993. 'Are "family-supportive" Employer Policies Relevant to Men?', in J. Hood, ed., *Men, Work and Family*, pp. 217–37. Newbury Park, CA: Sage.

Ranson, G. 1998. 'Education, Work and Family Decision Making: Finding the "right time" to Have a Baby', *Canadian Review of Sociology and Anthropology* 35, 4: 517–33.

———. 2000. 'The Best of Both Worlds? Work, Family Life and the Retention of Women in Engineering'. Paper presented at the 8th annual conference of the Canadian Coalition of Women in Engineering, Science, Trades and Technology, St. John's, Newfoundland, 6–8 July.

———. 2001. 'Men at Work: Change—or No Change?—in the Era of the "new father"', *Men and Masculinities* 4, 1: 3–26.

Rapoport, R., and L. Bailyn. 1996. *Relinking Life and Work: Toward a Better Future*. New York: Ford Foundation.

Rothman, B. 1994. 'Beyond Mothers and Fathers: Ideology in a Patriarchal Society', in E.N. Glenn, G. Chang, and L.R. Forcie, eds, *Mothering: Ideology, Experience and Agency*, pp. 139–57. New York: Routledge.

Rubin, J. 1997. 'Gender, Equality and the Culture of Organizational Assessment', *Gender, Work and Organization* 4, 1: 24–34.

Smith, D. 1987. *The Everyday World as Problematic: A Feminist Sociology*. Toronto: University of Toronto Press.

Snitow, A. 1990. 'A Gender Diary', in M. Hirsch and E.F. Keller, eds, *Conflicts in Feminism*. New York: Routledge.

Wajcman, J. 1991. *Feminism Confronts Technology*. Cambridge: Polity Press.

———. 1996. 'The Domestic Basis for the Managerial Career', *Sociological Review* 44, 4: 609–29.

———. 1998. *Managing Like a Man*. University Park, PA: Pennsylvania State University Press.

CHAPTER 16

Can Women's Social Networks Migrate?

Janet W. Salaf and Arent Greve[1]

Introduction: Work and Family Networks

With the globalization of production and services, professionals from Asia increasingly migrate to enrich their work experiences and their family economies in new countries (Castells, 1989; Sassen, 1991). These moves often disrupt their professional employment and family support networks, which they must mobilize anew (Portes and Borocz, 1989; Levitt and Schiller, 2003). Our 'Immigration from China' project explores how social networks bridge settlement of professionals who immigrated to Canada in the skilled worker category. We look for those features in their social networks that they share with others and those which are distinctly rooted in dual-career families. This paper analyzes how migration alters the family support system, how couples adapt to reduced social capital for childcare, and how this impedes career opportunities of skilled women in particular.

Typical People's Republic of China (PRC) immigrants to Canada are married professionals who apply to immigrate based on their skills, without having been offered jobs or preceded by other family members. In China, they had built collegial social networks during their education and careers (Lin, Ensel, and Vaughn, 1981). After immigration to Canada, to get appropriate positions they search for local work-related network partners that are rooted in the occupation, not in kinship or the ethnic enclave (Gold, 2001; Poros, 2001).

Family needs also require social network support but of a different sort. Professionals are likely to marry other professionals, and both want to develop their careers. To do so, parents with young children draw on complex support systems, which, unlike job networks, are based on kinship. Like other migrants, they also have to mobilize family-related social networks over immense physical distances (Hondagneu-Sotelo and Avila, 1997).

SOCIAL NEWTOWRKS: MIGRATION AND SOCIAL SUPPORT

Social networks play diverse functions in international migration (Portes and Borocz, 1989; Delechat, 2001). International migrants depend on social networks to find a job, start a business, or other career needs (Min, 1988; Burt, 1992). In addition to career exigencies, new arrivals need to find a place to live, get information and advice, emotional support, and help with childcare from others, the topic of this paper (Preston and Man, 1999; Willis and Yeoh, 2000; Parrenas, 2001; Man, 2002).

Depending on the resources that the network contacts can offer, they can provide different types of support, but one contact can rarely cover a broad range of services. Furthermore, different forms of social networks give diverse kinds of assistance over time (Poros, 2001). Therefore, people need a variety of contacts to get the kind of support they need. Childcare is one of many services that people can get through their social networks. However, this delicate type of service involves

considerable trust, and only a few members of a social network can offer the different types of assistance that childcare encompasses. This can be seen when we discuss types of relations and social networks that offer these resources.

LIFE COURSE STRUCTURE

Because the biggest demands from work and family come at the same time, a crucial problem for dual-career couples is balancing their work and family careers. State-legislated family policies to support social reproduction often fail to provide effective support to dual-career families. Few countries effectively organize public childcare and employment to support dual-career families. Those that do may favour some sections of the work force with childcare more than others (Moen and Firebaugh, 1994; Buchmann and Charles, 1995).

It is typically women who try to mesh these dual work–family demands. Women may adopt sequential work and family courses, focusing more on each role at different times. They might first study, then raise children, then return to the labour force. This staggered approach often runs against the demands of expected professional career sequences. Simultaneous roles allow attention to both family and career courses. Here, role conflict takes a toll on women's ability to do both without substantial help (Moen and Yu, 1999; Walter, Heinz, and Verma, 2001). Men commonly adjust their family life to their careers, while wives employ long-term, reciprocal support strategies to bridge formal and informal structures and attain work and family goals.

The difficulties that PRC immigrants to Canada encounter when they transfer between two different social contexts are central to their reconstructing work and family lives as new immigrants. Social structures, typical ways of building careers, and state family policies designed to support social reproduction differ from one setting to another and entail considerable readjustments. Without flexible informal social networks, parents have trouble bridging formal structures, and women assume most of this integrating work.

WORK–FAMILY ROLES IN CHINA

Educated Chinese women have public and private roles that are both sequential and simultaneous (Giele, 1998). The education of young Chinese professionals and skilled workers is sequential, determined by examinations that lead from one stage to the next. State educational and job placement systems—and their own performance and interests—channel the educated elite into their adult roles. In force when most of our respondents got their first jobs, this system began to change in the 1980s following the introduction of a private labour market with great consequences for their careers (Bian, 1994; Nee and Matthews, 1996). After graduation from college, they find jobs and begin to build careers. They marry and bear a child within the first year (Whyte and Parish, 1984; Robinson, 1985). Having few children is a political requirement, allowing them to devote themselves to work. The family is now seen as a smaller, leaner, even residual unit, whose tasks have lessened (Croll, Kane, and Davin, 1985).

Women and men remain in the labour force throughout their working lives. Educated women have made inroads into demanding professional, administrative, and skilled manual occupations, although assignments are gendered and males and females work in different sectors (Ngo, 2000). With the market reforms, successful professional and skilled workers increasingly earn high incomes, rewarding women for remaining on the job (Meng and Kidd, 1997).

Women take on the primary responsibility for child rearing and other caring roles. While they downplay their careers when it conflicts with their families, institutional and personal support systems help ease balancing simultaneous careers and work family roles (Moen and Yu, 1999; Zhan and Montgomery, 2003). Chinese family policy helps parents combine public and private roles. The city and the largest state work units operate daycare and nursery school places. Although there are institutional shortages, there are adequate places for professional dual-career families. Moreover, with flexible hours, parents can use around-the-clock services.

Mutual obligations between family members also provide social capital to ease the meshing of work–family systems. These norms are traced back to the patrilineal Chinese family. Respect for broad family obligations continues but is more mutual and negotiated today, giving family members a range of social supporters (Whyte and Parish, 1984). Each generation expects to benefit in the long run from mutual assistance (Yang, 1996). The elder generation wants to help professional sons and daughters, substantial earners in the family, meet their work responsibilities. The professional wife's job earning potential is worth more than the time she might spend at household and other reproductive chores. At the same time, children are the whole family's responsibility (Chen, Short, and Entwisle, 2000).

Many parents of our elite couples were themselves professionals who worked in the urban state sector and retired early while still in good health. With small families themselves, grandparents are not overwhelmed with care requests. Co-residence also contributes to shared reproductive tasks. There was no private housing market until the mid-1980s, and housing—provided by their work unit—was in short supply (Walder, 1986). Couples delayed marriage until they had an apartment or accepted living with the older generation, who often had better housing than the younger generation. The seniors first give young mothers childcare help; later, they receive personal care (Zhan and Montgomery, 2003). As a result, in the 1980s, an estimated 25 per cent of younger parents lived together with their own parents (Davis, 1993; Chen et al., 2000).

In these ways, features of the wider context ease reciprocal care between generations. If proximity, social norms, and structures underlay the social exchanges between female generations, how do transnational migrants get the help they need to work from kin?

WORK–FAMILY ROLES IN CANADA

North Americans integrate their work and family life courses in diverse patterns. Women go in and out of school and paid work at different times (Gerson, 1985; Giele, 1998; Partridge, in press). Jones, Marsden, and Tepperman (1990) point out that Canadian women adapt to paid work by individualizing their life patterns, including an increasingly fluid movement between adult statuses in domestic work, full-time and part-time work, and education.

Earlier cohorts of educated women returned to work after their children were older, often in new careers (Ginzberg, 1967). Professionally trained women today postpone having children until finishing their training. They may then stay in the labour force, finding other caregivers, paying for nannies—often new immigrants of colour, work part-time, or telework (Parrenas, 2001).

Lack of state commitment to childcare facilities contributes to this fluidity. Due to the incoherent and costly early childhood education system, Canadian childcare has become largely the private responsibility of parents (Doherty, Rose, Friendly, Lero, and Hope, 1995; Vanier Institute of the Family, 2000). Parents engage in considerable private strategizing in order to combine professional work and family roles (Hochschild, 1990). Much of this is the work of women.

Methods

To understand how they reconnect social networks to do their employment and family roles, we studied 50 dual-career couples from China over time. We contacted approximately half of our sample through a large NGO immigration agency in Toronto. The other half was composed of 'snowball' contacts, introduced by the original sample. While our small sample cannot represent the many Chinese immigrants in Toronto, our respondents are typical of emigrants from China's urban centers (Liang, 2001; Statistics Canada, 2001). With dependents to support, all needed to earn money immediately. We excluded those that originally came on student visas and investment immigrants who do not immediately enter the labour force.

Participants averaged 35 years of age at immigration, most with BA degrees or higher. Two-thirds have careers in engineering, medicine, accountancy, and computer science. Men, somewhat better educated, were concentrated in engineering and computer fields. Women were also well-trained and working in careers in accounting, computers, engineering, humanities, and medicine.

In China, these parents had only a single child, as dictated to the urban elite, and had a second child while living outside China. Over half the parents, with children 10 and under, have to find childcare in order to work.

We interviewed couples in their native language. In the first three-hour session, we gathered material on the husband's and wife's work, family histories, other personal experiences, and their social networks. Follow-up interviews and phone calls brought us up-to-date on these topics. We translated the taped interviews and analyzed them for themes, using N-Vivo, a qualitative software package. The text draws on our latest information for the respondents, unless otherwise noted. We maintained contact with nearly all respondents through December 2002 and continued to correspond with many through December 2003. In this paper, we quote directly from their comments, giving them pseudonyms and adding their gender in brackets after the comments.

Work–Family Roles in China and Canada

SOCIAL SUPPORT FOR WORK–FAMILY ROLES IN CHINA

These parents met their range of childcare needs through complex patterns of family obligations and institutional care in China. If their elders are available, the young couples initially turn to them. Seventy-one per cent of the couples received substantial childcare help from their seniors. Grandparents might take over the entire childcare burden to help their children build their professional careers. It was a recognized career advancement if their child stayed behind with its grandparents.

Getting help for further study

The help received went well beyond occasional babysitting. Although they finished their basic training before marriage, several returned to school for postgraduate studies. Wives' increased dual burden brought several family members into play.

Cheng Li (M) was a metallurgical engineer whose parents were retired teachers. First an engineer in a large public metal works, he transferred to a trading firm in charge of technical products. When the firm went downhill, Cheng Li returned to school for an MSc in another city. Throughout, his wife, Xing Ying, who worked as an administrative assistant, remained in her in-law's home to get help with family. Her own mother, a retired factory worker, was ill and could not care for grandchildren. Xing Ying explained: 'We could have gotten our own flat if we wanted (from the enterprise). But how could I take care of my baby on my own? I needed the help of my mother-in-law.' Xing Ying's mother-in-law continued to care for the little girl in China for two years after the couple moved to Canada. With her burden reduced, Xing Ying became a student and reoriented her career.

Studying abroad created even more demands on their kin. When his son was four-years-old, Chen Hung (M) won a coveted job in the Office of the Japanese architecture branch where he worked. His wife Ying Ying visited for a year, leaving their son in Beijing. Unable to find work in Tokyo, she returned to Beijing. A year later, she went to Holland to take an MSc in Computer Sciences.

The whole family reunited in Toronto several years later. Throughout the couple's overseas sojourns, Chen Hung's mother cared for her grandson.

Some co-ordinated their housing, further studies, and child bearing plans in an all-round support system. Liuma (F), a doctor married to Zhu Ji, an electrical engineer, lived with Liuma's parents after marriage, until Liuma's father, a plant director, arranged a nearby apartment for them. When Liuma had a son, she moved back to her parents' home, hired a babysitter, and her mother also helped after work. Liuma's family continued their help for a year after the couple immigrated to Canada and could get on their feet. She recalled, 'I never felt the burden of raising a child!'

Multiplexity

Our couples could rarely designate one grandparent to take responsibility throughout the child's early years. Grandmothers have their own life course and it was not always possible to meet patrilineal goals. As a result, most combined helpers from either side, or both, at different times. The main caregiver was usually a grandparent, the second a grandparent on the other side, or a servant. Arrangements were flexible. If they sent their child to nursery school, they might use fewer helpers. If they delayed school until kindergarten, they drew on more helpers. Of the 32 parents that gave help to their grandchildren, two-thirds were the wife's parents.

For example, QuPing (F), with a BA in social science, and her husband, Hu, a computer scientist, grew up in Beijing, and got good private firm jobs in Shenzhen. After their son was born, Hu's mother came to care for the baby. At the same time, she brought her youngest son, a recent graduate, to look for a job in Shenzhen with Hu's help. When QuPing's son was two and a half years old, he was sent to Beijing, where QuPing thought schools were better, and lived with QuPing's parents. But the boy could not adjust to the nursery school routine and returned to Shenzhen. QuPing took care of him, sent him to school in the morning, and fetched him after work. Servants were hard to find, and QuPing was afraid of bringing a stranger into her home. The many services available made it easy for QuPing to handle her household responsibilities after her child returned from school. 'There wasn't so much household work to do, so I could handle it. When we returned home late, we could easily find a place to grab a bite.'

CARING FOR THEIR OWN CHILDREN

Nine per cent of our couples, primarily those with no elders available, took primary responsibility for their child. The amount of time they spent on the job was central to how they combined work and family roles. When both spouses held state sector posts, they often had a more relaxed schedule. In contrast, professional mothers who worked long hours could not squeeze in much childcare. Conditions in the private sector were especially demanding.

For instance, Hung's (F) son was born during her light teaching stint in a Communist Party College, and flexible job freed her to care for her child for a year. When her son turned two, Hung's mother had retired from her factory job and helped look after her grandson. When, by the third year, he was old enough for nursery school, Hung and her husband shared responsibility for dropping him off and picking him up.

Many private sector and some state jobs required long hours or travel. Xu Fang (F) and her husband helped manage a branch of Xu Fang's family's private paint products firm. She '. . . didn't have Saturday or Sunday free, every day was busy.' She hired two people to take care of him.

SCALING BACK

With overall responsibility for their children, despite the help of others, many women altered their professional goals. Some wives deliberately slowed their careers, taking jobs that did not demand long hours and travel or transferred to more flexible jobs to care for their children. Reluctant to leave the stable state sector, fewer

moved over to private sector jobs. For instance, a couple, both engineers, grew up in large peasant households and met when both were assigned to the same factory in Beijing, far from their families. The wife recalled,

> Both of us needed to work and no one helped us to take care of our child, so I shifted to teach in a secondary technical school. Because there were winter and summer holidays, it was more convenient for me to look after a child. I didn't totally give up my major, but used it just in a supplementary way.

Education was another example; many had further training after they had married, including all the PhDs (four men, one woman). While their husbands returned to school, wives maintained the family, enabling their husbands to have both a family and career. Nevertheless, wives still continued their careers.

Wives quit their formal employment entirely and cared for their children in only three cases. However, working from home, they continued to use their professional skills in the private market. For instance, one woman quit her engineering job when one of her twin sons fell and broke his arm. She traded stocks from home, while caring for her toddlers.

INSTITUTIONAL CARE

A minority of our respondents that used state daycare facilities for very young infants and toddlers did so when there were no kin available.

School was often strict, instilling moral training, and requiring much independence. Parents wanted their children to have intimacy and personal care. Moreover, they did not want to deny the older generation the chance to care for a grandchild. Hence, most placed their children in formal childcare institutions only after they were three or older.

Few women were on their own while caring for their children. The majority drew on their social capital. They expected to work, and their kin expected to help them work as a boost to the family earnings and future. Most got help from their personal relations or others connected through them. Past that, they could draw on the state-run crèches for childcare. By supplementing kin support with their own work and scaling back on their demanding jobs, they carried work and family responsibilities first sequentially, then simultaneously.

Social Support for Work–Family Roles in Canada

From positions of relative gender equality, where they were embedded in structures that backed their careers and family roles, wives have trouble gaining professional acknowledgment abroad. They have to get Canadian professional certification, which in several cases entails doing most of the education they have over again. They also bear much of the family responsibilities. No longer in a sequential stage as in China, if they have young children to care for, they have heavy simultaneous roles. Although their kin relations are far away, building supportive social networks for their reproductive roles is central to their career edifice, and it is their double burden.

THEIR EXPERIENCES AS NEW IMMIGRANTS IN CANADA

Foreign earned credentials are rarely recognized by Canadian organizations. Few immigrants locate well-paying jobs, and most revise their career goals (Spitze, 1984; Basran and Zong, 1998; Salaff, Greve, and Xu, 2002). Eighty-four of our 100 respondents have experienced downward mobility compared to their position in China.

With their professional credentials and experiences unrecognized, they need to retrain. Their choice is dyadic, both parents' skills need upgrading, both are responsible for their child and need to combine their household resources. Couples decide whether both should try to break into the labour force at the same time,

each carrying simultaneous roles, caring for their children, working, and retraining. Or should they negotiate a sequential life course—going to school full-time, finding alternative care for their child, and then getting a suitable job?

By engaging in sequential roles in turn, one spouse works full-time, even at a minimum wage job, to support the family while the other returns to school to upgrade the credentials needed to adapt to the local labour market. They then switch. When the wife's English proficiency is better than her husband's and the job she seeks does not need long-term re-accreditation, she may be the first to try. If her English is worse and she has trouble fitting her technical and professional job experiences into the acceptable Canadian jobs for women, she waits. Most working parents compromise by scaling back, reducing their goals, changing jobs slowly, finding help where they can, and building new relationships in Canada—turning acquaintances into multiplex relations (Hochschild, 1990).

Most commonly, the wife's career is placed second. Without a way to care for a child, longer to go to upgrade her degree, wives are more likely to work at low-paying jobs. They shape their job search around their responsibilities to the home and hence their child's age figures in couples' plans. To suit their family roles, those with young children take short-term, English as a Second Language (ESL) courses (a non-degree program) while their children are at school. Short-term accounting courses improve their skills and get them entry-level jobs. By going to school part-time, women combine homemaking, reproductive labour, and job preparation.

Lian (F), a former accountant, weaves her ESL study with her son's primary school hours:

> How many hours do I study at school? Every-day I send my son to school at 8:30, then I go to my school from 9:15 AM till 2:45 PM. When I get home, I study 10–20 minutes, then I go to pick up my son.

DEVELOPING NEW SUPPORTS

Those with young children share their childcare responsibilities with kin, friends, and neighbours. Migration has not severed their family relations (Boyd, 1989), and kin are the most important support for those that are upgrading their skills. Just under half had children who were born since 1993 (and are under age 10 at time of writing). Of these, 63 per cent receive care for their children from kin, a proportion close to that in China. The child's grandparents immigrate or apply for shorter-term visitors' visas to help. Parents send infants and toddlers back to China to be reared by their grandparents. Parents plan for the children to remain in China for the two years they need to take courses to re-certify in professional fields, fetching the youngster back in time to enroll in primary school in Toronto.

Immigrant mothers also mobilize friends for backup care. Former colleagues have an established base for trust. They meet others, in their course of every day life, who are embedded in similar networks and share a common background, which conveys cultural similarity. These form the new multiplex networks.

Wei Yang (F) has her new roommate as backup support for her 10-year-old daughter. Although in China she was a major in Chinese literature and is a former Vice-Principal of a high school, Wei Yang cannot get a similar job in Canada. Her husband is an 'astronaut' who manages his computer sales business in Beijing. He visits several times a year, leaving childcare entirely to the wife. A virtual sole parent, Wei Yang is reluctant to return to school or take a demanding full-time job. She first tutored her daughter and other youngsters part-time in Chinese, as a service to the Chinese community. She next sold products part-time in a multilevel marketing position. Wei Yang finally found full-time work at a Chinese job agency, as a receptionist. Her daughter, now accustomed to Toronto, walks to the nearby primary school on her own. Wei Yang's family sublets a room of a 2-bedroom high-rise flat from another Chinese immigrant woman, with a daughter of the same age. Her roommate watches out for Wei Yang's child after school. Unlikely to regain a supervisory position at the level she had left in China, Wei Yang works with what is available in a Chinese environment, turning to sales and service work in the Chinese community. She finds social capital from her Chinese roommate: at age 10, her child does not need a lot of care, and her roommate helps out when needed.

Ying Ying (F) took up an invitation to live temporarily at a friend's that turned into a longer-term responsibility.

> Our first summer in Toronto, my husband's friend—whose wife was still in China—invited us to stay at their place (we had just arrived and had no place to live). After a few days, their son got chicken pox. My son got it, too. So the whole summer I was busy taking care of the two boys.

Although it is part of their social capital, they cannot turn to friends for the even longer-term support needed to return to school to re-qualify for professional positions. In this manner, neighbours stand in for each other and become social capital. Many negotiate exchanges with neighbours for routine help, such as when women with a neighbour with the same aged toddler share childcare. Neighbours are also likely to give emergency help. But there are limits to what friends and neighbours can and are willing to do on a long-term basis.

CHILDREN'S ROLES

Children play a role in the family restructuring as well. Some parents send their child to be cared for by its grandparents. Others give up the hope for a professional job for reinvented motherhood. In the end, their children grow up quickly and help the parents.

No longer part of an on-site three-generational household, without additional family help, mothers bear considerable household burdens

(Clarkberg and Moen, 2001). Parents demand a lot from their children, justifying coming abroad as a benefit for the youngsters. Their children take on an immigration burden, becoming independent, working hard, and assuming the reason for having left China. Children care for themselves and the family more than they had done in China. Teenagers get their first part-time jobs and they help out in the family business. They study hard; several parents proudly informed us that their child had gotten into the gifted primary school program. Older children were accepted into universities with scholarships.

A few examples show how children manage on their own. Wei Yang's (F) younger daughter goes to the neighbourhood school on her own. Ying Ying's (F) teenage son makes his own lunch in the microwave. On his summer holiday from his computer engineering studies, Jiang Jing's (M) son works in a factory and fills in the family store in the evenings.

> Q: You work at the same shift as your husband, so what about your daughter?
>
> Lei Min (F; with demonstrable pride): We prepare dinner for her and bring our dinner to work. She can take care of herself. She's very independent. My husband said he didn't shed a sad tear over the hard life here, but when I told him that she got second in her class during the first semester although her English was still not so good, his happy tears mixed with the sweat of his labouring job.

When Lei Min opened a hostel for new immigrants in her home, her 14-year-old daughter spent the summer greeting guests.

INTENSIFYING FAMILY ROLES

Some women find new family roles. In contrast to China, where bearing a second child was politically damaging for those with high standing,

in Canada, two children are 'natural'. Six of the couples had a second child in Canada. Nearly all with a second child had first borne a daughter.

Hen Rong (F), a former accountant in China, became a textile labourer in Toronto. Becoming pregnant, her kin and friends pressured the couple to give birth to the second child. 'This is your last chance,' her mother admonished her pregnant daughter. Her mother had cared for the couple's eldest daughter, and the couple sponsored her to immigrate. The older woman beamed as she toted the baby boy around.

A former pharmacist, now a sales clerk, justified her second pregnancy by what she saw around her, she said, 'We see Canadians around us having a child, and so decided it was natural.' Unable to resume her profession, she finds a new role in intensified motherhood. Her church members celebrated the pregnancy with showers and gifts.

The second child not only meets a long cherished value of bearing a son for the family. The newborn turns an aborted career, with a confusing prognosis, into the respected career of motherhood. None of the new mothers re-established their careers. Without childcare support in the new location, gender roles may become entrenched (Willis and Yeoh, 2000; Lee, Chan, Bradby, and Green, 2002).

Discussion

Transnational migration affects women and men in gender-specific ways and places a heavier load of responsibility on women's shoulders. This occurs both in the home and in the host countries, but migration makes this integration work difficult. Women assume more work because they undertake the meshing of work and family systems. Taken-for-granted work institutions, retirement schemes, and formal and informal childcare are rarely well integrated. When they do not easily come together, women's personal actions make these arrangements run in an expected manner. Women must organize support that requires creative reorganization of their social capital, under the new conditions.

Because work and family institutions are organized differently in every country, when catapulted into the new social system, new immigrants' experiences conflict in timing of work and family life courses. In China, professionals completed training before bearing and rearing children, following the sequential life course model. Most drew on multiplex ties to make work–family obligations function while they built their careers. They also obtained public institutional support for childcare, thus lessening the many activities they had to do simultaneously.

Arriving as professionals in Canada, where their qualifications are not recognized, with small children to care for and a household to run, they have heavy burdens. They must both re-qualify and mobilize support for their family roles at the same time. The formal and informal institutions, and personally constructed arrangements that provide childcare support, differ from those in China. When the social arrangements in Canada do not match their needs, women either leave the labour force or call on previous agreements, turning to their multiplex arrangements. They may bring their parents to Canada or send their children to China. For many, social capital is transnational.

Transnational motherhood is not limited to the working-class poor but also is known by middle-class, highly educated Chinese. Professional, career-oriented Chinese immigrants command a future promise of good resources and earnings for their wider families if they get support. They bring their mothers and mothers-in-law or send their children back to China. For some women, this support lets them reconstitute their careers. Others suffer considerable downward professional mobility. Transnational social capital facilitates but does not guarantee a rejuvenated career.

Work–family role conflicts are public issues needing institutional solutions, but few countries define them this way (Mills, 1957; Folbre, 2001). Societies rarely acknowledge the informal work that people do to mesh institutional structures. People draw on personal relations to resolve inconsistent demands. The plight of international migrants outlines the problems encountered in using personal solutions to meet public issues.

Note

1. We acknowledge gratefully the support of the 'migration from China' project by The Social Sciences and Humanities Council of Canada. Several centres provided generous homes for our research team. The Centre for Urban and Community Studies, University of Toronto, The Centre for Asian Studies, The University of Hong Kong provided us with helpful support. We wish to thank Stephanie Tang and staff of the CICS for their unstinting help, the many people who generously shared their views and experiences with us. Lynn Xu, Su Zhang, Yan Liu, Ada Choi, Tracy Kennedy, He Huang, and Heather Jiang supplied talented research assistance for this paper. Eleonore Kofinan, Evie Tastsoglou, and an anonymous reader for Women's Studies International Forum gave helpful suggestions.

References

Basran, G.S., and L. Zong. 1998. 'Devaluation of Foreign Credentials as Perceived by Visible Minority Professional Immigrants', *Canadian Ethnic Studies* 30, 3: 7–23.

Bian, Y. 1994. *Work and Inequality in Urban China*. New York: SUNY Press.

Boyd, M. 1989. 'Family and Personal Networks in International Migration: Recent Developments and New Agendas', *International Migration Review* 23: 638–70.

Buchmann, M., and M. Charles. 1995. 'Organizational and Institutional in the Process of Gender

Stratification: Comparing Social Arrangements in Six European Countries', *International Journal of Sociology* 25: 66–95.

Burt, R.S. 1992. *Structural Holes*. Cambridge, MA: Harvard University Press.

Castells, M. 1989. *The Informational City*. Oxford, UK: Blackwell.

Chen, F., S.E. Short, and B. Entwisle. 2000. 'The Impact of Grandparental Proximity on Maternal Childcare in China', *Population Research and Policy Review* 19: 571–90.

Clarkberg, M., and P. Moen. 2001. 'Understanding the Time-squeeze: Married Couples' Preferred and Actual Work-hour Strategies', *American Behavioral Scientist* 44: 1115–136.

Croll, E., P. Kane, and D. Davin, eds. 1985. *Chinas One Child Family Policy*. London: Macmillan.

Davis, D. 1993. 'Financial Security of Urban Retirees', *Journal of Cross-cultural Gerontology* 8: 179–95.

Delechat, C. 2001. 'International Migration Dynamics: The Role of Experience and Social Networks', *Labour* 15: 457–86.

Doherty, G., R. Rose, M. Friendly, D. Lero, and S. Hope. 1995. *Childcare: Canada Can't Work Without It*. Toronto: Irwin.

Folbre, N. 2001. *The Invisible Heart: Economics and Family Values*. New York: The New Press.

Gerson, K. 1985. *Hard Choices: How Women Decide about Work, Career, and Motherhood*. Berkeley, CA: University of California Press.

Giele, J.Z. 1998. 'Innovation in the Typical Life Course', in G.H. Elder and J. Giele, eds, *Methods of Life Course Research: Qualitative and Quantitative Approaches*, pp. 231–63. Thousand Oaks, CA: Sage Publications.

Ginzberg, E. 1967. *Life Styles of Educated Women*. New York: Columbia University Press.

Gold, S.J. 2001. 'Gender, Class, and Network: Social Structure and Migration Patterns among Transnational Israelis', *Global Networks* 1: 57–78

Heinz, W.R., H.Kruger, and A. Verma, eds. 2001. *Restructuring Work and the Life Course*. Toronto: University of Toronto Press.

Hochschild, A.R. 1990. *The Second Shift*. New York: Avon.

Hondagneu-Sotelo, P., and E. Avila. 1997. '"I'm here, but I'm there": The Meanings of Latina Transnational Motherhood', *Gender and Society* 2: 548–71.

Jones, C.L., L. Marsden, and L. Tepperman. 1990. *Lives of Their Own: The Individualization of Women's Lives*. Don Mills, ON: Oxford University Press.

Lee, M., A. Chan, H. Bradby, and G. Green. 2002. 'Chinese Migrant Women and Families in Britain', *Women's Studies International Forum* 25: 607–18.

Levitt, P., and N.G. Schiller. 2003. *Transnational Perspectives on Migration: Conceptualizing Simultaneity*. CMD Working Paper #03-09j. The Center for Migration and Migration and Development Working Paper Series. Princeton, NJ: Princeton University.

Liang, Z. 2001. 'Demography of Illicit Migration from China: A Sending Country's Perspective', *Sociological Forum* 16: 677–701.

Lin, N., W.M. Ensel, and J.C. Vaughn. 1981. 'Social Resources and the Strength of Weak Ties: Structural Factors in Occupational Status Attainment', *American Sociological Review* 46: 393–405.

Man, G. 2002. 'Globalization and the Erosion of the Welfare State: Effects on Chinese Immigrant Women', *Canadian Woman Studies* 21/22, 4/1: 26–32.

Meng, X., and M.P. Kidd. 1997. 'Labor Market Reform and the Changing Structure of Wage Determination in China's State Sector during the 1980s', *Journal of Comparative Economics* 25: 403–21.

Mills, C.W. 1957. *The Sociological Imagination*. New York: Oxford University Press.

Min, P.G. 1988. *Ethnic Business Enterprise: Korean Small Business in Atlanta*. New York: Center for Migration Studies.

Moen, P., and F.M. Firebaugh. 1994. 'Family Policies and Effective Families: A Life Course Perspective', *The International Journal of Sociology and Social Policy* 14: 29–52.

Moen, P., and Y. Yu. 1999. 'Having it All: Overall Work/Life Success in Two-earner Families', *Research in the Sociology of Work* 7: 109–39.

Nee, V., and R. Matthews. 1996. 'Market Transition and Societal Transformation in Reforming State Socialism', *Annual Review of Sociology* 22: 401–35.

Ngo, H. 2000. 'Trends in Occupational Sex Segregation in Urban China'. Paper delivered at the annual meeting of the NACSA, Washington, DC.

Parrenas, R.S. 2001. 'Mothering From a Distance:

Emotions, Gender, and Inter-generational Relations in Filipino Transnational Families', *Feminist Studies* 27: 361–90.

Partridge, M. In press. *Managing the Struggle: Career Strategies of University-educated Women*. Toronto: University of Toronto Press.

Poros, M.V. 2001. 'The Role of Migrant Networks in Linking Local Labour Markets: The Case of Asian Indian Migration to New York and London', *Global Networks* 1: 243–59.

Portes, A., and J. Borocz. 1989. 'Contemporary Immigration: Theoretical Perspectives on Its Determinants and Modes of Incorporation', *International Migration Review* 23: 606–30.

Preston, V., and G. Man. 1999. 'Employment Experiences of Chinese Immigrant Women: An Exploration of Diversity', *Canadian Woman Studies* 19, 3: 115–22.

Robinson, J.C. 1985. 'Of Women and Washing Machines: Employment, Housework, and the Reproduction of Motherhood in Socialist China', *The China Quarterly* 101: 32–57.

Salaff, J.W., A. Greve, and L. Xu. 2002. 'Paths Into the Economy: Structural Barriers and the Job Hunt for Professional PRC Migrants in Canada', *International Journal of Human Resource Management* 13: 450–64.

Sassen, S. 1991. *The Global City: New York, London, and Tokyo*. Princeton, NJ: Princeton University Press.

Spitze, G. 1984. 'The Effect of Family Migration on Wives' Employment: How Long Does it Last?', *Social Science Quarterly* 46: 21–36.

Statistics Canada. 2001. *Facts and Figures: Immigration Overview 2001*. Available at http://www.cic.gc.ca./english/pdf/pub/facts2001.pdf (accessed 22 September 2002).

Vanier Institute of the Family. 2000. *Profiling Canada's Families: II*. Ottawa. Available at http://www.vifamily.calpubs/p2.htm (accessed 22 September 2002).

Walder, A.G. 1986. *Communist Neo-traditionalism: Work and Authority in Chinese Industry*. Berkeley, CA: University of California Press.

Whyte, M.K., and W.L. Parish. 1984. *Urban Life in Contemporary China*. Chicago: University of Chicago Press.

Willis, K., and B. Yeoh. 2000. 'Gender and Transnational Household Strategies: Singaporean Migration to China', *Regional Studies* 34: 253–64.

Yang, H. 1996. 'The Distributive Norm of Monetary Support to Older Parents: A Look at a Township in China', *Journal of Marriage and the Family* 58: 404–14.

Zhan, H.J., and R.J.V. Montgomery. 2003. 'Gender and Elder Care in China: The Influence of Filial Piety and Structural Constraints', *Gender and Society* 17: 209–29.

CHAPTER 17

Household Labour and the Routine Production of Gender

Scott Coltrane

Motherhood is often perceived as the quintessence of womanhood. The everyday tasks of mothering are taken to be 'natural' expressions of femininity, and the routine care of home and children is seen to provide opportunities for women to express and reaffirm their gendered relation to men and to the world. The traditional tasks of fatherhood, in contrast, are limited to begetting, protecting, and providing for children. While fathers typically derive a gendered sense of self from these activities, their masculinity is even more dependent on *not* doing the things that mothers do. What happens, then, when fathers share with mothers those tasks that we define as expressing the true nature of womanhood?

This chapter describes how a sample of 20 dual-earner couples talk about sharing housework and childcare. Since marriage is one of the least scripted or most undefined interaction situations, the marital conversation is particularly important to a couple's shared sense of reality. I investigate these parents' construction of gender by examining their talk about negotiations over who does what around the house; how these divisions of labour influence their perceptions of self and other; how they conceive of gender-appropriate behaviour; and how they handle inconsistencies between their own views and those of the people around them. Drawing on the parents' accounts of the planning, allocation, and performance of childcare and housework, I illustrate how gender is produced through everyday practices and how adults are socialized by routine activity.

Gender as an Accomplishment

Candace West and Don Zimmerman (1987) suggest that gender is a routine, methodical, and recurring accomplishment. 'Doing gender' involves a complex of socially guided perceptual, interactional, and micropolitical activities that cast particular pursuits as expressions of masculine and feminine 'natures'. Rather than viewing gender as a property of individuals, West and Zimmerman conceive of it as an emergent feature of social situations that results from and legitimates gender inequality. Similarly, Sarah Fenstermaker Berk (1985: 204, emphasis in original) suggests that housework and child care

> can become the occasion for producing commodities (e.g., clean children, clean laundry, and new light switches) and a reaffirmation of

one's *gendered* relation to the work and to the world. In short, the 'shoulds' of gender ideals are fused with the 'musts' of efficient household production. The result may be something resembling a 'gendered' household-production function.

If appropriately doing gender serves to sustain and legitimate existing gender relations, would inappropriate gender activity challenge that legitimacy? Or, as West and Zimmerman (1987: 146) suggest, when people fail to do gender appropriately, are their individual characters, motives, and predispositions called into question? If doing gender is unavoidable and people are held accountable for its production, how might people initiate and sustain atypical gender behaviours?

By investigating how couples share childcare and housework, I explore (1) the sorts of dyadic and group interactions that facilitate the sharing of household labour; (2) how couples describe the requirements of parenting and how they evaluate men's developing capacities for nurturing; and (3) the impact of sharing domestic labour on conceptions of gender.

The Sample

To find couples who shared childcare, I initially contacted schools and day care centres in several suburban California communities. Using snowball-sampling techniques, I selected 20 moderate- to middle-income dual-earner couples with children. To compensate for gaps in the existing literature and to enhance comparisons between sample families, I included couples if they were the biological parents of at least two school-aged children, they were both employed at least half-time, and both identified the father as assuming significant responsibility for routine childcare. I observed families in their homes and interviewed fathers and mothers separately at least once and as many as five times. I recorded the interviews and transcribed them for coding and constant comparative analysis.

The parents were primarily in their late thirties and had been living together for an average of ten years. All wives and 17 of 20 husbands attended some college and most couples married later and had children later than others in their birth cohort. The median age at marriage for the mothers was 23; for fathers, 26. Median age at first birth for mothers was 27; for fathers, 30. Fifteen of 20 fathers were at least one year older than their wives. Median gross annual income was $40,000, with three families under $25,000 and three over $65,000. Sixteen of the couples had two children and four had three children. Over two-thirds of the families had both sons and daughters, but four families had two sons and no daughters, and two families had two daughters and no sons. The children's ages ranged from four to fourteen, with 80 per cent between the ages of five and eleven and with a median age of seven.

Mothers were more likely than fathers to hold professional or technical jobs, although most were employed in female-dominated occupations with relatively limited upward mobility and moderate pay. Over three-quarters held jobs in the 'helping' professions: seven mothers were nurses, five were teachers, and four were social workers or counselors. Other occupations for the mothers were administrator, laboratory technician, filmmaker, and bookbinder. Sample fathers held both blue-collar and white collar jobs, with concentrations in construction (3), maintenance (2), sales (3), business (3), teaching (3), delivery (4), and computers (2). Like most dual-earner wives, sample mothers earned, on average, less than half of what their husband's did, and worked an average of eight fewer hours per week. Eleven mothers (55 per cent), but only five fathers (25 per cent) were employed less than 40 hours per week. In nine of 20 families, mothers were employed at least as many hours as fathers, but in only four families did the mother's earnings approach or exceed those of her husband.

Developing Shared Parenting

Two-thirds of the parents indicated that current divisions of labour were accomplished by making minor practical adjustments to what they perceived as an already fairly equal division of labour. A common sentiment was expressed by one father who commented:

> Since we've both always been working since we've been married, we've typically shared everything as far as all the working—I mean all the housework responsibilities as well as child care responsibilities. So it's a pattern that was set up before the kids were even thought of.

Nevertheless, a full three-quarters of the couples reported that the mother performed much more of the early infant care. All of the mothers and only about half of the fathers reported that they initially reduced their hours of employment after having children. About a third of the fathers said they increased their employment hours to compensate for the loss of income that resulted from their wives taking time off work before or after the births of their children.

In talking about becoming parents, most of the fathers stressed the importance of their involvement in conception decisions, the birth process, and early infant care to later assumption of child-care duties. Most couples planned the births of their children jointly and intentionally. Eighty per cent reported that they mutually decided to have children, with two couples reporting that the wife desired children more than the husband and two reporting that the husband was more eager than the wife to become a parent. For many families, the husband's commitment to participate fully in childrearing was a precondition of the birth decision. One mother described how she and her husband decided to have children.

> Shared parenting was sort of part of the decision. When we decided to have children,

we realized that we were both going to be involved with our work, so it was part of the plan from the very beginning. As a matter of fact, I thought that we only could have the one and he convinced me that we could handle two and promised to really help (laughs), which he really has, but two children is a lot more work than you realize (laughs).

By promising to assume partial responsibility for childrearing, most husbands influenced their wives' initial decision to have children, the subsequent decision to have another child, and the decision of whether and when to return to work. Almost all of the mothers indicated that they had always assumed that they would have children, and most also assumed that they would return to paid employment before the children were in school. Half of the mothers did return to work within six months of the birth of their first child.

All but one of the fathers were present at the births of their children and most talked about the importance of the birth experience, using terms like 'incredible', 'magical', 'moving', 'wonderful', and 'exciting'. While most claimed that they played an important part in the birth process by providing emotional support to their wives or acting as labour coaches, a few considered their involvement to be inconsequential. Comments included, 'I felt a little bit necessary and a lot unnecessary,' and 'I didn't bug her too much and I might have helped a little.' Three quarters of the fathers reported that they were 'very involved' with their newborns, even though the mother provided most of the daily care for the first few months. Over two-thirds of the mothers breastfed their infants. Half of the fathers reported that they got up in the night to soothe their babies, and many described their early infant care experience in terms that mothers typically use to describe 'bonding' with newborns. The intensity of father–infant interaction was discussed by fathers as enabling them to experience a new and different level of intimacy and was depicted as 'deep emotional trust', 'very

interior', 'drawing me in', and 'making it difficult to deal with the outside world'.

About half of the fathers referred to the experience of being involved in the delivery and in early infant care as a necessary part of their assuming responsibility for later childcare. Many described a process in which the actual performance of care-taking duties provided them with the self-confidence and skills to feel that they knew what they were doing. They described their time alone with the baby as especially helpful in building their sense of competence as a shared primary caretaker. One man said,

> I felt I needed to start from the beginning. Then I learned how to walk them at night and not be totally p.o.'ed at them and not feel that it was an infringement. It was something I *got* to do in some sense, along with changing diapers and all these things. It was certainly not repulsive and in some ways I really liked it a lot. It was not something innate, it was something to be learned. I managed to start at the beginning. If you *don't* start at the beginning then you're sort of left behind.

This father, like almost all of the others, talked about having to learn how to nurture and care for his children. He also stressed how important it was to 'start at the beginning'. While all fathers intentionally shared routine childcare as the children approached school age, only half of the fathers attempted to assume a major share of daily infant care, and only five couples described the father as an equal caregiver for children under one year old. These early caregiving fathers described their involvement in infant care as explicitly planned:

> She nursed both of them completely, for at least five or six months. So, my role was—we agreed on this—my role was the other direct intervention, like changing, and getting them up and walking them, and putting them back to sleep. For instance, she would nurse them

but I would bring them to the bed afterward and change them if necessary, and get them back to sleep. . . . I really initiated those other kinds of care aspects so that I could be involved. I continued that on through infant and toddler and preschool classes that we would go to, even though I would usually be the only father there.

This man's wife offered a similar account, commenting that 'except for breast-feeding, he always provided the same things that I did—the emotional closeness and the attention.'

Another early caregiving father described how he and his wife 'very consciously' attempted to equalize the amount of time they spent with their children when they were infants: 'In both cases we very consciously made the decision that we wanted it to be a mutual process, so that from the start we shared, and all I didn't do was breast-feed. And I really would say that was the only distinction.' His wife also described their infant care arrangements as 'equal', and commented that other people did not comprehend the extent of his participation:

I think that nobody really understood that Jennifer had two mothers. The burden of proof was always on me that he was literally being a mother. He wasn't nursing, but he was getting up in the night to bring her to me, to change her poop, which is a lot more energy than nursing in the middle of the night. You have to get up and do all that, I mean get awake. So his sleep was interrupted, and yet within a week or two, at his work situation, it was expected that he was back to normal, and he never went back to normal. He was part of the same family that I was.

This was the only couple who talked about instituting, for a limited time, an explicit record-keeping system to ensure that they shared child care equally.

[Father]: We were committed to the principle of sharing and we would have schedules, keep hours, so that we had a pretty good sense that we were even, both in terms of the commitment to the principle as well as we wanted to in fact be equal. We would keep records in a log—one might say in a real compulsive way—so that we knew what had happened when the other person was on.

[Mother]: When the second one came we tried to keep to the log of hours and very quickly we threw it out completely. It was too complex.

Practicality and Flexibility

Both early- and later-sharing families identified practical considerations and flexibility as keys to equitable divisions of household labour. Most did not have explicit records or schedules for childcare or housework. For example, one early-involved father reported that practical divisions of labour evolved 'naturally':

Whoever cooks doesn't have to do the dishes. If for some reason she cooks and I don't do the dishes, she'll say something about it, certainly. Even though we never explicitly agreed that's how we do it, that's how we do it. The person who doesn't cook does the dishes. We don't even know who's going to cook a lot of the time. We just get it that we can do it. We act in good faith.

Couples who did not begin sharing routine childcare until after infancy were even more likely to describe their division of labour as practical solutions to shortages of time. For example, one mother described sharing household tasks as 'the only logical thing to do', and her husband said, 'It's the only practical way we could do it.' Other fathers describe practical and flexible arrangements based on the constraints of employment scheduling:

Her work schedule is more demanding and takes up a lot of evening time, so I think I do a lot of the every day routines, and she does a lot of the less frequent things. Like I might do more of the cooking and meal preparation, but she is the one that does the grocery shopping. An awful lot of what gets done gets done because the person is home first. That's been our standing rule for who fixes dinner. Typically, I get home before she does so I fix dinner, but that isn't a fixed rule. She gets home first, then she fixes dinner. Making the beds and doing the laundry just falls on me because I've got more time during the day to do it. And the yardwork and cuttin' all the wood, I do that. And so I'm endin' up doin' more around here than her just because I think I've got more time.

While mothers were more likely than fathers to report that talk was an important part of sharing household labour, most couples reported that they spent little time planning or arguing about who was going to do what around the house. Typical procedures for allocating domestic chores were described as 'ad hoc,' illustrated by one mother's discussion of cooking:

> Things with us have happened pretty easily as far as what gets done by who. It happened without having to have a schedule or deciding—you know—like cooking. We never decided that he would do all the cooking; it just kind of ended up that way. Every once in a while when he doesn't feel like cooking he'll say, 'Would you cook tonight?' 'Sure, fine.' But normally I don't offer to cook. I say, 'What are we having for dinner?'

In general, divisions of labour in sample families were described as flexible and changing. One mother talked about how routine adjustments in task allocation were satisfying to her: 'Once you're comfortable in your roles and division of tasks for a few months then it seems like the needs change a little bit and you have to change a little bit and you have to regroup. That's what keeps it interesting. I think that's why it's satisfying.'

Underlying Ideology

While ad hoc divisions of labour were described as being practical solutions to time shortages, there were two major ideological underpinnings to the sharing of housework and childcare: child-centeredness and equity ideals. While those who attempted to share infant care tended to have more elaborate vocabularies for talking about these issues, later sharing couples also referred to them. For instance, all couples provided accounts that focused on the sanctity of childhood and most stressed the impossibility of mothers 'doing it all'.

Couples were child-centered in that they placed a high value on their children's well-being, defined parenting as an important and serious undertaking, and organized most of their non-employed hours around their children. For instance, one father described how his social life revolved around his children:

> Basically if the other people don't have kids and if they aren't involved with the kids, then we aren't involved with them. It's as simple as that. The guys I know at work that are single or don't have children my age don't come over because then we have nothing in common. They're kind of the central driving force in my life.

While about half of the couples (11 of 20) had paid for ongoing out-of-home childcare, and three-quarters had regularly used some form of paid childcare, most of the parents said that they spent more time with their children than the other dual-earner parents in their neighbourhoods. One father commented that he and his wife had structured their lives around personally taking care of their children:

An awful lot of the way we've structured our lives has been based around our reluctance to have someone else raise our children. We just really didn't want the kids to be raised from 7:30 in the morning 'till 4:30 or 5:00 in the afternoon by somebody else. So we've structured the last ten years around that issue.

Many parents also advocated treating children as inexperienced equals or 'little people', rather than as inferior beings in need of authoritarian training. For example, an ex-military father employed in computer research stated, 'We don't discipline much. Generally the way it works is kind of like bargaining. They know that there are consequences to whatever actions they take, and we try and make sure they know what the consequences are before they have a chance to take the action.' Another father described his moral stance concerning children's rights:

> I'm not assuming—when I'm talking about parent–child stuff—that there's an inequality. Yes, there are a lot of differences in terms of time spent in this world, but our assumption has been, with both children, that we're peers. And so that's how we are with them. So, if they say something and they're holding fast to some position, we do not say, 'You do this because we're the parent and you're the child.'

About half of the parents talked directly about such equity ideals as applied to children.

Concerning women's rights, 80 per cent of fathers and 90 per cent of mothers agreed that women were disadvantaged in our society, but only two mothers and one father mentioned equal rights or the women's movement as motivators for sharing household labour. Most did not identify themselves as feminists, and a few offered derogatory comments about 'those women's libbers'. Nevertheless, almost all parents indicated that no one should be forced to perform a specific task because they were a man or a woman. This implicit equity ideal was evidenced by mothers and fathers using time availability, rather than gender, to assign most household tasks.

Divisions of Household Labour

Contributions to 64 household tasks were assessed by having fathers and mothers each sort cards on a five-point scale to indicate who most often performed them (see Table 17.1). Frequently performed tasks, such as meal preparation, laundry, sweeping, or putting children to bed, were judged for the two weeks preceding the interviews. Less frequently performed tasks, such as window washing, tax preparation, or car repair, were judged as to who typically performed them.

Some differences occurred between mothers' and fathers' accounts of household task allocation, but there was general agreement on who did what.

Table 17.1 shows that in the majority of families, most household tasks were seen as shared. Thirty-seven of 64 tasks (58 per cent), including all direct childcare, most household business, meal preparation, kitchen clean-up, and about half of other housecleaning tasks were reported to be shared about equally by fathers and mothers. Nevertheless, almost a quarter (15) of the tasks were performed principally by the mothers, including most clothes care, meal planning, kinkeeping, and some of the more onerous repetitive housecleaning. Just under one-fifth (12) of the tasks were performed principally by the fathers. These included the majority of the occasional outside chores such as home repair, car maintenance, lawn care, and taking out the trash. As a group, sample couples can thus be characterized as sharing an unusually high proportion of housework and childcare, but still partially conforming to a traditional division of household labour. The fathers and mothers in this study are pioneers in that they divided household tasks differently than their parents did, differently from most others in their age cohort, and from most families studied in time-use research.

Table 17.1 Household tasks by person most often performing them

	Mother More	Fathers and Mother Equally	Father More
Cleaning			
	Mopping	Vacuuming	Taking out trash
	Sweeping	Cleaning tub/shower	Cleaning porch
	Dusting	Making beds	
	Cleaning bathroom sink	Picking up toys	
	Cleaning toilet	Tidying living room	
		Hanging up clothes	
		Washing windows	
		Spring cleaning	
Cooking			
	Planning menus	Preparing lunch	Preparing breakfast
	Grocery shopping	Cooking dinner	
	Baking	Making snacks	
		Washing dishes	
		Putting dishes away	
		Wiping kitchen counters	
		Putting food away	
Clothes			
	Laundry	Shoe care	
	Hand laundry		
	Ironing		
	Sewing		
	Buying clothes		
Household			
		Running errands	Household repairs
		Decorating	Exterior painting
		Interior painting	Car maintenance
		General yardwork	Car repair
		Gardening	Washing car
			Watering lawn
			Mowing lawn
			Cleaning rain gutters
Finance, Social			
	Writing or phoning	Deciding major purchases	Investments
	relatives/friends	Paying bills	
		Preparing taxes	
		Handling insurance	
		Planning couple dates	

Table 17.1 continued

	Mother More	Fathers and Mother Equally	Father More
Children			
	Arranging baby-sitters	Waking children	
		Helping children dress	
		Helping children bathe	
		Putting children to bed	
		Supervising children	
		Disciplining children	
		Driving children	
		Taking children to doctor	
		Caring for sick children	
		Playing with children	
		Planning outings	

Note: Tasks were sorted separately by fathers and mothers according to relative frequency of performance: (1) Mother mostly or always, (2) Mother more than father, (3) Father and mother about equal, (4) Father more than mother, (5) Father mostly or always. For each task a mean ranking by couple was computed with 1.00–2.49 = Mother, 2.50–3.50 = Shared, 3.51–5.0 = Father. If over 50 per cent of families ranked a task as performed by one spouse more than the other, the task is listed under that spouse, otherwise tasks are listed as shared. N = 20 couples.

Managing versus Helping

Household divisions of labour in these families also can be described in terms of who takes responsibility for planning and initiating various tasks. In every family there were at least six frequently performed household chores over which the mother retained almost exclusive managerial control. That is, mothers noticed when the chore needed doing and made sure that someone adequately performed it. In general, mothers were more likely than fathers to act as managers for cooking, cleaning, and childcare, but over half of the couples shared responsibility in these areas. In all households the father was responsible for initiating and managing at least a few chores traditionally performed by mothers.

Based on participants' accounts of strategies for allocating household labour, I classified twelve couples as sharing responsibility for household labour and eight couples as reflecting manager–helper dynamics. Helper husbands often waited to be told what to do, when to do it, and how it should be done. While they invariably expressed a desire to perform their 'fair share' of housekeeping and child-rearing, they were less likely than the other fathers to assume responsibility for anticipating and planning these activities. Manager–helper couples sometimes referred to the fathers' contributions as 'helping' the mother.

When asked what they liked most about their husband's housework, about half of the mothers focused on their husband's self-responsibility: voluntarily doing work without being prodded. They commented, 'He does the everyday stuff' and 'I don't have to ask him.' The other mothers praised their husbands for particular skills with comments such as 'I love his spaghetti' or 'He's great at cleaning the bathroom.' In spite of such praise, three-fourths of the mothers said that what bothered them most about their husband's housework was the need to remind him to perform certain tasks, and some complained of having to 'train him' to correctly perform the chores. About a third of the fathers complained that their wives either didn't notice when things should be done or that *their* standards were too low. Although the extent of domestic task sharing varied considerably among couples, 90 per cent of both mothers and fathers independently reported that their divisions of labour were 'fair'.

Some mothers found it difficult to share authority for household management. For instance, one mother said, 'There's a certain control you have when you do the shopping and the cooking and I don't know if I'm ready to relinquish that control.' Another mother who shares most childcare and housework with her husband admitted that 'in general, household organization is something that I think I take over.' In discussing how they divide housework, she commented on how she notices more than her husband does:

> He does what he sees needs to be done. That would include basic cleaning kinds of things. However, there are some detailed kinds of things that he doesn't see that I feel need to be done, and in those cases I have to ask him to do things. He thinks some of the details are less important and I'm not sure, that might be a difference between men and women.

Like many of the mothers who maintained a managerial position in the household, this mother attributed an observed difference in domestic perceptiveness to an essential difference between women and men. By contrast, mothers who did not act as household managers were unlikely to link housecleaning styles to essential gender differences.

Many mothers talked about adjusting their housecleaning standards over the course of their marriage and trying to feel less responsible for being 'the perfect homemaker'. By partially relinquishing managerial duties and accepting their husband's housecleaning standards, some mothers reported that they were able to do less daily housework and focus more on occasional, thorough cleaning or adding 'finishing touches'. A mother with two nursing jobs whose husband delivered newspapers commented:

> He'll handle the surface things no problem, and I get down and do the nitty gritty. And I do it when it bugs me or when I have the time. It's not anything that we talk about usually. Sometimes if I feel like things are piling up, he'll say 'Well, make me a list,' and I will. And he'll do it. There are some things that he just doesn't notice and that's fine: he handles the day-to-day stuff. He'll do things, like for me cleaning off the table—for him it's getting everything off it; for me it's putting the table-cloth on, putting the flowers on, putting the candles on. That's the kind of stuff I do and I like that; it's not that I want him to start.

This list-making mother illustrates that responsibility for managing housework sometimes remained in the mother's domain, even if the father performed more of the actual tasks.

Responsibility for managing childcare, on the other hand, was more likely to be shared. Planning and initiating 'direct' childcare, including supervision, discipline and play, was typically an equal enterprise. Sharing responsibility for 'indirect' childcare, including clothing, cleaning, and feeding, was less common, but was still shared in over half of the families. When they cooked, cleaned, or tended to the children, fathers in these families did not talk of 'helping' the mother; they spoke of fulfilling their responsibilities as equal partners and parents. For example, one father described how he and his wife divided both direct and indirect child care:

> My philosophy is that they are my children and everything is my responsibility, and I think she approaches it the same way too. So when something needs to be done, it's whoever is

close does it . . . whoever it is convenient for. And we do keep a sense of what the other's recent efforts are, and try to provide some balance, but without actually counting how many times you've done this and I've done that.

In spite of reported efforts to relinquish total control over managing home and children, mothers were more likely than fathers to report that they would be embarrassed if unexpected company came over and the house was a mess (80 per cent versus 60 per cent). When asked to compare themselves directly to their spouse, almost two-thirds of both mothers and fathers reported that the mother would be more embarrassed than the father. Some mothers reported emotional reactions to the house being a mess that were similar to those they experienced when their husbands 'dressed the kids funny'. The women were more likely to focus on the children 'looking nice', particularly when they were going to be seen in public. Mothers' greater embarrassment over the kemptness of home or children might reflect their sense of mothering as part of women's essential nature.

Adult Socialization through Childrearing

Parents shared in creating and sustaining a world-view through the performance and evaluation of childrearing. Most reported that parenting was their primary topic of conversation, exemplified by one father's comment: 'That's what we mostly discuss when we're not with our kids—either when we're going to sleep or when we have time alone—is how we feel about how we're taking care of them.' Others commented that their spouse helped them to recognize unwanted patterns of interaction by focusing on parenting practices. For instance, one father remarked,

I'm not sure I could do it as a one-parent family, cause I wouldn't have the person, the other person saying, 'Hey, look at that, that's so much like what you do with your own family.' In a one-parent family, you don't have that, you don't have the other person putting out that stuff, you have to find it all out on your own and I'm not sure you can.

Usually the father was described as being transformed by the parenting experience and developing increased sensitivity. This was especially true of discourse between parents who were trying to convert a more traditional division of family labour into a more egalitarian one. A self-employed construction worker said his level of concern for child safety was heightened after he rearranged his work to do half of the parenting:

There's a difference in being at the park with the kids since we went on the schedule. Before it was, like, 'Sure, jump off the jungle bars.' But when you're totally responsible for them, and you know that if they sprained an ankle or something you have to pick up the slack, it's like you have more investment in the kid and you don't want to see them hurt and you don't want to see them crying. I find myself being a lot more cautious.

Mothers also reported that their husbands began to notice subtle cues from the children as a result of being with them on a regular basis. The wife of the construction worker quoted above commented that she had not anticipated many of the changes that emerged from sharing routine childcare.

I used to worry about the kids a lot more. I would say in the last year it's evened itself out quite a bit. That was an interesting kind of thing in sharing that started to happen that I hadn't anticipated. I suppose when you go into this your expectations about what will happen—that you won't take your kids to day care, that they'll be with their dad, and they'll get certain things from their dad and won't that be nice, and he won't have to worry about his hours—but then it starts creeping into other areas that you didn't have any way of knowing it was going to have an impact. When he began to raise issues about the kids or check in on them at school when they were sick, I thought, 'Well, that's my job, what are you talking about that for?' or, 'Oh my god. I didn't notice that!' Where did he get the intuitive sense to know what needed to be done? It wasn't there before. A whole lot of visible things happened.

Increased sensitivity on the part of the fathers, and their enhanced competence as parents, was typically evaluated by adopting a vocabulary of motives and feelings similar to the mothers', created and sustained through an ongoing dialogue about the children: a dialogue that grew out of the routine child care practices. Another mother described how her husband had 'the right temperament' for parenting, but had to learn how to notice the little things that she felt her daughters needed:

When it comes to the two of us as parents, I feel that my husband's parenting skills are probably superior to mine, just because of his calm rationale. But maybe that's not what little girls need all the time. He doesn't tend to be the one that tells them how gorgeous they look when they dress up, which they really like, and I see these things, I see when they're putting in a little extra effort. He's getting better as we grow in our relationship, as the kids grow in their relationship with him.

Like many fathers in this study, this one was characterized as developing sensitivity to the children by relying on interactions with his wife. She 'see things' which he has to learn to recognize. Thus, while he may have 'superior' parenting skills, he must learn something subtle from her. His reliance on her expertise suggests that his 'calm rationale'

is insufficient to make him 'maternal' in the way that she is. Her ability to notice things, and his inattention to them, serves to render them both accountable: parenting remains an essential part of her nature, but is a learned capacity for him. Couples talked about fathers being socialized, as adults, to become nurturing parents. This talking with their wives about childcare helped husbands construct and sustain images of themselves as competent fathers.

Greater paternal competence was also reported to enhance marital interaction. Fathers were often characterized as paying increased attention to emotional cues from their wives and engaging in more reciprocal communication. Taking responsibility for routine household labour offered some men the opportunity to better understand their mother's lives as well. For instance, one involved father who did most of the housework suggested that he could sometimes derive pleasure from cleaning the bathroom or picking up a sock if he looked at it as an act of caring for his family:

It makes it a different job, to place it in a context of being an expression of caring about a collective life together. It's at that moment that I'm maybe closest to understanding what my mother and other women of my mother's generation, and other women now, have felt about being housewives and being at home, being themselves. I think I emotionally understand the satisfaction and the gratification of being a homemaker.

More frequently, however, sharing childcare and housework helped fathers understand its drudgery. One father who is employed as a carpenter explained how assuming more responsibility for housework motivated him to encourage his wife to buy whatever she needs to make housework easier.

It was real interesting when I started doing more housework. Being in construction, when

I needed a tool, I bought the tool. And when I vacuum floors, I look at this piece of shit, I mean I can't vacuum the floor with this and feel good about it, it's not doing a good job. So I get a good vacuum system. So I have more appreciation for housecleaning. When I clean the tubs, I want something that is going to clean the tubs; I don't want to work extra hard. You know I have a kind of sponge to use for cleaning the tubs. So I have more of an appreciation for what she had to do. I tell her 'If you know of something that's going to make it easier, let's get it.'

Most sample fathers reported that performance of childcare, in and of itself, increased their commitment to both parenting and housework. All of the fathers had been involved in some housework before the birth of their children, but many indicated that their awareness and performance of housework increased in conjunction with their involvement in parenting. They reported that as they spent more time in the house alone with their children, they assumed more responsibility for cooking and cleaning. Fathers also noted that as they became more involved in the daily aspects of parenting, and in the face of their wives' absence and relinquishment of total responsibility for housekeeping, they became more aware that certain tasks needed doing and they were more likely to perform them. This was conditioned by the amount of time fathers spent on the job, but more than half reported that they increased their contributions to household labour when their children were under ten years old. This did not always mean that fathers' relative proportion of household tasks increased, because mothers were also doing more in response to an expanding total household workload.

Gender Attributions

Approximately half of both mothers and fathers volunteered that men and women brought some-

thing unique to childcare, and many stressed that they did not consider their own parenting skills to be identical to those of their spouse. One mother whose husband had recently increased the amount of time he spent with their school-aged children commented: 'Anybody can slap together a cream cheese and cucumber sandwich and a glass of milk and a few chips and call it lunch, but the ability to see that your child is troubled about something, or to be able to help them work through a conflict with a friend, that is really much different.' A list-making mother who provided less childcare and did less housework than her husband described herself as 'more intimate and gentle', and her husband as 'rough and out there'. Like many others she emphasized that mothers and fathers provide 'a balance' for their children. She described how she had to come to terms with her expectations that her husband would 'mother' the way that she did:

One of the things that I found I was expecting from him when he started doing so much here and I was gone so much, I was expecting him to mother the kids. And you know, I had to get over that one pretty quick and really accept him doing the things the way he did them as his way, and that being just fine with me. He wasn't mothering the kids, he was fathering the kids. It was just that he was the role of the mother as far as the chores and all that stuff.

A mother who managed and performed most of the housework and childcare used different reasoning to make similar claims about essential differences between women and men. In contrast to the mothers quoted above, this mother suggested that men could nurture, but not perform daily childcare:

Nurturance is one thing, actual care is another thing. I think if a father had to—like all of a sudden the wife was gone, he could nurture it with the love that it needed. But he might not change the diapers often enough, or he might not give 'em a bath often enough and he might not think of the perfect food to feed. But as far as nurturing, I think he's capable of caring . . . If the situation is the mother is there and he didn't have to, then he would trust the woman to.

This mother concluded, 'The woman has it more in her genes to be more equipped for nurturing.' Thus many of the manager–helper couples legitimated their divisions of labour and reaffirmed the 'naturalness' of essential gender differences.

Parents who equally shared the responsibility for direct and indirect childcare, on the other hand, were more likely to see similarities in their relationships with their children. They all reported that their children were emotionally 'close' to both parents. When asked who his children went to when they were hurt or upset, one early- and equal-sharing father commented: 'They'll go to either of us, that is pretty indistinguishable.' Mothers and fathers who equally shared most direct childcare reported that their children typically called for the parent with whom they had most recently spent time, and frequently called her mother 'daddy' or the father 'mommy,' using the gendered form to signify 'parent'. Most often, parents indicated that their children would turn to 'whoever's closest' or 'whoever they've been with', thus linking physical closeness with emotional closeness. In-home observations of family interactions confirmed such reports.

The central feature of these and other parental accounts is that shared activities formed an emotional connection between parent and child. Shared activities were also instrumental in constructing images of fathers as competent, nurturing caregivers. Two-thirds of both mothers and fathers expressed the belief that men could care for children's emotional needs as well as women. When asked whether men, in general, could nurture like women, mothers used their husbands as examples. One said, 'I don't neces-

sarily think that that skill comes with a sex type. Some women nurture better than others, some men nurture better than other men. I think that those skills can come when either person is willing to have the confidence and commitment to prioritize them.'

However, the parents who were the most successful at sharing childcare were the most likely to claim that men could nurture like women. Those who sustained manager–helper dynamics in childcare tended to invoke the images of 'maternal instincts' and alluded to natural differences between men and women. In contrast, more equal divisions of household labour were typically accompanied by an ideology of gender *similarity* rather than gender difference. The direction of causality is twofold: (1) those who believed that men could nurture like women seriously attempted to share all aspects of child care, and (2) the successful practice of sharing child care facilitated the development of beliefs that men could nurture like women.

Normalizing Atypical Behaviour

Mothers and fathers reported that women friends, most of whom were in more traditional marriages or were single, idealized their shared-parenting arrangements. About two-thirds of sample mothers reported that their women friends told them that they were extremely fortunate, and labelled their husbands 'wonderful', 'fantastic', 'incredible', or otherwise out of the ordinary. Some mothers said that women friends were 'jealous', 'envious', or 'amazed', and that they 'admired' and 'supported' their efforts at sharing domestic chores.

Both mothers and fathers said that the father received more credit for his family involvement than the mother did, because it was expected that she would perform childcare and housework. Since parenting is assumed to be 'only natural' for women, fathers were frequently praised for performing a task that would go unnoticed if a mother had performed it:

I think I get less praise because people automatically assume that, you know, the mother's *supposed* to do the childcare. And he gets a lot of praise because he's the visible one. Oh, I think that he gets far more praise. I can bust my butt at that school and all he has to do is show up in the parking lot and everybody's all *gah gah* over him. I don't get resentful about that—I think it's funny and I think it's sad.

While the fathers admitted that they enjoyed such praise, many indicated that they did not take these direct or implied compliments very seriously.

I get more credit than she does, because it's so unusual that the father's at home and involved in the family. I realize what it is: it's prejudice. The strokes feel real nice, but I don't take them too seriously. I'm sort of proud of it in a way that I don't really like. It's nothing to be proud of, except that I'm glad to be doing it and I think it's kind of neat because it hasn't been the style traditionally. I kind of like that, but I know that it means nothing.

These comments reveal that fathers appreciated praise, but actively discounted compliments received from those in dissimilar situations. The fathers' everyday parenting experiences led them to view parenthood as drudgery as well as fulfillment. They described their sense of parental responsibility as taken-for-granted and did not consider it to be out of the ordinary or something worthy of special praise. Fathers sometimes reported being puzzled by compliments from their wives' acquaintances and judged them to be inappropriate. When I asked one what kinds of reactions he received when his children were infants, he said,

They all thought it was really wonderful. They thought she'd really appreciate how wonderful it was and how different that was for her to

father. They'd say, 'You ought to know how lucky you are, he's doing so much.' I just felt like I'm doing what any person should do. Just like shouldn't anybody be this interested in their child? No big deal.

Another father said he resented all the special attention he received when he was out with his infant son:

Constant going shopping and having women stop me and say 'Oh it's so good to see you fathers.' I was no longer an individual: I was this generic father who was now a liberated father who could take care of his child. I actually didn't like it. I felt after a while that I wanted the time and the quality of my relationship with my child at that point, what was visible in public, to simply be accepted as what you do. It didn't strike me as worthy of recognition, and it pissed me off a lot that women in particular would show this sort of appreciation, which I think is well-intentioned, but which also tended to put a frame around the whole thing as though somehow this was an experience that could be extracted from one's regular life. It wasn't. It was going shopping with my son in a snuggly or on the backpack was what I was doing. It wasn't somehow this event that always had to be called attention to.

Thus fathers discounted and normalized extreme reactions to their divisions of labour and interpreted them in a way that supported the 'natural' character of what they were doing.

One mother commented on a pattern that was typically mentioned by both parents: domestic divisions of labour were 'normal' to those who were attempting something similar, and 'amazing' to those who were not: 'All the local friends here think it's amazing. They call him "Mr Mom" and tell me how lucky I am. I'm waiting for someone to tell him how lucky *he* is. I have several friends at work who have very similar arrangements and they just feel that it's normal.'

Because fathers assumed traditional mothering functions, they often had more social contact with mothers than with other fathers. They talked about being the only fathers at children's lessons, parent classes and meetings, at the laundromat, or in the market. One father said it took mothers there a while before they believed he really shared a range of household tasks.

> At first they ask me, 'Is this your day off?' And I say, 'If it's the day off for me, why isn't it the day off for you?' 'Well, I work 24 hours a day!' And I say, 'Yeah, right. I got my wash done and hung out and the beds made.' It takes the mother a couple of times to realize that I really do that stuff.

In general, fathers resisted attempts by other people to compare them to traditional fathers, and often compared themselves directly to their wives, or to other mothers.

Fathers tended to be employed in occupations predominantly composed of men, and in those settings were often discouraged from talking about family or children. Several fathers reported that people at their place of employment could not understand why they did 'women's work', and a few mentioned that coworkers would be disappointed when they would repeatedly turn down invitations to go out 'with the boys' for a drink. One of three self-employed carpenters in the study said that he would sometimes conceal that he was leaving work to do something with his children because he worried about negative reactions from employers or coworkers:

> I would say reactions that we've got—in business, like if I leave a job somewhere that I'm on and mention that I'm going to coach soccer, my son's soccer game, yeah. I have felt people kind of stiffen, like, I was more shirking my job, you know, such a small thing to leave

work for, getting home, racing home for. I got to the point with some people where I didn't necessarily mention what I was leaving for, just because I didn't need for them to think that I was being irresponsible about their work, I mean, I just decided it wasn't their business. If I didn't know them well enough to feel that they were supportive. I would just say, 'I have to leave early today'—never lie, if they asked me a question. I'd tell them the answer—but not volunteer it. And, maybe in some cases, I feel like, you know, you really have to be a little careful about being too *groovy* too, that what it is that you're doing is just so wonderful. 'I'm a father, I'm going to go be with my children.' It isn't like that, you know. I don't do it for what people think of me; I do it because I enjoy it.

Some fathers said coworkers perceived their talk of spending time with their children as indications that they were not 'serious' about their work. They reported receiving indirect messages that *providing* for the family was primary and *being with* the family was secondary. Fathers avoided negative workplace sanctions by selectively revealing the extent of their family involvement.

Many fathers selected their current jobs because the work schedule was flexible, or so they could take time off to care for their children. For instance, even though most fathers worked full-time, two-thirds had some daytime hours off, as exemplified by teachers, mail carriers, and self-employed carpenters. Similarly, most fathers avoided extra, work-related tasks or overtime hours in order to maximize time spent with their children. One computer technician said that he was prepared to accept possible imputations of non-seriousness:

> I kind of tend to choose my jobs. When I go to a job interview, I explain to people that I have a family and the family's very important to me. Some companies expect you to work a lot of overtime or work weekends, and I told them

that I don't have to accept that sort of thing. I may not have gotten all the jobs I ever might have had because of it, but it's something that I bring up at the job interview and let them know that my family comes first.

The same father admitted that it is sometimes a 'blessing' that his wife works evenings at a local hospital, because it allows him to justify leaving his job on time:

At five o'clock or five thirty at night, when there are a lot of people that are still going to be at work for an hour or two more. I go 'Adios!' [laughs]. I mean, I *can't* stay. I've gotta pick up the kids. And there are times when I feel real guilty about leaving my fellow workers behind when I know they're gonna be there for another hour or so. About a block from work I go 'God, this is great!' [laughs].

Over half of the study participants also indicated that their own mothers or fathers reacted negatively to their divisions of labour. Parents were described as 'confused', 'bemused', and 'befuddled', and it was said that they 'lack understanding' or 'think it's a little strange'. One mother reported that her parents and in-laws wouldn't 'dare to criticize' their situation because 'times have changed', but she sensed their underlying worry and concern:

I think both sides of the family think it's fine because it's popular now. They don't dare—I mean if we were doing this thirty years ago, they would dare to criticize. In a way, now they don't. I think both sides feel it's a little strange. I thought my mom was totally sympathetic and no problem, but when I was going to go away for a week and my husband was going to take care of the kids, she said something to my sister about how she didn't think I should do it. There's a little underlying tension about it, I think.

Other study participants reported that disagreements with parents were common, particularly if they revolved around trying to change childrearing practices their own parents had used.

Many couples reported that initial negative reactions from parents turned more positive over time as they saw that the children were 'turning out all right', that the couple was still together after an average of ten years, and that the men were still employed. This last point, that parents were primarily concerned with their son's or son-in-law's provider responsibilities, highlights how observers typically evaluated the couple's task sharing. A number of study participants mentioned that they thought their parents wanted the wife to quit work and stay home with the children and that the husband should 'make up the difference'. Most mentioned, however, that parents were more concerned that the husband continue to be the provider than they were that the wife made 'extra money' or that the husband 'helped out' at home.

In the beginning there was a real strong sense that I was in the space of my husband's duty. That came from his parents pretty strongly. The only way that they have been able to come to grips with this in any fashion is because he has also been financially successful. If he had decided, you know, 'Outside work is not for me, I'm going to stay home with the kids and she's going to work.' I think there would have been a whole lot more talk than there was. I think it's because he did both and was successful that it was okay.

Another mother noted that parental acceptance of shared parenting did not necessarily entail acceptance of the woman as provider:

There is a funny dynamic that happens. It's not really about childcare, where I don't think in our families—with our parents—I don't get enough credit for being the breadwinner.

Well they're still critical of him for not earning as much money as I do. In a way they've accepted him as being an active parenting father more than they've accepted me being a breadwinner.

Here again, the 'essential nature' of men is taken to be that of provider. If the men remain providers, they are still accountable as men, even if they take an active part in childcare.

Discussion

This brief exploration into the social construction of shared parenting in 20 dual-earner families illustrates how more equal domestic gender relations arise and under what conditions they flourish. All couples described flexible and practical task-allocation procedures that were responses to shortages of time. All families were child-centered in that they placed a high value on their children's well-being, defined parenting as an important and serious undertaking, and organized most of their non-employed time around their children. Besides being well-educated and delaying childbearing until their late twenties or early thirties, couples who shared most of the responsibility for household labour tended to involve the father in routine child care from the children's early infancy. As Sara Ruddick (1982) has noted, the everyday aspects of child care and housework help share ways of thinking, feeling, and acting that become associated with what it means to be a mother. My findings suggest that when domestic activities are equally shared, 'maternal thinking' develops in fathers, too, and the social meaning of gender begins to change. This de-emphasizes notions of gender as personality and locates it in social interaction.

To treat gender as the 'cause' of household division of labour overlooks its emergent character and fails to acknowledge how it is in fact implicated in precisely such routine practices.

References

Berk, S.F. 1985. *The Gender Factory*. New York: Plenum.

Ruddick, S. 1982. 'Maternal Thinking', in B. Thorne and M. Yalom, eds, *Rethinking the Family*, pp. 76–94. New York: Longman.

West, C., and D.H. Zimmerman. 1987. 'Doing Gender', *Gender & Society* 1: 125–51.

QUESTIONS FOR CRITICAL THOUGHT

1. What is your vision of ideal family life? Would your parents, siblings, and peers share that vision?

2. Both Ranson and Preston, et al. suggest, in different ways, that taking care of children is at odds with the demands of paid work, especially for women. Do you share their implicit pessimism about combining childcare and paid work?

3. The domestic division of labour still favours men with more leisure time than women, despite significant changes in recent decades. Why don't men do more around the house? What are the costs and rewards—for both men and women—of a lopsided distribution of household work?

4. Can you foresee a future in which all Canadian families will be shared-care families as described by Coltrane? What social changes would have to happen for this to become a reality?

5. Think about a parent with whom you share a gender. In what ways do you think your life will be different from his or hers? In what ways would you like your life to be different from his or hers?

PART V

The Gendered Classroom

Along with the family, educational institutions—from primary schools to second-ary schools, colleges, universities, and professional schools—are central arenas in which gender is reproduced. Students learn more than the formal curriculum—they learn what the society considers appropriate behaviour for men and women. And for adults, educational institutions are gendered workplaces, where the inequalities found in other institutions are also found.

From the earliest grades, students' experiences in the classroom differ by gender. Boys are more likely to interrupt, to be called upon by teachers, and to have any misbehaviour overlooked. Girls are more likely to remain obedient and quiet and to be steered away from math and science. As Myra and David Sadker, Lynn Fox, and Melinda Salata show, in this summary of the findings of their path-breaking book, *Failing at Fairness*, every arena of elementary and secondary education reproduces both gender difference and gender inequality. Ellen Jordan and Angela Cowan explore the ways in which children's play reinforces traditional gender stereotypes, showing that gender boundaries may be enforced even more rigidly on the playground than in the classroom.

Most of you who are reading this book have left primary and secondary schooling behind, and are currently immersed in postsecondary education. Your experiences as students may resonate with the work of both Tracey Lindberg and Brenda Beagan, who investigate everyday life in and out of the classroom. Lindberg and Beagan examine different types of education, but both find that the experience of being a student is profoundly shaped not just by gender but also by other social identities. Gender is by no means the only factor that shapes students' experiences of belonging or not belonging in school, but works in combination with other aspects of personal identity based in social categories such as race, class, and sexuality.

Schools may be sites of inequity and discrimination, but educational institutions are also sites where received ideas about gender can be challenged or transformed, particularly at postsecondary levels. Dorothy Smith's classic essay on women's perspec-tives in sociology is an example of transformative scholarship at its best, demonstrating how attention to gender and to the differences produced by gender can radically change the questions that researchers and scholars ask, and the answers that they produce.

CHAPTER 18

Gender Equity in the Classroom: The Unfinished Agenda

Myra Sadker, David Sadker, Lynn Fox, and Melinda Salata

In my science class the teacher never calls on me, and I feel like I don't exist. The other night I had a dream that I vanished (Sadker and Sadker, 1994).

Our interviews with female students have taught us that it is not just in science class that girls report the 'disappearing syndrome' referred to above. Female voices are also less likely to be heard in history and math classes, girls' names are less likely to be seen on lists of national merit finalists, and women's contributions infrequently appear in school textbooks. Twenty years after the passage of Title IX in the United States—the law prohibiting gender discrimination in American schools—and it is clear that most girls continue to receive a second-class education.

The very notion that women should be educated at all is a relatively recent development in North American history. It was not until late in the nineteenth century that the concept of educating girls beyond elementary school took hold. Even as women were gradually allowed to enter high school and college, the guiding principle in education was separate and unequal. Well into the twentieth century, boys and girls were assigned to sex-segregated classes and prepared for very different roles in life.

In 1833 Oberlin was the first college in the United States to admit women; but these early female college students were offered less rigorous courses and required to wait on male students and wash their clothes. Over the next several decades, only a few colleges followed suit in opening their doors to women. During the nineteenth century, a number of forward-thinking philanthropists and educators founded postsecondary schools for women—Mount Holyoke, Vassar, and the other seven-sister colleges. It was only in the aftermath of the Civil War that co-education became more prevalent on campuses across the United States, but economics, rather than equity, was the driving force. Since the casualties of war meant the loss of male students and their tuition dollars, many universities turned to women to fill classrooms and replace lost revenues. In 1870 two-thirds of all universities still barred women. By 1900 more than two-thirds admitted them. But the spread of co-education did not occur without a struggle. As late as the 1970s the all-male Ivy League colleges did not admit women, and even now the state-supported Virginia Military Institute fights to maintain both its all-male status and its state funding.

Cycle of Loss

Today, most female and male students attend the same schools, sit in the same classrooms, and read the same books but the legacy of inequity continues beneath the veneer of equal access. Although the school door is finally open and girls are inside the building, they remain second-class citizens.

In the early elementary school years, girls are ahead of boys academically, achieving higher standardized test scores in every area but science. By middle school, however, the test scores of female students begin a downward spiral that continues through high school, college, and even graduate school. Women consistently score lower than men on the Graduate Record Exams as well as on entrance tests for law, business, and medical schools. As a group, women are the only students who actually lose ground the longer they stay in school.

Ironically, falling female performance on tests is not mirrored by lower grades. Some have argued that women's grade-point averages are inflated because they tend not to take the allegedly more rigorous courses, such as advanced mathematics and physics. Another hypothesis suggests that female students get better grades in secondary school and college as a reward for effort and better behaviour rather than a mastery of the material. Another possibility is that the standardized tests do not adequately measure what female students know and what they are really able to do. Whatever the reason, course grades and test grades paint very different academic pictures.

Lower test scores handicap girls in the competition for places at elite colleges. On average, girls score 50 to 60 points less than boys on the Scholastic Aptitude Test (SAT)—recently renamed the Scholastic Assessment Test—which is required for admission to most colleges. Test scores also unlock scholarship money at 85 per cent of private colleges and 90 per cent of the public ones. For example, in 1991, boys scored so much higher on the Preliminary SAT/National Merit Scholarship Qualifying Test (PSAT/NMSQT) that they were nominated for two-thirds of the Merit Scholarships— 18,000 boys compared to 8,000 girls in 1991.

The drop in test scores begins around the same time that another deeply troubling loss occurs in the lives of girls: self-esteem. There is a precipitous decline from elementary school to high school. Entering middle school, girls begin what is often the most turbulent period in their young lives. According to a national survey sponsored by the American Association of University Women, 60 per cent of elementary school girls agreed with the statement 'I'm happy the way I am,' while only 37 per cent still agreed in middle school. By high

school, the level had dropped an astonishing 31 points to 29 per cent, with fewer than three out of every 10 girls feeling good about themselves. According to the survey, the decline is far less dramatic for boys: 67 per cent report being happy with themselves in elementary school, and this drops to 46 per cent in high school.

Recent research points to the relationship between academic achievement and self-esteem. Students who do well in school feel better about themselves; and in turn, they then feel more capable. For most female students, this connection has a negative twist and a cycle of loss is put into motion. As girls feel less good about themselves, their academic performance declines, and this poor performance further erodes their confidence. This pattern is particularly powerful in math and science classes, with only 18 per cent of middle school girls describing themselves as good in these subjects, down from 31 per cent in elementary school. It is not surprising that the testing gap between boys and girls is particularly wide in math and science.

Inequity in Instruction

During the past decade, Myra and David Sadker have investigated verbal interaction patterns in elementary, secondary, and college classrooms in a variety of settings and subject areas. In addition, they have interviewed students and teachers across the country. In their new book, *Failing at Fairness: How America's Schools Cheat Girls*, they expose the micro-inequities that occur daily in classrooms across the United States—and they show how this imbalance in attention results in the lowering of girls' achievement and self esteem. Consider the following:

- From grade school to graduate school, girls receive less teacher attention and less useful teacher feedback.
- Girls talk significantly less than boys do in class. In elementary and secondary school,

they are eight times less likely to call out comments. When they do, they are often reminded to raise their hands while similar behaviour by boys is accepted.

- Girls rarely see mention of the contributions of women in the curricula; most textbooks continue to report male worlds.
- Too frequently female students become targets of unwanted sexual attention from male peers and sometimes even from administrators and teachers.

From omission in textbooks to inappropriate sexual comments to bias in teacher behaviour, girls experience a powerful and often disabling education climate. A high school student from an affluent Northeastern high school describes her own painful experience:

My English teacher asks the class, 'What is the purpose of the visit to Johannesburg?' . . . I know the answer, but I contemplate whether I should answer the question. The boys in the back are going to tease me like they harass all the other girls in our class . . . I want to tell them to shut up. But I stand alone. All of the other girls don't even let themselves be bold. Perhaps they are all content to be molded into society's image of what a girl should be like—submissive, sweet, feminine . . . In my ninth period class, I am actually afraid—of what [the boys] might say . . . As my frustration builds, I promise myself that I will yell back at them. I say that everyday . . . and I never do it (Kim, 1993).

Teachers not only call on male students more frequently than on females; they also allow boys to call out more often. This imbalance in instructional attention is greatest at the college level. Our research shows that approximately one-half of the students in college classrooms are silent, having no interaction whatsoever with the professor. Two-thirds of these silent students are women.

This verbal domination is further heightened by the gender segregation of many of today's classes. Sometimes teachers seat girls and boys in different sections of the room, but more often students segregate themselves. Approximately one-half of the elementary and high school classrooms and one-third of the co-educational college classrooms that the Sadkers visited are sex-segregated. As male students talk and call out more, teachers are drawn to the noisier male sections of the class, a development that further silences girls.

Not only do male students interact more with the teacher but at all levels of schooling they receive a higher quality of interaction. Using four categories of teacher responses to student participation—praise, acceptance, remediation, and criticism—the Sadkers' studies found that more than 50 per cent of all teacher responses are mere acceptances, such as 'OK' and 'uh huh'. These non-specific reactions offer little instructional feedback. Teachers use remediation more than 30 per cent of the time, helping students correct or improve answers by asking probing questions or by phrases such as 'Try again'. Only 10 per cent of the time do teachers actually praise students, and they criticize them even less. Although praise, remediation, and criticism provide more useful information to students than the neutral acknowledgment of an 'OK', these clearer, more precise teacher comments are more often directed to boys.

Who gets taught—and how—has profound consequences. Student participation in the classroom enhances learning and self-esteem. Thus, boys gain an educational advantage over girls by claiming a greater share of the teacher's time and attention. This is particularly noteworthy in science classes, where, according to the AAUW report, *How Schools Shortchange Girls*, boys perform 79 per cent of all student-assisted demonstrations. When girls talk less and do less, it is little wonder that they learn less. Even when directing their attention to girls, teachers sometimes short-circuit the learning process. For example, teachers frequently explain how to focus a microscope to boys but simply adjust the microscope for the girls. Boys learn the skill; girls learn to ask for assistance.

When female students do speak in class, they often preface their statements with self-deprecating remarks such as, 'I'm not sure this is right,' or 'This probably isn't what you're looking for.' Even when offering excellent responses, female students may begin with this self-criticism. Such tentative forms of speech project a sense of academic uncertainty and self-doubt—almost a tacit admission of lesser status in the classroom.

Women are not only quiet in classrooms; they are also missing from the pages of textbooks. For example, history textbooks currently in use at middle and high schools offer little more than 2 per cent of their space to women. Studies of music textbooks have found that 70 per cent of the figures shown are male. A recent content analysis of five secondary school science textbooks revealed that more than two-thirds of all drawings were of male figures and that not a single female scientist was depicted. Furthermore, all five books used the male body as the model for the human body, a practice that continues even in medical school texts. At the college level, too, women rarely see themselves reflected in what they study. For example, the two-volume *Norton Anthology of English Literature* devotes less than 15 per cent of its pages to the works of women. Interestingly, there was greater representation of women in the first edition of the anthology in 1962 than in the fifth edition published in 1986.

Presence and Power

Not only are women hidden in the curriculum and quiet in the classroom, they are also less visible in other school locations. Even as early as the elementary grades, considered by some to be a distinctly feminine environment, boys tend to take over the territory. At recess time on playgrounds across the country, boys grab bats and balls as they fan out over the schoolyard for their games. Girls are likely to be left on the sideline—watching. In secondary school, male students become an even more powerful presence. In *Failing at Fairness*, high school teachers and students tell these stories:

> A rural school district in Wisconsin still has the practice of having the cheerleaders (all girls, of course) clean the mats for the wrestling team before each meet. They are called the 'Mat Maidens'.

> In our local high school, boys' sports teams received much more support from the school system and the community. The boys' team got shoes, jackets, and played on the best-maintained grounds. The girls' softball team received no clothes and nobody took care of our fields. Cheerleaders did not cheer for us. When we played, the bleachers were mostly empty.

Sports are not the only fields where women lose ground. In many secondary schools, mathematics, science, and computer technology remain male domains. In the past, girls were actively discouraged or even prohibited from taking the advanced courses in these fields. One woman, now a college professor, recalls her high school physics class:

> I was the only girl in the class. The teacher often told off-color jokes and when he did he would tell me to the leave the room. My great regret today is that I actually did it.

Today, we hope such explicitly offensive behaviour is rare, yet counsellors and teachers continue to harbour lower expectations for girls and are less likely to encourage them to take advanced classes in math and science. It is only later in life that women realize the price they paid for avoiding these courses as they are screened out of lucrative careers in science and technology.

By the time they reach college, male students' control of the environment is visible. Male students are more likely to hold positions of student leadership on campus and to play in heavily funded sports programs. College presidents and deans are usually men, as are most tenured professors. In a sense, a 'glass wall' divides today's college campus. On one side of the glass wall are men, comprising 70 per cent of all students majoring in chemistry, physics, and computer science. The percentage is even higher in engineering. While the 'hard sciences' flourish on the men's side of the campus, the women's side of the glass wall is where education, psychology, and foreign languages are taught. These gender walls not only separate programs, they also indicate social standing. Departments with higher male enrollment carry greater campus prestige and their faculty are often paid higher salaries.

These gender differences can be seen outside academic programs, in peer relationships both at college and in high school. In 1993 a national survey sponsored by the AAUW and reported in *Hostile Hallways* found that 76 per cent of male students and 85 per cent of female students in the typical high school had experienced sexual harassment. What differed dramatically for girls and boys was not the occurrence of unwanted touching or profane remarks but their reaction to them. Only 28 per cent of the boys, compared to 70 per cent of the girls, said they were upset by these experiences. For 33 per cent of the girls, the encounters were so troubling that they did not want to talk in class or even go to school. On college campuses problems range from sexist comments and sexual propositions to physical assault. Consider the following incidents:

- A UCLA fraternity manual found its way into a campus magazine. Along with the history and by-laws were songs the pledges were supposed to memorize. The lyrics described sexual scenes that were bizarre, graphic, and sadistic.

- One fraternity on a New England campus hosted 'pig parties' where the man bringing the female date voted the ugliest won.
- A toga party on the campus of another elite liberal arts college used, for decoration, the torso of a female mannequin hung from the balcony and splattered with paint to look like blood. A sign below suggested the female body was available for sex.

When one gender is consistently treated as less important and less valuable, the seeds of contempt take root and violence can be the result.

Strategies for Change

One of the ironies of gender bias in schools is that so much of its goes unnoticed by educators. While personally committed to fairness, many are unable to see the micro-inequities that surround them. The research on student–teacher interactions led the Sadkers to develop training programs to enable teachers and administrators to detect this bias and create equitable teaching methods. Program evaluations indicate that biased teaching patterns can be changed, and teachers can achieve equity in verbal interactions with their students. Research shows that for elementary and secondary schoolteachers, as well as college professors, this training leads not only to more equitable teaching but to more effective teaching as well.

During the 1970s, content analysis research showed women missing from schoolbooks. Publishers issued guidelines for equity and vowed to reform. But recent studies show that not all publishing companies have lived up to the promise of their guidelines. The curriculum continues to present a predominately male model of the world. Once again publishers and authors must be urged to incorporate women into school texts. Teachers and students need to become aware of the vast amount of excellent children's literature, including biographies that feature resourceful girls and strong women. *Failing at Fairness* includes an extensive list of these resources for both elementary and secondary schools.

In postsecondary education, faculty members typically select instructional materials on the basis of individual preference. Many instructors would benefit from programs that alert them to well-written, gender-fair books in their academic fields. And individual professors can enhance their own lectures and discussions by including works by and about women.

Education institutions at every level have a responsibility for students in and beyond the classroom. Harassing and intimidating behaviours that formerly might have been excused with the comment 'boys will be boys' are now often seen as less excusable and less acceptable. Many schools offer workshops for students and faculty to help eliminate sexual harassment. While controversy surrounds the exact definition of sexual harassment, the education community must take this issue seriously and devise strategies to keep the learning environment open to all.

After centuries of struggle, women have finally made their way into our colleges and graduate schools, only to discover that access does not guarantee equity. Walls of subtle bias continue to create different education environments, channelling women and men toward separate and unequal futures. To complete the agenda for equity, we must transform our education institutions and empower female students for full participation in society.

References

Sadker, M., and D. Sadker. 1994. *Failing at Fairness: How America's Schools Cheat Girls*. New York: Charles Scribner's Sons.

Kim, L. 1993. 'Boys Will Be Boys . . . Right?', *The Lance* (Livingston High School) 32 (June): 5.

CHAPTER 19

Warrior Narratives in the Kindergarten Classroom: Renegotiating the Social Contract?

Ellen Jordan and Angela Cowan

Since the beginning of second wave feminism, the separation between the public (masculine) world of politics and the economy and the private (feminine) world of the family and personal life has been seen as highly significant in establishing gender difference and inequality (Eisenstein, 1984). Twenty years of feminist research and speculation have refined our understanding of this divide and how it has been developed and reproduced. One particularly striking and influential account is given by Carole Pateman in her book *The Sexual Contract* (1988).

Pateman's broad argument is that in the modern world, the world since the Enlightenment, a 'civil society' has been established. In this civil society, patriarchy has been replaced by a fratriarchy, which is equally male and oppressive of women. Men now rule not as fathers but as brothers, able to compete with one another, but presenting a united front against those outside the group. It is the brothers who control the public world of the state, politics, and the economy. Women have been given token access to this world because the discourses of liberty and universalism made this difficult to refuse, but to take part they must conform to the rules established to suit the brothers.

This public world in which the brothers operate together is conceptualized as separate from the personal and emotional. One is a realm where there is little physicality—everything is done rationally, bureaucratically, according to contracts that the brothers accept as legitimate. Violence in this realm is severely controlled by agents of the state, except that the brothers are sometimes called upon for the supreme sacrifice of dying to preserve freedom. The social contract redefines the brawling and feuding long seen as essential characteristics of masculinity as deviant, even criminal, while the rest of physicality—sexuality, reproduction of the body, daily and intergenerationally—is left in the private sphere. Pateman quotes Robert Unger, 'The dichotomy of the public and private life is still another corollary of the separation of understanding and desire. . . . When reasoning, [men] belong to a public world. . . . When desiring, however, men are private beings' (Pateman, 1989: 48).

This is now widely accepted as the way men understand and experience their world. On the other hand, almost no attempt has been made to look at how it is that they take these views on board, or why the public/private divide is so much more deeply entrenched in men's lived experience than in women's. This article looks at one strand in the complex web of experiences through which this is achieved. A major site where this occurs is the school, one of the institutions particularly characteristic of the civil society that emerged with the Enlightenment (Foucault, 1980: 55–7). The school does not deliberately condition boys and not girls into this dichotomy, but it is, we believe, a site where what Giddens (1984: 10–3)

has called a 'cycle of practice' introduces little boys to the public/private division.

The article is based on weekly observations in a kindergarten classroom. We examine what happens in the early days of school when the children encounter the expectations of the school with their already established conceptions of gender. The early months of school are a period when a great deal of negotiating between the children's personal agendas and the teacher's expectations has to take place, where a great deal of what Genovese (1972) has described as accommodation and resistance must be involved.

In this article, we focus on a particular contest, which, although never specifically stated, is central to the children's accommodation to school: little boys' determination to explore certain narratives of masculinity with which they are already familiar—guns, fighting, fast cars—and the teacher's attempts to outlaw their importation into the classroom setting. We argue that what occurs is a contest between two definitions of masculinity: what we have chosen to call 'warrior narratives' and the discourses of civil society—rationality, responsibility, and decorum—that are the basis of school discipline.

By 'warrior narratives', we mean narratives that assume that violence is legitimate and justified when it occurs within a struggle between good and evil. There is a tradition of such narratives, stretching from Hercules and Beowulf to Superman and Dirty Harry, where the male is depicted as the warrior, the knight-errant, the superhero, the good guy (usually called a 'goody' by Australian children), often supported by brothers in arms, and always opposed to some evil figure, such as a monster, a giant, a villain, a criminal, or, very simply, in Australian parlance, a 'baddy'. There is also a connection, it is now often suggested, between these narratives and the activity that has come to epitomize the physical expression of masculinity in the modern era: sport (Duthie, 1980; Crosset, 1990; Messner, 1992). It is as sport that the physicality and desire usually lived out in the private sphere are permitted a ritualized public presence. Even though the violence once characteristic of the warrior has, in civil society and as part of the social contract, become the prerogative of the state, it can still be reenacted symbolically in countless sporting encounters. The mantle of the warrior is inherited by the sportsman.

The school discipline that seeks to outlaw these narratives is, we would suggest, very much a product of modernity. Bowles and Gintis have argued that 'the structure of social relations in education not only inures the student to the discipline of the work place, but develops the types of personal demeanor, modes of self-presentation, self-image, and social-class identifications which are the crucial ingredients of job adequacy' (1976: 131). The school is seeking to introduce the children to the behaviour appropriate to the civil society of the modern world.

An accommodation does eventually take place, this article argues, through a recognition of the split between the public and the private. Most boys learn to accept that the way to power and respectability is through acceptance of the conventions of civil society. They also learn that warrior narratives are not a part of this world; they can only be experienced symbolically as fantasy or sport. The outcome, we will suggest, is that little boys learn that these narratives must be left behind in the private world of desire when they participate in the public world of reason.

The Study

The school where this study was conducted serves an old-established suburb in a country town in New South Wales, Australia. The children are predominantly Australian born and English speaking, but come from socioeconomic backgrounds ranging from professional to welfare recipient. We carried out this research in a classroom run by a teacher who is widely acknowledged as one of the finest and most successful kindergarten teachers in our region. She is an admired practitioner of free play, process writing, and creativity. There was no gender definition of games in her classroom. Groups composed of both girls and boys had turns at playing in the Doll Corner, in the Construction Area, and on the Car Mat.

The research method used was non-participant observation, the classic mode for the sociological study of children in schools (Burgess 1984; Thorne 1986; Goodenough 1987). The group of children described came to school for the first time in February 1993. The observation sessions began within a fortnight of the children entering school and were conducted during 'free activity' time, a period lasting for about an hour. At first we observed twice a week, but then settled to a weekly visit, although there were some weeks when it was inconvenient for the teacher to accommodate an observer.

The observation was non-interactive. The observer stationed herself as unobtrusively as possible, usually seated on a kindergarten-sized chair, near one of the play stations. She made pencil notes of events, with particular attention to accurately recording the words spoken by the children, and wrote up detailed narratives from the notes, supplemented by memory, on reaching home. She discouraged attention from the children by rising and leaving the area if she was drawn by them into any interaction.

This project thus employed a methodology that was ethnographic and open-ended. It was nevertheless guided by certain theories, drawn from the work on gender of Jean Anyon, Barrie Thorne, and R.W. Connell, of the nature of social interaction and its part in creating personal identity and in reproducing the structures of a society.

Anyon has adapted the conceptions of accommodation and resistance developed by Genovese (1972) to understanding how women live with gender. Genovese argued that slaves in the American South accommodated to their contradictory situation by using certain of its aspects, for example, exposure to the Christian religion, to validate a sense of self-worth and dignity. Christian beliefs then allowed them to take a critical view of slavery, which in turn legitimated certain forms of resistance (Anyon, 1983). Anyon lists a variety of ways in which women accommodate to and resist prescriptions of appropriate feminine behaviour, arguing for a significant level of choice and agency (Anyon, 1983).

Thorne argues that the processes of social life, the form and nature of the interactions, as well as the choices of the actors, should be the object of analysis. She writes, 'In this book I begin not with individuals, although they certainly appear in the account, but with *group life*—with social relations, the organization and meanings of social situations, the collective practices through which children ad adults create and recreate gender in their daily interactions' (1993: 4).

These daily interactions, Connell (1987) has suggested mesh to form what Giddens (1984) has called 'cyclical practices'. Daily interactions are neither random nor specific to particular locations. They are repeated and recreated in similar settings throughout a society. Similar needs recur, similar discourses are available, and so similar solutions to problems are adopted; thus, actions performed and discourses adopted to achieve particular ends in particular situations have the unintended consequence of producing uniformities of gendered behaviour in individuals.

In looking at the patterns of accommodation and resistance that emerge when the warrior narratives that little boys have adapted from television encounter the discipline of the classroom, we believe we have uncovered one of the cyclical practices of modernity that reveal the social contract to these boys.

Warrior Narratives in the Doll Corner

In the first weeks of the children's school experience, the Doll Corner was the area where the most elaborate acting out of warrior narratives was observed. The Doll Corner in this classroom was a small room with a glass-panelled door opening off the main area. Its furnishings—stove, sink, dolls' cots, and so on—were an attempt at a literal re-creation of a domestic setting, revealing the school's definition of children's play as a preparation for adult life. It was an area where the acting out of 'pretend' games was acceptable.

Much of the boys' play in the area was domestic:

Jimmy and Tyler were jointly ironing a tablecloth. 'Look at the sheet is burnt, I've burnt it,' declared Tyler, waving the toy iron above his head. 'I'm telling Mrs Sandison,' said Jimmy worriedly. 'No, I tricked you. It's not really burnt. See,' explained Tyler, showing Jimmy the black pattern on the cloth (23 February 1993).

'Where is the baby, the baby boy?' Justin asked, as he helped Harvey and Malcolm settle some restless teddy babies. 'Give them some potion.' Justin pretended to force feed a teddy, asking 'Do you want to drink this potion?' (4 March 1993).

On the other hand, there were attempts from the beginning by some of the boys and one of the girls to use this area for non-domestic games and, in the case of the boys, for games based on warrior narratives, involving fighting, destruction, goodies, and baddies.

The play started off quietly, Winston cuddled a teddy bear, then settled it in a bed. Just as Winston tucked in his bear, Mac snatched the teddy out of bed and swung it around his head in circles. 'Don't hurt him, give him back,' pleaded Winston, trying vainly to retrieve the teddy. The two boys were circling the small table in the center of the room. As he ran, Mac started to karate chop the teddy on the arm, and then threw it on the floor and jumped on it. He then snatched up a plastic knife, 'This is a sword. Ted is dead. They all are.' He sliced the knife across the teddy's tummy, repeating the action on the bodies of two stuffed dogs. Winston grabbed the two dogs, and with a dog in each hand, staged a dog fight. 'They are alive again' (10 February 1993).

Three boys were busily stuffing teddies into the cupboard through the sink opening. 'They're in jail. They can't escape,' said Malcolm. 'Let's pour water over them.' 'Don't do that. It'll hurt them,' shouted Winston, rushing into the Doll Corner. 'Go away, Winston. You're not in our group,' said Malcolm (12 February 1993).

The boys even imported goodies and baddies into a classic ghost scenario initiated by one of the girls:

'I'm the father,' Tyler declared. 'I'm the mother,' said Alanna. 'Let's pretend it's a stormy night and I'm afraid. Let's pretend a ghost has come to steal the dog.' Tyler nodded and placed the sheet over his head. Tyler moaned, 'ooooOOOOOOOOAHHHH!!!' and moved his outstretched arms toward Alanna. Jamie joined the game and grabbed a sheet from the doll's cradle, 'I'm the goody ghost.' 'So am I,' said Tyler. They giggled and wrestled each other to the floor. 'No! you're the baddy ghost,' said Jamie. Meanwhile, Alanna was making ghostly noises and moving around the boys. 'Did you like the game? Let's play it again,' she suggested (23 February 1993).

In the first two incidents, there was some conflict between the narratives being invoked by Winston and those used by the other boys. For Winston, the stuffed toys were the weak whom he must protect knight-errant style. For the other boys, they could be set up as the baddies whom it was legitimate for the hero to attack. Both were versions of a warrior narrative.

The gender difference in the use of these narratives has been noted by a number of observers (Paley, 1984; Clark, 1989; Thorne, 1993).

Whereas even the most timid, least physically aggressive boys—Winston in this study is typical—are drawn to identifying with the heroes of these narratives, girls show almost no interest in them at this early age. The strong-willed and assertive girls in our study, as in others (Clark, 1990; Walkerdine, 1990), sought power by commandeering the role of mother, teacher, or shopkeeper, while even the highly imaginative Alanna, although she enlivened the more mundane fantasies of the other children with ghosts, old widow women, and magical mirrors, seems not to have been attracted by warrior heroes.[1]

Warrior narratives, it would seem, have a powerful attraction for little boys, which they lack for little girls. Why and how this occurs remains unexplored in early childhood research, perhaps because data for such an explanation are not available to those doing research in institutional settings. Those undertaking ethnographic research in preschools find the warrior narratives already in possession in these sites (Paley, 1984; Davies, 1989). In this research, gender difference in the appeal of warrior narratives has to be taken as a given—the data gathered are not suitable for constructing theories of origins; thus, the task of determining an explanation would seem to lie within the province of those investigating and theorizing gender differentiation during infancy, and perhaps, specifically, of those working in the tradition of feminist psychoanalysis pioneered by Dinnerstein (1977) and Chodorow (1978). Nevertheless, even though the cause may remain obscure, there can be little argument that in the English-speaking world for at least the last hundred years—think of Tom Sawyer playing Robin Hood and the pirates and Indians in J.M. Barrie's *Peter Pan*—boys have built these narratives into their conceptions of the masculine.

Accommodation through *Bricolage*

The school classroom, even one as committed to freedom and self-actualization as this, makes little provision for the enactment of these narratives. The classroom equipment invites children to play house, farm, and shop, to construct cities and roads, and to journey through them with toy cars, but there is no overt invitation to explore warrior narratives.

In the first few weeks of school, the little boys un-self-consciously set about redressing this omission. The method they used was what is known as *bricolage*—the transformation of objects from one use to another for symbolic purposes (Hebdige, 1979). The first site was the Doll Corner. Our records for the early weeks contain a number of examples of boys rejecting the usages ascribed to the various Doll Corner objects by the teacher and by the makers of equipment and assigning a different meaning to them. This became evident very early with their use of the toy baby carriages (called 'prams' in Australia). For the girls, the baby carriages were just that, but for many of the boys they very quickly became surrogate cars:

> Mac threw a doll into the largest pram in the Doll Corner. He walked the pram out past a group of his friends who were playing 'crashes' on the Car Mat. Three of the five boys turned and watched him wheeling the pram toward the classroom door. Mac performed a sharp three-point turn; raced his pram past the Car Mat group, striking one boy on the head with the pram wheel (10 February 1993).

> 'Brrrrmmmmmm, brrrrrmmmmm,' Tyler's revving engine noises grew louder as he rocked the pram back and forth with sharp jerking movements. The engine noise grew quieter as he left the Doll Corner and wheeled the pram around the classroom. He started to run with the pram when the teacher could not observe him (23 March 1993).

The boys transformed other objects into masculine appurtenances: knives and tongs became weapons, the dolls' beds became boats, and so on.

Mac tried to engage Winston in a sword fight using Doll Corner plastic knives. Winston backed away, but Mac persisted. Winston took a knife but continued to back away from Mac. He then put down the knife, and ran away half-screaming (semi-seriously, unsure of the situation) for his teacher (10 February 1993).

In the literature on youth subcultures, bricolage is seen as a characteristic of modes of resistance. Hebdige writes:

> It is through the distinctive rituals of consumption, through style, that the subculture at once reveals its 'secret' identity and communicates its forbidden meanings. It is predominantly the way commodities are used in subculture which mark the subculture off from more orthodox cultural formations. . . . The concept of *bricolage* can be used to explain how subcultural styles are constructed (1979: 103).

In these early weeks, however, the boys did not appear to be aware that they were doing anything more than establishing an accommodation between their needs and the classroom environment.

This mode of accommodation was rejected by the teacher, however, who practiced a gentle, but steady, discouragement of such bricolage. Even though the objects in this space are not really irons, beds, and cooking pots, she made strong efforts to assert their cultural meaning, instructing the children in the 'proper' use of the equipment and attempting to control their behaviour by questions like 'Would you do that with a tea towel in your house?' 'Cats never climb up on the benches in *my* house.' It was thus impressed upon the children that warrior narratives were inappropriate in this space.

The children, our observations suggest, accepted her guidance, and we found no importation of warrior narratives into the Doll Corner after the first few weeks. There were a number of elaborate and exciting narratives devised, but they were all to some degree related to the domestic environment. For example, on April 20, Justin and Nigel used one of the baby carriages as a four-wheel drive, packed it with equipment and went off for a camping trip, setting out a picnic with Doll Corner tablecloths, knives, forks, and plates when they arrived. On May 18, Matthew, Malcolm, Nigel, and Jonathan were dogs being fed in the Doll Corner. They then complained of the flies, and Jonathan picked up the toy telephone and said, 'Flycatcher! Flycatcher! Come and catch some flies. They are everywhere.' On June 1, the following was recorded:

'We don't want our nappies [diapers] changed,' Aaron informed Celia, the mum in the game. 'I'm poohing all over your clothes mum,' Mac declared, as he grunted and positioned himself over the dress-up box. Celia cast a despairing glance in Mac's direction, and went on dressing a doll. 'I am too; poohing all over your clothes mum,' said Aaron. 'Now mum will have to clean it all up and change my nappy,' he informed Mac, giggling. He turned to the dad [Nigel], and said in a baby voice, 'Goo-goo; give him [Mac] the feather duster.' 'No! give him the feather duster; he did the longest one all over the clothes,' Mac said to Nigel (1 June 1993).

Although exciting and imaginative games continued, the bricolage virtually disappeared from the Doll Corner. The intention of the designer of the Doll Corner equipment was increasingly respected. Food for the camping trip was bought from the shop the teacher had set up and consumed using the Doll Corner equipment. The space invaded by flies was a domestic space, and appropriate means, calling in expert help by telephone, were used to deal with the problem. Chairs and tables were chairs and tables, clothes were clothes and could be fouled by appropriate inhabitants of a domestic space, babies. Only the

baby carriages continued to have an ambiguous status, to maintain the ability to be transformed into vehicles of other kinds.

The warrior narratives—sword play, baddies in jail, pirates, and so on—did not vanish from the boys' imaginative world, but, as the later observations show, the site gradually moved from the Doll Corner to the Construction Area and the Car Mat. By the third week in March (that is, after about six weeks at school), the observer noticed the boys consistently using the construction toys to develop these narratives. The bricolage was now restricted to the more amorphously defined construction materials.

Tyler was busy constructing an object out of five pieces of plastic straw (clever sticks). 'This is a water pistol. Everyone's gonna get wet,' he cried as he moved into the Doll Corner pretending to wet people. The game shifted to guns and bullets between Tyler and two other boys. 'I've got a bigger gun,' Roger said, showing off his square block object. 'Mine's more longer. Ehehehehehehehe, got you,' Winston yelled to Roger, brandishing a plastic straw gun. 'I'll kill your gun,' Mac said, pushing Winston's gun away. 'No Mac. You broke it. No,' cried Winston (23 March 1993).

Two of the boys picked up swords made out of blue- and red-colored plastic squares they had displayed on the cupboard. 'This is my sword,' Jamie explained to Tyler. 'My jumper [sweater] holds it in. Whichever color is at the bottom, well that's the color it shoots out. Whoever is bad, we shoot with power out of it.' 'Come on Tyler,' he went on. 'Get your sword. Let's go get some baddies' (30 March 1993).

The toy cars on the Car Mat were also pressed into the service of warrior narratives:

Justin, Brendan, and Jonathan were busy on the Car Mat. The game involved police cars that were chasing baddies who had drunk 'too much beers'. Justin explained to Jonathan why his car had the word 'DOG' written on the front. 'These are different police cars, for catching robbers taking money' (4 March 1993).

Three boys, Harvey, Maurice, and Marshall, were on the Car Mat. 'Here comes the baddies,' Harvey shouted, spinning a toy car around the mat. 'Crasssshhhhh everywhere.' He crashed his car into the other boys' cars and they responded with laughter. 'I killed a baddie everyone,' said Maurice, crashing his cars into another group of cars (24 May 1993).

The boys were proposing a new accommodation, a new adaptation of classroom materials to the needs of their warrior narratives.

Classroom Rules and Resistance

Once again the teacher would not accept the accommodation proposed. Warrior narratives provoked what she considered inappropriate public behaviour in the miniature civil society of her classroom. Her aim was to create a 'free' environment where children could work independently, learn at their own pace, and explore their own interests, but creating such an environment involved its own form of social contract, its own version of the state's appropriation of violence. From the very first day, she began to establish a series of classroom rules that imposed constraints on violent or disruptive activity.

The belief underlying her practice was that firmly established classroom rules make genuine free play possible, rather than restricting the range of play opportunities. Her emphasis on 'proper' use of equipment was intended to stop it being damaged and consequently withdrawn from use. She had rules of 'no running' and 'no shouting' that allowed children to work and play safely on the floor of the classroom, even though

other children were using equipment or toys that demanded movement, and ensured that the noise level was low enough for children to talk at length to one another as part of their games.

One of the outcomes of these rules was the virtual outlawing of a whole series of games that groups of children usually want to initiate when they are playing together, games of speed and body contact, of gross motor self-expression and skill. This prohibition affected both girls and boys and was justified by setting up a version of public and private spaces: The classroom was not the proper place for such activities, they 'belong' in the playground.[2] The combined experience of many teachers has shown that it is almost impossible for children to play games involving car crashes and guns without violating these rules; therefore, in this classroom, as in many others (Paley, 1984), these games were in effect banned.

These rules were then policed by the children themselves, as the following interchange shows:

'Eeeeeeheeeeeeheeeeh!' Tyler leapt about the room. A couple of girls were saying, 'Stop it Tyler' but he persisted. Jane warned, 'You're not allowed to have guns.' Tyler responded saying, 'It's not a gun. It's a water pistol, and that's not a gun.' 'Not allowed to have water pistol guns,' Tony reiterated to Tyler. 'Yes, it's a water pistol,' shouted Tyler. Jane informed the teacher, who responded stating, 'NO GUNS, even if they are water pistols.' Tyler made a spear out of Clever Sticks, straight after the banning of gun play (23 March 1993).

The boys, however, were not prepared to abandon their warrior narratives. Unlike gross motor activities such as wrestling and football, they were not prepared to see them relegated to the playground, but the limitations on their expression and the teacher disapproval they evoked led the boys to explore them surreptitiously; they found ways of introducing them that did not violate rules about running and shouting.

As time passed, the games became less visible. The warrior narratives were not so much acted out as talked through, using the toy cars and the construction materials as a prompt and a basis:

Tyler was showing his plastic straw construction to Luke. 'This is a Samurai Man and this is his hat. A Samurai Man fights in Japan and they fight with the Ninja. The bad guys who use cannons and guns. My Samurai is captain of the Samurai and he is going to kill the sergeant of the bad guys. He is going to sneak up on him with a knife and kill him' (1 June 1993).

Malcolm and Aaron had built boats with Lego blocks and were explaining the various components to Roger. 'This ship can go faster,' Malcolm explained. 'He [a plastic man] is the boss of the ship. Mine is a goody boat. They are not baddies.' 'Mine's a steam shovel boat. It has wheels,' said Aaron. 'There it goes in the river and it has to go to a big shed where all the steam shovels are stopping' (11 June 1993).

It also became apparent that there was something covert about this play. The cars were crashed quietly. The guns were being transformed into water pistols. Swords were concealed under jumpers and only used when the teacher's back was turned. When the constructed objects were displayed to the class, their potential as players in a fighting game was concealed under a more mundane description. For example:

Prior to the free play, the children were taking turns to explain the Clever Stick and Lego Block constructions they had made the previous afternoon. I listened to Tyler describe his Lego robot to the class: 'This is a transformer robot. It can do things and turn into everything.' During free play, Tyler played with the same robot explaining its capacities to

Winston: 'This is a terminator ship. It can kill. It can turn into a robot and the top pops off' (23 March 1993).

Children even protested to one another that they were not making weapons, 'This isn't a gun, it's a lookout,' 'This isn't a place for bullets, it's for petrol.'

The warrior narratives, it would seem, went underground and became part of a 'deviant' masculine subculture with the characteristic 'secret' identity and hidden meanings (Hebdige, 1979). The boys were no longer seeking accommodation but practicing hidden resistance. The classroom, they were learning, was not a place where it was acceptable to explore their gender identity through fantasy.

This, however, was a message that only the boys were receiving. The girls' gender-specific fantasies (Paley, 1984; Davies, 1989) of nurturing and self-display—mothers, nurses, brides, princesses—were accommodated easily within the classroom. They could be played out without contravening the rules of the miniature civil society. Although certain delightful activities—eating, running, hugging, and kissing (Best, 1983)—might be excluded from this public sphere, they were not ones by means of which their femininity, and thus their subjectivity, their conception of the self, was defined.

Masculinity, the School Regime, and the Social Contract

We suggest that this conflict between warrior narratives and school rules is likely to form part of the experience of most boys growing up in the industrialized world. The commitment to such narratives was not only nearly 100 per cent among the boys we observed, but similar commitment is, as was argued above, common in other sites. On the other hand, the pressure to preserve a decorous classroom is strong in all teachers (with the possible exception of those teaching in 'alternative' schools) and has been since the beginnings of compulsory education. Indeed, it is only in classrooms where there is the balance of freedom and constraint we observed that such narratives are likely to surface at all. In more formal situations, they would be defined as deviant and forced underground from the boys' first entry into school.

If this is a widely recurring pattern, the question then arises: Is it of little significance or is it what Giddens (1984) would call one of the 'cyclical practices' that reproduce the structures of our society? The answer really depends on how little boys 'read' the outlawing of their warrior narratives. If they see it as simply one of the broad constraints of school against which they are continually negotiating, then perhaps it has no significance. If, on the other hand, it has in their minds a crucial connection to the definition of gender, to the creation of their own masculine identity, to where they position particular sites and practices on a masculine to feminine continuum, then the ostracism of warrior narratives may mean that they define the school environment as feminine.

There is considerable evidence that some primary school children do in fact make this categorization (Best, 1983; Brophy, 1985; Clark, 1990), and we suggest here that the outlawry of the masculine narrative contributes to this. Research by Willis (1977) and Walker (1988) in high schools has revealed a culture of resistance based on definitions of masculinity as *antagonistic* to the demands of the school, which are construed as feminine by the resisters. It might therefore seem plausible to see the underground perpetuation of the warrior narrative as an early expression of this resistance and one that gives some legitimacy to the resisters' claims that the school is feminine.

Is the school regime that outlaws the warrior narratives really feminine? We would argue, rather, that the regime being imposed is based on a male ideal, an outcome of the Enlightenment and compulsory schooling. Michel Foucault has pointed out that the development of this particular regime in schools coincided with the emergence of the prison, the hospital, the army barracks, and the factory (Foucault, 1980). Although teachers in the first years of school are predominantly female, the regime they impose is perpetuated by male teachers (Brophy, 1985), and this preference is endorsed by powerful and influential males in the society at large. The kind of demeanor and self-management that teachers are trying to inculcate in the early school years is the behaviour expected in male-dominated public arenas like boardrooms, courtrooms, and union mass meetings.[3]

Connell (1989) and Willis (1977) provide evidence that by adolescence, boys from all classes, particularly if they are ambitious, come to regard acquiescence in the school's demands as compatible with constructing a masculine identity. Connell writes:

> Some working class boys embrace a project of mobility in which they construct a masculinity organized around themes of rationality and responsibility. This is closely connected with the 'certification' function of the upper levels of the education system and to a key form of masculinity among professionals (1989: 291).

Rationality and responsibility are, as Weber argued long ago, the primary characteristics of the modern society theorized by the Enlightenment thinkers as based on a social contract. This prized rationality has been converted in practice into a bureaucratized legal system where 'responsible' acceptance by the population of the rules of civil society obviates the need for individuals to use physical violence in gaining their ends or protecting their rights, and where, if such violence is necessary, it is exercised by the state (Weber, 1978). In civil society, the warrior is obsolete, his activities redefined bureaucratically and performed by the police and the military.

The teacher in whose classroom our observation was conducted demonstrated a strong commitment to rationality and responsibility. For example, she devoted a great deal of time to showing that there was a cause and effect link between the behaviour forbidden by her classroom rules and classroom accidents. Each time an accident occurred, she asked the children to determine the cause of the accident, its result, and how it could have been prevented. The implication throughout was that children must take responsibility for the outcomes of their actions.

Mac accidentally struck a boy, who was lying on the floor, in the head with a pram wheel. He was screaming around with a pram, the victim was playing on the Car Mat and lying down to obtain a bird's eye view of a car crash. Mac rushed past the group and collected Justin on the side of the head. Tears and confusion ensued. The teacher's reaction was to see to Justin, then stop all play and gain children's attention, speaking first to Mac and Justin plus Justin's group:

T.   How did Justin get hurt?
M.   [No answer]
T.   Mac, what happened?
M.   I was wheeling the pram and Justin was in the way.
T.   Were you running?
M.   I was wheeling the pram.

The teacher now addresses the whole class:

T.   Stop working everyone, eyes to me and listen. Someone has just been hurt because someone didn't remember the classroom rules. What are they, Harvey?

(Harvey was listening intently and she wanted someone who could answer the question at this point).

H.   No running in the classroom.
T.   Why?

Other children offer an answer.

Chn.   Because someone will get hurt.
T.   Yes, and that is what happened. Mac was going too quickly with the pram and Justin was injured. Now how can we stop this happening next time?
Chn.   No running in the classroom, only walk (10 February 1993).

Malcolm, walking, bumped Winston on the head with a construction toy. The teacher intervened.

T.   [To Malcolm and Winston] What happened?
W.   Malcolm hit me on the head.
M.   But it was an accident. I didn't mean it. I didn't really hurt him.
T.   How did it happen?
M.   It was an accident.
W.   He [Malcolm] hit me.
T.   Malcolm, I know you didn't mean to hurt Winston, so how did it happen?
M.   I didn't mean it.
T.   I know you didn't mean it, Malcolm, but why did Winston get hurt?
Chn.   Malcolm was running.
M.   No I wasn't.
T.   See where everyone was sitting? There is hardly enough room for children to walk. Children working on the floor must remember to leave a walking path so that other children can move safely around the room. Otherwise someone will be hurt, and that's what has happened today (23 February 1993).

This public-sphere masculinity of rationality and responsibility, of civil society, of the social contract is not the masculinity that the boys are bringing into the classroom through their warrior narratives. They are using a different, much older version—not the male as responsible citizen, the producer, and consumer who keeps the capitalist system going, the breadwinner, and caring father of a family. Their earliest vision of masculinity is the male as warrior, the bonded male who goes out with his mates and meets the dangers of the world, the male who attacks and defeats other males characterized as baddies, the male who turns the natural products of the earth into weapons to carry out these purposes.

We would argue, nevertheless, that those boys who aspire to become one of the brothers who wield power in the public world of civil society ultimately realize that conformity to rationality and responsibility, to the demands of the school, is the price they must pay. They realize that although the girls can expect one day to become the brides and mothers of their pretend games, the boys will never, except perhaps in time of war, be allowed to act out the part of warrior hero in reality.

On the other hand, the school softens the transition for them by endorsing and encouraging the classic modern transformation and domestication of the warrior narrative, sport (Connell, 1987; Messner, 1992). In the school where this observation was conducted, large playground areas are set aside for lunchtime cricket, soccer, and basketball; by the age of seven, most boys are joining in these games. The message is conveyed to them that if they behave like citizens in the classroom, they can become warriors on the sports oval.

Gradually, we would suggest, little boys get the message that resistance is not the only way to live out warrior masculinity. If they accept a public/private division of life, it can be accommodated within the private sphere; thus, it becomes possible for those boys who aspire to respectability, figuring in civil society as one of the brothers, to accept that the school regime and its expectations are masculine and to reject the attempts of the 'resisters' to define it (and them) as feminine. They adopt the masculinity of rationality and responsibility as that appropriate to the public sphere, while the earlier, deeply appealing masculinity of the warrior narratives can still be

experienced through symbolic reenactment on the sports field.

Conclusion

We are not, of course, suggesting that this is the only way in which the public/private division becomes part of the lived awareness of little boys. We do, however, believe that we have teased out one strand of the manner in which they encounter it. We have suggested that the classroom is a major site where little boys are introduced to the masculinity of rationality and responsibility characteristic of the brothers in civil society; we have been looking at a 'cycle of practice' where, in classroom after classroom, generation after generation, the mode of masculinity typified in the warrior narratives is first driven underground and then transferred to the sports field. We are, we would suggest, seeing renegotiated for each generation and in each boy's own life the conception of the 'social contract' that is characteristic of the era of modernity, of the Enlightenment, of democracy, and of capitalism. We are watching reenacted the transformation of violence and power as exercised by body over body, to control through surveillance and rules (Foucault, 1977, 1984), the move from domination by individual superiors to acquiescence in a public sphere of decorum and rationality (Pateman, 1988).

Yet, this is a social *contract*, and there is another side to the bargain. Although they learn that they must give up their warrior narratives of masculinity in the public sphere, where rationality and responsibility hold sway, they also learn that in return they may preserve them in the private realm of desire as fantasy, as bricolage, as a symbolic survival that is appropriate to the spaces of leisure and self-indulgence, the playground, the backyard, the television set, the sports field. Although this is too large an issue to be explored in detail here, there may even be a reenactment in the school setting of what Pateman (1988) has defined as the sexual contract, the male right to dominate women in return for accepting the constraints of civil society. Is this, perhaps, established for both boys and girls by means of the endemic misogyny—invasion of girls' space (Thorne, 1986, 1993), overt expressions of aversion and disgust (Goodenough, 1987; D'Arcy, 1990), disparaging sexual innuendo (Best, 1983; Goodenough, 1987; Clark, 1990)—noted by so many observers in the classrooms and playgrounds of modernity? Are girls being contained by the boys' actions within a more restricted, ultimately a private, sphere because, in the boys' eyes, they have not earned access to the public sphere by sharing their ordeal of repression, resistance, and ultimate symbolic accommodation of their gender-defining fantasies?

Notes

The research on which this article is based was funded by the Research Management Committee of the University of Newcastle. The observation was conducted at East Maitland Public School and the authors would like to thank the principal, teachers, and children involved for making our observer so welcome.

1. Some ethnographic studies describe a 'tomboy' who wants to join in the boys' games (Best, 1983; Davies, 1989; Thorne, 1993), although in our experience, such girls are rare, rarer even than the boys who play by choice with girls. The girls' rejection of the warrior narratives does not appear to be simply the result of the fact that the characters are usually men. Bronwyn Davies, when she read the role-reversal story *Rita the Rescuer* to preschoolers, found that many boys identified strongly with Rita ('they flex their muscles to show how strong they are and fall to wrestling each other on the floor to display their strength'), whereas for most girls, Rita remained 'other' (Davies, 1989: 57–8).

2. This would seem to reverse the usual parallel of outdoor/indoor with public/private. This further suggests that the everyday equation of 'public' with 'visible' may not be appropriate for the specialized use of the term in sociological discussions of the public/private division. Behaviour in the street may be more visible than what goes on in a courtroom, but it is nevertheless acceptable for the street behaviour to be, to a greater degree, personal, private, and driven by 'desire'.

3. There are some groups of men who continue to reject these modes of modernity throughout their lives. Andrew Metcalfe, in his study of an Australian mining community, has identified two broad categories of miner, the 'respectable', and the 'larrikin' (an Australian slang expression carrying implications of non-conformism, irreverence, and impudence). The first are committed to the procedural decorums of union meetings, sporting and hobby clubs, welfare groups, and so on; the others relate more strongly to the less disciplined masculinity of the pub, the brawl, and the racetrack (Metcalfe, 1988). This distinction is very similar to that noted by Paul Willis in England between the 'ear'oles' and the 'lads' in a working-class secondary school (Willis, 1977). It needs to be noted that this is not a *class* difference and that demographically the groups are identical. What distinguishes them is, as Metcalfe points out, their relative commitment to the respectable modes of accommodation and resistance characteristic of civil society of larrikin modes with a much longer history, perhaps even their acceptance or rejection of the social contract.

References

Anyon, J. 1983. 'Intersections of Gender and Class: Accommodation and Resistance by Working-class and Affluent Females to Contradictory Sex-role Ideologies', in S. Walker and L. Barton, eds, *Gender, Class and Education*. Barcombe, Sussex: Falmer.

Best, R. 1983. *We've All Got Scars: What Girls and Boys Learn in Elementary School*. Bloomington: Indiana University Press.

Bowles, S., and H. Gintis. 1976. *Schooling in Capitalist America: Educational Reform and the Contradictions of Economic Life*. London: Routledge and Kegan Paul.

Brophy, J.E. 1985. 'Interactions of Male and Female Students with Male and Female Teachers', in L.C. Wilkinson and C.B. Marrett, eds, *Gender Influences in Classroom Interaction*. New York: Academic Press.

Burgess, R.G., ed. 1984. *The Research Process in Educational Settings: Ten Case Studies*. Lewes: Falmer.

Chodorow, N. 1978. *The Reproduction of Mothering: Psychoanalysis and the Sociology of Gender*. Berkeley: University of California Press.

Clark, M. 1989. 'Anastasia is a Normal Developer because She is Unique', *Oxford Review of Education* 15: 243–55.

———. 1990. *The Great Divide: Gender in the Primary School*. Melbourne: Curriculum Corporation.

Connell, R.W. 1987. *Gender and Power: Society, the Person and Sexual Politics*. Sydney: Allen and Unwin.

———. 1989. 'Cool Guys, Swots and Wimps: The Interplay of Masculinity and Education', *Oxford Review of Education* 15: 291–303.

Crosset, T. 1990. 'Masculinity, Sexuality, and the Development of Early Modern Sport', in M.E. Messner and D.F. Sabo, eds, *Sport, Men and the Gender Order*. Champaign, IL: Human Kinetics Books.

D'Arcy, S. 1990. 'Towards a Non-sexist Primary Classroom', in E. Tutchell, ed., *Dolls and Dungarees: Gender Issues in the Primary School Curriculum*. Milton Keynes: Open University Press.

Davies, B. 1989. *Frogs and Snails and Feminist Tales: Preschool Children and Gender*. Sydney: Allen and Unwin.

Dinnerstein, M. 1977. *The Mermaid and the Minotaur: Sexual Arrangements and Human Malaise*. New York: Harper and Row.

Duthie, J.H. 1980. 'Athletics: The Ritual of a Technological Society?', in H.B. Schwartzman, ed., *Play and Culture*. West Point, NY: Leisure.

Eisenstein, H. 1984. *Contemporary Feminist Thought*. London: Unwin Paperbacks.

Foucault, M. 1977. *Discipline and Punish: The Birth of the Prison*, A. Sheridan, trans. New York: Pantheon.

———. 1980. 'Body/power', in C. Gordon, ed., *power/knowledge: Selected Interviews and Other Writings 1972–1977*. Brighton: Harvester.

———. 1984. 'Truth and Power', in P. Rabinow, *The Foucault Reader*. New York: Pantheon.

Genovese, E.E. 1972. *Roll, Jordan, Roll: The World the Slaves Made*. New York: Pantheon.

Giddens, A. 1984. *The Constitution of Society. Outline of the Theory of Structuration*. Berkeley: University of California Press.

Goodenough, Ruth Gallagher. 1987. 'Small Group Culture and the Emergence of Sexist Behaviour: A Comparative Study of Four Children's Groups', in G. Spindler and L. Spindler, eds, *Interpretive Ethnography of Education*. Hillsdale, NJ: Lawrence Erlbaum.

Hebdige, D. 1979. *Subculture: The Meaning of Style*. London: Methuen.

Messner, M.E. 1992. *Power at Play: Sports and the Problem of Masculinity*. Boston: Beacon.

Metcalfe, A. 1988. *For Freedom and Dignity: Historical Agency and Class Structure in the Coalfields of NSW.* Sydney: Allen and Unwin.

Paley, V.G. 1984. *Boys and Girls: Superheroes in the Doll Corner*. Chicago: University of Chicago Press.

Pateman, C. 1988. *The Sexual Contract*. Oxford: Polity.

———. 1989. 'The Fraternal Social Contract', in *The Disorder of Women*. Cambridge: Polity.

Thorne, B. 1986. 'Girls and Boys Together . . . But Mostly Apart: Gender Arrangements in Elementary Schools', in W.W. Hartup and Z. Rubin, eds, *Relationships and Development*. Hillsdale, NJ: Lawrence Erlbaum.

———. 1993. *Gender Play: Girls and Boys in School*. New Brunswick, NJ: Rutgers University Press.

Walker, J.C. 1988. *Louts and Legends: Male Youth Culture in an Inner-city School*. Sydney: Allen and Unwin.

Walkerdine, V. 1990. *Schoolgirl Fictions*. London: Verso.

Weber, M. 1978. *Selections in Translation*. W.G. Runciman, ed. and E. Matthews, trans. Cambridge: Cambridge University Press.

Willis, P. 1977. *Learning to Labour: How Working Class Kids Get Working Class Jobs*. Farnborough: Saxon House.

CHAPTER 20

What Do You Call an Indian Women with a Law Degree? Nine Aboriginal Women at the University of Saskatchewan College of Law Speak Out

Tracey Lindberg

I write this paper with an unsteady hand and with my heart beating in my head.[1] It is a very difficult thing to do—to evaluate legal education as it has affected First Nations women in the College of Law. I feel liberated since I am finally able to write as I want to with heart, spirit, and mind. I speak as an Indian. I speak as a woman. I speak as an Indian woman. I begin with a story.

I didn't go to Grace Adam's funeral. I didn't think I could talk to her family. She had four daughters and one son—the most giving and the strongest person, and a very lonely person. I'm not quite sure where I fit in. All I know is that they loved everyone, cared for the Earth, and celebrated the Creator.

She was an amazing woman, you know—one of the first Indian women in the province of Saskatchewan to graduate form Lebret Residential School, one of the first Indian women to obtain a university degree, one of the best teachers in the province. She was the closest many of us had come to meeting pure goodness. This woman typified for me what education for First Nations people could be like. She studied hard, learned new information, and adapted it to apply understandings of 'Indianness'. Learning was not limited to her formal education. She continued learning for the rest of her life. Her time spent at university was just a part of it. She taught her children

traditional values and skills and let them learn formal education when they entered their learning phase. She was the most Indian person I had ever met. She worked hard in a world filled with much more enmity towards Indian woman than I will ever know. She always gave, constantly worked for change, and believed each person had value.

I want so much to describe effectively the story of being an Indian woman in a non-Indian, male educational setting. I want the story to be true and strong. I want it to reflect that I am here because of Grace Adam. My daughters may come here because of me. My story involves much beauty and celebration. Yet, it is written with somewhat more cynicism and bitterness than existed three years ago when I first began this journey.

First Nations women are best at telling the stories of our first days:

> I overhead two women in the back of Torts discussing who was and was not Indian in the classroom. The assessment was based purely on physical attributes. More distressing and painful than that was the fact that we were objectified and examined like some foreign entity in 'their' class. I was hurt, alone and labeled by women I was to spend the next three years with. I remember that every time I speak with either of them.

Nine Aboriginal women,[2] including myself, have chosen to share our experiences in law school. I am fortunate to be the person compiling and presenting these experiences. The majority of Aboriginal women in the College of Law at the University of Saskatchewan are over 25 years of age. Three of the respondents are Métis women. The remainder are Treaty Indian women representing Indian Nations. Many have children. The few of us without partners or children are a distinct minority. The support system we provide for each other extends to the community as well. Many of us have met previously (through the Native Law Summer Program, employment, and political or social organizations). This support has been an undeniable factor in our continued success and presence in law school.

> I am fortunate because I know I can rely on the other Indian people I met through the summer program. It is not academic support. The presence of other Indian people I the college makes me feel visible. I thought I would vanish in law school . . . somehow become White. With other Aboriginal people here I am constantly reminded that I am here for many important and good reasons.

The contributors to this article co-operated with the knowledge that their statements and understandings would be compiled and presented as an assessment of legal education in Saskatchewan as it affects Aboriginal women. Our comments have been edited as little as possible to ensure that the truth, beauty, and, at times, rawness, are fully evident. It may hurt to read these pages. This pain is reflective of the anger and silent screaming that some of us have had to bear and suppress. These pages are also filled with support, strength, and wisdom. It will feel good to read them. Of the women polled, the majority state that they are glad to be law students. We offer our comments, critiques, and feelings not as a negative allegory of our experiences, but as an expression of our

understandings of legal education. As 'outsiders' (Sheppard and Westpahl, 1992), we are able to see patterns of belief or behaviour that are difficult to detect for those immersed in the college.

Our view necessarily includes a careful examination of the accommodation of Aboriginal women in the curriculum, class teachings, materials, and understandings of law school.[3] The comments were solicited by questionnaires distributed by hand to each Aboriginal woman in the college. Participants were given the option of answering anonymously or meeting with the author to discuss their responses. Most chose to discuss the questionnaire in person.

We leave the following words to you and to your interpretation. The onus of learning about Indian and Aboriginal peoples too often comes to lie on those who are being defined. We hope our words will aid in your learning. We will facilitate your knowledge, but you must take responsibility for your own education.

Aboriginal women come to law school for a variety of reasons:

> [I came to law school] on a dare from someone.

> I was particularly optimistic. I came here to change everyone's views about Indians. I mean it. I would change professorial teaching styles, the textbooks, non-Indian students and even the laws! I was going to teach the world about an alternative mode of justice. I guess I really didn't come here to learn.

> I came to law school because I've always wanted to be a lawyer. If I am going to make a difference in the world—a law degree will help me.

> For career reasons. A law degree offers many choices.

> Because of the way I was treated by males in the justice system.

I was arrested once protesting at Indian Affairs. When I was begin photographed and fingerprinted I asked the officer in charge why this process was being used. He said, 'Because you'll be back.' I kept that in my head while I wrote the LSAT and when I applied to law school.

There are times when as Aboriginal women, we find ourselves alienated from the learning processes. Many of the Aboriginal women interviewed found that, in part, the alienation was related to perceptions of their race based on physical attributes:

I am able to be perceived as an Aboriginal person. This affects me in two very major ways: I cannot be a member of the very real boys club; I am to be an expert on all Aboriginal groups and all Aboriginal concerns.

I am perceived and received as a First Nations female. Therefore, my interaction is based on who I am.

[Other's perception of me as a First Nation member] has kept me form interacting with certain people in the college. You get vibes from some people so you in turn treat them as invisible as well. Once you do that I find some of these people take notice and are annoyed by it, probably because I am not a visible minority.

I find that my look limits somewhat the people who associate with me. It is not chic or trendy to befriend an Aboriginal. I enter each situation open to new ideas and people. I request the same. I find that I do not receive this. I think there are probably all sorts of stereotypes and concerns that come with this brown skin. We are all affirmative action, we are all from reserves on a scholarship, who had a great GPA. I feel proud of how I look but

I am distressed at being a brown page in their [other law students'] previously written book of experiences. I sometimes feel like I am on the outside looking in.

In many situations, we associate with, and locate near, other Aboriginal people. In many cases, the group that provides the most support includes Aboriginal peoples. The majority of Aboriginal women at the College of Law do not separate gender from origin. Aboriginal women make up a strong portion of the circle. We perform an important role in racial and cultural self-determination. Therefore, issues of racism and community wellness are often our major concern.

Sisterhood in the college, in many cases, is a secondary concern to nationhood. As Aboriginal people, we find ourselves in the position of being a bridge between two worlds. Our interaction, therefore, takes place with many people of differing world views, including Aboriginal and non-Aboriginal people. Since our support within the college varies, some of us interact principally with other Aboriginal students.

Aboriginal women in the college find it difficult to stay connected. Many of us study with, or socialize predominantly with, Aboriginal males in the college. Many of the males are single with no dependants or have partners who assume the childcare responsibilities. We associate with other Aboriginal people in situations where we need support: exam periods, community and family concerns, and assignment due dates. This behaviour is known as taking comfort into the room with you (Monture, 1986).

The support I received from Aboriginals whether male or female is moral and personal. [We are all concerned with] how to make the system work for us and who and what can work for us (the oppressed).

I find myself drawn to minority group members (lesbians, gays, other First Nations members). I was never a very strong femin-ist, but there is merit to a somewhat common oppressive background. I find the Aboriginal men found their voices a lot easier than Aboriginal women in the college. I have only been present during one incident of an Aboriginal woman speaking out in class. It seems like we are the first to be asked for our opinions on Aboriginal issues and dismissed in many other situations.

In my Advanced Constitutional Law class the professor announced we were to have a dis-cussion the next day on First Nations consti-tutional concerns. As he read the reading list I felt more and more depressed and I couldn't figure out why. Another woman in class asked why all the assigned readings were written by non-Aboriginal males. I wanted to hug her. She made sure that I didn't disappear in that class.

There is a general sense that we [all law students] share a common experience, but I received support specifically from both Aboriginal men and women both academic-ally and personally and I cherish it.

My main support in the college from Aborig-inals has come from Aboriginal men. We keep each other sane at exam time and can discuss issues of race and even gender that are lacking in class. Aboriginal women are important to my life at law school and in general—but there is no one woman who has been a support group for school. They are good friends and good sounding boards for life though.

I have been told that women were created out of the bone of a buffalo—this is how integral Aboriginal women are to life. We were created with strength in mind—sinewy and rare. We were not made as a mate for one person, nor are we made from one person. Our strength supports

all life. Because of this, we have distinct roles as Aboriginal women. We each have the same responsibilities to protect the children and their children.

However, every Aboriginal woman does not consider this gender differentiation—this femin-ine side of the earth—to mean that we must join together for that reason alone.

I feel that Aboriginal women in law school are not as connected to one another as they should be; outside of law school, I have managed to maintain contact and communication with the Aboriginal organizations and attend and par-ticipate in events such as conferences, social events and so forth.

There are so few of us that it is hard to bond just on the basis of race. All people of all cultures have interesting and complicated histories. I think we tend to connect with the people who are the most like us. This includes more than race and gender. While I certainly fell connected to all the Aboriginal students, as a single female with no dependants I share many traits and characteristics of other single females in the college.

I am connected to some Aboriginal students and not to others—applies to women or men.

In some classes I sit with Aboriginal students . . . our interaction is distinct because of shared experiences and confidences.

Another reason identified for this strong affili-ating with Aboriginal people lies in the fact that almost all of the Aboriginal women interviewed found that non-Aboriginal students' knowledge of Aboriginal issues and understandings was quite low. This is the result of an education system that does not convey the understandings, needs, and legal positions of Aboriginal peoples and systems to the people who most need to understand it—non-Aboriginal students.[4]

In my world, you have to deal with Aboriginal people everyday. I do not understand why this is not so in a college professing to be on the cutting edge of society. Aboriginal women possess untold stories and understandings. We come from areas where there is a 100 per cent Aboriginal population. We come from homes where families raised eight children. We have concepts of property and self-determination that could make others richer through the telling. I think that as Aboriginal women we have a story that is both the same as, and different from, shared. Most of us have found that the majority of the college's students are empathetic and open-minded towards Aboriginal issues, and we believe that they are 'fertile ground' for planting new seeds of knowledge about Aboriginal people.

I have found two people in the college who are constantly trying to understand, to really get around the concept of Aboriginal rights. They do this not for curiosity, for classroom purposes, or to settle their fears. They do this because they respect Aboriginal people and accept that the responsibility for keeping Aboriginal peoples and issues alive is their concern as well.

I have heard the only two women on a hockey trip called 'clan mothers' as a joke in the college newspaper. I just found the objectification so thoughtless and unkind . . . I couldn't bring myself to mention it.

Most people recognize that a great deal of this knowledge deficit could be minimized if professors, administrators, and other staff realized that teaching from a variety of perspectives is beneficial to classroom settings. In many Aboriginal communities, elders and teachers bear a great responsibility of ensuring that the people/students are well prepared for life. This includes stories of other cultures, their understandings, and the importance of respect for all people. What kind of lives are Aboriginal law students being prepared for?

I have had two completely awful contacts with college professors. In the first, one of my professors was unable to defuse a potentially damaging conversation about Aboriginal women. One of the students commented that 'Indian men only hit Indian women when they are drunk.' This was said in a jovial and accepting tone. Several other women in the class spoke for me as I was incoherent with weariness and pain. In the second situation, a professor questioned two of eleven presentations in a class belligerently and very condescendingly. The two presentations were both on issues of Aboriginal title that adopted a point of view that differed with that of the professor. Only one faculty member was sympathetic to my concern. Other comments I received from the faculty were 'Professor X is one of the most sympathetic professors in the college', 'Professor X is just brusque,' and the advice I received was to 'write your best paper' based on the presentation. Although the professor was approached eventually I am disillusioned with the process of taking professors to task for their behaviour.

The general impression was that there were some 'informed' professors, yet many others who were unable to convey to their classes that Aboriginal issues were often distinct and very much a reality. In the few instances where Aboriginal issues were discussed, the possibility of a female interpretation was often ignored. We found ourselves immersed in invisibility. Aboriginal issues and concerns, we believe, would be considered more seriously and addressed more frequently if there was an Aboriginal faculty member on staff.

This problem of little or no attention to gender resulted in two widely talked about class discussions in the College of Law last year. In one discussion, Aboriginal men spoke for all Aboriginal people, necessitating the request by Aboriginal women in the class that there be an opportunity for the concerns of Aboriginal women to be expressed by themselves. The other discussion, which took place in a small-group seminar class on Aboriginal law, involved a similar exclusion of Aboriginal women from the debate. In each situation, the distinct concerns of Aboriginal women were initially addressed only by Aboriginal men. In response, Aboriginal women found their voices and insisted that there were distinct issues that affected Aboriginal women.

The issue of gender differences in Aboriginal communities has become a subject that both Aboriginal and non-Aboriginal people prefer not to discuss. The truth is that women have always had a separate and equal position in politics, labour, and familial tasks. Equality as an ideal has different meanings for Aboriginal people. Aboriginal women are an essential and important part of the circle, the continuity of life. We are a part of fire, of water. We are elemental and essentially intrinsic to the continuance of life. We have our roles, different and the same, which match perfectly with those of our men. Yet somehow we are overlooked. We are elemental, and we need to reclaim our place. We are women. We are Aboriginal. But to draw a sharp line between these two characteristics makes sense only in theorist' minds.

> Aboriginal politics demands a role for Aboriginal women. I think that the Aboriginal community is slow to get the message of the importance of women's roles and involvement in society and especially in politics. As with everything else, women see problems and solutions from a different perspective—which is just as valid and as important. We need a voice, and a political voice often carries farther.

> I never see us as a Women's Struggle. Sisterhood, to me, most often will be secondary to nationhood. We have an unclaimed seat at the circle of Aboriginal politics. This is something we have tried and tried to discuss with other Aboriginal people. It seems the only time that Aboriginal political issues come to the forefront is when there is perceived infighting. I hope that Aboriginal issues from a women's perspective will soon be addressed. I am not yet willing to confer authority upon women's groups to speak for us.

It is widely recognized that many non-Aboriginal people do not think about, understand, or define reality in the same way that some Aboriginal people do (Monture, 1986). Certain situations and class discussions include introductory information that introduces and explains differing perspective. For example, in an environmental law class, it is made clear that corporations have different perspectives than other entities in society. The corporations' perspective is often alluded to. However, though this courtesy is extended to a fictional entity, it is not extended to Aboriginal people very often. It is even more rarely extended to Aboriginal women. As Aboriginal women, we enter our criminal law classes with the knowledge that the majority of female offenders in this province are Aboriginal women. We also recognize that there Aboriginal women prisoners are pre-judged as 'violent, uncontrollable, and unmanageable' in some prisons (Sugar and Fox, 1990). Yet I have never heard an introductory lecture on systemic discrimination. There are many ways for a professor to convey that Aboriginal women don't matter and that includes silence (Boyle, 1986).[5] I have never once heard the term 'institutionalized racism', cross a professor's lips. Yet I sit, I read, and I wonder each time we discuss an Aboriginal offender: what is everyone in this room thinking? It is not a good feeling. I feel indignant, angry, and afraid. I hope everyone in the room who is aware of these issues knows that I am Indian. I want no one to notice me and everyone to notice me. I hope no one will make a painful statement. It is an open wound to my being. This is my personhood

(Monture, 1986), and we are dismembering it. Its main organs are taken out: the facts, the issues, and the ratio.

It is difficult to find the strengths in a college where many of us feel alienated, separate, and invisibly brown. Many of us only participate in seminar or limited-enrolment classes. Theory classes also encourage different perspectives, and many upper-year Aboriginal women feel comfortable speaking out in these classes. Large classes where the professor uses a Socratic teaching style were widely criticized as intimidating, [and] uncomfortable.

There is a great deal of uncertainly that surrounds us as Aboriginal in law school. We have few predecessors to look for advice. None of us are second-generation lawyers. Some of us are the daughters and granddaughters of trappers. Coming to law school is similar to moving to a foreign country, learning a new culture and language. We proceed by trial and error. As a result, we are often quiet, sometimes ill at ease, and occasionally frightened.

> In property when Aboriginal title was starting I did not know how the class would respond; I felt responsible for the whole Aboriginal people—but it turned out okay and there was no need to defend my people.

> I am never comfortable when called upon. It doesn't matter how well I am prepared. I will offer information when I feel there is a point that needs to be raised. I never speak just to comment on a case or give my opinion. If there is an alternate way to interpret a situation I will try to bring that up.

> I try really hared to make sure I am prepared. This whole 'lazy Indian' image really is alive and at work in this college. It is especially evident in the statements I have heard regarding Aboriginal people in the part-time program.

We find ourselves making choices based on a complex set of values. These values, it seems, are based upon how connected we are with the Aboriginal communities of interest to which we belong. In turn, this connection is based on our goals for the future. In establishing goals, all the Aboriginal women who responded stated that their connection to their communities of interest was central in goal determination and occupational choice:

> I will work in any capacity to facilitate the advancement of Aboriginal self-determination. I hope this does not leave me in an urban centre, but realistically it might. I want to take my information and training and better educate myself in traditional learning (teachings of the community, elders, and other involved in self-determination).

> I plan to stay in Saskatoon and work with the community here.

> If not to my reserve, to other Native communities.

> I feel best about speaking at Bridging Week in front of all the first year students. I told them that I know we are called squaws and that when some people see us they think 'squaw'. I am proudest of telling them to see people, not colours, and to think Indian person—not Indian. I have tried my best to eradicate labeling and naming.

It is very evident among most of my Aboriginal women colleagues that law school is a portion of their lives and not the entirety of it. We are very proud of balancing family, partners, careers, community, and studies. The balance most of us accomplish is welcome and sometimes difficult to achieve. All but one of the respondents have familial support and obligations in addition to their studies. Balancing becomes an implicit and important part of our lives as family and community shift positions in our web of responsibilities.

I feel terribly guilty for not committing any time to social or cultural concerns (like I did before law school).

I had to miss conferences, ceremonies, and elders talks that I love to go to—for something that I am not even sure that I like.

[I make time for] spiritual and extended family, children's social well-being, which call for frequent trips to Regina and rez. Lots of time, money, and support are required, not to mention family emergencies.

[There is pressure on an Aboriginal woman that there is not on an Aboriginal man], women are still expected to do it all but I need a wife too. Not in the sexual sense but someone to do all or at least some of my duties.

Considering the funding conditions put on me by Indian Affairs I have no choice but to go full-time to get full funding. Otherwise it would be full-time work and part-time studies.

Overt racism is something that few of the Aboriginal women had actually seen, heard, or experienced from law school peers. Yet a very strong majority of the women interviewed believed that there were racial slurs and understandings at work in the College of Law.

I heard one male student jokingly saying that he was from [an urban centre with a very high Aboriginal population] and that because he was from that town it was okay if he transgressed the limits of the law because it was all relative. He stated that he could not be penalized because 'he only shot one or two

Indians.' I did not say a word. It is too scary to approach someone who feels confident enough about that belief to say it in a normal tone of voice.

I am quite sure there are [racist statements] in the college.

I am not likely to be made privy to the confidences of people who dislike other people on the basis of skin colour. My friends have told me of a few instances. It is hard to sleep sometimes.

Yet, as Aboriginal women we have an ongoing responsibility to seven unborn generations of children. This responsibility includes making sure that they do not have to bear this weight. It includes ensuring that barriers that barriers that existed for us as Aboriginal women are knocked down so that our children do not have to break them down. It is in this spirit that the Aboriginal women in the University of Saskatchewan College of Law mad their recommendations in the questionnaire.

There is a perception in law school that Aboriginal people in law school are not there on our merits. We are taking the spot of deserving candidates. We are lower achievers and undeserving of a position in the college. All people should compete for spaces on the same basis. These prejudiced views extend to and touch every Aboriginal woman who goes to law school. Patricia Monture wrote of this sentiment:

Remembering back to my first day of law school, I was confronted in the lounge by another student, who with some hostility explained that perhaps one of his friends was not present because of me. And this made him angry because the only reason I could have reached the hallowed halls of the law school was by virtue of a special access program (Monture, 1990).

I have found this to be true in my experience as well.

Many of the legal concepts that we learn in law school are contrary to Aboriginal traditional notions of justice. All of the contributors to the questionnaire are in agreement that the Canadian legal system has a duty to respect Aboriginal peoples. This respect can be fostered by:

> displaying genuine commitment to and support of our dreams and aspirations of self-determination and by the willingness to listen to and implement the innovative idea conveyed by First Nations people in response to issues that directly affect us as a nation.

There is also concern regarding the exclusion of Aboriginal people and, particularly, Aboriginal women, from the curriculum. In my first year, my only memorable experiences with Aboriginal people in the justice system were confined to a duress defense (because Aboriginal people are, of course, unable to fully comprehend the complexities of a contract) and a drug trafficking offence. As future lawyers, we all depend narrowly on our experiences in law school as a basis for future understanding and learning. I trust the ability of others to exclude information that is culturally biased, but I question all people's abilities to include information that is excluded. This includes hypotheticals that incorporate Aboriginal women as well as Aboriginal men. I have been present in two classes where there were serious attempts to linguistically include women in hypotheticals (Boyle, 1986). My pride and the feelings of inclusion were very strong. I felt my invisibility by exclusion warp for a moment. I was the same as, and different from, every person in the room. I felt included and important. It is such a small thing, but it chips away at the massive base of oppression.

We are always Aboriginal. We are always women. We are not allowed the luxury of turning our pain on and off (Monture, 1986).[6] But we bear it and we proceed. More importantly, we succeed. Many of the Aboriginal women currently in law school still consider themselves very attuned to the needs and goals of the Aboriginal community. In addition, there are more Aboriginal women in the University of Saskatchewan College of Law at this time than in any year in recent memory. We succeed in the management of studies, community interaction, and family. There can be no greater success story than that.

The essence of this paper is this: we have accepted the responsibility of educating ourselves. We have risen to the challenge of remaining Aboriginal in the search for knowledge in a system that challenges our make-up. We respect the wisdom that we have gained. We honour the teachers who have tried to change a vision of their world in order to include other worlds. We have found ourselves immersed in a value system that is strange and foreign to many of us. We have struggled academically, personally, and in innumerable other ways to include, or at least to respect, your vision of the world. It is your turn.

True success in law school includes ensuring that parity, fairness, and respect are maintained at all times. It is your turn to ensure that the infliction of racism, the appropriation of pain, and the disrespect of alternative viewpoints and understandings ends. Patricia Monture wrote of this responsibility:

> When are those of you who inflict racism, who appropriate pain, who speak with no knowledge or respect when you ought to listen and accept, going to take hared looks at yourself instead of at me. How can you continue to look at me to carry what is your responsibility? And when I speak and the brutality of my experience hurts you, you hide behind your hurt. You point the finger at me and you claim I hurt you. I will not carry your responsibility anymore. Your pain is unfortunate. But do not look at me to soften it. Look to yourself (1986: 168).

We persevere and we struggle on. For many of us, the most difficult aspect of our experience is dealing with the ignorance of others. For Aboriginal women who are law students, as it was for Grace Adam, the struggle is a hared-fought one.

We do not, in all cases, reject our legal education. We do, however, refuse to bear the burdens of a system that will not evolve. We continue to break the path initially walked by women like Grace Adam—our Women.

Notes

1. Because there are so few of us, many Aboriginal academics and professionals must play multiple roles in the achievement of our goals. Telling this story was important enough that I wanted to undertake to gather the stories, but I also wanted to be one of the voices that was heard. I do not profess to be impartial as I am a participant. I do not profess to be apolitical as this is personal and, as such, politicized.

2. The phrase 'Aboriginal women' is utilized throughout this article to indicate the distinct and multi-facial component and also the cultural affinity, of the respondents. This may yield a certain homogeneity that is by no means indicative of our multiplicity of experiences, understandings, or feelings about law school. However, the term does encompass the unity of nations that binds the respondents together.

3. This examination is based, in great part, on the approach taken by Catherine Weiss and Louise Melling, 'The Legal Education of Twenty Women', *Stanford Law Review* 40 (1988): 1299. We adapted and revised the questionnaire used

in that article (Ibid., Appendix A at 1360). In particular, we employed terms of racial specificity and of race/gender duality. Our questionnaire is contained in the appendix to this article.

4. Mari Matsuda has written that: 'a system that ignores outsiders' perspectives artificially restricts and stultifies the scholarly imagination.' Mari Matsuda, 'Affirmative Action and Legal Knowledge: Planting Seeds in Plowed-Up Ground' *Harvard Women's Legal Journal* 2 (1988): 1 at 3.

5. Boyle discusses silence after a pro-woman comment is made. I think it is relevant that complete silence regarding any issue that concerns all students dismisses certain defined groups of people.

6. At a conference that Monture attended, she heard of a discussion where an individual stated that 'the pain of minority people is like television, we can turn it on and off as we want to.' This is a luxury that Aboriginal people are usually not allowed.

References

Boyle, C. 1986. 'Teaching Law As If Women Really Mattered or What About the Washroom?', *Canadian Journal of Women and the Law* 2, 1: 96 at 99.

Matsuda, M. 1988. 'Affirmative Action and Legal Knowledge: Planting Seeds in Plowed-Up Ground', *Harvard Women's Legal Journal* 2: 1 at 3.

Monture, P.A. 1986. 'Ka-Nin-Geh-Heh-E-Sa-Nonh-Yah-Gah', *Canadian Journal of Women and the Law* 2, 1: 159 at 161.

———. 1990. 'Now That the Door Is Open: First Nations and the Law School Experience' *Queen's Law Journal* 15: 179 at 205.

Sugar, F., and L. Fox. 1990. 'Nistum Peyako Seht'wanin Iskwewak: Breaking Chains', *Canadian Journal of Women and the Law* 3, 2: 465 at 469.

Sheppard, C., and S. Westpahl. 1992. 'Equity and the University: Learning From Women's Experience', *Canadian Journal of Women and the Law* 5, 1: 8.

Weiss, C., and L. Melling. 1988. 'The Legal Education of Twenty Women', *Stanford Law Review* 40: 1299.

CHAPTER 21

Micro Inequities and Everyday Inequalities: 'Race', Gender, Sexuality, and Class in Medical School[1]

Brenda Beagan

Elements in the students' background do not exert any decisive influence . . . in medical school. Such background factors may have indirect influence in many ways, but the problems of the student role are so pressing . . . that the perspectives developed are much more apt to reflect the pressures of the immediate school situation than of ideas associated with prior roles and experiences (Becker et al., 1961: 47).

In this passage from *Boys in White*, a classic study of medical professional socialization, Howard Becker and his colleagues insist that social characteristics such as gender, 'race',[2] culture, social class, sexual orientation, and religion have little or no impact on medical student experiences. Social differences become background variables in the face of an overwhelming medical student culture. In their study, conducted in 1956–7, about 5 per cent of the students in any class were women and 5 per cent to 7 per cent were non-white (1961: 60).[3] They really were *boys* in white—in fact they were *white* boys in white.

Over the next 40 years the profile of the typical North American medical school class changed considerably. By 1993, 42 per cent of medical students in the United States were women (Bickel and Kopriva, 1993). In Canada, women's proportion of medical school classes increased from 9 per cent in 1957–8 to 49 per cent by 1997–8

(Association of Canadian Medical Colleges, 1998). By 1991–2 African American, Native American, Mexican American, Puerto Rican, other Hispanic, and Asian or Pacific Islander students made up 27 per cent of all medical students in the United States (Jonas et al., 1992; c.f., Foster, 1996). In Canada statistics on the 'race' of medical students are not available. As well, medical students are somewhat older and better educated upon entry than they were in previous years (Gray and Reudy, 1998: 1047). Evidence also indicates there are more openly-identified gay/lesbian/bisexual medical students. There are currently gay and lesbian student caucuses in medical schools, a Canadian gay and lesbian medical student e-mail list, a gay and lesbian committee of the American Medical Student Association (Oriel et al., 1996), and recent journal articles addressing the concerns of gays and lesbians in medicine (Wallick et al., 1992; Rose, 1994; Cook et al., 1995; Oriel et al., 1996; Druzin et al., 1998; Klamen et al., 1999; Risdon et al., 2000).

In short, the medical student population is far less homogeneous than when Becker et al. (1961) conducted their research 40 years ago.[4] What is the impact of this increased diversity in the student population? Linda Grant (1988) suggests that who you are when you enter medicine affects the extent to which you 'fit in' during medical school. She argues that all schools have their own 'latent culture', which dictates the boundaries of appropriate behaviour: 'Those who share the latent culture have a sense of belonging; those who do not may feel alienated and marginal' (Grant, 1988: 109).

Current research supports this position. Women medical students, for example, perceive more gender discrimination than do male students and are substantially more likely to be sexually harassed by clinicians, faculty, and/or patients (Grant, 1988; Dickstein, 1993; Hostler and Gressard, 1993; Komaromy et al., 1993; Bickel, 1994; Moscarello et al., 1994; Schulte and Kay, 1994; Bickel and Ruffin, 1995; Bergen et al., 1996). Studies have documented 'micro-inequities' (Haslett and Lipman, 1997) based in gender, including gender-exclusive language, absence of parental leave policies, gender-biased illustrations in medical texts, sexist jokes in class and at school social events, male students being called doctor while women are not, women being mistaken for nurses, being called 'girls', being ignored by instructors (Dickstein, 1993; Lenhart, 1993; Bickel, 1994; Kirk, 1994; Mendelsohn et al., 1994; Guyatt et al., 1997). Taken together all of these factors lead to a gendered climate in medical school that may cause women to feel less welcome, more marginal.

Similarly, racial or ethnic harassment and discrimination have been experienced by 20 per cent of medical students (Baldwin et al., 1991) and 23 per cent of residents (Baldwin et al., 1994) in the United States.[5] There is less evidence about the more subtle processes that might construct a racialized medical school climate, nevertheless one recent ethnography of a British medical school depicts a high degree of racial segregation in extra-curricular activities, suggesting the marginalization of students of colour (Sinclair, 1997). Not surprisingly, perhaps, racialized minority students tend to have higher attrition rates than white students, take longer to complete undergraduate training, and are more likely to switch specialties or drop out of residency programs (Lee, 1992; Babbott et al., 1994; Campos-Outcalt et al., 1994; McManus et al., 1996).

Class-based cultural norms that may predominate in medical training remain under examined. In a Canadian study with 80 medical students one of the two who self-identified as working-class joked that the hardest thing for him to learn at medical school was 'the wine and cheeses' (Haas and Shaffir, 1987: 23).

Recent investigations into the impact of sexual orientation in medical school suggest that homophobic attitudes are as prevalent among medical students and faculty members as in the general population (Klamen et al., 1999). Thus students who identify as gay, lesbian, or bisexual may feel more marginalized in medical school than do heterosexually-identified students. National surveys found 40 per cent of general internists and 50 per cent of internal medicine residents witnessed homophobic[6] remarks by fellow physicians, nurses, other health care workers, and patients (Cook et al., 1995; vanIneveld et al., 1996). An American study found that although 67 per cent of family practice residency program directors showed attitudes supportive to gay men and lesbians, 25 per cent would rank residency applicants lower if they were known to be gay or lesbian (Oriel et al., 1996). In addition, 46 per cent of the gay/lesbian/bisexual students surveyed had experienced discrimination based on sexual orientation during medical school, and most hid or planned to hide their homosexuality during their residency application process.

Most medical schools today have an institutional commitment to equality, which has led to the reduction or eradication of overt discrimination in admissions (Cole, 1986) and to the establishment of policies and procedures to address harassment and discrimination. Even in the absence of blatant discrimination, however, an institution may have an overall climate that welcomes some participants more than others. The research presented here sought to investigate the micro level interactional processes through which the dominant culture of an institution may be conveyed, with attendant messages of inclusion and exclusion. This study did not set out to determine the *existence* of social inequalities based on gender, 'race', class, and sexual orientation; instead it explicates processes through which, in one particular educational institution, such inequalities are enacted.

Research Methods and Participants

In this study three complementary strategies were employed: A survey of an entire third-year class (123 students) at one medical school; interviews with 25 students from that class; and interviews with 23 faculty members from the same medical school.[7] In a traditional medical curriculum the third year is a key transition point for students as they move out of the classrooms and into the hospital wards and clinics (Becker et al., 1961; Coombs, 1978; Broadhead, 1983; Haas and Shaffir, 1987; Konner, 1987). The increased interactions with staff and patients reflect the students back to themselves as 'doctors' (Coombs, 1978: 227; Konner, 1987; Shapiro, 1987). Such interactions can simultaneously enforce gendered and racialized notions of who fits best with common ideas of 'doctor' by refusing to reinforce some students' emerging self-conceptions as physicians (Gamble, 1990; Rucker, 1992; Dickstein, 1993; Lenhart, 1993; Bickel, 1994; Kirk, 1994; Mendelsohn et al., 1994; Blackstock, 1996).

The characteristics of students who completed the survey are indicated in Table 21.1. The sample was highly heterogeneous. Half the respondents had no religious affiliation (51 per cent) while the remainder were Christian (36 per cent), Sikh (6 per cent), Hindu (3 per cent) and Jewish (3 per cent). Twenty respondents (28 per cent) considered themselves members of minority groups, almost all identifying as Asian, Chinese, Indo-Canadian, and South Asian. The 25 students interviewed were slightly less heterogeneous; most were of European Canadian heritage and they were more likely to be married or living with a partner. The class from which these samples were taken was 48 per cent female and approximately 66 per cent Caucasian, 22 per cent Asian, 11 per cent Indo-Canadian, and 1 per cent African heritage.[8]

The purposive sample of faculty members and administrators tended to be male and of European heritage—not unlike the majority of faculty in this school. The length of time working at this medical school ranged from 3 to 29 years, averaging 15 years. Five were academic faculty teaching the basic sciences;[9] the rest were clinical faculty.[10] Ten faculty members had administrative positions.

Everyday Inequalities and Micro Inequities

The notion of everyday inequalities is useful for understanding the micro level processes through which inequities of racism, sexism, heterosexism, and classism are experienced and perpetuated in Canadian society, where most citizens express commitment to democratic principles of justice, equality, tolerance, and fairness. Studying the contrasts between America and the Netherlands, Dutch sociologist Philomena Essed developed the concept of 'everyday racism', a form of racism distinctively structured in 'practices that infiltrate everyday life and become part of what is see as "normal" by the dominant group', even in the context of formal commitment to equality (1991: 288).

Recent work has begun to develop analyses that parallel Essed's everyday racism in other areas, particularly gender and sexuality. Nijole Benokraitis (1997a) has edited a collection of case studies analyzing what she terms 'subtle sexism'. By this she means the 'unequal and harmful treatment of women' that has been internalized 'as "normal", "natural", or "acceptable"' (Benokraitis, 1997b: 11). It can be intentional or unintentional and, as Lisa Frehill found in her study of engineering, it is consistent with normative expectations of male–female interactions: 'Although subtle sexist behaviour may be unintentional or "friendly", it still reinforces the boundaries between men and women' (1997: 126).

In their case study of women in law, Haslett and Lipman (1997) outline instances of hostile humour, isolation, diminishing, devaluation,

Table 21.1 Characteristics of the samples

Characteristic	Student survey sample (N = 72)	Student interviews sample (N = 25)	Faculty interviews sample (N = 23)
Gender			
Female	36 (50%)	14 (56%)	5 (22%)
Male	36 (50%)	11 (44%)	18 (78%)
Age			
Mean age	27 years	28 years	51 years
Range	24–40 years	23–40 years	36–67 years
Race/Ethnicity*			
Euro-Canadian	38 (53%)	18 (72%)	23 (100%)
Asian	15 (21%)	6 (24%)	
South Asian	6 (8%)		
Jewish	2 (3%)	1 (4%)	
Aboriginal	1 (1%)		
Not given	10 (14%)		
First Language			
English	52 (72%)	23 (92%)	21 (91%)
Not English	20 (28%)	2 (8%)	2 (9%)
Social class background**			
Upper/Upper-Middle	36 (50%)	14 (56%)	
Lower-Middle	23 (32%)	6 (24%)	
Working/Poor	11 (15%)	5 (20%)	
Other	2 (3%)		
Sexual orientation			
Heterosexual	71 (99%)	24 (96%)	13 (56%)
Homosexual	1 (1%)	1 (4%)	2 (9%)
Unknown			8 (35%)

*　Includes 'Canadian', British, Scottish, Irish, American, German, Scandinavian, Polish, Italian, Portuguese, Oceanic. Asian includes Chinese, Japanese, Korean, Taiwanese, Indonesian, Malaysian. South Asian includes Indian, Punjabi, Pakistani.
**　Self-described

and discouragement that cumulatively exclude women; rendering them less confident and productive. As was the case with everyday racism, the power of these practices, which Haslett and Lipman term 'micro inequities', lies in their repetition and 'aggregate burden'.

> Taken individually, each instance of an innuendo or hostile humor may strike one as being minor and not worth 'calling someone on it'; however, the daily, cumulative burden of continuously experiencing such micro inequities is significant . . . Over time . . . micro inequities constitute a formidable barrier to performance, productivity, and advancement (Haslett and Lipman, 1997: 51).

The individually trivial nature of such practices makes them particularly difficult to address effectively.

The perpetuation of structural arrangements of inequality is accomplished through 'ongoing, everyday, taken-far-granted practices that are rooted in cultural habit' (O'Brien, 1998: 25). Understanding, then, demands inquiry focused on the interactional processes that perpetually alter or counter existing structural arrangements. Inquiry must focus on the ways even those of us committed to equality practice inequality in our everyday interactions. The research presented here is an illustration of such inquiry. It investigates the everyday inequalities and micro inequities through which the dominant culture of one medical school is maintained despite an institutional commitment to equality of opportunity.

Everyday Racism

In interviews, both faculty and students generally indicated that 'race' and racism really are not issues in medical school. Nonetheless, many students then went on to describe racist incidents, most of which occurred during rural practice placements or elective rotations in other schools: 'People there were quite racist against Natives.'

Mark[11]: Last summer when we did a rural practice elective out in the community I heard a few things about East Indian students who had trouble with the more redneck kind of attitudes. Older, white people in the communities might say something offensive.

In keeping with the notion of everyday racism, overt racist incidents were not very common, yet 'race' appears to affect the extent to which students feel they fit in during medical school, with 45 per cent of 'minority' students indicating they 'fit in' well, compared with 58 per cent of non-minority students. Racialized minority students were slightly more likely than others to agree that 'race' affects how students are treated by other medical staff, and that it affects the degree of respect from patients. The day-to-day importance of 'race' and culture were also highest for minority students. Furthermore, 25 per cent of students who identi-

fied as members of minority groups indicated that their racial or cultural background had a negative effect on their experiences of medical school, compared to only 4 per cent of non-minority students. Interestingly, minority students were also more likely to indicate that their race/culture had a positive impact; in contrast 84 per cent of non-minority students experienced their race as neutral. In interviews students explained that being Chinese is often an advantage in a city with a large Chinese patient population.

The most apparent form of everyday racism was racist jokes. About half (52 per cent) of the survey respondents indicated they heard 'offensive jokes' in medical school; the most common category of such jokes was those concerning 'race or ethnicity' (see Table 21.2).[12] For example:

Sean: This guy had gone through the windshield of his car and they made some comment about, 'Oh, he was DWC. And I said, what's DWC? And they said, 'Driving While Chinese'. And that was the first day I was there. And that's on the wards, and walking along the halls, so anybody could hear it. One of the residents said that to a doctor and the doctor laughed and said, 'Oh, that was a good one. I never heard that before.'

As Nancy indicates, it can be very awkward for students to deal with racist comments when they come from attending physicians or senior residents who are in a position of power over students.

Nancy: We had a Native man come in and told us he wasn't feeling well or whatever. And we went into the other room and the doctor said, 'So do you think this is a dumb Indian or a smart Indian?' And I went, 'What?!' . . . This is a person I'm supposed to be learning from so I can't say, 'What kind of a stupid questions are you asking me here?!' I've got to be with him for another three weeks and try and get a reference letter out of him, so I can't cut him down.

Table 21.2 Survey findings concerning offensive jokes

Question: What type of jokes do you hear in medical school that you find offensive?

Jokes about:	Frequency
Ethnic/racial groups	22
Gender	19
Particular patient types	19
Gays and lesbians	14
Height or weight	12
Religious groups	10
Cadavers	7
'Crude' topics	3
Age	2

Two white students suggested they heard more overt racism than did students from racialized minority groups, since they were 'included in all the jokes' and were assumed to be like-minded because they are white: 'I was supposed to be one of them.'

Everyday Sexism

Neither male nor female students, on average, thought gender had much impact on their experiences of medical school, although the day-to-day importance of gender was greatest for women. Women also demonstrate more polarization than men; 54 per cent of women said gender is important to how they think about themselves, while a significant minority (23 per cent) said it was very unimportant. A certain ambiguity became apparent in the interviews, where most students stated that gender is really not an issue in medical school; classes are almost exactly gender balanced and everyone gets treated similarly. Having said this, however, most women and some men then went on to give examples of how gender does make a difference, ranging from quite blatant

sexism and sexual harassment to a more subtle climate of gendered expectations that may make things intangibly easier for male students.

One woman was in a small clinical group with three male classmates; they were greeted every day by the attending physician with, 'Good morning, gentlemen.' Again, in the terms of everyday sexism, this minor, perhaps trivial incident may have a cumulative effect over time, conveying a repeated message of marginalization. Other students described incidents of outright sexual harassment. For example, when one woman was serving as a model patient for a demonstration the male clinician inappropriately fondled and commented on her buttocks in front of the whole class.

Far more subtle is the impact of an overall gendered climate, a series of gendered assumptions and expectations that can make life in medical school more comfortable and inviting for male students. One woman described 'low level slightly irritating stuff', that is 'just somehow not inclusive or something, or not valuing me the way I would.' For example, students confront a lingering societal assumption that doctor = man. Two male students suggested this assumption facilitates rapport with patients and eases their way through the medical hierarchy.

Mark: Perhaps I bond better with the students and the residents and the staff members just because I come from the same background as the other doctors do . . . I've often felt, because I fit like a stereotyped white that patients might see me as a bit more trustworthy. A bit more what they'd like to see. Who they want to see.

This assumption that doctors are male may be reinforced by the fact that women students are less likely to be called doctor by other health care staff or by patients. Both students and faculty reported that women students and clinicians are still frequently mistaken for nurses. Fifty-seven per cent of the women surveyed were occasionally or regularly called doctor by someone other than family or friends, compared with 78 per cent of the men; 14 per cent of the women were *never* called doctor compared with 0 per cent of the men, Again, though being called 'Miss' while your male peers are called 'doctor' is in itself trivial, the effect can be cumulative. Perhaps consequently, almost half (6 of 14) of the women students interviewed indicated that they do not identify themselves as medical students in casual social settings outside school lest they be seen as putting on airs. None of the male students indicated this.

Constructing a professional appearance is another key element of medical socialization (Beagan, 2001), and one that is highly gendered. Both male and female survey respondents had concerns about their appearances. While male students dealt with those concerns by shaving, wearing a shirt with a collar, perhaps adding a tie, women's concerns were both more extensive and more complex. Women worried about style, accessories, body shapes, hair and make-up, about looking well-dressed without appearing too provocative, too feminine or simply incompetent: 'Is it professional enough? Competent looking? . . . I do not want to appear sexy on the job' (Survey comment, female). In the interviews, both women students and clinicians talked about dressing to earn respect; deliberately constructing an image that conveys desired messages. In contrast, the men took this for granted.

One of the most obvious areas where gender affects medical education *is* in students' choice of future career directions. Women were under-represented among those considering anesthesiology, surgery, and internal medicine all highly paid specialties. Women were over-represented among those considering obstetrics and gynecology, psychiatry, family medicine, and pediatrics, some of the lowest paid fields of medicine. Some faculty members argued that unless there are active moves to keep women out of specific specialties gender is not an issue. Indeed for 89 per cent of male students, gender was *not* an important considera-

tion when choosing their future specialty; for 43 per cent of women it *was* an important or very important factor (see Table 21.3).

One specialty, surgery, illustrates the complexity of gendering institutional climates. Only 28 per cent of women surveyed were considering surgery or surgical subspecialties. Students commented on the absence of women role-models, and described surgery as 'a man's world', a macho field.

> *Becky*: It's still fairly intimidating for females to go into. . . . It's really sort of old-school, very male oriented, a boy's club. And I think that as a female I wouldn't cope well in that. Lots of guys, if there's a woman there they won't do their usual jokes and banter between them. Or if they *do* do it, then you have to stand there and listen to it, which I wouldn't really want to either.

Even the material realities of an operating room contribute to the masculine climate of surgery, as one male surgeon outlined (c.f., Cassell, 1996).

In addition to a masculine atmosphere several women students ruled out surgery because they could not see how the long hours and intense call schedule would fit with having a family. Women rated parental and marital status as far more important considerations in career choice than did male students (see Table 21.3). Virtually every woman interviewed had concerns about fitting together career and family life, which guided them away from some specialties and toward others.

> *Nancy*: I worry about balancing my family life. I worry about when I'm going to have children. How I'm going to put my children and my husband into a full-time career, with him having a full-time career. I don't want to have children who know their nanny better than they know me. I'm in that position that I think a lot of women are in, of wanting to be able to do it all and

Table 21.3 Gender-related concerns in specially considerations

Question: How important are the following factors to you in choosing your future specialty? (I = Not important, 5 = Very important)

	1	2	3	4	5
Gender					
Female %	26	14	17	31	12
Male %	67	22	8	3	0
$\lambda = 0.26$					
Parental status					
Female %	9	3	11	23	54
Male %	19	14	14	31	22
$\lambda = 0.17$					
Marital or relationship status					
Female %	9	3	6	37	46
Male %	19	6	17	36	22
$\lambda = 0.14$					

feeling inadequate when you can't. Wanting to be a full-time mom and have a nice house and be able to keep it up and do the grocery shopping and do the laundry and still work full-time and be there for all your patients and also be a good wife to your husband. And I know something's got to give and I'm not sure where it's going to be. I hope it's not my children.

While the women students were almost universally concerned with how a career would fit with expected family roles, virtually none of the men interviewed had thought about this.

Again, as was the case with everyday racism, the point is not that women face unusually high levels of sexism in medical school. Rather, this research illustrates the subtle processes of everyday sexism, interactional processes that construct the role of medical student or physician as somewhat more suited to a man than a woman. Women have to work to construct a professional appearance, to look feminine yet competent, to earn respect.

Women students choose career paths that avoid overly masculinized environments, opting for lower paid specialties that will allow them to be good wives and mothers without sacrificing their careers. When attending physicians routinely call women medical students 'Miss' while addressing their male peers as 'doctor', and when patients routinely call women students 'nurse', those trivial incidents occur *on top* of a pattern of micro inequities (Haslett and Lipman, 1997), as part of daily processes of gendering medicine.

Everyday Heterosexism

The experience of being identifiably gay or lesbian in this medical school seemed to depend a great deal on the dominant tone of each class. Being openly gay might lead to isolation one year, while the next entering class might be very supportive of an openly gay classmate. The two clinicians interviewed who identified as gay said their sexual orientation had been a source of difficulty and marginalization for them in medical school. They had to decide how 'out' to be, and how much to suppress that part of their identity. They both see gay and lesbian students today facing similar struggles.

The one gay student who responded to the survey noted that his sexual orientation is a source of great stress. One aspect of that stress is homophobia expressed by other medical personnel. Students and physicians indicated that jokes about gays and lesbians were common.

While there are some sanctions for staff who make harassing comments, homophobic comments from patients leave students with little recourse. One clinician indicated that students just have to learn to handle it.

> Dr E: As a physician you will be called the 'F-word' [fag]. You will be told that you're going to get punched if you don't leave. And if you're gay or of different orientation, they might tell you, 'Hey, you take it in the ass and I'm not gonna talk to you.' It will happen. And I think it's part of [students'] education—how to deal with it.

As was the case with racist jokes and comments, students are placed in a particularly awkward position when homophobic jokes or slurs come from their patients.

Students may also face some degree of homophobia from their classmates.[13] Two students identified their heterosexuality as an advantage, commenting that it would be difficult to be gay or lesbian in their class.

> Robin: I see huge homophobia. I'm not gay, but out of a hundred and twenty people, statistically there's gonna be a few gay or lesbian people in my class. And no one will admit to it. . . . They obviously don't feel comfortable saying that. . . . One of my colleagues in first year had someone scribble 'fag' on his nametag on his desk. . . .

> I think people try to avoid standing out in any way and I guess one way to stand out is to be gay.

It only takes a few instances such as that described by Robin to have an effect. Even if just a few students are vocally homophobic, that may be sufficient to cause gay and lesbian students in the class to feel unsafe.

Students and faculty who identified as gay described leading highly segregated lives during medical school, keeping their school lives separate from their lives in gay and lesbian community. Several faculty members argued that this segregation and 'closeting' is a necessary survival strategy, as being out can be costly in terms of desired jobs. One gay clinician described a student coming out gradually by his third year of medical school, 'then slipping back in during fourth year, because he was afraid—and, I hate to say it . . . my feeling is that he's probably right. If he were gay and out he probably wouldn't get into a surgical residency' (c.f. Oriel et al., 1996). Even if the risks of being out are more perceived than real, one clinician pointed out that 'you're giving up an awful lot if you're wrong, if you feel that, "Gee they would accept me," and find out they won't.' Finally, one faculty member suggested sexual orientation may even influence residency choices, as he sees gay and lesbian students trying to identify which fields might be safest for them to be out (c.f., Risdon, Cook, and Willms, 2000). Again, this process, like the process of women students choosing not to enter surgery, is one of self-elimination. The realm of the possible becomes defined through cultural habit, excluding some options from consideration.

> Jason: What I've experienced is a lot of—not overt homophobia, well, a *little* overt homophobia, especially by a vocal sect in the class. . . . Among the teaching faculty there's some homophobia, just underneath the surface. They never come out

and say it, they're always politically correct, but you know it's there. Fellow students—I guess that's one of the reasons why I also feel more distant from a lot of people in the class. . . . If somebody talks about what they did on the weekend, if I did party I'm not going to tell them that I went to one of the gay bars.

Again, what is described here is not an unusually high degree of homophobia or heterosexism, nor even a set of hostile practices *intended* to exclude, discriminate, or harm. It is, rather, the experience of not quite fitting in with the dominant culture that surrounds you, of being marginalized. Everyday heterosexism, like everyday racism and sexism, is not life-threatening—although gay and lesbian students never know when it might be accompanied by a more virulent homophobia. From the simple assumption that everyone around you is heterosexual, to teasing about (hetero)sex at school social gatherings, to laughing at or making homophobic jokes, to not challenging homophobic remarks, to declining residency applications from openly gay students (Oriel et al., 1996), again the micro inequities of everyday heterosexism consist of the repetition of numerous small practices.

Everyday Classism

In Canada, the extremes of poverty and wealth are mitigated by our redistributive social welfare system. Widely accessible student loans mean university education—including medical education—and subsequent upward mobility are available to anyone willing to incur that level of debt. But social class is not just about money. Class also operates on the more subtle level of cultural capital and social capital: knowing the right people, being able to make the right sort of small talk, having the right hobbies and playing the right sports, knowing the right fork to use, and having the right clothes, accent, and demeanour.

Students from working class or impoverished families also described a significant struggle to construct the professional appearance expected in medicine. The 'right look' felt wrong for them. One woman noted that the very first time she felt she actually belonged in medical school was during a third-year elective in a clinic for low-income patients: 'I had the thrill of my lifetime at the Clinic. I could just dress in what's in my closet and not feel bad about it. And I could talk my natural way. And I *totally* fit in over there!'

There was considerable agreement among students and faculty that students from upper- or upper-middle-class backgrounds, especially the children of doctors, find it easiest to fit in at medical school and may adopt a student physician identity more readily. A third (31 per cent) of the students surveyed agreed that, 'students who come from upper-class backgrounds find it easier to fit in during medical training'—a belief held most strongly by students from working-class and impoverished family backgrounds. Poor and working-class students were more likely to believe their class background had a negative impact during medical school. One student wrote simply: 'I cannot relate to many of my classmates who come from very wealthy, AngloSaxon backgrounds' (Survey comment).

Two clinicians who came from working-class families said they never fit in during medical school and they continue to feel marginalized as physicians.

> *Dr P.:* [One] reason that I had a very difficult time [in medical school] is that I come from a working-class family, the only person in my extended family to finish high-school, to go to university. . . . That puts me in a very difference spot than the upper-middle-class white male, whose father was a doctor, who like the medical school, who was part of the 'in group' at the school and who is now part of the 'in group' as faculty.

One clinician was moved to tears during our interview when she recognized that the extreme isolation she felt as a working-class medical student 30 years ago has never really lessened.

Conclusions

This research in a single Canadian medical school illustrates the complexity of everyday racism, classism, sexism, and heterosexism. Well beyond blatant forms of discrimination (practices already targeted by formal anti-discrimination policies and procedures) more covert and more subtle forms of marginalization maintain and reproduce an institutional climate that is more welcoming to some participants than others. Micro level everyday practices of inclusion and exclusion cumulatively convey messages about who does and who does not truly belong. The interactional processes of everyday inequalities maintain hierarchies even within this group of relatively elite students and faculty.

As Jodi O'Brien (1998) suggests, the practices of everyday inequalities are often mindless, unknowing, and habitual. The power of these micro inequities is that they are seen as normal, natural, or acceptable. The majority of the participants in this research would say that gender, 'race', sexual orientation, and class are not issues in their medical school. In a society imbued with belief in meritocracy, these students and faculty have made it very near the top. They have a vested interest in denying categorically based injustices in favour of individual merit and equal opportunity. Yet the fact that the micro inequities illustrated here are at odds with the equality of opportunity expressly endorsed by the institution does not make them less, damaging for marginalized and alienated students.

In contrast it suggests that ensuring equality of opportunity is not enough. Simply getting in to a school, an occupation, or a profession in which members of your social group have historically been under-represented, does not ensure that your experience there will be equitable. There may still be significant barriers to full participation. In his examination of a Canadian aboriginal teacher education program, Rick Hesch (1994: 201) argues that although students construct the program to meet their own needs as best they can, they do so in the face of 'fundamentally punishing conditions' that serve to limit their achievements. Those punishing conditions arise in the intersection of institutional expectations about students' roles with socio-cultural expectations about their private lives; there is a privileging of particular class-based and Eurocentric forms of knowledge that implicitly marginalizes the or pushes them toward assimilation. Similarly, although medical education provides an avenue for members of subordinated social groups to achieve upward mobility, in doing so they confront an institution that privileges particular cultural habits and knowledge forms. It simultaneously reproduces the inclusions and exclusions of racism, sexism, heterosexism, and classism. That institutional climate is maintained through daily subtle practices whose effects taken individually may be considered trivial, but taken cumulatively convey a message about who does and who does not belong. What remains to be seen in further research is what impact—if any—these micro inequities and everyday inequalities and their messages of marginality have on medical practitioners in their work lives.

Notes

1. I would like to thank Bethan Lloyd for comments on earlier versions of this work, and the anonymous *CJS* reviewers for their detailed reading and helpful comments. The research was supported by doctoral fellowships from the Social Sciences and Humanities Research Council of Canada, and the Izaak Killam Memorial Foundation.

2. The term 'race' is enclosed in quotation marks to indicate its status as a social construct rather than an ontologically valid category. Social constructs are nonetheless real in their consequences. The routine use of the term 'race' as if it actually exists in our daily social worlds makes it difficult to investigate the social relations of racialization without reference to the term—even as that helps to perpetuate its presumed validity.

3. Calculated based on the descriptive statistics given by Becker et al.: 'each class contains a number of women, ordinarily around five . . . as well as a small number of American Negroes, possibly four or five' (1961: 60). They give the entering class size for one year, 1958, as 94 new students (1961: 53). Assuming class sizes are fairly constant, I estimate the percentages above.

4. Yet even very recent research has failed to problematize the impact of social differences among students, perpetuating the image of a generic medical student (e.g., Sinclair, 1997).

5. This research is bolstered by a growing body of personal accounts about racism in medical school (Blackstock, 1996; Gamble, 1990; Rucker, 1992). Research on the experiences of racialized minority students in Canada is virtually non-existent.

6. By 'homophobia' I mean fear and hatred of or, more mildly, hostility and condemnation directed toward people known or believed to be gay, lesbian, or bisexual. By 'heterosexism' I mean the overwhelming assumption that the world is and must be heterosexual, and the systemic display of power and privilege that establish heterosexuality as the irrefutable norm—by extension establishing homosexuality as deviance. Heterosexism centres on oblivion about/denial of the very existence of gays and lesbians. Homophobia is a more active form of intolerance and hostility.

7. The medical school where the research was conducted is not identified. This was an agreement made with the administration of the school in order to gain access to the research site. That decontextualizes the research and leaves the degree of generalizability to other medical schools an empirical question. The school followed a traditional undergraduate curriculum and was located in a large Canadian city with a racially and ethnically diverse population.

8. Subjective assessment of class photos shows that since the early 1980s about 30 per cent of each class at this school would be considered 'visible minority' students.

9. They represented anatomy, biochemistry, physiology, and pharmacology.

10. Their clinical areas included renal, pulmonary, pediatrics and pediatric oncology, medical genetics, family practice, surgery, neurology, ethics, internal medicine, infectious disease, endocrinology, anesthesia, and psychiatry.

11. All names used are pseudonyms.

12. Unfortunately, we cannot know from the data whether they had heard one such joke or heard them daily.

13. Again, whether the level of homophobia in medical school is higher or lower than in the rest of the society is not the point. The point is simply that students who identify as, or are identified as, gay or lesbian have distinctive experiences in medical school in part because they have to deal with homophobia from patients, staff, faculty, and classmates. It makes their experience of school different from that of students identified as heterosexual.

References

Association of Canadian Medical Colleges. 1998. *Canadian Medical Education Statistics* 20.

Baldwin, D.C., Jr., S.R. Daugherty, and B.D. Rowley. 1994. 'Emotional Impact of Medical School and Residency', *Academic Medicine* 69 Supplement: S19–21.

Baldwin, D.C., S.R. Daugherty, and E.J. Eckenfels. 1991. 'Student Perceptions of Mistreatment and Harassment During Medical School: A Survey in 10 United States Schools', *Western Journal of Medicine* 155: 140–5.

Beagan, B.L. 2001. 'Even if I don't know what I'm

doing I can make it *look* like I know what I'm doing': Becoming a Doctor in the 1990s', *Canadian Review of Sociology and Anthropology* 39, 3: 275–92.

Becker, H.S., B. Geer, A.L. Strauss, and E.C. Hughes. 1961. *Boys in White: Student Culture in Medical School*. Chicago: University of Chicago Press.

Benokraitis, N.E., ed. 1997a. *Subtle Sexism: Current Practice and Prospects For Change*. Thousand Oaks, CA: Sage.

———. 1997b. 'Sex Discrimination in the 21st Century', in N.V. Benokraitis, ed., *Subtle Sexism: Current Practice and Prospects For Change*, pp. 5–33. Thousand Oaks, CA: Sage.

Bergen, M.R., C.M. Guarino, and C.D. Jacobs. 1996. 'A Climate Survey for Medical Students', *Evaluation and the Health Professions* 19: 30–47.

Bickel, J. 1994. 'Special Needs and Affinities of Women Medical Students', in E.S. More and M.A. Milligan, eds, *The Empathetic Practitioner: Empathy, Gender and Medicine*, pp. 237–49. New Brunswick, NJ: Rutgers Press.

Bickel, J. and A. Ruffin. 1995. 'Gender-Associated Differences in Matriculating and Graduating Medical Students', *Academic Medicine* 70: 552–9.

Bickel, J., and P.R. Kopriva. 1993. 'A Statistical Perspective on Gender in Medicine', *Journal of the American Medical Women's Association* 48: 141–4.

Blackstock, D.G. 1996. 'A Black Woman in Medicine', in D. Wear, ed., *Women in Medical Education: An Anthology of Experience*, pp. 75–80. New York, SUNY Press.

Broadhead, R. 1983. *The Private Lives and Professional Identities of Medical Students*. New Brunswick, NJ: Transaction.

Cassel, J. 1996. 'The Woman in the Surgeon's Body: Understanding Difference', *American Anthropologist* 98: 41–53.

Cole, S. 1986. 'Sex Discrimination and Admission to Medical School, 1929–1984', *American Journal of Sociology* 92: 549–67.

Cook, D.I., L.E. Griffith, M. Cohen, G.H., Guyatt, and B. O'Brien. 1995. 'Discrimination and Abuse Experienced by General Internists in Canada', *Journal of General Internal Medicine* 10: 565–72.

Coombs, R.H. 1978. *Mastering Medicine*. New York: Free Press.

Dickstein, L.J. 1993. 'Gender Bias in Medical Education: Twenty Vignettes and Recommended Responses', *Journal of the American Medical Women's Association* 48: 152–62.

Druzin, P., I. Shrier, M. Yacowar, and M. Rossognol. 1998. 'Discrimination Against Gay, Lesbian and Bisexual Family Physicians By Patients', *Canadian Medical Association Journal* 158: 593–7.

Essed, P. 1991. *Understanding Everyday Racism: An Interdisciplinary Theory*. New York: Sage.

Foster, H.W. 1996. 'Reaching Parity for Minority Medical Residents: A Possibility or a Pipe Dream?', *Journal of the National Medical Association* 88: 17–21.

Frehill. L.M. 1997. 'Subtle Sexism in Engineering', in N.V. Benokraitis, ed., *Subtle Sexism: Current Practice and Prospects For Change*, pp. 117–35. Thousand Oaks, CA: Sage.

Gamble, V.N. 1990. 'On Becoming a Physician: A Dream Not Deferred', in E.C. White, ed., *The Black Women's Health Book: Speaking for Ourselves*, pp. 52–64. Seattle, WA: Seal Press.

Grant, L. 1988. 'The Gender Climate of Medical School: Perspectives of Women and Men Students', *Journal of the American Medical Women's Association* 43: 109–19.

Gray, J.D., and J. Reudy. 1998. 'Undergraduate and Postgraduate Medical Education in Canada', *Canadian Medical Association Journal* 58: 1047–50.

Guyatt, G.H., D.J. Cook, L. Griffith, S.D. Walter, C. Risdon, and J. Liukus. 1997. 'Attitudes Toward the Use of Gender-Inclusive Language Among Residency Trainees', *Canadian Medical Association Journal* 156: 1289–93.

Haas, J., and W. Shaffir. 1987. *Becoming Doctors: The Adoption of a Cloak of Competence*. Greenwich, CN: JAI Press.

Haslett, B.B., and S. Lipman. 1997. 'Micro Inequities: Up Close and Personal', in N.V. Benokraitis, ed., *Subtle Sexism: Current Practice and Prospects for Change*, pp. 34–53. Thousand Oaks, CA: Sage.

Hesch, R. 1994. 'Cultural Production and Cultural Reproduction in Aboriginal Preservice Teacher Education', in L. Erwin and D. MacLennan, eds, *Sociology of Education in Canada: Critical Perspectives on Theory, Research and Practice*. Mississauga: Copp Clark Longman: 200–19.

Hostler, S.L., and R.R.P. Gressard. 1993. 'Perceptions of the Gender Fairness of the Medical Education Environment', *Journal of the American Medical Women's Association* 48: 51–4.

Jonas, H.S., S.A. Etzel, and B. Barzansky. 1992. 'Educational Programs in US Medical Schools', *Journal of the American Medical Association* 268: 1083–90.

Kirk, J. 1994. 'A Feminist Analysis of Women in Medical Schools', in B.S. Bolaria and H.D. Dickenson, eds, *Health, Illness, and Health Care in Canada, 2nd edition*, pp. 158–82. Toronto: Harcourt Brace.

Klamen, D.L, L.S. Grossman, and D.R. Kopacz. 1999. 'Medical Student Homophobia', *Journal of Homosexuality* 37: 53–63.

Komaromy, M., A.B. Bindman, R.J. Haber, and M.A. Sande. 1993. 'Sexual Harassment in Medical Training', *The New England Journal of Medicine* 328: 322–6.

Konner, M. 1987. *Becoming a Doctor: A Journey of Initiation in Medical School*. New York: Viking.

Lenhart, S. 1993. 'Gender Discrimination: A Health and Career Development Problem for Women Physicians', *Journal of the American Medical Women's Association* 4, 8: 155–9.

Mendelsohn, K.D., L.Z. Neiman, K. Isaacs, S. Lee, and S.P. Levison. 1994. 'Sex and Gender Bias in Anatomy and Physical Diagnosis Text Illustrations', *Journal of the American Medical Association* 272: 1267–70.

Moscarello, R., K.J. Margittai, and M. Rissi. 1994. 'Differences in Abuse Reported by Female and Male Canadian Medical Students', *Canadian Medical Association Journal* 150: 357–63.

O'Brien, J. 1998. 'Introduction: Differences and Inequities', in J. O'Brien and J.A. Howard, eds, *Everyday Iinqualities: Critical Inquiries*, pp. 1–39. Malden, MA: Blackwell.

Oriel, K.A., D.J. Madlon-Kay, D. Govaker, and D.J. Mersey. 1996. 'Gay and Lesbian Physicians in Training: Family Practice Program Directors' Attitudes and Students' Perceptions of Bias', *Family Medicine* 28: 720–5.

Risdon, C., D. Cook, and D. Willms. 2000. 'Gay and Lesbian Physicians in Training: A Qualitative Study', *Canadian Medical Association Journal* 162: 331–4.

Rose, L. 1994. 'Homophobia Among Doctors', *British Medical Journal* 308: 586–7.

Rucker, C.S. 1992. 'Wrestling with Ignorance', *Journal of the American Medical Association* 267: 2392.

Schulte, H.M., and J. Kay. 1994. 'Medical Students' Perceptions of Patient-Initiated Sexual Behavior', *Academic Medicine* 69: 842–6.

Shapiro, M. 1987. *Getting Doctored: Critical Reflections on Becoming a Physician*. Toronto, ON: Between the Lines.

Sinclair, S. 1997. *Making Doctors: An Institutional Apprenticeship*. New York: Berg.

vanIneveld, C.H., D.J. Cook, S.L. Kane, and D. King. 1996. 'Discrimination and Abuse in Internal Medicine Residency', *Journal of General Internal Medicine* 11: 401–5.

Wallick, M.M., K.M. Cambre, and M.H. Townsend. 1992. 'How the Topic of Homosexuality is Taught at US Medical Schools', *Academic Medicine* 67: 601–3.

CHAPTER22

Women's Perspective as a Radical Critique of Sociology[1]

Dorothy E. Smith

The women's movement has given us a sense of our right to have women's interests represented in sociology, rather than just receiving as authoritative the interests traditionally represented in a sociology put together by men. What can we make of this access to a social reality that was previously unavailable, was indeed repressed? What happens as we begin to relate to it in the terms of our discipline? We can of course think as many do merely of the addition of courses to the existing repertoire—courses on sex roles, on the social psychology of women, and perhaps somewhat different versions of the sociology of the family. But thinking more boldly, or perhaps just thinking the whole thing through a little further, might bring us to ask first how a sociology might look if it began from the point of view of women's traditional place in it and what happens to a sociology which attempts to deal seriously with that. Following this line of thought, I have found, has consequences larger than they seem at first.

How sociology is thought—its methods, conceptual schemes, and theories—had been based on the built up within, the male social universe (even when women have participated in its doing). It has taken for granted not just that scheme of relevance as an itemized inventory of issues or subject matters (industrial sociology, political sociology, social stratification, etc.) but also the fundamental social and political structures under which these become relevant and are ordered. There is a difficulty first then of a disjunction between how women find and experience the world beginning (though not necessarily ending up) from their place and the concepts and theoretical schemes available to think about it in. Thus in a graduate seminar last year, we discussed on one occasion the possibility of a women's sociology and two graduate students told us that in their view and their experience of functioning in experimental group situations, theories of the emergence of leadership in small groups, etc. just did not apply to what was happening as they experienced it. They could not find the correlates of the theory in their experiences.

A second difficulty is that the two worlds and the two bases of knowledge and experience don't stand in an equal relation. The world as it is constituted by men stands in authority over that of women. It is the part of the world from which our kind of society is governed and from which what happens to us begins. The domestic world stands

in a dependent relation to that other and its whole character is subordinate to it.

The two difficulties are related to one another in a special way. The effect of the second interacting with the first is to impose the concepts and terms in which the world of men is thought of as the concepts and terms in which women must thing their world. Hence in these terms women are alienated from their experience.When I speak here of governing or ruling I mean something more general than the notion of government as political organization. I refer rather to that total complex of activities differentiated into many spheres, by which our kind of society is ruled, managed, and administered. It includes that whole section which in the business world is called 'management'. It includes the professions. It includes of course government more conventionally defined and also the activities of those who are selecting, training, and indoctrinating those who provide and elaborate the procedures in which it is governed and develop methods for accounting for how it is done and predicting and analyzing its characteristic consequences and sequences of events, namely the business schools, the sociologists, the economists, etc. Theses are the institutions through which we are ruled and through which we, and I emphasize this we, participate in ruling.

Sociology then I conceive as much more than ideology, much more than a gloss on the enterprise that justifies and rationalizes it and at the same time as much less than 'science'. The governing of our kind of society is done in concepts and symbols. The contribution of sociology to this is that of working up the conceptual procedures, models, and methods by which the immediate and concrete features of experience can be read into the conceptual mode in which the governing is done. What is actually observed or what is systematically recovered by the sociologist from the actualities of what people say and do, must be transposed into the abstract mode. Sociology thus participates in and contributes to the formation and facilitation of this mode of action and plays a distinctive part in the work of transposing the actualities of people's lives and experience into the conceptual currency in which it is and can be governed.

As graduate students learning to become sociologists, we learn to think sociology as it is thought and to practice it as it is practiced. We learn that some topics are relevant and some are not. We learn to discard our experienced world as a source of reliable information or suggestions about the character of the world; to confine and focus our insights within the conceptual frameworks and relevances that are given in the discipline. Should we think other kinds of thoughts or experience the world in a different way or with edges and horizons that pass beyond the conceptual we must practice a discipline that discards them or find some procedure which makes it possible to sneak them in. We learn a way of thinking about the world that is recognizable to its practitioners as the sociological way of thinking.

We learn to practice the sociological subsumption of the actualities of ourselves and of other people. We find out how to treat the world as instances of a sociological body of knowledge. The procedure operates as a sort of conceptual imperialism. When we write a thesis or a paper, we learn that the first thing to do is to latch it on to the discipline at some point. This may be by showing how it is a problem within an existing theoretical and conceptual framework. The boundaries of enquiry are thus set within the framework of what is already established. Even when this becomes, as it happily often does, a ceremonial authorization of a project that has little to do with the theory used to authorize it, we still work within the vocabularies and within the conceptual boundaries of what we have come to know as 'the sociological perspective'.

An important set of procedures which serve to constitute the body of knowledge of the discipline as something which is separated from its practitioners are those known as 'objectivity'. The ethic of objectivity and the methods used in its practice are concerned primarily with the separation of the knower from what he knows and in particular with the separation of what is known from any interests, 'biases', etc., which he may have that are not the interests and concerns authorized by the discipline. I must emphasize that being interested in knowing something doesn't invalidate what is known. In the social sciences the pursuit of objectivity makes it possible for people to be paid to pursue a knowledge to which they are otherwise indifferent. What they feel and think about society can be taken apart from and kept out of what they are professionally or academically interested in.

The sociologist enters the conceptually ordered society when he goes to work. He enters it as a member and he enters it also as the mode in which he investigates it. He observes, analyzes, explains, and examines as if there were no problem in how that world becomes observable to him. He moves among the doings of organizations, governmental processes, bureaucracies, etc., as a person who is at home in that medium. The nature of that world itself, how it is known to him, and the conditions of its existence or his relation to it are not called into question. His methods of observation and inquiry extend into it as procedures that are essentially of the same order as those which bring about the phenomena with which he is concerned, or which he is concerned to bring under the jurisdiction of that order. His perspectives and interests may differ, but the substance is the same. He works with facts and information which have been worked up from actualities and appear in the form of documents, which are themselves the product of organizational processes, whether his own or administered by him, or of some other agency. He fits that information back into a framework of entities and organizational processes which he takes for granted as known, without asking how it is that he knows them or what are the social processes by which the phenomena which correspond to or provide the empirical events, acts, decision, etc., of the world, may be recognized.

He passes beyond the particular and immediate setting in which he is always located in the body (the office he writes in, the libraries he consults, the streets he travels, the home he returns to) without any sense of having made a transition. He works in the same medium as he studies.

But like everyone else he also exists in the body in the place in which it is. This is also then the place of his sensory organization of immediate experience, the place where his coordinates of here and now before and after are organized around himself as centre; the place where he confronts people face to face in the physical mode in which he expresses himself to them and they to him as more and other than either can speak. It is in this place that things smell. The irrelevant birds fly away in front of the window. Here he has indigestion. It is a place he dies in. Into this whether as the sounds of speech the scratchings on the surface of paper that he constitutes as document, or directly anything he knows of the world. It has to happen here somehow if he is the experience it at all.

Women are outside and subservient to this structure. They have a very specific relation to it that anchors them into the local and particular phase of the bifurcated world. For both traditionally and as a matter of occupational practices in our society, the governing conceptual mode is appropriated by men and the world organized in the natural attitude, the home, is appropriated by (or assigned to) women (Smith, 1973).

It is a condition of a man's being able to enter and become absorbed in the conceptual mode that he does not have to focus his activities and interests upon his bodily existence. If he is to participate fully in the abstract mode of the action, then he must be liberated also from having to attend to his needs, etc. in the concrete and particular. The organization of work and expectations in managerial and professional circles both constitutes and depends upon the alienation of man from his bodily and local existence. The structure of work and the structure of career take

for granted that these matters are provided for in such a way that they will not interfere with his action and participation in that world. Providing for the liberation from the Aristotelian categories of which Bierstedt speaks, is a woman who keeps house for him, bears and cares for his children, washes his clothes, looks after him when he is sick and generally provides for the logistics of his bodily existence.

The place of women then in relation to this mode of action is that where the work is done to create conditions that facilitate his occupation of the conceptual mode of consciousness. The meeting of a man's physical needs, the organization of his daily life, and even the consistency of expressive background, are made maximally congruent with his commitment. A similar relation exists for women who work in and around the professional and managerial scene. They do those things that give concrete form to the conceptual activities. They do the clerical work, the computer programming, the interviewing for the survey, the nursing, and the secretarial work. At almost every point women mediate for men the relation between the conceptual mode of action and the actual concrete forms in which it is and must be realized, and the actual material conditions upon which it depends.

Women sociologists stand at the centre of a contradiction in the relation of our discipline to our experience of the world. For women, the relation between ourselves as practicing sociologists and ourselves as working women is continually visible to us, a central feature of experience of the world, so that the bifurcation of consciousness becomes for us a daily chasm which is to be crossed, on the one side of which is this special conceptual activity of thought, research, teaching, and administration and on the other the world of concrete practical activities in keeping things clean, managing somehow the house and household and the children in a world in which the particularities of persons in their full organic immediacy (cleaning up the vomit, changing the diapers, as well as feeding) are inescapable. Even if we don't have that as a direct contingency in our lives, we are aware of that as something that our becoming may be inserted into as a possible predicate.

It is also present for us to discover that the discipline is not one which we enter and occupy on the same terms as men enter and occupy it. We do not fully appropriate its authority, i.e., the right to author and authorize the acts and knowing and thinking of the discipline as it is thought. We cannot therefore command the inner principles of our action. That remains lodged outside us. The frames of reference that order the terms upon which inquiry and discussion are conducted originate with men. The subjects of sociological sentences (if they are a subject) are male. The sociologist is 'he'. An alternative approach must somehow transcend this contradiction without re-entering Bierstedt's 'transcendental realm' (1966). Women's perspective, as I have analyzed it here, discredits sociology's claim to constitute an objective knowledge independent of the sociologist's situation. Its conceptual procedures, methods, and relevances are seen to organize its subject matter from a determinate position in society. This critical disclosure becomes the basis for an alternative way of thinking sociology. If sociology cannot avoid being situated, then sociology should take that as its beginning and build it into its methodological and theoretical strategies. As it is now, these separate a sociologically constructed world from that which is known in direct experience and it is precisely that separation which must be undone.

I am not proposing an immediate and radical transformation of the subject matter and methods of the discipline nor the junking of everything that has gone before. What I am suggesting is more in the nature of a reorganization that changes the relating of the sociologist to the object of her knowledge and changes also her problematic. This reorganization involves first placing the sociologist where she is actually situated, namely at the beginning of those acts by which she knows or will come to know; and second, making her direct experience of the everyday world the primary ground of her knowledge.

We would reject, it seems to me, a sociology aimed primarily at itself. We would not be interested in contributing to a body of knowledge the uses of which are not ours and the knower of whom are who knows whom, but generally make—particularly when it is not at all clear what it is that is constituted as knowledge in that relation. The professional sociologist's practice of thinking it as it is thought would have to be discarded. She would be constrained by the actualities of how it happens in her direct experience. Sociology would aim at offering to anyone a knowledge of the social organization and determinations of the properties and events of their directly experienced world. Its analyses would become part of our ordinary interpretations of the experienced world, just as our experience of the sun's sinking below the horizon is transformed by our knowledge that the world turns. (Yet from where we are it seems to sink and that must be accounted for.)

The only way of knowing a socially constructed world is knowing it from within. We can never stand outside it. A relation in which sociological phenomena are objectified and presented as external to and independent of the observer is itself a special social practice also known from within. The relation of observer and object of observation, of sociologist to 'subject', is a specialized social relationship. Even to be a stranger is to enter a world constituted from within as strange. The strangeness itself is the mode in which it is experienced.

When Jean Briggs (1970) made her ethnographic study of the ways in which an Eskimo people structure and express emotion, what she learned and observed emerged for her in the context of the actual developing relations between her and the family with whom she lived and other members of the group. Her account situates her knowledge in the context of those relationships. Affections, tensions, and quarrels were the living texture in which she learnt what she describes.

She makes it clear how this context structured her learning and how what she learnt and can speak of became observable to her. Briggs tells us what is normally discarded in the anthological or sociological telling. Although sociological inquiry is necessarily a social relation, we have learned to disattend our own part in it. We recover only the object of its knowledge as if that stood all by itself and of itself. Sociology does not provide for seeing that there are always two terms to this relation. An alternative sociology must be reflexive (Gouldner, 1971), i.e., one that preserves in it the presence, concerns, and experience of the sociologist as knower and discoverer.

To begin from direct experience and to return to it as a constraint or 'test' of the adequacy of a systematic knowledge is to begin from where we are located bodily. The actualities of our everyday world are already socially organized. Settings, equipment, 'environment', schedules, occasions, etc., as well as the enterprises and routines of actors are socially produced and concretely and symbolically organized prior to our practice. By beginning from her original and immediate knowledge of her world, sociology offers a way of making its socially organized properties first observable and then problematic.

Let me make it clear that when I speak of 'experience' I do not use the term as a synonym for 'perspective'. Nor in proposing a sociology grounded in the sociologist's actual experience, am I recommending the self-indulgence of inner exploration or any other enterprise with self as sole focus and object. Such subjectivist interpretations of 'experience' are themselves an aspect of that organization of consciousness which bifurcates it and transports us into mind country while stashing away the concrete conditions and practices upon which it depends. We can never escape the circles of our own hands if we accept that as our territory. Rather the sociologist's investigating of our directly experienced world as a problem is a mode of discovering or rediscovering the society from within. She begins from her own original but

tacit knowledge and from within the acts by which she brings it into her grasp in making it observable and in understanding how it works. She aims not at a reiteration of what she already (tacitly) knows, but at an exploration through that of what passes beyond it and is deeply implicated in how it is.

Our knowledge of the world is given to us in the modes we enter into relations with the object of knowledge. Riding a train not long ago in Ontario I saw a family of Indians, woman, man, and three children standing together on a spur above a river watching the train go by. There was (for me) that moment—the train those five people seen on the other side of the glass. I saw first that I could tell this incident as it was, but that telling as a description built in my position and my interpretations. I have called them a family; I have said they were watching the train. My understanding has already subsumed theirs. Everything may have been quite other for them. My description is privileged to stand as what actually happened, because theirs is not heard in the contexts in which I may speak. If we begin from the world as we actually experience it, it is at least possible to see that we are located and that what we know of the other is conditional upon that location as part of a relation comprehending the other's location also. There are and must be different experiences of the world and different bases of experience. We must not do away with them by taking advantage of our privileged speaking to construct a sociological version which we then impose upon them as their reality. We may not rewrite the other's world or impose upon it a conceptual framework which extracts from it what fits with our. Our conceptual procedures should be capable of explicating and analyzing the properties of their experienced world rather than administering it. Their reality, their varieties of experience must be an unconditional datum.

My experience in the train epitomizes a sociological relation. The observer is already separated from the world as it is experienced by those she observes. That separation is fundamental to the character of that experience. Once she becomes aware of how her world is put together as a practical everyday matter and of how her relations are shaped by its concrete conditions (even in so simple a matter as that she is sitting in the train and it travels, but those people standing on the spur do not) the sociologist is led into the discovery that she cannot understand the nature of there experienced world by staying within its ordinary boundaries of assumption and knowledge. To account for that moment on the train and for the relation between the two experiences (or more) and the two positions for which those experiences begin involved positing a total socio-economic order 'in back' of that moment. The coming together which makes the observation possible as well as how we were separated and drawn apart as well as how I now make use of that here—these properties are determined elsewhere than in that relation itself.

Further, how our knowledge of the world is mediated to us becomes a problem. It is a problem in knowing how that world is organized for us prior to our participation as knowers in that process. As intellectuals we ordinarily receive it as a media world, of documents, images, journals, books, and talk, as well as in other symbolic modes. We discard as an essential focus of our practice other ways of knowing. Accounting for that mode of knowing and the social organization which sets it up for us again leads us back into an analysis of the total socio-economic order of which it is part. It is not possible to account for one's directly experienced world or how it is related to the worlds which others directly experience who are differently placed by remaining within the boundaries of the former.

If we address the problem of the conditions as well as the perceived forms and organization of immediate experience, we should include in it the events as they actually happen or the ordinary material world which we encounter as a matter of fact—the urban renewal project which uproots 400 families; how it is to live on welfare as an ordinary daily practice; cities as the actual physical structures in which we move; the organization of academic occasions such as that in which this paper originated. When we examine them, we find that there are many aspects of how these things come about of which we have little as sociologists to say. We have a sense that the events which enter our experience originate somewhere in a human intention, but we are unable to track back to find it and to find out how it got from there to here. Or take this room in which I work or that room in which you are reading and treat that as a problem. If we think about the conditions of our activity here, we could track back to how it is that there are chairs, table, walls, our clothing, our presence; how these places (your and mine) are cleaned and maintained, etc. There are human activities, intentions, and relations that are not apparent as such in the actual material conditions of our work. The social organization of the setting is not wholly available to us in its appearance. We bypass in the immediacy of the specific practical activity, a complex division of labour that is an essential pre-condition to it. Such pre-conditions are fundamentally mysterious to us and present us with problems in grasping social relations in our kind of society with which sociology is ill equipped to deal.

The incomprehensibility of the determinations of our immediate local world is for women a particularly striking metaphor. It recovers an inner organization in common with their typical relation to the world. For women's activities and existence are determined outside them and beyond the world which is their 'place'. They are oriented by their training and by the daily practices which confirm it, towards the demands and initiations an authority of others. But more than that, the very organization of the world which has been assigned to them as the primary locus of their being is determined by and subordinate to the corporate organization of society (Smith, 1973). Thus as I have expressed her relation to sociology, its logic lies elsewhere. She lacks the inner principle of her own activity. She does not grasp how it is put together because it is determined elsewhere than where she is. As a sociologist, then, the grasp and exploration of her own experience as a method of discovering society restores to her a centre that, in this enterprise at least, is wholly hers.

Notes

1. This paper was originally prepared for the meetings of the American Academy for the Advancement of Science (Pacific Division) Eugene, Oregon, June 1972. The original draft of this paper was typed by Jane Lemke and the final version by Mildred Brown. I am indebted to both of them.

References

Briggs, J.L. 1970. *Never in Anger*. Cambridge, MA: Harvard University Press.

Bierstedi, R. 1966. 'Sociology and General Education', in C.H. Page, ed., *Sociology and Contemporary Education*. New York: Random House.

Gouldner, A. 1971. *The Coming Crisis in Western Sociology*. London: Heninemann Educational Books.

Smith, D.E. 1973. 'Women, the Family and Corporate Capitalism', in M.L. Stephenson, ed., *Women in Canada*. Toronto: Newpress.

QUESTIONS FOR CRITICAL THOUGHT

1. In your experience of formal education, have you seen evidence of the inclusion of women's perspectives, as Smith advocates, or their exclusion? Or both?

2. Educational institutions include not only classrooms and curriculums, but also locker rooms, cliques, playgrounds, and other sites of informal education about what gender means. What did you learn about gender at school outside of the classroom?

3. One proposed solution to the problem of gender polarization in schools is the creation of same-sex schools. Would you send your son or daughter to a same-sex school? What would be some of the advantages? What about disadvantages?

4. Is there a connection between gender inequities and other kinds of 'micro-inequities', as discussed by both Beagan and Lindberg?

5. If young children's play is reinforcing gender stereotypes, as is the case in the settings investigated by Jordan and Cowan, should parents or educators be concerned? Should we try to explicitly 'teach' gender equality?

PART VI

The Gendered Workplace

Perhaps the most dramatic social change in industrial countries in the twentieth century was the entry of women into the workplace. The nineteenth-century ideology of 'separate spheres'—the breadwinner husband and the homemaker wife—has slowly and steadily evaporated. While only 20 per cent of women, and only 4 per cent of married women, worked outside the home in 1900, more than 75 per cent did so by 1995, including 60 per cent of married women. In the first decade of the twenty-first century, 80 per cent of the new entrants into the labour force will be women, minorities, and immigrants.

Despite the collapse of the doctrine of separate spheres—work and home—the workplace remains a dramatically divided world where women and men rarely do the same jobs in the same place for the same pay. Occupational sex segregation, persistent sex discrimination, and wage disparities are all significant problems faced by working women. As Barbara Reskin's article demonstrates, workplace inequality is one of the most persistent and pernicious forms of gender discrimination. Joan Acker's chapter explores paid work and workplaces as examples of the much broader class of gendered organizations.

The gendering of organizations implies that certain sexes are 'right' or 'wrong' for certain types of jobs. In recent years, women have made significant inroads into career areas that were formerly bastions of masculinity, such as medicine or law. Men, however, have been much less likely to 'desegregate' female-dominated occupations such as nursery-school teaching or cosmetology. For those men who do enter female-dominated fields, negotiating the pitfalls of being the 'wrong' sex for the job means finding one's professional way through a minefield of gender and sexuality, as Joan Evans discusses. The male nurses in Evans's work judge themselves, and are judged by others, by their adherence to or deviation from a feminized norm of caring.

Workplace experiences are marked by race and class (among other social categories), which combine with gender to produce distinctive forms of masculinity and femininity. Pamela Sugiman looks backwards to the shop floors of Ontario auto manufacturing plants in the 1940s. She demonstrates how ideas about gender and masculinity combined with racialized hierarchies within the plants to produce experiences and careers for black men that were very different from those of either their white or female colleagues. Black men were able to find work in the auto plants and solidarity in the labour union at a time when women, white or black, faced major obstacles; but institutionalized racism meant that they were never treated as fully equal to white men.

For most people, 'work' and 'home' are separate, and the challenges in one realm do not dominate life in the other. However, for some workers, their home is their workplace. Bernadette Stiell and Kim England examine the lives of live-in domestic workers, for whom the wall dividing home from work has collapsed. Although these female workers live in close quarters with their same-gender employers, hierarchies based on class and racial categories overshadow their physical proximity and their gender commonalities, just as in Sugiman's auto plants.

CHAPTER 23

Bringing the Men Back In: Sex Differentiation and the Devaluation of Women's Work

Barbara F. Reskin

One of the most enduring manifestations of sex inequality in industrial and postindustrial societies is the wage gap. In 1986, as in 1957, among full-time workers in the United States, men earned 50 per cent more per hour than did women. This disparity translated to $8,000 a year in median earnings, an all-time high bonus for being male. Most sociologists agree that the major cause of the wage gap is the segregation of women and men into different kinds of work. Whether or not women freely choose the occupations in which they are concentrated, the outcome is the same: the more proportionately female an occupation, the lower its average wages. The high level of job segregation means that the 1963 law stipulating equal pay for equal work did little to reduce the wage gap.

This 'causal model'—that the segregation of women and men into different occupations causes the wage gap—implies two possible remedies. One is to equalize men and women on the causal variable—occupation—by ensuring women's access to traditionally male occupations. The other is to replace occupation with a causal variable on which women and men differ less, by instituting comparable-worth pay policies that compensate workers for the 'worth' of their job regardless of its sex composition.

I contend, however, that the preceding explanation of the wage gap is incorrect because it omits variables responsible for the difference between women and men in their distribution across occupations. If a causal model is incorrect, the remedies it implies may be ineffective. Lieberson's (1985: 185) critique of causal analysis as it is commonly practiced explicates the problem by distinguishing between *superficial* (or surface) causes that *appear* to give rise to a particular outcome and *basic* causes that *actually* produce the outcome. For example, he cites the belief that the black–white income gap is due to educational differences and thus can be reduced by reducing the educational disparity. As Lieberson pointed out, this analysis misses the fact that 'the dominant group . . . uses its dominance to advance its own position' (166), so that eliminating race differences in education is unlikely to reduce racial inequality in income because whites will find another way to maintain their income advantage. In other words, what appears in this example to be both the outcome variable (the black–white income gap) and the imputed causal variable (the black–white educational disparity) may stem from the same basic cause (whites' attempt to maintain their economic advantage). If so, then if the disparity in education were eliminated, some other factor would arise to produce the same economic consequence.

Dominant groups remain privileged because they write the rules, and the rules they write 'enable them *to continue to write the rules*' (Lieberson, 1985: 167, emphasis added). As a result, they can change the rules to thwart challenges to their position. Consider the following example. Because Asian American students tend to outscore occidentals on standard admissions tests, they are increasingly over-represented in some university programs. Some universities have allegedly responded by imposing quotas for Asian students or weighing more heavily admissions criteria on which they believe Asian Americans do less well.

How can one tell whether a variable is a superficial or a basic cause of some outcome? Lieberson offered a straightforward test: Does a change in that variable lead to a change in the outcome? Applying this rule to the prevailing causal theory of the wage gap, we find that between 1970 and 1980 the index of occupational sex segregation declined by 10 per cent, but the wage gap for full-time workers declined by just under 2 per cent. Although the meaning may be equivocal, this finding is consistent with other evidence that attributing the wage gap to job segregation misses its basic cause: men's propensity to maintain their privileges. This claim is neither novel nor specific to men. Marxist and conflict theory have long recognized that dominant groups act to preserve their position. Like other dominant groups, men are reluctant to give up their advantages (Goode, 1982). To avoid having to do so, they construct 'rules' for distributing rewards that guarantee them the lion's share (see also Epstein, 1985: 30). In the past, men cited their need as household heads for a 'family wage' and designated women as secondary earners. Today, when millions of women who head households would benefit from such a rule, occupation has supplanted it as the principle for assigning wages.

Neoclassical economic theory holds that the market is the mechanism through which wages are set, but markets are merely systems of rules that dominant groups establish for their own purposes. When other groups, such as labour unions, amassed enough power, they modified the 'market' principle. Steinberg (1987) observed that when consulted in making comparable-worth adjustments, male-dominated unions tended to support management over changes that would raise women's salaries.

In sum, the basic cause of the income gap is not sex segregation but men's desire to preserve their advantaged position and their ability to do so by establishing rules to distribute valued resources in their favour. Figure 23.1 represents this more complete causal model. Note that currently segregation is a superficial cause of the income gap, in part through 'crowding', but that some other distributional system such as comparable-worth pay could replace it with the same effect.

Figure 23.1 Heuristic model of the wage gap

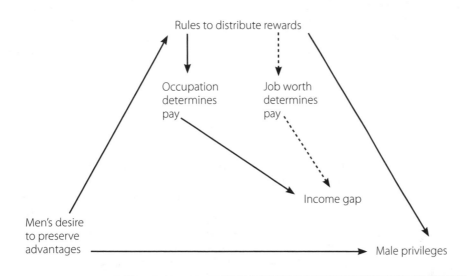

With respect to income, this model implies that men will resist efforts to close the wage gap. Resistance will include opposing equalizing women's access to jobs because integration would equalize women and men on the current superficial cause of the wage gap—occupation. Men may also try to preserve job segregation because it is a central mechanism through which they retain their dominance in other spheres, and because many people learn to prefer the company of others like them. My theory also implies that men will resist efforts to replace occupation with alternative principles for assigning pay that would mitigate segregation's effect on women's wages (as pay equity purports to do).

Before I offer evidence for these claims, let us examine how dominant groups in general and men in particular maintain their privileged position. I formulate my analysis with reference to dominant groups to emphasize that the processes I discuss are not specific to sex classes. It also follows that, were women the dominant sex, the claims I make about men's behaviour should hold for women.

Differentiation, Devaluation, and Hierarchy

Differentiation—the practice of distinguishing categories based on some attribute—is the fundamental process in hierarchical systems, a logical necessity for differential evaluation and differential rewards. But differentiation involves much more than merely acting on a pre-existing difference. In a hierarchical context, differentiation assumes, amplifies, and even creates psychological and behavioural differences in order to ensure that the subordinate group differs from the dominant group, 'because the systematically differential delivery of benefits and deprivations require[s] making no mistake about who was who' (MacKinnon, 1987: 40) and because 'differences are inequality's post hoc excuse' (MacKinnon, 1987: 8).

Differentiated status characteristics influence evaluations of people's behaviour and their overall worth. In hierarchical systems in which differentiation takes the form of an Aristotelian dichotomy, individuals are classified as either A ('the subject') or Not-A ('the other'). But these two classes are not construed as natural opposites that both have positive qualities; instead, A's characteristics are valued as normal or good and Not-A's as without value or negative.

The official response to the influx of south- and central-eastern European immigrants to the United States early in the twentieth century, when people assumed that each European country represented a distinct biological race, illustrates differentiation's central role in dominance systems. A congressionally mandated immigration commission concluded that 'innate, ineradicable race distinctions separated groups of men from one another' and agreed on the necessity of classifying these races to know which were most worthy of survival. The immediate problem was to ascertain 'whether there may not be certain races that are inferior to other races . . . to discover some test to show whether some may be better fitted for American citizenship than others' (Lieberson, 1980: 2–26).

Thus differentiation in all its forms supports dominance systems by demonstrating that superordinate and subordinate groups differ in essential ways and that such differences are natural and even desirable.

'SEX DIFFERENTIATION' VERSUS 'GENDER DIFFERENTIATION': A NOTE ON TERMINOLOGY

Scholars speak of both 'sex' and 'gender' differentiation: the former when biological sex or the 'sex category' into which people are placed at birth is the *basis for* classification and differential treatment; the latter to refer to the *result* of that differential treatment. In order to emphasize that the initial biological difference (mediated through sex category) is the basis for differential treatment, I use the terms *sex differentiation* and *sex segregation*. This usage should not obscure the fact that the process of converting sex category into gender is a social one or that most differences that are assumed to distinguish the sexes are socially created. I agree with Kessler and McKenna (1978) that the 'gender attribution process' assumes dimorphism and seeks evidence of it to justify classifying people as male and female and treating them unequally. This article examines how and why those differences are produced.

SEX DIFFERENTIATION AND DEVALUATION

Probably no system of social differentiation is as extensive as that based on sex category. Its prevalence led anthropologist Gayle Rubin to claim that there is 'a taboo against the sameness of men and women, a taboo dividing the sexes into two mutually exclusive categories, a taboo which exacerbates the biological differences between the sexes and thereby *creates* gender' (1975: 178). Moreover, although femaleness is not always devalued, its deviation from maleness in a culture that reserves virtues for men has meant the devaluation of women. Bleier's research on biological scientists' study of sex differences illustrates this point: the 'search for the truth about differences, [implies] that difference means *different from the white male norm and, therefore, inferior'* (1987: 2, emphasis added). In consequence, men's activities are typically valued above women's, regardless of their content or importance for group survival, and both sexes come to devalue women's efforts. Thus it should be no surprise that women's occupations pay less at least partly *because* women do them.

In short, differentiation is the sine qua non of dominance systems. Because of its importance, it is achieved through myriad ways:

> To go for a walk with one's eyes open is enough to demonstrate that humanity is

divided into two classes of individuals whose clothes, faces, bodies, smiles, gaits, interests and occupations are manifestly different (de Beauvoir, 1953: xiv).

We differentiate groups in their location, appearance, and behaviour, and in the tasks they do. Now let us turn to how these mechanisms operate to differentiate women and men.

Physical Segregation

Dominant groups differentiate subordinate groups by physically isolating them—in ghettos, nurseries, segregated living quarters, and so on. Physical segregation fosters unequal treatment, because physically separate people can be treated differently and because it spares members of the dominant group the knowledge of the disparity and hides it from the subordinate group. Although women and men are integrated in some spheres, physical separation continues to differentiate them.

Cohn's (1985) vivid account of women's physical segregation in the British Foreign Office in the nineteenth century illustrates the extent to which organizations have gone to separate the sexes. The Foreign Office hid its first female typists in an attic, but it failed to rescind the requirement that workers collect their pay on the ground floor. When payday came, managers evacuated the corridors, shut all the doors, and then sent the women running down the attic stairs to get their checks and back up again. Only after they were out of sight were the corridors reopened to men.

This account raises the question of *why* managers segregate working men and women. What licentiousness did the Foreign Office fear would occur in integrated hallways? Contemporary answers are markedly similar to turn-of-the-century fears. Compare the scenario expressed in a 1923 editorial in the *Journal of Accountancy* ('any attempt at heterogeneous personnel [in after-hours auditing of banks] would hamper progress and lead to infinite embarrassment'

[151]) with recent reactions to the prospect of women integrating police patrol cars, coal mines, and merchant marine vessels (e.g., Martin, 1980). At or just below the surface lies the specter of sexual liaisons. For years, McDonald's founder Ray Kroc forbade franchisees to hire women counter workers because they would attract 'the wrong type' of customers. The US Army ended sex-integrated basic training to 'facilitate toughening goals', and the Air Force reevaluated whether women could serve on two-person Minuteman missile-silo teams because 'it could lead to stress.'

My thesis offers a more parsimonious alternative to these ad hoc explanations—men resist allowing women and men to work together *as equals* because doing so undermines differentiation and hence male dominance.

Behavioural Differentiation

People's behaviour is differentiated on their status-group membership in far too many ways for me to review the differences adequately here. I concentrate in this section on differentiation of behaviours that occur in the workplace: task differentiation and social differentiation.

Task differentiation assigns work according to group membership. It was expressed in the extreme in traditional Hindu society in which caste virtually determined life work. Task assignment based on sex category—the sexual division of labour—both prescribes and proscribes assorted tasks to each sex, and modern societies still assign men and women different roles in domestic work, labour-market work, and emotional and interpersonal work. Task differentiation generally assigns to lower-status groups the least desirable, most poorly rewarded work: menial, tedious, and degraded tasks, such as cleaning, disposing of waste, and caring for the dying. This practice symbolizes and legitimates the subordinate group's low status, while making it appear to have an affinity for these undesirable tasks. As an added benefit, members of the dominant group don't have to do them! Important to discussions of the wage gap, because modern law and custom permit unequal pay for different work, task differentiation justifies paying the subordinate group lower wages, thereby ensuring their economic inferiority. Women's assignment to childcare, viewed as unskilled work in our society, illustrates these patterns. Women are said to have a 'natural talent' for it and similar work; men are relieved from doing it; society obtains free or cheap childcare; and women are handicapped in competing with men. As researchers have shown, sex-based task differentiation of both non-market and market work legitimates women's lower pay, hinders women's ability to succeed in traditionally male enterprises, and, in general, reinforces men's hegemony.

Social differentiation is achieved through norms that set dominant and subordinate groups apart in their appearance (sumptuary rules) or behaviour. When applied to sex, Goffman's (1976) concept of 'gender display' encompasses both. Sumptuary rules require certain modes of dress, diet, or life-style of members of subordinate groups as emblems of their inferior status, and reserve other modes to distinguish the dominant group. For example, Rollins (1985) discovered that white female employers preferred black domestic employees to dress shabbily to exaggerate their economic inferiority. Sex-specific sumptuary rules are epitomized in norms that dictate divergent dress styles that often exaggerate physical sex differences and sometimes even incapacitate women. An extreme example is the *burqua* fundamentalist Muslim women wear as a symbol of their status and as a portable system of segregation.

Etiquette rules support differentiation by requiring subordinate group members to display ritualized deference toward dominants. Relations between enlistees and officers or female domestic workers and their employers illustrate their role. Although typically it is the subordinate group that must defer, gender etiquette that requires middle- and upper-class men to display deference to women of the same classes preserves

differentiation by highlighting women's differentness. Women who do not express gratitude or who refuse to accept the deference are faced with hostility, shattering the fiction that women hold the preferred position.

Physical segregation, behavioural differentiation, social separation, and even hierarchy are functional alternatives for satisfying the need for differentiation in domination systems. For example, when their physical integration with the dominant group means that a subordinate group's status differences might otherwise be invisible, special dress is usually required of them, as servants are required to wear uniforms. Physical separation can even compensate for the absence of hierarchy, a point acknowledged in the black folk saying that southern whites don't care how close blacks get if they don't get too high, and northern whites don't care how high blacks get if they don't get too close.

This substitutability explains why men will tolerate women in predominantly male work settings if they work in 'women's' jobs and accept women doing 'men's' jobs in traditionally female settings, but resist women doing traditionally male jobs in male work settings. Physical proximity per se is not threatening as long as another form of differentiation sets women apart. But the absence of *any* form of differentiation precludes devaluation and unequal rewards and hence threatens the sex-gender hierarchy. Because of the centrality of differentiation in domination systems, dominant groups have a considerable stake in maintaining it.

Dominants' Response to Challenges

Dominants respond to subordinates' challenges by citing the group differences that supposedly warrant differential treatment. Serious challenges often give rise to attempts to demonstrate biological differences scientifically.

The nineteenth-century antislavery and women's rights movements led reputable scientists to try to prove that women's and blacks' brains were underdeveloped. The Great Migration to the United States in the first two decades of the twentieth century fueled a eugenics movement that purported to establish scientifically the inferiority of south- and central-eastern Europeans. The civil rights movement of the 1960s stimulated renewed efforts to establish racial differences in intelligence. And we are once again witnessing a spate of allegedly scientific research seeking a biological basis for presumed sex differences in cognitive ability and, specifically, for boys' higher average scores on math questions in some standardized tests. As Bleier pointed out, 'The implication if not purposes of [such] research is to demonstrate that the structure of society faithfully reflects the natural order of things.' According to Bleier, reputable journals have published studies that violate accepted standards of proof, and the scientific press has given dubious findings considerable attention (as in the news story in *Science* that asked, 'Is There a Male Math Gene?'). Although subsequently these studies have been discredited, the debate serves its purpose by focusing attention on how groups differ.

Men's Response to Occupational Integration

An influx of women into male spheres threatens the differentiation of men and women, and men resist. One response is to bar women's entry. Women have had to turn to the courts to win entry into Little League sports, college dining clubs, private professional clubs, and the Rotary. Recently, University of North Carolina trustees decried the fact that women are now a majority of UNC students, and some proposed changing the weights for certain admission criteria to restore the male majority. Twice since a shortage of male recruits forced the army to lift its quota on women, it has reduced the number of jobs open to women. Numerous studies have documented men's resistance to women entering 'their' jobs. Sometimes the resistance is simply exclusion; at other times it is subtle barriers that block women's advancement or open harassment. Now that more women hold managerial jobs, one hears of 'a glass ceiling' that bars middle-management women from top-level positions, and Kanter (1987) claimed that organizations are changing the rules of what one must do to reach the top in order to make it more difficult for women to succeed.

My thesis implies that men will respond to women's challenge in the workplace by emphasizing how they differ from men. Especially common are reminders of women's 'natural' roles as wife, mother, or sexual partner. Witness the recent—and subsequently disputed—claims that women who postponed marriage and childbearing to establish their careers had a negligible chance of finding husbands and were running the risk that their 'biological clocks' would prevent pregnancy, and accounts of women dropping out of middle management to spend more time with their children.

Men who cannot bar women from 'male' jobs can still preserve differentiation in other spheres. Their attempts to do so may explain why so few husbands of wage-working women share housework, as well as elucidating Wharton and Baron's (1987) finding that among men working in sex-integrated jobs, those whose wives were employed were more dissatisfied than unmarried men or men married to homemakers.

Another response to women's challenge is to weaken the mechanisms that have helped women advance in the workplace. Since 1980, the Reagan administration has sought to undermine equal-opportunity programs and affirmative-action regulations, and the campaign has partly succeeded. Efforts to dilute or eliminate Equal Employment Opportunity (EEO) programs are advanced by claims that sex inequality has disappeared (or that men now experience 'reverse discrimination'). For example, the *New York Times* recently described the Department of Commerce announcement that women now compose the majority in professional occupations as a 'historic milestone', adding that 'the barriers have fallen.'

The Illusion of Occupational Integration

If male resistance is so pervasive, how can we explain the drop in the index of occupational sex segregation in the 1970s and women's disproportionate gains in a modest number of male-dominated occupations? In order to answer this question, Patricia Roos and I embarked on a study of the changing sex composition of occupations. The results of our case studies of a dozen traditionally male occupations in which women made disproportionate statistical gains during the 1970s cast doubt on whether many women can advance economically through job integration.

The case studies revealed two general patterns. First, within many occupations nominally being integrated, men and women remain highly segregated, with men concentrated in the highest-status and best-paying jobs. For example, although women's representation in baking grew from 25 per cent in 1970 to 41 per cent in 1980, men continue to dominate production baking. The increase in women bakers is due almost wholly to their concentration in proliferating 'in-store' bakeries. Although women now make up the majority of residential real estate salespersons, men still monopolize commercial sales.

The second pattern shows that women often gained access to these occupations after changes in work content and declines in autonomy or rewards made the work less attractive to men. In some occupations, the growth of functions already socially labelled as 'women's work' (e.g., clerical, communications, or emotional work) spurred the change. For example, computerization and the ensuing clericalization prompted women's entry into typesetting and composing and insurance adjusting and examining. An increasing emphasis on communicating and interpersonal or emotional work contributed to women's gains in insurance sales, insurance adjusting and examining, systems analysis, public relations, and bank and financial management.

Brief summaries of our findings for two occupations illustrate these processes. First, women's disproportionate gains in pharmacy have been largely confined to the retail sector (male pharmacists work disproportionately in research and management) and occurred after retail pharmacists lost professional status and entrepreneurial opportunities. After drug manufacturers took over the compounding of drugs, pharmacists increasingly resembled retail sales clerks; their primary duties became dispensing and record keeping. As chain and discount store pharmacies supplanted independently owned pharmacies, retail pharmacy no longer offered a chance to own one's own business, reducing another traditional attraction for men. The resulting shortages of male pharmacy graduates eased women's access to training programs and retail jobs.

Second, book editing illustrates how declining autonomy and occupational prestige contributed to feminization of an occupation. For most of the twentieth century, the cultural image of publishing attracted bright young men and women despite very low wages. But during the 1970s, multinational conglomerates entered book publishing, with profound results. Their emphasis on the bottom line robbed publishing of its cultural aura, and the search for blockbusters brought a greater role for marketing people in acquisition decisions, thereby eroding editorial autonomy. As a result, editing could no longer compete effectively for talented men who could choose from better opportunities. Because women's occupational choices are more limited than men's, editing still attracted them, and the occupation's sex composition shifted accordingly.

In sum, although sex integration appears to have occurred in the 1970s among census-designated detailed occupations, our findings indicate that within these occupations, women are segregated into certain specialties or work settings and that they gained entry because various changes made the occupations less attractive to men. The nominal integration that occurred in the 1970s often masks within-occupation segregation or presages resegregation of traditionally male occupations as women's work. In short, the workplace is still overwhelmingly differentiated by sex. Moreover, our preliminary results suggest that real incomes in the occupations we are studying declined during the 1970s; so reducing segregation at the occupational level appears to have been relatively ineffective in reducing the wage gap—and certainly not the remedy many experts predicted. This brings us to the other possible remedy for the wage gap—comparable worth.

Implications for Comparable Worth

The comparable-worth movement calls for equal pay for work of equal worth. Worth is usually determined by job-evaluation studies that measure the skill, effort, and responsibility required, but in practice, assessing worth often turns on how to conceptualize and measure skill.

Although some objective criteria exist for assessing skill (e.g., how long it takes a worker to learn the job, typically the designation of work as skilled is socially negotiated. Workers are most likely to win it when they control social resources that permit them to press their claims, such as a monopoly over a labour supply or authority based on their personal characteristics such as education, training, or sex. As a result, the evaluation of 'skill' is shaped by and confounded with workers' sex.

Groups use the same power that enabled them to define their work as skilled to restrict competition by excluding women (among others) from training for and practicing their trade or profession, as Millicent Fawcett recognized almost a hundred years ago when she declared, 'Equal pay for equal work is a fraud for women.' Because men use their power to keep women 'from obtaining equal skills, their work [cannot be] equal' (Hartmann, 1976: 157). Roos's (1986) case history of the effect of technological change on women's employment in typesetting illustrates

these points. When a Linotype machine was developed that 'female typists could operate', the International Typographical Union (ITU) used its labour monopoly to force employers to agree to hire as operators only skilled printers who knew *all* aspects of the trade. By denying women access to apprenticeships or other channels to become fully skilled and limiting the job of operating the Linotype to highly skilled printers, the ITU effectively barred women from the new Linotype jobs. In short, the ITU used its monopoly power both to restrict women's access to skills and credentials and to define its members as 'uniquely skilled' to operate the Linotype.

Excluded from occupations male workers define as skilled, women are often unable, for several reasons, to press the claim that work in traditionally female occupations is skilled. First, as I have shown, the devaluation of women's work leads whatever work women do to be seen as unskilled. Second, women's powerlessness prevents their successfully defining their work—caring for children, entering data, assembling microelectronic circuits—as skilled. Third, because many female-dominated occupations require workers to acquire skills before employment, skill acquisition is less visible and hence unlikely to be socially credited. Fourth, the scarcity of apprenticeship programs for women's jobs and women's exclusion from other programs denies women a credential society recognizes as denoting skill. Finally, 'much of women's work involves recognizing and responding to subtle cues' (Feldberg, 1984: 321), but the notion of 'women's intuition' permits men to define such skills as inborn and hence not meriting compensation. Thus women are both kept from acquiring socially valued skills and not credited for those they do acquire. As a result, the sex of the majority of workers in an occupation influences whether or not their work is classified as skilled.

In view of these patterns, how effective can comparable worth be in reducing the wage gap? As with the Equal Pay Act, implementing it has symbolic value. Moreover, it would bar employers from underpaying women relative to their job-evaluation scores, the practice alleged in *AFSCME v. Washington State* (1985). But setting salaries according to an occupation's worth will reduce the wage gap only to the extent that (1) women have access to tasks that society values, (2) evaluators do not take workers' sex into account in determining a job's worth, and (3) implementers do not sacrifice equity to other political agendas.

Neither of the first two conditions holds. As I have shown, men already dominate jobs society deems skilled. Moreover, the tendency to devalue women's work is embedded in job-evaluation techniques that define job worth; so such techniques may yield biased evaluations of traditionally female jobs and lower their job-evaluation scores. Beyond these difficulties is the problem of good-faith implementation. Acker (1987), Brenner (1987), and Steinberg (1987) have documented the problems in implementing comparable-worth pay adjustments. According to Steinberg (1987: 8), New York State's proposed compensation model *negatively* values working with difficult clients, work performed in historically female and minority jobs (in other words, workers lose pay for doing it!), and Massachusetts plans to establish separate comparable-worth plans across sex-segregated bargaining units. For these reasons, the magnitude of comparable-worth adjustments have been about half of what experts expected—only 5–15 per cent of salaries (Steinberg, 1987).

Moreover, to the extent that equity adjustments significantly raise salaries in women's jobs, men can use their power to monopolize them. It is no accident that the men who integrated the female semi-professions moved rapidly to the top. The recent experience of athletic directors provides an additional illustration. Title IX required college athletic programs to eliminate disparities in resources between women's and men's programs including salaries. Within ten years the proportion of coaches for women's programs who were male grew from 10 per cent to 50 per cent. Finally, men

as the primary implementers of job evaluation have a second line of defense—they can and do subvert the process of job evaluation.

Conclusion

Integrating men's jobs and implementing comparable-worth programs have helped some women economically and, more fully implemented, would help others. But neither strategy can be broadly effective because both are premised on a flawed causal model of the pay gap that assigns primary responsibility to job segregation. A theory that purports to explain unequal outcomes without examining the dominant group's stake in maintaining them is incomplete. Like other dominant groups, men make rules that preserve their privileges. With respect to earnings, the current rule—that one's job or occupation determines one's pay—has maintained white men's economic advantage because men and women and whites and non-whites are differently distributed across jobs.

Changing the allocation principle from occupation to job worth would help non-whites and women if occupation were the pay gap's basic cause. But it is not. As long as a dominant group wants to subordinate others' interests to its own and is able to do so, the outcome—distributing more income to men than women—is, in a sense, its own cause, and tinkering with superficial causes will not substantially alter the outcome. Either the rule that one's occupation determines one's wages exists *because* men and women hold different occupations, or men and women hold different occupations because we allocate wages according to one's occupation. Obviously the dominant group will resist attempts to change the rules. In *Lemon v. City and County of Denver* (1980), the court called comparable worth 'pregnant with the possibility of disrupting the entire economic system' (Steinberg, 1987). 'Disrupting the entire white-male dominance system' would have been closer to the mark.

If men's desire to preserve their privileges is the basic cause of the wage gap, then how can we bring about change? The beneficiaries of hierarchical reward systems yield their privileges only when failing to yield is more costly than yielding. Increasing the costs men pay to maintain the status quo or rewarding men for dividing resources more equitably may reduce their resistance.

As individuals, many men will gain economically if their partners earn higher wages. Of course, these men stand to lose whatever advantages come from out-earning one's partner. But more important than individual adjustments are those achieved through organizations that have the power to impose rewards and penalties. Firms that recognize their economic stake in treating women equitably (or can be pressed by women employees or EEO agencies to act as if they do) can be an important source of pressure on male employees. Employers have effectively used various incentives to overcome resistance to affirmative action (e.g., rewarding supervisors for treating women fairly [Shaeffer and Lynton, 1979; Walshok, 1981]). Employers are most likely to use such mechanisms if they believe that regulatory agencies are enforcing equal-opportunity rules. We can attack men's resistance through political pressure on employers, the regulatory agencies that monitor them, and branches of government that establish and fund such agencies.

Analyses of sex inequality in the 1980s implicitly advance a no-fault concept of institutionalized discrimination rather than fixing any responsibility on men. But men *are* the dominant group, the makers and the beneficiaries of the rules. Of course, most men do not consciously oppose equality for women or try to thwart women's progress. When men and women work together, both can gain, as occurred when the largely male blue-collar union supported the striking Yale clerical and technical workers. But as a rule, this silent majority avoids the fray, leaving the field to those who do resist to act on behalf of all men. It is time to bring men back into our theories of economic inequality. To do so does not imply that women are passive agents. The gains we have made in the last two decades in the struggle for economic equality—redefining the kinds of work women can do, reshaping young people's aspirations, and amassing popular support for pay equity despite opponents' attempt to write it off as a 'loony tune' idea—stand as testimony to the contrary. Just as the causal model I propose views the dominant group's self-interest as the source of unequal outcomes, so too does it see subordinate groups as the agents of change.

References

Acker, J. 1987. 'Sex Bias in Job Evaluation: A Comparable-Worth Issue', in C. Bose and g. Spitze, eds, *Ingredients for Women's Employment Policy*, pp. 183–96. Albany, NY: SUNY Press.

AFSCME v. State of Washington. 1985. 770 F.2d 1401. 9th Circuit.

Bleier, R. 1987. 'Gender Ideology: The Medical and Scientific Construction of Women'. Lecture presented at the University of Illinois, Urbana.

Brenner, J. 1987. 'Feminist Political Discourses: Radical vs. Liberal Approaches to the Feminization of Poverty and Comparable Worth', *Gender & Society* 1: 447–65.

Cohn, S. 1985. *The Process of Occupational Sex Typing*. Philadelphia: Temple University Press.

de Beauvoir, S. 1953. *The Second Sex*. New York: Knopf.

Epstein, C.F. 1985. 'Ideal Roles and Real Roles or the Fallacy of Misplaced Dichotomy', *Research on Social Stratification and Mobility* 4: 29–51.

Feldberg, R.L. 1984. 'Comparable Worth: Toward Theory and Practice in the U.S.', *Signs: Journal of Women in Culture and Society* 10: 311–28.

Goffman, E. 1976. 'Gender Display', *Studies in the Anthropology of Visual Communication* 3: 69–77.

Goode, W.C. 1964. *The Family*. Englewood Cliffs, NJ: Prentice Hall.

Hartmann, H. 1976. 'Capitalism, Patriarchy, and Job Segregation by Sex', *Signs: Journal of Women in Culture and Society* 1 (Part 2): 137–69.

Kanter, R.M. 1987. 'Men and Women of the Change Master Corporation (1977–1987 and Beyond): Dilemmas and Consequences of Innovations of Organizational Structure'. Paper presented at Annual Meetings, Academy of Management, New Orleans.

Kessler, S., and W. McKenna. 1978. *Gender: An Ethnomethodological Approach*. New York: John Wiley.

Lieberson, S. 1980. *A Piece of the Pie*. Berkeley, CA: University of California Press.

———. 1985. *Making It Count*. Berkeley, CA: University of California Press.

MacKinnon, C. 1987. *Feminism Unmodified*. Cambridge, MA: Harvard University Press.

Martin, S.E. 1980. *Breaking and Entering*. Berkeley, CA: University of California Press.

Rollins, J. 1985. *Between Women*. Philadelphia, PA: Temple University Press.

Roos, P.A. 1986. 'Women in the Composing Room: Technology and Organization as the Determin-ants of Social Change'. Paper presented at Annual Meetings, American Sociological Association, New York.

Rubin, G. 1975. 'The Traffic in Women: Notes on the "Political Economy" of Sex', in R.R. Reiter, *Toward an Anthropology of Women,* pp. 157–210. New York: Monthly Review Press.

Shaeffer, R.G., and E.F. Lynton. 1979. *Corporate Experience in Improving Women's Job Opportunities*. Report no. 755. New York: The Conference Board.

Steiger, T. 1987. 'Female Employment Gains and Sex Segregation: The Case of Bakers'. Paper presented at Annual Meetings, American Sociological Association, Chicago.

Steinberg, R.J. 1987. 'Radical Challenges in a Liberal World: The Mixed Successes of Comparable Worth', *Gender & Society* 1: 466–75.

Walshok, M.L. 1981. 'Some Innovations in Industrial Apprenticeship at General Motors', in V.M. Briggs, Jr, and F. Foltman, eds, *Apprenticeship Research: Emerging Findings and Future Trends*, pp. 173–82. Ithaca: New York State School of Industrial Relations.

CHAPTER 24

Hierarchies, Jobs, Bodies: A Theory of Gendered Organizations

Joan Acker

Most of us spend most of our days in work organizations that are almost always dominated by men. The most powerful organizational positions are almost entirely occupied by men, with the exception of the occasional biological female who acts as a social man. Power at the national and world level is located in all-male enclaves at the pinnacle of large state and economic organizations. These facts are not news, although sociologists paid no attention to them until feminism came along to point out the problematic nature of the obvious. Writers on organizations and organizational theory now include some consideration of women and gender, but their treatment is usually cursory, and male domination is, on the whole, not analyzed and not explained.

Among feminist social scientists there are some outstanding contributions on women and organizations, such as the work of Kanter (1977), Feldberg and Glenn (1979), MacKinnon (1979), and Ferguson (1984). In addition, there have been theoretical and empirical investigations of particular aspects of organizational structure and process, and women's situations have been studied using traditional organizational ideas. Moreover, the very rich literature, popular and scholarly, on women and work contains much material on work organizations. However, most of this new knowledge has not been brought together in a systematic feminist theory of organizations.

A systematic theory of gender and organizations is needed for a number of reasons. First, the gender segregation of work, including divisions between paid and unpaid work, is partly created through organizational practices. Second, and related to gender segregation, income and status inequality between women and men is also partly created in organizational processes; understanding these processes is necessary for understanding gender inequality. Third, organizations are one arena in which widely disseminated cultural images of gender are invented and reproduced. Knowledge of cultural production is important for understanding gender construction. Fourth, some aspects of individual gender identity, perhaps particularly masculinity, are also products of organizational processes and pressures. Fifth, an important feminist project is to make large-scale organizations more democratic and more supportive of humane goals.

In this article, I begin by speculating about why feminist scholars have not debated organizational theory. I then look briefly at how those feminist scholars who have paid attention to organizations have conceptualized them. In the main part of the article, I examine organizations as gendered processes in which both gender and sexuality have been obscured through a gender-neutral, asexual discourse, and suggest some of the ways that gender, the body, and sexuality are part of the processes of control in work organizations. Finally, I point to some directions for feminist theory about this ubiquitous human invention.

Why So Little Feminist Debate on Organizations?

The early radical feminist critique of sexism denounced bureaucracy and hierarchy as male-created and male-dominated structures of control that oppress women. The easiest answer to the 'why so little debate' question is that the link between masculinity and organizational power was so obvious that no debate was needed. However, experiences in the feminist movement suggest that the questions are not exhausted by recognizing male power.

Part of the feminist project was to create non-hierarchical, egalitarian organizations that would demonstrate the possibilities of non-patriarchal ways of working. Although many feminist organizations survived, few retained this radical-democratic form. Others succumbed to the same sorts of pressures that have undermined other utopian experiments with alternative work forms, yet analyses of feminist efforts to create alternative organizations were not followed by debates about the feasibility of non-patriarchal, non-hierarchical organization or the relationship of organizations and gender. Perhaps one of the reasons was that the reality was embarrassing; women failing to cooperate with each other, taking power and using it in oppressive ways, creating their own structures of status and reward were at odds with other images of women as nurturing and supportive.

Another reason for feminist theorists' scant attention to conceptualizing organizations probably lies in the nature of the concepts and models at hand. As Dorothy Smith (1979) has argued, the available discourses on organizations, the way that organizational sociology is defined as an area or domain 'is grounded in the working worlds and relations of men, whose experience and interests arise in the course of and in relation to participation in the ruling apparatus of this society' (148). Concepts developed to answer managerial questions, such as how to achieve organizational efficiency, were irrelevant to feminist questions, such as why women are always concentrated at the bottom of organizational structures.

Critical perspectives on organizations, with the notable exception of some of the studies of the labour process, although focusing on control, power, exploitation, and how these relations might be changed, have ignored women and have been insensitive to the implications of gender for their own goals. The active debate on work democracy, the area of organizational exploration closest to feminist concerns about oppressive structures, has been almost untouched by feminist insights. For example, Carole Pateman's influential book, *Participation and Democratic Theory* (1970), critical in shaping the discussions on democratic organization in the 1970s, did not consider women or gender. More recently, Pateman (1983a, 1983b, 1988) has examined the fundamental ideas of democracy from a feminist perspective, and other feminist political scientists have criticized theories of democracy, but on the whole, their work is isolated from the main discourse on work organization and democracy.

Empirical research on work democracy has also ignored women and gender. For example, in the 1980s, many male Swedish researchers saw little relation between questions of democracy and gender equality with a few exceptions. Other examples are studies of Mondragon, a community in the Spanish Basque country, which is probably the most famous attempt at democratic ownership, control, and organization. Until Sally Hacker's feminist study (1987), researchers who went to Mondragon to see this model of work democracy failed to note the situation of women and asked no questions about gender. In sum, the absence of women and gender from theoretical and empirical studies about work democracy provided little material for feminist theorizing.

Another impediment to feminist theorizing is that the available discourses conceptualize organizations as gender neutral. Both traditional and critical approaches to organizations originate in the male, abstract intellectual domain and take as reality the world as seen from that standpoint. As a relational phenomenon, gender is difficult to see when only the masculine is present. Since men in organizations take their behaviour and perspectives to represent the human, organizational structures and processes are theorized as gender neutral. When it is acknowledged that women and men are affected differently by organizations, it is argued that gendered attitudes and behaviour are brought into (and contaminate) essentially gender-neutral structures. This view of organizations separates structures from the people in them.

Current theories of organization also ignore sexuality. Certainly, a gender-neutral structure is also asexual. If sexuality is a core component of the production of gender identity, gender images, and gender inequality, organizational theory that is blind to sexuality does not immediately offer avenues into the comprehension of gender domination. Catharine MacKinnon's (1982) compelling argument that sexual domination of women is embedded within legal organizations has not to date become part of mainstream discussions. Rather, behaviours such as sexual harassment are viewed as deviations of gendered actors, not, as MacKinnon (1979) might argue, as components of organizational structure.

Feminist Analyses of Organizations

The treatment of women and gender most assimilated into the literature on organizations is Rosabeth Moss Kanter's *Men and Women of the Corporation* (1977). Kanter sets out to show that gender differences in organizational behaviour are due to structure rather than to characteristics of women and men as individuals (1977: 291–2). She argues that the problems women have in large organizations are consequences of their structural placement, crowded in dead-end jobs at the bottom and exposed as tokens at the top. Gender enters the picture through organizational roles that 'carry characteristic images of the kinds of people that should occupy them' (250). Here, Kanter recognizes the presence of gender in early models of organizations:

> A 'masculine ethic' of rationality and reason can be identified in the early image of managers. This 'masculine ethic' elevates the traits assumed to belong to men with educational advantages to necessities for effective organizations: a tough-minded approach to problems; analytic abilities to abstract and plan; a capacity to set aside personal, emotional considerations in the interests of task accomplishment; a cognitive superiority in problemsolving and decision making (1974: 43).

Identifying the central problem of seeming gender neutrality, Kanter observes: 'While organizations were being defined as sex-neutral machines, masculine principles were dominating their authority structures' (1977: 46).

In spite of these insights, organizational structure, not gender, is the focus of Kanter's analysis. In posing the argument as structure *or* gender, Kanter also implicitly posits gender as standing outside of structure, and she fails to follow up her own observations about masculinity and organizations (1977: 22). Kanter's analysis of the effects of organizational position applies as well to men in low-status positions. Her analysis of the effect of numbers, or the situation of the 'token' worker, applies also to men as minorities in women-predominant organizations, but fails to account for gender differences in the situation of the token. In contrast to the token woman, white men

in women-dominated workplaces are likely to be positively evaluated and to be rapidly promoted to positions of greater authority. The specificity of male dominance is absent in Kanter's argument, even though she presents a great deal of material that illuminates gender and male dominance.

Another approach, using Kanter's insights but building on the theoretical work of Hartmann (1976), is the argument that organizations have a dual structure, bureaucracy and patriarchy (Ressner, 1987). Ressner argues that bureaucracy has its own dynamic, and gender enters through patriarchy, a more or less autonomous structure, that exists alongside the bureaucratic structure. The analysis of two hierarchies facilitates and clarifies the discussion of women's experiences of discrimination, exclusion, segregation, and low wages. However, this approach has all the problems of two systems theories of women's oppression: the central theory of bureaucratic or organizational structure is unexamined, and patriarchy is added to allow the theorist to deal with women. Like Kanter, Ressner's approach implicitly accepts the assumption of mainstream organizational theory that organizations are gender-neutral social phenomena.

Ferguson, in *The Feminist Case Against Bureaucracy* (1984), develops a radical feminist critique of bureaucracy as an organization of oppressive male power, arguing that it is both mystified and constructed through an abstract discourse on rationality, rules, and procedures. Thus, in contrast to the implicit arguments of Kanter and Ressner, Ferguson views bureaucracy itself as a construction of male domination. In response to this overwhelming organization of power, bureaucrats, workers, and clients are all 'feminized', as they develop ways of managing their powerlessness that at the same time perpetuate their dependence. Ferguson argues further that feminist discourse, rooted in women's experiences of caring and nurturing outside bureaucracy's control, provides a ground for opposition to bureaucracy and for the development of alternative ways of organizing society.

However, there are problems with Ferguson's theoretical formulation. Her argument that feminization is a metaphor for bureaucratization not only uses a stereotype of femininity as oppressed, weak, and passive, but also, by equating the experience of male and female clients, women workers, and male bureaucrats, obscures the specificity of women's experiences and the connections between masculinity and power. Ferguson builds on Foucault's (1979) analysis of power as widely diffused and constituted through discourse, and the problems in her analysis have their origin in Foucault, who also fails to place gender in his analysis of power. What results is a disembodied, and consequently gender-neutral, bureaucracy as the oppressor. That is, of course, not a new vision of bureaucracy, but it is one in which gender enters only as analogy, rather than as a complex component of processes of control and domination.

In sum, some of the best feminist attempts to theorize about gender and organizations have been trapped within the constraints of definitions of the theoretical domain that cast organizations as gender neutral and asexual. These theories take us only part of the way to understanding how deeply embedded gender is in organizations. There is ample empirical evidence: We know now that gender segregation is an amazingly persistent pattern and that the gender identity of jobs and occupations is repeatedly reproduced, often in new forms. The reconstruction of gender segregation is an integral part of the dynamic of technological and organizational change. Individual men and particular groups of men do not always win in these processes, but masculinity always seems to symbolize self-respect for men at the bottom and power for men at the top, while confirming for both their gender's superiority. Theories that posit organization and bureaucracy as gender neutral cannot adequately account for this continual gendered structuring. We need different theoretical strategies that examine organizations as gendered processes in which sexuality also plays a part.

Organization as Gendered Processes

The idea that social structure and social processes are gendered has slowly emerged in diverse areas of feminist discourse. Feminists have elaborated gender as a concept to mean more than a socially constructed, binary identity and image. This turn to gender as an analytic category is an attempt to find new avenues into the dense and complicated problem of explaining the extraordinary persistence through history and across societies of the subordination of women. Scott, for example, defines gender as follows: 'The core of the definition rests on an integral connection between two propositions; gender is a constitutive element of social relationships based on perceived differences between the sexes, and gender is a primary way of signifying relationships of power' (1986: 1067).

New approaches to the study of waged work, particularly studies of the labour process, see organizations as gendered, not as gender neutral, and conceptualize organizations as one of the locations of the inextricably intertwined production of both gender and class relations. Examining class and gender, I have argued that class is constructed through gender and that class relations are always gendered.

The structure of the labour market, relations in the workplace, the control of the work process, and the underlying wage relation are always affected by symbols of gender, processes of gender identity, and material inequalities between women and men. These processes are complexly related to and powerfully support the reproduction of the class structure. Here, I will focus on the interface of gender and organizations, assuming the simultaneous presence of class relations.

To say that an organization, or any other analytic unit, is gendered means that advantage and disadvantage, exploitation and control, action and emotion, meaning and identity, are patterned through and in terms of a distinction between male and female, masculine and feminine. Gender is not an addition to ongoing processes, conceived as gender neutral. Rather, it is an integral part of those processes, which cannot be properly understood without an analysis of gender. Gendering occurs in at least five interacting processes that, although analytically distinct, are, in practice, parts of the same reality.

First is the construction of divisions along lines of gender—divisions of labour, of allowed behaviours, of locations in physical space, of power, including the institutionalized means of maintaining the divisions in the structures of labour markets, the family, the state. Such divisions in work organizations are well documented as well as often obvious to casual observers. Although there are great variations in the patterns and extent of gender division, men are almost always in the highest positions of organizational power. Managers' decisions often initiate gender divisions, and organizational practices maintain them—although they also take on new forms with changes in technology and the labour process. For example, Cynthia Cockburn (1983, 1985) has shown how the introduction of new technology in a number of industries was accompanied by a reorganization, but not abolition, of the gendered division of labour that left the technology in men's control and maintained the definition of skilled work as men's work and unskilled work as women's work.

Second is the construction of symbols and images that explain, express, reinforce, or sometimes oppose those divisions. These have many sources or forms in language, ideology, popular and high culture, dress, the press, and television. For example, as Kanter (1975), among others, has noted, the image of the top manager or the business leader is an image of successful, forceful masculinity. In Cockburn's studies, men workers' images of masculinity linked their gender with

their technical skills; the possibility that women might also obtain such skills represented a threat to that masculinity.

The third set of processes that produce gendered social structures, including organizations, are interactions between women and men, women and women, men and men, including all those patterns that enact dominance and submission. For example, conversation analysis shows how gender differences in interruptions, turn taking, and setting the topic of discussion recreate gender inequality in the flow of ordinary talk. Although much of this research has used experimental groups, qualitative accounts of organizational life record the same phenomena: Men are the actors, women the emotional support.

Fourth, these processes help to produce gendered components of individual identity, which may include consciousness of the existence of the other three aspects of gender, such as, in organizations, choice of appropriate work, language use, clothing, and presentation of self as a gendered member of an organization.

Finally, gender is implicated in the fundamental, ongoing processes of creating and conceptualizing social structures. Gender is obviously a basic constitutive element in family and kinship, but, less obviously, it helps to frame the underlying relations of other structures, including complex organizations. Gender is a constitutive element in organizational logic, or the underlying assumptions and practices that construct most contemporary work organizations. Organizational logic appears to be gender neutral; gender-neutral theories of bureaucracy and organizations employ and give expression to this logic. However, underlying both academic theories and practical guides for managers is a gendered substructure that is reproduced daily in practical work activities and, somewhat less frequently, in the writings of organizational theorists.

Organizational logic has material forms in written work rules, labour contracts, managerial directives, and other documentary tools for running large organizations, including systems of job evaluation widely used in the comparable-worth strategy of feminists. Job evaluation is accomplished through the use and interpretation of documents that describe jobs and how they are to be evaluated. These documents contain symbolic indicators of structure; the ways that they are interpreted and talked about in the process of job evaluation reveals the underlying organizational logic. I base the following theoretical discussion on my observations of organizational logic in action in the job-evaluation component of a comparable-worth project.

Job evaluation is a management tool used in every industrial country, capitalist and socialist, to rationalize the organizational hierarchy and to help in setting equitable wages. Although there are many different systems of job evaluation, the underlying rationales are similar enough so that the observation of one system can provide a window into a common organizational mode of thinking and practice.

In job evaluation, the content of jobs is described and jobs are compared on criteria of knowledge, skill, complexity, effort, and working conditions. The particular system I observed was built incrementally over many years to reflect the assessment of managers about the job components for which they were willing to pay. Thus today this system can be taken as composed of residues of these judgments, which are a set of decision rules that, when followed, reproduce managerial values. But these rules are also the imagery out of which managers construct and reconstruct their organizations. The rules of job evaluation, which help to determine pay differences between jobs, are not simply a compilation of managers' values or sets of beliefs, but are the underlying logic or organization that provides at least part of the blueprint for its structure. Every time that job evaluation is used, that structure is created or reinforced.

Job evaluation evaluates jobs, not their incumbents. The job is the basic unit in a work organization's hierarchy, a description of a set of tasks, competencies, and responsibilities represented as a position on an organizational chart. A job is separate from people. It is an empty slot, a reification that must continually be reconstructed, for positions exist only as scraps of paper until people fill them. The rationale for evaluating jobs as devoid of actual workers reveals further the organizational logic—the intent is to assess the characteristics of the job, not of their incumbents who may vary in skill, industriousness, and commitment. Human beings are to be motivated, managed, and chosen to fit the job. The job exists as a thing apart.

Every job has a place in the hierarchy, another essential element in organizational logic. Hierarchies, like jobs, are devoid of actual workers and based on abstract differentiations. Hierarchy is taken for granted; only its particular form is at issue. Job evaluation is based on the assumption that workers in general see hierarchy as an acceptable principle, and the final test of the evaluation of any particular job is whether its place in the hierarchy looks reasonable. The ranking of jobs within an organization must make sense to managers, but it is also important that most workers accept the ranking as just in order for the system of evaluation is to contribute to orderly working relationships.

Organizational logic assumes a congruence between responsibility, job complexity, and hierarchical position. For example, a lower-level position, the level of most jobs filled predominantly by women, must have equally low levels of complexity and responsibility. Complexity and responsibility are defined in terms of managerial and professional tasks. The childcare worker's responsibility for other human beings or the complexity facing the secretary who serves six different, temperamental bosses can only be minimally counted if the congruence between position level, responsibility, and complexity is to be preserved. In addition, the logic holds that two jobs at different hierarchical levels cannot be responsible for the same outcome; as a consequence, for example, tasks delegated to a secretary by a manager will not raise her hierarchical level because such tasks are still his responsibility, even though she has the practical responsibility to see that they are done. Levels of skill, complexity, and responsibility, all used in constructing hierarchy, are conceptualized as existing independently of any concrete worker.

In organizational logic, both jobs and hierarchies are abstract categories that have no occupants, no human bodies, and no gender. However, an abstract job can exist—can be transformed into a concrete instance—only if there is a worker. In organizational logic, filling the abstract job is a disembodied worker who exists only for the work. Such a hypothetical worker cannot have other imperatives of existence that impinge upon the job. At the very least, outside imperatives cannot be included within the definition of the job. Too many obligations outside the boundaries of the job would make a worker unsuited for the position. The closest the disembodied worker doing the abstract job comes to a real worker is the male worker whose life centres on his full-time, life-long job, while his wife or another woman takes care of his personal needs and his children. While the realities of life in industrial capitalism never allowed all men to live out this ideal, it was the goal for labour unions and the image of the worker in social and economic theory. The woman worker, assumed to have legitimate obligations other than those required by the job, did not fit with the abstract job.

The concept 'a job' is thus implicitly a gendered concept, even though organizational logic presents it as gender neutral. 'A job' already contains the gender-based division of labour and the separation between the public and the private sphere. The concept of 'a job' assumes a particular gendered organization of domestic life

and social production. It is an example of what Dorothy Smith has called 'the gender subtext of the rational and impersonal' (1988: 4).

Hierarchies are gendered because they also are constructed on these underlying assumptions: Those who are committed to paid employment are 'naturally' more suited to responsibility and authority; those who must divide their commitments are in the lower ranks. In addition, principles of hierarchy, as exemplified in most existing job-evaluation systems, have been derived from already existing gendered structures. Management consultants working with managers to build methods of consistently evaluating jobs and rationalizing pay and job classifications developed the best-known systems. For example, all managers with similar levels of responsibility in the firm should have similar pay. Job-evaluation systems were intended to reflect the values of managers and to produce a believable ranking of jobs based on those values. Such rankings would not deviate substantially from rankings already in place that contain gender typing and gender segregation of jobs and the clustering of women workers in the lowest and the most poorly paid jobs. The concrete value judgments that constitute conventional job evaluation are designed to replicate such structures. Replication is achieved in many ways; for example, skills in managing money, more often found in men's than in women's jobs, frequently receive more points than skills in dealing with clients or human relations skills, more often found in women's than in men's jobs.

The gender-neutral status of 'a job' and of the organizational theories of which it is a part depend upon the assumption that the worker is abstract and disembodied, although in actuality both the concept of 'a job' and real workers are deeply gendered and 'bodied'. Carole Pateman (1986), in a discussion of women and political theory, similarly points out that the most fundamental abstraction in the concept of liberal individualism is 'the abstraction of the "individual" from the body. In order for the individual to appear in liberal theory as a universal figure, who represents anyone and everyone, the individual must be disembodied' (8). If the individual were not abstracted from bodily attributes, it would be clear that the individual represents one sex and one gender, not a universal being. The political fiction of the universal 'individual' or 'citizen', fundamental to ideas of democracy and contract, excluded women, judging them lacking in the capacities necessary for participation in civil society. Although women now have the rights of citizens in democratic states, they still stand in an ambiguous relationship to the universal individual who is 'constructed from a male body so that his identity is always masculine' (Pateman, 1988: 223). The worker with 'a job' is the same universal 'individual' who in actual social reality is a man. The concept of a universal worker excludes and marginalizes women who cannot, almost by definition, achieve the qualities of a real worker because to do so is to become like a man.

Organizational Control, Gender, and the Body

The abstract, bodiless worker, who occupies the abstract, gender-neutral job has no sexuality, no emotions, and does not procreate. The absence of sexuality, emotionality, and procreation in organizational logic and organizational theory is an additional element that both obscures and helps to reproduce the underlying gender relations.

New work on sexuality in organizations, often indebted to Foucault (1979), suggests that this silence on sexuality may have historical roots in the development of large, all-male organizations that are the primary locations of societal power. The history of modern organizations includes, among other processes, the suppression of sexuality in the interests of organization and the conceptual exclusion of the body as a concrete living whole.

In a review of historical evidence on sexuality in early modern organizations, Burrell (1984: 98) suggests that 'the suppression of sexuality is one of the first tasks the bureaucracy sets itself.' Long before the emergence of the very large factory of the nineteenth century, other large organizations, such as armies and monasteries, which had allowed certain kinds of limited participation of women, were more and more excluding women and attempting to banish sexuality in the interests of control of members and the organization's activities. Active sexuality was the enemy of orderly procedures, and excluding women from certain areas of activity may have been, at least in part, a way to control sexuality. As Burrell (1984) points out, the exclusion of women did not eliminate homosexuality, which has always been an element in the life of large all-male organizations, particularly if members spend all of their time in the organization. Insistence on heterosexuality or celibacy were ways to control homosexuality. But heterosexuality had to be practiced outside the organization, whether it was an army or a capitalist workplace. Thus the attempts to banish sexuality from the workplace were part of the wider process that differentiated the home, the location of legitimate sexual activity, from the place of capitalist production. The concept of the disembodied job symbolizes this separation of work and sexuality.

Similarly, there is no place within the disembodied job or the gender-neutral organization for other 'bodied' processes, such as human reproduction or the free expression of emotions. Sexuality, procreation, and emotions all intrude upon and disrupt the ideal functioning of the organization, which tries to control such interferences. However, as argued above, the abstract worker is actually a man, and it is the man's body, its sexuality, minimal responsibility in procreation, and conventional control of emotions that pervades work and organizational processes. Women's bodies—female sexuality, their ability to procreate and their pregnancy, breast-feeding, and childcare, menstruation, and mythic 'emotionality'—are suspect, stigmatized, and used as grounds for control and exclusion.

The ranking of women's jobs is often justified on the basis of women's identification with childbearing and domestic life. They are devalued because women are assumed to be unable to conform to the demands of the abstract job. Gender segregation at work is also sometimes openly justified by the necessity to control sexuality, and women may be barred from types of work, such as skilled blue-collar work or top management, where most workers are men, on the grounds that potentially disruptive sexual liaisons should be avoided. On the other hand, the gendered definition of some jobs 'includes sexualization of the woman worker as a part of the job' (MacKinnon, 1979: 18). These are often jobs that serve men, such as secretaries, or a largely male public.

The maintenance of gendered hierarchy is achieved partly through such often-tacit controls based on arguments about women's reproduction, emotionality, and sexuality, helping to legitimate the organizational structures created through abstract, intellectualized techniques. More overt controls, such as sexual harassment, relegating childbearing women to lower-level mobility tracks, and penalizing (or rewarding) their emotion management also conform to and reinforce hierarchy. MacKinnon (1979), on the basis of an extensive analysis of legal cases, argues that the willingness to tolerate sexual harassment is often a condition of the job, both a consequence and a cause of gender hierarchy.

While women's bodies are ruled out of order, or sexualized and objectified, in work organizations, men's bodies are not. Indeed, male sexual imagery pervades organizational metaphors and language, helping to give form to work activities. For example, the military and the male world of sports are considered valuable training for organizational success and provide images for teamwork, campaigns, and tough competition.

The symbolic expression of male sexuality may be used as a means of control over male workers, too, allowed or even encouraged within the bounds of the work situation to create cohesion or alleviate stress. Management approval of pornographic pictures in the locker room or support for all-male work and play groups where casual talk is about sexual exploits or sports are examples. These symbolic expressions of male dominance also act as significant controls over women in work organizations because they are per se excluded from the informal bonding men produce with the 'body talk' of sex and sports.

Symbolically, a certain kind of male heterosexual sexuality plays an important part in legitimating organizational power. Connell (1987) calls this hegemonic masculinity, emphasizing that it is formed around dominance over women and in opposition to other masculinities, although its exact content changes as historical conditions change. Currently, hegemonic masculinity is typified by the image of the strong, technically competent, authoritative leader who is sexually potent and attractive, has a family, and has his emotions under control. Images of male sexual function and patriarchal paternalism may also be embedded in notions of what the manager does when he leads his organization. Women's bodies cannot be adapted to hegemonic masculinity; to function at the top of male hierarchies requires that women render irrelevant everything that makes them women.

The image of the masculine organizational leader could be expanded, without altering its basic elements, to include other qualities also needed, according to many management experts, in contemporary organizations, such as flexibility and sensitivity to the capacities and needs of subordinates. Such qualities are not necessarily the symbolic monopoly of women. For example, the wise and experienced coach is empathetic and supportive to his individual players and flexibly leads his team against devious opposition tactics to victory.

The connections between organizational power and men's sexuality may be even more deeply embedded in organizational processes. Sally Hacker (1989) argues that eroticism and technology have common roots in human sensual pleasure and that for the engineer or the skilled worker, and probably for many other kinds of workers, there is a powerful erotic element in work processes. The pleasures of technology, Hacker continues, become harnessed to domination, and passion becomes directed toward power over nature, the machine, and other people, particularly women, in the work hierarchy. Hacker believes that men lose a great deal in this transformation of the erotic into domination, but they also win in other ways. For example, many men gain economically from the organizational gender hierarchy. As Crompton and Jones (1984) point out, men's career opportunities in white-collar work depend on the barriers that deny those opportunities to women. If the mass of female clerical workers were able to compete with men in such work, promotion probabilities for men would be drastically reduced.

Class relations as well as gender relations are reproduced in organizations. Critical, but non-feminist, perspectives on work organizations argue that rational-technical systems for organizing work, such as job classification and evaluation systems and detailed specifications of how work is to be done, are parts of pervasive systems of control that help to maintain class relations. The abstract 'job', devoid of a human body, is a basic unit in such systems of control. The positing of a job as an abstract category, separate from the worker, is an essential move in creating jobs as mechanisms of compulsion and control over work processes. Rational-technical, ostensibly gender-neutral, control systems are built upon and conceal a gendered substructure (Smith, 1988) in which men's bodies fill the abstract jobs. Use of such abstract systems continually reproduces the underlying gender assumptions and

the subordinated or excluded place of women. Gender processes, including the manipulation and management of women's and men's sexuality, procreation, and emotion, are part of the control processes of organizations, maintaining not only gender stratification but contributing also to maintaining class and, possibly, race and ethnic relations. Is the abstract worker white as well as male? Are white-male-dominated organizations also built on underlying assumptions about the proper place of people with different skin colours? Are racial differences produced by organizational practices as gender differences are?

Conclusion

Feminists wanting to theorize about organizations face a difficult task because of the deeply embedded gendering of both organizational processes and theory. Commonsense notions, such as jobs and positions, which constitute the units managers use in making organizations and some theorists use in making theory, are posited upon the prior exclusion of women. This underlying construction of a way of thinking is not simply an error, but part of processes of organization. This exclusion in turn creates fundamental inadequacies in theorizing about gender-neutral systems of positions to be filled. Creating more adequate theory may come only as organizations are transformed in ways that dissolve the concept of the abstract job and restore the absent female body.

Such a transformation would be radical in practice because it would probably require the end of organizations as they exist today, along with a redefinition of work and work relations. The rhythm and timing of work would be adapted to the rhythms of life outside of work. Caring work would be just as important and well rewarded as any other; having a baby or taking care of a sick mother would be as valued as making an automobile or designing computer software.

Hierarchy would be abolished, and workers would run things themselves. Of course, women and men would share equally in different kinds of work. Perhaps there would be some communal or collective form of organization where work and intimate relations are closely related, children learn in places close to working adults, and workmates, lovers, and friends are all part of the same group. Utopian writers and experimenters have left us many possible models (Hacker, 1989). But this brief listing begs many questions, perhaps the most important of which is how, given the present organization of economy and technology and the pervasive, powerful, and impersonal textually mediated relations of ruling (Smith, 1988), so radical a change could come about.

Feminist research and theorizing, by continuing to puzzle out how gender provides the subtext for arrangements of subordination, can make some contributions to a future in which collective action to do what needs doing—producing goods, caring for people, disposing of the garbage—is organized so that dominance, control, and subordination, particularly the subordination of women, are eradicated, or at least minimized, in our organization life.

References

Burrell, G. 1984. 'Sex and Organizational Analysis', *Organization Studies* 5: 97–118.

Cockburn, C. 1983. *Brothers: Male Dominance and Technological Change*. London: Pluto Press.

———. 1985. *Machinery of Dominance*. London: Pluto Press.

Connell, R.W. 1987. *Gender and Power*. Stanford, CA: Stanford University Press.

Crompton, R., and G. Jones. 1984. *White-collar Proletariat: Deskilling and Gender in Clerical Work*. Philadelphia: Temple University Press.

Feldberg, R., and E.N. Glenn. 1979. 'Male and Female: Job versus Gender Models in the Sociology of Work', *Social Problems* 26: 524–38.

Ferguson, K.E. 1984. *The Feminist Case Against Bureaucracy*. Philadelphia: Temple University Press.

Foucault, M. 1979. *The History of Sexuality*, Vol. 1. London: Allen Lane.

Hacker, S. 1987. 'Women Workers in the Mondragon System of Industrial Cooperatives', *Gender & Society* 1: 358–79.

———. 1989. *Pleasure, Power and Technology*. Boston: Unwin Hyman.

Hartmann, H. 1976. 'Capitalism, Patriarchy and Job Segregation by Sex', *Signs* 1: 137–70.

Kanter, R.M. 1975. 'Women and the Structure of Organizations: Explorations in Theory and Behavior', in R. Kanter and M. Millman, eds, *Another Voice*. New York: Doubleday.

———. 1977. *Men and Women of the Corporation*. New York: Basic Books.

MacKinnon, C.A. 1979. *Sexual Harassment of Working Women*. New Haven, CT: Yale University Press.

———. 1982. 'Feminism, Marxism, Method and the State: An Agenda for Theory', *Signs* 7: 515–44.

Pateman, C. 1970. *Participation and Democratic Theory*. Cambridge: Cambridge University Press.

———. 1983a. 'Feminist Critiques of the Public–Private Dichotomy', in S.I. Benn and G. F. Gaus, eds, *Public and Private in Social Life*. Beckenham, Kent: Croom Helm.

———. 1983b. 'Feminism and Democracy', in G. Duncan, ed., *Democratic Theory and Practice*. Cambridge: Cambridge University Press.

———. 1986. 'Introduction: The Theoretical Subversiveness of Feminism', in C. Pateman and E. Gross, *Feminist Challenges*. Winchester, MA: Allen & Unwin.

———. 1988. *The Sexual Contract*. Cambridge, MA: Polity.

Ressner, U. 1986. 'Review of K. Ferguson, *The Feminist Case Against Bureaucracy*', *Economic and Industrial Democracy* 7: 130–4.

———. 1987. *The Hidden Hierarchy*. Aldershot: Gower.

Scott, J. 1986. 'Gender: A Useful Category of Historical Analysis', *American Historical Review* 91: 1053–75.

Smith, D.E. 1979. 'A Sociology for Women', in J.A. Sherman and E.T. Beck, *The Prism of Sex: Essays in the Sociology of Knowledge*. Madison: University of Wisconsin Press.

———. 1988. *The Everyday World as Problematic*. Boston: Northeastern University Press.

CHAPTER 25

Cautious Caregivers: Gender Stereotypes and the Sexualization of Men Nurses' Touch

Joan A. Evans

Introduction

Caring for and about others is historically associated with women and nursing, and more than any other quality it captures the process and goal of nurses' work (MacDougall, 1997). Despite this association, men are now entering the profession in record numbers (Halloran and Welton, 1994; Zurlinden 1998) and challenging the stereotype that men are inappropriate in the caregiver role or incapable of providing compassionate and sensitive care. The nursing literature suggests that the desire to be of help and care for others is a major reason men chose nursing as a career (Taylor et al., 1983; Skevington and Dawkes, 1988; Galbraith, 1991; Cyr, 1992; Kelly et al., 1996; MacDougall, 1997). Once in the profession, however, prevailing gender stereotypes of men as sexual aggressors and men nurses as gay, negatively influence the ability of men nurses to develop comfortable and trusting relationships with their patients (Mathieson, 1991; Lodge et al., 1997). The sexualization of men nurses' touch provides insight into how gender stereotypes create discomfort and suspicion on the part of patients. This, in turn, impacts on men nurses' perceptions of their own safety while performing intimate and caregiving tasks. This situation ultimately impacts on the ability of men nurses to perform the very work they came into nursing to do.

The Study

AIM

The overall aim of this research was to explore the experience of men nurses and the gendered and sexed relations that structure different experiences for women and men in the same profession. The definition of masculinity used in this study is based on Connell's (1987) sociology of masculinity work. Meanings of masculinity are demonstrated through practices that capture the performative nature of gender. Connell's definition moves us away from the essentialist notion that a relatively stable masculine essence exists that defines men and differentiates them from a feminine essence that defines women (Petersen, 1998).

When theorizing about men and masculinity, we now talk of masculinities, rather than masculinity (Connell, 1987, 1995; Hearn and Morgan, 1990) because masculinity is not uniform. This concept is reflected in the notion of hegemony and the dominance in society of certain forms and practices of masculinity. Men nurses, by virtue of their participation in 'women's work', may not measure up to the hegemonic standard as evidenced by the stigma of homosexuality that surrounds them.

METHOD

Participants

Eight men Registered Nurses practicing in the province of Nova Scotia, Canada were selected to participate in this research using a convenience sampling technique. Because men are a highly visible minority in nursing, demographic data have been purposefully kept vague to protect the identities of the participants. Their ages ranged from late-20s to mid-50s, and years of nursing practice ranged from 7 to 32 years. Areas of nursing practice included community health nursing, mental health nursing, medical-surgical and general duty nursing. Three participants were in a leadership role; two had a baccalaureate degree. Six participants were married, and two lived with a partner. One participant was an 'out' gay man. Data were collected in 1998 in two rounds of semi-structured interviews.

Findings

The theme of men nurses as cautious caregivers emerged as one of four themes that characterized the experience of participants. The findings presented offer insight into the experience of men in nursing, but are not intended to be generalizable.

AFFIRMATION OF CARING

The participants in this research affirmed the importance of caring and traits such as compassion, empathy, and honesty as those that gave meaning to their lives as nurses. They generally also supported the perception that men and women nurses' caring styles were not the same. As one participant noted, 'We have our ways of

getting it across without putting that female bent or lean on it.' Participants did not agree, however, on the ways in which women's and men's expressions of caring differed and they expressed conflicting opinions about whether men nurses were more task-orientated, more gentle, or more caring. One participant characterized the difference between women and men nurses by describing women's caring as 'warm fuzzies' and more 'touchy feelie'. These were not necessarily negative descriptors; however, most participants commented that men nurses generally used touch less than their women colleagues.

For most participants, humour and camaraderie were identified as important expressions of their caring practice. Humour in particular, added warmth and helped patients relax and feel more comfortable with them as men. Despite an acknowledgement that humour needed to be patient-specific, its character and purpose was different when it was used with men patients and in the presence of men only. In such instances, humour was described as important in relieving male anxiety. It was also a comfortable approach to men patients and a way to be more of a friend or 'buddy' to them. Men patients in turn joked with men nurses and enjoyed the freedom of sharing things with another man that a woman might find inappropriate or offensive. The masculine nature of such humour is evidenced by its 'male only' character as 'when a female staff would come in, we wouldn't continue on with it.'

THE PROBLEMATIC NATURE OF MEN NURSES' TOUCH

Touch was one expression of caring that all participants identified as important, if not central, to their practice as nurses. Touch was also acknowledged, however, to be a practice that sometimes did not come naturally to them as men. One participant described his hands as 'rough hands' before he became a nurse. Another spoke of the newness of touching people 'because that wasn't part of my existence to that point'. Despite the newness of some caring expressions, touching and comforting others was acknowledged to be rewarding for participants and patients.

Whether the purpose of touch is to perform a procedure or provide comfort, an overriding theme is that for men nurses touching patients, particularly women patients, is potentially dangerous. Participants voiced concern that women patients might be uncomfortable and/or misinterpret their touch—a situation that in turn might lead to accusations of inappropriate behaviour or sexual molestation. The fear of misunderstandings and accusations related to touching patients resulted in participants being cautious and vigilant: 'I have to be careful what I'm doing . . . because of the possibility of somebody saying that I did something wrong, or rape, or I touched her wrong—that's always there.' Another participant commented that: 'You are very vulnerable, particularly if you're alone—and even in a ward situation. You have to be very careful that you assess the situation and know that this might be an inappropriate place to touch.'

The perception that men nurses are unable to defend themselves against patient accusations of inappropriate behaviour compounded participants' sense of themselves as vulnerable caregivers. As pointed out by one participant, 'It's my word against theirs.' Another participant who acknowledged the difficulty of defending himself commented that there were situations where he deemed it was too unsafe to touch.

ASSESSING WHEN IT IS SAFE TO TOUCH

Knowing when it is safe to touch and what the touch should consist of is based on a careful assessment of each patient situation. When the patient was a man, decisions regarding touch were guided by an accepted masculine norm, or what one participant referred to as a 'code' of understanding. This code is illustrated by the comment, 'Large men don't wash a healthy man's back—code'.

How far participants could go before violating the 'code' or crossing the line was dependent on the illness acuity of the male patient. As one noted, 'if you are sick, you don't mind a guy being there, you don't care who is doing anything.' It was also influenced by the age of the patient as participants generally described feeling more comfortable with older men who were less 'macho' and more receptive to expressions of compassion. They were less comfortable touching young people, particularly teens, who they perceived were more preoccupied with the possibility that a man nurse might be gay.

Participants commented that despite it being acceptable for women nurses to touch men and women patients, it was not as acceptable for men nurses to do the same. This aura of unacceptability was noted to impact not only on patients' perceptions of men nurses' touch, but also women nurses' perceptions. One participant commented that a woman colleague reported him to a supervisor when he reassured a distraught, partially dressed woman patient by putting his hand on her shoulder. Another was accused of molesting a newborn boy by the father who discovered him changing the baby's diaper. Incidents such as these left a lasting impression and reminded participants that touching patients was potentially dangerous work.

STRATEGIZING TO PROTECT ONESELF FROM ACCUSATIONS

As a result of the fear of being wrongfully accused of inappropriate touch, participants described six strategies they used to reduce this risk.

Strategy no. 1: Taking the time to build trust before touching. This was particularly important when interacting with women patients.

Strategy no. 2: Maintaining a degree of formality by shaking the hand of a patient. This set the tone of the interaction and provided an opportunity to assess patient comfort.

Strategy no. 3: Projecting the traditional image of a nurse to legitimize the role of men as nurses. This included wearing a white uniform.

Strategy no. 4: Working in teams with women colleagues in situations deemed to be unsafe. Such situations included checking female patients on night shifts, entering a room with teenage girls, or performing a procedure on a female that required intimate touching.

Strategy no. 5: Delegating tasks that required intimate touching of women patients. Participants traded off tasks with women nurses to ensure patient comfort and their own safety.

Strategy no. 6: Modifying procedural techniques to minimize patient exposure and the need for intimate touching. One participant commented that he might try to convince a female patient that the best intramuscular injection site was the thigh, 'not the butt'.

Discussion

GOING AGAINST THE GRAIN: MEN CAREGIVERS

Despite research that suggests men choose careers in nursing to help others (Taylor et al., 1983; Skevington and Dawkes, 1988; Cyr, 1992; Kelly et al., 1996; MacDougall, 1997), men nurses tend to gravitate to nursing specialties that require less intimate patient touching (Williams, 1989, 1995; Kauppinen-Toropainen and Lammi, 1993). The participants in this study support this tendency, and only two currently worked at the bedside in a role that required intimate caregiving. The remaining six, despite having worked at the bedside, were now in positions that required less touching and more psychological patient care. In some of these positions, however, participants continued to express vulnerability. This was especially so for those in psychiatry: 'Touch takes on a whole new meaning that it didn't have in medicine or in med-surg . . . It's never straight forward here. If I have someone who I know has a full-blown personality disorder, I won't even be caught in the same room alone with them.'

In order to avoid uncomfortable situations, men nurses distance themselves from traditional nursing roles and the caring ideology of nursing (Egeland and Brown, 1989; Kauppinen-Toropainen and Lammi, 1993). They are also tracked into elite specialty and leadership positions considered more congruent with prevailing notions of masculinity (Williams, 1995; Evans, 1997). The result is that power and prestige tend to be associated with small numbers of men in the profession (Porter, 1992; Ryan and Porter, 1993; Villeneuve, 1994). At the heart of this situation are gender stereotypes and the belief that men are inappropriate in caregiver roles.

FEMINIZATION OF CARING

Participant accounts draw attention to differences between societal and nursing expectations of men in relation to expressions of caring. They spoke of the newness of touching with caring hands and learning to feel comfortable touching others. The need to learn to care and/or develop comfort with expressions of caring previously not practised, is supported in the nursing literature. In a study of 20 men nursing students in a baccalaureate nursing program, Paterson et al. (1996) found that men nursing students feared they would never be able to touch clients or openly display emotions because they had learned all their lives that such behaviours were effeminate and emasculating (32). Similarly, Streubert (1994) reported that men nursing students were confronted with the task of having to learn caring skills that were unique to them. They consequently struggled with the need to consciously to divest themselves of their macho image as they learned to express caring in sensitive and demonstrative ways that women educators and nurses expected (Paterson et al., 1996).

Research conducted by Okrainec (1994) further highlights the notion that men and women judge the caring practices of men against a feminine norm. Okrainec surveyed 117 men and 121 women nursing students in the province of Alberta, Canada and reported that 25 per cent of both men and women felt that women were superior in caring; 20 per cent of men and 25 per cent, of women rated women superior to men in terms of empathy (104); and 50 per cent of men and 66 per cent of women rated women superior to men in ability to express feelings (103). Differences in perceptions between women and men students are noteworthy, given Okrainec's comment that most men and women nursing students thought that a caring attitude was equal in both sexes.

In the absence of an acknowledgement that expressions of caring include a wide range of possible behaviours that reflect the personalities of individual nurses and specifics of each client situation, theorizing about caring will be likely to continue to be based on stereotypical notions of masculine and feminine behaviours. Even more problematic, men nurses' expressions of caring will continue to be conceptualized as unique or special because they either fall outside the masculine stereotype, or conversely, within the feminine one. The implication of such stereotyping is that it perpetuates an artificial separation of the masculine and feminine and polarizes masculinity and femininity.

MAINTAINING MASCULINITY

For men in patriarchal culture, perpetuating the polarization of masculinity and femininity is an important practice of masculinity, as the maintenance of masculinity is predicated on the separation of all that is male and masculine from all that is female (Williams, 1989). Williams (1989) and Kauppinen-Toropainen and Lammi (1993) suggest that, for men nurses, this separation is accomplished by emphasizing different caring styles as a means of distinguishing the contribution of men nurses from that of women.

Maintaining masculinity through humour

Participants in this study demonstrate how humour as a practice of caring also constitutes a practice of masculinity. Participants commented that many of the jokes they shared with men clients were bawdy and sexist in nature and not appropriate for women. In this context, the practice of humour and its 'male only' character can be understood to be an important means of (re)affirming masculinity. This conclusion is supported by ethnographic research about the role of humour in young men in two British schools. Researchers Kehily and Nayak (1997) suggest that humorous exchanges among young men have an unfeminine and exclusively 'straight' character to them and are constitutive of heterosexual masculine identities. As such, humorous exchanges among men can also be conceptualized as practices of male bonding, as 'men recognize and reinforce one another's bona fide membership in the male gender' and remind one another that 'they were not born women' (Frank, 1992: 57).

Sexualization of men nurses' touch

Men learn early in their nursing career that, despite being in an occupation that requires compassion and caring, touch as an expression of that compassion and caring exposes them to the risk of misinterpretation and accusations of inappropriate behaviour (Glasper and Campbell, 1994; Paterson et al., 1996). Unlike women's touch, which is considered a natural extension of women's traditional caregiver role, men's touch is surrounded with suspicion that implies that men nurses' motives for touching are not care-oriented, but sexual in nature.

Participants in this study were well aware of their vulnerability when they touched patients. Similarly, Streubert (1994) found that men nursing students dreaded how women clients might feel about having them as nurses. They consequently struggled with learning appropriate ways to care and touch that would avoid the problem of clients thinking that a man was seducing them (Paterson et al., 1996). Several practices described by participants indicate that, with experience, men nurses can and do develop strategies that allow them to care for patients and ensure their own safety. Such strategies reflect the notion that men who see themselves operating outside the hegemony of masculinity are fine-tuned to the necessary practices to protect themselves (Frank, 1992).

The sexualization of men nurses' touch is particularly evident in the area of obstetric nursing, where the nature of touch is extremely intimate. Situations in which obstetric or gynecological women patients refuse to be cared for by men nurses or men nursing students provide valuable insight into the sexualized character of men nurses' touch. An ethnographic study by Morin et al. (1999) of 32 women obstetric patients revealed that most women were accepting of men nurses. Those women who refused them, however, cited reasons that were often sexual in nature.

An interesting observation by Morin et al. (1999) is that men nurses who are older, married, and have children are generally more accepted as caregivers by women patients (85). This can be attributed to perceptions by women patients that such qualities make men nurses sexually safer and hence more comfortable to be around. Continuing with this line of theorizing, it follows that practices which contribute to the perception of men nurses as sexually safe would be employed by them to put women patients at ease. This conclusion may be evidenced by men nurses' practice of wearing a traditional nurse uniform. Mangan (1994) suggests that the nursing uniform strengthens and promotes the image of men as conforming

to the expectations of the larger nursing group. This association may be important in helping men nurses project a genuine desire to care for others as one means of reducing the risk of accusations of inappropriate touch.

Discussion

GENDER STEREOTYPES: A NO-WIN SITUATION

The need for men nurses to project conformity in relation to a traditional nursing image may not apply to all patient populations. In situations where men nurses provide intimate care to men, sexual safety for men patients may depend on the degree to which men nurses project hegemonic masculinity. The nurse uniform, because it projects a feminine image, may consequently have a negative influence on the acceptance of men nurses by men patients. It is interesting to note that only two of the participants in this research wore a nurse uniform. Both worked at the bedside in positions that required intimate patient touching.

For most participants, the need to minimize suspicions of gayness and project a masculine identity with men patients was facilitated by a 'code' of understanding among men that was grounded in the heterosexist or homophobic principle that men do not touch other men without a legitimate need. The concept of need, as pointed out by participants, was complex and depended on factors such as patient age and illness acuity. They mentioned that they were more comfortable touching men who were acutely ill because they were too sick to care about what anyone did to them. They also found that older men were more comfortable being touched by another man because they were less macho.

MEN NURSES AS FAILED CAREGIVERS

The stigma associated with the stereotype of men nurses as gay is compounded by the stereotype that gay men are also sexual deviants and sexual predators (Levine, 1992). In situations where men nurses provide intimate care to children, the sexualization of men's touch consequently assumes a more sinister character that fuels suspicion that men nurses are pedophiles. Glasper and Campbell (1994) suggest that any intimate procedure conducted by men nurses on children is now suspicious as a result of a British nurse being convicted of sexually assaulting a child in his care. An interesting observation in light of this situation is that the behaviour of one man nurse has not been attributed to an individual deviation, but to all men nurses as a group.

The notion of blaming all men nurses for the transgressions of a few is also raised by Bush (1976). She notes the tendency of some patients to blame individual men nurses when they are perceived to fail in the performance of a technical skill. When a man nurse is perceived to fail in an affective area, however, men nurses as a group are blamed. This situation can be understood as a consequence of traditional gender stereotypes and the belief that men are inappropriate and unable to function as well as women in caring roles.

Conclusion

The gendered nature of men nurses' caring interactions reveals the ways in which gender stereotypes create contradictory and complex situations of acceptance, rejection, and suspicion of men as nurturers and caregivers. Here the stereotype of men as sexual aggressors creates suspicion that

men are at the bedside for reasons other than a genuine desire to help others. When this stereotype is compounded by the stereotype that men nurses are gay, the caring practices of men nurses are viewed with suspicion in situations where there is intimate touching, not only of women patients, but of men and children as well. In each of these patient situations, men nurses are caught up in complex and contradictory gender relations that situate them in stigmatizing roles vulnerable to accusations of inappropriate touch.

Gender relations are complex and do not lend themselves to 'quick fixes' or recommendations that are easily implemented. The challenge in nursing is to acknowledge the power and pervasiveness of gender relations and the role they play in all nurses' lives. The answer to reducing the suspicion that surrounds men nurses' caring practice lies in challenging prevailing gender stereotypes that situate men in deviant positions when they do not conform to the hegemonic masculine standard. This challenge cannot be taken up by women nurses or men nurses alone. Meaningful change will need to be grounded in an ethos of alliance-building between women nurses and men nurses. This alliance-building needs to begin with dialogue in our nursing classrooms and workplaces if we are to begin to reveal the gendered nature of our thinking, our practices, and our institutions in the interests of revaluing caring and interpersonal skills that challenge hegemonic masculinity.

References

Connell, R.W. 1987. *Gender and Power. Society, the Person and Sexual Politics*. Stanford, CA: Stanford University Press.
———. 1995. *Masculinities*. Cambridge: Polity.

Cyr, J. 1992. 'Males in Nursing', *Nursing Managements* 23: 54–5.
Egeland, J., and J. Brown. 1989. 'Men in Nursing: Their Fields of Employment, Preferred Fields of

Practice and Role Strain', *Health Services Research* 24: 693–707.

Evans, J. (1997). 'Men in Nursing: Issues of Gender Segregation and Hidden Advantage', *Journal of Advanced Nursing* 26: 226–31.

Frank, B. 1992. 'Straight/Strait Jackets for Masculinity: Educating for "Real" Men', *Atlantis* 18: 47–59.

Galbraith, M. 1991. 'Attracting Men to Nursing: What Will They Find Important in Their Career', *Journal of Nursing Education* 30: 182–6.

Glasper, A., and S. Campbell. 1994. 'Beyond the Clothier Inquiry', *Nursing Standard* 8: 18–19.

Halloran, E., and J. Welton. 1994. 'Why Aren't There More Men in Nursing' in J. McCloskey and H. Grace, eds, *Current Issues in Nursing, 4th edn*, pp, 683–91. Toronto: Moshy.

Hearn, J., and D. Morgan. 1990. 'Men, Masculinities and Social Theory', in J. Hearn and D. Morgan, eds., *Men, Masculinities and Social Theory*, pp. 1–18. Boston: Unwin-Hyman.

Kauppinen-Toropainen, K., and J. Lammi. 1993. 'Men in Female-dominated Occupations: A Cross Cultural Comparison', in C. Williams, ed., *Doing 'Women's Work'*, pp. 91–112. London: Sage.

Kehily, M.J., and A. Navak. 1997. 'Lads and Laughter: Humor and the Production of Heterosexual Hierarchies', *Gender and Education* 9: 69–87.

Kelly, N., M. Shoemaker, and T. Steele. 1996. 'The Experience of Being a Male Student Nurse', *Journal of Nursing Education* 35: 170–4.

Levine, M. 1992. 'The Status of Gay Men in the Workplace', in M. Kimmel and M. Messner, eds, *In Men's Lives*, 2nd edn, pp. 251–66. Toronto: Maxwell MacMillan Canada.

Lodge, N., J. Mallett, P. Blake, and I. Fryatt. 1997. 'A Study to Ascertain Gynecological Patients' Perceived Levels of Endorsement with Physical and Psychological Care Given by Female and Male Nurses', *Journal of Advanced Nursing* 25: 893–907.

MacDougall, G. 1997. 'Caring—A Masculine Perspective', *Journal of Advanced Nursing* 25, 809–13.

Mangan, P. 1994. 'Private Lives', *Nursing Times* 90: 60–4.

Mathieson, E. 1991. 'A Question of Gender', *Nursing Times* 87: 31–2.

Morin, K., B. Patterson, B. Kurtz, and B. Brzowski. 1999. 'Mothers' Responses to Care Given by Male Nursing Students During and After Birth', *Image: Journal or Nursing Scholarship* 31: 83–7.

Okrainec, G. 1994. 'Perceptions of Nursing Education Held by Male Nursing Students', *Western Journal or Nursing Research* 16: 94–107.

Paterson, B., S. Tschikota, M. Crawford, M. Saydak, P. Venkatesh, and T. Aronowitz. 1996. 'Learning to Care: Gender Issues for Male Nursing Students', *Canadian Journal of Nursing Research* 28: 25–39.

Petersen, A. 1998. *Unmasking the Masculine: Men and 'Identity' in a Skeptical Age*. London: Sage.

Porter, S. 1992. 'Women in a Women's Job: The Gendered Experience of Nurses', *Sociology of Health and Illness* 14: 510–27.

Ryan, S., and S. Porter. 1993. 'Men in Nursing: A Cautionary Comparative Critique', *Nursing Outlook* 41: 262–7.

Skevington, S., and D. Dawkes. 1988. 'Fred Nightingale', *Nursing Times* 84: 49–51.

Streubert, H. 1994. 'Male Nursing Students' Perceptions of Clinical Experience', *Nurse Educator* 19: 28–32.

Taylor, E., R. Dwiggins, M. Albert, and J. Dearner. 1983. 'Male Nurses: What They Think About Themselves—and Others', *RN* 46: 61–4.

Villeneuve, M. 1994. 'Recruiting and Retaining Men in Nursing: A Review of the Literature', *Journal of Professional Nursing* 10: 217–28.

Williams, C. 1989. *Gender Differences at Work: Women and Men in Nontraditional Occupations*. Berkeley, CA: University of California Press.

———. 1995. 'Hidden Advantages for Men in Nursing', *Nursing Administration Quarterly* 19: 63–70.

Zurlinden, J. 1998. 'Are Men a Step Higher on the Nursing Ladder of Success?', *Nursing Spectrum* 10A: 4–5, 12.

CHAPTER 26

Privilege and Oppression: The Configuration of Race, Gender, and Class in Southern Ontario Auto Plants, 1939 to 1949[1]

Pamela Sugiman

This paper offers an examination of the ways in which the matrix of race, gender, and class has structured the automobile manufacturing industry of southern Ontario, a work setting that has long been racialized and gendered. Since the beginnings of the industry, white men have dominated the auto-manufacturing workforce. Anyone who was not white and male was in the minority, different, an intruder, treated as unequal. In the auto plants of southern Ontario, two such 'minorities' existed. One, small groups of women, many of whom were born in Canada of Anglo-Celtic and Eastern European descent, worked in McKinnon Industries of St Catharines, Ontario and the General Motors Company of Canada's (GM) manufacturing facility in Oshawa, Ontario.[2] Two, even smaller pockets of black men, mostly Canadian-born, were concentrated in janitorial jobs and various types of foundry work in McKinnon Industries and the Ford Motor Company of Canada, as well as some smaller auto foundries in Windsor.[3]

In earlier research, I documented the experiences of white, women auto workers, tracing changes in both their position in the industry and their perceptions and politics over the course of several decades (Sugiman, 1994). This study is an attempt to reconstruct a small part of the lives of black men, on the job and in their union, at a time when their numerical presence in the auto plants was at its peak, throughout the Second World War and into the post-war period.[4] It is based on a review of union documents, as well as the

oral testimonies of twelve black men who were employed in the industry during these years.[5]

In spite of the scant numbers of black men in the plants, auto manufacturers drew on widespread cultural beliefs about race and gender, and exploited and reinforced the structural inequalities that working-class blacks faced in wartime southern Ontario. Employers manipulated these beliefs in hiring workers, allocating them to jobs, and establishing the terms of their employment. In doing so, management was central to the construction of difference among workers—a notable achievement given the striking social homogeneity of the workforce as a whole.

An understanding of the social meaning of racial and sexual difference is central to an analysis of the workplace, working people, and their struggles. When we recognize these differences, we uncover many parallel, but separate working-class realities. The distinctive experiences of black men in the industry can be attributed to the particular ways in which race, gender, and class, both as subjectivities and social processes, have converged at different moments and touched the lives of workers, as well as shaped the larger historical scenario.

Constructing Difference Among Auto Workers

Though data on the demographic composition of auto plants in Canada is based largely on anecdotal evidence, it is undeniable that employers used race and sex as criteria in filling jobs. Prior to the Second World War, in the pre-union period, sizeable communities of black families lived in the auto towns of St Catharines and Windsor. St Catharines, a small city near Niagara Falls, was the home of McKinnon Industries. Windsor, a mid-sized city that is situated across the river from Detroit, was the location of the Ford Motor Company of Canada, Chrysler Canada, and a number of affiliated auto foundries such as Auto Specialties, Walker Metal Products, and Malleable Iron.

Despite the strong presence of the auto companies in their communities, however, most blacks understood that auto employment was unattainable to them. Before the Second World War, only a handful of blacks worked in auto.[6]

With the outbreak of the Second World War, employers were forced to alter their hiring policies in response to stepped-up production demands and the temporary departure of many prime age, white, male employees. Thus, the doors to the auto plants opened a crack for some of those workers who had long been on the outside. For instance, during this time, Ford hired a number of Chinese men in its Windsor plant. Proud of this move, company publicists featured a photograph of each of their 56 Chinese workers in its monthly magazine, *Ford Times*. Ford described the employment of these men as a patriotic gesture in the context of war.[7]

None of the companies, however, offered employment to black women. According to a report by Lyle Talbot, former Ford employee and president of the anti-racist organization, the Windsor Council on Group Relations, at a time when many employers badly needed to replenish their diminishing supply of workers, 'the doors of virtually every factory in the Windsor area were closed tight against coloured girls and women.'[8] The Second World War 'broke the barrier' for 'coloured *men*' only (Interview #12, 1995).

Richard Nicholson worked in the foundry in St Catharines for 36 years. He remembers his entry into the company:

I heard the rumour . . . that McKinnon Industries was hiring blacks. . . . They were looking for *coloured people* to work in the foundry so I went down there to Ontario Street and 'bingo!' I got hired right away because I was a big lad and everything (emphasis added).

'Foundries Is Made For Black Men'

Auto makers took special measures to locate black male labourers largely because they wanted them to fill the most undesirable jobs in the plants—jobs that few white men wanted. In the auto plants of Ontario, racial segregation was never enforced as a matter of company policy nor was it written into collective agreements (as it had been in the US). Yet management used informal, unspoken means of exclusion to place blacks in one of three areas: the heat treat, the powerhouse, or the foundry. Within various departments or divisions, some black men could also find work as janitors. According to Lyle Talbot, who temporarily worked in each of these jobs, they were all bad places to be. The powerhouse was dirty.

> [T]hey'd get all kinds of soot from the smoke. . . . In the powerhouse, there was a big pile of coal out in the yard, and big transformers that were run by coal, heat. Black men worked in a tunnel where the coal was brought in on a conveyor from the coal pile into the big furnaces that generated the heat for the power. The men had to make sure that the coal did not fall off the conveyor going through.

The 'heat treat's the same thing', Talbot added. This is where they treated the metal with heat in long ovens. The worst of the three areas, however, was the foundry—'where all the heavy, slugging, dirty work' went on.[9] The vast majority of the black workforce was situated in the foundry.[10] And there, along with Armenians, they typically performed the least desirable job of iron pouring.

The men poured their own iron and you had to go out and shift the moulds—had a plate on top about that thick and go on top of the moulds for them to pour the iron. Sometimes they'd be pouring and the mould would be bad and as they poured in the iron would burst out the side and sometimes, as soon as that iron, just a drop, would hit . . . the concrete it would look like fireworks (Interview #12, 1995).

GM worker Richard Nicholson commented on the relationship between race and job allocation:

In 1938 . . . when I went to General Motors, they hired us blacks for one reason. They didn't lie to you. When they hired me, they told me . . . 'We got a job for you in the foundry. It's a hot job. It's a hard job.' . . . [T]hey kept calling in blacks, more blacks. They would've hired more blacks if they could have got 'em because that was where you were supposed to be—right there in the foundry.

Compounding the labour force requirements of auto manufacturers and the dire economic straits of most black workers, employers upheld a particular vision of black masculinity that rested in part on the belief that a 'coloured man' was most suited to hard, dirty, and physically demanding jobs.[11] Before foundries became highly automated, many of the operations required enormous physical strength (lifting castings and pouring iron, for example). And the dominant cultural image of a black man was that of a strong, robust, and muscular worker. Moreover, foundry work was performed at extraordinarily high temperatures and thus demanded tremendous physical stamina. Some company officials claimed that coloured men, in particular, could endure these excesses because of a genetic predisposition to withstand heat (Interview #1, 1990; Interview #7, 1994). According to auto worker Cassell Smith,

At that time the foundry there was smoky and dusty and the workers they'd get in there wouldn't stay long. . . . So they decided, we [black men] could stand it . . . that was the purpose of it because they figured, being black, you know, you could stand the heat . . . that they're all the same . . . people in Africa stand a lot of heat.

Exhibiting a racialized paternalism, some managers publicly showcased 'their' hard-working black employees. In doing so, they presented black masculinity in a hyperbolic form—using a racial stereotype to magnify the image of the unskilled working man.[12] In the eyes of some observers in the plants, these men were little more than powerful, labouring bodies. GM foundry employee Richard Nicholson recounted,

. . . quite a few white people come over and watch you work. Take pictures. They've got pictures of me down there now. Take pictures of us doing this heavy job. And they'd just sit back and say, 'Look at them guys work!' Visitors . . . the foremen or the general foreman [would] bring people in and say, 'Let's show you how we do it—how our boys do it.' They all look at one another and they used to be taking pictures of us guys all the time—the kind of work we was doin' (Interview #1, 1990).

These men were highlighted for displaying manly brawn and to some extent they themselves expressed pride in their ability to perform work that involved remarkably high levels of physical exertion.[13] Yet at the same time, black men were objectified by employers. Managers who put the men on public display for performing hard, dirty, hazardous labour—work that they had little choice but to perform—paradoxically reinforced the notion that black males possessed a heightened masculinity while at the same time they emasculated these men in denying their 'humanness', in constructing them as 'beasts of burden'. Employers contributed to the construction of a racialized masculinity, a masculinity that embodied racial and class subordination.

The Privileges of Manhood

Being a man, however, did bring with it some privileges. It was because of their *sex* that these men were hired in the auto industry. As noted, even during the Second World War, black women faced formidable obstacles in finding any kind of factory employment in Windsor and elsewhere in Canada. Their sexual status furthermore ensured that black men would possess specific job rights, rights that were denied the small numbers of white women who had been allowed to work in some auto plants largely because of their privilege as a race.

Assumed to be breadwinners, black men held departmental, and ultimately plant-wide seniority rights, received the same wages and piece rates, and in theory, could occupy the same job classifications as all other male auto workers. There is no evidence that during these years, any of the local collective agreements between the UAW and the Big Three auto makers in Canada openly made distinctions among workers on the basis of *race*. GM worker Richard Nicholson explained that in the past, differences in monetary rewards among the male workforce were based on an employee's family responsibilities only:

> The white boys I worked with and the black boys, we'd always see one another's cheque. . . . We all get the same [pay] . . . The only difference would be in deductions. If you have more kids than the other guy, you have a dollar or two more because they didn't take as much money off ya.

Married or single, male auto workers received higher than average wages for working-class men because of the successful efforts of the UAW to secure a family wage. The family wage demand was premised on the assumption that workers (men only) must be paid a relatively high rate because of their responsibility, as head of a household, for the economic welfare of a wife and children.[14] It was this ideology of the male breadwinner that in turn provided the rationale for women's lower rates of pay. In the words of Windsor-based auto worker Howard Olbey, in the Ford Motor Company, 'it was all man to man.'

In this particular historic context, and specifically in this sphere of social life—the paid work setting—the social meaning of gender (manhood) and race (blackness), and their configuration, permitted the elevation of black men to the *formal status* of white working-class men.

'We're All Brothers With the Union'

The vehicle by which all male auto workers secured various rights and entitlements in the workplace was the UAW, and there was a strong connection between belonging to the union and being a working-class man. Masculine bonds strengthened union ties and, in turn, union affiliation and masculinized class-based allegiances played an important part in reinforcing gender-based solidarities among these groups of men. Indeed, it is difficult to disentangle unionism from 'brotherhood' during these years. The industrial trade union was very much a masculine institution, not only because the vast majority of UAW members and leaders were men, but also because these men built their unionism around a place in the sexual division of familial labour, recreational pursuits, cultural forms of expression, strategies of resistance, and a political agenda that spoke to many of the shared experiences of working-class men (Sugiman, 1994).

Women auto workers clearly expressed strong loyalties to the union. They played an important part in building the UAW. Though female members were underrepresented in the UAW leadership, seldom held an elected position, and rarely voiced their views in local union forums, they regularly attended union meetings and faithfully performed their duty as 'foot soldiers' in the early strikes and sit-downs. Notwithstanding these loyalties, however, most women felt marginalized in union politics and subordinate to their UAW brothers. Women auto workers viewed the UAW of the 1940s as a distinctly masculine enterprise. 'That was men,' one woman auto worker matter-of-factly said about the union (as cited in Sugiman, 1994).

Black men, too, had an ambivalent relationship to the UAW. Afterall, white men dominated the upper echelons of the union bureaucracy, few of whom challenged the informal discriminatory measures that kept black workers in perilous foundry jobs and out of the preferred skilled trades.[15] Yet black men's awareness of racist undercurrents within the labour movement did not diminish their strong commitment to industrial unionism and (unlike women members) they became actively involved in mainstream union politics at the local level. In fact, during the Second World War, their level of UAW office-holding was notably high in proportion to their numbers in the plants.

The union allegiances of black men were strengthened by the UAW International's ideological commitment to racial equality as a basic principle of industrial unionism. For decades, the discussion of race among Canadian workers has been dominated, and perhaps inhibited, by this largely American discourse.[16] In response to the persistent demands of African American rank and file workers (Boyle, 1995), heightened racial strife in UAW-organized plants, locals, and in American cities generally, as well as the passage of US federal civil rights legislation during the war and post-war years,[17] the UAW International office took a clear stand against racial discrimination.[18] During the 1940s, the union created an International Fair Employment Practices and Anti-Discrimination Department (FEPC), made local FEPCs mandatory,

and appointed a (limited) number of women and black men on the International staff, mainly in fair practices, organizing, and education departments.[19]

To the UAW, racial discrimination was a serious matter with clear moral, political, and economic ramifications. First, UAW discourse on race was highly moralistic, and was expressed in passionate, emotional language. Appealing to workers' basic sense of right and wrong, and underscoring the moral authority of industrial unionism, official UAW statements espoused an essential immorality of racism in industry. In policy statements and public addresses, UAW International leaders posited racial discrimination as 'cancerous', 'evil', 'infectious', a 'poison', and 'an act against humanity'.[20] They argued that any good trade unionist should take a stand against racism as a matter of good conscience, and out of a commitment to one of the most fundamental philosophies of their union—that of 'brotherhood'.

UAW records contain a series of diatribes by leaders asserting that it was 'illogical' and 'stupid' for trade unionists to foster or maintain racial divisions between workers because of the potential impact of such divisions on the economic security of white male workers, the future bargaining power of the union, and labour solidarity.[21]

Most black workers believed that the union contract could be used as a tool to protect their rights, in spite of the actions or inaction, prejudices or indifference, of individual men. The collective agreement was a tool for the achievement of a better life, a measure of dignity, and equal opportunity at work—an instrument that, when pressured, some (white) union leaders would put to use. According to John Milben, a foundry worker for thirty-one years, '[t]he union was a hundred percent behind us . . . Fairness. We're all brothers with the union.'

Race, Brotherhood, and Resistance

From the beginnings of the auto industry in Canada, employers have contributed to the *construction of difference* within the working class. These differences were based on race, gender, and family status, as well as skill. While auto manufacturers hired white male breadwinners to fill the vast majority of jobs in the industry, they also recruited extremely small numbers of black men (and white women) to perform work that many white men either rejected or were temporarily unavailable to perform. While these two groups of workers met a need on the part of capitalists, management clearly regarded each as marginal to the industry, different, and unequal to the core workforce. Both black men and white women were defined as the 'other', a socially-created category that was itself broken down along lines of race and gender.

The history of black men in auto work is one of many contradictions. Such contradictions are the outcome of the changing configuration of race, gender, and social class. While black men were intruders in the homogeneous white world of the auto plants, their status as wage-earning men/union brothers accorded them various rights and entitlements that were denied (white) women workers. The social and political implications of race in these settings permitted black men to be elevated to the formal status of white men, a status that was based on gender privilege, and class, and gender solidarities.

Formal equal rights in union contracts (equal wages and equal seniority rights), though, did not shield black men from face-to-face indignities on the plant floor, nor did they protect the men from the hazards of working in bad jobs, or the economic impact of stunted opportunities within the firm. Gender and class shaped the content of the racism that these men experienced; they did not protect them from it.

Race and gender shape working-class experience. Whiteness and masculinity were undeniably central features of auto work. The primacy of one of these constructs over the others has sometimes been debated, but this is not at issue here for there is no neat formula that can be consistently applied to understand their alliance. It is more useful to observe how the racialization of gender and the gendering of race have changed over time, and have taken on meaning in different spheres of social existence. When we examine the ever-changing nexus of race, gender and class, we understand the relationship not merely as one of multiple oppressions, but as something more complex—one in which people can be simultaneously victims and agents; privileged and oppressed.

Notes

1. This is a revised version of a paper presented at the Annual Meeting of the American Historical Association, 2–5 January 1997. For comments on earlier drafts of this paper, I would like to thank Robert Storey, Joan Sangster, and Alice Kessler-Harris, and four anonymous reviewers for *Labour/Le Travail*. Thanks also to Hassan Yussuff, students in the CAW Workers of Colour Leadership Training Programme, and the many workers who graciously agreed to share with me their stories. This research was funded by an Arts Research Board grant and a Labour Studies Programme research grant at McMaster University.

2. McKinnon Industries was originally a subsidiary of General Motors and later became a General Motors plant.

3. Small numbers of Armenian, Chinese, and Chinese-Canadian workers were also employed in the southern Ontario auto industry during the Second World War. However, I have chosen to focus here on black workers because they represented the largest minority, with the longest history in the plants.

4. Unlike their American counterparts, these workers were so few in number, so seemingly marginal to either the company or the union, that their unique histories have never been

traced. Paradoxically, they are workers whose difference made them highly visible in the workplace; yet this difference has rendered them largely invisible in Canadian labour history. Currently, there are no published scholarly accounts of the ways in which race has been used in structuring the auto industry in Canada. In comparison, one can find a number of studies of gender and race relations in the American auto industry, as well as in the UAW International Office, and regional and local UAW offices in the United States. See for example, K. Tucker Anderson, 'Last Hired, First Fired: Black Women Workers during World War II', *Journal of American History* 69, 1 (June 1982): 82–97; L. Bailer, 'Negro Labor in the American Automobile Industry', Unpublished PhD Dissertation, University of Michigan, 1943; K. Boyle, '"There are No Union Sorrows That the Union Can't Heal": The Struggle for Racial Equality in the United Automobile Workers, 1940–1960', *Labor History* 36, 1 (Winter 1995): 5–23; N. Gabin, *Feminism in the Labor Movement: Women and the United Automobile Workers, 1935–1975* (Ithaca, NY: Cornell University Press, 1990); J.A. Geschwender, 'The League of Revolutionary Black Workers: Problems Confronting Black Marxist-Leninist Organizations', *Journal of Ethnic Studies* 2, 3 (Fall 1974): 1–23; sections in S. Jefferys, *Management and Managed: Fifty Years of Crisis at Chrysler* (New York: Cambridge University Press, 1986); sections in Alex Lichtenstein, 'Labor Radicalism, Race Relations, and Anticommunism in Miami During the 1940s', Paper presented at the Annual Meeting of the Organization of American Historians, Washington, DC, 30 March 1995; M. May, 'The Historical Problem of the Family Wage: The Ford Motor Company and the Five Dollar Day', *Feminist Studies* 8, 2 (Summer 1982): 399–424; A. Meier, and E. Rudwick, *Black Detroit and the Rise of the UAW* (New York: Oxford University Press, 1979); R. Milkman, *Gender at Work: The Dynamics of Job Segregation by Sex during World War II* (Urbana: University of Illinois Press, 1987); B.J. Widick, 'Black Workers: Double

Discontents', in B. Widick, ed., *Auto Work and Its Discontents* (Baltimore: John Hopkins University Press, 1976), 52–60.

5. It was extremely difficult to locate black men who had worked in the auto industry during the period of study. Given the harsh conditions of their work, a sizeable number of these workers left the auto industry after the Second World War. Also, many of the men who remained in the plants suffered from serious health problems such as silicosis. Man of these men had died before this project was undertaken. By the time all the interviews for this study were completed, several participants had died.

6. White women too have had a long presence in the auto industry, and likewise they constituted a small minority. Of the Big Three auto makers, General Motors consistently employed the largest number of females. In 1918, women comprised less than 6 per cent of GM's total hourly workforce. But between 1942 and 1943, the number of women employees increased dramatically. In 1942, GM's Oshawa plant employed only 200 women, but by March 1943, this figure had risen to 400 out of a total workforce of 4,000. Rapid expansion of production as well as growing wartime labour shortages drew even more women into McKinnon Industries. According to UAW estimates, the female workforce in McKinnon rose from 600 in 1942 to 1,200 out of a total workforce of 4,500 in 1943. Where previously women had made up about 8 per cent of the total personnel, their proportion increased to 25 per cent.

7. 'Gung Ho', *Ford Times* 3, 5 (October 1943): 12–14; 'Heart Strings Stretch From Windsor 'Round the World . . .', *Ford Times* 2, 2 (November 1942): 3–4. In contrast, in June 1944, the National Selective Service of Canada (NSS) requested that McKinnon Industries employ a small number of Japanese Canadian men. One Japanese Canadian man had already been employed in the foundry. However, the UAW Local 199 Bargaining Committee opposed the hiring of Canadian-born 'Japs', and recommended that the matter be taken up with both

the NSS and the company and that it be discussed further by District Council 26. Archives of Labor and Urban Affairs (ALUA), Box 11, UAW Region 7 Toronto Sub-Regional Office, Local 199 Report to District Council 26 Meeting, Minutes (June 1944), 8–11.

8. Lyle Talbot Private Collection, untitled document (March 1950). During the Second World War, a small group of black persons based in Toronto challenged the discriminatory practices of the National Selective Service in recruiting workers for essential war industries. See J.W. Walker, *Racial Discrimination in Canada: The Black Experience*, Canadian Historical Association Booklet 41 (Ottawa 1985), 17.

This stands in contrast to the situation in the United States. In the US, labour market shortages during the Second World War were so great, and the black population much more sizeable than in Canada, that both black women and men began to get jobs in the auto industry. For example, Chrysler went from 0 black women to approximately 5,000 in April 1945. See B. Widick, 'Black Workers: Double Discontents', 93. In the mid-1960s one black female was employed in Chrysler Canada's administrative office. In Oshawa, the home of General Motors of Canada, there was no black community from which to draw workers.

9. For a discussion of foundry work in early twentieth century Canada, see C. Heron, 'The Craftsman: Hamilton's Metal Workers in the Early Twentieth Century', *Labour/Le Travailleur* 6 (Autumn 1980): 7–48. Decoufle and Wood examine mortality patterns among workers in a grey iron foundry for the period 1938 to 1967. The authors highlight the connection between foundry employment and race. P. Decoufle and D.J. Wood, 'Mortality Patterns Among Workers in a Gray Iron Foundry', *American Journal of Epidemiology* 109, 6 (1979): 667–75; see also, E.S. Gibson, R.H. Martin, and J.N. Lockington, 'Lung Cancer Mortality in a Steel Foundry', *Journal of Occupational Medicine* 19, 12 (December 1977): 807–12.

10. Black men in the US were also concentrated in foundry work, as well as wet-sanding operations, material handling, and janitorial assignments. See K. Boyle, '"There Are No Sorrows"', 8; B. Widick, 'Black Workers: Double Discontents', 53.

11. For a discussion of race and images of masculinity in the contemporary period, see among others, R. Staples, 'Masculinity and Race: The Dual Dilemma of Black Men', *Journal of Social Issues* 34, 1 (1978): 169–83.

12. This idea was articulated by *Labour/Le Travail* reviewer #2.

13. In his account of metal workers in Hamilton, Ontario during the early twentieth century, Heron argues that the pride of moulders in steel foundries 'fed on the physical demands of the work, which was notoriously heavy, dirty, and unhealthy'. See C. Heron, 'The Craftsman', 11.

14. For a more detailed discussion of the family wage, see B. Bradbury, *Working Families: Age, Gender, and Daily Survival in Industrializing Montreal* (Toronto: McClelland and Stewart, 1993), chapter 3; N. Gabin, *Feminism in the Labor Movement*; M. May, 'Bread before Roses: American Workingmen, Labor Unions, and the Family Wage', in R. Milkman, ed., *Women, Work, and Protest: A Century of U.S. Women's Labor History* (Boston: Routledge and Keegan Paul, 1985), 1–21; R. Milkman, *Gender at Work*; J. Parr, *The Gender of Breadwinners: Women, Men, and Change in Two Industrial Towns, 1880–1950* (Toronto: University of Toronto Press, 1990); B. Palmer, *Working-Class Experience: Rethinking the History of Canadian Labour, 1800—1991* (Toronto: McClelland and Stewart, 1992).

15. The level of participation of workers of colour, however, dropped in the following decades. To this day, workers of colour remain underrepresented in the Canadian Auto Workers Union, especially in local office.

16. Although racism was a reality in Canada, the experience of Canadian auto workers was distinctive. As noted, blacks constituted a tiny minority in Canadian UAW plants relative to American firms, particularly in comparison to US cities such as Detroit. Thus, in Canada, there

was no strong and politically powerful contingency to fight for racial equality. Furthermore, this small group of workers was concentrated in a very narrow range of jobs. Likewise, they were minorities within their communities. Importantly, because of the hidden nature of the discrimination they faced, because racism in Canadian auto plants was less extreme and less overt than in the United States, many people believed that race discrimination was exclusively an American problem. See for example, L.E. Talbot, 'The Distinctive Character of Racism in Canada', MA thesis, University of Windsor (1982); James W. St.G. Walker, *Racial Discrimination in Canada: The Black Experience*, Canadian Historical Association Historical Booklet 41 (Ottawa 1985). UAW Canadian Region leaders therefore seldom addressed the issue of race. For this reason, the focus of this discussion is the resistance activities of rank and file workers themselves.

17. For example, on 25 June 1941, the US government issued Presidential Executive Order 8802, which reaffirmed the policy of full participation in defense programmes by all persons regardless of race, creed, colour, or national origin. See ALUA, UAW Research Department Collection, Box 9, File: 9–24, Discrimination Against Negroes in Employment, 1942–7, 'Executive Order 8802.'

18. For example, ALUA, Emil Mazey Collection, Box 11, File: 11-6, FEPC, 1946-47-2, 'William Oliver to All Local Union Officers and Fair Practices Committees' (4 September 1947); ALUA, Emil Mazey Collection, Box 11, File: 11-6, FEPC, 1946-47-2, 'Fair Practices and Anti-Discrimination Department Article 25'.

19. For example, ALUA, UAW Canadian Region Series III Collection, Box 70, File: 7, District Council, 1940, 'Minutes, District Council 26 Meeting' (13–14 January 1940); ALUA, George Addes Collection, Box 82, File: 82-24, 'Order Creating UAW-CIO Fair Practices Committee'.

Created in 1944, the overriding goal of the Fair Practices and Anti-Discrimination Department was to unite workers, regardless of religion, race, creed, colour, political affiliation, or nationality. It was to accomplish this aim by addressing workers' complaints of discrimination, publicizing UAW no-discrimination policies and guidelines for handling discrimination cases, setting up and activizing local FEPCs, conducting workplace audits to determine composition by sex and race in the plants, and educating workers through various programmes, conferences, radio addresses, and the Department's monthly publication, *Ammunition*.

20. See for example, ALUA, UAW Research Department Collection, Box 9, File: 9-24, Discrimination Against Negroes in Employment, 1942–47, 'R.J. Thomas to All UAW-CIO Executive Board Members and Department Heads, November 25, 1943'; ALUA, UAW Research Department Collection, Box 18, File: Minorities, 1942-47, 1 of 2, 'UAW Fight Against Intolerance', Address by George W. Crockett, Director, UAW-CIO Fair Practices Committee 4 November, 1945.

21. For example, ALUA, UAW Research Department Collection, Box 11, File: 11-20, Fair Practices and Anti-Discrimination Department, 1947–58, 'Summer School Course in Workers Education'; ALUA, Emil Mazey Collection, Box 11, File: 11-6, FEPC, 1946-47-2, 'First Annual Summary of Activities of the International UAW-CIO Fair Practices Committee'; 'UAW Seeks to Prevent Hiring Discrimination', *Michigan Chronicle*, 8 September 1945.

References

Boyle, K. 1995. '"There are No Union Sorrows That the Union Can't Heal": The Struggle for Racial Equality in the United Automobile Workers, 1940–1960', *Labor History* 36, 1 (Winter): 5–23.

Sugiman, P. 1994. *Labour's Dilemma: The Gender Politics of Workers in Canada, 1937–1979*. Toronto: University of Toronto Press.

CHAPTER 27

Domestic Distinctions: Constructing Difference among Paid Domestic Workers in Toronto[1]

Bernadette Stiell and Kim England

Have you seen the movie *Mary Poppins*? There's a song that says that if you can find the good things, then everything else is OK. What she says is actually amazing. The kids love it too. It's my theme song to keep me going sometimes. That is our song, the nanny song. 'You find the fun and the job's a game.' That's exactly it, 'a spoonful of sugar helps the medicine go down', that's it literally, and figuratively speaking. A pat on the back goes a long way. But I didn't get that at all. That's the reason why I was unhappy [with her previous employer] (Silke, a 30-year-old German woman employed as a 'domestic worker in Toronto).

Silke came to Toronto in 1986 to work as a nanny. She is one of more than 90,000 women who have arrived in Canada over the past 15 years under two federal government programs (the Foreign Domestic Movement program, 1981–92, and the Live-in Caregivers Program, 1992 to the present). These programs require that domestic workers/caregivers be 'live-ins' at their employer's homes for their first two years in Canada. Silke had a difficult relationship with her employer, partly as a result of the contradictions and ambiguities associated with her 'workplace' being her employer's 'home'. In this paper we explore how paid domestic workers in Toronto, including Silke, negotiate the dynamics of their employer–employee relation.

As in Canada as a whole, live-in paid domestic work in Toronto is usually the work of migrant or immigrant women, especially 'third world' women of colour. However, most employers are white. Thus, our investigation of the employer–employee work relation hinges on an exploration of difference and diversity. Recent discussions in feminist studies stress the simultaneous and inseparable operation of various social relations of difference. In other words, social relations of difference are not merely additive; instead the experience of one transforms the experience of the others. Taken together, gender, 'race'/ethnicity, class, and so on form interlocking, relational systems of oppression and privilege within which there are a multiplicity of identities, which in turn gain meaning in relation to other identifies (Spelman, 1988; hooks, 1989; Hill-Collins, 1990; McDowell, 1991; Kobayashi and Peake, 1994; Ruddick, 1996). In this paper we explore the experiential pluralities of women in paid domestic work.

Towards a Household Geography of Paid Domestic Work

BLURRING THE 'PUBLIC'/'PRIVATE' AND 'HOME'/'WORK' DIVIDES

Since 1981, Canada's federal policies have strictly stipulated that foreign domestic workers can only enter Canada if they 'live-in' for 2 years. Various advocacy groups have lobbied to remove the live-in requirement, but the government insists that the demand is only for live-in domestic workers, and that live-out jobs in domestic work can be easily filled by workers already in Canada (Employment and Immigration Canada, 1991, 1992). Live-in domestic work represents a peculiar form of paid employment and employer–employee relations. First and foremost, the domestic worker's 'workplace' is her employer's home, with its high degree of personalism in a 'private' (as opposed to the more usual 'public') domain of work. So, live-in paid domestic work blurs the boundaries between 'home' and 'work' and 'public' and 'private', which in turn complicates the employer–employee relation. Secondly, the work relation is shaped by intimacy, affective labour, ideologies of the family, as well as public discourse about 'good mothering'. It is a work relation summarized by the notion that it is a 'labour of love' and that paid domestic workers are Like One of the Family (Childress, 1956).[2] Thirdly, that the boundary of public and private is blurred and even undefined, means that live-in domestic work can lead to exploitation (Rollins, 1985; Colen, 1989; Arat-Koç, 1992; Ng, 1993; Bakan and Stasiulis, 1994; Gregson and Lowe, 1994; Thornton-Dill, 1994). For example, Arat-Koç and Villasin (1990) found that 65 per cent of the domestic workers they surveyed in the Toronto area were routinely required to work overtime, 44 per cent of whom received no compensation.

When an employee is legally required to live-in as part of her job, work relations are complicated by antagonisms and ambiguities based on the merging of public 'work' and private 'home' spheres, and the emotional complexities of trying to simultaneously maintain both a personal relationship and a work relationship.

The literature on the experience of paid domestic workers highlights a set of commonalities. It tends to be characterized by oppressive material conditions, including isolation, loneliness, powerlessness, and invisibility. Even for the live-out domestic workers (who form the focus of many non-Canadian studies), exploitation is a frequent experience, imposed by long working hours, unpaid overtime, and limited time off. For some domestic workers, working in what

they see as a low-status occupation means that stigma, low self-esteem, and low self-worth are also relatively common. In part, these experiences relate to the asymmetrical power relations between the domestic worker and her employer (Cock, 1980; Gaitskell et al., 1984; Rollins, 1985; Glenn, 1986, 1992; Bradshaw-Camball and Cohen, 1988; Colen, 1989; Romero, 1992; Thornton-Dill, 1994; Mattingley, 1996). The characteristics and experiences of domestic work are further exacerbated when the domestic worker is 'living in'. Certainly, significant improvement in work experience is reported when the 'live-in' arrangement is removed (Colen, 1989; Romero, 1992). This is clearly the case in the US where the trend towards live-out, 'day-work', multiple employers and more formal work schedules has decreased the intensity of isolation, dependence and exploitation which are still features of live-in domestic work in Canada.

In Canada, at least, there is evidence that strongly suggests that paid domestic work has become racialized. Key to the process of racialization is the ideology that a domestic worker's relative worth is judged relative to the poverty (or wealth) of her country of origin. European women seem to be accorded more prestige than 'third world' women. Moreover, it seems that Europeans may receive higher pay, better treatment, and be regarded as 'nannies' in the strictest sense of doing mainly childcare. 'Third world' women may receive less pay and be treated less well, while being deemed 'domestics' who are expected to do extensive housework as well as childcare (Arat-Koç, 1992; Bakan and Stasiulis, 1994, 1995).

EMPLOYER–EMPLOYEE RELATIONS

Previous studies indicate that women are more likely to hire domestic workers if they are unable to negotiate an equitable division of domestic labour with their male partners (Rollins, 1985; Hertz, 1986; Arat-Koç, 1992; Ng, 1993; Gregson and Lowe, 1994). In other words, despite the growth in women's employment, women continue to be largely responsible for domestic work whether as paid domestic workers, or as 'managers' of domestic workers they hire. However, the gender commonality between employer and employee is often marked by myriad differences. For example, that immigrant women of colour are over-represented among domestic workers is naturalized as their being predisposed to domestic work (Rollins, 1985; Glenn, 1992; Macklin, 1992; Ng, 1993; Bakan and Stasiulis, 1995). Macklin (1992) demonstrates this point with the example of Mary, the white Canadian employer of Delia, a Filipina domestic worker:

> Mary (can) objectify Delia in various ways that are influenced, but not precluded, by gender. For example, Mary can hardly claim that Delia is ideally suited to domestic work because she is a woman without impugning herself, but she can fall back on Filipino women being 'naturally' hard working, subservient, loyal, tidy housekeepers and 'good with children'. In this context, race, ethnicity and culture conjoin with sex to create a sub-category of women whose subordination other women can rationalize by projecting onto them the stereotypical 'feminine' qualities that patriarchy has used against women generally (1992: 754).

Of course, not all employer–employee relations in paid domestic work are exploitative and abusive. Bradshaw-Camball and Cohen (1988) suggest that the range and variety of employer–employee relations can be placed along two intersecting continua: one representing the domestic worker's 'sense of self-worth', the other representing the employer's 'concern with equity and fairness'. So, for instance, potentially exploitative work relations may result from an employer with little 'concern with equity and fairness' employing a domestic worker with a low 'sense of self-worth'. The employer's and domestic worker's location on these continua are mediated by issues of identity. Employers of domestic workers in Toronto are

more likely to be white and middle-class and, most commonly, Anglophone. On the other hand, domestic workers are frequently of a different 'race'/ethnicity, country of origin, immigration/citizenship status, and language, and these differences can alter the complexion of employer–employee relations.

In this paper, we take the first word/third world dichotomy as a starting point. However, we want to avoid an over-emphasis on the fixed and oppositional categories of black/white dichotomy of 'race'. This is particularly important in the case of foreign domestic workers in Canada, because if the more subtle differences of language are not accentuated, Filipinas might not be differentiated from Afro-Caribbeans (the two largest groups of foreign domestic workers in Canada). In light of the diversity among Canada's foreign domestic workers, we look at a number of groups of paid domestic workers in Toronto. Our analysis highlights the simultaneous operation of systems of difference (gender, 'race'/ethnicity, class, language, and so on) that texture the experience of paid domestic workers, and emphasizes that within these interlocking systems there are a range of locations with varying degrees of power and marginality.

Background to the Study

The empirical portion of our paper is based on our collaborative analysis of 18 lengthy, in-depth interviews conducted by Bernadette with women who were, or had been, paid domestic workers in Toronto (see Table 27.1; the women are identified by pseudonyms). The women were reached through notices in the offices of INTERCEDE and 'snow-balling'. The women interviewed came from nine countries of origin—Canada, England, France, Germany, Hungary, Eire, Jamaica, Philippines, and Thailand. In no way do we contend that this small sample is representative of all domestic workers in Toronto; rather, we believe these 18 women reflect some of the diverse identifies and experiences of this varied group of workers. The

Table 27.1 Characteristics of domestic workers interviewed

Pseudonym	Country of origin	'Race'	First language	Age (years)	Marital status	Children	Year of arrival	Immigration status	Live-in or live-out
Barb	Canada	White	English	24	Singles	0	N/A	Citizen	Live-in
Kath	England	White	English	22	Single	0	1989	Open	Live-in
Karen	England	White	English	23	Single	0	1993	Temp	Live-in
Sue	England	White	English	23	Single	0	1993	Temp	Live-in
Maryse	France	White	French	27	Single	0	1991	Temp	Live-in
Ingrid	Germany	White	German	29	Single	0	1991	Temp	Live-out
Silke	Germany	White	German	30	Single	0	1986	Landed	Live-out
Alena	Hungary	White	Hungarian	26	Single	0	1991	Open	Live-in
Anna	Hungary	White	Hungarian	27	Divorced	0	1990	Open	Live-out
Maggie	Eire	White	English	29	Single	0	1986	Landed	Line-in
Cynthia	Jamaica	Non-white	English	30	Single	0	1991	Temp	Live-in
Felicity	Jamaica	Non-white	English	35	Married	2	1992	Temp	Live-in
Edith	Philippines	Non-white	Tagalog	50s	Single	0	1986	Landed	House-keeper, live-out
Joan	Philippines	Non-white	Tagalog	32	Married	1	1987	Landed	Cashier[*]
Jocie	Philippines	Non-white	Tagalog	34	Single	0	1989	Open	Live-in
Naomi	Philippines	Non-white	Tagalog	28	Single	0	1991	Open	Live-in
Wilma	Philippines	Non-white	Tagalog	30	Single	0	1990	Open	Cashier[*]
Amy	Thailand	Non-white	Thai	30	Single	0	1989	Landed	Cashier[*]

*   Woman with open/landed immigrant status who no longer works as a paid domestic worker.

majority of the women were in their twenties and thirties, all but two were single (the two who were married were also the only ones with children). One was Canadian, five were landed immigrants; of the others, five were on open permits (an immigration status between a temporary work permit and landed immigrant), and seven were on temporary work permits. Most of the women were live-ins, but three were live-outs and another three (who were no longer on temporary work permits) had recently left paid domestic work.

I (Bernadette) conducted the interviews, and quickly realized that my own identity was a significant factor in the subtle and not too subtle interactions between myself and the participants. My country of origin (England), language and accent (south-east English), 'race' and culture (British West Indian), education (graduate student at the University of Toronto), and, of course, gender, all to some extent affected the negotiation of the 'betweenness' of the researcher–researched relationship. I was able to relate with great ease with the English and Irish women. We chatted quite generally about our shared experience of being 'Anglos' in Canada. There were also partial points of connection between the Jamaican women and myself in terms of a shared 'West Indian' identity—they disclosed a number of experiences and opinions that I do not believe they would have so readily revealed to a Canadian or white English interviewer. At the same time, however, there were occasions when I realized they had assumed rather too much common ground and I was unable to appreciate fully the more subtle nuances of everything they said because I am not Jamaican. Perhaps the greatest social distance was between the Filipina women and myself, which was in part due to a lack of shared language fluency and my unfamiliarity with their culture (all the interviews were conducted in English).

Employer–Employee Relations and the Construction of Difference

A number of major themes emerged from the interviews regarding the relationship between the paid domestic workers and their middle-class employers. In particular, we look at the domestic workers' experiences of living-in, being 'one of the family' and the degree of respect, dignity, and self-worth they feel. We not only consider these experiences around issues of class and 'race'/ethnicity, but in terms of domestic workers' immigration/citizenship status, country of origin (or nationality), and language.

LIVING-IN

Living-in means you are on call 24 hours a day. Living-in means if (the employers) feel like going to a party at 10 o'clock, then that's OK, the nanny's there. And you don't get paid for that (Felicity, Jamaican).

More than any other issue that emerged from the interviews, the living-in requirement was unanimously cited as being especially problematic. However, this was not the case for every woman interviewed. As a white, Anglophone Canadian, Barb was not required to live-in. She saw living-in as an opportunity to live away from her parents that enabled her to continue living in a comfortable middle-class home (something she could not afford if she was in a different occupation). Regardless of their motivations for coming to Canada or their long-term immigration goals, all the women who entered Canada as domestic workers/caregivers were legally required to live-in their employer's home for their first two years in Canada. Corroborating previous studies, we found that regardless of their identities, most of the women interviewed felt that they had experienced some level of exploitation through excessively long working hours, overtime without pay, restricted days off, or performing tasks outside their contract—all of which they attributed wholly or partially to their living-in. As Joan (Filipina) and Felicity (Jamaican) put it:

When you live-in they can demand a lot, because they see that you're there. In the night, if they want something to eat or drink, they will call you. As long as they are awake, then you have to stay awake with them too (Joan, Filipina).

I knew it wasn't going to be easy living in someone else's home. What I didn't prepare myself for was the subtle abuses. . . . Living-in means they come in at 5:30 pm, but you keep the kids until they've finished supper. Then you clean up, after you clean up, they might decide they want to go for ice cream or coffee, but you are still working. When you even mention that you're supposed to get overtime pay, they say 'You're a trouble-maker.' They say no one has ever asked for that before (Felicity, Jamaican).

Although exploitation was a general feeling, it is interesting to observe the ways in which different groups of domestic workers experienced these problems and how they were able to deal with them. One important issue was the perceived need to remain in an unsuitable job. When the English NNEB-trained[3] nannies reported enduring poor working or living conditions it was usually in their first job, which was often arranged before their arrival in Canada. These jobs often fell short of their expectations, but they remained with these employers in the pursuit of a good reference for their next job. As Kath described:

My first job changed, that's why I was only there for a year. It was awful. They changed a lot of things once I got here . . . they wanted a housekeeper and they took the car away from me, extended my hours, but that just wasn't on. When I tried to talk to them about it they said they'd deal with it later, but later never came. When you're at college they drum it into you that you have to do your first year, you have to get that experience and then a good reference. They don't tell you how easy it is to get another job over here. So I stuck it out, I was unhappy, but I did it (Kath, English).

For a number of the 'third world' women, it was their desire to apply for landed immigrant status that may have led them to put up with intolerable conditions and treatment from their employers. In a number of instances, domestic work provided much-needed remittance to support children and relatives in their homeland. Changing jobs entailed bureaucratic delays, considerable expense, and could reduce their chances of being viewed as reliable and hard-working when they came to submit their application for landed-immigrant status. Lack of freedom to change jobs, negotiate with employers or even complain about their treatment was expressed by a number of 'third world' women, including Cynthia and Jocie:

Each time you have to change jobs, you pay Immigration $100 . . . It doesn't look good on your record—that's why a lot of people take the abuse, you can't be bothered changing this and that. And then the probability of you meeting someone who is decent is 0.000000 up to infinity 1 (Cynthia, Jamaican).

There's less problem [with Filipinas], because they don't complain. Even though they get into trouble, they just stay quiet. You know why? Because they don't want to get bad record from government. They want their immigration status (Jocie, Filipina).

For most, living-in contributed to the feelings of isolation and loneliness associated with their job. Joan (a Filipina carer of an elderly couple) remarked that 'when you live-in, you feel lonely, when you don't see anybody, just this old couple';

and Amy (Thai) said that: 'My first employer never made me feel as if their home was mine. I missed my family. I became very lonesome and they wouldn't allow my friends to visit.' Many of the domestic workers said that they felt like an intruder in their employer's house. For example, paid domestic workers are often segregated to selected areas of the household at specific times of the day—a practice that Romero (1992) terms 'spatial deference' (also see Glenn, 1992). Cynthia (Jamaican) illustrated this concept when she talked of her employer's insistence on family privacy extending to making Cynthia wait until they had finished eating the meal that she had prepared, before 'crawling out of my room to get something to eat'. Of course, 'spatial deference' highlights the use of space to reinforce the invisibility expected of domestic workers when their services were not required; and the 'non-person', invisible identity domestic workers are expected to assume emphasizes the significance of geography at the household scale.

Typically, the women resented living-in because it often engendered a feeling of being trapped and also impinged upon their independence as adults. This was summed up by Joyce (Filipina): 'I'm living under someone else's rules' and Ingrid (German): 'I don't have to tell them where I'm going or what I'm doing all the time, but they ask anyway.' Such feelings were exacerbated by the family's lack of respect for the domestic worker's privacy and space, especially when they have to share a bathroom, or if their bedrooms are all on the same floor. Immigration Canada states that employers should 'provide accommodation which ensures privacy, such as a private room with a lock on the door,' for which room and board is deducted monthly (Employment and Immigration Canada, 1992). Six of the women said that in at least one job they had bedroom doors without locks, which sometimes resulted in members of the family entering without knocking. Generally, living-in was less resented in more equitable, respectful employer–employee relationships, and the more privacy and freedom the women had, the more content they tended to be living-in. Once in a 'good job', compromises were less frequent and usually compensated, and/or appreciated.

'LIKE ONE OF THE FAMILY'?

You're supposed to feel so privileged to be part of their family that you overlook everything else (Cynthia, Jamaican).

The interviews indicated that 'living-in' was an almost uniformly problematic experience for the women, but that the experiences of being 'like one of the family' was less even. The emotional involvement of domestic workers in private households can result in mutual friendships with the employers. Rollins (1985) even uses the term 'maternalism' to convey the highly gendered and personal nature of this type of work relation, where women's supportive, nurturing roles alter the power dynamic. While nationality, 'race'/ethnicity, and class differences are very significant, the extent and way in which personalism is experienced obviously also depends on the personalities of the individual domestic worker and her employer. However, we think the interviews suggest that more equitable, mutually supportive, and respectful relationships were most often experienced where there was greater similarity in the identities of the domestic worker and her employer.

More than any other group, the white Anglophones (Canadian, English, and Irish) reported having more informal and symmetrical relationships with their employers, sometimes describing their employers as 'friends', or feeling that they are considered to be 'like one of the family'. As Barb (Canadian) told Bernadette:

Sometimes we go from being like best friends to employer–employee. There's a line you can't cross when you're in this job. It's kinda weird, sometimes you're really good friends, and sometimes you can just say the wrong thing,

if you are not in the friendship mode (Barb, Canadian).

However, being 'like one of the family' was also interpreted by some of the woman as a means of extracting further unpaid physical and affective labour, without the genuine caring and respect associated with familial relationships. Gregson and Lowe (1994) describe such relations as false kinship ties. Felicity expresses her disdain at what she felt were false displays of affection and kinship from her white employer:

What I can't deal with is the idea that because I mop their floors, I'm stupid. They can do anything they want to me. They don't have to respect you, but they come with this disguise, 'Oh, you're part of the family.' They hug you. I don't want to be hugged! For God's sake, I'm your employee, treat me like an employee! I don't want to be hugged. But that's their way of trying to outsmart you. It's emotional blackmail. You're meant to think, 'This nice white lady, she's hugging me.' Then I'm supposed to take everything they dish out. I don't want that. I just want to be respected as a worker, with an employer–employee relationship (Felicity, Jamaican).

Both Jamaican women with whom Bernadette spoke objected to what they considered to be a patronizing emotional association. Their comments also reflect Rollins' (1985) and Romero's (1992) observations that personalism across racial lines is often advantageous to the employer. Women of colour can become safe confidants for their middle class, white employers, as they each tend to have entirely different social networks. The inherent power relation means that the middle-class, white employer need not fear rebuttal, disapproval or rejection.

Of course, no matter how symmetrical the employer–employee relationship, there still remains a status differential in terms of the work relation. Maryse (French) came to Canada as a nanny to learn English. In her first job she had difficulties based on her language ability. However, in her present job, class has emerged as a prominent factor in her relationship with her employer, who does not have a paid job outside the home:

> She's not from a rich family, but, because she's married to a neuro-surgeon, she feels she must live a good life . . . she's not a bad person, she's just snobby, and because of that it makes a big difference. She's a woman, she says 'It's because I pay (you) I need everything, you have to give me everything.' And she's really demanding. When she wants something, she wants it now. She's just like a spoilt kid (Maryse, French).

We see the intersection of gender and class as very evident here. Asymmetric power relations are enforced because Maryse's employer feels that she should be able to purchase obedience through her husband's class position and her status as his wife. The gendered character of the domestic division of labour also comes into play as the employer sees herself as paying Maryse to do 'her' chores. Moreover, it seems to us that the deference inherent in this type of work relation may have placed the employer in a position of power not otherwise available to her as a 'housewife'. This power differential seemed to have been internalized by Maryse who said: 'You feel like a real slave . . . I feel extremely humiliated sometimes. I know I shouldn't take it that way, but its the way I feel'.

The introduction of 'race'/ethnicity differences into an already asymmetrical relationship multiplies the subtleties of those differences already inherent in class difference. Cynthia and Felicity (Jamaicans) both told Bernadette that they had experienced racism (as well as classism), often in quite overt and complex ways. Felicity maintained that racism was fundamental to explaining her situation, although she clearly understood that it is impossible to untangle 'race' from other structures of differentiation.

Sometimes when they treat you badly, it's because you're black, and they really just don't have any respect for you as a human being, no matter how educated, well-spoken, and no matter how good you are with the kids. But it's also because they pay you to be in their house that makes it even worse, you become nothing in their eyes. I can't tell you why, there are so many reasons, but they happen together, we come as one package. . . . They just abuse, abuse, abuse you. It doesn't matter how intelligent you may appear to be, they just look at you as a black helper. . . . Colour doesn't have any respect for class. They will still see you as a helper, no matter what (Felicity, Jamaican).

In short, intimacy, affective labour, and a high degree of personalism often veil the asymmetrical class relation associated with paid domestic employment. However, we think the interviews also reveal that the class relation is constructed in relation to interlocking systems of 'race'/ethnicity and gender.

RESPECT, DIGNITY, AND SELF-WORTH

> I'm pretty well respected . . . what you say goes, and they're willing to come around to what you want. Well this one (her current employer), more than the first one. They know what you're capable of. She's always had NNEBs. She knows what to expect (Kath, English).

Respect and dignity are fundamental to a person's feeling of self-worth and self-esteem, and are important in defining the dynamics of the social relations of paid domestic work. It does seem that the degree of respect experienced by different groups of domestic workers is highly variable and nuanced, with the overriding significant factor being the precise nature of each employer–employee relation—the attitude of the employer to her employee, and the ability of each domestic worker to be assertive in a given situation. The relative presence or absence of respect in the employer–employee work relation can also indicate the level of asymmetry in the power relation. Bradshaw-Camball and Cohen's (1988) concepts of the employer's 'concern with equity and fairness' versus the employee's 'sense of self-worth' are useful here.

As a white, Anglophone Canadian, Barb shared the same citizenship and (at least in terms of her family background) class position as her employer. So, relative to the foreign domestic workers Bernadette interviewed, Barb experienced the most symmetrical power relations with her employer.

> My dad is not poor. I am not a poor person, I'm basically pretty privileged. My boss finds it weird that I'm on the same social scale as she is. I'm not impressed by the car she drives, or the house she lives in, so in a way that is different. I'm Canadian, I speak near-perfect English, and I'm educated . . . (our relationship) is pretty good. Having me was a bit of an adjustment because she was used to having a Filipina nanny, and to have someone who understands everything she says to me, and someone who's not going to fight her exactly, but not meekly let her walk all over me, was a big change for her. Sometimes we have our altercations over it. Other than that she really likes me, and I really like her (Barb, Canadian).

Barb's confident and assertive personality must be placed in the broader context of her identity. Barb makes the interconnections between numerous systems of difference when explaining her reasonably symmetrical work relation. She does not stress her class background alone. Her country of origin (including its relative wealth), citizenship, language, and education intersect to construct her relatively privileged position. Indeed, the openly contested nature of this work relation appears to have presented more challenges for Barb's employer, who had been in a position of clear authority and control with her previous Filipina

employee. As Barb put it: 'The difference with me is that I have more choice, more freedom. Tomorrow if I think "well, screw you", I can walk out the door and go home.' Barb became a nanny because she 'loves kids', but she only saw her job as 'something to do for now'. We argue that Barb's secure social, economic, and political status as a Canadian, without immigration or employment restrictions, helped create a much more equitable power relation between her and her employer.

The other groups of foreign domestic workers seldom expressed the same level of friendship with, or respect from their employers. English language difficulties can distance non-Anglophone domestic workers (even those from Europe) from the mutual respect or intimacy of personal friendship. Although they often talked about respect and mutuality, the non-Anglophone domestic workers also talked of being made to feel 'stupid' because of language and communication difficulties:

> These employers respect me, they respect what I have to say about the children, what I think should happen. They respect me (but sometimes) I think they must think that we are pretty stupid. . . . They really underestimated my intelligence, which is really insulting (Silke, German).

However, it seemed to us that the non-Anglophone Europeans often challenged their employers when they 'underestimated their intelligence'. As Anna (Hungarian) told Bernadette, 'If your English is not that great, they think you're as stupid as your English is. But the first time you show that you are not, they know it!' We feel it is important to differentiate between East and West Europeans. For instance, Anna and Alena (Hungarians) experienced further degrees of isolation and alienation based on their transition from a socialist background to the Western culture of Canada. Alena felt that her employer had been especially neglectful of her responsibilities towards her foreign employee, and was insensitive to Alena's 'culture shock'. She felt that this, combined with her feelings of powerlessness and her employer's apparent lack of respect for her needs, prevented Alena from objecting to her employer's demands for emotional support:

> She's a single mother, when she comes home after a hard day, I am her spouse! When she talks to me about her troubles, all her hard times at work, somewhere behind that (is) 'what an easy life you've got'. Sometimes she wants to comfort me and say 'I know how hard your day can be', but basically, I know what she thinks. Many times we ended up talking, imagine, I am desperate to get to my room . . . I am willing to listen to her, but I'm very bothered by the fact that I'm paid there (and) she's still the boss actually, no matter how friendly she is. (And the) fact that she can use those things against you (in day-to-day confrontations and negotiations, or even with Employment and Immigration Canada), if I start talking about my problems (Alena, Hungarian).

This situation is clearly not a mutually supportive emotional relationship. The asymmetric power relation is obvious, and it is only the emotional needs of the employer that are being met, with little consideration for the boundaries of the work relation, or Alena's personal needs.

'Race'/ethnicity differences further reinforced feelings of language inferiority, particularly if the employers did not seem to respect their employees efforts to learn English. Moreover, having their intellect demeaned was a particularly familiar experience for the Thai and Filipina women, as Amy (Thai) and Joan (Filipina) show:

> I didn't get on well with my employer. I couldn't speak English well. After seven months things got better, but they think you are stupid because you can't speak English,

so they over-work you, they think you don't know the rules. . . . I was so upset when I heard them call me stupid. That made me determined to learn to speak English (Amy, Thai).

The interviews are full of statements that illustrate that the stereotype of the uneducated, poor, 'third world' domestic worker of colour, who cannot speak English is so persuasive and potent that it can lead to their educational achievements or middle-class background being discounted. Joan described her previous job:

> At my last employer, her daughter—she were talking to me, asking me about life in the Philippines. . . . And I was telling her, I never worked as a domestic back home. All of my family are educated, all the children and everything. And she felt that because she was not educated, she was just a high school graduate, working in Bell Canada, she felt like I am over her. She said to me, even though you are educated, they don't acknowledge your education here and you still belong to poor country. That's what she told me! I don't say anything, because I think I hurt her feelings in some way. She had to find some way to put me down. I just don't say anything. I feel bad, but I just don't say anything. I just keep quiet (Joan, Filipina).

It is evident that Joan disrupted and challenged the 'third world domestic' stereotype. This family member re-asserted an asymmetric power relation by re-constructing Joan as a 'third word domestic' by discounting her worth, achievements and background as 'inferior' to her own.

As with personalism, a 'sense of self-worth' is dependant on a number of structural factors, including 'race'/ethnicity, class, education, and training, as well as other factors such as personality, life experience, support networks and family responsibilities. Similarly, the employer's 'concern with equity and fairness' can also be related to her own and her employee's identity, personality, and life experiences. Overall, the interviews indicated to us that the white Anglophones generally appeared to have a higher degree of confidence and a stronger 'sense of self-worth', enabling them to be more assertive, while non-Anglophones and women of colour experienced increasing degrees of difficulty in negotiating their position and gaining their employer's respect.

Conclusions

Our paper illustrates how paid domestic workers' experiences of the employer–employee relation are mediated through an interlocking, relational system of difference, particularly gender, class, 'race'/ethnicity, immigration/citizenship status, and language. Commonalities of gender and occupation shared by domestic workers are cross-cut by locations of privilege and marginality in terms of class, citizenship/immigration status, 'race'/ethnicity, country of origin, training, and language. The most privileged was the white, Anglophone Canadian who experienced the most freedom, choice, and power, which meant she had a much more secure, symmetrical relationship with her employer compared to many of her foreign counterparts. Of the foreign domestic workers interviewed, the specific articulation of systems

of difference led to a range of experiences of the extent of asymmetry in employer–employee power relations, with the greatest symmetry tending to be in those situations where the employee and employer held more similar positions in the social relations of difference.

However, we also want to emphasize that many of the women interviewed shared a number of common concerns. Almost all the domestic workers had, at some stage, experienced difficulties related to living-in, especially in dealing with employers who frequently demanded additional duties not stated on their contracts. But those who are less marginalized tended to be better able to negotiate these situations. Their locations in the systems of difference often related to their 'sense of self-worth' in terms of their occupation and their experience of respect. One result tended to be that Anglophone 'nannies', unlike 'third world' 'domestic workers' were more likely to find jobs with better hours and less or no housework.

We have attempted to provide insights into the dynamic, complex, and interrelated character of the processes that shape employer–employee relations marked by the antagonisms, contradictions, and ambiguities associated with a 'workplace' being someone else's 'home'. We have stressed that specific articulations of difference (as well as the specific context and the individual personalities involved) produce difference constellations of experiences of live-in paid domestic work.

Notes

1. We thank the staff and volunteers of INTERCEDE for their time and access to their resources. We also thank women who participated in this research: they are identified by pseudonyms. We are grateful to Kevin Cox, Nancy Duncan, Linda McDowell, Lynn Staeheli and the three reviewers for their helpful comments on an earlier version of this paper. Bernadette Stiell was partly funded by the Canadian Memorial Foundation.

2. Alice Childress's book is a fictional account that draws on lived experiences from the everyday lives of African American domestic workers.
3. The NNEB (National Nursery Examination Board) diploma is offered only in Britain. It is a two-year, post-secondary training program and is one of the most widely recognized qualifications in childcare.

References

Arat-koç, S. 1992. 'In the Privacy of Our Own Home: Foreign Domestic Workers as Solution to the Crisis of the Domestic Sphere in Canada', in M.P. Connelly and P. Armstrong, eds, *Feminism in Action: Studies in Political Economy*, pp. 149–75. Toronto: Canadian Studies Press.

Arat-koç, S., and F. Villansin. 1990. 'Report and Recommendations on the Foreign Domestic Movement Program'. Submitted to the Ministry of Employment and Immigration on behalf of INTERCEDE, Toronto Organization for Domestic Workers' Rights.

Bakan, A.B., and D. Stasiulis. 1994. 'Foreign Domestic Worker Policy in Canada and the Social Boundaries of Modern Citizenship', *Science and Society* 58: 7–33.

———. 1995. 'Making the Match: Domestic Placement Agencies and the Racialization of Women's Household Work', *Signs* 20: 303–35.

Bradshaw-Cambrall, P., and R. Cohen. 1988. 'Feminists: Explorers or Exploiters', *Women and Environments* 11: 8–10.

Childress, A. 1956. *Like One of the Family*. Brooklyn, NY: Independence.

Cock, J. 1980. *Maids and Madams: A Study in the Politics of Exploitation*. Johannesburg: Raven Press.

Colen, S. 1989. '"Just a little respect": West Indian Domestic Workers in New York City', in E.M. Chaney and M.G. Castro, eds, *Muchachas No More: Household Workers in Latin America and the Caribbean*, pp. 171–94. Philadelphia: Temple University Press.

Employment and Immigration Canada. 1991. *Foreign Domestic Workers: Preliminary Statistical Highlight Report*. Ottawa: Employment and Immigration Canada.

———. 1992. *The Live-in Caregiver Program: Information for Employers and Live-in Caregivers from Abroad*. Ottawa: Employment and Immigration Canada.

Gaitskell, D., J. Kimble, M. Manconachie, and E. Unterhalther. 1984. 'Class, Race, and Gender: Domestic Workers in South Africa', *Review of African Political Economy* 27/28: 86–108.

Glenn, E.N. 1986. *Issei, Nisei, War Bride: Three Generations of Japanese American Women and Domestic Service*. Philadelphia: Temple University Press.

———. 1992. 'From Servitude to Service Work: Historical Continuities in the Racial Division of Paid Reproductive Labor', *Signs* 18: 1–43.

Gregson, N., and M. Lowe. 1994. *Servicing the Middle Classes: Class, Gender and Waged Domestic Work in Contemporary Britain*. London and New York: Routledge.

Hertz, R. 1986. *More Equal Than Others: Women and Men in Dual-career Marriages*. Berkeley, CA: University of California Press.

Hill-Collins, P. 1990. *Black Feminist Thought: Knowledge, Consciousness and the Politics of Empowerment*. London and New York: Routledge.

hooks, b. 1989. *Talking Back—Thinking Feminist, Thinking Black*. Boston: South End Press.

Kobayashi, A., and L. Peake. 1994. 'Unnatural Discourse: 'Race' and Gender in Geography', *Gender, Place and Culture* 1: 225–43.

Macklin, A. 1992. 'Foreign Domestic Worker: Surrogate Housewife or Mail Order Bride?', *McGill Law Journal* 37: 681–760.

Mattingley, D. 1996. 'Domestic Service, Migration, and Local Labor Markets on the US–Mexican Border', PhD dissertation. Graduate School of Geography, Clark University, Worcester, MA.

McDowell, L. 1991. 'The Baby and the Bath Water: Diversity, Deconstruction and Feminist Theory in Geography', *Geoforum* 22: 123–33.

Ng, R. 1993. 'Racism, Sexism, and Immigrant Women', in B. Sadra, L. Code, and L. Dorney, eds, *Changing Patterns: Women in Canada*, pp. 279–301. Toronto: McClelland and Stewart.

Rollins, J. 1985. *Between Women: Domestics and Their Employers*. Philadelphia: Temple University Press.

Romero, M. 1992. *Maid in the USA*. London and New York: Routledge.

Ruddick, S. 1996. 'Constructing Difference in Public Spaces: Race, Class, and Gender as Interlocking Systems', *Urban Geography* 17: 132–51.

Spelman, E. 1988. *Inessential Woman: Problems of Exclusion in Feminist Thought*. Boston: Beacon Books.

Thornton-Dill, B. 1994. *Across Boundaries of Class and Race: An Exploration of the Relationship Between Work and Family among Black Female Domestic Servants*. New York: Garland Publishing.

QUESTIONS FOR CRITICAL THOUGHT

1. Are you currently training for a particular type of work, or do you have a particular career in mind? Do you expect that your gender will influence your success in this career?

2. If you work with people of different genders, whether in a part-time or full-time job, how do you think gender might affect workplace experiences? If your workplace is dominated by one gender, why is that the case?

3. Why do you think women still make less money in their paid jobs than men? Is it because of individual choices or systematic barriers? Or both? Or neither?

4. The male nurses that Evans studied were clearly considered unusual for working in a field dominated by women. Are there any kinds of work that you think would be difficult for you, or that you would not want to take, because of your gender?

5. What workplaces have you encountered as a worker, customer, or visitor that are dominated by one sex or the other? What workplaces have you encountered that are more equally divided between the sexes?

PART VII | The Gendered Body

Perhaps nothing is more deceptive than the 'naturalness' of our bodies. We experience what happens to our bodies, and what happens *in* our bodies, as utterly natural, physical phenomena.

Yet to the social scientist, nothing could be farther from the truth. Our bodies are themselves shaped and created, and interpreted and understood by us, in entirely gendered ways. How we look, what we feel, and what we think about how our bodies look and feel, are partially the results of the ways our society defines how bodies should look and feel. Thus, for example, cultural standards of beauty, musculature, and aesthetics are constantly changing—and with them change our feelings about how we look when compared to these images.

Take, for example, women's notions of beauty. Fortunes are made by companies that purvey the beauty myth—as feminist writer Naomi Wolf called it—and remind women that they do not measure up to these cultural standards, and then provide products that will help them try. By such logic, women who experience eating disorders are not deviant non-conformists, but rather over-conformists to unrealizable norms of femininity. Feminist philosopher Susan Bordo's essay reminds us of the ways in which the types of female bodies valorized in contemporary North American society articulate with particular forms of femininity.

While many people feel pressured to consume body-enhancing products, for a minority, their bodies are themselves the products. For example, the figure skaters described by Karen McGarry are used to 'sell' excitement, beauty, and Canadian pride. In order to do this, their bodies must be easily readable as both gender-normative and hetero-normative. The skaters and other entrepreneurs of the body experience an intensified form of the same pressures which 'ordinary' men and women confront.

However, 'ordinary' men and women are not merely passive templates, uncritically receiving and accepting cultural messages about 'good' and 'bad' bodies. Pamela Wakewich's work shows how people can, and do, create their own ideas about what it means to have a 'good' body, ideas which have more to do with health and well-being than with unrealizable standards of beauty.

At the most fundamental level of assumptions about bodies, both social and medical scientists are beginning to question the relationship between gender and bodily sex, and even to question whether the standard two-sex framework for understanding bodies has any basis. As Ann Fausto-Sterling suggests, transgendered people, intersexed people, and people with ambiguous genitalia complicate prevailing assumptions that gender adheres to specific body types.

CHAPTER 28

The Body and the Reproduction of Femininity[1]

Susan Bordo

Reconstructing Feminist Discourse on the Body

The body—what we eat, how we dress, and the daily rituals to which we attend—is a medium of culture. The body, as anthropologist Mary Douglas has argued, is a powerful symbolic form, a surface on which the central rules, hierarchies, and even metaphysical commitments of a culture are inscribed and thus reinforced through the concrete language of the body (Douglas, 1966, 1982). The body may also operate as a metaphor for culture. From quarters as diverse as Plato and Hobbes to French feminist Luce Irigaray, an imagination of body morphology has provided a blueprint for diagnosis and/or vision of social and political life.

The body is not only a *text* of culture. It is also, as anthropologist Pierre Bourdieu and philosopher Michel Foucault (among others) have argued, a *practical*, direct locus of social control. Banally, through table manners and toilet habits, through seemingly trivial routines, rules, and practices, culture is 'made body', as Bourdieu puts it—converted into automatic, habitual activity. As

such it is put 'beyond the grasp of consciousness . . . [untouchable] by voluntary, deliberate transformations' (Bourdieu, 1977: 94). Our conscious politics, social commitments, and strivings for change may be undermined and betrayed by the life of our bodies—not the craving, instinctual body imagined by Plato, Augustine, and Freud, but what Foucault calls the 'docile body', regulated by the norms of cultural life.[2]

Throughout his later 'genealogical' works (*Discipline and Punish*, *The History of Sexuality*), Foucault constantly reminds us of the primacy of practice over belief. Not chiefly through ideology, but through the organization and regulation of the time, space, and movements of our daily lives, our bodies are trained, shaped, and impressed with the stamp of prevailing historical forms of selfhood, desire, masculinity, and femininity. Such an emphasis casts a dark and disquieting shadow across the contemporary scene. Women, as study after study shows, are spending more time on the management and discipline of our bodies than we have in a long, long time. In a decade marked by a reopening of the public arena to women, the intensification of such regimens appears diversionary and subverting. Through the pursuit of an ever-changing, homogenizing, elusive ideal of femininity—a pursuit without a terminus, requiring that women constantly attend to minute and often whimsical changes in fashion—female bodies become docile bodies—bodies whose forces and energies are habituated to external regulation, subjection, transformation, and 'improvement'. Through the exacting and normalizing disciplines of diet, makeup, and dress—central organizing principles of time and space in the day of many women—we are rendered less socially oriented and more centripetally focused on self-modification. Through these disciplines, we continue to memorize on our bodies the feel and conviction of lack, of insufficiency, of never being good enough. At the farthest extremes, the practices of femininity may lead us to utter demoralization, debilitation, and death.

Viewed historically, the discipline and normalization of the female body—perhaps the only gender oppression that exercises itself, although to different degrees and in different forms, across age, race, class, and sexual orientation—has to be acknowledged as an amazingly durable and flexible strategy of social control. In our own era, it is difficult to avoid the recognition that the contemporary preoccupation with appearance, which still affects women far more powerfully than men, even in our narcissistic and visually-oriented culture, may function as a backlash phenomenon, reasserting existing gender configurations against any attempts to shift or transform power relations.[3] Surely we are in the throes of this backlash today. In newspapers and magazines we daily encounter stories that promote traditional gender relations and prey on anxieties about change: stories about latch-key children, abuse in daycare centres, the 'new woman's' troubles with men, her lack of marriageability, and so on. A dominant visual theme in teenage magazines involves women hiding in the shadows of men, seeking solace in their arms, willingly contracting the space they occupy. The last, of course, also describes our contemporary aesthetic ideal for women, an ideal whose obsessive pursuit has become the central torment of many women's lives. In such an era we desperately need an effective political discourse about the female body, a discourse adequate to an analysis of the insidious, and often paradoxical, pathways of modern social control.

Developing such a discourse requires reconstructing the feminist paradigm of the late 1960s and early 1970s, with its political categories of oppressors and oppressed, villains and victims. Here I believe that a feminist appropriation of some of Foucault's later concepts can prove useful. Following Foucault, we must first abandon the idea of power as something possessed by one group and levelled against another; we must instead think of the network of practices, institutions, and technologies that sustain positions of dominance and subordination in a particular domain.

Second, we need an analytics adequate to describe a power whose central mechanisms are not repressive, but *constitutive*: 'a power bent on generating forces, making them grow, and ordering them, rather than one dedicated to impeding them, making them submit, or destroying them.' Particularly in the realm of femininity, where so much depends on the seemingly willing acceptance of various norms and practices, we need an analysis of power 'from below', as Foucault puts it; for example, of the mechanisms that shape and proliferate—rather than repress—desire, generate and focus our energies, construct our conceptions of normalcy and deviance (Foucault, 1980).

And, third, we need a discourse that will enable us to account for the subversion of potential rebellion, a discourse that, while insisting on the necessity of objective analysis of power relations, social hierarchy, political backlash, and so forth, will nonetheless allow us to confront the mechanisms by which the subject at times becomes enmeshed in collusion with forces that sustain her own oppression.

This essay will not attempt to produce a general theory along these lines. Rather, my focus will be the analysis of one particular arena where the interplay of these dynamics is striking and perhaps exemplary. It is a limited and unusual arena—that of a group of gender-related and historically localized disorders: hysteria, agoraphobia, and anorexia nervosa.[4] I recognize that these disorders have also historically been class- and race-biased, largely (although not exclusively) occurring among white middle- and upper-middle-class women. Nonetheless, anorexia, hysteria, and agoraphobia may provide a paradigm of one way in which potential resistance is not merely undercut but *utilized* in the maintenance and reproduction of existing power relations.[5]

The central mechanism I will describe involves a transformation (or, if you wish, duality) of meaning, through which conditions that are objectively (and, on one level, experientially) constraining, enslaving, and even murderous, come to be experienced as liberating, transforming, and life-giving. I offer this analysis, although limited to a specific domain, as an example of how various contemporary critical discourses may be joined to yield an understanding of the subtle and often unwitting role played by our bodies in the symbolization and reproduction of gender.

The Body as a Text of Femininity

The continuum between female disorder and 'normal' feminine practice is sharply revealed through a close reading of those disorders to which women have been particularly vulnerable. These, of course, have varied historically: neurasthenia and hysteria in the second half of the nineteenth century; agoraphobia and, most dramatically, anorexia nervosa and bulimia in the second half of the twentieth century. This is not to say that anorectics did not exist in the nineteenth century—many cases were described, usually in the context of diagnoses of hysteria (Showalter, 1985: 128–

9)—or that women no longer suffer from classical hysterical symptoms in the twentieth century. But the taking up of eating disorders on a mass scale is as unique to the culture of the 1980s as the epidemic of hysteria was to the Victorian era.[6]

The symptomatology of these disorders reveals itself as textuality. Loss of mobility, loss of voice, inability to leave the home, feeding others while starving oneself, taking up space, and whittling down the space one's body takes up—all have symbolic meaning, all have *political* meaning under the varying rules governing the historical construction of gender. Working within this framework, we see that whether we look at hysteria, agoraphobia, or anorexia, we find the body of the sufferer deeply inscribed with an ideological construction of femininity emblematic of the period in question. The construction, of course, is always homogenizing and normalizing, erasing racial, class, and other differences and insisting that all women aspire to a coercive, standardized ideal. Strikingly, in these disorders the construction of femininity is written in disturbingly concrete, hyperbolic terms: exaggerated, extremely literal, at times virtually caricatured presentations of the ruling feminine mystique. The bodies of disordered women in this way offer themselves as an aggressively graphic text for the interpreter—a text that insists, actually demands, that it be read as a cultural statement, a statement about gender.

Both nineteenth-century male physicians and twentieth-century feminist critics have seen, in the symptoms of neurasthenia and hysteria (syndromes that became increasingly less differentiated as the century wore on), an exaggeration of stereotypically feminine traits. The nineteenth-century 'lady' was idealized in terms of delicacy and dreaminess, sexual passivity, and a charmingly labile and capricious emotionality (Vicinus, 1972, x–xi). Such notions were formalized and scientized in the work of male theorists from Acton and Krafft-Ebing to Freud, who described 'normal', mature femininity in such terms.[7] In this context, the dissociations, the drifting and fogging of perception, the nervous tremors and faints, the anesthesias, and the extreme mutability of symptomatology associated with nineteenth-century female disorders can be seen to be concretizations of the feminine mystique of the period, produced according to rules that governed the prevailing construction of femininity. Doctors described what came to be known as the hysterical personality as 'impressionable, suggestible, and narcissistic; highly labile, their moods changing suddenly, dramatically, and seemingly for inconsequential reasons. . . egocentric in the extreme . . . essentially asexual and not uncommonly frigid' (Smith-Rosenberg, 1985: 203)—all characteristics normative of femininity in this era. As Elaine Showalter points out, the term *hysterical* itself became almost interchangeable with the term *feminine* in the literature of the period (Showalter, 1985: 129).

The hysteric's embodiment of the feminine mystique of her era, however, seems subtle and ineffable compared to the ingenious literalism of agoraphobia and anorexia. In the context of our culture this literalism makes sense. With the advent of movies and television, the rules for femininity have come to be culturally transmitted more and more through standardized visual images. As a result, femininity itself has come to be largely a matter of constructing, in the manner described by Erving Goffman, the appropriate surface presentation of the self (Goffman, 1959). We are no longer given verbal descriptions or exemplars of what a lady is or of what femininity consists. Rather, we learn the rules directly through bodily discourse: through images that tell us what clothes, body shape, facial expression, movements, and behaviour are required.

In agoraphobia and, even more dramatically, in anorexia, the disorder presents itself as a virtual, though tragic, parody of twentieth-century constructions of femininity. The 1950s and early 1960s, when agoraphobia first began to escalate among women, was a period of reassertion

of domesticity and dependency as the feminine ideal. *Career woman* became a dirty word, much more so than it had been during the war, when the economy depended on women's willingness to do 'men's work'. The reigning ideology of femininity, so well described by Betty Friedan and perfectly captured in the movies and television shows of the era, was childlike, non-assertive, helpless without a man, 'content in a world of bedroom and kitchen, sex, babies and home' (Friedan, 1962: 36). The housebound agoraphobic lives this construction of femininity literally. 'You want me in this home? You'll have me in this home—with a vengeance!' The point, upon which many therapists have commented, does not need belabouring. Agoraphobia, as I.G. Fodor has put it, seems 'the logical—albeit extreme—extension of the cultural sex-role stereotype for women' in this era (Fodor, 1974: 119; see also Brehony, 1983).

The emaciated body of the anorectic, of course, immediately presents itself as a caricature of the contemporary ideal of hyper-slenderness for women, an ideal that, despite the game resistance of racial and ethnic difference, has become the norm for women today. But slenderness is only the tip of the iceberg, for slenderness itself requires interpretation. 'C'est le sens qui fait vendre', said Barthes, speaking of clothing styles—it is meaning that makes the sale (Culler, 1983: 74). So, too, it is meaning that makes the body admirable. To the degree that anorexia may be said to be 'about' slenderness, it is about slenderness as a citadel of contemporary and historical meaning, not as an empty fashion ideal. As such, the interpretation of slenderness yields multiple readings, some related to gender, some not. For the purposes of this essay I will offer an abbreviated, gender-focused reading. But I must stress that this reading illuminates only partially, and that many other currents not discussed here—economic, psychosocial, and historical, as well as ethnic and class dimensions—figure prominently.[9]

We begin with the painfully literal inscription, on the anorectic's body, of the rules governing

Figure 28.1

Figure 28.2

the construction of contemporary femininity. That construction is a double bind that legislates contradictory ideals and directives. On the one hand, our culture still widely advertises domestic conceptions of femininity, the ideological moorings for a rigorously dualistic sexual division of labour that casts woman as chief emotional and physical nurturer. The rules for this construction of femininity (and I speak here in a language both symbolic and literal) require that women learn to feed others, not the self, and to construe any desires for self-nurturance and self-feeding as greedy and excessive.[10] Thus, women must develop a totally other-oriented emotional economy. In this economy, the control of female appetite for food is merely the most concrete expression of the general rule governing the construction of femininity: that female hunger—for

public power, for independence, for sexual gratification—be contained, and the public space that women be allowed to take up be circumscribed, limited. Figure 28.1, which appeared in a women's magazine fashion spread, dramatically illustrates the degree to which slenderness, set off against the resurgent muscularity and bulk of the current male body-ideal, carries connotations of fragility and lack of power in the face of a decisive male occupation of social space. On the body of the anorexic woman such rules are grimly and deeply etched.

On the other hand, even as young women today continue to be taught traditionally 'feminine' virtues, to the degree that the professional arena is open to them they must also learn to embody the 'masculine' language and values of that arena—self-control, determination, cool, emotional

Figure 28.3

discipline, mastery, and so on. Female bodies now speak symbolically of this necessity in their slender spare shape and the currently fashionable men's-wear look. (A contemporary clothing line's clever mirror-image logo, shown in Figure 28.2, offers women's fashions for the 'New Man', with the model posed to suggest phallic confidence combined with female allure.) Our bodies, too, as we trudge to the gym every day and fiercely resist both our hungers and our desire to soothe ourselves, are becoming more and more practiced at the 'male' virtues of control and self-mastery. Figure 28.3 illustrates this contemporary equation of physical discipline with becoming the 'captain' of one's soul. The anorectic pursues these virtues with single-minded, unswerving dedication. 'Energy, discipline, my own power will keep me going,' says ex-anorectic Aimee Liu, recreating her anorexic days. 'I need nothing and no one else. . . . I will be master of my own body, if nothing else, I vow' (Lie, 1979: 123).

The ideal of slenderness, then, and the diet and exercise regimens that have become inseparable from it offer the illusion of meeting, through the body, the contradictory demands of the contemporary ideology of femininity. Popular images reflect this dual demand. In a single issue of *Complete Woman* magazine, two articles appear, one on 'Feminine Intuition', the other asking, 'Are You the New Macho Woman?' In *Vision Quest*, the young male hero falls in love with the heroine, as he says, because 'she has all the best things I like in girls and all the best things I like in guys,' that is, she's tough and cool, but warm and alluring. In the enormously popular *Aliens*, the heroine's personality has been deliberately constructed, with near-comic book explicitness, to embody traditional nurturant femininity alongside breathtaking macho prowess and control; Sigourney Weaver, the actress who portrays her, has called the character 'Rambolina'.

In the pursuit of slenderness and the denial of appetite the traditional construction of femininity intersects with the new requirement for women to embody the 'masculine' values of the public arena. The anorectic, as I have argued, embodies this intersection, this double bind, in a particularly painful and graphic way.[11] I mean *double bind* quite literally here. 'Masculinity' and 'femininity', at least since the nineteenth century and arguably before, have been constructed through a process of mutual exclusion. One cannot simply add the historically feminine virtues to the historically masculine ones to yield a New Woman, a New Man, a new ethics, or a new culture. Even on the screen or on television, embodied in created characters like the *Aliens* heroine, the result is a parody. Unfortunately, in this image-bedazzled culture, we find it increasingly difficult to discriminate between parodies and possibilities for the self. Explored as a possibility for the self, the 'androgynous' ideal ultimately exposes its internal contradiction and becomes a war that tears the subject in two—a war explicitly thematized, by many anorectics, as a battle between male and female sides of the self.

Protest and Retreat in the Same Gesture

In hysteria, agoraphobia, and anorexia, then, the woman's body may be viewed as a surface on which conventional constructions of femininity are exposed starkly to view, through their inscription in extreme or hyperliteral form. They are written, of course, in languages of horrible suffering. It is as though these bodies are speaking to us of the pathology and violence that lurks just around the corner, waiting at the horizon of 'normal' femininity. It is no wonder that a steady motif in the feminist literature on female disorder is that of pathology as embodied *protest*—unconscious, inchoate, and counterproductive protest without an effective language, voice, or politics, but protest nonetheless.

American and French feminists alike have heard the hysteric speaking a language of protest, even or perhaps especially when she was mute. Dianne Hunter interprets Anna O.'s aphasia, which manifested itself in an inability to speak her native German, as a rebellion against the linguistic and cultural rules of the father and a return to the 'mother-tongue': the semiotic babble of infancy, the language of the body. For Hunter, and for a number of other feminists working with Lacanian categories, the return to the semiotic level is both regressive and, as Hunter puts it, an 'expressive' communication 'addressed to patriarchal thought', 'a self-repudiating form of feminine discourse in which the body signifies what social conditions make it impossible to state linguistically' (Hunter, 1985: 114). 'The hysterics are accusing; they are pointing,' writes Catherine Clément in *The Newly Born Woman*; they make a 'mockery of culture' (Clément and Cixous, 1986: 42). In the same volume, Hélène Cixous speaks of 'those wonderful hysterics, who subjected Freud to so many voluptuous moments too shameful to mention, bombarding his mosaic statute/law of Moses with their carnal, passionate body-words, haunting him with their inaudible thundering denunciations.' For Cixous, Dora, who so frustrated Freud, is 'the core example of the protesting force in women' (Clément and Cixous, 1986: 95). The literature of protest includes functional as well as symbolic approaches.

Robert Seidenberg and Karen DeCrow, for example, describe agoraphobia as a 'strike' against

'the renunciations usually demanded of women' and the expectations of housewifely functions such as shopping, driving the children to school, accompanying their husband to social events (1983: 31). Carroll Smith-Rosenberg presents a similar analysis of hysteria, arguing that by preventing the woman from functioning in the wifely role of caretaker of others, of 'ministering angel' to husband and children, hysteria 'became one way in which conventional women could express—in most cases unconsciously—dissatisfaction with one or several aspects of their lives' (1985: 208). A number of feminist writers, among whom Susie Orbach is the most articulate and forceful, have interpreted anorexia as a species of unconscious feminist protest. The anorectic is engaged in a 'hunger strike', as Orbach calls it, stressing that this is a political discourse, in which the action of food refusal and dramatic transformation of body size 'expresses with [the] body what [the anorectic] is unable to tell us with words'—her indictment of a culture that disdains and suppresses female hunger, makes women ashamed of their appetites and needs, and demands that women constantly work on the transformation of their body (Orbach, 1985).[12]

The anorectic, of course, is unaware that she is making a political statement. She may, indeed, be hostile to feminism and any other critical perspectives that she views as disputing her own autonomy and control or questioning the cultural ideals around which her life is organized. Through embodied rather than deliberate demonstration she exposes and indicts those ideals, precisely by pursuing them to the point at which their destructive potential is revealed for all to see.

The same gesture that expresses protest, moreover, can also signal retreat; this, indeed, may be part of the symptom's attraction. Kim Chernin, for example, argues that the debilitating anorexic fixation, by halting or mitigating personal development, assuages this generation's guilt and separation anxiety over the prospect of surpassing our mothers, of living less circumscribed, freer lives (Chernin, 1985). Agoraphobia, too, which often develops shortly after marriage, clearly functions in many cases as a way to cement dependency and attachment in the face of unacceptable stirrings of dissatisfaction and restlessness.

Although we may talk meaningfully of protest, then, I want to emphasize the counterproductive, tragically self-defeating (indeed, self-deconstructing) nature of that protest. Functionally, the symptoms of these disorders isolate, weaken, and undermine the sufferers; at the same time they turn the life of the body into an all-absorbing fetish, beside which all other objects of attention pale into unreality. On the symbolic level, too, the protest collapses into its opposite and proclaims the utter capitulation of the subject to the contracted female world. The muteness of hysterics and their return to the level of pure, primary bodily expressivity have been interpreted, as we have seen, as rejecting the symbolic order of the patriarchy and recovering a lost world of semiotic, maternal value. But *at the same time*, of course, muteness is the condition of the silent, uncomplaining woman—an ideal of patriarchal culture. Protesting the stifling of the female voice through one's own voicelessness—that is, employing the language of femininity to protest the conditions of the female world—will always involve ambiguities of this sort. Perhaps this is why symptoms crystallized from the language of femininity are so perfectly suited to express the dilemmas of middle-class and upper-middle-class women living in periods poised on the edge of gender change, women who have the social and material resources to carry the traditional construction of femininity to symbolic excess but who also confront the anxieties of new possibilities. The late nineteenth century, the post-Second World War period, and the late twentieth century are all periods in which gender becomes an issue to be discussed and in which discourse proliferates about 'the Woman Question', 'the New Woman', 'What Women Want', 'What Femininity Is'.

Collusion, Resistance, and the Body

The pathologies of female protest function, paradoxically, as if in collusion with the cultural conditions that produce them, reproducing rather than transforming precisely that which is being protested. In this connection, the fact that hysteria and anorexia have peaked during historical periods of cultural backlash against attempts at reorganization and redefinition of male and female roles is significant. Female pathology reveals itself here as an extremely interesting social formation through which one source of potential for resistance and rebellion is pressed into the service of maintaining the established order.

In our attempt to explain this formation, objective accounts of power relations fail us. For whatever the objective social conditions are that create a pathology, the symptoms themselves must still be produced (however unconsciously or inadvertently) by the subject. That is, the individual must invest the body with meanings of various sorts. Only by examining this productive process on the part of the subject can we, as Mark Poster has put it, 'illuminate the mechanisms of domination in the processes through which meaning is produced in everyday life'; that is, only then can we see how the desires and dreams of the subject become implicated in the matrix of power relations (Poster, 1984: 28).

Here, examining the context in which the anorexic syndrome is produced may be illuminating. Anorexia will erupt, typically, in the course of what begins as a fairly moderate diet regime, undertaken because someone—often the father—has made a casual critical remark. Anorexia *begins in*, emerges out of, what is, in our time, conventional feminine practice. In the course of that practice, for any number of individual reasons, the practice is pushed a little beyond the parameters of moderate dieting. The young woman discovers what it feels like to crave and want and need and yet, through the exercise of her own will, to triumph over that need. In the process, a new realm of meanings is discovered, a range of values and possibilities that Western culture has traditionally coded as 'male' and rarely made available to women: an ethic and aesthetic of self-mastery and self-transcendence, expertise, and power over others through the example of superior will and control. The experience is intoxicating and habit-forming.

At school the anorectic discovers that her steadily shrinking body is admired, not so much as an aesthetic or sexual object, but for the strength of will and self-control it projects. At home she discovers, in the inevitable battles her parents fight to get her to eat, that her actions have enormous power over the lives of those around her. As her body begins to lose its traditional feminine curves, its breasts and hips and rounded stomach, it begins to feel and look more like a spare, lanky male body, and she begins to feel untouchable, out of reach of hurt, 'invulnerable, clean and hard as the bones etched into my silhouette', as one student described it in her journal. She despises, in particular, all those parts of her body that continue to mark her as female. 'If only I could eliminate [my breasts],' says Liu, 'cut them off if need be' (1979: 99). For her, as for many anorectics, the breasts represent a bovine, unconscious, vulnerable side of the self. Liu's body symbolism is thoroughly continuous with dominant cultural associations. Brett Silverstein's studies on the 'Possible Causes of the Thin Standard of Bodily Attractiveness for Women' (1986) testify empirically to what is obvious from every comedy routine involving a dramatically shapely woman: namely, our cultural association of curvaceousness with incompetence. The anorectic is also quite aware, of course, of the social and sexual vulnerability involved in having a female body; many, in fact, were sexually abused as children.

Through her anorexia, by contrast, she has unexpectedly discovered an entry into the privileged male world, a way to become what is valued in our culture, a way to become safe, to rise above

it all—for her, they are the same thing. She has discovered this, paradoxically, by pursuing conventional feminine behaviour—in this case, the discipline of perfecting the body as an object—to excess. At this point of excess, the conventionally feminine deconstructs, we might say, into its opposite and opens onto those values our culture has coded as male. No wonder anorexia is experienced as liberating and that the anorectic will fight family, friends, and therapists in an effort to hold onto it—fight them to the death, if need be. The anorectic's experience of power is, of course, deeply and dangerously illusory. To reshape one's body into a male body is *not* to put on male power and privilege. To *feel* autonomous and free while harnessing body and soul to an obsessive body-practice is to serve, not transform, a social order that limits female possibilities. And, of course, for the female to become male is only for her to locate herself on the other side of a disfiguring opposition. The new 'power look' of female body-building, which encourages women to develop the same hulk-like, triangular shape that has been the norm for male body-builders, is no less determined by a hierarchical, dualistic construction of gender than was the conventionally 'feminine' norm that tyrannized female body-builders such as Bev Francis for years.

Although the specific cultural practices and meanings are different, similar mechanisms, I suspect, are at work in hysteria and agoraphobia. In these cases too, the language of femininity, when pushed to excess—when shouted and asserted, when disruptive and demanding—deconstructs into its opposite and makes available to the woman an illusory experience of power previously forbidden to her by virtue of her gender. In the case of nineteenth-century femininity, the forbidden experience may have been the bursting of fetters—particularly moral and emotional fetters. John Conolly, the asylum reformer, recommended institutionalization for women who 'want that restraint over the passions without which the female character is lost' (Showalter, 1985: 48). Hysterics often infuriated male doctors by their lack of precisely this quality. S. Weir Mitchell described these patients as 'the despair of physicians', whose 'despotic selfishness wrecks the constitution of nurses and devoted relatives, and in unconscious or half-conscious self-indulgence destroys the comfort of everyone around them' (Smith-Rosenberg, 1985: 207). It must have given the Victorian patient some illicit pleasure to be viewed as capable of such disruption of the staid nineteenth-century household. A similar form of power, I believe, is part of the experience of agoraphobia.

This does not mean that the primary reality of these disorders is not one of pain and entrapment. Anorexia, too, clearly contains a dimension of physical addiction to the biochemical effects of starvation. But whatever the physiology involved, the ways in which the subject understands and thematizes her experience cannot be reduced to a mechanical process. The anorectic's ability to live with minimal food intake allows her to feel powerful and worthy of admiration in a 'world', as Susie Orbach describes it, 'from which at the most profound level [she] feels excluded' and unvalued (1985: 103). The literature on both anorexia and hysteria is strewn with battles of will between the sufferer and those trying to 'cure' her; the latter, as Orbach points out, very rarely understand that the psychic values she is fighting for are often more important to the woman than life itself.

Textuality, Praxis, and the Body

The 'solutions' offered by anorexia, hysteria, and agoraphobia, I have suggested, develop out of the practice of femininity itself, the pursuit of which is still presented as the chief route to acceptance and success for women in our culture. Too aggressively pursued, that practice leads to its own undoing, in one sense. For if femininity is, as Susan Brownmiller has said, at its core a 'tradition of imposed limitations' (1984: 14), then an unwillingness to limit oneself, even in the pursuit of femininity, breaks the rules. But, of course, in another sense the rules remain fully in place. The sufferer becomes wedded to an obsessive practice, unable to make any effective change in her life. She remains, as Toril Moi has put it, 'gagged and chained to [the] feminine role', a reproducer of the docile body of femininity (1985: 192).

This tension between the psychological meaning of a disorder, which may enact fantasies of rebellion and embody a language of protest, and the practical life of the disordered body, which may utterly defeat rebellion and subvert protest, may be obscured by too exclusive a focus on the symbolic dimension and insufficient attention to praxis. As we have seen in the case of some Lacanian feminist readings of hysteria, the result of this can be a one-sided interpretation that romanticizes the hysteric's symbolic subversion of the phallocentric order while confined to her bed. This is not to say that confinement in bed has a transparent, univocal meaning—in powerlessness, debilitation, dependency, and so forth. The 'practical' body is no brute biological or material entity. It, too, is a culturally mediated form; its activities are subject to interpretation and description. The shift to the practical dimension is not a turn to biology or nature, but to another 'register', as Foucault puts it, of the cultural body, the register of the 'useful body' rather than the 'intelligible body' (Foucault, 1979: 136). The distinction can prove useful, I believe, to feminist discourse.

The intelligible body includes our scientific, philosophic, and aesthetic representations of the body—our cultural *conceptions* of the body, norms of beauty, models of health, and so forth. But the same representations may also be seen as forming a set of *practical* rules and regulations through which the living body is 'trained, shaped, obeys, responds', becoming, in short, a socially adapted and 'useful body' (Foucault, 1979: 136). Consider this particularly clear and appropriate example: the nineteenth-century hourglass figure, emphasizing breasts and hips against a wasp waist, was an intelligible *symbolic* form, representing a domestic, sexualized ideal of femininity. The sharp cultural contrast between the female and the male form, made possible by the use of corsets and bustles, reflected, in symbolic terms, the dualistic division of social and economic life into clearly defined male and female spheres. At the same time, to achieve the specified look, a particular feminine *praxis* was required—straitlacing, minimal eating, and reduced mobility—rendering the female body unfit to perform activities outside its designated sphere. This, in Foucauldian terms, would be the 'useful body' corresponding to the aesthetic norm.

The intelligible body and the useful body are two arenas of the same discourse; they often mirror and support each other, as in the above illustration. Another example can be found in the seventeenth-century philosophic conception of the body as a machine, mirroring an increasingly more automated productive machinery of labour. But the two bodies may also contradict and mock each other. A range of contemporary representations and images, as noted earlier, have coded the transcendence of female appetite and its public display in the slenderness ideal in terms of power, will, mastery, and the possibilities of success in the professional arena. These associations are carried visually by the slender superwomen of prime-time television and popular movies and promoted explicitly in advertisements and articles appearing routinely in women's fashion magazines, diet books, and weight-training publications. Yet the thousands of slender girls and women who strive to embody these images and who in that service suffer from eating disorders, exercise compulsions, and continual self-scrutiny and self-castigation are anything *but* the 'masters' of their lives.

Exposure and productive cultural analysis of such contradictory and mystifying relations between image and practice are possible only if

the analysis includes attention to and interpretation of the 'useful' or, as I prefer to call it, the practical body. Such attention, although often in inchoate and theoretically unsophisticated form, was central to the beginnings of the contemporary feminist movement. In the late 1960s and early 1970s the objectification of the female body was a serious political issue. All the cultural paraphernalia of femininity, of learning to please visually and sexually through the practices of the body—media imagery, beauty pageants, high heels, girdles, makeup, simulated orgasm—were seen as crucial in maintaining gender domination.

Disquietingly, for the feminists of the present decade, such focus on the politics of feminine praxis, although still maintained in the work of individual feminists, is no longer a centerpiece of feminist cultural critique.[13] On the popular front, we find *Ms* magazine presenting issues on fitness and 'style', the rhetoric reconstructed for the 1980s to pitch 'self-expression' and 'power'. Although feminist theory surely has the tools, it has not provided a critical discourse to dismantle and demystify this rhetoric. The work of French feminists has provided a powerful framework for understanding the inscription of phallocentric, dualistic culture on gendered bodies, but it has offered very little in the way of concrete analyses of the female body as a locus of practical cultural control. Among feminist theorists in this country, the study of cultural representations of the female body has flourished, and it has often been brilliantly illuminating and instrumental to a feminist rereading of culture.[14] But the study of cultural representations alone, divorced from consideration of their relation to the practical lives of bodies, can obscure and mislead.

Here, Helena Mitchie's significantly titled *The Flesh Made Word* offers a striking example. Examining nineteenth-century representations of women, appetite, and eating, Mitchie draws fascinating and astute metaphorical connections between female eating and female sexuality. Female hunger, she argues, and I agree, 'figures unspeakable desires for sexuality and power' (1987: 13). The Victorian novel's 'representational taboo' against depicting women eating (an activity, apparently, that only 'happens offstage', as Mitchie puts it) thus functions as a 'code' for the suppression of female sexuality, as does the general cultural requirement, exhibited in etiquette and sex manuals of the day, that the well-bred woman eat little and delicately. The same coding is drawn on, Mitchie argues, in contemporary feminist 'inversions' of Victorian values, inversions that celebrate female sexuality and power through images exulting in female eating and female hunger, depicting it explicitly, lushly, and joyfully.

Despite the fact that Mitchie's analysis centres on issues concerning women's hunger, food, and eating practices, she makes no mention of the grave eating disorders that surfaced in the late nineteenth century and that are ravaging the lives of young women today. The practical arena of women dieting, fasting, straitlacing, and so forth is, to a certain extent, implicit in her examination of Victorian gender ideology. But when Mitchie turns, at the end of her study, to consider contemporary feminist literature celebrating female eating and female hunger, the absence of even a passing glance at how women are *actually* managing their hungers today leaves her analysis adrift, lacking any concrete social moorings. Mitchie's sole focus is on the inevitable failure of feminist literature to escape 'phallic representational codes' (1987: 149). But the feminist celebration of the female

body did not merely deconstruct on the written page or canvas. Largely located in the feminist counterculture of the 1970s, it has been culturally displaced by a very different contemporary reality. Its celebration of female flesh now presents itself in jarring dissonance with the fact that women, feminists included, are starving themselves to death in our culture.

This is not to deny the benefits of diet, exercise, and other forms of body management. Rather, I view our bodies as a site of struggle, where we must *work* to keep our daily practices in the service of resistance to gender domination, not in the service of docility and gender normalization. This work requires, I believe, a determinedly skeptical attitude toward the routes of seeming liberation and pleasure offered by our culture. It also demands an awareness of the often contradictory relations between image and practice, between rhetoric and reality. Popular representations, as we have seen, may forcefully employ the rhetoric and symbolism of empowerment, personal freedom, 'having it all'. Yet female bodies, pursuing these ideals, may find themselves as distracted, depressed, and physically ill as female bodies in the nineteenth century were made when pursuing a feminine ideal of dependency, domesticity, and delicacy. The recognition and analysis of such contradictions, and of all the other collusions, subversions, and enticements through which culture enjoins the aid of our bodies in the reproduction of gender, require that we restore a concern for female praxis to its formerly central place in feminist politics.

Notes

1. Early versions of this essay, under various titles, were delivered at the philosophy department of the State University of New York at Stony Brook, the University of Massachusetts conference on Histories of Sexuality, and the twenty-first annual conference for the Society of Phenomenology and Existential Philosophy.

I thank all those who commented and provided encouragement on those occasions. The essay was revised and originally published in Alison Jaggar and Susan Bordo, eds, *Gender/Body/ Knowledge: Feminist Reconstructions of Being and Knowing* (New Brunswick: Rutgers University Press, 1989).

2. On docility, see Michel Foucault, *Discipline and Punish* (New York: Vintage, 1979), 135–69. For a Foucauldian analysis of feminine practice, see Sandra Bartky, 'Foucault, Femininity, and the Modernization of Patriarchal Power', in her *Femininity and Domination* (New York: Routledge, 1990); see also Susan Brownmiller, *Femininity* (New York: Ballantine, 1984).

3. During the late 1970s and 1980s, male concern over appearance undeniably increased. Study after study confirms, however, that there is still a large gender gap in this area. Research conducted at the University of Pennsylvania in 1985 found men to be generally satisfied with their appearance, often, in fact, 'distorting their perceptions [of themselves] in a positive, self-aggrandizing way' ('Dislike of Own Bodies Found Common Among Women', *New York Times*, 19 March 1985: C1). Women, however, were found to exhibit extreme negative assessments and distortions of body perception. Other studies have suggested that women are judged more harshly than men when they deviate from dominant social standards of attractiveness. Thomas Cash et al., in 'The Great American Shape-Up', *Psychology Today* (April 1986): 34, report that although the situation for men has changed, the situation for women has more than proportionally worsened. Citing results from 30,000 responses to a 1985 survey of perceptions of body image and comparing similar responses to a 1972 questionnaire, they report that the 1985 respondents were considerably more dissatisfied with their bodies than the 1972 respondents, and they note a marked intensification of concern among men. Among the 1985 group, the group most dissatisfied of all with their appearance, however, were teenage women. Women today constitute by far the largest number of consumers of diet products, attenders of spas and diet centers, and subjects of intestinal by-pass and other fat-reduction operations.

4. On the gendered and historical nature of these disorders: the number of female to male hysterics has been estimated at anywhere from 2:1 to 4:1, and as many as 80 per cent of all agoraphobics are female (Annette Brodsky and Rachel Hare-Mustin, *Women and Psychotherapy* [New York: Guilford Press, 1980], 116, 122). Although more cases of male eating disorders have been reported in the late eighties and early nineties, it is estimated that close to 90 per cent of all anorectics are female (Paul Garfinkel and David Garner, *Anorexia Nervosa: A Multidimensional Perspective* [New York: Brunner/Mazel, 1982], 112–13). For a sophisticated account of female psychopathology, with particular attention to nineteenth-century disorders but, unfortunately, little mention of agoraphobia or eating disorders, see Elaine Showalter, *The Female Malady: Women, Madness and English Culture, 1830–1980* (New York: Pantheon, 1985). For a discussion of social and gender issues in agoraphobia, see Robert Seidenberg and Karen DeCrow, *Women Who Marry Houses: Panic and Protest in Agoraphobia* (New York: McGraw-Hill, 1983). On the history of anorexia nervosa, see Joan Jacobs Brumberg, *Fasting Girls: The Emergence of Anorexia Nervosa as a Modern Disease* (Cambridge: Harvard University Press, 1988).

5. In constructing such a paradigm I do not pretend to do justice to any of these disorders in its individual complexity. My aim is to chart some points of intersection, to describe some similar patterns, as they emerge through a particular reading of the phenomenon—a political reading, if you will.

6. On the epidemic of hysteria and neurasthenia, see Showalter, *The Female Malady;* Carroll Smith-Rosenberg, 'The Hysterical Woman: Sex Roles and Role Conflict in Nineteenth-Century America', in her *Disorderly Conduct: Visions of Gender in Victorian America* (Oxford: Oxford University Press, 1985).

7. See Carol Nadelson and Malkah Notman, *The Female Patient* (New York: Plenum, 1982), 5; E.M. Sigsworth and T.J. Wyke, 'A Study of Victorian Prostitution and Venereal Disease', in Vicinus, *Suffer and Be Still*, 82. For more general discussions, see Peter Gay, *The Bourgeois Experience: Victoria to Freud*. Vol. 1: *Education of the Senses* (New York: Oxford University Press,

1984), esp. 109–68; Showalter, *The Female Malady*, esp. 121–44. The delicate lady, an ideal that had very strong class connotations (as does slenderness today), is not the only conception of femininity to be found in Victorian cultures. But it was arguably the single most powerful ideological representation of femininity in that era, affecting women of all classes, including those without the material means to realize the ideal fully. See Helena Mitchie, *The Flesh Made Word* (New York: Oxford, 1987), for discussions of the control of female appetite and Victorian constructions of femininity.

8. Betty Friedan, *The Feminine Mystique* (New York: Dell, 1962), 36. The theme song of one such show ran, in part, 'I married Joan . . . What a girl . . . what a whirl . . . what a life! I married Joan . . . What a mind . . . love is blind . . . what a wife!'

9. For other interpretive perspectives on the slenderness ideal, see 'Reading the Slender Body' in this volume; Kim Chernin, *The Obsession: Reflections on the Tyranny of Slenderness* (New York: Harper and Row, 1981); Susie Orbach, *Hunger Strike: The Anorectic's Struggle as a Metaphor for Our Age* (New York: W.W. Norton, 1985).

10. See 'Hunger as Ideology', in this volume, for a discussion of how this construction of femininity is reproduced in contemporary commercials and advertisements concerning food, eating, and cooking.

11. Striking, in connection with this, is Catherine Steiner-Adair's 1984 study of high-school women, which reveals a dramatic association between problems with food and body image and emulation of the cool, professionally 'together' and gorgeous superwoman. On the basis of a series of interviews, the high schoolers were classified into two groups: one expressed skepticism over the superwoman ideal, the other thoroughly aspired to it. Later administrations of diagnostic tests revealed that 94 per cent of the pro-superwoman group fell into the eating-disordered range of the scale. Of the other group, 100 per cent fell into the non-eating-disordered range. Media images notwith-

standing, young women today appear to sense, either consciously or through their bodies, the impossibility of simultaneously meeting the demands of two spheres whose values have been historically defined in utter opposition to each other.

12. When we look into the many autobiographies and case studies of hysterics, anorectics, and agoraphobics, we find that these are indeed the sorts of women one might expect to be frustrated by the constraints of a specified female role. Sigmund Freud and Joseph Breuer, in *Studies on Hysteria* (New York: Avon, 1966), and Freud, in the later *Dora: An Analysis of a Case of Hysteria* (New York: Macmillan, 1963), constantly remark on the ambitiousness, independence, intellectual ability, and creative strivings of their patients. We know, moreover, that many women who later became leading social activists and feminists of the nineteenth century were among those who fell ill with hysteria and neurasthenia. It has become a virtual cliché that the typical anorectic is a perfectionist, driven to excel in all areas of her life. Though less prominently, a similar theme runs throughout the literature on agoraphobia.

One must keep in mind that in drawing on case studies, one is relying on the perceptions of other acculturated individuals. One suspects, for example, that the popular portrait of the anorectic as a relentless over-achiever may be coloured by the lingering or perhaps resurgent Victorianism of our culture's attitudes toward ambitious women. One does not escape this hermeneutic problem by turning to autobiography. But in autobiography one is at least dealing with social constructions and attitudes that animate the subject's own psychic reality. In this regard the autobiographical literature on anorexia, drawn on in a variety of places in this volume, is strikingly full of anxiety about the domestic world and other themes that suggest deep rebellion against traditional notions of femininity.

13. A focus on the politics of sexualization and objectification remains central to the anti-

pornography movement (e.g., in the work of Andrea Dworkin, Catherine MacKinnon). Feminists exploring the politics of appearance include Sandra Bartky, Susan Brownmiller, Wendy Chapkis, Kim Chernin, and Susie Orbach. And a developing feminist interest in the work of Michel Foucault has begun to produce a poststructuralist feminism oriented toward practice; see, for example, Irene Diamond and Lee Quinby, *Feminism and Foucault: Reflections on Resistance* (Boston: Northeastern University Press, 1988).

14. See, for example, Susan Suleiman, ed., *The Female Body in Western Culture* (Cambridge: Harvard University Press, 1986).

References

Bourdieu, P. 1977. *Outline of a Theory of Practice.* Cambridge: Cambridge University Press.

Brehony, K. 1983. 'Women and Agoraphobia', in V. Franks and E. Rothblum, eds, *The Stereotyping of Women.* New York: Springer.

Brownmiller, S. 1984. *Femininity.* New York: Ballantine.

Chernin, K. 1985. *The Hungry Self: Women, Eating, and Identity.* New York: Harper and Row.

Clément, C., and Cixous, H. 1986. *The Newly Born Woman*, B. Wing, trans. Minneapolis: University of Minnesota Press.

Culler, J. 1983. *Roland Barthes.* New York: Oxford University Press.

Douglas, M. 1966. *Purity and Danger.* London: Routledge and Kegan Paul.

———. 1982. *Natural Symbols.* New York: Pantheon.

Fodor, I.G. 1974. 'The Phobic Syndrome in Women', in V. Franks and V. Burtle, eds, *Women in Therapy.* New York: Brunner/Mazel.

Foucault, M. 1979. *Discipline and Punish.* New York: Vintage.

———. 1980. *The History of Sexuality.* Volume 1: *An Introduction.* New York: Vintage.

Friedan, B. 1962. *The Feminine Mystique.* New York: Dell.

Goffman, E. 1959. *The Presentation of the Self in Everyday Life.* Garden City, NJ: Anchor Doubleday.

Hunter, D. 1985. 'Hysteria, Psychoanalysis and Feminism', in S. Garner, C. Kahane, and M. Sprenger, eds, *The (M)Other Tongue.* Ithaca, NY: Cornell University Press.

Liu, A. 1979. *Solitaire.* New York: Harper and Row.

Mitchie, H. 1987. *The Flesh Made Word.* New York: Oxford University Press.

Moi, T. 1985. 'Representations of Patriarchy: Sex and Epistemology in Freud's Dora', in C. Bernheimer and C. Kahane, eds, *In Dora's Case: Freud—Hysteria—Feminism.* New York: Columbia University Press.

Orbach, S. 1985. *Hunger Strike: The Anorectic's Struggle as a Metaphor for Our Age.* New York: W.W. Norton.

Poster, M. 1984. *Foucault, Marxism, and History.* Cambridge: Polity Press.

Showalter, E. 1985. *The Female Malady: Women, Madness and English Culture, 1830–1980.* New York: Pantheon.

Siedenberg, R., and K. DeCrow. 1983. *Women Who Marry Houses: Panic and Protest in Agoraphobia.* New York: McGraw-Hill.

Silverstein, B. 1986. 'Possible Causes of the Thin Standard of Bodily Attractiveness for Women', *International Journal of Eating Disorders* 5: 907–16.

Smith-Rosenberg, C. 1985. 'The Hysterical Woman: Sex Roles and Role Conflict in Nineteenth-Century America', in C. Smith-Rosenberg, *Disorderly Conduct: Visions of Gender in Victorian America.* Oxford: Oxford University Press.

Vicinus, M. 1972. 'Introduction: The Perfect Victorian Lady', in M. Vicinus, *Suffer and Be Still: Women in the Victorian Age*, pp. x–xi. Bloomington: Indiana University Press.

CHAPTER 29

Mass Media and Gender Identity in High Performance Canadian Figure Skating

Karen McGarry

Introduction

This paper is based upon qualitative, anthropological fieldwork conducted between 2000 and 2002 among Canadian journalists, high performance (i.e., National, World, and Olympic level) figure skaters, coaches, sponsors, and others involved in the production of mediated representations of figure skating for mainstream Canadian television networks and other print media. With the permission of various organizations, I conducted participant observation and field work in skating arenas and in the media centres of major competitions to understand the role of figure skating in shaping a sense of Canadian national identity. As standard practice in anthropology, the names of those interviewed are withheld to protect their anonymity. The goal of this paper is to highlight the role of the media in promoting particular gendered images of figure skaters for public consumption, thereby drawing attention to two issues: (1) the socially constructed nature of various representations of men and women in the sport, and; (2) the ways in which particular gendered images of sports figures are promoted in the interests of nationalism.

Figure Skating, the Media, and Canadian Culture

Figure skating is viewed by many Canadians as an integral part of Canadian culture. Records of ice-skating date back to at least the 1700s, and figure skating, along with hockey, receives prime-time television coverage on major Canadian television networks. Figure skating, in fact, is ranked second only to hockey in terms of television spectatorship, government funding, and corporate sponsorship (Skate Canada, 2002). Its popularity among fans is heightened by the fact that since the 1940s, Canadians have won more than 500 international medals, making it one of the nation's most competitively successful amateur sports. Skaters such as Elvis Stojko, Kurt Browning, Elizabeth Manley, Barbara Ann Scott, Toller Cranston, and Jamie Salé and David Pelletier, to name a few, have become household names and national icons in Canada.

Given figure skating's high spectatorship levels, it is not surprising that Skate Canada, the sport's amateur governing body, and CTV, Canada's self-declared 'official figure skating network' have opportunistically marketed figure skating as a distinctly 'Canadian' sport and a sport of national significance:

> Figure Skating is a sport of national significance to Canadians and is part of our heritage. Canadians have excelled in figure skating, achieving international success and celebrity status (Skate Canada Fact Sheet, 2002).

> It's part of our Canadian heritage. That's why CTV—'Canada's Figure Skating Network'—is committed to bringing you the best figure skating in the world. CTV has been partnered with the sport since 1961, and makes figure skating its core sports property (CTV website, 16 July 2001).

For Skate Canada and its top skaters, sponsorships are relatively easy to obtain (in comparison with other amateur sports). In fact, Skate Canada has become a primarily self-sustaining organization over the years, thanks mainly to lucrative sponsorship opportunities. While the organization continues to receive government funding, this represents a small portion (7 per cent) of its annual operating budget (Skate Canada, 2002). This means that the task of promoting a sense of national identity among Canadians has, in the case of figure skating, moved increasingly into the hands of non-state actors, and particularly the mass media and its sponsors and advertisers. Throughout my research, I learned that there exist powerful alliances of interest between skating sponsors and various Canadian media outlets, both of which have a vested economic interest in promoting various national representations that appeal to entertainment spectacles. These alliances, in turn, indirectly influence the gendered representations upheld for Canadian audiences. For example, at one event, I talked with a television sports network executive from a major media outlet. Very excited to be there, she had this to say about her company's agreement with Skate Canada:

> *Executive:* When they [Skate Canada] approached us, we were excited to be a part of it all. We were looking for the best sports ambassadors for Canada to support. What's better than figure skating? They're good, clean-cut kids. We're proud too of our association with skating and our advertisers have really supported Elvis Stojko over the years.
>
> *Karen:* What was it about Elvis that makes him appealing?
>
> *Executive:* He's successful and a champion. And he's such a strong, masculine presence.

Top skaters recognize the importance of their sport to the country, and they rarely doubt that their image will not be promoted favourably. Their bodies have become commodified to the point where, as one skater confidently told me, 'I'm not trying to be arrogant here, but they [the network] would have my people [his sponsors] down their throats if I got criticized. I'm worth a lot to them.' In many ways then, figure skating represents an opportunity for understanding how the Canadian media and television, in conjunction with advertisers, influence the production of gendered, commodified identities on ice, and in doing so, produce highly specific gendered bodily representations of the nation.

Gender and Figure Skating

The gendered categories of 'masculinity' and 'femininity' are socially constructed concepts and societal ideals about an appropriate masculine or feminine behaviour vary spatially, from culture to culture, and temporally, depending upon various socio-historical circumstances (e.g., Butler, 1990). In other words, what is considered 'socially appropriate' behaviour for a female or male (today) is not the same as a century ago. Given the lucrative sponsorship potential of the sport, it is not surprising that the Canadian mainstream media and its sponsors and advertisers have sought to endorse 'clean cut', mainstream, heterosexual images of masculinity and femininity for public consumption.

While figure skating is rumoured to have the highest proportion of homosexual men of any amateur competitive sport (Pronger, 1999), it is ironically a sport in which men must exhibit the most blatantly heterosexual signs to be successful and to receive commercial endorsements. Since the late 1980s, Skate Canada, the media, and its sponsors have made a concerted effort to de-emphasize figure skating's balletic heritage, a tradition that was strengthened in the 1970s by skaters such as Canadian Olympian Toller Cranston, an openly homosexual competitor who introduced flamboyant costumes, cosmetics, ballet, and choreography into men's skating. Male homosexuality, it seems, is considered a financial liability to the sport. In 1998, for example, the two-time Olympic silver medallist, Brian Orser, was 'outed' in the media during a palimony lawsuit. Orser was devastated by the media exposure and claimed that such allegations of homosexuality would threaten his economic livelihood. Similarly, at the 2001 World Championships in Vancouver when a well-known male Canadian skater was contacted by a gay magazine about the possibility of doing a feature story on him, he was told by Skate Canada that he must decline the request. As one coach said to me, 'that is not the sort of picture that Skate Canada wants to paint for the country, especially in an international forum.' Every effort is made to construct such skaters as heterosexual.

The heterosexual masculine images of World Champion skaters like Kurt Browning and Elvis Stojko were endorsed enthusiastically in the media throughout the 1990s, a point also noted by Adams (1997). Usually skating to rock and roll music, or adopting the traditionally masculine personas of characters like ninjas, Scottish warriors, or karate experts, Stojko was constructed in the media as 'Canada's Terminator'. At one competition I attended, I watched Stojko warm up backstage with balletic exercises, but the camera technician, who was instructed to film Stojko's pre-competitive routine, waited until he decided to jog to film him. As he said to me, 'Elvis is such a macho guy; we want to show that side of him.' By emphasizing male skaters' athletic abilities in media portrayals, links are made between the supposed 'strength' of the male figure skating body, and the 'strength' of the nation. As one sponsor said to me, 'we want to promote strong images of our male skaters to show the Americans and other nations that we are an important force to contend with.' The bottom line is that images of male heterosexuality sell to a broader, and hence more lucrative, spectator demographic.

Similar sorts of gender expectations and pressures exist for Canada's female skaters. Women are expected to emulate a soft, delicate femininity reminiscent of, as one coach told me, 'an Audrey Hepburn or Grace Kelly era'. The competitive future of female skaters who fail to project such images may, in some cases, be threatened. One female skater I spoke with, for example, told me that, subsequent to a competition, she was informed by a judge that her earring (she had three piercings in each ear), her nose ring, and her weight, were 'unfeminine' and that she might fare better in the future should she comport herself 'more accordingly and ladylike'. She also suggested that the skater should lose five pounds, as this would make her more attractive to the media.

Clearly then, the gendered images performed in figure skating are culturally constructed images, oftentimes produced in conjunction with the media. Some skaters I spoke with, for instance, informed me that they consult their agents and media organizations for input before deciding upon their annual costume and program themes.

Social Implications / Conclusion

The gendered images favoured in figure skating are important to discuss here because they have a variety of negative consequences for the sport. First, the persistence of idealized representations of gender can lead to the onset of debilitating emotional and physical disabilities among skaters. For women in particular, figure skating is notorious for the existence of eating disorders and a variety of other physical and psychological ailments (e.g., Ryan, 1995; Davis 1997) as a result of the desire to achieve an 'idealized femininity'. The narrow range of opportunities for gendered identities also hampers the individual creative talents and artistic abilities of skaters, coaches, and choreographers, many of whom feel limited in the range of options available. Also, it is somewhat surprising, in the supposedly tolerant, multicultural, and inclusive environment of a nation like Canada, that such a rigid and narrow definition of gendered identities is accepted and promoted (oftentimes unconsciously) for public consumption. Clearly, this is a growing concern within the sport due to the increasing power and hegemony of the mainstream media and its powerful position in shaping modern identities. As nation-states gradually begin to lose control over the production of national identities in increasingly globalized contexts, non-state entities like the mass media are taking over or supplanting the state's role in nation-building. As this article has suggested, this has important connotations for the future of increasingly mediated sports like figure skating, where the bodies of skaters are heavily commodified and mainstream representations of national bodies dominate.

References

Adams, M. 1997. 'To be an Ordinary Hero: Male Figure Skaters and the Ideology of Gender', *Avante* 3, 3: 93–110.

Butler, J. 1990. *Gender Trouble: Feminism and the Subversion of Identity*. New York: Routledge.

CTV. 2001. *CTV and Figure Skating*. Available at http://www.ctv.ca/sport (accessed 16 July 2001).

Davis, C. 1997. 'Eating Disorders and Hyperactivity: A Psycho-biological Perspective', *Canadian Journal of Psychiatry* 42: 168–75.

Pronger, B. 1999. *The Arena of Masculinity: Sport, Homosexuality, and the Meaning of Sex*. New York: St Martin's Press.

Ryan, J. 1995. *Little Girls in Pretty Boxes: The Making and Breaking of Elite Gymnasts and Figure Skaters*. New York: Doubleday.

Skate Canada. 2002. *Skate Canada Fact Sheet*. Ottawa: Skate Canada.

CHAPTER 30

Contours of Everyday Life: Women's Reflections on Embodiment and Health Over Time

Pamela Wakewich

Written on the body is a secret code only visible in certain lights; the accumulations of a lifetime gather there. In places the palimpsest is so heavily worked that the letters feels like Braille. I keep my body rolled up away from prying eyes. Never unfold too much, tell the whole story.
—Jeanette Winterson, *Written on the Body*

People have to inhabit their bodies, and their physical identity is part of themselves. Particularly as they grow older, they have a need to account for this identity, to draw together all that they have experienced. This body is their inheritance, it is the result of the events of their life, and it is their constraint.
—Mildred Blaxter, 'The Causes of Disease: Women Talking'

While efforts to incorporate the body into social theory have become prolific in the past decade, it is only recently that writers have begun to explore the ways in which people actively constitute and experience the body in everyday life.[1] Analysts have tended to focus upon representations of the female body in the professional discourses of medicine and science or the popular discourses of media and advertising, and to presume a direct link between these representations and women's experiences of the body.[2] Even where authors seek to present alternative frameworks, their analysis generally remain framed by the scientific and bio-medical categories and language that they wish to challenge. Body and identity are presented as static notions with the presumption that they remain fixed and homogenous through time and place.

A similar limitation is evident in much contemporary feminist literature that addresses the relationship between media and women's body image dissatisfaction. Largely influenced by writers like Foucault, analysts have carefully documented the ways in which media and advertising serve to promote and normalize disciplinary practices of the female body towards the achievement of unhealthy ideals. Susan Bordo's much cited essay 'Reading the Slender Body' brilliantly deconstructs the pathologized, individuated image that both medicine and media present us with—the woman who 'succeeds' in achieving these ideals only to damage her own health and perhaps risk her life in the process. Bordo's analysis clearly shows the importance of seeing the 'everyday-ness' of these disciplinary practices and how they inscribe on the surface (and increasingly the interior) of women's bodies the 'bulimic personality' of contemporary American capitalist society. This society requires, at one and the same time, unrestrained consumption to achieve health and happiness and intense repression of desire and body boundaries to meet narrowly prescribed moral and cultural standards (Bordo, 1990).

Yet Bordo's analysis, along with those of many others who address this topic, leaves us with little, if any, indication of how women 'read' and respond to—or perhaps even resist—these dominant ideals. We get little sense of the extent to which these dominant ideals may or may not be significant or predominant in women's identity construction and how this may shift over time and in different social contexts, as well as in relation to other aspects of the multiple-subject positions women hold (such as class, ethnicity, age, sexuality, regional identity, and so on).

Studying Health and Body Perceptions in Northwestern Ontario

These concerns were the points of departure for a research project that I conducted in northwestern Ontario between 1996 and 1999. Comparing the experiences of white working-class and middle-class women and men, I explored how ideas about health and the body are shaped and reshaped over time, as well as how identities of gender, class, sexuality, culture, region (in this case 'north-ern-ness') are constituted within and through discourses on health and the body.[3] The decision to interview both women and men was in part motivated by my desire to 'de-problematize' the female body, a problem that is evident in many current medico-scientific and feminist analyses.

In conducting this research, I used techniques of feminist oral history to elicit what Barbara Duden calls 'bio-logies', or body stories, in order to bring into view the everyday processes and social relations through which ideas about health and the body are constituted and experienced.[4]

My research was carried out in the city of Thunder Bay, in northwestern Ontario, a community whose own identity is in many ways negotiated and liminal.[5] By 'liminal', I mean it is at once northern (officially considered part of the provincial north), and yet not northern (being located only 50 kilometres from the American border). It is urban (having a population of some 120,000), and yet rural (being physically isolated from other large centres by at least a full day's drive in either direction). It is an important regional business and service centre, and yet residents feel largely ignored and insignificant in provincial terms. Its population is culturally diverse, comprising a mix of various Northern and Eastern European roots, a significant First Nations population as well as recent migrants from Latin America and South East Asia and yet conformity of style, speech, and even behaviour is valued and remarked upon. As several of the women interviewed noted, straying too far from the accepted norms of dress and appearance may meet with social sanctions such as public commentary or ridicule. Although the primary resource industries (such as the paper mills and grain elevators) are no longer as significant to the local economy as they one were, and even though women make up an increasingly large share of the city's labour force, the city maintains an image in the eyes of both residents and outsiders of being a 'lunch-bucket' or 'working-man's' town (Dunk, 1991).

Interviews were conducted with forty women and men between the ages of 30 and 65. In choosing this age range, I anticipated that participants would be old enough to have a 'history' of body experiences to reflect upon, and yet young enough to not be preoccupied with significant gerontological concerns. To address the dimension of social class, equal numbers of working-class and middle-class women and men were included. As Robert Crawford's research on working-class notions of health and white middle-class discourses on AIDS has suggested (Crawford, 1994), attentiveness to class enables a comparison of both gender and class discourses on the language and representation of health and the body, and the extent to which they are invoked in the constitution of identity. For working-class women, I expected that there might not be a distinctly positive association between the nature of work and body image. The exigencies of work, family, and limited income experienced by working-class women might be seen as antithetical to the possibility of 'cultivating' the ideal female body

promoted by popular cultural representations. My interest here was to examine whether working-class women define their health and body experiences in relation to the middle-class norms represented in popular culture and medico-scientific discourse on the 'healthy' body, or whether alternative identities are constructed.

The 20 women interviewed ranged in age from 33–53, with a median age of 43. Sixteen of the women were currently married, one was living common-law, another was single, and two were divorced. All but five of the women had children or dependents living at home. Some of these children were in their late teens and early twenties; however, the women still thought of them as dependents financially, emotionally and in terms of household labour. The working-class women's occupations included clerical work, grocery clerk, letter carrier, homemaker, babysitter, kitchen worker, union representative, and diploma nurses. The middle-class women's occupations included nurse administrators, lawyer, teacher, university professor, homemaker, small business owner/workers and office administrator. Four of the women combined part-time work with primary childcare responsibilities, while the remainder were employed full-time, and most reported some additional responsibility for children or dependents. Nine of the women had more than one paid occupation—either a combination of part-time jobs, or a full-time job and a part-time job (such as union representative).

In broad terms, the interviews focused on the participants' past and current perceptions of health and embodiment with particular attention to the ways in which these have changed or remained stable through the course of their lives. Interviews explored the role of body image in the women's perceptions of health and well-being, construction of self and 'other', and the significance attributed to popular culture, family socialization, employment, medical interactions, and other aspects of the social environment in shaping ideas about health and the body.

The interview schedule focused on four main themes: (1) background information on family, education, employment and social class; (2) definitions of health; (3) gender, work, family, and leisure, and their relationship to health and identity; and (4) ideas about body and body image, and their relationship to gender, work, family, health, and identity.

Defining Health and Healthiness

For the majority of the women interviewed, ideas about health and body image are intimately interlinked and have changed over their lives. For many, ideas about health and healthiness have evolved from a more conventional biomedical notion of health as the absence of disease (adhered to at an earlier age), to the assessment of well-being in more environmental or holistic terms. The women's notions of health discuss levels of physical energy, comfort in carrying out and balancing multiple roles, satisfaction with quality of work and family relations, and concerns about time for self and leisure.

When asked whether her idea of what it is to be healthy had always been the same, Carol, a 41-year-old university professor, responded this way: 'No. I'd say now, getting older that . . . there is no doubt that my sense of health is becoming much less separate from how I look, and much more to do with how I feel.' Laura, a 43-year-old nurse administrator and part-time graduate student, said, 'Probably as I have grown older my expectations for being healthy have actually increased rather than decreased . . . To me now, being healthy does not just mean being free of disease or not on any medication, but being in the best state I can be in, mentally and physically.' Janet, also 43 and a teaching administrator, agreed that her notions of health had changed over time. As she notes: 'I used to think before that you had to be like five foot five, 120 pounds [and] go to the gym everyday. That was my image of what it was to be healthy. I think now it's more like how you feel on

the inside. Mentally, as well as physically. The two kind of go together.' Similarly, Debbie, a 44-year-old clerical worker responded, 'I don't think that I thought about stress when I was [younger]. I don't think that I thought about assessing my health I that way. It is different now.'

The women generally evaluated their health in terms of coping with multiple roles and the quality of family relations.[6] In contrast to many of the men who discussed the importance of physical endurance and a perceived sense of strength when evaluating their appearance, and several expressed a sentiment of being 'overweight' even though they generally felt healthy.

Behaviours associated with staying healthy had also changed over the course of the women's lives. Many indicated that they did little consciously to stay healthy when they were younger, but now were much more conscientious about eating well, getting regular exercise, and rest. For most, time was the more important constraint to achieving optimal health. They cited the difficulties of finding time for themselves (for leisure or exercise) while juggling multiple work and family roles.

Reflecting on her past and present health practices in response to my question 'Do you consider yourself a healthy person?' Mildred, a 49-year-old co-owner/worker in a small family business, replied:

> Sigh . . . well, I would like to think I was. There certainly was a time when I had a lot more time to spend on getting myself that way, [such as] all the time [we were] raising the children and everything. I still make all our own bread and pastries, cookies and those things. I think that counts. I buy meat from the farmer that I know doesn't use steroids or penicillin. We raise our own chickens, eggs and stuff like that. I try working at it. I try to get exercise. Years ago I got tons more than I do now. I would have to say the working thing has just cramped my style considerably. I'm overweight, of course, and I don't get as

much exercise as I should. Years ago when I was home I would walk for three hours a day. I love walking. I love being outside. I also feel at times, I've narrowed it down, I know what it is—it is nature deprivation. I feel nature deprivation if I don't get outside enough—you know, the less you do [exercise], the less you can do it. You get home and you're tired. You don't fell like going out.

I asked Mildred, 'When would you say you used to do more? Was it when your kids were younger?' and she replied:

Yeah. And I babysat, and I was at home. We had the business out of the house for a while too. When we started doing it [establishing the business], the transitional period, I could just be out more. It was easier to do it . . . If I could afford somebody full time [to help with the business], I would be out of there in a flash. I would be home feeding the chickens and raising the pigs and things like that. Because that's what I enjoy doing.

Several of the women indicated that they didn't have a sense of entitlement of 'time off'. Women with younger children generally built their own leisure pursuits around activities that could include their children. Terri, a professional who had been very athletic in her youth, expressed frustration at trying to get a 'workout' for herself while doing activates with her children. Having recognized that the desires to spend time with her children and to exercise for herself were working at cross-purposes, she temporarily 'resolved' the issue by putting her own needs on hold until the children were older.

Class differences were also apparent in the women's definitions of health over the life course. Many middle-class women identified with current 'healthiest' discourses that emphasize health as an individual phenomenon, and blamed themselves for failing to live up to the ideals of dietary and

exercise regimes promoted in public health rhetoric. Ironically, even those who were professionals identified structural elements such as the exigencies of the double-work day and an unequal division of labour in the home as the major impediments to self-care. Working-class women tended to evaluate and discuss their own health in relational, rather than individual, terms. They assessed their own health in terms of their self-sufficiency and their ability to serve others (their family members, for example).

In general, the women were attentive to, and aware of, body image issues through the course of their lives, yet the importance and meanings attributed to them had changed significantly for most.[7] Many had previously dieted and monitored their weight carefully as adolescents and in their early twenties, yet most had abandoned these practices, either due to a sense of frustration with their lack of success, or emptily as a form of resistance to what they perceived as inappropriate medicalization and monitoring of their bodies by parents, doctors, partners and others.

Laura, a 50-year-old clothing store owner and mother of two grown children, described how her ideas of body image and being healthy have changed over time in this way:

I guess I was, as a baby boomer, probably on the leading edge of anorexia and bulimia and all that kind of stuff. I never had bulimia, but I'm sure I was one of the first anorexics [and this] was never diagnosed. Just from trying to starve yourself because society said you should be a thin person. If you weren't [thin] you felt you should be, so you tried anything to get there. That has changed for me drastically I'm not unhealthy and I'm certain my body image is no longer an issue [for me]. If somebody doesn't like me because I am heavy that's their problem, not mine.

When I asked Laura whether there was something specific that changed her notion of health, she said:

I think it was just finding out just after having my son that I couldn't starve myself every day. And why the heck should I have to—to be somebody else's image of what I should be? As long as I'm a good mother and a good person. Being in the [business of running a clothing store for large women] has certainly helped that too . . . if you're clean and your makeup's on and your clothes are nice and you keep yourself looking good, that's what people see.

Most of the women talked about having multiple body images. They emphasized the fluidity and contextualness of their own perceptions. Body image was different at home and in public spaces, in the company of friends and with strangers, at times of healthiness and during illness episodes, and often between work and leisure. Karen, a 33-year-old health administrator, described body image in he following way: 'It's how you perceive yourself. How I perceive myself is not just my physical being. It's whether I am confident in a certain situation of feeling secure. It does change if you are in a situation that you don't feel as confident [in].'

Debbie pointed out that her consciousness of body image is affected by whether she is in the company of women or of men. She states: 'I think I am more aware of what I look like and how I am perceived when I am with a bunch of women. Men are, even though you like to think men are fussy—they aren't fussy, they don't care. Women are much more critical. I think I worry about it more when I an with a bunch of women.' Marg, a 45-year-old office administrator similarly observe: 'I think it's different I different settings . . . Okay, for instance when I'm dressed nicer and I look good. When I'm dressed in sloppy clothes around the house. . . . I don't feel to powerful.'

For many of the women, different body images were also related to the quality of relationships with their partners or their peer group. Rita, a 43-year-old small business owner who had divorced and remarried, described a very different sense of body image with her new partner whom she

described as 'comfortable with me as I am'. Laura indicated that comfort with her body shifts in relation to contact with a group of female friends who are extremely physically active and concerned about appearance. Louise, a 38-year-old homemaker with three school-age children, described herself as a 'borderline' anorexic in adolescence, but had overcome this during her early twenties. She found the weigh-in and fundus[8] measurement during routine pregnancy checkups very anxiety-provoking; it created for her a negative shift in body image that has taken many years to resolve.

The women's notions of body image were fluid and changing over time. Often defined as body shape or physical appearance in adolescence, for some, body image expanded to a larger sense of 'presentation of self' (Goffman, 1959) as they aged. For professional and business women this incorporated not only appearance and styles of dress—or 'dressing for success' as many described it—but also a sense of self-confidence, a feeling of accomplishment or skill in their field of work, and an improved sense of healthiness over time. For many of the working-class women, being successfully relied upon by others and being seen as coping were important aspects of the assessment of body image. Some of their responses expressed a kind of idealization of a 'northern' (almost akin to pioneer) women for whom strength and endurance were key dimensions of a positive body image.

Consciousness of the body was also described as situational and, again, varied along class and gender lines. Many of the women indicated that they were not conscious of their bodies on an on-going basis. A few women who were particularly concerned about weight described their bodies as constraints (as the opening quote form Blaxter suggests), which they had difficulty transcending. However, most others indicated that body consciousness was situational, brought on by a particularly serious or sudden illness episode, by concerns about what to wear to a particular social event (for example, a class reunion or family gathering), by travelling to a large urban centre like

Toronto where consciousness and monitoring of appearance seems more evident, or by shopping for clothing—especially the painful annual new bathing suit ritual. For many of the women, body consciousness and anxiety were also heightened by medical concerns encounters (even routine checkups) that frequently raised concerns about unhealthy weight, independent of a women's own assessment of her state of healthiness.

Media and Other Representations of the Female Body and Health

Responses to predominant media images of the idealized female body had also changed in the women's reflections. They differed on opinions about the extent to which ideals of slenderness and feminine beauty were more predominant or widely circulated today than when they were younger. Many remembered routinely reading or 'studying' the teen magazines of their youth, such as *Seventeen*, often with a sense of regret that the products and fashions advertised were not readily available in the North. While many continue to be avid magazine reader, the choice of magazines has changed from teen magazines to ones such as *Canadian Living* or *Woman's Day*, and the appeal cited was as much the recipes and advice columns as the clothing and fashion images.

When asked how they respond to or whether they 'see' themselves in the images of women presented in these magazines, most indicated a strong sense that the images were largely unreal and sometimes almost amusing in their absurdity. A few noted an increased representation of 'real' or average women in the magazines in recent years. They found this trend appealing and felt they paid much more attention to these ads or pictures because they could get a sense of how clothes might really look on them.

Medical information and advice columns in the magazines were frequently read by the women and taken much more seriously than fashion layouts. Many of the women found these columns

to be an important source of personal and family health information and said they discussed them with friends. But even this information could be dismissed or resisted if the women didn't feel that it matched their own perspective.

Body and body image were seldom discussed in individual terms, but rather almost always constituted in relational terms. Constructing the self was done in relation to a constructed 'other'. Thus, norms or expectations of femininity were contrasted with norms of masculinity (and vice versa); middle-class concerns about presentation of self and success were presented as opposite to stereotypes of a working class lack of care or lack of discipline; and working-class concerns about the lack of time and money to pursue idealized health and body images were construed in relation to the presumption of generic middle-class investment in, and resources available to, achieve those ideals.

Contemporary senses of health and body image were referential to past notions and ideals and often made efforts to present an integrated or coherent history of embodiment. In some instance, where particularly troubling experiences of violence—such as sexual abuse or social stigma—were part of a woman's past, her efforts at providing an integrated narrative were contradictory or incomplete. The strong resonances of past experiences showed though the narrative surface, giving a texture much like the 'palimpsest' that Winterson's opening quote to this chapter so eloquently describes.

These observations suggest that women's ideas about body and body image are fluid and contextual. They are shaped and re-shaped over time and placed in relation to other aspects of identity and subjectivity. Ideas about the body are interlinked with notions of health and well-being and evolve in relation to both individual and collective experiences. Science, medicine and media may play an important role in shaping and normalizing our ideals and behaviours—particularly in our younger years—but they are often ignored or actively resisted when the images they present us with fail to match our own evolving sense of health or well-being. Thus the analysis and incorporation of body and embodiment in social theory and feminist research must attend to the fluidity and contextualness of women's experiences, and explore their constitution and reconstitution in specific times and places with particular attention to the quality and nature of the social relations in which they are shaped.

Notes

1. See, for example, Kathy Davis, ed., *Embodied Practices: Feminist Perspectives on the Body* (London: Sage, 1997); Frigga Haug, ed., *Female Sexualization* (London: Verso, 1987); Nicole Sault, ed., *Many Mirrors: Body Image and Social Relations* (New Brunswick, NJ: Rutgers University Press, 1994); and Sue Scott and David Morgan, ed., *Body Matters* (London: The Falmer Press, 1993).

2. See Diane Barthel, *Putting on Appearance* (Philadelphia: Temple University Press, 1988); Susan Bordo, 'Reading the Slender Body', in Mary Jacobus and Evelyn Fox Keller, eds, *Body/Politics: Women and the Discourses of Science* (London: Routledge, 1990), 83–112; and Susie Orbach, *Hunger Strike: The Anorectic's Struggle as a Metaphor for Our Age* (New York: W.W. Northon, 1986).

3. This paper is drawn from portions of my PhD dissertation, 'Contours of Everyday Life: Reflections on Health and Embodiment Over the Life Course' (University of Warwick, UK, 2000). To study the ways in which ideas about health and embodiment change over the life course, I conducted in-depth interviews with forty working-and middle-class women and men in northwestern Ontario. Interviewing both women and men allowed a close comparison of the similarities and differences of women and men's experiences of health and embodiment, and the extent to which these were a potential source of gender consciousness.

   All but two of the respondents were 'white'. I use the term 'white' here as a social construct following Richard Dyer, *White* (London: Routledge, 1997) and Ruth Frankenberg, *White Women, Race Matters: The Social Construction of Whiteness* (Minneapolis: University of Minnesota Press, 1993). While the research sample reflects the ethnic diversity of the region, as other analysts have noted, the primary distinction recognized by local residents is that between First Nations, or Aboriginal Peoples, and 'whites'. See, for example, Thomas Dunk, *It's a Working Man's Town: Male Working-Class Culture in Northwestern Ontario* (Montreal: McGill-Queen's University Press, 1991). The dissertation includes an analysis of the terrain and interpretations of 'whiteness' as it is both visible and invisible in the participants' narratives of 'healthy selves' and 'unhealthy others'.

4. Barbara Duden, *The Woman Beneath the Skin*, uses the concept of 'bio-logies' or body stories to describe the changing understandings and representations of the body evident in the narratives given to eighteenth-century German physician Johannes Storch by his clients over the course of his professional relationship with them.

5. Liminality is valued by postmodern researchers because studying liminal or 'in-between' categories highlights the ways in which differences are marked by people and given 'presence' or value within a particular culture or subculture. See Sonya Andermahr, Terry Lovell, and Carol Wolkowitz, *A Concise Glossary of Feminist Theory* (London: Arnold, 1997) for a discussion of the use of liminality in post-modern research.

6. A similar point is raised by Nickie Charles and Vivienne Walters in their analysis of age and gender in South Wales' women's accounts of health. They point out, 'women's accounts demonstrate that their experiences and explanations of health, while showing certain commonalities, vary with age and stage in the life cycle and are shaped by wider structural changes in employment patterns and gendered divisions of labour.'

Thus structural and cultural changes shape the discourses that women call upon when talking about health and illness . . .' 'Age and Gender in Women's Accounts of Their Health: Interviews with Women in South Wales', *Sociology of Health and Illness* 20 (1998): 348.

7. By contrast, many of the men found it much harder to reflect on 'body' history and required more prompting to make connections between a sense of embodiment and specific activities or instances of their youth. Most often, they talked about embodiment in terms of success or endurance in sporting activities, the ability to do physical labour (especially for working-class men) or in relation to illness of self or appearance norms. Those who did were primarily middle-class men who discussed presentation of self in terms of their leadership image at work and their embodiment of corporate imagery.

8. The fundus is the top of the uterus. Its changing position is measured throughout the pregnancy to assess the growth and position of the baby.

References

Blaxter, M. 1983. 'The Causes of Disease: Women Talking', *Social Science and Medicine* 17: 69.

Bordo, S. 1990. 'Reading the Slender Body', in M. Jacobus and E. Fox Keller, eds, *Body/Politics: Women and the Discourses of Science*, pp. 83–112. London: Routledge.

Charles, N., and V. Walters. 1998. 'Age and Gender in Women's Accounts of Their Health: Interviews with Women in South Wales', *Sociology of Health and Illness* 20: 348.

Crawford, R. 1994. 'The Boundaries of the Self and the Unhealthy Other: Reflections on Health, Culture and AIDS', *Social Science and Medicine* 38: 1347–65.

Dunk, T. 1991. *It's a Working Man's Town: Male Working-Class Culture in Northwestern Ontario*. Montreal: McGill-Queen's University Press.

Goffman, E. 1959. *The Presentation of Self in Everyday Life*. Garden City, NY: Doubleday.

Winterson, J. 1994. *Written on the Body*. New York: Vintage Books.

CHAPTER 31

The Five Sexes: Why Male and Female Are Not Enough

Anne Fausto-Sterling

In 1843 Levi Suydam, a 23-year-old resident of Salisbury, Connecticut, asked the town board of selectmen to validate his right to vote as a Whig in a hotly contested local election. The request raised a flurry of objections from the opposition party, for reasons that must be rare in the annals of American democracy: it was said that Suydam was more female than male and thus (some 80 years before suffrage was extended to women) could not be allowed to cast a ballot. To settle the dispute a physician, one William James Barry, was brought in to examine Suydam. And, presumably upon encountering a phallus, the good doctor declared the prospective voter male. With Suydam safely in their column the Whigs won the election by a majority of one.

Barry's diagnosis, however, turned out to be somewhat premature. Within a few days he discovered that, phallus notwithstanding, Suydam menstruated regularly and had a vaginal opening. Both his/her physique and his/her mental predispositions were more complex than was first suspected. S/he had narrow shoulders and broad hips and felt occasional sexual yearnings for women. Suydam's 'feminine propensities, such as a fondness for gay colors, for pieces of calico, comparing and placing them together, and an aversion for bodily labor, and an inability to perform the same, were remarked by many,' Barry later wrote. It is not clear whether Suydam lost or retained the vote, or whether the election results were reversed.

Western culture is deeply committed to the idea that there are only two sexes. Even language refuses other possibilities; thus to write about Levi Suydam I have had to invent conventions—*s/he* and *his/her*—to denote someone who is clearly neither male nor female or who is perhaps both sexes at once. Legally, too, every adult is either man or woman, and the difference, of course, is not trivial. For Suydam it meant the franchise; today it means being available for, or exempt from, draft registration, as well as being subject, in various ways, to a number of laws governing marriage, the family, and human intimacy. In many parts of the United States, for instance, two people legally registered as men cannot have sexual relations without violating anti-sodomy statutes.

But if the state and the legal system have an interest in maintaining a two-party sexual system, they are in defiance of nature. For biologically speaking, there are many gradations running from female to male; and depending on how one calls the shots, one can argue that along that spectrum lie at least five sexes—and perhaps even more.

For some time medical investigators have recognized the concept of the intersexual body. But the standard medical literature uses the term *intersex* as a catch-all for three major subgroups with some mixture of male and female characteristics:

the so-called true hermaphrodites, whom I call herms, who possess one testis and one ovary (the sperm- and egg-producing vessels, or gonads); the male pseudohermaphrodites (the 'merms'), who have testes and some aspects of the female genitalia but no ovaries; and the female pseudohermaphrodites (the 'ferms'), who have ovaries and some aspects of the male genitalia but lack testes. Each of those categories is in itself complex; the percentage of male and female characteristics, for instance, can vary enormously among members of the same subgroup. Moreover, the inner lives of the people in each subgroup—their special needs and their problems, attractions, and repulsions—have gone unexplored by science. But on the basis of what is known about them I suggest that the three intersexes, herm, merm, and ferm, deserve to be considered additional sexes each in its own right. Indeed, I would argue further that sex is a vast, infinitely malleable continuum that defies the constraints of even five categories.

Not surprisingly, it is extremely difficult to estimate the frequency of intersexuality, much less the frequency of each of the three additional sexes: it is not the sort of information one volunteers on a job application. The psychologist John Money of Johns Hopkins University, a specialist in the study of congenital sexual-organ defects, suggests intersexuals may constitute as many as 4 per cent of births. As I point out to my students at Brown University, in a student body of about 6,000 that fraction, if correct, implies there may be as many as 240 intersexuals on campus—surely enough to form a minority caucus of some kind.

In reality though, few such students would make it as far as Brown in sexually diverse form. Recent advances in physiology and surgical technology now enable physicians to catch most intersexuals at the moment of birth. Almost at once such infants are entered into a program of hormonal and surgical management so that they can slip quietly into society as 'normal' heterosexual males or females. I emphasize that the motive is in no way conspiratorial. The aims of the policy are genuinely humanitarian, reflecting the wish that people be able to 'fit in' both physically and psychologically. In the medical community, however, the assumptions behind that wish—that there be only two sexes, that heterosexuality alone is normal, that there is one true model of psychological health—have gone virtually unexamined.

The word *hermaphrodite* comes from the Greek names Hermes, variously known as the messenger of the gods, the patron of music, the controller of dreams, or the protector of livestock, and Aphrodite, the goddess of sexual love and beauty. According to Greek mythology, those two gods parented Hermaphroditus, who at age fifteen became half male and half female when his body fused with the body of a nymph he fell in love with. In some true hermaphrodites the testis and the ovary grow separately but bilaterally; in others they grow together within the same organ, forming an ovotestis. Not infrequently, at least one of the gonads functions quite well, producing either sperm cells or eggs, as well as functional levels of the sex hormones—androgens or estrogens. Although in theory it might be possible for a true hermaphrodite to become both father and mother to a child, in practice the appropriate ducts and tubes are not configured so that egg and sperm can meet.

In contrast with the true hermaphrodites, the pseudohermaphrodites possess two gonads of the same kind along with the usual male (XY) or female (XX) chromosomal makeup. But their external genitalia and secondary sex characteristics do not match their chromosomes. Thus merms have testes and XY chromosomes, yet they also have a vagina and a clitoris, and at puberty they often develop breasts. They do not menstruate, however. Ferms have ovaries, two X chromosomes and sometimes a uterus, but they also have at least partly masculine external genitalia. Without medical intervention they can develop beards, deep voices and adult-size penises.

Intersexuality itself is old news. Hermaphrodites, for instance, are often featured in stories about human origins. Early biblical scholars believed Adam began life as a hermaphrodite and later divided into two people—a male and a female—after falling from grace. According to Plato there once were three sexes—male, female, and hermaphrodite—but the third sex was lost with time.

Both the Talmud and the Tosefta, the Jewish books of law, list extensive regulations for people of mixed sex. The Tosefta expressly forbids hermaphrodites to inherit their fathers' estates (like daughters), to seclude themselves with women (like sons), or to shave (like men). When hermaphrodites menstruate they must be isolated from men (like women); they are disqualified from serving as witnesses or as priests (like women), but the laws of pederasty apply to them.

In Europe a pattern emerged by the end of the Middle Ages that, in a sense, has lasted to the present day: hermaphrodites were compelled to choose an established gender role and stick with it. The penalty for transgression was often death. Thus in the 1600s a Scottish hermaphrodite living as a woman was buried alive after impregnating his/her master's daughter.

For questions of inheritance, legitimacy, paternity, succession to title, and eligibility for certain professions to be determined, modern Anglo-Saxon legal systems require that newborns be registered as either male or female. In the United States today state laws govern sex determination. Illinois permits adults to change the sex recorded on their birth certificates should a physician attest to having performed the appropriate surgery. The New York Academy of Medicine, on the other hand, has taken an opposite view. In spite of surgical alterations of the external genitalia, the academy argued in 1966, the chromosomal sex remains the same. By that measure, a person's wish to conceal his or her original sex cannot outweigh the public interest in protection against fraud.

During this century the medical community has completed what the legal world began—the complete erasure of any form of embodied sex that does not conform to a male–female, hetero-sexual pattern. Ironically, a more sophisticated knowledge of the complexity of sexual systems has led to the repression of such intricacy.

In 1937 the urologist Hugh H. Young of Johns Hopkins University published a volume titled *Genital Abnormalities, Hermaphroditism and Related Adrenal Diseases*. The book is remarkable for its erudition, scientific insight, and open-mindedness. In it Young drew together a wealth of carefully documented case histories to demonstrate and study the medical treatment of such 'accidents of birth'. Young did not pass judgment on the people he studied, nor did he attempt to coerce into treatment those intersexuals who rejected that option. And he showed unusual even-handedness in referring to those people who had had sexual experiences as both men and women as 'practicing hermaphrodites'.

One of Young's more interesting cases was a hermaphrodite named Emma who had grown up as a female. Emma had both a penis-size clitoris and a vagina, which made it possible for him/her to have 'normal' heterosexual sex with both men and women. As a teenager Emma had had sex with a number of girls to whom s/he was deeply attracted; but at the age of nineteen s/he had married a man. Unfortunately, he had given Emma little sexual pleasure (though he had had no complaints), and so throughout that marriage and subsequent ones Emma had kept girlfriends on the side. With some frequency s/he had pleasurable sex with them. Young describes his subject as appearing 'to be quite content and even happy'. In conversation Emma occasionally told him of his/her wish to be a man, a circumstance Young said would be relatively easy to bring about. But Emma's reply strikes a heroic blow for self-interest:

> Would you have to remove that vagina? I don't know about that because that's my meal ticket. If you did that, I would have to quit my husband and go to work, so I think I'll keep it and stay as I am. My husband supports me

well, and even though I don't have any sexual pleasure with him, I do have lots with my girlfriends.

Yet even as Young was illuminating intersexuality with the light of scientific reason, he was beginning its suppression. For his book is also an extended treatise on the most modern surgical and hormonal methods of changing intersexuals into either males or females. Young may have differed from his successors in being less judgmental and controlling of the patients and their families, but he nonetheless supplied the foundation on which current intervention practices were built.

By 1969, when the English physicians Christopher J. Dewhurst and Ronald R. Gordon wrote *The Intersexual Disorders*, medical and surgical approaches to intersexuality had neared a state of rigid uniformity. It is hardly surprising that such a hardening of opinion took place in the era of the feminine mystique—of the post-Second World War flight to the suburbs and the strict division of family roles according to sex. That the medical consensus was not quite universal (or perhaps that it seemed poised to break apart again) can be gleaned from the near-hysterical tone of Dewhurst and Gordon's book, which contrasts markedly with the calm reason of Young's founding work. Consider their opening description of an inter-sexual newborn:

> One can only attempt to imagine the anguish of the parents. That a newborn should have a deformity . . . [affecting] so fundamental an issue as the very sex of the child . . . is a tragic event which immediately conjures up visions of a hopeless psychological misfit doomed to live always as a sexual freak in loneliness and frustration.

Dewhurst and Gordon warned that such a miserable fate would, indeed, be a baby's lot should the case be improperly managed; 'but fortunately,' they wrote, 'with correct management the outlook is infinitely better than the poor parents—emotionally stunned by the event—or indeed anyone without special knowledge could ever imagine.'

Scientific dogma has held fast to the assumption that without medical care hermaphrodites are doomed to a life of misery. Yet there are few empirical studies to back up that assumption, and some of the same research gathered to build a case for medical treatment contradicts it. Francies Benton, another of Young's practicing hermaphrodites, 'had not worried over his condition, did not wish to be changed, and was enjoying life'. The same could be said of Emma, the opportunistic hausfrau. Even Dewhurst and Gordon, adamant about the psychological importance of treating intersexuals at the infant stage, acknowledged great success in 'changing the sex' of older patients. They reported on twenty cases of children reclassified into a different sex after the supposedly critical age of eighteen months. They asserted that all the reclassifications were 'successful,' and they wondered then whether re-registration could be 'recommended more readily than [had] been suggested so far'.

The treatment of intersexuality in this century provides a clear example of what the French historian Michel Foucault has called biopower. The knowledge developed in biochemistry, embryology, endocrinology, psychology, and surgery has enabled physicians to control the very sex of the human body. The multiple contradictions in that kind of power call for some scrutiny. On the one hand, the medical 'management' of intersexuality certainly developed as part of an attempt to free people from perceived psychological pain (though whether the pain was the patient's, the parents', or the physician's is unclear). And if one accepts the assumption that in a sex-divided culture people can realize their greatest potential for happiness and productivity only if they are sure they belong to one of only two acknowledged sexes, modern medicine has been extremely successful.

On the other hand, the same medical accomplishments can be read not as progress but as a mode of discipline. Hermaphrodites have unruly bodies. They do not fall naturally into a binary classification; only a surgical shoehorn can put them there. But why should we care if a 'woman', defined as one who has breasts, a vagina, a uterus and ovaries, and who menstruates, also has a clitoris large enough to penetrate the vagina of another woman? Why should we care if there are people whose biological equipment enables them to have sex 'naturally' with both men and women? The answers seem to lie in a cultural need to maintain clear distinctions between the sexes. Society mandates the control of intersexual bodies because they blur and bridge the great divide. Inasmuch as hermaphrodites literally embody both sexes, they challenge traditional beliefs about sexual difference: they possess the irritating ability to live sometimes as one sex and sometimes the other, and they raise the spectre of homosexuality.

But what if things were altogether different? Imagine a world in which the same knowledge that has enabled medicine to intervene in the management of intersexual patients has been placed at the service of multiple sexualities. Imagine that the sexes have multiplied beyond currently imaginable limits. It would have to be a world of shared powers. Patient and physician, parent and child, male and female, heterosexual and homosexual—all those oppositions and others would have to be dissolved as sources of division. A new ethic of medical treatment would arise, one that would permit ambiguity in a culture that had overcome sexual division. The central mission of medical treatment would be to preserve life. Thus hermaphrodites would be concerned primarily not about whether they can conform to society but about whether they might develop potentially life-threatening conditions—hernias, gonadal tumours, salt imbalances caused by adrenal malfunctions—that sometimes accompany hermaphroditic development. In my ideal world, medical intervention for intersexuals would take place only rarely before the age of

reason; subsequent treatment would be a cooperative venture between physician, patient, and other
advisers trained in issues of gender multiplicity.

I do not pretend that the transition to my
utopia would be smooth. Sex, even the supposedly
'normal', heterosexual kind, continues to cause
untold anxieties in Western society. And certainly
a culture that has yet to come to grips—religiously
and, in some states, legally—with the ancient and
relatively uncomplicated reality of homosexual
love will not readily embrace intersexuality. No
doubt the most troublesome arena by far would
be the rearing of children. Parents, at least since
the Victorian era, have fretted, sometimes to the
point of outright denial, over the fact that their
children are sexual beings.

All that and more amply explains why intersexual children are generally squeezed into one
of the two prevailing sexual categories. But what
would be the psychological consequences of
taking the alternative road—raising children
as unabashed intersexuals? On the surface, that
tack seems fraught with peril. What, for example,
would happen to the intersexual child amid the
unrelenting cruelty of the schoolyard? When the
time came to shower in gym class, what horrors
and humiliations would await the intersexual as
his/her anatomy was displayed in all its nontraditional glory? In whose gym class would s/he
register to begin with? What bathroom would

s/he use? And how on earth would Mom and Dad
help shepherd him/her through the minefield of
puberty?

In the past 30 years those questions have been
ignored, as the scientific community has, with
remarkable unanimity, avoided contemplating
the alternative route of unimpeded intersexuality. But modern investigators tend to overlook a
substantial body of case histories, most of them
compiled between 1930 and 1960, before surgical
intervention became rampant. Almost without
exception, those reports describe children who
grew up knowing they were intersexual (though
they did not advertise it) and adjusted to their
unusual status. Some of the studies are richly
detailed—described at the level of gym-class
showering (which most intersexuals avoided
without incident); in any event, there is not a
psychotic or a suicide in the lot.

Still, the nuances of socialization among intersexuals cry out for more sophisticated analysis.
Clearly, before my vision of sexual multiplicity can
be realized, the first openly intersexual children
and their parents will have to be brave pioneers
who will bear the brunt of society's growing pains.
But in the long view—though it could take generations to achieve—the prize might be a society
in which sexuality is something to be celebrated
for its subtleties and not something to be feared
or ridiculed.

QUESTIONS FOR CRITICAL THOUGHT

1. Fausto-Sterling describes a 'utopia' in which intersexuality would be not be viewed as a deviation from the two-sex model for human bodies, but accepted as just one of the many physical manifestations of being human. How would this utopia be different from the world you live in today?

2. Bordo emphasizes the impact of media on the body image of young women, while the women Wakewich interviewed do not appear to base their own body image on what they see in media. How influential are the representations of male and female bodies we see in magazines, on TV, and on the Internet? What other forces influence how people think about their bodies?

3. How much do you depend on the appearances of bodies to shape your interactions with other people? What would life be like for someone whose body was not easily identifiable as belonging to one gender or the other?

4. Do you think there is one dominant or hegemonic ideal of beauty for women today? What about for men?

5. McGarry describes a group of people who function as 'public bodies'—whose physical appearance is made available as a product to be consumed by the public. Think of other 'public bodies'. Do all 'public bodies' share any common traits?

PART VIII

Gendered Intimacies

Nowhere are the differences between women and men more pronounced than in our intimate lives; our experiences of love, friendship, and sexuality. It is in our intimate relationships that it so often feels like men and women are truly from different planets.

The very definitions of emotional intimacy bear the mark of gender. As Francesca Cancian argues, the ideal of love has been 'feminized' since the nineteenth century. No longer is love the arduous pining or the sober shouldering of familial responsibility; today, love is expressed as the ability to sustain emotional commitment and connection—a 'feminine' definition of love.

The impact of these gendered definitions of love, friendship, and intimacy ripples through our intimate lives. Ritch C. Savin-Williams finds that gender is often a crucial variable in understanding the different trajectories of friendships and dating relationships among gay, lesbian, and bisexual youth.

But gender is not necessarily destiny when it comes to intimacy. In heterosexual relationships, we find a mixed pattern of convergence and divergence between men and women in terms of the way they experience love and sex. As Lily Tsui and Elena Nicoladis demonstrate in their study of first intercourse experiences among Canadian university students, men and women have much more similar experiences of first intercourse than the men-are-from-Mars-women-are-from-Venus model of gender difference might lead us to expect. Melanie Beres develops this theme further, suggesting that men and women use very similar presumptions and discourses to shape their experience of heterosexual casual sex—although, as Beres argues, these discourses tend to position men as active sexual pursuers and women as more passive participants in sexual activities. Nonetheless, some women manage to find ways to meet their own sexual desires, even without overtly challenging dominant ways of thinking about sex.

While Tsui, Nicoladis, and Beres focus on interpersonal experiences of sexuality, Angus McLaren and Arlene Tigar McLaren remind us that all heterosexuality takes place within broad social constraints. Their historical work takes us back to a time which may seem almost unimaginable for university students today—a time when it was very difficult, if not impossible, to have heterosexual sex without having babies. For much of the last two centuries in Canada, birth control was ineffective, inaccessible, or illegal, a state of affairs which created tremendous tension for heterosexually active women (and men), whether married or unmarried. Drawing on the letters desperate women and men wrote to Marie Stopes, a well-known campaigner for accessible contraception, the McLarens depict the enormous impact that contraception has on sexuality in Canada, and on the gender-differentiated distribution of risks and benefits for men and women to engage in heterosexual sex.

CHAPTER 32

The Feminization of Love

Francesca M. Cancian

A feminized and incomplete perspective on love predominates in the United States. We identify love with emotional expression and talking about feelings, aspects of love that women prefer and in which women tend to be more skilled than men. At the same time we often ignore the instrumental and physical aspects of love that men prefer, such as providing help, sharing activities, and sex. This feminized perspective leads us to believe that women are much more capable of love than men and that the way to make relationships more loving is for men to become more like women. This paper proposes an alternative, androgynous perspective on love, one based on the premise that love is both instrumental and expressive. From this perspective, the way to make relationships more loving is for women and men to reject polarized gender roles and integrate 'masculine' and 'feminine' styles of love.

The Two Perspectives

'Love is active, doing something for your good even if it bothers me' says a fundamentalist Christian. 'Love is sharing, the real sharing of feelings' says a divorced secretary who is in love again. In ancient Greece, the ideal love was the adoration of a man for a beautiful young boy who was his lover. In the thirteenth century, the exemplar of love was the chaste devotion of a knight for another man's wife. In Puritan New England, love between husband and wife was the ideal, and in Victorian times, the asexual devotion of a mother for her child seemed the essence of love. My purpose is to focus on one kind of love: long-term heterosexual love in the contemporary United States.

What is a useful definition of enduring love between a woman and a man? One guideline for a definition comes from the prototypes of enduring love—the relations between committed lovers, husband and wife, parent and child. These relationships combine care and assistance with physical and emotional closeness. Studies of attachment between infants and their mothers emphasize the importance of being protected and fed as well as touched and held. In marriage, according to most family sociologists, both practical help and affection are part of enduring love, or 'the affection we feel for those with whom our lives are deeply intertwined' (Walster and Walster,

1978: 9).[1] Our own informal observations often point in the same direction: if we consider the relationships that are the prototypes of enduring love, it seems that what we really mean by love is some combination of instrumental and expressive qualities.

Historical studies provide a second guideline for defining enduring love, specifically between a woman and a man. In pre-capitalist America, such love was a complex whole that included work and feelings. Then it was split into feminine and masculine fragments by the separation of home and workplace. This historical analysis implies that affection, material help, and routine cooperation all are parts of enduring love.

Consistent with these guidelines, my working definition of enduring love between adults is a relationship wherein a small number of people are affectionate and emotionally committed to each other, define their collective well-being as a major goal, and feel obliged to provide care and practical assistance for each other. People who love each other also usually share physical contact; they communicate with each other frequently and cooperate in some routine tasks of daily life. My discussion is of enduring heterosexual love only; I will for the sake of simplicity refer to it as 'love'.

In contrast to this broad definition of love, the narrower, feminized definition dominates both contemporary scholarship and public opinion. Most scholars who study love, intimacy, or close friendship focus on qualities that are stereotypically feminine, such as talking about feelings. For example, Abraham Maslow defines love as 'a feeling of tenderness and affection with great enjoyment, happiness, satisfaction, elation and even ecstasy'. Among healthy individuals, he says, 'there is a growing intimacy and honesty and self-expression' (Maslow, 1970: 182–3). Zick Rubin's 'Love Scale', designed to measure the degree of passionate love as opposed to 'like', includes questions about confiding in each other, longing to be together, and sexual attraction, as well as caring for each other. Studies of friendship usually distinguish

close friends from acquaintances on the basis of how much personal information is disclosed, and many recent studies of married couples and lovers emphasize communication and self-disclosure. A recent book on marital love by Lillian Rubin focuses on intimacy, which she defines as 'reciprocal expression of feeling and thought, not out of fear or dependent need, but out of a wish to know another's inner life and to be able to share one's own' (Rubin, 1983: 90).[2] She argues that intimacy is distinct from nurturance or care taking and that men are usually unable to be intimate.

Among the general public, love is also defined primarily as expressing feelings and verbal disclosure, not as instrumental help. This is especially true among the more affluent; poorer people are more likely than they to see practical help and financial assistance as a sign of love. In a study conducted in 1980, 130 adults from a wide range of social classes and ethnic backgrounds were interviewed about the qualities that make a good love relationship. The most frequent response referred to honest and open communication. Being caring and supportive and being tolerant and understanding were the other qualities most often mentioned. Similar results were reported from Ann Swidler's study of an affluent suburb: the dominant conception of love stressed communicating feelings, working on the relationship, and self-development. Finally, a contemporary dictionary defines love as 'strong affection for another arising out of kinship or personal ties' and as attraction based on sexual desire, affection, and tenderness.

These contemporary definitions of love clearly focus on qualities that are seen as feminine in our culture. A study of gender roles in 1968 found that warmth, expressiveness, and talkativeness were seen as appropriate for women and not for men. In 1978 the core features of gender stereotypes were unchanged although fewer qualities were seen as appropriate for only one sex. Expressing tender feelings, being gentle, and being aware of the feelings of others were still ideal qualities for women and not for men. The desirable qualities for men and not for women included being independent, unemotional, and interested in sex. The only component perceived as masculine in popular definitions of love is interest in sex.

The two approaches to defining love—one broad, encompassing instrumental and affective qualities, one narrow, including only the affective qualities—inform the two different perspectives on love. According to the androgynous perspective, both gender roles contain elements of love. The feminine role does not include all of the major ways of loving; some aspects of love come from the masculine role, such as sex and providing material help, and some, such as cooperating in daily tasks, are associated with neither gender role. In contrast, the feminized perspective on love implies that all of the elements of love are included in the feminine role. The capacity to love is divided by gender. Women can love and men cannot.

Some Feminist Interpretations

Feminist scholars are divided on the question of love and gender. Supporters of the feminized perspective seem most influential at present. Nancy Chodorow's psychoanalytic theory has been especially influential in promoting a feminized perspective on love among social scientists studying close relationships. Chodorow's argument—in greatly simplified form—is that as infants, both boys and girls have strong identification and intimate attachments with their mothers. Since boys grow up to be men, they must repress this early identification, and in the process they repress their capacity for intimacy. Girls retain their early identification since they will grow up to be women, and throughout their lives females see themselves as connected to others. As a result of this process, Chodorow argues, 'girls come to define and experience themselves as continuous with others; . . . boys come to define themselves as more separate and distinct' (1978: 169).[3] This theory implies that love is feminine—women

are more open to love than men—and that this gender difference will remain as long as women are the primary caretakers of infants.

Scholars have used Chodorow's theory to develop the idea that love and attachment are fundamental parts of women's personalities but not of men's. Carol Gilligan's influential book on female personality development asserts that women define their identity 'by a standard of responsibility and care'. The predominant female image is 'a network of connection, a web of relationships that is sustained by a process of communication'. In contrast, males favour a 'hierarchical ordering, with its imagery of winning and losing and the potential for violence which it contains'. 'Although the world of the self that men describe at times includes "people" and "deep attachments", no particular person or relationship is mentioned. . . . Thus the male "I" is defined in separation' (Gilligan, 1982: 159–61).[4]

A feminized conception of love can be supported by other theories as well. In past decades, for example, such a conception developed from Talcott Parsons's theory of the benefits to the nuclear family of women's specializing in expressive action and men's specializing in instrumental action. Among contemporary social scientists, the strongest support for the feminized perspective comes from such psychological theories as Chodorow's.

On the other hand, feminist historians have developed an incisive critique of the feminized perspective on love. Mary Ryan and other social historians have analyzed how the separation of home and workplace in the nineteenth century polarized gender roles and feminized love. Their argument, in simplified form, begins with the observation that in the colonial era the family household was the arena for economic production, affection, and social welfare. The integration of activities in the family produced a certain integration of expressive and instrumental traits in the personalities of men and women. Both women and men were expected to be hard working, modest, and loving toward their spouses and children, and the concept of love included instrumental cooperation as well as expression of feelings. In Ryan's words, 'When early Americans spoke of love they were not withdrawing into a female byway of human experience. Domestic affection, like sex and economics, was not segregated into male and female spheres.' There was a 'reciprocal ideal of conjugal love' that 'grew out of the day-to-day cooperation, sharing, and closeness of the diversified home economy'.[5]

Economic production gradually moved out of the home and became separated from personal relationships as capitalism expanded. Husbands increasingly worked for wages in factories and shops while wives stayed at home to care for the family. This division of labour gave women more experience with close relationships and intensified women's economic dependence on men. As the daily activities of men and women grew further apart, a new worldview emerged that exaggerated the differences between the personal, loving, feminine sphere of the home and the impersonal, powerful, masculine sphere of the workplace. Work became identified with what men do for money while love became identified with women's activities at home. As a result, the conception of love shifted toward emphasizing tenderness, powerlessness, and the expression of emotion.

This partial and feminized conception of love persisted into the twentieth century as the division of labour remained stable: the workplace remained impersonal and separated from the home, and married women continued to be excluded from paid employment. According to this historical explanation, one might expect a change in the conception of love since the 1940s, as growing numbers of wives took jobs. However, women's persistent responsibility for childcare and housework, and their lower wages, might explain a continued feminized conception of love.

Like the historical critiques, some psychological studies of gender also imply that our current conception of love is distorted and needs to be integrated with qualities associated with the masculine role. For example, Jean Baker Miller argues that women's ways of loving—their need to be attached to a man and to serve others—result from women's powerlessness, and that a better way of loving would integrate power with women's style of love (Miller, 1976).[6] The importance of combining activities and personality traits that have been split apart by gender is also a frequent theme in the human potential movement. These historical and psychological works emphasize the flexibility of gender roles and the inadequacy of a concept of love that includes only the feminine half of human qualities. In contrast, theories like Chodorow's emphasize the rigidity of gender differences after childhood and define love in terms of feminine qualities. The two theoretical approaches are not as inconsistent as my simplified sketches may suggest, and many scholars combine them; however, the two approaches have different implications for empirical research.

Evidence on Women's 'Superiority' in Love

A large number of studies show that women are more interested and more skilled in love than men. However, most of these studies use biased measures based on feminine styles of loving, such as verbal self-disclosure, emotional expression, and willingness to report that one has close relationships. When less biased measures are used, the differences between women and men are often small.

Women have a greater number of close relationships than men. At all stages of the life cycle, women see their relatives more often. Men and women report closer relations with their mothers than with their fathers and are generally closer to female kin. Thus an average Yale man in the 1970s talked about himself more with his mother than with his father and was more satisfied with his relationship with his mother. His most frequent grievance against his father was that his father gave too little of himself and was cold and uninvolved; his grievance against his mother was that she gave too much of herself and was alternately overprotective and punitive.

Throughout their lives, women are more likely to have a confidant—a person to whom one discloses personal experiences and feelings. Girls prefer to be with one friend or a small group, while boys usually play competitive games in large groups. Men usually get together with friends to play sports or do some other activity, while women get together explicitly to talk and to be together.

Men seem isolated, given their weak ties with their families and friends. Among blue-collar couples interviewed in 1950, 64 per cent of the husbands had no confidants other than their spouses, compared to 24 per cent of the wives. The predominantly upper-middle-class men interviewed by Daniel Levinson in the 1970s were no less isolated. Levinson concludes that 'close friendship with a man or a woman is rarely experienced by American men' (1978: 335). Apparently, most men have no loving relationships besides those with wife or lover; and given the estrangement that often occurs in marriages, many men may have no loving relationship at all.

Several psychologists have suggested that there is a natural reversal of these roles in middle age, as men become more concerned with relationships and women turn toward independence and achievement; but there seems to be no evidence showing that men's relationships become more numerous or more intimate after middle age, and some evidence to the contrary.

Women are also more skilled than men in talking about relationships. Whether working class or middle class, women value talking about feelings and relationships and disclose more than men about personal experiences. Men who deviate and talk a lot about their personal experiences are commonly defined as feminine and maladjusted. Working-class wives prefer to talk about themselves, their close relationships with family and friends, and their homes, while their husbands prefer to talk about cars, sports, work, and politics. College students express the same gender-specific preferences.

Men do talk more about one area of personal experience: their victories and achievements; but talking about success is associated with power, not intimacy. Women say more about their fears and disappointments, and it is disclosure of such weaknesses that usually is interpreted as a sign of intimacy. Women are also more accepting of the expression of intense feelings, including love, sadness, and fear, and they are more skilled in interpreting other people's emotions.

Finally, in their leisure time, women are drawn to topics of love and human entanglements while men are drawn to competition among men. Women's preferences in television viewing run to daytime soap operas, or if they are more educated, the high-brow soap operas on educational channels, while most men like to watch competitive and often aggressive sports. Reading-tastes show the same pattern. Women read novels and magazine articles about love, while men's magazines feature stories about men's adventures and encounters with death.

However, this evidence on women's greater involvement and skill in love is not as strong as it appears. Part of the reason that men seem so much less loving than women is that their behaviour is measured with a feminine ruler. Much of this research considers only the kinds of loving behaviour that are associated with the feminine role and rarely compares women and men in terms of qualities associated with the masculine role. When less biased measures are used, the behaviour of men and women is often quite similar. For example, in a careful study of kinship relations among young adults in a southern city, Bert Adams found that women were much more likely than men to say that their parents and relatives were very important to their lives (58 per cent of women and 37 per cent of men). In measures of actual contact with relatives, though, there were much smaller differences: 88 per cent of women and 81 per cent of men whose parents lived in the same city saw their parents weekly. Adams concluded that 'differences between males and females in relations with parents are discernible primarily in the subjective sphere; contact frequencies are quite similar' (1968: 169).

The differences between the sexes can be small even when biased measures are used. For example, Marjorie Lowenthal and Clayton Haven reported the finding, later widely quoted, that elderly women were more likely than elderly men to have a friend with whom they could talk about their personal troubles—clearly a measure of a traditionally feminine behaviour. The figures revealed that 81 per cent of the married women and 74 per cent of the married men had confidants—not a sizable difference (Lowenthal and Haven, 1968). On the other hand, whatever the measure, virtually all such studies find that women are more involved in close relationships than men, even if the difference is small.

In sum, women are only moderately superior to men in love: they have more close relationships and care more about them, and they seem to be more skilled at love, especially those aspects of love that involve expressing feelings and being vulnerable. This does not mean that men are separate and unconcerned with close relationships, however. When national surveys ask people what is most important in their lives, women tend to put family bonds first while men put family bonds first or second, along with work. For both sexes, love is clearly very important.

Evidence on the Masculine Style of Love

Men tend to have a distinctive style of love that focuses on practical help, shared physical activities, spending time together, and sex. The major elements of the masculine style of love emerged in Margaret Reedy's study of 102 married couples in the late 1970s. She showed individuals statements describing aspects of love and asked them to rate how well the statements described their marriages. On the whole, husband and wife had similar views of their marriage, but several sex differences emerged. Practical help and spending time together were more important to men. The men were more likely to give high ratings to such statements as: 'When she needs help I help her,' and 'She would rather spend her time with me than with anyone else.' Men also described themselves more often as sexually attracted and endorsed such statements as: 'I get physically excited and aroused just thinking about her.' In addition, emotional security was less important to men than to women, and men were less likely to describe the relationship as secure, safe, and comforting.[7] Another study in the late 1970s showed a similar pattern among young, highly educated couples. The husbands gave greater emphasis to feeling responsible for the partner's well-being and putting the spouse's needs first, as well as to spending time together. The wives gave greater importance to emotional involvement and verbal self-disclosure but also were more concerned than the men about maintaining their separate activities and their independence.

The difference between men and women in their views of the significance of practical help was demonstrated in a study in which seven couples recorded their interactions for several days. They noted how pleasant their relations were and counted how often the spouse did a helpful chore, such as cooking a good meal or repairing a faucet, and how often the spouse expressed acceptance or affection. The social scientists doing the study used a feminized definition of love. They labelled practical help as 'instrumental behaviour' and expressions of acceptance or affection as 'affectionate behaviour,' thereby denying the affectionate aspect of practical help. The wives seemed to be using the same scheme; they thought their marital relations were pleasant that day if their husbands had directed a lot of affectionate behaviour to them, regardless of their husbands' positive instrumental behaviour. The husbands' enjoyment of their marital relations, on the other hand, depended on their wives' instrumental actions, not on their expressions of affection. The men actually saw instrumental actions as affection. One husband who was told by the researchers to increase his affectionate behaviour toward his wife decided to wash her car and was surprised when neither his wife nor the researchers accepted that as an 'affectionate' act.

The masculine view of instrumental help as loving behaviour is clearly expressed by a husband discussing his wife's complaints about his lack of communication: 'What does she want? Proof? She's got it, hasn't she? Would I be knocking myself out to get things for her—like to keep up this house—if I didn't love her? Why does a man do things like that if not because he loves his wife and kids? I swear, I can't figure what she wants.' His wife, who has a feminine orientation to love, says something very different: 'It is not enough that he supports us and takes care of us. I appreciate that, but I want him to share things with me. I need for him to tell me his feelings' (Rubin, 1976: 147). Many working-class women agree with men that a man's job is something he does out of love for his family (Rubin, 1976),[8] but middle-class women and social scientists rarely recognize men's practical help as a form of love. (Indeed, among upper-middle-class men whose jobs offer a great deal of intrinsic gratification, their belief that they are 'doing it for the family' may seem somewhat self-serving.)

Other differences between men's and women's styles of love involve sex. Men seem to separate sex and love while women connect them, but paradoxically, sexual intercourse seems to be the most meaningful way of giving and receiving love for many men. A 29-year-old carpenter who had been married for three years said that, after sex, 'I feel so close to her and the kids. We feel like a real family then. I don't talk to her very often, I guess,

but somehow I feel we have really communicated after we have made love' (Garlich, 1982).

Because sexual intimacy is the only recognized 'masculine' way of expressing love, the recent trend toward viewing sex as a way for men and women to express mutual intimacy is an important challenge to the feminization of love. However, the connection between sexuality and love is undermined both by the 'sexual revolution' definition of sex as a form of casual recreation and by the view of male sexuality as a weapon—as in rape—with which men dominate and punish women.

Another paradoxical feature of men's style of love is that men have a more romantic attitude toward their partners than do women. In Reedy's study, men were more likely to select statements like 'we are perfect for each other.' In a survey of college students, 65 per cent of the men but only 24 per cent of the women said that, even if a relationship had all of the other qualities they desired, they would not marry unless they were in love. The common view of this phenomenon focuses on women. The view is that women marry for money and status and so see marriage as instrumentally, rather than emotionally, desirable. This of course is at odds with women's greater concern with self-disclosure and emotional intimacy and lesser concern with instrumental help. A better way to explain men's greater romanticism might be to focus on men. One such possible explanation is that men do not feel responsible for 'working on' the emotional aspects of a relationship, and therefore see love as magically and perfectly present or absent. This is consistent with men's relative lack of concern with affective interaction and greater concern with instrumental help.

In sum, there is a masculine style of love. Except for romanticism, men's style fits the popularly conceived masculine role of being the powerful provider. From the androgynous perspective, the practical help and physical activities included in this role are as much a part of love as the expression of feelings. The feminized perspective cannot account for this masculine style of love; nor can it explain why women and men are so close in the degrees to which they are loving.

Negative Consequences of the Feminization of Love

The division of gender roles in our society that contributes to the two separate styles of love is reinforced by the feminized perspective and leads to political and moral problems that would be mitigated with a more androgynous approach to love. The feminized perspective works against some of the key values and goals of feminists and humanists by contributing to the devaluation and exploitation of women.

It is especially striking how the differences between men's and women's styles of love reinforce men's power over women. Men's style involves giving women important resources, such as money and protection that men control and women believe they need, and ignoring the resources that women control and men need. Thus men's dependency on women remains covert and repressed, while women's dependency on men is overt and exaggerated; and it is overt dependency that creates power, according to social exchange theory. The feminized perspective on love reinforces this power differential by leading to the belief that women need love more than do men, which is implied in the association of love with the feminine role. The effect of this belief is to intensify the asymmetrical dependency of women on men. In fact, however, evidence on the high death rates of unmarried men suggests that men need love at least as much as do women.

Sexual relations can also reinforce male dominance insofar as the man takes the initiative and intercourse is defined either as his 'taking' pleasure or as his being skilled at 'giving' pleasure, either way giving him control. The man's power advantage is further strengthened if the couple assumes that the man's sexual needs can be filled by any attractive woman while the woman's sexual needs can be filled only by the man she loves.

On the other hand, women's preferred ways of loving seem incompatible with control. They involve admitting dependency and sharing or losing control, and being emotionally intense. Further, the intimate talk about personal troubles that appeals to women requires of a couple a mutual vulnerability, a willingness to see oneself as weak and in need of support. It is true that a woman, like a man, can gain some power by providing her partner with services, such as understanding, sex, or cooking; but this power is largely unrecognized because the man's dependency on such services is not overt. The couple may even see these services as her duty or as her response to his requests (or demands).

The identification of love with expressing feelings also contributes to the lack of recognition of women's power by obscuring the instrumental, active component of women's love just as it obscures the loving aspect of men's work. In a culture that glorifies instrumental achievement, this identification devalues both women and love. In reality, a major way by which women are loving is in the clearly instrumental activities associated with caring for others, such as preparing meals, washing clothes, and providing care during illness; but because of our focus on the expressive side of love, this caring work of women is either ignored or redefined as expressing feelings. Thus, from the feminized perspective on love, childcare is a subtle communication of attitudes, not work. A wife washing her husband's shirt is seen as expressing love, even though a husband washing his wife's car is seen as doing a job.

Gilligan, in her critique of theories of human development, shows the way in which devaluing love is linked to devaluing women. Basic to most psychological theories of development is the idea that a healthy person develops from a dependent child to an autonomous, independent adult. As Gilligan comments, 'Development itself comes to be identified with separation, and attachments appear to be developmental impediments' (1982: 12–13). Thus women, who emphasize attachment, are judged to be developmentally retarded or insufficiently individuated.

The pervasiveness of this image was documented in a well-known study of mental health professionals who were asked to describe mental health, femininity, and masculinity. They associated both mental health and masculinity with independence, rationality, and dominance. Qualities concerning attachment, such as being tactful, gentle, or aware of the feelings of others, they associated with femininity but not with mental health (Broverman, et al., 1970).

Another negative consequence of a feminized perspective on love is that it legitimates impersonal, exploitive relations in the workplace and the community. The ideology of separate spheres that developed in the nineteenth century contrasted the harsh, immoral marketplace with the warm and loving home and implied that this contrast is acceptable. Defining love as expressive, feminine, and divorced from productive activity maintains this ideology. If personal relationships and love are reserved for women and the home, then it is acceptable for a manager to underpay workers or for a community to ignore a needy family. Such behaviour is not unloving; it is businesslike or shows a respect for privacy. The ideology of separate spheres also implies that men are properly judged by their instrumental and economic achievements and that poor or unsuccessful men are failures who may deserve a hard life. Levinson (1978) presents a conception of masculine development itself as centering on achieving an occupational dream.

Finally, the feminization of love intensifies the conflicts over intimacy between women and men in close relationships. One of the most common conflicts is that the woman wants more closeness and verbal contact while the man withdraws and wants less pressure. Her need for more closeness is partly the result of the feminization of love, which encourages her to be more emotionally dependent on him. Because love is feminine, he in turn may feel controlled during intimate contact. Intimacy

is her 'turf', an area where she sets the rules and expectations. Talking about the relationship, as she wants, may well feel to him like taking a test that she made up and that he will fail. He is likely to react by withdrawing, causing her to intensify her efforts to get closer. The feminization of love thus can lead to a vicious cycle of conflict where neither partner feels in control or gets what she or he wants.

Conclusion

The values of improving the status of women and humanizing the public sphere are shared by many of the scholars who support a feminized conception of love; and they, too, explain the conflicts in close relationships in terms of polarized gender roles. Nancy Chodorow, Lillian Rubin, and Carol Gilligan have addressed these issues in detail and with great insight in their research. However, by arguing that women's identity is based on attachment while men's identity is based on separation, they reinforce the distinction between feminine expressiveness and masculine instrumentality, revive the ideology of separate spheres, and legitimate the popular idea that only women know the right way to love. They also suggest that there is no way to overcome the rigidity of gender roles other than by pursuing the goal of men and women becoming equally involved in infant care. In contrast, an androgynous perspective on love challenges the identification of women and love with being expressive, powerless, and non-productive and the identification of men with being instrumental, powerful, and productive. It rejects the ideology of separate spheres and validates masculine as well as feminine styles of love. This viewpoint suggests that progress could be made by means of a variety of social changes, including men doing childcare, relations at work becoming more personal and nurturant, and cultural conceptions of love and gender becoming more androgynous. Changes that equalize power within close relationships by equalizing the economic and emotional dependency between men and women may be especially important in moving toward androgynous love.

The validity of an androgynous definition of love cannot be 'proven'; the view that informs the androgynous perspective is that both the feminine style of love (characterized by emotional closeness and verbal self-disclosure) and the masculine style of love (characterized by instrumental help and sex) represent necessary parts of a good love relationship. Who is more loving: a couple who confide most of their experiences to each other but rarely cooperate or give each other practical help, or a couple who help each other through many crises and cooperate in running a household but rarely discuss their personal experiences? Both relationships are limited. Most people would probably choose a combination: a relationship that integrates feminine and masculine styles of loving, an androgynous love.

Notes

1. See John Bowlby, *Attachment and Loss* (New York: Basic Books, 1969), on mother–infant attachment. The quotation is from Elaine Walster and G. William Walster, *A New Look at Love* (Reading, MA: Addison-Wesley Publishing Co., 1978), 9. Conceptions of love and adjustment used by family sociologists are reviewed in Robert Lewis and Graham Spanier, 'Theorizing about the Quality and Stability of Marriage' in *Contemporary Theories about the Family*, W. Burr, R. Hill, F. Nye, and I. Reiss, eds (New York: Free Press, 1979), 268–94.

2. Zick Rubin's scale is described in his article 'Measurement of Romantic Love,' *Journal of Personality and Social Psychology* 16, 2 (1970): 265–73.

3. Dorothy Dinnerstein presents a similar theory in *The Mermaid and the Minotaur: Sexual Arrangements and Human Malaise* (New York: Harper & Row, 1976). Freudian and biological dispositional theories about women's nurturance are surveyed in Jean Stockard and Miriam Johnson, *Sex Roles* (Englewood Cliffs, NJ: Prentice-Hall, Inc., 1980).

4. See also L. Rubin, *Intimate Strangers* (New York: Harper & Row, 1983).

5. I have drawn most heavily on Mary Ryan, *Womanhood in America,* 2nd ed. (New York: New Viewpoints, 1978), and *The Cradle of the Middle Class: The Family in Oneida County, N.Y., 1790–1865* (New York: Cambridge University Press, 1981); Barbara Ehrenreich and Deidre English, *For Her Own Good: 150 Years of Experts Advice to Women* (New York: Anchor Books, 1978); Barbara Welter, 'The Cult of True Womanhood: 1820–1860', *American Quarterly* 18, 2 (1966): 151–74.

6. There are, of course, many exceptions to Miller's generalization, e.g., women who need to be independent or who need an attachment with a woman.

7. Margaret Reedy, 'Age and Sex Differences in Personal Needs and the Nature of Love' (PhD diss. University of Southern California, 1977). Unlike most studies, Reedy did not find that women emphasized communication more than men. Her subjects were upper-middle-class couples who seemed to be very much in love.

8. See L. Rubin, *Worlds of Pain* (New York: Basic Books, 1976); also see Richard Sennett and Jonathan Cobb, *Hidden Injuries of Class* (New York: Vintage, 1973).

References

Adams, B. 1968. *Kinship in an Urban Setting*. Chicago: Markham Publishing Co.

Broverman, I., F. Clarkson, P. Rosenkrantz, and S. Vogel. 1970. 'Sex-Role Stereotypes and Clinical Judgments of Mental Health', *Journal of Consulting Psychology* 34, 1: 1–7.

Chodorow, N. 1978. *The Reproduction of Mothering*. Berkeley: University of California Press.

Garlich, C. 1982. 'Interviews of Married Couples'. University of California: Irvine, School of Social Sciences.

Gilligan, C. 1982. *In a Different Voice*. Cambridge, MA: Harvard University Press.

Levinson, D. 1978. *The Seasons of a Man's Life*. New York: Alfred A. Knopf.

Lowenthal, M., and C. Haven. 1968. 'Interaction and Adaptation: Intimacy as a Critical Variable', *American Sociological Review* 22, 4: 20–30.

Maslow, A. 1970. *Motivation and Personality,* 2nd ed. New York: Harper & Row.

Miller, J.B. 1976. *Toward a New Psychology of Women*. Boston: Beacon Press.

Rubin, L. 1976. *Worlds of Pain*. New York: Basic Books.

———. 1983. *Intimate Strangers*. New York: Harper & Row.

Rubin, Z. 1970. 'Measurement of Romantic Love', *Journal of Personality and Social Psychology* 16, 2: 265–73.

Walster, E., and G.W. Walster. 1978. *A New Look at Love*. Reading, MA: Addison-Wesley Publishing Co.

CHAPTER 33

Dating and Romantic Relationships among Gay, Lesbian, and Bisexual Youths

Ritch C. Savin-Williams

The Importance of Dating and Romance

According to Scarf (1987), the developmental significance of an intimate relationship is to help us 'contact archaic, dimly perceived and yet powerfully meaningful aspects of our inner selves' (79). We desire closeness within the context of a trusting, intimate relationship. Attachment theory posits that humans are prewired for loving and for developing strongly felt emotional attachments (Bowlby, 1973). When established, we experience safety, security, and nurturance. Early attachments, including those in infancy, are thought to circumscribe an internal blueprint that profoundly affects future relationships, such as the establishment of intimate friendships and romances in adolescence and adulthood (Hazan and Shaver, 1987).

Developmentally, dating is a means by which romantic relationships are practiced, pursued, and established. It serves a number of important functions, such as entertainment, recreation, and socialization, which assist participants in developing appropriate means of interacting. It also enhances peer group status and facilitates the selection of a mate (Skipper and Nass, 1966). Adolescents who are most confident in their dating abilities begin dating during early adolescence, date frequently, are satisfied with their dating, and are most likely to become involved in a 'committed' dating relationship (Herold, 1979).

The establishment of romantic relationships is important for youths regardless of sexual orientation. Isay (1989) noted that falling in love was a critical factor in helping his gay clients feel comfortable with their gay identity and that 'the self-affirming value of a mutual relationship over time cannot be overemphasized' (50). Browning regarded lesbian love relationships as an opportunity to enhance:

. . . the development of the individual's adult identity by validating her personhood, reinforcing that she deserves to receive and give love. A relationship can also be a source of tremendous emotional support as the woman explores her goals, values, and relationship to the world (1987: 51).

Because dating experience increases the likelihood that an intimate romantic relationship will evolve, the absence of this opportunity may have long-term repercussions. Malyon noted some of the reverberations:

Their most charged sexual desires are usually seen as perverted, and their deepest feelings of psychological attachment are regarded as unacceptable. This social disapproval interferes with the preintimacy involvement that fosters the evolution of maturity and self-respect in the domain of object relations (1981: 326).

Culture's Devaluation of Same-sex Relationships

Relatively speaking, our culture is far more willing to turn a blind eye to sexual than to romantic relationships among same-sex adolescent partners. Same-sex activity may appear 'temporary', an experiment, a phase, or a perverted source of fun. But falling in love with someone of the same gender and maintaining a sustained emotional involvement with that person implies an irreversible deviancy at worst and a bad decision at best. In our homes, schools, religious institutions, and media, we teach that intense relationships after early adolescence among members of the same sex 'should' raise the concern of good parents, good friends, and good teachers. One result is that youths of all sexual orientations may become frightened of developing close friendships with same-sex peers. They fear that these friendships will be viewed as sexually intimate.

It is hardly surprising that a sexual-minority adolescent can easily become 'the loneliest person . . . in the typical high school of today' (Norton, 1976: 376):

For the homosexual-identified student, high school is often a lonely place where, from every vantage point, there are couples: couples holding hands as they enter school; couples dissolving into an endless wet kiss between school bells; couples exchanging rings with ephemeral vows of devotion and love (Sears, 1991: 326–7).

The separation of a youth's homoerotic passion from the socially sanctioned act of heterosexual dating can generate self-doubt, anger, and resentment, and can ultimately retard or distort the development of interpersonal intimacy during the adolescent years. Thus, many youths never consider same-sex dating to be a reasonable option, except in their fantasies. Scientific and clinical writings that ignore same-sex romance and dating among youth contribute to this conspiracy of silence. Sexual-minority youth struggle with issues of identity and intimacy because important impediments rooted in our cultural values and attitudes deter them from dating those they love and instead mandate that they date those they cannot love.

Empirical Studies of Same-sex Romantic Relationships among Youth

Until the last several years same-sex relationships among sexual-minority youths were seldom recognized in the empirical, scientific literature. With the recent visibility of gay, bisexual, and lesbian youths in the culture at large, social and behavioural scientists are beginning to conduct research focusing on various developmental processes of such youths, including their sexuality and intimacy.

Bisexual, lesbian, and gay youths, whether in Detroit, Minneapolis, Pennsylvania, New York, or the Netherlands, report that they desire to have long-lasting, committed same-sex romantic relationships in their future (Sanders, 1980; Savin-Williams, 1990; D'Augelli, 1991). According to Silverstein (1981), establishing a romantic relationship with a same-sex partner helps one to feel 'chosen', to resolve issues of sexual identity, and to feel more complete. Indeed, those who are in a long-term love relationship generally have high levels of self-esteem and self-acceptance.[1]

Although there are few published studies of teens that focus primarily on their same-sex dating or romantic relationships, there are suggestive data that debunk the myth in our culture that gays, lesbians, and bisexuals neither want nor maintain steady, loving same-sex relationships. In two studies of gay and bisexual male youths, same-sex relationships are regarded as highly desirable. Among 29 Minnesota youths, 10 had a steady male partner at the time of the interview, 11 had been in a same-sex relationship, and, most tellingly, all but 2 hoped for a steady male partner in their future (Remafedi, 1987). For these youths, many of whom were living independently with friends or on the street, being in a long-term relationship was considered to be an ideal state. With a college-age sample of 61 males, D'Augelli (1991) reported similar results. One half of his sample was 'partnered', and their most troubling mental health concern was termination of a close relationship, ranking just ahead of telling parents about their homosexuality.

The difficulty, however, is to maintain a visible same-sex romance in high school. Sears (1991) interviewed 36 Southern late adolescent and young adult lesbians, gays, and bisexuals. He discovered that although nearly everyone had heterosexually dated in high school, very few dated a member of the same sex during that time. Because of concerns about secrecy and the lack of social support, most same-sex romances involved little emotional commitment and were of short duration. None were overt.

Research with over 300 gay, bisexual, and lesbian youths between the ages of 14 and 23 years (Savin-Williams, 1990) supports the finding that sexual-minority youths have romantic relationships during adolescence and young adulthood. Almost 90 per cent of the females and two-thirds of the males reported that they have had a romantic relationship. Of the total number of romances listed, 60 per cent were with same-sex partners. The male youths were slightly more likely than lesbian and bisexual female youths to begin their romantic career with a same-sex, rather than an opposite-sex partner.

In the same study, the lesbians and bisexual females who had a high proportion of same-sex romances were most likely to be 'out' to others. However, their self-esteem level was essentially the same as those who had a high percentage of heterosexual relationships. If she began same-sex dating early, during adolescence, then a lesbian or bisexual female also tended to be in a current relationship and to experience long-lasting romances. Gay and bisexual male youths who had a large percentage of adolescent romantic relationships with boys had high self-esteem. They were more likely to be publicly 'out' to friends and family if they had had a large number of romances. Boys who initiated same-sex romances at an early age were more likely to report that they have had long-term and multiple same-sex relationships.

The findings from these studies are admittedly sparse and do not provide the depth and insight that are needed to help us better understand the experience of being in a same-sex romantic relationship. They do illustrate that youths have same-sex romances while in high school. Where there is desire, some youths will find a way. Sexually active same-sex friendships may evolve into romantic relationships (Savin-Williams, 1995), and those most publicly out are most likely to have had adolescent same-sex romances. Certainly, most lesbian, gay, and bisexual youths value the importance of a same-sex, lifelong, committed relationship in their adult years.

Perhaps the primary issue is not the absence of same-sex romances during adolescence, but the hidden nature of the romances. They are seldom recognized and rarely supported or celebrated. The research data offer little information regarding the psychological impact of not being involved in a same-sex romantic relationship or of having to hide such a relationship when it exists. For this, one must turn to stories of the personal struggles of adolescents.

Personal Struggles

Youths who have same-sex romances during their adolescence face a severe struggle to have these relationships acknowledged and supported. Gibson (1989) noted the troubling contradictions:

> The first romantic involvements of lesbian and gay male youth are a source of great joy to them in affirming their sexual identity, providing them with support, and assuring them that they too can experience love. However, society places extreme hardships on these relationships that make them difficult to establish and maintain (130).

A significant number of youths, perhaps those feeling most insecure regarding their sexual identity, may fantasize about being sexually intimate with a same-sex partner but have little hope that it could in fact become a reality. One youth, Lawrence, reported this feeling in his coming-out story:

> While growing up, love was something I watched other people experience and enjoy. . . . The countless men I secretly loved and fantasized about were only in private, empty dreams in which love was never

returned. I seemed to be the only person in the world with no need for love and companionship. . . . Throughout high school and college I had no way to meet people of the same sex and sexual orientation. These were more years of isolation and secrecy. I saw what other guys my age did, listened to what they said and how they felt. I was expected to be part of a world with which I had nothing in common (Curtis, 1988: 109–10).

A young lesbian, Diane, recalled that 'love of women was never a possibility that I even realized could be. You loved your mother and your aunts, and you had girlfriends for a while. Someday, though, you would always meet a man' (Stanley and Wolfe, 1980: 47). Girls dated boys and not other girls. Because she did not want to date boys, she did not date.

Another youth knew he had homoerotic attractions, but he never fathomed that they could be expressed to the boy that he most admired, his high school soccer teammate. It took alcohol and the right situation:

> I knew I was checking out the guys in the shower after soccer practice. I thought of myself as hetero who had the urge for males. I fought it, said it was a phase. And then it happened.
>
> Derek was my best friend. After soccer practice the fall of our junior year we celebrated both making the 'A' team by getting really drunk. We were just fooling around and suddenly our pants were off. I was so scared I stayed out of school for three days but we kept being friends and nothing was said until a year later when I came out to everyone and he came up to me with these tears and asked if he made me homosexual (Savin-Williams, 1995).

It is never easy for youths to directly confront the mores of peers whose values and attitudes are routinely supported by the culture. Nearly all youths know implicitly the rules of socially appropriate behaviour and the consequences of nonconformity. This single, most influential barrier to same-sex dating, the threat posed by peers, can have severe repercussions. The penalty for crossing the line of 'normalcy' can result in emotional and physical pain.

Peer Harassment as a Barrier to Dating

Price (1982) concluded, 'Adolescents can be very cruel to others who are different, who do not conform to the expectations of the peer group' (472). Very little has changed in the last decade. For example, 17-year-old actor Ryan Phillippe worried about the consequences on his family and friends if he played a gay teen on ABC's soap opera *One Life to Live* (Gable, 1992: 3D). David Ruffin, 19, of Ferndale, Michigan, explained why he boycotted his high school senior prom: 'The kids could tell I was different from them, and I think I was different because I was gay. And when you're dealing with young people, different means not cool' (Bruni, 1992: 10A).

Unlike heterosexual dating, little social advantage, such as peer popularity or acceptance, is gained by holding hands and kissing a same-sex peer in school hallways, shopping malls, or synagogues. Lies are spun to protect secrets and to avoid peer harassment. One lesbian youth, Kim, felt that she had to be an actress around her friends. She lied to friends by creating 'Andrew' when she was dating 'Andrea' over the weekend (Bruni, 1992).

To avoid harassment, sexual minority adolescents may monitor their interpersonal interactions. They may wonder, 'Am I standing too close?' or 'Do I appear too happy to see him(her)?' (Anderson, 1987). Hetrick and Martin (1987) found that youths are often apprehensive to show 'friendship for a friend of the same sex for fear of being misunderstood or giving away their secretly held sexual orientation' (31). If erotic desires

become aroused and threaten expression, youths may seek to terminate same-sex friendships rather than risk revealing their secret. For many adolescents, especially bisexual youths, relationships with the other sex may be easier to develop. The appeal of such relationships is that peers will view the youths as heterosexual, thus peer acceptance will be enhanced and the threat of harassment and rejection will be reduced. The result is that some sexual-minority youths feel inherently 'fake' and they therefore retreat from becoming intimate with others. Although they may meet the implicit and explicit demands of their culture, it is at a cost—their sense of authenticity.

Faking It: Heterosexual Sex and Dating

Retrospective data from gay, bisexual, and lesbian adults reveal the extent to which heterosexual dating and sex are commonplace during the adolescent and young adult years (Schafer, 1976; Bell and Weinberg, 1978; Troiden and Goode, 1980). These might be one-night stands, brief romances, or long-term relationships. Across various studies, nearly two-thirds of gay men and three-quarters of lesbians report having had heterosexual sex in their past. Motivations include fun, curiosity, denial of homoerotic feelings, and pressure to conform to society's insistence on heterosexual norms and behaviours. Even though heterosexual sex often results in a low level of sexual gratification, it is deemed a necessary sacrifice to meet the expectations of peers and, by extension, receive their approval. Only later, as adults, when they have the opportunity to compare these heterosexual relationships with same-sex ones do they fully realize that which they had missed during their younger years.

Several studies with lesbian, bisexual, and gay adolescents document the extent to which they are sexually involved with opposite-sex partners. Few gay and bisexual [male] youth had *extensive* sexual contact with females, even among those who began heterosexual sex at an early age. Sex with one or two girls was usually considered 'quite enough'. Not infrequently these girls were best friends who expressed a romantic or sexual interest in the gay boys. The male youths liked the girls, but they preferred friendships rather than sexual relations. One youth expressed this dilemma:

> She was a year older and we had been friends for a long time before beginning dating. It was a date with the full thing: dinner, theater, alcohol, making out, sex. At her house and I think we both came during intercourse. I was disappointed because it was such hard work—not physically I mean but emotionally. Later on in my masturbation my fantasies were never of her. We did it once more in high school and then once more when we were in college. I labelled it love but not sexual love. I really wanted them to occur together. It all ended when I labelled myself gay (Savin-Williams, 1995).

An even greater percentage of lesbian and bisexual female adolescents engaged in heterosexual sexual experiences—2 of every 3 (Herdt and Boxer, 1993), 3 of every 4 (Sears, 1991), and 8 of every 10 (Savin-Williams, 1990). Heterosexual activity began as early as second grade and as late as senior year in high school. Few of these girls, however, had extensive sex with boys—usually with two or three boys within the context of dating. Eighteen-year-old Kimba noted that she went through a heterosexual stage:

> . . . trying to figure out what was so great about guys sexually. I still don't understand. I guess that, for straights, it is like it is for me when I am with a woman. . . . I experimented in whatever ways I thought would make a difference, but it was no go. My closest friends are guys; there is caring and closeness between us (Heron, 1983: 82).

Georgina also tried to follow a heterosexual script:

> In sixth and seventh grades you start wearing makeup, you start getting your hair cut, you start liking boys—you start thinking about letting them 'French kiss' you. I did all those major things. But, I still didn't feel very satisfied with myself. I remember I never really wanted to be intimate with any guy. I always wanted to be their best friend (Sears, 1991: 327).

One young lesbian, Lisa, found herself 'having sex with boys to prove I wasn't gay. Maybe I was even trying to prove it to myself! I didn't enjoy having sex with boys' (Heron, 1983: 76). These three lesbian youths forfeited a sense of authenticity, intimacy, and love because they were taught that emotional intimacy can only be achieved with members of the other sex.

The reasons sexual-minority adolescents gave as to why they engaged in heterosexual sex were similar to those reported in retrospective studies by adults. The youths needed to test whether their heterosexual attractions were as strong as their homoerotic ones—thus attempting to disconfirm their homosexuality—and to mask their homosexuality so as to win peer- and self-acceptance and to avoid peer rejection. Many youths believed that they could not really know whether they were lesbian, gay, bisexual, or heterosexual without first experiencing heterosexual sex. For many, however, heterosexual activities consisted of sex without feelings that they tried to enjoy without much success (Herdt and Boxer, 1993). Heterosexual sex felt unnatural because it lacked the desired emotional intensity. One young gay youth reported:

> We'd been dating for three months. I was 15 and she, a year or so older. We had petted previously and so she planned this event. We attempted intercourse in her barn, but I

was too nervous. I didn't feel good afterwards because it was not successful. We did it every week for a month or so. It was fun but it wasn't a big deal. But then I did not have a great lust or drive. This was just normal I guess. It gave me something to do to tell the other guys who were always bragging (Savin-Williams, 1995).

Similarly, Kimberly always had a steady heterosexual relationship: 'It was like I was just going through the motions. It was expected of me, so I did it. I'd kiss him or embrace him but it was like I was just there. He was probably enjoying it, but I wasn't' (Sears, 1991: 327).

Jacob, an African American adolescent, dated the prettiest girls in his school in order to maintain his image: 'It was more like President Reagan entertaining heads of state. It's expected of you when you're in a certain position' (Sears, 1991: 126–7). Another Southern male youth, Grant, used 'group dates' to reinforce his heterosexual image. Rumours that he was gay were squelched because his jock friends came to his defense: 'He's not a fag. He has a girlfriend' (Sears, 1991: 328).

These and other personal stories of youths vividly recount the use of heterosexual sex and dating as a cover for an emerging same-sex or bisexual identity. Dating provides opportunities to temporarily 'pass' as straight until the meaning of homoerotic feelings are resolved or youths find a safe haven to be lesbian or gay. Heterosexual sex and dating may be less pleasurable than same-sex encounters, but many sexual-minority youths feel that the former are the only safe, acceptable options.

Impediments and Consequences

The difficulties inherent in dating same-sex partners during adolescence are monumental. First is the fundamental difficulty of finding a suitable partner. The vast majority of lesbian, bisexual, and gay youths are closeted, not out to themselves, let alone to others. A second barrier is the consequences of same-sex dating, such as verbal and physical harassment from peers. A third impediment is the lack of public recognition or 'celebration' of those who are romantically involved with a member of the same gender. Thus, same-sex dating remains hidden and mysterious, something that is either ridiculed, condemned, or ignored.

The consequences of an exclusively heterosexually oriented atmosphere in the peer social world can be severe and enduring. An adolescent may feel isolated and socially excluded from the world of peers. Sex with others of the same gender may be associated exclusively with anonymous, guilt-ridden encounters, handicapping the ability to develop healthy intimate relationships in adulthood. Denied the opportunity for romantic involvement with someone of the same sex, a youth may suffer impaired self-esteem that reinforces the belief that one is unworthy of love, affection, and intimacy. One youth, Rick, even doubted his ability to love:

When I started my senior year, I was still unclear about my sexuality. I had dated women with increasing frequency, but never felt love for any of them. I discovered that I could perform sexually with a woman, but heterosexual experiences were not satisfying emotionally. I felt neither love nor emotional oneness with women. Indeed, I had concluded that I was incapable of human love (Heron, 1983: 95–6).

If youths are to take advantage of opportunities to explore their erotic sexuality, it is sometimes, at least for males, confined to clandestine sexual encounters, void of romance, affection, and intimacy but replete with misgivings, anonymity, and guilt.

Ted was 21 and me, 16. It was New Year's Eve and it was a swimming pool party at my rich friend's house. Not sure why Ted was there but he really came on to me, even putting his arm around me in front of everyone. I wasn't ready for that but I liked it. New Year's Day, every time Ted looked at me I looked away because I thought it was obvious that we had had sex. It did clarify things for me. It didn't feel like I was cheating on [my girlfriend] Beth because the sex felt so different, so right (Savin-Williams, 1995).

A gay youth may have genital contact with another boy without ever kissing him because to do so would be too meaningful. Remafedi (1990) found this escape from intimacy to be very damaging: 'Without appropriate opportunities for peer dating and socialization, gay youth frequently eschew intimacy altogether and resort to transient and anonymous sexual encounters with adults' (1173). One consequence is the increased risk for contracting sexually transmitted diseases, including HIV. This is particularly risky for youths who turn to prostitution to meet their intimacy needs (Coleman, 1989).

When youths eventually match their erotic and intimacy needs, they may be surprised with the results. This was Jacob's experience (Sears, 1991) when he fell in love with Warren, an African American senior who also sang in the choir. Sex quickly evolved into 'an emotional thing'. Jacob explained: 'He got to the point of telling me he loved me. That was the first time anybody ever said any thing like that. It was kind of hard to believe that even after sex there are really feelings' (127).

Equally common, however, especially among closeted youths, is that lesbian, bisexual, and gay teens may experience a poverty of intimacy in their lives and considerable social and emotional isolation. One youth, Grant, enjoyed occasional sex with a star football player, but he was devastated by the subsequent exclusion the athlete meted out to him: 'We would see each other and barely speak but after school we'd see each other a lot. He had his image that he had to keep up and,

since it was rumored that I was gay, he didn't want to get a close identity with me' (Sears, 1991: 330).

Largely because of negative peer prohibitions and the lack of social support and recognition, same-sex romances that are initiated have difficulty flourishing. Irwin met Benji in the eighth grade and was immediately attracted to him (Sears, 1991). They shared interests in music and academics and enjoyed long conversations, playing music, and riding in the country-side. Eventually, their attractions for each other were expressed and a romantic, sexual relationship began. Although Irwin was in love with Benji, their relationship soon ended because it was no match for the social pressures and personal goals that conflicted with Irwin being in a same-sex relationship.

Georgina's relationship with Kay began dramatically with intense feelings that were at times ambivalent for both of them. At one point she overheard Kay praying, 'Dear Lord, forgive me for the way I am' (Sears, 1991: 333). Georgina's parents demanded that she end her 'friendship' with Kay. Georgina told classmates they were just 'good friends' and began dating boys as a cover. Despite her love for Kay, the relationship ended when Georgina's boyfriend told her that no one liked her because she hung around 'that dyke, Kay'. In retrospect, Georgina wished: 'If everybody would have accepted everybody, I would have stayed with Kay' (334).

Given this situation, lesbian, bisexual, and gay youths in same-sex relationships may place unreasonable and ultimately destructive demands on each other. For example, they may expect that the relationship will resolve all fears of loneliness and isolation and validate all aspects of their personal identity (Browning, 1987).

A Success Story

A vivid account of how a same-sex romantic relationship can empower a youth is depicted in the seminal autobiography of Aaron Fricke (1981),

Reflections of a Rock Lobster. He fell in love with a classmate, Paul:

> With Paul's help, I started to challenge all the prejudice I had encountered during 16 1/2 years of life. Sure, it was scary to think that half my classmates might hate me if they knew my secret, but from Paul's example I knew it was possible to one day be strong and face them without apprehension (Fricke, 1981: 44).

Through Paul, Aaron became more resilient and self-confident:

> His strengths were my strengths. . . . I realized that my feelings for him were unlike anything I had felt before. The sense of camaraderie was familiar from other friendships; the deep spiritual love I felt for Paul was new. So was the openness, the sense of communication with another (Fricke, 1981: 45).

Life gained significance. He wrote poems. He planned a future. He learned to express both kindness and strength. Aaron was in love, with another boy. But no guidelines or models existed on how best to express these feelings:

> Heterosexuals learn early in life what behavior is expected of them. They get practice in their early teens having crushes, talking to their friends about their feelings, going on first dates and to chaperoned parties, and figuring out their feelings. Paul and I hadn't gotten all that practice; our relationship was formed without much of a model to base it on. It was the first time either of us had been in love like this and we spent much of our time just figuring out what that meant for us (Fricke, 1981: 46).

Eventually, after a court case that received national attention, Aaron won the right to take Paul to the senior prom as his date. This victory was relatively minor compared to the self-respect, authenticity, and pride in being gay that their relationship won for each of them.

Final Reflections

As a clinical and developmental psychologist, I find it disheartening to observe our culture ignoring and condemning sexual-minority youth. One consequence is that myths and stereotypes are perpetuated that interfere with or prevent youths from developing intimate same-sex relationships with those to whom they are erotically and emotionally attracted. Separating passion from affection, engaging in sex with strangers in impersonal and sometimes unsafe places, and finding alienation rather than intimacy in those relationships are not conducive to psychological health. In one study the most common reason given for initial suicide attempts by lesbians and gay men was relationship problems (Bell and Weinberg, 1978).

A youth's limited ability to meet other bisexual, lesbian, and gay adolescents compounds a sense of isolation and alienation. Crushes may develop on 'unknowing friends, teachers, and peers. These are often cases of unrequited love with the youth never revealing their true feelings' (Gibson, 1989: 131).

Sexual-minority youths need the validation of those around them as they attempt to develop a personal integrity and to discover those similar to themselves. How long can gay, bisexual, and lesbian adolescents maintain their charades before they encounter difficulty separating the pretensions from the realities? Many 'use' heterosexual dating to blind themselves and others. By so doing they attempt to disconfirm to themselves the growing encroachment of their homoerotic attractions while escaping derogatory name calling and gaining peer status and prestige. The incidence of heterosexual sex and relationships in the adolescence of gay men and lesbians attests to these desires.

Future generations of adolescents will no doubt find it easier to establish same-sex relationships. This is due in part to the dramatic increase in the visibility that adult same-sex relationships have received during the last few years. Domestic partnership ordinances in several cities and counties, victories for spousal equivalency rights in businesses, court cases addressing adoption by lesbian couples, challenges to marriage laws by several male couples, the dramatic story of the life partnership of Karen Thompson and Sharon Kowalski, and the marriage of former Mr Universe Bob Paris to male Supermodel Rod Jackson raise public awareness of same-sex romantic relationships. Even Ann Landers (1992) is spreading the word. In a column, an 18-year-old gay teen from Santa Barbara requested that girls quit hitting on him because, as he explained, 'I have a very special friend who is a student at the local university . . . and [we] are very happy with each other' (Landers, 1992: 2B).

A decade after Aaron Fricke fought for and won the right to take his boyfriend to the prom, a dozen lesbian, gay, and bisexual youths in the Detroit-Ann Arbor area arranged to have their own prom. Most felt excluded from the traditional high school prom, which they considered 'a final, bitter postscript to painful years of feeling left out' (Bruni, 1992: 10A). Seventeen-year-old Brenda said, 'I want to feel rich for one moment. I want to feel all glamorous, just for one night' (Bruni, 1992: 10A). Going to the 'Fantasy' prom was a celebration that created a sense of pride, a connection with other sexual-minority teens, and a chance to dance—'two girls together, unguarded and unashamed, in the middle of a room filled with teenagers just like them' (Bruni, 1992: 10A). One year later, I attended this prom with my life partner and the number of youths in attendance had increased six-fold.

We need to listen to youths such as Aaron, Diane, and Georgina, to hear their concerns, insights, and solutions. Most of all, we need to end the invisibility of same-sex romantic relationships. It is easily within our power to enhance the well being of millions of youths, including 'Billy Joe', a character in a famous Bobbie Gentry song. If Billy Joe had seen an option to a heterosexual life style, he might have considered an alternative to ending his life by jumping off the Tallahatchie Bridge.

Note

1. The causal pathway, however, is unclear (Savin-Williams, 1990). That is, being in a same-sex romance may build positive self-regard, but it may also be true that those with high self-esteem are more likely to form love relationships and to stay in them.

References

Anderson, D. 1987. 'Family and Peer Relations of Gay Adolescents', in S.C. Geinstein, ed., *Adolescent Psychiatry: Developmental and Clinical Studies: Vol. 14*, pp. 162–78. Chicago: The University of Chicago Press.

Bell, A.P., and M.S. Weinberg. 1978. *Homosexualities: A Study of Diversity among Men and Women*. New York: Simon & Schuster.

Bowlby, J. 1973. *Attachment and Loss: Vol. 2. Separation*. New York: Basic Books.

Browning, C. 1987. 'Therapeutic Issues and Intervention Strategies with Young Adult Lesbian Clients: A Developmental Approach', *Journal of Homosexuality* 14: 45–52.

Bruni, F. 1992. 'A Prom Night of Their Own to Dance, Laugh, Reminisce', *Detroit Free Press*, 22 May: 1A, 10A.

Coleman, E. 1989. 'The Development of Male Prostitution Activity among Gay and Bisexual Adolescents', *Journal of Homosexuality* 17: 131–49.

Curtis, W., ed. 1988. *Revelations: A Collection of Gay Male Coming Out Stories*. Boston: Alyson.

D'Augelli, A.R. 1991. 'Gay Men in College: Identity Processes and Adaptations', *Journal of College Student Development* 32: 140–6.

Fricke, A. 1981. *Reflections of a Rock Lobster: A Story About Growing Up Gay*. Boston: Alyson.

Gable, D. 1992, June 2. '"Life" Story Looks at Roots of Homophobia', *USA Today*, 2 June: 3D.

Gibson, P. 1989. 'Gay Male and Lesbian Youth Suicide', in M.R. Feinleib, ed., *Report of the Secretary's Task Force on Youth Suicide, Vol. 3: Prevention and Interventions in Youth Suicide (3-1103-142)*. Rockville, MD: US Department of Health and Human Services.

Hazan, C., and P. Shaver. 1987. 'Romantic Love Conceptualized as an Attachment Process', *Journal of Personality and Social Psychology* 52: 511–24.

Herdt, G., and A. Boxer. 1993. *Children of Horizons: How Gay and Lesbian Teens are Leading a New Way Out of the Closet*. Boston: Beacon.

Herold, E.S. 1979. 'Variables Influencing the Dating Adjustment of University Students', *Journal of Youth and Adolescence* 8: 73–9.

Heron, A., ed. 1983. *One Teenager in Ten*. Boston: Alyson.

Hetrick, E.S., and A.D. Martin. 1987. 'Developmental Issues and Their Resolution for Gay and Lesbian Adolescents', *Journal of Homosexuality* 14: 25–44.

Isay, R.A. 1989. *Being Homosexual: Gay Men and Their Development*. New York: Avon.

Landers, A. 1992. 'Gay Teen Tired of Advances from Sexually Aggressive Girls', *Detroit Free Press*, 26 May: 2B.

Malyon, A.K. 1981. 'The Homosexual Adolescent: Developmental Issues and Social Bias', *Child Welfare* 60: 321–30.

Norton, J.L. 1976. 'The Homosexual and Counseling', *Personnel and Guidance Journal* 54: 374–7.

Price, J.H. 1982. 'High School Students' Attitudes toward Homosexuality', *Journal of School Health* 52: 469–74.

Remafedi, G. 1987. 'Male Homosexuality: The Adolescent's Perspective', *Pediatrics* 79: 326–30.

———. 1990. 'Fundamental Issues in the Care of Homosexual Youth', *Adolescent Medicine* 74: 1169–79.

Sanders, G. 1980. 'Homosexualities in the Netherlands', *Alternative Lifestyles* 3: 278–311.

Savin-Williams, R.C. 1990. *Gay and Lesbian Youth: Expressions of Identity*. New York: Hemisphere.

———. 1994. 'Dating Those You Can't Love and Loving Those You Can't Date', in R. Montemayor, G.R. Adams, and T.P. Gullotta, eds, *Personal Relationships during Adolescence: Vol 6. Advances in Adolescent Development*, pp. 196–215. Newbury Park, CA: Sage.

———. 1995. *Sex and Sexual Identity among Gay and Bisexual Males*. Manuscript in preparation, Cornell University, Ithaca, NY.

Scarf, M. 1987. *Intimate Partners: Patterns in Love and Marriage*. New York: Random House.

Schafer, S. 1976. 'Sexual and Social Problems of Lesbians', *Journal of Sex Research* 12: 50–69.

Sears, J.T. 1991. *Growing Up Gay in the South: Race, Gender, and Journeys of the Spirit*. New York: Harrington Park Press.

Silverstein, C. 1981. *Man to Man: Gay Couples in America*. New York: William Morrow.

Skipper, J.K., Jr, and G. Nass. 1966. 'Dating Behavior: A Framework for Analysis and an Illustration', *Journal of Marriage and the Family* 27: 412–20.

Stanley, J.P., and S.J. Wolfe, eds. 1980. *The Coming Out Stories*. New York: Persephone.

Troiden, R.R., and E. Goode. 1980. 'Variables Related to the Acquisition of a Gay Identity', *Journal of Homosexuality* 5: 383–92.

CHAPTER 34

Losing It: Similarities and Differences in First Intercourse Experiences of Men and Women[1]

Lily Tsui and Elena Nicoladis

Introduction

Historically, a woman's virginity was crucial to marriage in terms of both honour and value; women who were found not to be virgins on their wedding night (often determined by the presence of blood at first intercourse) were seen as worthless in many cultures. In contrast, 'proof' of male virginity is unavailable physically and less important culturally. Such differences in how virginity has been perceived in society have created an environment in which men and women may have different perceptions of first intercourse and its meanings.

Quantitative studies have demonstrated gender differences in both attitudes toward and actual experience of first intercourse. For example, Carpenter (2001) found that women were twice as likely as men to think of their virginity as a gift to a future partner (61 per cent versus 36 per cent), while men were three times more likely than women to view their virginity as a stigma (57 per cent versus 21 per cent). Darling, Davidson, and Passarello (1992) found that a greater percentage of men than women perceived their first intercourse to be physiologically satisfying (81 per cent versus 28 per cent) and psychologically satisfying (67 per cent versus 28 per cent).

Qualitative studies based on feminist analyses of power differences between men and women have suggested possible explanations for such findings. For example, young adults' accounts of first sexual intercourse reveal that men gain an affirmation of manhood through first intercourse. It is thus primarily a young man's moment that marks his 'coming of age' or his entry into manhood (Holland, Ramazanoglu, Sharpe, and Thomson, 2000). However, the dependence on women for this validation of men has taken on multiple social meanings, many of which are viewed by feminist thinkers as embedded in a patriarchal culture.

Holland et al. (2000) found that young men's accounts of first intercourse were mostly concerned with their own performance, orgasm, and sense of having reached a landmark. Their partners' pleasure or orgasm was seen as 'icing on the cake'. The problem with young men having this construction of first intercourse is that it leaves young women to cope with first intercourse experiences that may fail to meet their own expectations to affirm feelings of love and romance (Holland et al., 2000). In this view, sex differences in first intercourse experiences have their basis in different perceptions of its meaning and in constructions of sexuality.

Burr (2001) argues that the contemporary construction of men's sexuality as 'active, dynamic, powerful, and, potentially uncontrollable' also portrays women's sexuality as essentially passive. In this construction, sex for women is not about active participation but about something that is received (Darling et al., 1992). Women may thus be seen as dependent on men for introducing them to the physical pleasure aspects of sexual activities because conventional femininity demands that a woman appear to be sexually unknowing, to desire not just sex but a relationship, to let sex 'happen' without requesting it, to trust, to love, and to make men happy (Holland et al., 2000). Traditional dating scenarios reinforced this perspective in that the woman was expected to wait for the man to ask her out and the man was expected to handle details of cost, transportation, and activity (Allgeier and Royster, 1991).

Social discourses around sexuality, and particularly female sexuality, reflect and influence personal and educational perspectives on first intercourse. Fine (1997) identifies three such discourses. The first discourse, sexuality as violence, instills fear of sex by focusing on abuse, incest, and other negative outcomes of sexual activity. The second discourse, sexuality as victimization, identifies females as subject to the pressuring tendencies of male sexuality and focuses attention on the risk of women 'being used' or coerced and thus on ways to avoid the physical, social, and emotional risks of sexual intimacy. Messages related to unintended pregnancy and sexually transmitted infections (STIs) may reinforce notions of risk and are used by some to pressure for classroom priority on strategies to avoid sex, 'saying no', and 'abstinence only' approaches to sexuality education. In this context, Fine's third discourse, sexuality as individual morality, would value women's choice about sexuality as long as the choice is premarital abstinence. Such discourses, Fine suggests, lead to a construction of sexuality where the male is in search of desire and the female is in search of protection. Largely absent from public sexual education is a fourth discourse, sexuality as desire. Fine notes that

> The naming of desire, pleasure, or sexual entitlement, particularly for females, barely exists in the formal agenda of public schooling on sexuality . . . a genuine discourse of desire would invite adolescents to explore what feels good and bad, desirable and undesirable,

grounded in experiences, needs, and limits (Fine, 1997).

THE PRESENT STUDY

Given the questions implicit in these background observations, the present study sought to identify university students' perspectives on various aspects of their first experience of consensual heterosexual sexual intercourse. The questionnaire designed for this purpose dealt with precursors to, experience of, and subsequent feelings about first intercourse. Students who had not had intercourse answered selected questions based on their expectations.

Apart from the anticipation arising from the literature review that men's and women's experiences would differ and that men's would be more positive, we refrained from making more specific hypotheses. This reticence was due to our perception that the literature had given a clearer picture of what to ask than what to expect. We consider the study to be a descriptive and exploratory step in determining if and how women's and men's experiences of first intercourse differ and to what extent the findings reflect the various constructions of sexuality portrayed in the literature.

Method

QUESTIONNAIRE

Respondents who had experienced first intercourse answered questions about the context of their first intercourse, preparations prior to intercourse, actual circumstances of first intercourse, and feelings afterward. Those who had not experienced consensual first intercourse were asked about their expectations of first intercourse including preparation, anticipation of pain, orgasm, etc. The questionnaire is presented in Appendix A.

DEFINITIONS

This study defined first intercourse as the first time the person had consensual heterosexual

Table 34.1 Mean age and relationship status of participants and their partners at time of participants' first intercourse

	Men	Women
Age of Participant and Partner at First Intercourse		
Participant's Age	17.31	17.04*
Partner's Age	17.6	18.41*

*Difference for women and partners siginificatn p < .001; n: men (63), partners (60); women (135), partners (130)

	Men	Women
Relationship Status with First Intercourse Partner		
Couple	83%	85%
Other Relationship	17%	15%
Length of Relationship and Time Known		
Mean Length of Relationship	5.74 months* (SD = 5.46)	8.14 months* (SD = 7.89)
Time Known Regardless of Relationship	26 months ns	34 months ns

*Difference approaches significance at p = 0.51

intercourse. The four participants whose first experience of sexual intercourse happened in the context of a sexual assault therefore did not provide answers about their first intercourse based on this experience but rather on their first consensual experience, if that had occurred. If they had not had consensual intercourse, their responses were based on their expectations regarding first intercourse, as were those of others who had not had consensual intercourse.

Participants

Among the 358 introductory psychology undergraduate students who participated (114 men, 244 women), the mean age was 19.4 years (SD = 2.32, range 17–38). Participants who had not had intercourse were slightly but significantly younger on average that those who had (19.0 versus 19.73 years respectively) t(356) = 2.99; p = .002. Most participants were born in Canada (79 per cent). Grouping of free-response items on cultural background yielded six categories: 'Canadian' (30 per

cent); 'European' (39 per cent); 'Asian' (18 per cent); 'Middle Eastern' (4 per cent); and 'Other' (10 per cent). Religious affiliation grouped into five categories: 'Christian (not Catholic)' (33 per cent); 'Catholic' (31 per cent); 'Hindu/Sikh/Muslim' (9 per cent); 'Buddhist/Taoist' (3 per cent); and 'No religious affiliation' (25 per cent).

Based on the definition of first intercourse as the first experience of consensual sexual intercourse, 55.6 per cent (n = 199) of the sample had experienced first intercourse and 44.4 per cent (n = 159) had not. Men and women did not differ in this respect (44.7 per cent of men and 44.3 per cent of women had not had first intercourse).

Results

Contextual variables of first intercourse

Age at first intercourse
All but one participant could recall their age at first intercourse. Mean age for first intercourse

Table 34.2 Participants' perception of being in love at time of first intercourse and in retrospect

	'In Love' at time of first intercourse? (%)		'In Love' in hindsight? (%)	
	Men (n = 63)	Women (n = 136)	Men (n = 63)	Women (n = 136)
Yes	43	63	41	47
No	35	25	48	42
Not sure	22	12	11	11
χ^2(2, N = 199)		7.78*	ns	

* p = .02
ns indicates not significant

was 17.13 years (*SD* = 1.65; range 13–28) with no significant difference between the sexes (17.04 for women and 17.31 for men; see Table 34.1 for all age-related data).

Partner's age at participant's first intercourse
On average, women had first intercourse with partners who were significantly older than they were (mean of 17.04 years for women and 18.41 years for their partners) (*t*(132) = −6.01, *p* < .001, *d* = −1.38) whereas mean age at first intercourse for men (17.31 years) did not differ from that of their partners (17.6 years; see Table 34.1).

Relationship to partner at time of first intercourse
The great majority of both women and men (84 per cent overall) said they were in a couple/romantic relationship with their first intercourse partner while 16 per cent were not in a romantic relationship. There was no significant sex difference in relationship status at first intercourse (see Table 34.1).

Duration of relationship with partner prior to first intercourse
Among the 84 per cent of participants who were in a relationship at the time of first intercourse, mean relationship duration was 7.4 months (*SD* = 7.29 months, range = less than one month to 36 months) with men approaching a significantly

greater likelihood of having shorter duration than women (5.74 months for men, 8.14 months for women) (*t*(163) = 1.97, p = .051, d = −2.40). On average, all participants had known their partner for 31 months (*SD*= 39.5; range was less than one month to 2 years) with no significant difference between the sexes in this respect (see Table 34.1).

Intercourse experience of participant's first partner
Just over half of the participants reported that they were the first person with whom their partner had intercourse (52.3 per cent). The sexes did not differ in this respect.

Perceptions of being in love at first intercourse and in hindsight
Women were significantly more likely than men to report that they were in love with their partner at the time of first intercourse (63 per cent and 43 per cent respectively) (χ^2(2, N = 199) = 7.78 , p = .02). This difference was not present in hindsight (47 per cent and 41 per cent respectively) with men appearing to move from 'unsure' to 'no' and women from 'yes' to 'no' (see Table 34.2).

Decision to have intercourse
Participants were asked whether the decision to have first intercourse was mutual or whether one partner took the lead. While 57 per cent of men and 61 per cent of women said the decision was

Table 34.3 Participant perceptions of their and their partners' role in decision to have first intercourse

Participants	Mutual Decision	Male Partner Suggested	Female Partner Suggested
Men (n = 63)	57%	25%	18%
Women (n = 136)	61%	31%	8%
χ^2(2, N = 199)		12.53, p = .002*	

*   When the decision was not identified as mutual, men were significantly more likely to have been the ones who suggested intercourse.

mutual, Chi-squared analysis showed a significant effect of gender on the decision to have first intercourse (see Table 34.3). In cases where women did not report a mutual decision, 79 per cent assigned the initiative to their partner and 21 per cent to themselves; for men, 42 per cent assigned the initiative to their partners, and 42 per cent to themselves (calculated from data in Table 34.3). Since these students were not reporting on first intercourse with other respondents, it is not possible to determine whether these sex differences in perception of who initiated would also be seen within couples.

Discussions prior to first intercourse
Among the six pre-intercourse discussion items listed in Table 34.4, participants were most likely to have discussed having sexual intercourse and condom use (63–73 per cent), somewhat less likely to have discussed other methods of birth control (48–58 per cent) and most unlikely to have discussed sexually transmitted infections, possible outcomes of pregnancy, and emotional implications of intercourse for them (32–40 per cent). The sexes did not differ significantly on any of these items (see Table 34.4).

Circumstances associated with first intercourse
Nine items in Table 34.4 assessed different aspects of the participants' actual first intercourse

experience. Although less than half of respondents indicated that first intercourse had occurred when they expected it to (41 per cent of males, 46 per cent of females), condom use at first intercourse was common (75–80 per cent). Alcohol use by self or partner was less common (14–21 per cent) and drug use by self or partner was rare (0–2 per cent). The sexes did not differ on any of these items (see Table 34.4).

Women were much more likely than men to report pain at first intercourse (52 per cent versus 5 per cent), much less likely than men to report orgasm at first intercourse (12 per cent versus 76 per cent), and more likely to report partner orgasm than were men (73 per cent versus 32 per cent). Each of these differences was statistically significant (see Table 34.4). We did not ask about prior orgasm history of women in our sample but note that our female participants appear less likely to have had orgasm at first intercourse (12 per cent) than was reported by our male respondents of their first intercourse partners (32 per cent; see Table 34.4).

Feelings and outcomes after first intercourse
Men were significantly more likely than women to report feeling physically satisfied after first intercourse (62 per cent versus 35 per cent). However, the sexes did not differ on reports of emotional satisfaction (56 per cent and 54 per cent), having

Table 34.4 Participants 'yes' responses to questions about prior discussion, circumstances of, and follow-up to first intercourse (%)

	Men (n = 63)	Women (n = 136)	$\chi^2(1, 199)$
Pre-Intercourse Discussion			
Having intercourse	76	74	ns
Condom use	63	73	ns
Other methods of birth control	58	48	ns
Sexually transmitted infection	33	32	ns
Outcomes if pregnancy were to occur	33	37	ns
Emotional implications	33	40	ns
Circumstances Associated with First Intercourse			
Did intercourse occur when expected?	41	46	ns
Was a condom used?	75	80	ns
Were you drinking?	19	21	ns
Was your partner drinking?	14	18	ns
Were you using any drugs?	0	0	ns
Was your partner using any drugs?	2	2	ns
Was first intercourse painful?	5	52	41.49*
Did you have an orgasm?	76	12	81.91*
Did your partner have an orgasm?	32	73	30.18*
Feelings / Outcomes Subsequent to First Intercourse			
Physical satisfaction	62	35	12.39*
Emotional satisfaction	56	54	ns
Sex again with same partner?	87	89	ns
Stayed a couple or became a couple after?	83	86	ns
Pregnancy occur?	0	0	–

* $p < 001$
ns indicates not significant

had sex again with the same partner (87 per cent and 89 per cent), or staying as or becoming a couple after first intercourse (83 per cent and 86 per cent). None of the respondents reported pregnancy as a consequence of first intercourse. Men and women were similar in the extent to which they reported no regrets about first intercourse (76 per cent and 72 per cent) and in their perception that they had first intercourse at 'the right age' (63 per cent and 65 per cent; see Table 34.4).

Overall assessment of first intercourse experience
Participants were asked to give an overall 'rating' of their first intercourse experience based on six options (see Table 34.5). There was no statistically significant sex difference in these overall assessments with 72 per cent of men and 61 per cent of women rating the experience as either perfect, very good, or good in contrast to the 11 per cent and 13 per cent respectively who recalled their first intercourse as either 'bad' or 'very bad'.

Table 34.5 Participants' overall ratings of their first intercourse experience (%)

Response	Men (n = 63)	Women (n = 136)	Total
Perfect, wouldn't change a thing	14	19	18
Very good	29	19	22
Good	29	23	25
Neither good or bad	18	26	23
Bad	8	10	10
Very bad	3	3	3

Slightly less than one quarter of all respondents chose the 'neither good nor bad' option.

Expectations of first intercourse among participants who had not had intercourse

Participants who had not had intercourse (n = 159) answered 9 items from Table 34.4 based on their expectations of first intercourse. There responses are reported in the first two columns of Table 34.6. Students who had not had intercourse did not generally consider it important that their first intercourse partner would also have not had intercourse (36 per cent of men and 29 per cent of women said yes). We did not ask about current relationship status and thus cannot determine how many students in this subsample might, at the time of the study, have been in a relationship with an eventual first intercourse partner.

With respect to their expectations of discussion of particular topics prior to first intercourse, the sexes in this non-intercourse group differed significantly in their expectations about discussing methods of birth control other than condoms $\chi^2(2, N= 156) = 10.65$, p = .005. Women were more likely than men to expect such discussion (77 per cent versus 53 per cent respectively; see Table 34.6) and men more often unsure (41 per cent versus 17 per cent respectively). Men and women who had not had intercourse also differed significantly in their expectations about prior discussion of STIs, $\chi^2(2, N = 157) = 8.17$, p = .017

(57 per cent of women expected such discussion versus 36 per cent of men; 36 per cent of women and 46 per cent of men were unsure or did not know).

The sexes also differed in their expectation of pain at first intercourse, $\chi^2(2, N = 157) = 69.01$, p < .001, with a smaller percentage of men (4 per cent) than women (34 per cent) expecting to experience pain. Men and women also differed in expectations about their own and their future partner's likelihood of having orgasm at first intercourse, $\chi^2(2, N = 156) = 39.44$, p < .001, and $\chi^2(2, N = 156) = 7.80$, p = .020 respectively.

Comparison of expectations of participants who had not had intercourse with actual experiences of those who had first intercourse

Table 34.6 also provides an opportunity to compare the first intercourse expectations of the participants who had not had intercourse with the first intercourse experiences of those who had. A comparison of the experiences of the latter with the expectations of the former invites speculation about the extent to which expectations may or may not match experience. For example, women who had not had intercourse appeared more likely to expect pre-intercourse discussion of birth control methods other than condoms (77 per cent) than was actually experienced by women who had first intercourse (48 per cent). The expected sex difference on this item experienced by those who had intercourse was in the reverse direction to that

Table 34.6 Expectations of first intercourse among students who had not had intercourse and a comparison with those who had

Responses	First Intercourse Expectations (students who had not had intercourse)		Reported First Intercourse Experiences (students who had had intercourse)	
	Men (n = 51)	Women (n = 108)	Men (n = 63)	Women (n = 136)
Partners not having had intercourse before is important?	36	29		
Pre-Intercourse Discussion				
Discuss having intercourse	60	66	76	74
Discuss condom use	70	83	63	73
Discuss other methods of birth control	53	77	58	48
Discuss STIs	36	57	33	32
Discuss pregnancy	55	53	33	37
Discuss emotional implications	33	44	33	40
Physical Expectations				
Pain at first intercourse	4	34	5	52
Personal experience of orgasm	58	11	76	12
Partner's experience of orgasm	22	28	32	73

expected by those who had not. In the relation to the pre-intercourse discussion items as a whole, the trend appears to be for women who have not had intercourse to have higher expectations for such discussion than occurred in practice for those who had. Women's expectation of their own orgasm at first intercourse (11 per cent) matched that of women who had intercourse (12 per cent) but women's expectation of their partner's orgasm (28 per cent) was lower than that reported about their partners by women who had had intercourse (73 per cent; see Table 34.6).

Discussion

In contrast to other studies that highlighted differences between the sexes in their experience of first intercourse (Darling et al., 1992; Cohen and Shotland, 1996; Guggino, 1997; Holland et al., 2000; Carpenter, 2001), the present findings indicate that, with some exceptions, women's and men's reports of the experience were quite similar. The average age at first intercourse was the same for both sexes. Men and women were equally likely to have had first intercourse within the context of a romantic relationship, to have known their first intercourse partner for the same average length of time, and to have had a first partner who had previous intercourse experience. Women were as likely as men to report activities indicating that they had discussed preparations for and other aspects of first intercourse. In a majority of cases the decision to have first intercourse was a mutual one. On average, men and women gave similar responses to questions about condom use (usually), alcohol use (seldom), drug use (almost never) and whether first intercourse was expected. The finding that 75 per cent of men and 80 per cent of women reported condom use at first intercourse is consistent with the relatively high levels of protection against unintended pregnancy and STI at first intercourse reported in other recent Canadian studies of young adults (e.g., Hampton, Smith, Jeffrey, and McWatters, 2001). In addition, the sexes did not differ significantly in their evaluation of their feelings and follow-up to first intercourse in relation to emotional satisfaction, subsequent intercourse with first partner, regret, timing, and overall rating.

The women and men in our study who had not had intercourse were also similar to each other on such items as whether it was important that their first partner had also not previously had intercourse (about one-third said yes) and on their expectation of discussion in advance of condom use (high) and possible outcomes if unintended pregnancy were to occur (slightly over half).

The degree of gender similarity in this sample of university students may not represent accurately what is going on in the general population. However, it is also possible that this sample reflects a shift in the sexual practice of young people towards more equally balanced engagement in discussions and decisions related to sexual activity in general and first intercourse in particular. Since the limited research that has been done on first intercourse experience is from the United States, it has been tempting to assume that the Canadian population is similar. However, strongly conservative political and religious influences in the US may reflect an environment that has been more hostile than Canada to premarital sexual activity and hence to the education that would support more informed, and perhaps egalitarian, decision-making and experiences surrounding first intercourse.

Some of our findings do suggest gender differences in which men appear to have greater influence on sexual interactions in heterosexual relationships, at least when it comes to first intercourse. The greater age differences between women and their first intercourse partners could result in men having more power and control in the sexual relationship. On the other hand this could simply be a reflection of our society's tendency for younger women to be drawn to older partners and vice versa. The fact that men had known their first intercourse partners for a shorter period of time than women is consistent with Cohen and Shotland's (1996) report that men consider sexual intercourse acceptable earlier in a dating relationship than do women. Among the approximately 40 per cent of women and men in our study who said first intercourse had not been a 'mutual decision', women were significantly more likely to say that their partner had suggested intercourse than were men. This fits with the traditional dating scenario in which men are more likely to take initiative with the sexual aspects of romantic relationships. However, our questions did not explore what these students meant by their partner 'taking the initiative' nor did they explore other aspects of relationship dynamics.

On average, women were more likely than men to believe that they were in love at first intercourse (men were more likely to be unsure). These views converged in retrospect with both sexes being equally likely to believe that they were not in love. The greater tendency for women to believe they were in love at first intercourse may reflect greater internalization by women than men of the feeling that sex is about love. There may be a parallel here in the finding of Quackenbush, Strassberg, and Tumer (1995) that the inclusion of romance in erotica can serve as a relationship buffer that make erotic material more acceptable to women. Similarly, the belief that they are 'in love' might be viewed as the relationship buffer necessary for some women to justify first intercourse.

We think these findings have important implications for sexual health education although we are also aware that the study has a number of limitations that invite cautious interpretation of the results. The study was conducted on a convenience sample of introductory psychology students and cannot be generalized to other populations including students who did not go to university or who left school early. The questionnaire was designed for this study and has not been validated. Participants were only asked about consensual first intercourse and not about other sexual activities such as oral sex. Thus, the study cannot shed light on participants' prior sexual behaviour or on the attitudes that may have shaped their perceptions of their first intercourse experience. That being said, socially constructed gender differences appear to permeate all levels of society and to that extent the findings may well have useful applications for educators and health professionals.

Note

1. We would like to thank Jenn Mitchell, Kim Scott, and Hanna Wajda for their assistance in conducting this study. This research is partially supported by SSHRC funding to the second author.

References

Allgeir, E.R., and B.J.T. Royster. 1991. 'New Approaches to Dating and Sexuality', in E. Grauerholz and M.A. Koralewski, eds, *Sexual Coercion: A Sourcebook On Its Nature, Causes, and Prevention*, pp. 133–47. Lexington, MA: Lexington Books.

Burr, J. 2001. 'Women Have It. Men Want It. What Is It? Constructions of Sexuality in Rape Discourse', *Psychology, Evolution, & Gender* 3: 103–7.

Carpenter, L.M. 2001. 'The Ambiguity of "having sex": The Subjective Experience of Virginity Loss in the United States', *The Journal of Sex Research* 38: 127–39.

Cohen, L.L., and R.L. Shotland. 1996. 'Timing of First Sexual Intercourse in a Relationship: Expectations, Experiences, and Perceptions of Others', *The Journal of Sex Research* 33: 291–9.

Darling, C.A., J.K. Davidson, and L.C. Passarello. 1992. 'The Mystique of First Intercourse among College Youth: The Role of Partners, Contraceptive Practices, and Psychological Reactions', *Journal of Youth and Adolescence* 21: 97–117.

Fine, M. 1997. 'Sexuality, Schooling, and Adolescent Females: The Missing Discourse of Desire', in M.M. Gergen and S.N. Davis, eds, *Toward a New Psychology of Gender*, pp. 375–402. New York, NY: Routledge.

Guggino, J.M., and J.J., Jr., Ponzetti. 1997. 'Gender Differences in Affective Reactions to First Coitus', *Journal of Adolescence* 20: 189–200.

Hampton, M.R, P. Smith, B. Jeffery, and B. McWatters. 2001. 'Sexual Experience, Contraception, and STI Prevention among High School Students: Results from a Canadian Urban Centre', *The Canadian Journal of Human Sexuality* 10: 111–26.

Holland, J., C. Ramazanoglu, S. Sharpe, and R. Thomson. 2000. 'Deconstructing Virginity—Young People's Accounts of First Sex', *Sexual and Relationship Therapy* 15: 221–32.

Quackenbush, D.M., D.S. Strassberg, and C.W. Turner. 1995. 'Gender Effects of Romantic Themes in Erotica', *Archives of Sexual Behavior* 24: 21–35.

Appendix A: Survey items and response categories

Questions	Response Categories

Relationship to Partner

Were you a couple at the time?   Yes / Now

Did you consider yourself to be 'in love' with this person at the time
when you had intercourse?   Yes / No / Not Sure

Looking back, do you think you were actually 'in love' with this person when you had
intercourse, regardless of your answer to the last question?   Yes / No / Not Sure

How long had you known this person in total, regardless of changes in your
relationship to this person?   ____ months and ___ years

Were you the first person with whom your partner has had intercourse?   Yes / No

What is your relationship to this
person now?   Partner or Spouse / Friend / Acquaintance / No relationship / Other

Preparations Prior to Intercourse

Did you and your partner talk about having intercourse beforehand?   Yes / No / Not Sure

Did you and your partner discuss condom use before having first intercourse?   Yes / No / Not Sure

Did you and your partner discuss other methods of birth control before having
first intercourse?   Yes / No / Not Sure

Did you and your partner discuss STIs before having first intercourse?   Yes / No / Not Sure

Did you and your partner discuss what to do if you / your partner became pregnant
before having first intercourse?   Yes / No / Not Sure

Did you and your partner discuss the emotional implications of having intercourse before
having first intercourse?   Yes / No / Not Sure

Do you think that you and your partner
decided to have intercourse together,
or did one of you take the lead?   Decided together / You took the initiative / Partner took the initiative

Circumstances of First Intercourse

Did first intercourse occur when you expected it to?   Yes / No / Not Sure

Where did you have intercourse for the first time?   Your home / Partner's home / Hotel or motel / Vehicle / Other

Did you / your partner use a condom?   Yes / No

Did you / your partner use any other form of contraceptive?   Yes / No

At the time you had intercourse, was there alcohol in your system?   Yes / No / Don't remember or know

Was there alcohol in your partner's system?   Yes / No / Don't remember or know

Were you on any drugs?   Yes / No / Don't Remember or Know

Was your partner on any drugs?   Yes / No / Don't Remember or Know

Did you find your first intercourse experience to be physically painful
in any way?   Yes / No / Not Sure

Did you achieve orgasm?   Yes / Not / Not Sure / Don't Remember

Did your partner achieve orgasm?   Yes / Not / Not Sure / Don't Remember

Feelings / Outcomes Subsequent to First Intercourse

Did you feel physically satisfied with your first intercourse experience?	Yes / No / Not Sure
Did you feel emotionally satisfied with your first intercourse experience?	Yes / No / Not Sure
Did you and this particular partner ever have sex again?	Yes / No / Don't Remember
Did you and this partner stay together as a couple, or, if you were not a couple at the time you had intercourse, did you and this partner become a couple?	Yes / No
Do you regret having shared your first intercourse experience with this person?	Yes / No / Don't Remember
Looking back, what do you think about the timing of your first intercourse experience?	I was about the right age / I was too young / I was too old / Not Sure
Did you or your partner become pregnant as a result of your first intercourse experience?	Yes / No / I don't know
Did you or your partner get an STI as a result of your first intercourse experience?	Yes, I caught something from him or her / Yes, s / he caught something from me / No / Not Sure
Overall, how would you rate your first intercourse experience?	Perfect, wouldn't change a thing / Very Good / Good / Neither Good or Bad / Bad / Very Bad

Expectations About First Intercourse by Respondents who had not had Intercourse

Will it be important to you that the person with whom you have intercourse for the first time is also having intercourse for the first time?	Yes / Maybe / No / Don't Know
Do you think you and your future partner will talk about having intercourse beforehand?	Yes / Maybe / No / Don't Know
Do you think you and your future partner will discuss condom use before having first intercourse?	Yes / Maybe / No / Don't Know
Do you think you and your future partner will discuss other methods of birth control before having first intercourse?	Yes / Maybe / No / Don't Know
Do you think you and your future partner will discuss STI's before having first intercourse?	Yes / Maybe / No / Don't Know
Do you think you and your future partner will discuss what to do if you / your partner became pregnant after having first intercourse?	Yes / Maybe / No / Don't Know
Do you think you and your future partner will discuss the emotional implications of having first intercourse before having first intercourse?	Yes / Maybe / No / Don't Know
Do you think your first intercourse experience will be physically painful in any way?	Yes / Maybe / No / Don't Know
Do you think you will achieve orgasm at first intercourse?	Yes / Maybe / No / Don't Know
Do you think your future partner will achieve orgasm at first intercourse?	Yes / Maybe / No / Don't Know

CHAPTER 35

'It just happens': Negotiating Casual Heterosexual Sex

Melanie Beres

In the summer of 2005, Melanie Beres spent several months in Jasper, Alberta, interviewing young people who had come to Jasper for seasonal work in the tourist industry. Her intent was to understand the negotiating of sexual consent in short-term heterosexual encounters ('hooking up' or 'one night stands'). Beres chose Jasper because of the dense population of transients and seasonal workers. The youth culture that grew up around this population perceived recreational sex as a common activity. In this chapter, Beres discusses the different ways in which men and women in Jasper talk about casual sex, and how they depict the process of consenting to a sexual encounter.

I begin this chapter by highlighting ways that the negotiation of casual sex in Jasper is dominated by discourses that privilege male sexual desire. I discuss the three discourses of heterosexuality as outlined by Hollway (1984) and I argue for a fourth discourse within casual sex; I label it the 'it just happens' discourse. Through this discourse casual sex is constructed as something that 'just happens' and is beyond the control of the partners. I end with an analysis of the ways that women find spaces of power and agency within these discourses. Women do this by placing limits on casual sex, disrupting the 'coital imperative', and taking the typically 'male' position within the discourse and actively seeking casual sex.

The (Male) Models of Heterosexual Casual Sex in Jasper

'IT JUST HAPPENS' DISCOURSE

When I approached young adults in Jasper (YAJs) and told them about my study I explained that I was interested in learning about how casual sex happens in Jasper, and how partners communicate their willingness to participate in casual sex. I began interviews by asking them about their lives in Jasper and about their past dating and sexual experiences. At some point during the interview I inevitably asked some version of the question 'How does casual sex happen?' or 'How do two people come to the understanding that they are going to have sex?'. At this point many of the participants stopped and stared at me with perplexed looks on their faces. I interpreted their reactions as saying 'Have you never had sex?'. The presumption seemed to be that if I had sex at some point, then I would have known how it happened. The answer would have been obvious. The answer (of course) is that 'it just happens'. Almost all of the women and a few of the men responded with some version of this statement.

Samantha: So you're like kind of like making eye contact, smiling at each other, and then all of a sudden we're like standing by each other talking. And just like . . . I don't know how it happened but we like; all of a sudden we were . . . (laughs) . . . we were just like talking and we were talking about that and like he started kissing me and we went back to my house. And it wasn't even a question of 'would you like to come to my house?'. You know what I mean? It was just like that.

That's what happened. (laughs) And then in the middle of it, it was just like, oh my God!

Anne: He, he just kissed me. Like he just, we were holding hands and dancing then he kissed me and I kissed him back and then it just . . . Yeah, we were hugging and kissing. I was, it was not . . . I don't know, it just happened.

James: That's a really interesting question, because you don't really, I don't really analyze how it happens really, it just kind of happens.

This discourse of 'it just happens' reflects a sense that there is a force greater than and external to the two people involved in casual sex that is ultimately responsible for instigating sex. By using this discourse it seems more acceptable for women (and men?) to engage in casual sex. By saying that it 'just happens' women are relinquishing responsibility for engaging in casual sex. Anne expresses this sense by saying that she 'felt a little less of a slut if it wasn't something I really intended on doing, it just happened.' Anne's comment also highlights her negotiation of the good girl/bad girl dichotomy. In order to maintain her 'good girl' image of herself, it is only acceptable to engage in casual sex that is 'accidental'. By adopting this discourse, women are relinquishing themselves and their male partners of responsibility. It suggests that men are just as susceptible to this force as women. There is no recognition that their male partner may have orchestrated the casual sex in any way. Gwen provides a particularly poignant example.

Yeah. And then so, yeah, and then he just kept talking. Like we didn't dance or anything. We just sat by the bar and talked for like two hours and he just kept feeding me drinks. (laughs) But he was just drinking just as much as I was

so it wasn't that big of a deal. So every time I'd get a drink, he would get a drink. And um . . . yeah, and then . . . And then I went to the washroom and then when I came out, he wasn't there. It was like okay, I'm just going to go home. And then I was walking outside and he like got a cab and stuff. And he was like do you need a ride? Like I'll give you a cab and I'll give you a ride home. And then like sure, whatever. It was raining. It was ugly out. And then um. . . his friend was with him too and he said well why don't you just come over for a couple of beer? And I was like okay, I don't have to work until 3:30 the next day. I can do that. And um . . . so I went over. We had some beer. And then I was like okay, I'm going to go home. And he was like well no, let's just talk for a bit. And I was like okay, and then one thing led to another . . .

The way that Gwen tells the story, she sees it as a series of events that took place, finishing with 'and one thing led to another'. She does not see the man's behaviour as orchestrating her going home with him for casual sex. She dismisses his buying her lots of drinks, because he too is drinking. She does not think anything of him arranging a cab for her, or asking her home. She does not say anything to imply that his actions may have been planned—that he may be buying her alcohol to get her drunk so she would be more likely to go home with him. She ends the story with 'and one thing led to another' implying that neither one of them was in control of what was happening.

Most participants, especially women, expressed a sense that one thing led to another, rather than expressing an intent or interest in engaging in casual sex. James is one of the few men who also express this sense of 'it just happens'.

It's just something that happens, and you don't really know how it happened, but it happened. And ah, I've never had an experience where it's happened and then she's been like 'I really didn't want that to happen' which I'm very thankful for. But you know, you go to an after party or something, right like you're already just hard-core making out on the dance floor lets say, right and you're doing dry humping and bumping and grinding and hanging off each other as you leave the bar. You get to the guy's party house or wherever you're at right, you're sitting around. The next thing you know, nobody's in the room and you're lying on each other and one thing leads to another. Right like, that's really the only way to put it, you start making out that leads to nakedness that leads to sex.

James was thankful that no woman has ever told him afterwards that she did not want to have sex. He said this as though he cannot control the situation or outcome—as though he has no access to the woman's comfort levels, interests, or desires. If sex can just happen, and he has no control over what happens, he then has no control over any potential consequences of the interaction. This use of the 'it just happens' discourse assumes that they are not responsible for negotiating casual sex. This results in a failure for men to take responsibility for their actions and the potential for these actions to create harm.

Agnes, among others, connected the 'it just happens' discourse with alcohol. 'Alcohol is a huge key, like huge, and it really makes you, it really limits you, your ability to make good, clear, conscious decisions.' I spoke with only one person who said that most often his casual sex hook-ups occur in the absence of alcohol, often with people he meets in coffee shops or on the street. All other participants mentioned that alcohol plays an important part in their casual sex experiences. When I asked Susan how casual sex happens, alcohol was the first thing she mentioned.

Go to the bar. Start buying other people drinks and start drinking yourself. It's really really . . . it's all related to alcohol, I think. And for a lot

of other people drugs, but I don't see that side of it because I've never been a part of that side of it. Um, but yeah, well it depends, well as a girl if that's what you're looking for when you come to Jasper. You dress really skanky and you get out on the dance floor and you drink lots. And there's gonna be a guy there. Guaranteed.

Many others mentioned being drunk as a necessary component of casual sex.

> *Teresa:* Yeah, we were, we were both pretty drunk. We were outside having a cigarette and I leaned over and kissed him. I was like, come on, you can sleep at my place tonight. So we walked home. I lived like not even a block away from the bar that we both worked at. And, and um . . . got inside . . . I put on a tee shirt and a pair of boxers. He was in his shorts. He was in there and apparently I had my own shirt off and both of our own shorts off within about half an hour and it was completely not an issue and it doesn't surprise me whatsoever cause he was very, very attractive.

While a few men commented that moderating the amount of alcohol was important when they are interested in casual sex, no women expressed similar sentiments. Women did not limit alcohol when they engaged in casual sex, and were much less likely to be able to maintain a level of control during the interaction. The alcohol can then be used as an excuse for how or why sex 'just happened'. The discourse of 'it just happens' creates a version of casual sex where the illusion is that neither partner is responsible. By positioning themselves within this discourse women can then feel like 'good girls' who do not actively seek sex; they are 'not slutty'. Women are also taking responsibility off their male partners. Men are not viewed as controlling sex, or as orchestrating the interaction. The sex just happened; the men were not in control over what took place any more than the women.

MALE SEXUAL DRIVE DISCOURSE

While most women and a few men began talking about casual sex through the 'it just happens' discourse, this was not the only way that hookups were conceptualized.

Many men said they went out to parties or bars with an intention of hooking up, and they pay particular attention to what types of things women may want in men, or particular things to do to get women interested in them. For these men, casual sex does not just happen; it is something that they have to work for, and something they practice. Robert, a bouncer in one of the local bars said that he often sees men going from one group of women to another until they find someone willing to talk with them. Don said that he approaches a lot of women when he's looking for sex and that he knows he will get turned down frequently.

This fits in with what Hollway (1984) describes as the male sexual drive discourse in which men's sex drive is insatiable and that women's role in sexual activity is to be passive and go along with men's desires. Within this discourse men are sexual subjects acting in ways to fulfill their desire for sex. Through this discourse men also secure their masculinity, by reinforcing their ever-present sex drive. Conversely, women are positioned as sexual objects, necessary for men to satiate their desire for sex without any desires of their own. Men reported many strategies that they used in order to find a sexual partner. For instance, some men said that they will often approach many women, with the idea that the more women they approach, the greater the likelihood that they will find one who will have sex with them.

Even once men were in conversation, or dancing with a particular woman, it was important for them to continue to monitor women's behaviours in ways that would increase the chance of 'getting laid'. For instance, it was important that women should feel as though that the situation was not threatening, and to feel comfortable and cared for.

> Don: You just give her a sense of security like, making them the focal point, and just looking out for them like, just simple sayings like, like obviously getting the door for them, like putting on their jacket but like actually pulling their hair back so it doesn't go under their jacket, like little things like that, and just looking out for them, even if it's just like creating some space for them, like in a crowded club or something like that just little things like that seemed to go a long way . . . you have to really play it by ear because it can be overdone . . . you have to give her her space and be relaxed then the same time just be conscientious and make her feel comfortable, you know offer them like something to drink, right. I'm not saying offering them a shot or something like that, but like can I get you a drink, would you like my jacket, are you cold, and something like that.

Don is very deliberate in his approach with women; he sees himself in pursuit of sex and sees it as challenging to get women to have sex with him. He is quite aware of his actions and how they may help him reach his goal. While on the surface he seems concerned about women's comfort level, this is a means to an end, a way to get women to go to bed with him.

Don took up the male sexual drive discourse throughout his interview. When I first met him, he had just recently moved to Jasper, and had a girlfriend still living in their hometown. During the interview Don said that it was 'inevitable' that he would have casual sex during his time in Jasper. He seemed to believe that his sex drive was insatiable and it would be futile to resist his desire for casual sex. Don articulated his approach to women quite clearly and it was obvious that he thought carefully about how to approach women to get what he wants. He made references to the importance of 'knowing how to court a woman properly' and 'knowing your arts well'. By these he meant that it is important for men to know the right away to approach women and talk to them, to make them feel comfortable, and to build a sense of trust.

In order to satiate his 'natural' sexual desires, Don learned and implemented specific strategies that enabled him to have casual sex. In this version of the male sexual drive discourse Don positioned himself in a way that relinquishes both partners from responsibility. Here, Don accepts that he is responsible for learning how to quench his ever-present desire. His drive is 'natural' and thus it is 'inevitable' that he must have casual sex throughout the summer, however by becoming skilled at the 'arts' of 'courting' he increases the likelihood and frequency that he will be able to satisfy these desires.

He talked in detail about monitoring women's behaviour to gauge their comfort level and willingness to have sex. In particular, a woman's breathing was very important.

It is all about the girl's breathing, and that's like, a lot of guys don't realize that, but that's like, that's your like light signal that's your red, yellow, green, right there it's her breathing and just playing that off and so you just gradually sort of progress things forward to taking off clothes.

For Don, it was important that he maintain control over the situation and over casual sex. He talked positively about situations where women initiated casual sex, as long as the woman was not too direct.

The odd time that I get approached by a girl it works, like it's nice to see a girl of confidence

and stuff like that but you can't be too direct because then it's just too easy, it kills it, like you know unless I was just slumming it you know, and going for raunchy sex.

Several other men talked in similar ways about women who are actively seeking sex.

Colin: If they come on too strong, then you can kind of tell that they're kinda skanky. But if they come on sort of in a shy manner, then, then it's a good thing. Good cause it gives you room to open them up. You know what I mean? Like you've got to make them feel comfortable obviously or else it's just going to be stupid and suck . . . If they're really aggressive, it's just like no; I don't want to do this. Cause it's not really giving you a challenge. Cause if they're really aggressive, it's just like well okay, I'll just take my shorts off and let's go.

Thus, the chase becomes a 'natural' part of casual sex, and courtship and seduction becomes the property of men.

A key component to the male sexual drive discourse is that men maintain control of the sexual experience. Overly sexually aggressive women threaten this control, men find this intimidating, and the women are then labelled 'slutty'.

Women were far less likely to articulate ways that casual sex happens. Even in cases where the women were interested in particular men, women waited for men to initiate contact.

Samantha: It's usually the guy who makes the first move I guess, towards me if they can see I'm attracted to them or whatever.

Even when women initiate sex, they still take up the male sexual drive discourse by assuming that the men will be willing to engage in sex.

Agnes: And I think it's more the girl to . . . be the one that decides whether or not it's going to happen because from my experiences, there's not very many times when a guy won't have sex. In fact, more often than not, that's all they're in it for is and not like looking for a relationship or just somebody to snuggle with.

Men also articulated this aspect of the male sexual drive discourse. When I asked men how they indicated their willingness for sex to their partners, many responded by saying that they do not have to demonstrate willingness.

Colin: I just like I'm, I'm a guy. I'm ready, willing and able anywhere anytime.

Gary: I think it's probably pretty rare that the guy says stop. I mean, I don't know with other guys for sure but . . . from, from what I know, then I say that the guy's not going to say stop. Unless there's something else like he has a girlfriend or something like that.

This male sexual drive discourse was the discourse most frequently referred to by both women and men as they talked about casual sex. The male sexual drive discourse is different from the 'it just happens' discourse in that both men and women who take up this discourse recognize that men actively pursue casual sex. This is viewed as the 'normal' and 'natural' way to do engage in casual sex. It remained unquestioned by all but one female participant.

Stacy: It's, it's so unfair that it's really assumed in our society that it's the guy's job to [initiate sex]. You know what I mean. It's the guy's job to invite the girl out on a date. It's the guy's job to initiate this. It's the guy's job to initiate that. Yeah, it's the guy's job to initiate sex. It's the

guy's job to do everything. The girl's kind of the passive like you know? Passive partner who goes along with everything or doesn't. But is always like you know, things happen to her, she doesn't, you know what I mean? . . . Like don't treat me like some idiot! Like some damsel in fucking distress. So I think that that goes a long way into the bedroom too where like I don't expect him, you know what I mean? Like I'm willing to go out on a limb and face rejection, you know what I mean?

HAVE/HOLD DISCOURSE

While the male sexual drive discourse was the most frequently taken up, other discourses described by Hollway (1984) were alluded to by participants. Many women and a few men took up the have/hold discourse, which Hollway describes as the belief that sex comes with a committed and ongoing relationship. In this discourse women are positioned as the sexual subjects who were trying to establish a committed relationship with a man. Men are positioned as the objects of this discourse. Thus the have/hold discourse works with the male sexual drive discourse; men are attempting to satiate their sexual desires, and women participate in sex to build and maintain a committed relationship.

It was surprising to see this discourse taken up when women and men were talking about casual sex. Although both women and men were aware that many casual sex experiences do not lead to lasting and committed relationships, some women reported that one reason they engage in casual sex is because they may be interested in a relationship. Samantha and Agnes both said that some of the partners they chose were people they were interested in developing a relationship with. Most of these casual sex experiences did not lead to a relationship.

Agnes said that she learnt that if she wanted a relationship that she should not sleep with a man the first night they are together because she found that after she slept with a man on the first 'date', he would no longer speak to her.

> We ended up sleeping together and woke up the next morning, and we slept together again and then he like, never talked to me after that. And we were supposed to hang out on New Year's Eve together, cuz it was like two nights after that and umm, I phoned him on New Year's Eve, and asked him what he was doing, and he was like 'oh I think I'm just going to stay home'. He totally blew me off.

As a result, Agnes made a rule for herself and lets men know that she will not have sex with them right away. She will, though, have sex with them on the second date. By staying around for a second night, they demonstrated a certain level of interest or commitment. Unfortunately, she found that waiting until the second night they were together did not change the end result.

> I ended up hooking up with this friend of mine, but now I like have this thing where I won't sleep with guys on the first date, just because I don't like the feeling of being used the next day and for me that's a really big thing, and so, but this guy . . . we hooked up one night and then, I wouldn't sleep with him, so the next night, he ended up spending the night and I slept with him and then he never talked to me again. And so now, like even that little theory of mine, is totally like . . . blown out the window.

Agnes told stories about hooking up with people for casual sex, and said 'I'm totally, like, fine to have casual sex with people, but like if they're under one impression and I'm under another and it's not the same then that kind of makes me mad.' In Agnes's version of this discourse, she is looking for more than just one night of sex. This commitment does not have to be in the form of an exclusive and romantic relationship. It could also be a casual affair that lasts several weeks.

Agnes is not the only woman who spoke of similar ideas. Jane recounts a story where she met a man she was interested in. At first she thinks he is a real 'gentleman' because he does not try to sleep with her the first night they are together. They did, however, have sex the second night they were together. Afterwards she was angry because he is no longer speaking to her. She called him a 'really big slut' and a liar. She sees his actions as being dishonest because for her, having sex with someone is a sign that there is at least some interest and some commitment.

Even for some women who actively sought out one-night-stands, their subject position was at least partially constructed through the have/hold discourse. After seeking out casual sex with a particular man Anne turned off her answering machine and purposely spent a lot of time out of the house for the following few days. She did not want to know if he had called or not.

> So it was not like I was expecting anything out of it, but I still, I do have like, like, I had like little fantasies about him, like staying or something like that, or like us continuing the relationship, so there must be, and I went into it totally like chasing him. I just wanted to have, to basically have casual sex, but I still have the future flashes.

Anne has purposely tried to disregard and shed the have/hold discourse and went out looking for a one-night-stand. Yet she still finds that she has what she calls 'future flashes' and that she fantasizes about a possible future with the man. She also mentioned a few times that she saw no reason why they could not be friends, or at least talk with one another after having casual sex.

> I had one one-night-stand . . . and I just, I thought, like okay, well, you have sex with someone, and to me it doesn't matter, like sex

. . . ok, I never felt like a slut when I do it, so I don't see other people . . . like I can never imagine other people thinking of me as a slut, but like, so I thought that we could just hang out with these guys afterwards and be friends, but it's weird, like once you've done the act, it's, there's like very like a lack of interest . . . How are you supposed to meet anybody in this stupid town to hang out with, you know what I mean?

Here Anne takes up a different form of the have/hold discourse. She is not concerned with creating or maintaining a sexual or romantic relationship. However, she expects that she should be able to maintain a friendly relationship with men with whom she has had sex. She views the men as potential people to hang out with and party with, people who can be part of her larger social network. She resents that most often after she has sex with them, she is excluded from their social network.

Men do not take up this discourse as it relates to casual sex. Almost all the men expected not to engage in any sort of relationship with someone after they had sex, unless there was a relationship established before they had sex. A few men mentioned that they would delay having sex with a woman if they wanted to have a relationship with her.

Colin: Well if you have a connection with this person and you're super attracted to them and you can see yourself being with them, then you won't fuck them the first date. Like if you really want a relationship with them, you're not going to spoil it by screwing them.

Don: Like a really good one is going home to smoke pot or to do blow but like I've cut blow out of my life, that was like a high school thing. But like blow's really good because it shows that you really wanna talk to them because when you do a lot of blow your dick is like a limp

spaghetti, and it's just like useless for sex and so shows that you care about conversation and bullshit like that.

For men, the have/hold discourse comes into play only when they want to develop a relationship with a woman, whereas for women, they often take it up whenever they are engaging in casual sex.

This discourse operates along with the male sexual drive discourse to enable casual sex among YAJs in Jasper. Men engage in casual sex because of their 'natural' and insatiable drive for sexual gratification. Conversely, women participate in casual sex with the hope of developing a lasting and committed relationship.

SEXUAL PERMISSIVENESS DISCOURSE

Both men and women deployed the sexual permissiveness discourse, according to which casual sexual activity is considered normal and expected. Many of the men and women I spoke with were surprised at how many women in Jasper initiate and seek out casual sex. Robert said, 'When I lived in [another province], it was the guys. But like here, it's anybody who's you know, guys or girls making the first move for sure.'

There was a sense that in Jasper it is a lot more acceptable for women to want casual sex, compared to other places.

Agnes: When I was in high school, somebody who like had casual sex and slept with a lot of people was called a slut. But I seldom ever hear that term. And I don't know if people have just grown up to realize that yeah, casual sex is something that you do when you get older. Like you know, just cause you sleep with a couple of people doesn't make you a bad person or a slut for it. And I don't see that [in Jasper] at all.

Casual sex for women is accepted, rather than stigmatized, in Jasper (although if they are 'too' assertive or aggressive they risk being labelled a slut). Without this discourse, and the feeling that it is acceptable for women to have casual sex, it would be much more difficult for men to find willing partners. This discourse, while on the surface seems to support women's sexual desires, is necessary for men to engage in a lot of casual sex. This discourse can also obscure sexual double standards. It appears as though it is acceptable for both women and men to engage in casual sex. However, this is only acceptable if they are engaging in a 'masculine' version of casual sex and if women are adhering to normative constructions of femininity created through the male sexual drive discourse.

WOMEN'S SEXUAL AGENCY

The discourses discussed above create depictions of casual sex that benefit male sexual desires and needs and are subject to male initiation. However, within these discourses women carve out spaces to exercise agency over their own sexuality and engage in heterosexual casual sex. Women create different degrees of agency during their casual sex experiences. First, women take advantage of the perception that more men are interested in casual sex than women, and therefore women have more choice about with whom they have sex. Second, women exercise agency by interrupting sexual activity before they engage in casual sex. Third, they actively seek out and orchestrate casual sex to satisfy their own sexual desires.

Women exercise agency by taking advantage of the perception that there are a lot more men seeking casual sex than there are women, creating a situation where women have a lot of choice regarding with whom they go home.

> *Teresa*: There's so many men looking for sex that, you know, women really have their pick and choose of the litter. If they're just looking a one-night-stand [the men I've talked to] said that you

really have to stick out like a sore thumb or like be right there.

Men and women sometimes argue that women have more power than men when it comes to casual sex, because they have the power of choice. Jane says that 'girls have a lot of power in whether they go home with a man or not. Guys just kind of take their chance and hope they get lucky.' If women are looking for casual sex it is much easier for them to find someone with whom to go home. In a sense they are taking advantage of the male sexual drive discourse and using it to their advantage to have casual sex when they desire it.

Additionally, women exercise agency within and around the male sexual drive discourse by placing limits on the sexual activity—getting what they want out of it and stopping the interaction when they are satisfied. Agnes says that 'I think too because the girl ultimately usually decides on . . . if there's going to be sex or not.' Thus, while casual sex operates on the presumption of a male model of sexuality women and men perceive that women act as the 'gatekeepers' and determine whether or not casual sex will happen.

Men, as well as women, reported that women often act as limit-setters. Tim mentioned that sometimes women will be totally 'into making out', but they will not let him take off their pants. He reads this as an indication that they are menstruating; he suggests that many women get particularly 'horny' while they are menstruating. Regardless of whether or not these women are menstruating, taking up this strategy, or going along with his suggestion that they are menstruating gives them a chance to engage in casual sexual activity that does not lead to penetration. James mentioned similar strategies used by a few women.

> Like, you'll be with the girl and you'll be making out and she'll stop and be like, you know, 'I really like you but I don't wanna go all the way because of this reason.' Right, like,

there are still virgins out there, believe it or not, who are like, saving themselves for marriage, it's a really romantic concept that I really still enjoy, but you . . . it's a rarity I'll say . . . but they'll still have tonnes and tonnes of fun, but they just won't go all the way.

By being up front and telling men their limits, these women are opening up possibilities for casual sexual activity that do not include penetration. James mentioned that often they would engage in oral sex or genital touching. When men mentioned these strategies, they did not mind that the women were placing limits on sexual activity. James mentioned later on that 'realistically again, you know, a lot of them are tourists they're not gonna be around the next day, so you have bad luck that night you always go out to couple nights later and maybe your luck's changed.' If one woman is not willing to participate fully in a male model of casual sex that includes sexual penetration, then another one will be later on.

Thus, these women are able to negotiate the 'coital imperative' (Jackson, 1984) of heterosexual sex by placing boundaries and limits around the sexual activity. This way, women are able to indirectly satisfy their own sexual desires while operating within normative heterosexual discourses. They do this without completely rejecting the coital imperative. By saying that they want to wait until marriage to have sex or that they are having their period, they imply that they would otherwise be willing to engage in intercourse and are recognizing the central role that intercourse plays in heterosexual relations.

While the women I interviewed did not talk about strategies that included claiming they were menstruating or that they wanted to remain virgins, many of them mentioned setting limits as a way to ensure control over their casual sex.

Agnes: I just don't let it happen. I say no, like when they try to go that direction, I'm

like 'no, I don't sleep with guys on the first date.'

Many women have a sense that they are in control of placing limits on sexual activity. Of course they do have to be careful how they approach setting these limits.

Laurie: Well I guess, I would just, I don't know, I guess I would try to keep it kind of light and stuff, cause I don't want to piss them off right? Some guys could be weird and psycho (laughs) and so, I don't know I'd probably try to keep it light, put clothes on or whatever if I took my clothes off, and be like, 'oh, can you go?' or 'I'm gonna go home' or whatever.

While women exercised agency by setting limits and interrupting sexual activity prior to penetration, the reaction of the men they were with varied. In the examples discussed above the women's excuses were considered 'legitimate' by the men. However, if a man did not consider the excuses 'legitimate' he often became frustrated and women were labeled 'teases'. These consequences acted as constraints and attempted to limit women's access to these strategies to create their own agency.

While many women set sexual limits, others reported orchestrating their own casual sex experiences focused on their own pleasure. Anne's story is a good example of this type of agency and of the tension between a male-oriented discursive construction of heterosexual casual sex and women's space for agency within that discourse. Anne carefully sought out and chose a man to have casual sex with.

He's not young young, he's 19, but like I haven't been with a 19-year-old guy since I was 17, so it was really weird, but um it's so sad but it seems to safer to me, to go for someone who wasn't like, living in Jasper for so long, than for someone new and innocent, it sounds so dirty! (laughs) . . . but its that attitude. Like he was a really good-looking boy, but he probably didn't know how good-looking quite yet you know what I mean . . . and I knew when I met him that he was like, how old he was and I knew he was leaving in August.

Anne carefully chose a man whose social position enabled her more control over the situation. She liked the idea that Jack was young and new to Jasper. To her, this meant that he was likely not very experienced and that he had not yet developed an attitude like many other men she met in Jasper. This gave her greater control over the situation. She went out with Jack and a few friends one night to go partying. Both of them got quite drunk, but the whole night she was focused on getting him to go home with her. At one point they tried to go to a different bar, but Jack was so drunk that the bouncers would not let him in; he said that he would just go home.

I was like, no, the whole point of going out with you guys is because of you, you can't go home, so, but I didn't say that, I'm like oh no no no, we can't leave one person out that's so wrong. And I asked the bouncer if we take him to park and he sobers up can we come back in an hour, and they said as long as he can walk straight or something like that then we'll let him in. So that, so we ended up doing that.

Anne ensured that Jack would stay with the rest of the group until the end of the night so she could take him home with her. They did end up back at that bar. Anne and Jack were dancing and kissing on the dance floor. One of Jack's friends was leaving the bar and came up and shook Jack's hand to congratulate him on successfully picking up Anne.

Like when the guy shook the guy's hand and like I don't care cause like, congratulations to me too, you know mean, that was my goal for the night, to go home with him. So like, and then we did, and he is so much fun.

Anne felt that she too should be congratulated; she was taking up the typically male role in casual sex. She took up the active role seeking sex, and he took on the more passive role by going along with it. When they did end up back at her place she was concerned about him, and his willingness to participate in sex.

I know I wanted to have sex, like that was something that was going to happen for me. But I did ask him because I kinda felt. . . just because I was so forward with it all the time, I just wanted to make sure he was along for the, like was there as well . . . Cause yeah, cause a lot of times I probably haven't been with the guy, and it just happened anyways, you just kind of follow along with the progression of things . . . Like I asked him before we had sex, are you sure you're okay with this? And he was like, yeah! Like what the fuck, like why are you asking that question?

She knew that she was not always really into the casual sex that took place previously, and she did not like the feeling that gave her. Therefore, she made a point of ensuring that Jack was a willing participant. Jack almost took offense to her question. Her question subverts the male sexual drive discourse by questioning his desire. He took this as also questioning his masculinity as framed within the male sexual drive discourse.

Throughout the sexual activity, Anne ensured that her desires would be met.

I don't mind like, like helping myself get off when I'm having sex cause some guys are good at it, some guys know how to do it and you don't have to worry about it, but some guys are totally clueless, especially, maybe not so experienced guys and so I don't have an issue at all with for me its for me and I know that I don't have a problem with I want to do this I want to do that . . . Like when I was with Jack I did say it I have no problem saying certain things like, like just stuff like getting on top, different positions and like can you move over here can you move over there.

Anne had no problem taking control over her sexual pleasure. During casual sex, she will pleasure herself if she is not getting what she wants from sex. She is also comfortable enough to ask for what she wants, a switch in position, or for Jack to shift to a different position. Anne uses her sense of agency to get what she wants, at the same time she recognizes that the model of casual sex is a male model and so she has learned how to temporarily manipulate the model to fit her desires.

> Like guys are assholes, I had no idea, no one told me, and it's not that I'm not angry at them, because I just see it, as that's the way they are, you just have to know that. I think girls should be given that knowledge, so that and then they can make their own decisions and what they want. If they want to participate in it or not, because sometimes I do, sometimes I'm like, I want to, and I'm up for it but you have to be really aware of what you're getting into, because you think it really hurt like otherwise.

She feels that now that she knows more about what casual sex is all about, she can choose when and how she participates in it. For Anne, casual sex is deliberately engaged in, which contrasts with many other women's experiences of casual sex as something that 'just happens'.

Women who take up sexual agency in this way move beyond the permissiveness discourse because they are not just giving themselves permission to participate in sex. They are creating experiences and situations to satisfy their own

sexual desires. They do this not by changing the dominant discourses that govern heterosexual casual sex, but by creating spaces within those discourses and subtly challenging them to allow them to cater to their own needs.

The negotiation of heterosexual casual sex is a nuanced process laden with hegemonic and often contradictory discourses. Often, there is the sense that casual sex is not really negotiated at all, that it just happens when two people are together at the bar drinking. Running parallel to this discourse are the male sexual drive discourse and the sexual permissiveness discourse. The male sexual drive discourse is used to create a model of casual sex governed by notions of male sexual desire as being ever-present and never satisfied. This discourse simultaneously silences women's sexual desires and assumes that women play a passive role in sexual relations. For casual sex to take place, the sexual permissiveness discourse is deployed, allowing women to desire and participate in sex as long as it is the version of sex in the male sexual drive discourse—that is penetrative sex with 'no strings attached'. A few women however, position themselves within the have/hold discourse and expect that after casual sex the possibility for a friendship or relationship still exists.

Within these discourses that privilege male desire, women have been able to carve out ways to negotiate casual sex that takes into consideration their own desires. Women will place limits on the sexual activity or leave after their needs have been met. Sometimes women will take an even more active role in designing and orchestrating their own casual sex experiences that satisfy their desires. Women are adapting by recognizing that casual sex is often controlled by male sexual desire, then choosing when and how they participate in casual sex to get their own desires met.

Conclusion

When discussing issues of casual sex, YAJs first turn to a discourse of 'it just happens' and suggest that casual sex is a serendipitous event. However, through their stories the male sexual drive discourse is the dominant discourse operating in this environment. Casual sex is driven by the assumption that men are perpetually in search of sex. Perhaps surprisingly, the women deploy the have/hold discourse and report that one reason they engage in casual sex is for the possibility of developing a relationship with their casual partner. Finally, casual sex is dependent on the sexual permissiveness discourse that suggests that casual sex is permissible for both women and men (at least within the confines of the male sexual drive discourse). Finally, within these discourses women exert power through their choice in partners, by setting limits and by taking what may be considered a typically masculine role and actively pursuing casual sex.

References

Hollway, W. 1984. 'Gender Difference and the Production of Subjectivity', in J. Henriques, W. Hollway, C. Urwin, C. Venn, and V. Walkerdine, eds, *Changing the Subject: Psychology, Social Regulation and Subjectivity*, pp. 227–63. New York: Routledge.

CHAPTER 36

The Bedroom and The State: Women's Struggle to Limit Their Fertility

Angus McLaren and Arlene Tigar McLaren

In the spring of 1908 the congregation of Toronto's St James's Cathedral was informed by the Reverend C. Ensor Sharp that the Almighty interested himself directly in the demographic details of Canada's declining birth rate.

> God abhors the spirit so prevalent nowadays which contemns [sic] motherhood. How it must grieve Him when He sees what we call race suicide; when he sees the problem of married life approached lightly and wantonly; based on nothing higher and nobler than mere luxury and gratification of passion (*Toronto Evening Telegram*, 26 March 1908: 9).

This fear of 'race suicide' to which Sharp referred had been popularized in North America by President Theodore Roosevelt, who stated, 'The woman who flinches from childbirth stands on a par with the soldier who drops his rifle and runs in battle.' This was only the most famous remark to be made by a generation of social observers who attributed the shrinking size of the Anglo-Saxon family to the 'selfishness' of women. By the turn of the century Canadians were well acquainted with such concerns. In the Canadian edition of Sylvanus Stall's *What a Young Man Ought to Know* (1897) the author expressed his horrors that many women married, not to bear children, but 'for the purpose of practically leading a life of legalized prostitution' (198). Crown Attorney J.W. Curry, KC, addressing the city pastors of Toronto in 1901, claimed that employment opportunities permitted women to avoid marriage or to fall back on 'crime', which led to a 'low birth rate' (*Toronto Globe*, 17 December 1901: 8). According

Table 36.1 General Fertility Rates, Canada and Selected Provinces, 1871 to 1931
(annual number of births per 1,000 women aged 15–49 years)

Year	Canada	Nova Scotia	Quebec	Ontario	Manitoba	Saskatchewan	British Columbia
1871	189	174	180	191	–	–	–
1881	160	148	173	149	366	–	202
1891	144	138	163	121	242	–	204
1901	145	132	160	108	209	550	184
1911	144	128	161	112	167	229	149
1921	120	105	155	98	125	135	84
1931	94	98	116	79	81	100	62

SOURCE: Jacque Henripin, *Trends and Factors of Fertility in Canada* (Ottawa, 1972), 21.

to Professor H.E. Armstong, speaking at the 1909 Winnipeg meeting of the British Association, all attempts to bring women into competition with men were dangerous, 'for she will inevitably cease to exercise her specific womanly functions with effect, so delicate is the adjustment of her mechanism' (*Manitoba Free Press*, 30 August 1909: 3). A contributor to the *Canadian Churchman* (1900) went so far as to assert that even the pressures of existing society encouraged, 'to put it bluntly, in nine cases out of ten, women to murder their unborn children' (29 November 1900: 724).

What exercised the imaginations of these writers was the belief that women were responsible for the fall in marital fertility [i.e. the decline in the number of children born per woman, which affected Canada at the beginning of the twentieth century, and which was interpreted as a moral and social crisis for the young nation]. In fact, this fall was only a symptom of the major social and economic transformations Canada was undergoing at the turn of the century. Later commentators were to speak of the confidence and optimism of the age, but any examination of the population discussion uncovers many expressions of fear and foreboding

As bizarre as these outbursts might first appear, they are nevertheless noteworthy because they point to one of the major social phenomena of Canadian history that has yet to be carefully examined—the decline of the birth rate. The most

dramatic decline took place in Ontario, falling by 44 per cent between 1871 and 1901; from 1881 to 1911, Ontario had the lowest fertility of any province. Even Quebec's general fertility rate dropped by 21 per cent between 1851 and 1921 while that of Canada as a whole fell by 41 per cent (Henripin, 1972: 21).[1] (See Table 36.1.)

Despite relatively stable marriage rates and improving fecundity, the birth rate of English-speaking families fell; hence, some form of birth control must have been used. Discovering exactly what form is a problem.[2] Traditional histories of birth control assume that the decline of fertility in the late nineteenth century in Europe and North America was due to the diffusion of some new knowledge or technique. It had to be recalled, however, that there were several traditional methods already available. To space births, Canadian families had long relied on simple continence and the margin of safety from conception provided when a woman was nursing.[3] In addition, two major methods of family restriction were to be used well into the twentieth century—coitus interruptus and self-induced abortion.

Contraceptive Practices in Canada

How would young Canadian couples of the 1890s seek to control their family size? The information available to them in published form was limited.

Section 179c of the 1892 Criminal Code (substituted with Section 207 in 1900) restricted writing on the subject.

> Everyone is guilty of an indictable offense and liable to two years' imprisonment who knowingly, without lawful excuse or justification, offers to sell, advertises, publishes and advertisement of or has for sale or disposal any medicine, drug or article intended or represented as a means of preventing conception or causing abortion.

Discussion of family limitation was restricted but it did take place. From the mass-produced medical and self-help literature, mostly of American origin, that circulated widely in Canada, it is clear that doctors and popular practitioners recognized the growing desire of the public to avoid overly large families.[4] Although respectable physicians would not countenance the use of 'mechanical' contraceptives they would on occasion advise the use of certain 'natural' means of control. The first means were simple continence—Emma F. Angell Drake in *What a Young Wife Ought to Know* (1908) recommended twin beds—and prolonged nursing, which was widely believed to provide protection against a subsequent conception (1908: 131 ff). The second advised natural method was restriction of intercourse to what was thought to be the 'safe period' in the woman's ovulation cycle. Unfortunately, the cycle was completely misunderstood and the so-called 'safe period' was mistakenly calculated to fall at mid-month. The correct cycle was not established until the 1920s, but in the meantime several generations of physicians vaunted the reliability of their schedule. Augustus K. Gardner, for example, in *Conjugal Sins Against the Laws and Health* (1874), advised waiting twelve days after the menses.

> This act of continence is healthy, moral and irreproachable. Then there need be no imperfection in the conjugal act, no fears, no shame, no disgust, no drawback to the joys which legitimately belong to a true married life. Thus excess is avoided, diseases diminished, and such a desirable limitation to the number of children, as is consistent with the peculiar nature of the individuals concerned, is effected (Gardner, 1874: 182–3).[5]

But what of the most reliable known forms of contraception in the nineteenth century—the sheath, douche, and pessary?[6] Doctors would not discuss their use because such appliances were associated in their minds with the libertine, the prostitute, and the midwife and were thus outside the realm of respectable medicine. The importance of the rhythm method and the reason why it was greeted by physicians with enthusiasm was that it was not tainted with such associations; it had been 'scientifically' determined and so offered a means by which the medical profession could claim to extend its expertise into the most intimate area of human life.

When one looks for references to 'mechanical' means of contraception one finds, because of both legal restrictions and medical distaste for the subject, little direct information. Women who did know about the prophylactic benefits of douching would, however, have been able to read between the lines in the advertisements for the 'Every Woman Marvel Whirling Spray', which offered, according to its producer, the Windsor Supply Company, the advantages of 'vaginal hygiene'. The company's advertisements appeared in such diverse publications as the T. Eaton Company catalogue, Jefferis and Nichols, *Searchlights on Health*, the Toronto *Daily Mail and Empire*, and even in the staid pages of the *Dominion Medical Monthly*. Of course, to be fully effective a douche would have to be used in conjunction with a pessary. Recipes for homemade ones concocted of coca butter, boric acid, and tannic acid found in private papers suggest that Canadian women were not slow in producing their own protective devices (Rasmussen, et al., 1976: 72).[7]

For men the most effective contraceptive was the sheath or condom. By the 1890s they were being mass-produced in Britain and the United States and distributed by druggists in Canadian urban centers. A sensational report on their easy availability was made in 1898 by the purity campaigner C.S. Clark in *Of Toronto the Good*.

> I saw a druggist's advertisement a short time ago in a Toronto paper with this significant line: *Rubber Goods* of ALL KINDS For Sale. There is not a boy in Toronto, I dare say, who does not know what that means. . . . A young fellow of sixteen once handed me a pasteboard coin, silvered over. When I mentioned to him that I saw nothing in the possession of such a coin, he laughed and told me to tear off the outside layer. I did so, and discovered one of the articles I have endeavoured to describe (1898: 127).[8]

What is noteworthy in Clark's report, however, is that such contraceptives were assumed to be employed not so much to control marital fertility as to permit extra- or premarital liaisons. They were no doubt used by some to control family size but their relatively high price, their association with venereal disease and prostitution, and the claims of doctors that they caused dangerous inflammation all restricted their employment. This, then, left coitus interruptus as the simplest and most widespread form of contraception. Doctors might condemn it as 'mutual masturbation' or 'conjugal onanism', but until well into the twentieth century it was the main way in which Canadian couples sought to 'cheat nature'.[9]

It is a commonplace assumption that the 'Roaring Twenties' witnessed a great surge in sexual freedom and experimentation. If this did in fact occur—which some historians deny—it took place without the aid of any new form of contraceptive protection. It is true that many servicemen were introduced to the use of the sheath while overseas during the First World War and that some

women were aware of Marie Stopes's popularization of the cervical cap in England and the Margaret Sanger's defence of the vaginal diaphragm in the United States (McLaren, 1978: 210). It is also true that Drs Ogino and Knaus's correct determination of the ovulation cycle was made in the late 1920s and with Roman Catholic approbation, publicized in the 1930s (Latz, 1932). But when one compares the effective forms of contraception available to the mass of the people in the 1890s to those to which they had access in the 1930s, one can detect no major advance. The birth rate was brought down, not because of any technological breakthrough, but because more couples intent on limited their fertility conscientiously employed traditional methods.

In response to such demands the 'feminine hygiene' industry became a multimillion-dollar business. In the United States it was estimated that in the 1930s $250 million a year was spent on such products; though figures on Canadian purchases are not available they likely were in the $12 million-a-year range (Reed, 1978).[10] In popular women's magazines such as *Chatelaine* the advertisements for such products as Lysol and Dettol intimated that they could be turned to contraceptive purposes: 'It used to be that feminine hygiene was not discussed. It was taboo. But today it is recognized as modern science's safeguard to health . . . very often to happiness' (*Grain Grower's Guide*, 1930: 19).[11] In addition to such douching products, the women's pages of the popular press were dotted with references to a variety of suppositories and soluble pessaries—Rendells, Norforms, Sani-tabs, Zonite, and Zonitors.[12] Rendells's suppositories, which were claimed to produce a swift and sure 'protective film', were in fact the only proven contraceptives (*Chatelaine*, March 1936: 48). The others, like the douches, could act as spermicidal agents but were often no more than vaginal deodorants. They were clearly passed off as contraceptives, however, guaranteed to protect 'marital happiness' or intended only for 'married women'.

Those who preferred a barrier method of birth control were assured by the guarded advertisements of the Novelty Rubber Co., the Sanitary Rubber Goods Co., the Paris Specialty Co., the National Specialty Co., the Federal Supply Co., and a host of other businesses that their orders could be filled.[13] Supreme Specialties of Regina, Saskatchewan, for example, sold—in addition to a number of pessaries and abortifacient pills—and extensive range of sheathes with such exotic names as: Canadian Royal Guards, Merry Widow, Japs, Excella-Never-Rips, Pretty Polly, and Ramses.[14]

The census data tells us the extent to which Canadians were limited their fertility and a short review of the traditional birth control methods tells us how they did it. To understand *why* they were employing contraceptives is a far more difficult issue. Fortunately, we have invaluable evidence on their motivations in the collections of letters written by Canadians to the birth controllers Marie Stopes and Margaret Sanger.[15] Stopes and Sanger received hundreds of letters from Canadians because, until at least the mid-1930s, the general assumption was made that no birth control movement existed in Canada. Both received requests for information on birth control and sexual counselling from doctors, ministers, nurses, and social workers, as well as from private individuals.

For the purpose of this chapter it is only necessary to draw on the Stopes correspondence.[16] Her typical Canadian correspondent was the woman who felt she had no one else to turn to. Marie Stopes, though thousands of miles away, was in effect a mother figure. One woman wrote in 1934, 'I might say I had no mother to whom I could go for advise [sic] hence a great ignorance on this subject' (Stopes Papers [CMAC], 23 November 1934). The assumption that mothers should provide their daughters with such information was also made by a Toronto woman, who wanted to know what to tell her eighteen year-old daughter, and by a Saskatoon writer, who said of her daughter: 'She has one Boy she has only be

[sic] Married 10 months and I hate to think of the future for her' (Stopes Papers [CMAC], 14 November 1934; 20 November 1934).

A frequent complaint was that clearly the better-off and well-informed knew how to avoid conceptions but that they were shrouding their methods in mystery. A number of these women hold doctors responsible for not providing the needed information. A correspondent in Tecumseh, Ontario, informed Stopes that after having two live births and one stillborn,

> . . . the Doctor attending advised us to avoid having any more: promising to give us birth control knowledge. This he did not do, and I did not care to bring the subject up again. But as I do wish to avoid the misery misunderstandings my other married friends are going through I am asking you to help me (Stopes Papers [CMAC], 5 June 1935).

More outspoken was a woman who exclaimed, 'really it seems almost wicked that Doctors are so "dumb" in both its uses.' She attributed their silence and ignorance to concern that a limitation of births would cut into their practices (Stopes Papers [CMAC], 9 November 1934).

Some women were completely ignorant of birth control (Stopes Papers [CMAC], 26 January 1935). Others, such as a Kendall, Ontario, woman, found that some purportedly effective methods did not work: 'I have used Lysol douches, also Quinine and cocoa butter pessaries. They were either unreliable or I did something incorrectly' (Stopes Papers [CMAC], 23 November 1934). Still others had heard of newer methods like the cap or pessary but wanted more information: did the pessary cause injury, would the condom lower sexual sensitivity, should a quinine pessary be used with the cap? (Stopes Papers [CMAC], 21 November 1934; 11 March 1935).

As might be expected, the main reason Stopes's correspondents wanted birth control information was to limit the size of their families. A Prince

Edward Island woman married nine years, with four children and one on the way, wrote: 'It seems that all my married life is spent either in having children or nursing them and it does pale on one no matter how much they like children' (Stopes Papers [CMAC], 15 January 1935).[17] A Dartmouth, Nova Scotia, mother, who after four years of marriage had two boys, pathetically begged:

> I am writing to you as a very ignorant married women to find out if I too may share your secret. . . . I am taking a great liberty I know but when one worries so from month to month to find a way out would be wonderful (Stopes Papers [CMAC], no date 1934).

After having given birth to eight children, an Oshawa woman informed Stopes, one could rationally appraise the moral issues raised by birth control.

> I am thirty-seven years of age and I feel that I have had enough children; indeed I think it is a bigger sin to bring children into the world when you haven't enough to keep them than it is to try to prevent them (Stopes Papers [CMAC], 25 November 1934).

But though most of the women who wrote Stopes already had large families whose size they wished to limit, some had only just begun their child-bearing careers and wanted birth control information so they could plan their families in a purposeful manner. A young married woman in Winnipeg simply wanted information on how to best assure a conception; a Welland, Ontario, mother who had one child and intended to postpone the birth of the second for some time asked: 'Could I get information on the best way to conceive a perfect child?' (Stopes Papers [CMAC], 25 September 1934).[18] Contraception was employed to plan, space, and limit births.

Although the opponents of birth control depicted the women who employed it as being indifferent to the importance of children and the family, the letters to Stopes tell a very different story. It was because these women took so seriously the roles of wife and mother that they were turning to professional counselors like Stopes to tell them how to respond to the new challenges of the twentieth century.[19] For example, a young Ontario woman wrote, 'I am about to be married and I am anxious that my married life will be as perfect as I can make it, and my fiancée is as anxious as I am that we enter into marriage intelligently' (Stopes Papers [CMAC], 22 November 1934). A Toronto woman, fearing that the unexpected arrival of her first child had damaged her marriage and that a second might destroy it, sent Stopes the plea, 'Can't you help me save our romance?' (Stopes Papers [CMAC], 12 November 1934).

What is especially striking in these letters is their writers' conviction that birth control, by ending the terrible anxiety of becoming pregnant, would restore sexual pleasure to their marriages and strengthen the marital bond. In a 10-page letter an Ontario woman told her tragic story of a life plagued by pregnancies and miscarriages. She faced each conception with anger and fear, her doctors told her to avoid pregnancy but did not say how, and, worst of all, 'my husband grew almost to fear his desire for me and I to loathe it' (Stopes Papers [CMAC], 15 November 1934). A Toronto woman related a similar tale. After the first birth she and her husband 'knew that we must be careful (horrible word in marriage)'. They used condoms, douches, and coitus interruptus, but all proved unsatisfactory and a second child arrived. The third pregnancy miscarried, because, as the woman admitted, 'Yes, I did try to bring it on. I was afraid' (Stopes Papers [CMAC], 14 November 1934).

She was afraid, as other correspondents were, that without being able to limit her fertility she would not be able to fill the demanding twentieth-century role of romantic wife and conscientious mother and possibly would lose her husband (Stopes Papers [CMAC], 10 November 1934).[20] A

Port Arthur woman who had three babies in four years lamented: 'I am tired and miserable most of the time, and certainly do not make an ideal wife and mother' (Stopes Papers [CMAC], 13 November 1934). In the interwar period the Canadian media subjected such women to a barrage of exhortations to become more devoted mothers and more appealing spouses. Never mentioned—but understood all the same—was the fact that only birth control would permit the inherently contradictory implications of the cult of domesticity to be resolved.[21]

Birth control was portrayed in these letters as very much a woman's responsibility. Although the opponents of family limitation frequently associated it with some sort of 'revolt' of women against male power, Stopes's correspondents frequently fretted about any inconveniences their husbands might have to suffer. A Toronto woman, while discussing with Stopes the employment by her husband of a condom, asked worriedly, 'I'll be frank. Doctor is it fair to him? . . . Will he in time weary of such interference?' (Stopes Papers [CMAC], 14 November 1934).[22] Few male correspondents expressed such concerns regarding their wives' contraceptive practices. One husband did tell Stopes of his worries:

> We have used rubber appliances but they seem to be to harsh and mechanical, we have also practiced withdrawal which cheats my wife of a perfect 'orgasm' and leaves her in a very nervous and exhausted condition for days (Stopes Papers [CMAC], 27 November 1934).

In most cases, however, the old assumption was maintained that since the woman faced the greatest risk she should bear the greater responsibility in birth control.

The letters written to Stopes, as valuable as they are, do not tell us everything about the motivations of those who had recourse to contraceptives. They are necessarily self-serving and make no mention of concerns that the writers may have felt Stopes would have disliked. For example, all the women said they had children or intended to have them; anyone who had read Stopes's work knew she was hostile to the notion of couples remaining childless for life. They tended to describe to Stopes their desire for a fulfilling sexual life in terms that she herself had done much to popularize. They downplayed the more mundane but basic causes for the fertility decline—the end of the economic rationality of the large family as child employment was restricted and education costs soared, the increased availability of employment for women in white-collar work and light industry, and the urgent concern, once the depression hit, to protect the family economy as best one could. Nevertheless, the letters, written principally by urban, English-speaking, middle-class Protestants, do confirm the demographers' argument that the Canadian fertility decline was marked by important class, religious, and ethnic differentials (Henripin, 1972). Most important of all, the letters offer precious insights into the lives of women attempting to exert some control over their reproductive functions.

Notes

1. See also John Davidson, 'The Census of Canada', *Economic Journal* 11 (1901): 595–602; W.J.A. Donald, 'The Growth and Distribution of Canadian Population', *Journal of Political Economy* 21 (1913): 296–312.
2. On statistical evidence that such controls were employed by the upper middle class from the 1850s, see Michael Katz, *The People of Hamilton,*

Canada West: Family and Class in a Mid-Nineteenth Century City (Cambridge, MA: Harvard University Press, 1975), 35; see also Lorne Tepperman, 'Ethnic Variations in Marriage and Fertility: Canada in 1871', *Canadian Review of Sociology and Anthropology* 9 (1974): 287–307. On the relative impact of delayed marriages, changes in proportion married, and birth control, see W.B. Hurd, 'The Decline in the Canadian Birth Rate', *Canadian Journal of Economics and Political Science* 3 (1937): 43–55.

3. See L.F. Bouvier, 'The Spacing of Births Among French Canadian Families: An Historical Approach', *Canadian Review of Sociology and Anthropology* 5 (1968): 17–26; Jacques Henripin, *La population canadienne au debut du XV/IIe siecle* (Paris: Presses Universitaires de France, 1954), 86–7.

4. See Michael Bliss, 'Pure Books on Avoided Subjects: Pre-Freudian Sexual Ideas in Canada', *Historical Papers* (1970): 89–108. For a specific example of the way in which information on 'sex hygiene' was brought from America to Canada, see Beatrice Brigden, 'One Woman's Campaign for Social Purity and Social Reform', in Richard Allen, ed., *The Social Gospel in Canada*. National Museum of Man Mercury Series. History Division Paper No.8 (Ottawa: National Museum of Canada, 1975), 36–62.

5. An additional reason for doctors' enthusiasm for the 'safe period' was the Vatican's tacit acceptance from the 1880s of this 'natural' form of control. See John T. Noonan, *Contraception: A History of its Treatment by Catholic Theologians and Canonists* (Cambridge, MA: Harvard University Press, 1965), 441–2.

6. For the development of contraceptives in the nineteenth century, see the notes in Angus McLaren, 'Contraception and the Working Classes: The Social Ideology of the English Birth Control Movement in Its Early Years', *Comparative Studies in Society and History*, 18 (1976), 236–51.

7. See also G. Kolischer, 'The Prevention of Conception', *Dominion Medical Monthly* 19 (1902): 116–19.

8. As examples of what Clark was talking about, see the advertisements of 'rubber goods' placed by F.E. Karn Ltd., 'The People's Popular Drug Store', in the Toronto *Daily Star*, and by Cyrus H. Bowes in the Victoria *Daily Colonist* of 1906.

9. For attacks on withdrawal, see Napheys, *The Physical Life of Women* (Toronto, no date), 97; Jefferis and Nichols, *Searchlights on Health: Light on Dark Corners* (Toronto, 1897), 244 ff; J.H. Kellogg, *Man, the Masterpiece* (London: Modern Medicine Publishing Company, 1903), 426.

That medical warnings against coitus interruptus were not taken seriously, at least by Canadians of Scottish ancestry, as suggested by the fact that the practice was jocularly referred to as 'getting off at Kilmarnock', that is, the last train stop before Glasgow (personal communication).

10. See also John Peel, 'The Manufacturing and Retailing of Contraceptives in England', *Population Studies* 17 (1963): 113–25; *Fortune* (February 1938): 83–114.

11. See also *Chatelaine*, March 1928: 59. For Dettol, see *Chatelaine*, October 1939: 36.

12. See *Chatelaine* for advertisements for Norforms (May 1936: 56); Sanitabs (January 1937: 38); Zonite (October 1928: 32); Zonitors (January 1940: 22).

13. See, for example, *The United Farmer*, 22 June 1934: 15, 6 July 1934: 15, 5 October 1934: 15, 9 November 1934: 15; *Grain Growers' Guide*, 1 January 1930: 19.

14. See advertisement in Marie Stopes to Supreme Specialties, 19 April 1935, Stopes Papers, Contemporary Medical Archives Centre, Wellcome Institute for the History of Medicine; hereafter Stopes Papers, CMAC.

15. On English correspondents, see Ruth Hall, *Dear Dr. Stopes: Sex in the 1920s* (London: Penguin, 1978); Ellen Holtzman, 'The Pursuit of Married Love: Women's Attitudes towards Sexuality and Marriage in Great Britain, 1918–1939', *Journal of Social History* 16 (1982): 39–51.

16. There are collections of Stopes papers in the British Museum and the Contemporary Medical Archives Centre. The latter contains an especially interesting file of Canadian letters, nearly all written after a story on Stopes had appeared in a November 1934, issue of the *Star Weekly*. These are the letters referred to in what follows. To protect the anonymity of Stopes's correspondents, we have not given their names.

17. See also A.G. to Stopes, 14 November 1934, and M.M. to Stopes, 27 November 1934.

18. M.W. to Stopes, 25 September 1934, Stopes Papers, British Museum.

19. On the role of the counsellor, see Jacques Donzelot, *The Policing of Families* (New York: Pantheon, 1979); Barbara Ehrenreich and Deidre English, *For Her Own Good* (Garden

City, NY: Anchor, 1978); Michel Foucault, *The History of Sexuality* (New York: Vintage, 1979); Christopher Lasch, *Haven in a Heartless World* (New York: W.W. Norton, 1977).

20. After clinics were established in Canada one doctor would write, 'There are birth control clinics where the proper information can be obtained. The domestic relations courts have found this one item to be the source of more marital difficulties than any other trouble that enters into life together.' Dr Anne B. Fisher, 'Live with a Man and Love It', *Chatelaine,* September 1937: 34.

21. See, for example, the Lysol ad in the *Manitoba Free Press*, 15 January 1927: 15: '. . . a woman's health and youthfulness need not fade with marriage. Modern science provides a simple protection. Sane habits of living, plus the *proper protection of feminine hygiene. . . . Preserve your health and youth with Lysol.'* On the discussion of the role of the 'Modern Mother', see *Chatelaine*, March 1931: 15, 69; December 1931: 13, 39–40; April 1933: 18, 74; May 1933: 2; June 1933: 22, 36, 44; Mary Vipond, 'The Image of Women in Mass Circulation Magazines in the 1920s', in Susan Mann Trofimenkoff and Alison Prentice, eds., *The Neglected Majority: Essays in Canadian Women's History* (Toronto: McClelland and Stewart, 1977), 116–24; Veronica Strong-Boag, 'Intruders in the Nursery: Childcare Professionals Reshape the Years One to Five, 1920–1940', in Joy Parr, ed., *Childhood and Family in Canadian Society* (Toronto: McClelland and Stewart, 1982), 160–79.

22. See also G.S. to Stopes, 9 November 1934, Stopes Papers, CMAC.

References

Canadian Churchman. 1900. 'Childless Marriages'. 29 November.

Chatelaine. 1936. March.

Clark, C.S. 1898. *Of Toronto the Good*. Montreal: The Toronto Publishing Company.

Drake, E.F.A. 1908. *What a Young Wife Ought to Know*. Toronto: Vir Publishing Company.

Gardner, A.K. 1874. *Conjugal Sins Against the Law of Life and Health*. New York: G.J. Moulton.

Grain Grower's Guide, 1930. 1 January.

Henripin, J. 1972. *Trends and Factors of Fertility in Canada*. Ottawa: Statistics Canada.

Latz, L.J. 1932. *The Rhythm of Sterility and Fertility in Women*. Chicago: Latz Foundation.

McLaren, A. 1978. *Birth Control in Nineteenth Century England*. New York: Holmes & Meier.

Manitoba Free Press. 1909. 30 August.

Rasmussen, L., et al. 1976. *A Harvest Yet to Reap*. Toronto: Women's Press.

Reed, J. 1978. *From Private Vice to Public Virtue: A History of the Birth Control Movement in America Since 1830*. New York: Basic Books.

Stall, S. 1897. *What a Young Man Ought to Know*. Toronto: Vir Publishing Company.

Stopes Papers, Contemporary Medical Archives Centre (CMAC). *Specific letters cited within the chapter*: R.C. to Stopes, no date 1934; M.W. to Stopes, 25 September 1934; G.S. to Stopes, 9 November 1934; J.D. to Stopes, 12 November 1934; W.M. to Stopes, 13 November 1934; G.H. to Stopes, 14 November 1934; R.R. to Stopes, 15 November 1934; D.L. to Stopes, 20 November 1934; J.H. to Stopes, 21 November 1934; I.A. to Stopes, 22 November 1934; J.D. to Stopes, 23 November 1934; J.B. to Stopes, 25 November 1934; I.S. to Stopes, 27 November 1934; J.M. to Stopes, 15 January 1935; I.S. to Stopes, 26 January 1935; S.S. to Stopes, 11 March 1935; J.G. to Stopes, 5 June 1935.

Toronto Evening Telegram. 1908. 26 March.

Toronto Globe. 1901. 17 December.

QUESTIONS FOR CRITICAL THOUGHT

1. Do you, or the people you know, 'measure love with a feminine yardstick', as Cancian suggests?

2. The McLarens' research finds that contraception—the ability to avoid getting pregnant—has had a major influence on the ways that men and women experience heterosexual sex in Canada. How does the availability of contraception change sex? Are you satisfied with the means of contraception currently available where you live?

3. Sexual relationships are intensely intimate, individualized, and personal, yet they exist within a gender-differentiated world. How does gender influence the ways that men and women experience sexual intimacy and closeness?

4. What role do same-gender friends play in your life? Do you have non-sexual friends of another gender? How is their role different than that of your same-gender friends?

5. In your experience, or in the experiences of people you know, are long-term, intimate relationships gendered differently from short-term, casual relationships?

PART IX

The Gender of Violence

F rom early childhood to old age, violence is perhaps the most obdurate, intractable gender difference we have observed. Men constitute 99 per cent of all persons arrested for rape; 88 per cent of those arrested for murder; 92 per cent of those arrested for robbery; 87 per cent for aggravated assault; 85 per cent of other assaults; 83 per cent of all family violence; 82 per cent of disorderly conduct. Men are overwhelmingly more violent than women. According to the US Department of Justice, nearly 90 per cent of all murder victims are murdered by men (*Uniform Crime Reports*, 1991: 17).

The National Academy of Sciences puts the case most starkly: 'The most consistent pattern with respect to gender is the extent to which male criminal participation in serious crimes at any age greatly exceeds that of females, regardless of source of data, crime type, level of involvement, or measure of participation.' 'Men are always and everywhere more likely than women to commit criminal acts,' write criminologists Michael Gottfredson and Travis Hirschi (1990: 145).

The equation of men and violence runs so deep that the notion of violent women—or 'nasty girls', as Christie Barron and Dany Lacombe put it—can evoke a moral panic and a sense that the natural order of things has been inverted. Barron and Lacombe dissect recent Canadian media hype about 'girls who kill', following the Reena Virk murder, and argue that there has not actually been any significant increase in girl violence.

As Barron and Lacombe show, the apparent incongruity of femininity and violence continues to fascinate commentators and pop-cultural analysts—another sign of how tightly violence and masculinity are bound together in contemporary culture. Yet how do we understand this association between masculinity and violence? Is it a biological fact of nature, caused by something inherent in male anatomy? Is it culturally universal? What can we do to prevent or at least ameliorate the problem of male violence?

If we look closely, we can find violence subtly, or not-so-subtly, implicated in the social construction of gender across a diverse range of settings. Carol Cohn's insightful essay examines the gendered language of masculine 'war-talk', in which the human tragedy of nuclear war preparation is masked behind discussions of kill ratios, body counts, and megaton delivery. Violence is also implicated in the social organization of gender when it is used to enforce the rigid gender binary, by punishing those who dare to step outside it, such as transgendered people. Vivian Namaste coined the term 'genderbashing' to describe the violence perpetrated on transgendered individuals, and argues that this form of violence is still largely invisible to the general public, even as violence against lesbians and gay men receives more and more attention.

Russell Dobash, R. Emerson Dobash, and their colleagues use a gendered power analysis to explain why men batter the women they say they love in far greater numbers than women hit men. They bring a sensible sobriety to current discussions that suggest women are just as likely to commit acts of violence against their husbands as men are against their wives.

Of course, once masculinity is identified as a risk factor for violence, we are left with the political question of what to do about it. Michael Kaufman describes the efforts of a brave group of men to stop male violence—starting from the belief that men can be honourable, strong, and assertive without taking out their frustrations on the women in their lives. Kaufman believes that men are the only ones who can end male violence, because men are the only ones who can create new, healthier meanings for masculinity.

References

Gottfredson, M., and T. Hirschi. 1990. *A General Theory of Crime*. Stanford, CA: Stanford University Press.
Uniform Crime Reports. 1991. Washington, DC: US Department of Justice.

CHAPTER 37

Moral Panic and the Nasty Girl

Christie Barron and Dany Lacombe

Female violence became a topic of much discussion in the mid 1990s in the wake of the gruesome sexual murders of teenagers by the infamous Ontario couple Paul Bernardo and Karla Homolka. But it was the murder of Reena Virk by a group of mostly female teens, in a suburb of Victoria in November 1997, which led Canadians to believe that something had gone terribly wrong with teenage girls. The belief that girl violence is rampant is a social construction. According to Statistics Canada, the annual youth charge rate for violent crime dropped 5 per cent in 1999, signaling a decline for the fourth year in a row (Statistics Canada, 2000). Moreover, Doob and Sprott (1998) have shown that the severity of youth violence did not change in the first half of the 1990s. Questioning the federal government's concern about the increase in girls' participation in violent and gang-related activities, Reitsma-Street (1999: 350) indicates that the number of girls charged for murder and attempted murder has been constant for the past twenty years and that such charges are infrequent. Although statistics indicate a phenomenal increase in the number of young women charged with minor or moderate assault over the past 10 years (from 710 charged under the *Juvenile Delinquents Act* in 1980 to 4,434 under the *Young Offenders Act* in 1995–6), several researchers indicate that the increase is more a reflection of the youth justice system's change in policy and charging practices than a 'real' change in behaviour (Doob and Sprott, 1998; Reitsma-Street, 1999). Yet the public continues to believe that youth violence, particularly girl violence, is increasing at an alarming rate and necessitates immediate attention (Chesney-Lind and Brown, 1999: 171). This perception begs the important question: Why, despite evidence to the contrary, are recent isolated incidents of female violence interpreted as a sign that today's girls have become increasingly 'nasty'?

We argue that the recent alarm over girl violence is the product of a moral panic that has had a significant impact on social, educational, and legal policy making. Drawing on the moral panic and risk society literature, as well as the work of Michel Foucault, this paper examines how the recent concern with girl violence emerged; what effects that concern has had on policy making in particularly and on society in general; and why the panic over young females is occurring today.

How the Nasty Girl Emerged

All moral panics identify and denounce a personal agent responsible for the condition that is generating widespread public concern. As Schissel explains, 'folk devils are inherently deviant and are presumed to be self-seeking, out of control and in danger of undermining the stability of society . . .' (1997: 30). Hence, during the 'warning phase' of a panic there are predictions of impending doom, sensitization to cues of danger, frequent overreactions, and rumours speculating about what is happening or what will happen (Cohen, 1980: 144–8). Subsequently, a large part of the public becomes sensitized to the threat, and, as in the case of the Nasty Girl, when confronted with an actual act of girl violence their perception of danger and risk solidifies.

It is not surprising, therefore, that the beating and murder of 14-year-old Reena Virk by a group of seven girls and one boy would become the event that provided evidence that girl violence had become a significant problem in Canada. On 14 November 1997, Virk, 'a pudgy East Indian girl trying desperately to fit in', (Cernetig, Laghi, Matas, and McInnes, 1997: A1) was on her way back to her foster home when friends asked her to join them under the bridge, a popular hangout. According to trial testimony, an argument broke out and accusations were directed at Virk for spreading rumours about one of the girls, talking to another's boyfriend, and rifling through the address book of another (Tafler, 1998: 20). The news that Virk was beaten to death by a youth group part of 'a teen subculture where girls pretending to be members of L.A. street gangs fight each other' shocked the country. According to *The Globe and Mail*, Reena's death became: 'A national tragedy' (Cernetig et al., 1997: A1).

Central to the creation of a climate of fear is statistical manipulation of crime data to establish the amplitude of girl violence. As journalist N. Nolan astutely recognizes in her analysis of the media reporting of the Virk case: 'experts and authors were appearing on TV and radio talk shows trumpeting—with the solemn self-importance that always accompanies adult laments about the various wickedness of youth—the shocking fact that, according to the Canadian Centre for Justice Statistics, crime by young girls had increased 200 per cent since 1986' (1998: 32). However, most articles failed to recognize that the increase was in reference to minor assaults, such as pushing or slapping, which did not cause serious injury. Doob and Sprott explain, '[o]ne would, we believe, have more confidence that this increase reflected a change in girls' behaviour if it were to have shown up in the 'most serious' category of assaults' (1998: 192).[1] At the time of Virk's murder, girls were still far less involved than boys in all levels of assault and only 4.5 per cent of youths charged with a homicide offence were female (1998: 192). Moreover, according to more recent official statistics, the rate of male youth crime is almost three times higher than the female rate and, in 1999, the violent crime rate dropped (–6.5 per cent) for female youths (Statistics Canada, 2000). Yet, inflated statistics about girl violence are usually assumed to be factual because, as Cohen (1980) explains, they are voiced by 'socially accredited experts' whose expertise alone serves to legitimize the moral panic.

Historically, as Klein (1995) details, female offenders were described by experts as masculinized monsters (Lombroso, 1920), insensitive and lacking moral values (Thomas, 1907), envious of men due to lack of a penis (Freud, 1933), psychologically maladjusted (Pollack, 1950) and promiscuous (Davis, 1961) (all as cited in Madriz, 1997: 26). Moreover, conceptions of morality increasingly became central to the identification and supervision of 'dangerous' females. As the legitimate guardians of the moral sphere, middle-class women, in particular, participated in social purity movements that succeeded in criminalizing females who used their sexuality to survive.

The reformers' efforts to rescue 'fallen women' and 'delinquent girls' from the harmful effects of industrial capitalism indicate how the bourgeois preoccupation with uplifting moral standards became central to the supervision of working-class girls.

Such reform movements also led to the establishment of child welfare agencies and the creation of juvenile justice systems. The youth criminal court evolved as a judicial parent or 'parens patriae' that signalled the increasing involvement of the state in regulating and rehabilitating adolescent behaviour (Geller, 1987: 116). Girls, in particular, were deemed vulnerable and were incarcerated for status offences for their own protection, both from themselves and others. In the mid-twentieth century, the popularization of psychology helped foster a shift in the understanding of unruly girls and women: from being inherently bad or immoral they became inherently mad (Faith and Jiwani, 2002: 87). As Myers and Sangster uncovered in their study of Canadian reform schools for girls from 1930–60, the 'girl problem' was construction by 'psychologists, penal workers, administrators and nuns whose preconceived expert knowledge about the nature of young women shaped their reconstructions of delinquent girls' rebellions within a language of irrationality, incredulity and pathology' (2001: 669).

Overall, the dominant idea throughout most of the twentieth century was that females who offend are rejecting their feminine role and are emulating their male counterpart. Consequently, many criminologists feared the impact of the 1960s women's movement on the feminine role.

Lacking from media analyses of female violence is the considerable impact of structural factors, including institutional racism, and economic and social inequality in the life of young female offenders and their victims. As Faith and Jiwani contend: 'Significantly absent in the range of explanations put forward by the media was

Reena Virk's marginalized positioning vis-à-vis those who had beaten and killed her. The issue of race and racism was either absent from the media discourse or presented in terms of her inability to fit in' (2002: 101–2). In a re-examination of her research data, Artz (2004) draws on social interdependence theory to acknowledge the importance of social structures in girls' use of violence because they 'provide us with clues as to how people may be interpreting self and world and how they may be morally positioned with regard to their actions' (Artz, 2004: 104).

In summary, we have drawn on the moral panic literature to examine the recent preoccupation with the violent girl. We argued that through distortion, exaggeration, and statistical manipulation of data, as well as expert evidence, the media was able to construct a new breed of female, the Nasty Girl, who has become one of our current folk devils. This construction is not without consequences: 'We want assurances that what happened to Reena couldn't happen to anybody else' asserts the popular magazine *Chatelaine*, because 'after all, next time it might be my daughter or yours who is the victim' (Martin, 1998: 71). In a climate of fear, Schissel (1997: 30) reminds us, it is easier 'for average citizens to become embroiled in the alarm over [folk devils] and to call for harsh justice'. Unfortunately, the reforms resorted to in a time of panic often fail to address the real source of public anxiety. It is to those reforms that we now turn.

The Effects of the Moral Panic on Policy Making

The panic over the Nasty Girl has had a significant impact on legal, educational, and social policy in Canada. The result has been an increase in both formal and informal mechanisms of control. While proposals for legal reform mostly consist of repressive measures targeted at delinquent youths, social and educational programs contain informal mechanisms of control targeting society more

generally. As we show in this section, proposals for reform are not only disciplinary mechanisms of power acting on the body of the individual delinquent, they are also part of the more recent governmental techniques of power which regulate and mange free individuals through the fostering of a culture of risk management, public safety, and security consciousness (Foucault, 1982; Cohen, 1985; O'Malley, 1996; Garland, 1997).

While harsh legal policy is aimed at incapacitating both violent boys and girls, informal mechanisms of control targeting young girls in particular have also resulted from the panic over girl violence. These mechanisms, however, did not emerge from within the centre of the criminal justice apparatus, rather they evolved at the margins of society, through the work of social agencies, activists, and experts who helped create a consensus about the problem of girl violence. This groundwork has produced new definitions of violence and new methods of controlling both young females and society in general.

The new rationality and concern actively seeks the participation of authorities in the informal control of girls. For example, Pepler and Sedighdeilami's caution that '[g]irls in families with violence, ineffective parenting, and high levels of conflict should be identified for supportive, interventions' (1998: iii) encourages school staff to observe and detect signs of risk in girls. The popular magazine *Today's Parent*, in an article entitled, 'When the Tough Get Going . . . the Going Gets Tough: How to Deal with Bullies', promotes parents becoming detectives through continuous observation of their children, since bullying is an 'underground activity'. Stuart Auty, president of the Canadian Safe School Network, is known to give parents his expert advice on how to steer children away from violence, including basic strategies such as 'knowing your kid, staying connected and providing them with opportunities to develop their self-esteem, as well as establishing limits and consequences when rules are broken' (cited in Martin, 1998: 77). While it is ironic that mainstream parental and educational advice is now repackaged as state-of-the-art technology to prevent bullying, we see in this strategy a sign of the current shift in crime control policy that Foucauldian scholars have identified as 'government-at-a-distance' (Rose and Miller, 1992; Garland, 1997).

As we know from Foucault's studies of the asylum, the prison and sexuality, power—which he also refers to as 'governmentality'—is better understood as a rationality evolving from the margins of society than as one concentrated exclusively in its centre, the state. It is in the interstice between the state and the individual, that is to say, in the social field occupied by the school, the hospital, the juvenile court, and social workers' and psychologists' offices, that different forms of rationality emerge and produce their disciplinary and regulatory effects onto the social body. Diverse professionals and agencies come together to govern the behaviour and mentality of both those who pose problems, such as the violent girl, and those they can enlist in the management of the violent girl. While the strategies of power produced in those 'centres of governance' (Garland, 1997: 179–80) have disciplinary effects meant to break and tame those at the receiving end, some act through the subjects for the purpose of creating a 'responsibilized autonomy' in them. For example, since Virk's death, expert advice encourages parents, teachers, and youth to change their behaviour and self- image to bring them into line with socially approved desires and identities, and, in the process, ensure the good functioning of the family and the school. The participation of these individuals in the management of the violent girl does not rely on force, but rests instead upon an alliance expert authorities, which is grounded in what Garland perceives as 'willingness of individuals—whether as family members, or workers, citizens—to exercise a 'responsibilized' autonomy, and to pursue interests and desires in ways which are socially approved and legally sanctioned' (1997: 180). This strategy of governmental power,

Garland continues, characterizes most current crime control policy:

> State authorities . . . seek to enlist other agencies arid individuals to form a chain of coordinated action that reaches into criminogenic situations, prompting crime-control conduct: on the part of 'responsibilized' actors (see Garland, 1996). Central to this strategy is the attempt to ensure that all the agencies and individuals who are in a position to contribute to these crime-reducing ends come to see it as being in their interests to do so. 'Government' is thus extended and enhanced by the creation of 'governors' and 'guardians' in the space between the state and the offender (Garland, 1997: 188).

Youths are particularly targeted by this strategy of power grounded in a 'responsibilized' autonomy. For example, as part of its 'Taking a Stand' program, the BC government made available a toll-free, province-wide phone number to 'prevent crime and violence and to offer youth a safe, confidential means to obtain information and help'. The 'Youth against Violence Line' wallet card distributed to schools invites young people to phone in and report incidents where they feel 'scared', 'threatened' or 'don't know what to do'. Similarly, the Police force of a suburb of Victoria, BC, launched a program named 'Solid Rock', in which police officers or actors perform skits to convince young people that teenagers who go to the authorities rather than putting up with bullies are not rats but exemplary, responsible citizens (McInnes, 1998: A4). We see in these well intentioned government programs an attempt to help youth become not only law-abiding citizens, but *homo prudens* (O'Malley, 1996) too, thus enticing them in the creation of a culture of risk management in which they learn to fear youth and think of themselves as potential victims (Ericson and Haggerty, 1997). These programs illustrate the profound change in current crime control policy

Garland foresaw: 'the new programmes of action are directed not towards individual offenders, but towards the conduct of potential victims, to vulnerable situations, and to those routines of everyday life which create criminal opportunities as an unintended byproduct' (Garland, 1996: 451). Hence, we need to understand the moral panic about the violent girl or youth in general as a process that leads not only to the containment and transformation of violent girls and boys, but also to the increased self-discipline and regulation of all youths, who learn to think of themselves as potential victims of bullying.'

To summarize, the policies and programs stemming from the moral panic about violent girls include repressive measures towards violent youth that are deployed by the crime-control apparatus. They also include more informal mechanisms of crime control directed at society, which are deployed by a 'government-at-a-distance'. While repressive measures stem from traditional crime-control agencies, such as the police or prisons, informal control operates rather indirectly or 'at a distance' by fostering the co-operation of non-state organizations and private individuals (Garland, 1997: 188). Through the actions of various experts involved in the fight against bullies, parents, teachers, young people and, specifically, girls are encouraged to become responsible and prudent individuals. To this effect, policies and programs seek to make them recognize their responsibility in reducing crime and persuade them to change their behaviour to reduce criminal opportunities (Garland, 1996: 453).

Why Is the Panic Happening Today?

Why did the reaction to girl violence take the particular form and intensity it did during the late 1990s? The moral panic literature emphasizes that, during a panic, the anxieties the public experiences are real, but their reaction is often misplaced. Hence, the object of the panic, the violent girl, is not always the source of people's anxiety.

In psychoanalytical terms, she is more likely to be the object of a projection, rather than the source of concern and fear. As one media article stated, the murder of Virk resulted in 'a profound self-examination and fear among Canadians that society's rules are undergoing unsettling change' (Mitchell, 1997: A1). This section attempts to situate the moral panic about girl-violence in its larger social and political context, in order, to uncover some of the anxieties that propelled it to become symbolically attached to aggressive girls. We follow this discussion with a brief examination of the way policies aimed at violent girls could better attempt to address the problems young girls face today.

We start our attempt at contextualizing the moral panic over the violent girl by examining the larger structural forces characterizing our present. According to Young (1999), the transition from modernity (the 'Golden Age' of the postwar period) to the present late modernity (late 1960s and onwards) resulted in significant structural and psychological changes that produced social anxieties. The shift primarily entailed a movement from an inclusive to an exclusive society: from a society that incorporated its members and enjoyed full (male) employment, rising affluence, stable families and conformity, to an exclusive society arising from changes in the labour force. These changes included a shift from a more social-based, communitarian labour force to one of individualism stemming from the new knowledge-based, technology, society. As late-modern society became increasingly characterized by plurality of values, self-reflexivity, multiculturalism, and scientific and political relativism, the solid foundation of modernity began to melt. Material certainty and shared values shattered, leaving us with a heightened sense of risk and uncertainties. In such a precarious climate, crime acquires a powerful symbolic value. If we could only control crime better, we would bring safety into one aspect of our disrupted lives. It is not surprising that our quest for security often translates into a projection of our fears onto specific scapegoats, who are made responsible for our feelings of insecurity.

What social anxieties are projected onto the violent girl today? What threat to societal values has she come to represent. In the wake of the Virk case, it was not difficult to find newspaper articles emphasizing the dangers of the rise in 'Girl Power'. A pullout section of the *Vancouver Province*, for example, had a picture of the petite head of the popular sitcom character Ally McBeal superimposed on the body of Rambo. Whiles she smiles innocently at the camera, her muscular arms are holding a machine gun. The caption reads: 'It's a girrrl's world: Yikes! It's only a matter of time before women take over' (Bacchus, 1998). Although Bacchus writes in a tongue-in-cheek manner, he outlines 'evidence' of a shift from patriarchy to matriarchy: the Spice Girls, Buffy the Vampire Slayer, angry chanteuses like Alanis Morissette, Xena, the Lilith Fair, the WNBA, Martha Stewart, Rosie O'Donnell, and the Women's Television Network. While Bacchus quickly clarifies that women have not achieved superiority or even equality in the workplace, the evidence of the shift to matriarchy he posits is in the form of a change 'in spirit'. The mantra of this spirit, Bacchus claims, is 'Go girl!' (Bacchus, 1998).

The media sensationalized the spirit of girl power by positing it as the cause of girl violence. Showing insightful reflexivity, Nolan suggests that '[f]ollowing long-standing misogynist traditions, they've made the assumption that the behaviour of a few reveals the brutality of all girls and that increased freedom for women—brought about specifically by feminism—is responsible for the supposed rise in young women's violence' (1998: 32). Girl power, the source of social anxieties, is the real nasty here; the moral panic over the statistically insignificant Nasty Girl is a projection of a desire to retrieve a patriarchal social order characterized by gender conformity.

While a segment of our society is increasingly worried about the ill effect of the spirit of girl power and engrossed in attacking popular culture

and in developing policies to transform all girls into good girls, another segment is capitalizing on girl power to rune a profit. 'Bad girls = big bucks' claims the *Vancouver Sun* (Todd, 2001: A17). It is not the first time folk devils become prey to commercial exploitation and are given a greater ethos than they originally possessed (Cohen, 1980: 140, 176). Today, young girls are implored by marketers and the media to dress like adults and to express sexual, aggressive confidence (Clark, 1999: 47). Under the headline 'Hollywood discovers girl power', *USA Today* acknowledges that 'where the girls are is where Hollywood wants to be' (Bacchus, 1998: B1). And whereas girls were previously sex symbols in the background of beverage advertisements, they are now staring down the camera lens as they 'growl': 'This is our beer' (Bacchus, 1998: B3).

The spirit of girl power is paradoxically what policies and programming for violent girls aim at transforming through the adoption of anger management skills based on a cognitive behavioural model. Programs that encourage control, empathy, self-esteem, communication, and social skills are important, yet they do little in addressing the wider social context in which girl power takes place, as well as the desire for autonomy and the consumerism it creates. These techniques assume individual pathology and are based on a punishment–correction model that has failed repeatedly to reform (Foucault, 1979). Moreover, while most current programs to curb girl-violence are founded on cognitive skills training and risk technologies, we also believe there has been insufficient critical evaluation of actuarial practices with youth. As Lupton (1999: 2) argues, the technico-scientific approach to risk ignores how 'risk' can be a socio-cultural phenomenon in its own right. In a study on girls incarcerated for violent offences in Saskatchewan, one of us questions if actuarial techniques depoliticize the process of social control by assisting in the efficient management of the offender, rather than addressing social conditions requiring reform (Barron, forthcoming).

An alternative approach to address violence would be to focus on gender, race, and class-specific initiatives that appeal to the realities of young females. Chesney-Lind and Brown (1999) argue that because girl violence differs from boy violence in magnitude and quality, the traditional approaches to treatment and models of law enforcement are inappropriate for girls. They, and others, call for programs that recognize factors that marginalize girls, including the extensiveness of girl victimization, and the complicating factors of culture, racism, and social and economic inequality, which may contribute to violent behaviour (Jiwani, 1998; Chesney-Lind and Brown, 1999; Jackson, 2004).

Conclusion

Discussing the construction of the Nasty Girl as a moral panic should not negate a search for positive reforms nor undermine the devastation resulting from rare acts of female aggression and violence. Although it can be argued that the call of gender-based programs would confirm the amplitude of girl violence, it cannot be denied that young females are incarcerated for violent acts and have different life experience and needs than those of males. Perhaps the most promising recommendations for female programming include giving girls a voice in program design, implementation and evaluation in order to address the wider context in which violence takes place. We maintain that, in addition to gender, the interlocking systems of oppression in young women's lives must be considered. Acknowledging and responding to the connections between racism, sexism, ableism, homophobia, and economic inequality is a challenge to the philosophical underpinnings of the criminal justice and education systems.

Note

1. Doob and Sprott also bring to our attention the problems associated with statistics on minor offences among youth by revealing how their increase is more related to institutional changes in reporting policies than in an actual increase in violence. For example, the Ontario Ministry of Education requested that education boards develop violence-prevention policies and implementation plans for reporting and recording violent incidents by September 1994. Increasingly, policies of 'zero tolerance' of violence in the schools mandate that all cases of violence be brought to court. According to Doob and Sprott, 'such policies can be expected to result in increased numbers of minor cases of violence—these are the cases that are likely to have been ignored in the past' (1998: 188).

References

Anon. 1996. 'When the Tough Get Going . . . the Going Gets Tough: How to Deal with Bullies', *Today's Parent* 13, 7: 66–70.

Anon. 1997. 'In Reena's World, Being a "Slut" Can Get you Killed', *Toronto Star*, 6 December: E1, E4.

Artz, S. 2004. 'Revisiting the Moral Domain: Using Social Interdependence Theory to Understand Adolescent Girls' Perspectives on the Use of Violence', in M. Moretti, C. Odgers, and J. Jackson, eds, *Girls and Aggression: Contributing Factors and Intervention Principles*, pp. 101–13. New York: Springer.

Bacchus, L. 1998. 'It's a Girrrl's World', *Vancouver Province*, 2 August: B1–B3.

Barron, C. (forthcoming). 'Nasty Girl: The Impact of the Risk Society on Female Young Offenders'. PhD dissertation, Simon Fraser University, School of Criminology, Burnaby, BC.

Cernetig, M., B. Laghi, R. Matas, and C. McInnes. 1997. 'Reena Virk's Short Life and Lonely Death; Swept Away: A 14 year-old Girl Beaten by the Very Teens She Wanted as Friends was Left to the Cold Salt-water', *The Globe and Mail*, 27 November: A1.

Chesney-Lind, M., and M. Brown. 1999. 'Girls and Violence: An Overview', in D. Flannery and C.R. Huff, eds, *Youth Violence: Prevention, Intervention and Social Policy*. Washington, DC: American Psychiatric Press.

Clark, A. 1999. 'How Teens Got the Power: Gen Y Has the Cash, the Cool—and a Burgeoning Consumer Culture', *Maclean's* 22 March: 42–9.

Cohen, S. 1980. *Folk Devils and Moral Panics: The Creation of the Mods and Rockers*. New York: St Martin's Press.

Cohen, S. 1985. *Visions of Social Control*. New York: Oxford University Press.

Doob, A., and J.B. Sprott. 1998. 'Is the "Quality" of Youth Violence Becoming More Serious?', *Canadian Journal of Criminology and Criminal Justice* 40, 2: 185–94.

Ericson, R., and K. Haggerty. 1997. *Policing the Risk Society*. Toronto: University of Toronto Press.

Faith, K., and Y. Jiwani. 2002. 'The Social Construction of "Dangerous" Girls and Women', in B. Schissel and C. Brooks, eds, *Marginality and Condemnation: An Introduction to Critical Criminology*, pp. 83–107. Halifax: Fernwood Publishing.

Foucault, M. 1979. *Discipline and Punish: The Birth of the Prison*. New York: Vintage Books.

———. 1982. *The Subject and Power*, 2nd ed., H.L. Dreyfus and P. Rabinow, eds. Chicago: Chicago University Press.

Garland, D. 1996. 'The Limits of the Sovereign State: Strategies of Crime Control in Contemporary Society', *British Journal of Criminology* 36, 4: 445–71.

———. 1997. '"Governmentality" and the Problem of Crime: Foucault, Criminology, Sociology', *Theoretical Criminology* 1, 2: 173–214.

Geller, G. 1987. '"Young Women in Conflict with the Law', in E. Adelberg and C. Currie, eds, *Too Few to Count: Canadian Women in Conflict with the Law*, pp. 113–26. Vancouver: Press Gang Publishers.

Jackson, M.A. 2004. 'Race, Gender, and Aggression: The Impact of Sociocultural Factors on Girls', in M. Moretti, C. Odgers, and J. Jackson, eds, *Girls and Aggression: Contributing Factors and Interven-*

tion Principles, pp. 82–99. New York: Kluwer Academic/Plenum Publishers.

Lupton, D. 1999. *Risk and Sociocultural Theory: New Directions and Perspectives*. Cambridge, UK: Cambridge University Press.

Madriz, E. 1997. *Nothing Bad Happens to Good Girls*. Berkeley, CA: University of California Press.

Martin, S. 1998. 'Murder in Victoria: Why did Reena Virk Die?', *Chatelaine*, May: 70–7.

McInnes, C. 1998. 'Police Probe Gang Assault of Nanaimo Teen', *The Globe and Mail*, 12 March: A4.

Mitchell, A. 1997. 'Virk's Death Triggers Painful Questions: Girls' Involvement "Exacerbates Rage"', *The Globe and Mail*, 28 Nov: A1, A8.

Myers, T., and J. Sangster. 2001. 'Retorts, Runaways and Riots: Patterns of Resistance in Canadian Reform Schools for Girls, 1930–60', *Journal of Social History* 34, 3: 669–97.

Nolan, N. 1998. 'Girl Crazy: After the Brutal Murder of Reena Virk, the Media Whipped the Country into a Frenzy Over a Supposed "Girl Crime Wave"', *This Magazine*, 31, 5 (March/April): 30–5.

O'Malley, P. 1996. 'Risk and Responsibility', in A. Barry, T. Osborne, and N. Rose, eds, *Foucault and Political Reason*, pp. 189–208. Chicago: Chicago University Press.

Pepler, D.J., and F. Sedighdeilami. 1998. *Aggressive Girls in Canada*. Working Papers. Hull, QC: Applied Research Branch, Strategic Policy, Human Resources Development Canada.

Reitsma-Street, M. 1999. 'Justice for Canadian Girls: A 1990s Update', *Canadian Journal of Criminology and Criminal Justice* 41, 3: 335–64.

Rose, N., and P. Miller. 1992. 'Political Power Beyond the State: Problematics of Government', *British Journal of Sociology* 43, 2: 173–205.

Schissel, B. 1997. *Blaming Children: Youth Crime, Moral Panics and the Politics of Hate*. Halifax: Fernwood Publishing.

Statistics Canada. 2000. 'Crime Statistics', *The Daily*. 18 July. Available at http://www.statcan.ca/Daily/English1000718/d000718a.htm.

Tafler, S. 1998. 'Who was Reena Virk?' *Saturday Night*, 113, 3: 15–22.

Todd, D. 2001. 'Bad Girls = Big Bucks', *The Vancouver Sun*, 26 January: A17.

Young, J. 1999. *The Exclusive Society*. London: Sage.

CHAPTER 38

Wars, Wimps, and Women: Talking Gender and Thinking War

Carol Cohn

I start with a true story, told to me by a white male physicist:

> Several colleagues and I were working on modeling counterforce attacks, trying to get realistic estimates of the number of immediate fatalities that would result from different deployments. At one point, we remodeled a particular attack, using slightly different assumptions, and found that instead of there being 36 million immediate fatalities, there would only be 30 million. And everybody was sitting around nodding, saying, 'Oh yeah, that's great, only 30 million,' when all of a sudden, I heard what we were saying. And I blurted out, 'Wait, I've just heard how we're talking—Only 30 million! Only 30 million human beings killed instantly?' Silence fell upon the room. Nobody said a word. They didn't even look at me. It was awful. I felt like a woman.

The physicist added that henceforth he was careful to never blurt out anything like that again.

During the early years of the Reagan presidency, in the era of the Evil Empire, the cold war, and loose talk in Washington about the possibility of fighting and 'prevailing' in a nuclear war, I went off to do participant observation in a community of North American nuclear defense intellectuals and security affairs analysts—a community virtually entirely composed of white men. They worked in universities, think tanks, and as advisers to government. They theorized about nuclear deterrence and arms control, and nuclear and conventional war fighting, about how to best translate military might into political power; in short, they created the discourse that underwrites American national security policy. The exact relation of their theories to American political and military practice is a complex and thorny one; the argument can be made, for example, that their ideas do not so much shape policy decisions as legitimate them after the fact. But one thing that is clear is that the body of language and thinking they have generated filters out to the military, politicians, and the public, and increasingly shapes how we talk and think about war. This was amply evident during the Gulf War: Gulf War 'news', as generated by the military briefers, reported by newscasters, and analyzed by the television networks' resident security experts, was marked by its use of the professional language of defense analysis, nearly to the exclusion of other ways of speaking.

My goal has been to understand something about how defense intellectuals think, and why they think that way. Despite the parsimonious appeal of ascribing the nuclear arms race to 'missile envy', I felt certain that masculinity was not a sufficient explanation of why men think about war in the ways that they do. Indeed, I found many ways to understand what these men were doing that had little or nothing to do with gender. But ultimately, the physicist's story and others like it made confronting the role of gender unavoidable. Thus, in this paper I will explore gender discourse, and its role in shaping nuclear and national security discourse.

I want to stress, this is not a paper about men and women, and what they are or are not like. I will not be claiming that men are aggressive and women peace loving. I will not even address the question of how men's and women's relations to war may differ, nor of the different propensities they may have to committing acts of violence. Neither will I pay more than passing attention to the question which so often crops up in discussions of war and gender, that is, would it be a more peaceful world if our national leaders were women? These questions are valid and important, and recent feminist discussion of them has been complex, interesting, and contentious. But my focus is elsewhere. I wish to direct attention away from gendered individuals and toward gendered discourses. My question is about the way that civilian defense analysts think about war, and the ways in which that thinking is shaped not by their maleness (or, in extremely rare instances, femaleness), but by the ways in which gender discourse intertwines with and permeates that thinking.

Let me be more specific about my terms. I use the term *gender* to refer to the constellation of meanings that a given culture assigns to biological sex differences. But more than that, I use gender to refer to a symbolic system, a central organizing discourse of culture, one that not only shapes how we experience and understand ourselves as men and women, but that also interweaves with other discourses and shapes *them*—and therefore shapes other aspects of our world—such as how nuclear weapons are thought about and deployed.

So when I talk about 'gender discourse', I am talking not only about words or language but about a system of meanings, of ways of thinking, images and words that first shape how we experience, understand, and represent ourselves as men and women, but that also do more than that; they shape many other aspects of our lives and culture. In this symbolic system, human characteristics are dichotomized, divided into pairs of polar opposites that are supposedly mutually exclusive: mind is opposed to body; culture to nature; thought to feeling; logic to intuition; objectivity to subjectivity; aggression to passivity; confrontation to accommodation; abstraction to particularity; public to private; political to personal, ad nauseam. In each case, the first term of the 'opposites' is associated with male, the second with female. And in each case, our society values the first over the second.

I break it into steps like this—analytically separating the *existence* of these groupings of binary oppositions, from the association of each group with a gender, from the valuing of one over the other, the so-called male over the so-called female, for two reasons: first, to try to make visible the fact that this system of dichotomies is encoding many meanings that may be quite unrelated to male and female bodies. Yet once that first step is made—the association of each side of those lists with a gender—gender now becomes tied to many other kinds of cultural representations. If a human activity, such as engineering, fits some of the characteristics, it becomes gendered.

My second reason for breaking it into those steps is to try to help make it clear that the meanings can flow in different directions; that is, in gender discourse, men and women are supposed to exemplify the characteristics on the lists. It also works in reverse, however; to evidence any of these characteristics—to be abstract, logical or dispassionate, for example—is not simply to be those things, but also to be manly. And to be manly is not simply to be manly, but also to be in the more highly valued position in the discourse. In other words, to exhibit a trait on that list is not neutral—it is not simply displaying some basic human characteristic. It also positions you in a discourse of gender. It associates you with a particular gender, and also with a higher or lower valuation.

In stressing that this is a *symbolic* system, I want first to emphasize that while real women and men do not really fit these gender 'ideals', the existence of this system of meaning affects all of us, nonetheless. Whether we want to or not, we see ourselves and others against its templates, we interpret our own and others' actions against it. A man who cries easily cannot avoid in some way confronting that he is likely to be seen as less than fully manly. A woman who is very aggressive and incisive may enjoy that quality in herself, but the fact of her aggressiveness does not exist by itself; she cannot avoid having her own and others' perceptions of that quality of hers, the meaning it has for people, being in some way mediated by the discourse of gender. Or, a different kind of example: Why does it mean one thing when George Bush gets teary-eyed in public, and something entirely different when Patricia Shroeder does? The same act is viewed through the lens of gender and is seen to mean two very different things.

Second, as gender discourse assigns gender to human characteristics, we can think of the discourse as something we are positioned *by*. If I say, for example, that a corporation should stop dumping toxic waste because it is damaging the creations of mother earth, (i.e., articulating a valuing and sentimental vision of nature), I am speaking in a manner associated with women, and our cultural discourse of gender positions me as female. As such I am then associated with the whole constellation of traits—irrational, emotional, subjective, and so forth—and I am in the devalued position. If, on the other hand, I say the corporation should stop dumping toxic wastes because I have calculated that it is causing $8.215 billion of damage to eight nonrenewable resources, which should be seen as equivalent to lowering the GDP by 0.15 per cent per annum, (i.e., using a rational, calculative mode of thought), the discourse positions me as masculine—rational, objective, logical, and so forth—the dominant, valued position.

But if we are positioned *by* discourses, we can also take different positions *within* them. Although I am female, and this would 'naturally' fall into the devalued term, I can choose to 'speak like a

man'—to be hard-nosed, realistic, unsentimental, dispassionate. Jeanne Kirkpatrick is a formidable example. While we can choose a position in a discourse, however, it means something different for a woman to 'speak like a man' than for a man to do so. It is heard differently.

One other note about my use of the term *gender discourse*: I am using it in the general sense to refer to the phenomenon of symbolically organizing the world in these gender-associated opposites. I do not mean to suggest that there is a single discourse defining a single set of gender ideals. In fact, there are many specific discourses of gender, which vary by race, class, ethnicity, locale, sexuality, nationality, and other factors. The masculinity idealized in the gender discourse of new Haitian immigrants is in some ways different from that of sixth-generation white Anglo-Saxon Protestant business executives, and both differ somewhat from that of white-male defense intellectuals and security analysts. One version of masculinity is mobilized and enforced in the armed forces in order to enable men to fight wars, while a somewhat different version of masculinity is drawn upon and expressed by abstract theoreticians of war.

Let us now return to the physicist who felt like a woman: what happened when he 'blurted out' his sudden awareness of the 'only 30 million' dead people? First, he was transgressing a code of professional conduct. In the civilian defense intellectuals' world, when you are in professional settings you do not discuss the bloody reality behind the calculations. It is not required that you be completely unaware of them in your outside life, or that you have no feelings about them, but it is required that you do not bring them to the foreground in the context of professional activities. There is a general awareness that you *could not* do your work if you did; in addition, most defense intellectuals believe that emotion and description of human reality distort the process required to think well about nuclear weapons and warfare.

So the physicist violated a behavioural norm, in and of itself a difficult thing to do because it threatens your relationships to and your standing with your colleagues.

But even worse than that, he demonstrated some of the characteristics on the 'female' side of the dichotomies—in his 'blurting' he was impulsive, uncontrolled, emotional, concrete, and attentive to human bodies, at the very least. Thus, he marked himself not only as unprofessional but as feminine, and this, in turn, was doubly threatening. It was not only a threat to his own sense of self as masculine, his gender identity, it also identified him with a devalued status—of a woman—or put him in the devalued or subordinate position in the discourse.

Thus, both his statement, 'I felt like a woman,' and his subsequent silence in that and other settings are completely understandable. To have the strength of character and courage to transgress the strictures of both professional and gender codes *and* to associate yourself with a lower status is very difficult.

This story is not simply about one individual, his feelings, and his actions; it is about the role of gender discourse. The impact of gender discourse in that room (and countless others like it) is that some things get left out. Certain ideas, concerns, interests, information, feelings, and meanings are marked in national security discourse as feminine, and are devalued. They are therefore, first, very difficult to *speak*, as exemplified by the physicist who felt like a woman. And second, they are very difficult to *hear*, to take in and work with seriously, even if they *are* said. For the others in the room, the way in which the physicist's comments were marked as female and devalued served to delegitimate them. It is almost as though they had become an accidental excrescence in the middle of the room. Embarrassed politeness demanded that they be ignored.

I must stress that this is not simply the product of the idiosyncratic personal composition of that particular room. In other professional settings, I have experienced the feeling that something terribly important is being left out and must be spoken; and yet, it has felt almost physically impossible to utter the words, almost as though they could not be pushed out into the smooth, cool, opaque air of the room.

What is it that cannot be spoken? First, any words that express an emotional awareness of the desperate human reality behind the sanitized abstractions of death and destruction—as in the physicist's sudden vision of 30 million rotting corpses. Similarly, weapons' effects may be spoken of only in the most clinical and abstract terms, leaving no room to imagine a seven-year-old boy with his flesh melting away from his bones or a toddler with her skin hanging down in strips. Voicing concern about the number of casualties in the enemy's armed forces, imagining the suffering of the killed and wounded young men, is out of bounds. (Within the military itself, it is permissible, even desirable, to attempt to minimize immediate civilian casualties if it is possible to do so without compromising military objectives, but as we learned in the Persian Gulf War, this is only an extremely limited enterprise; the planning and precision of military targeting does not admit of consideration of the cost in human lives of such actions as destroying power systems, or water and sewer systems, or highways and food distribution systems.) Psychological effects—on the soldiers fighting the war or on the citizens injured, or fearing for their own safety, or living through tremendous deprivation, or helplessly watching their babies die from diarrhea due to the lack of clean water—all of these are not to be talked about.

But it is not only particular subjects that are out of bounds. It is also tone of voice that counts. A speaking style that is identified as cool, dispassionate, and distanced is required. One that vibrates with the intensity of emotion almost always disqualifies the speaker, who is heard to sound like 'a hysterical housewife'.

What gets left out, then, is the emotional, the concrete, the particular, the human bodies and their vulnerability, human lives and their subjectivity—all of which are marked as feminine in the binary dichotomies of gender discourse. In other words, gender discourse informs and shapes nuclear and national security discourse, and in so doing creates silences and absences. It keeps things out of the room, unsaid, and keeps them ignored if they manage to get in. As such, it degrades our ability to think *well* and *fully* about nuclear weapons and national security, and shapes and limits the possible outcomes of our deliberations.

What becomes clear, then, is that defense intellectuals' standards of what constitutes 'good thinking' about weapons and security have not simply evolved out of trial and error; it is not that the history of nuclear discourse has been filled with exploration of other ideas, concerns, interests, information, questions, feelings, meanings, and stances which were then found to create distorted or poor thought. It is that these options have been *preempted* by gender discourse, and by the feelings evoked by living up to or transgressing gender codes.

To borrow a term from defense intellectuals, you might say that gender discourse becomes a 'preemptive deterrent' to certain kinds of thought. Let me give you another example of what I mean—another story, this one my own experience.

One Saturday morning I, two other women, and about 55 men gathered to play a war game designed by the RAND Corporation. Our 'controllers' (the people running the game) first divided us up into three sets of teams; there would be three simultaneous games being played, each pitting a Red Team against a Blue Team (I leave the reader to figure out which colour represents which country). All three women were put onto the same team, a Red Team.

The teams were then placed in different rooms so that we had no way of communicating with each other, except through our military actions (or lack of them) or by sending demands and responses to those demands via the controllers. There was no way to negotiate or to take actions other than military ones. (This was supposed to simulate reality.) The controllers then presented us with maps and pages covered with numbers representing each side's forces. We were also given a 'scenario', a situation of escalating tensions and military conflicts, starting in the Middle East and spreading to Central Europe. We were to decide what to do, the controllers would go back and forth between the two teams to relate the other team's actions, and periodically the controllers themselves would add something that would ratchet up the conflict—an announcement of an 'intercepted intelligence report' from the other side, the authenticity of which we had no way of judging.

Our Red Team was heavily into strategizing, attacking ground forces, and generally playing war. We also, at one point, decided that we were going to pull our troops out of Afghanistan, reasoning it was bad for us to have them there and that the Afghanis had the right to self-determination. At another point we removed some troops from Eastern Europe. I must add that later my team was accused of being wildly 'unrealistic'—this group of experts found the idea that the Soviet Union might voluntarily choose to pull troops out of Afghanistan and Eastern Europe utterly absurd. (It was about six months before Gorbachev actually did the same thing.)

Gradually our game escalated to nuclear war. The Blue Team used tactical nuclear weapons against our troops, but our Red Team decided, initially at least, against nuclear retaliation. When the game ended (at the end of the allotted time) our Red Team had 'lost the war' (meaning that we had political control over less territory than we had started with, although our homeland had remained completely unviolated and our civilian population safe).

In the debriefing afterwards, all six teams returned to one room and reported on their games. Since we had had absolutely no way to know why the other team had taken any of its actions, we now had the opportunity to find out what they had been thinking. A member of the team that had played against us said, 'Well, when he took his troops out of Afghanistan, I knew he was weak and I could push him around. And then, when we nuked him and he didn't nuke us back, I knew he was just such a wimp, I could take him for everything he's got and I nuked him again. He just wimped out.'

There are many different possible comments to make at this point. I will restrict myself to a couple. First, when the man from the Blue Team called me a wimp (which is what it felt like for each of us on the Red Team—a personal accusation), I felt silenced. My reality, the careful reasoning that had gone into my strategic and tactical choices, the intelligence, the politics, the morality—all of it just disappeared, completely invalidated. I could not explain the reasons for my actions, could not protest, 'Wait, you idiot, I didn't do it because I was weak, I did it because it made sense to do it that way, given my understandings of strategy and tactics, history and politics, my goals and my values.' The protestation would be met with knowing sneers. In this discourse, the coding of an act as wimpish is hegemonic. Its emotional heat and resonance is like a bath of sulfuric acid: it erases everything else.

'Acting like a wimp' is an *interpretation* of a person's acts (or, in national security discourse, a country's acts, an important distinction I will return to later). As with any other interpretation, it is a selection of one among many possible different ways to understand something—once the selection is made, the other possibilities recede into invisibility. In national security discourse, 'acting like a wimp'—being insufficiently masculine—is one of the most readily available interpretive codes. (You do not need to do participant observation in a community of defense intellectuals to know this—just look at the 'geopolitical analyses' in the media and on Capitol Hill of the way in which George Bush's military intervention in Panama and the Persian Gulf War finally allowed him to beat the 'wimp factor'.) You learn that someone is being a wimp if he perceives an international crisis as very dangerous and urges caution; if he thinks it might not be important to

have just as many weapons that are just as big as the other guy's; if he suggests that an attack should not necessarily be answered by an even more destructive counterattack; or, until recently, if he suggested that making unilateral arms reductions might be useful for our own security. All of these are 'wimping out'.

The prevalence of this particular interpretive code is another example of how gender discourse affects the quality of thinking within the national security community, first, because, as in the case of the physicist who 'felt like a woman', it is internalized to become a self-censor; there are things professionals simply will not *say* in groups, options they simply will not argue nor write about, because they know that to do so is to brand themselves as wimps. Thus, a whole range of inputs is left out, a whole series of options is foreclosed from their deliberations.

Equally, if not more damagingly, is the way in which this interpretive coding not only limits what is *said*, but even limits what is *thought*. 'He's a wimp' is a phrase that *stops* thought. When we were playing the game, once my opponent on the Blue Team 'recognized the fact that I was a wimp', that is, once he interpreted my team's actions through the lens of this common interpretive code in national security discourse, he *stopped thinking*; he stopped looking for ways to understand what we were doing. He did not ask, 'Why on earth would the Red Team do that? What does it tell me about them, about their motives and purposes and goals and capabilities? What does it tell me about their possible understandings of *my* actions, or of the situation they're in?' or any other of the many questions that might have enabled him to revise his own conception of the situation or perhaps achieve his goals at a far lower level of violence and destruction. Here, again, gender discourse acts as a preemptive deterrent to thought.

'Wimp' is, of course, not the only gendered pejorative used in the national security community; 'pussy' is another popular epithet, conjoining the imagery of harmless domesticated (read demasculinized) pets with contemptuous reference to women's genitals. In an informal setting, an analyst worrying about the other side's casualties, for example, might be asked, 'What kind of pussy are you, anyway?' It need not happen more than once or twice before everyone gets the message; they quickly learn not to raise the issue in their discussions. Attention to and care for the living, suffering, and dying of human beings (in this case, soldiers and their families and friends) is again banished from the discourse through the expedient means of genderbashing.

Other words are also used to impugn someone's masculinity and, in the process, to delegitimate his position and avoid thinking seriously about it. 'Those Krauts are a bunch of limp-dicked wimps' was the way one US defense intellectual dismissed the West German politicians who were concerned about popular opposition to Euromissile deployments. I have heard our NATO allies referred to as 'the Euro-fags' when they disagreed with American policy on such issues as the Contra War or the bombing of Libya. Labeling them 'fags' is an effective strategy; it immediately dismisses and trivializes their opposition to US policy by coding it as due to inadequate masculinity. In other words, the American analyst need not seriously confront the Europeans' arguments, since the Europeans' doubts about US policy obviously stem not from their reasoning but from the 'fact' that they 'just don't have the stones for war'. Here, again, gender discourse deters thought.

'Fag' imagery is not, of course, confined to the professional community of security analysts; it also appears in popular 'political' discourse. The Gulf War was replete with examples. American derision of Saddam Hussein included bumper stickers that read 'Saddam, Bend Over'. American soldiers reported that the 'USA' stenciled on their uniforms stood for 'Up Saddam's Ass'. A widely reprinted cartoon, surely one of the most multiply offensive that came out of the war, depicted Saddam bowing down in the Islamic posture of prayer, with a huge US missile, approximately five times the size of the prostrate figure, about to penetrate his upraised bottom. Over and over, defeat for the Iraqis was portrayed as humiliating anal penetration by the more powerful and manly United States.

Within the defense community discourse, manliness is equated not only with the ability to win a war (or to 'prevail', as some like to say when talking about nuclear war); it is also equated with the willingness (which they would call courage) to threaten and use force. During the Carter administration, for example, a well-known academic security affairs specialist was quoted as saying that 'under Jimmy Carter the United States is spreading its legs for the Soviet Union'. Once this image is evoked, how does rational discourse about the value of US policy proceed?

In 1989 and 1990, as Gorbachev presided over the withdrawal of Soviet forces from Eastern Europe, I heard some defense analysts sneeringly say things like, 'They're a bunch of pussies for pulling out of Eastern Europe.' This is extraordinary. Here they were, men who for years railed against Soviet domination of Eastern Europe. You would assume that if they were politically and ideologically consistent, if they were rational, they would be applauding the Soviet actions. Yet in their informal conversations, it was not their rational analyses that dominated their response, but the fact that for them, the decision for war, the willingness to use force, is cast as a question of masculinity—not prudence, thoughtfulness, efficacy, 'rational' cost-benefit calculation, or morality, but masculinity.

In the face of this equation, genuine political discourse disappears. One more example: After Iraq invaded Kuwait and President Bush hastily sent US forces to Saudi Arabia, there was a period in which the Bush administration struggled to find a convincing political justification for US military involvement and the security affairs community debated the political merit of US intervention. Then Bush set the deadline, January 16—high noon at the OK Corral—and as the day approached conversations changed. More of these centred on the question compellingly articulated by one defense intellectual as 'Does George Bush have the stones for war?' This, too, is utterly extraordinary. This was a time when crucial political questions abounded: Can the sanctions work if given more time? Just what vital interests does the United States actually have at stake? What would be the goals of military intervention? Could they be accomplished by other means? Is the difference between what sanctions might accomplish and what military violence might accomplish worth the greater cost in human suffering, human lives, even dollars? What will the long-term effects on the people of the region be? On the ecology? Given the apparent successes of Gorbachev's last-minute diplomacy and Hussein's series of nearly daily small concessions, can and should Bush put off the deadline? Does he have the strength to let another leader play a major role in solving the problem? Does he have the political flexibility to not fight, or is he hell-bent on war at all costs? And so on, ad infinitum. All of these disappear in the sulfuric acid test of the size of Mr Bush's private parts.

I want to return to the RAND war simulation story to make one other observation. First, it requires a true confession: *I was stung by being called a wimp.* Yes, I thought the remark was deeply inane, and it infuriated me. But even so, I was also stung. Let me hasten to add, this was not because my identity is very wrapped up with not being wimpish—it actually is not a term that normally figures very heavily in my self-image one way or the other. But it was impossible to be in that room, hear his comment and the snickering laughter with which it was met, and not to feel stung and humiliated.

Why? There I was, a woman and a feminist, not only contemptuous of the mentality that measures human beings by their degree of so-called wimpishness, but also someone for whom the term *wimp* does not have a deeply resonant personal meaning. How could it have affected me so much?

The answer lies in the role of the context within which I was experiencing myself—the discursive framework. For in that room I was not 'simply me', but I was a participant in a discourse, a shared set of words, concepts, symbols that constituted not only the linguistic possibilities available to us but also constituted *me* in that situation. This is not entirely true, of course. How I experienced myself was at least partly shaped by other experiences and other discursive frameworks—certainly those of feminist politics and anti-militarist politics; in fact, I would say those frameworks predominantly shaped my reactions. But that is quite different from saying 'I am a feminist, and that individual, psychological self simply moves encapsulated through the world being itself'—and therefore assuming that I am unaffected. No matter who else I was at that moment, I was unavoidably a participant in a discourse in which being a wimp has a meaning, and a deeply pejorative one at that. By calling me a wimp, my accuser on the Blue Team *positioned* me in that discourse, and I could not but feel the sting.

In other words, I am suggesting that national security discourse can be seen as having different positions within it—ones that are starkly gender coded; indeed, the enormous strength of their evocative power comes from gender. Thus, when you participate in conversation in that community, you do not simply choose what to say and how to say it; you advertently or inadvertently choose a position in the discourse. As a woman, I can choose the 'masculine' (thoughtful, rational, logical) position. If I do, I am seen as legitimate, but I limit what I can say. Or, I can say things that place me in the 'feminine' position—in which case no one will listen to me.

Finally, I would like to briefly explore a phenomenon I call the 'unitary masculine actor problem' in national security discourse. During the Persian Gulf War, many feminists probably noticed that both the military briefers and George Bush himself frequently used the singular masculine pronoun 'he' when referring to Iraq and Iraq's army. Someone not listening carefully could simply assume that 'he' referred to Saddam Hussein. Sometimes it did; much of the time it simply reflected the defense community's characteristic habit of calling opponents 'he' or 'the other guy'. A battalion commander, for example, was quoted as saying 'Saddam knows where we are and we know where he is. We will move a lot now to keep him off guard' (Hedges, 1991: A1). In these sentences, 'he' and 'him' appear to refer to Saddam Hussein. But, of course, the American forces had *no idea* where Saddam Hussein himself was; the singular masculine pronouns are actually being used to refer to the Iraqi military.

This linguistic move, frequently heard in discussions within the security affairs and defense communities, turns a complex state and set of forces into a singular male opponent. In fact, discussions that purport to be serious explorations of the strategy and tactics of war can have a tone that sounds more like the story of a sporting match, a fistfight, or a personal vendetta.

> I would want to suck him out into the desert as far as I could, and then pound him to death (Schwarzkopf, 1991b).

> Once we had taken out his eyes, we did what could be best described as the 'Hail Mary play' in football (Schwarzkopf, 1991a: 2).

> [I]f the adversary decides to embark on a very high roll, because he's frightened that something even worse is in the works, does grabbing him by the scruff of the neck and slapping him up the side of the head, does that make him behave better or is it plausible that it makes him behave even worse? (Transcript, 29 June 1987).

Most defense intellectuals would claim that using 'he' is just a convenient shorthand, without significant import or effects. I believe, however, that the effects of this usage are many and the

implications far-reaching. Here I will sketch just a few, starting first with the usage throughout defense discourse generally, and then coming back to the Gulf War in particular.

The use of 'he' distorts the analyst's understanding of the opposing state and the conflict in which they are engaged. When the analyst refers to the opposing state as 'he' or 'the other guy', the image evoked is that of a person, a unitary actor; yet states are not people. Nor are they unitary and unified. They comprise complex, multifaceted governmental and military apparatuses, each with opposing forces within it, each, in turn, with its own internal institutional dynamics, its own varied needs in relation to domestic politics, and so on. In other words, if the state is referred to and pictured as a unitary actor, what becomes unavailable to the analyst and policy-maker is a series of much more complex truths that might enable him to imagine many more policy options, many more ways to interact with that state.

If one kind of distortion of the state results from the image of the state as a person, a unitary actor, another can be seen to stem from the image of the state as a specifically *male* actor. Although states are almost uniformly run by men, states are not men; they are complex social institutions, and they act and react as such. Yet, when 'he' and 'the other guy' are used to refer to states, the words do not simply function as shorthand codes; instead, they have their own entailments, including assumptions about how men act, which just might be different from how states act, but which invisibly become assumed to be isomorphic with how states act.

It also entails emotional responses on the part of the speaker. The reference to the opposing state as 'he' evokes male competitive identity issues, as in, 'I'm not going to let him push me around,' or, 'I'm not going to let him get the best of me.' While these responses may or may not be adaptive for a barroom brawl, it is probably safe to say that they are less functional when trying to determine the best way for one state to respond to another state. Defense analysts and foreign policy experts can usually agree upon the supreme desirability of dispassionate, logical analysis and its ensuing rationally calculated action. Yet the emotions evoked by the portrayal of global conflict in the personalized terms of male competition must, at the very least, exert a strong pull in exactly the opposite direction.

A third problem is that even while the use of 'he' acts to personalize the conflict, it simultaneously abstracts both the opponent and the war itself. That is, the use of 'he' functions in very much the same way that discussions about 'Red' and 'Blue' do. It facilitates treating war within a kind of game-playing model, A against B, Red against Blue, he against me. For even while 'he' is evocative of male identity issues, it is also just an abstract piece to moved around on a game board, or, more appropriately, a computer screen.

That tension between personalization and abstraction was striking in Gulf War discourse. In the Gulf War, not only was 'he' frequently used to refer to the Iraqi military, but so was 'Saddam', as in 'Saddam really took a pounding today,' or 'Our goal remains the same: to liberate Kuwait by forcing Saddam Hussein out' (Cheney, 1991: A11). The personalization is obvious: in this locution, the US armed forces are not destroying a nation, killing people; instead, they (or George) are giving Saddam a good pounding, or bodily removing him from where he does not belong. Our emotional response is to get fired up about a bully getting his comeuppance.

Yet this personalization, this conflation of Iraq and Iraqi forces with Saddam himself, also abstracts: it functions to substitute in the mind's eye the abstraction of an implacably, impeccably evil enemy for the particular human beings, the men, women, and children being pounded, burned, torn, and eviscerated. A cartoon image of Saddam being ejected from Kuwait preempts the image of the blackened, charred, decomposing bodies of 19-year-old boys tossed in ditches by the side of the road, and the other concrete images of the acts of violence that constitute 'forcing Hussein [sic] out of Kuwait' (Scarry, 1984).[1] Paradoxical as it may seem, in personalizing the Iraqi army as Saddam, the individual human beings in Iraq were abstracted out of existence.

In summary, I have been exploring the way in which defense intellectuals talk to each other—the comments they make to each other, the particular usages that appear in their informal conversations or their lectures. In addition, I have occasionally left the professional community to draw upon public talk about the Gulf War. My analysis does *not* lead me to conclude that 'national security thinking is masculine'—that is, a separate, and different, discussion. Instead, I have tried to show that national security discourse is gendered, and that it matters. Gender discourse is interwoven through national security discourse. It sets fixed boundaries, and in so doing, it skews what is discussed and how it is thought about. It shapes expectations of other nations' actions, and in so doing it affects both our interpretations of international events and conceptions of how the United States should respond.

In a world where professionals pride themselves on their ability to engage in cool, rational, objective calculation while others around them are letting their thinking be sullied by emotion, the unacknowledged interweaving of gender discourse in security discourse allows men to not acknowledge that their pristine rational thought is in fact riddled with emotional response. In an 'objective' and 'universal' discourse that valorizes the 'masculine' and deauthorizes the 'feminine,' it is only the 'feminine' emotions that are noticed and labelled as emotions, and thus in need of banning from the analytic process. 'Masculine' emotions—such as feelings of aggression, competition, macho pride and swagger, or the sense of identity resting on carefully defended borders—are not so easily noticed and identified as emotions, and are instead invisibly folded into 'self-evident,' so-called realist paradigms and analyses. It is both the interweaving of gender discourse in national security thinking *and* the blindness to its presence and impact that have deleterious effects. Finally, the impact is to distort, degrade, and deter roundly rational, fully complex thought within the community of defense intellectuals and national security elites and, by extension, to cripple democratic deliberation about crucial matters of war and peace.

Note

1. Elaine Scarry explains that when an army is described as a single 'embodied combatant', injury, (as in Saddam's 'pounding'), may be referred to but is 'no longer recognizable or interpretable'. It is not only that Americans might be happy to imagine Saddam being pounded; we also on some level know that it is not really happening, and thus need not feel the pain of the wounded. We 'respond to the injury . . . as an imaginary wound to an imaginary body, despite the fact that that imaginary body is itself made up of thousands of real human bodies' (Scarry, 1984: 72).

References

Cheney, D. 1991. 'Excerpts from Briefing at Pentagon by Cheney and Powell', *New York Times*, 24 January.

Hedges, C. 1991. 'War is Vivid in the Gun Sights of the Sniper', *New York Times*, 3 February.

Scarry, E. 1984. *Body in Pain: The Making and Unmaking of the World*. New York: Oxford.

Schwarzkopf, N. 1991a. CENTCOM News Briefing.

Riyadh, Saudi Arabia, 27 February.

———. 1991b. National Public Radio broadcast. 8 February.

Transcript. 1987. Lecture on NATO and the Warsaw Pack. Summer Insititute on Regional Conflict and Global Security: The Nuclear Dimension, Madison, WI, 29 June.

CHAPTER 39

Genderbashing: Sexuality, Gender, and the Regulation of Public Space

Viviane K. Namaste

In North America, violence against lesbians, gay men, and bisexuals is escalating at an alarming rate. A survey conducted in 1986–7 by the Philadelphia Lesbian and Gay Task Force reports that violence against lesbians and gay men in that city had doubled since 1983–4 (as cited in Valentine, 1993: 409). The United States National and Lesbian Task Force (NGLTF) documents that incidents of violence against sexual minorities increased 127 per cent from 1988 to 1993 (NGLTF, 1994: 1).

Though scholars (Comstock, 1991; von Schultess, 1992; Valentine, 1993) and community activists (Hendricks, 1993) have increasingly addressed the issue of violence against lesbians and gay men, there remains very little reflection on the function of gender within these acts of aggression. In this chapter, I argue that a perceived transgression of normative sex/gender relations motivates much of the violence against sexual minorities, and that an assault on these 'transgressive' bodies is fundamentally concerned with policing gender presentation through public and private space. I also consider the implications of this research for transsexual and transgendered people. Given that the perception of gender dissidence informs acts of queerbashing, we can deduce that those individuals who live outside normative sex/gender relations will be most at risk for assault. Finally, I examine some of the ways in which educational strategies on violence separate gender and sexuality, and thus prevent a political response that accounts for the function of gender in queerbashing. Specific examples are taken from briefs presented in November 1993 to the Quebec Human Rights Commission's public hearing in Montreal on violence and discrimination against lesbians and gay men (Demczuk, 1993; Hendricks, 1993; Namaste, 1993; Pepper, 1993).[1] I demonstrate the ways in which gender and sexuality are separated, and thus how the issue of gender is foreclosed by certain gay male community activists.

Limits of Tolerance: Gender Norms and Gender Transgressions

'Gender' refers to the roles and meanings assigned to men and women based on their presumed biological sex (Mackie, 1983). It is a social function, neither timeless nor historical. For example, we generally associate the colour pink with girls and femininity and the colour blue with boys and masculinity. There is nothing inherent in either of these colours that links them to a particular gender: pink, or turquoise, could just as easily designate masculinity. Gender is also about what men and women are supposed to do in the world—men wear pants, have short hair, can

grow beards, and are considered more physically aggressive than women. Women can wear skirts, have longer hair, wear makeup, and are judged to be emotional. In Western societies, it is thought that there are only two genders—men and women (Ortner and Whitehead, 1981).

'Sexuality', in contrast, refers to the ways in which individuals organize their erotic and sexual lives. This is generally categorized into three separate areas: heterosexuals—individuals who have sexual relations with members of the opposite sex; homosexuals—those who have sexual relations with members of the same sex; and bisexuals—people who relate erotically to both men and women (Kinsey, Pomeroy, and Martin, 1948).

In Western societies, gender and sexuality get confused. For example, when a 15-year-old boy is assaulted and called a 'faggot', he is so labelled because he has mannerisms that are considered 'effeminate'. He may or may not be gay, but he is called a 'queer' because he does not fulfill his expected gender role. A young girl can be a tomboy until the age of 11 or so, but she must then live as a more 'dainty', 'feminine' person. If she does not, she may be called a 'dyke—again, regardless of how she actually defines her sexual identity. In both examples, the presentation of gender determines how these youths are received by their peers. When people shout 'faggot' at a 15-year-old boy, they really mean that he is not a 'masculine' man. Gender and sexuality are collapsed. As Rubin points out, the merging of gender and sexuality enables some feminist theorists to write about erotic desire (Rubin, 1984: 307).

The fusion of gender and sexuality has distinct implications for the problematic of violence. The connotations of the pejorative names used against individuals who are assaulted—names like 'sissy', 'faggot', 'dyke', 'man-hater', 'queer', and 'pervert'—suggest that an attack is justified not in reaction to one's sexual identity, but to one's gender presentation. Indeed, bashers do not characteristically inquire as to the sexual identity of their potential victims, but rather make this assumption on their own. On what basis do 'queerbashers' determine who is gay, lesbian, or bisexual?

Joseph Harry's research suggests that gender should be considered an important variable in queerbashing incidents (1982, 1990). Harry found that groups of assailants involved in these crimes relied on gender cues to ascertain sexual identity. If they judged a potential victim to be 'effeminate', for example, he was subject to attack. A related study confirms this hypothesis: 39 per cent of men surveyed who behaved in a 'feminine' manner had been physically assaulted, compared with 22 per cent of men who were 'masculine' and only 17 per cent of men who conducted themselves in a 'very masculine' fashion (Harry, 1982). According to this survey, males who are classified as 'effeminate' are more than twice as likely to experience physical violence than males who gender presentation corresponds to social norms. A study of anti-lesbian abuse in San Francisco indicates that 12 per cent of lesbians surveyed had been punched, kicked, or otherwise physically assaulted (von Schultess, 1992). Significantly, the only justification offered related to gender:

> [F]ourteen of the women said that the only explanation for incidents they had experienced was the fact that they had short hair and were wearing trousers and in most cases were in the company of another woman (Valentine, 1993: 409).

Women and men who transgress acceptable limits of self-presentation, then, are among those most at risk for assault. Assaults against men judged to be 'effeminate' or women deemed 'masculine' reveal the ways in which gender and sexuality are intertwined. Gender is used as a cue to locate lesbians and gay men. Though the perceived transgression of gender norms motivates bashing, this affects men and women differently. The gendered construction of space—both public and private—figures centrally in these acts of aggression.

Transsexual and Transgendered People and Violence

Despite the variety of gender identities available in transgender networks, and despite the prevalence of transgendered people in other cultures, most people in Western societies assume that there are only two sexes (males and females) and two genders (men and women) (Ortner and Whitehead, 1981; Devor, 1989; Bullough and Bullough, 1993; Herdt, 1994; Feinberg, 1996). For transsexual and/or transgendered people, this poses a significant problem: a person must choose the gender to which he/she belongs and behave accordingly. Because most people believe that there are only 'men' and 'women'; transgendered people need to live as one or the other in order to avoid verbal and physical harassment. In transgendered communities, this is known as the need to pass. Passing is about presenting yourself as a 'real' woman or a 'real' man—that is, as an individual whose 'original' sex is never suspected.[2] Passing means hiding the fact that you are transsexual and/or transgendered. Most people go to extraordinary lengths to live undetected as transsexuals. Electrolysis, voice therapy, the binding of breasts, mastectomy, and plastic surgery are some of the more common means employed to ensure that people pass successfully.

Given the cultural coding of gender into a binary framework, a high incidence of violence directed against TS/TG people is not surprising. Although there is very little data available on transgendered people as victims of violence, a 1992 study showed that 52 per cent of MTF transsexuals and 43 per cent of FTM transsexuals surveyed in London, England, had been physically assaulted (Tully, 1992: 266). Contrast these members with data from a 1989 American telephone poll, which revealed that 7 per cent of lesbians and gay men were victims of assault in the previous year (NGLTF, 1994). Although these samples represent two different countries, the statistical difference of violent incidents against gay/

lesbian and transgender individuals is remarkable and certainly suggests that gender plays a crucial role in the attacks generally referred to as 'gay-bashing'.

Although gender plays a central role in incidents of queerbashing, a collapse of gender and sexuality precludes a consideration of how this violence specifically affects transgendered people. Dorian Corey notes that contemporary gay anti-violence activists do not recognize the different ways aggression is, and has historically been, directed against transgendered people and gays:

> When the closet doors were shut [for gays, in the past], drag queens, of course, were out there anyways. We never had a closet. Let's face it, when you put on a dress and hit the world, you're declaring what you are. . . . These children that are supposedly straight looking, they're the ones getting bashed, so now [in the 1990s] they're protesting. The girls were always getting their assses kicked. It's just a thing of who you are and what you are (as quoted in Enigma, 1992: 35–6).

Transsexual activists have suggested that one of the ways we can respond to the function of gender in violence is by naming it directly. As an activist button proclaims, 'transsexuals get queerbashed too'. Activists also insist that we need to speak of *genderbashing*, not gaybashing. This discourse separates gender and sexuality, since their collapse prevents an appreciation of the specificity of violence against transsexual and transgendered people.

Sex Work and Transsexual/ Transgendered Public Space

'Transsexual and transgendered public space' refers to urban areas known for their transsexuals and transvestites, such as the Meat District on the border of New York's Greenwich Village, Santa Monica Boulevard in Los Angeles, or the Tenderloin in San Francisco. While gay male public space is defined through the presence of gay businesses and bars, transsexual public space reflects the areas of the city frequented by transsexual and transvestite sex workers.

Since gender and sexuality are not the same, it is not surprising that most cities have separate geographic areas known for transgendered people and lesbians/gays. Pat Califia articulates the differences between gay ghettoes and sex worker areas:

> Gay ghettos operate differently than other types of sex zones. They are more likely to be residential districts for gay men as well as places where they can find entertainment. Although johns still enter gay ghettos in quest of pleasurable activities not available within the nuclear family, they have better luck scoring if they camouflage themselves as residents of the area (1991: 14).

Because transgender areas are not tied to a notion of a resident (as in the case of gay ghettos), the ways in which the space can be defined varies. Although certain sections of the city are known for their transsexuals and transvestites, these people are usually only visible at night. New York's Meat Market District is so named because of its many meat-packaging warehouses. When these businesses close at the end of the day, transgendered sex workers come out to earn their livelihoods, and thus transform the meaning of the term 'meat' into one with explicit sexual connotations. Time of day and geographic space converge to establish a public transgender identity. For example, a Toronto sex worker interviewed in David Adkin's film *Out: Stories of Lesbian and Gay Youth* refers to the area where transgender prostitutes solicit clients as 'trannie town' (Adkin, 1993).

As Califia demonstrates, the recent emergence of gay ghettos has separated sexual minorities from transsexual prostitutes. Although bars catering to transgendered people are extremely rare, they are usually located in sex worker districts rather than in gay villages. In Montreal, for example, the transsexual/transvestite bar Café Cléopâtra is situated near the corner of Sainte-Catherine and Saint-Laurent streets, in the heart of the red-light district.[3] The bar is widely known for its prostitutes—it is a space not only where transgendered people can socialize, but where they can also earn their livings. Montreal police observe the establishment regularly. While recent years have not witnessed any official raids on the bar, it is common of officers to walk in, 'do the rounds', and inspect bar patrons, sex workers, and their prospective clinets.[4]

This police harassment of transgendered people relates to the laws against prostitution. In Canada, prostitution is entirely legal, but soliciting clients is not (*Pocket Criminal Code of Canada*, 1987: 118–19). Individual officers have enormous scrutiny in the interpretation of what constitutes 'solicitation': it may be a verbal agreement about sexual acts in exchange for financial compensation, or it may be a smile or glance directed at an undercover officer. While the latter instance would probably not be considered 'solicitation' in a court of law, officers still have the power to charge individuals with the crime and place them in custody at night (Scott, 1987). It is the communication of sexual desire that is criminalized in Canada, not sexual desire or its enactment per se. Not surprisingly, this legislation does not affect all sex workers equally. Cathy, the operator of an escort service, remarks that street prostitutes—those most visible in the public eye—are most affected by this law: 'escort services . . . have enjoyed . . . tolerance as we go tiptoeing around in the night, not bothering communities because we're not standing in people's front yards' (1987: 88–91). Research indicates that police use the soliciting law to harass prostitutes, following them down the street in a patrol car or stopping to talk with them during their work (Hankins and Gendron, nd).

Limits of Antiviolence Activism: Opposing Gender and Sexuality

Much of the activist response to violence against sexual and gender minorities has centered on the gay village of a particular city (see Hendricks, 1993). As most gay men are assaulted in areas demarcated as 'gay': this focus is useful. Yet such a strategy forecloses an investigation of gender and ignores the different experiences of lesbians, bisexual women, and transgendered people with respect to public space and violence. By emphasizing sexual identity, this discourse establishes an antiviolence agenda that is, at best, only somewhat useful. Consider the text of an educational poster produced by Montreal's police department (Service de police de la communauté urbaine de Montreal, or SPCUM): 'Being lesbian, gay, or bisexual is not a crime. Bashing is.' The slogan—which also appears on buttons produced by antiviolence activists in Toronto—addresses the perpetrators of violence directly, and in that, it is to be commended. Despite this direct address, however, the poster does not engage the cognitive processes at work that perpetrators use to determine who is gay, lesbian, or bisexual. In this discourse, identity is mobilized as the ground upon which acts of violence are established. People are bashed because they are gay, lesbian, or bisexual. But we have already seen that bashing occurs due to the perception of potential victims, and that compulsory sex/gender relations figure centrally in these acts of interpretation. In this light, educational materials that address the perpetrators of violence should focus on the interpretive processes these people use to locate queerbashing victims. Because gender is the primary mechanism through which this takes place, there is a desperate need for posters, pamphlets, and presentations that outline the ways in which a binary gender system is upheld, as well as the power relations concealed within it. Through a stress on being, rather than on the perception of doing, the

SPCUM poster reifies sexual identity and prevents a proper investigation of gender in the problematic of violence.

Implicitly, gender and sexuality are juxtaposed. This opposition can be witnessed in the brief presented by the SPCUM to the Quebec Human Rights Commission in association with its public hearings on violence and discrimination against lesbians and gay men (November 1993). In their brief to the commission, the SPCUM presented data on the prevalence of crime in District 33—the geographic area that includes (but is not limited to) the gay village. The borders of the village (René-Lévesque and Ontario, Amherst and Papineau) were compared to a similar section of the city—that demarcated by the streets René-Lévesque and Ontario (north/south axis) and Amherst and Saint-Laurent (east/west). The SPCUM was interested in comparing these two sections of District 33 in order to evaluate the frequency of violent incidents (thefts, sexual assault, harassment). The areas are proportional in size, each comprising about 20 per cent of the district. Moreover, they share certain similarities in terms of the businesses, bars, and people present:

> Tous deux sont dans l'axe de la rue Ste-Catherine, rue très fréquentée de jour comme de nuit et où l'on retrouve divers commerces, restaurants, bars et salles d'amusement. On y retrouve également des activités reliées à la vente et la consommation de stupéfiants, à la prostitution masculine et féminine contrôlée, en partie, par deux groupes des motards criminels. [Both include Sainte-Catherine street, which is busy both day and night, and where one can find a variety of businesses, restaurants, bars, and amusement halls. One can also find activities related to the sale and consumption of drugs, as well as male and female prostitution, which is controlled, in part, by two groups of criminal bikers.] (SPCUM, 1993).

The SPCUM data indicates that between November 1991 and October 1993, a total of 1,454 crimes were recorded for the gay village—approximately 18 per cent of the total number of reported crimes in District 33 (1993: 10–11). Given that the gay village comprises 20 per cent of the district, the study implies that incidents of violence and crime correspond proportionately to geography. (However, the brief does not address the population of the gay village in relation to that of the entire district, thus associating violence with city space rather than demographics.)

The SPCUM offers comparative data to legitimate this figure. The section of District 33 to which the gay village is compared indicates 2,774 incidents of violence over the same time period, a statistic that amounts to 34 per cent of the violence in the total district (1993: 11). Since the comparison territory is relatively equal in size to that of the gay village, it is suggested that violence and crime occur more frequently in this area than in the section of the city known to be populated by gay men. By demonstrating the ways in which crime in the gay village is statistically *below* the proportional incidents of violence in District 33, the SPCUM attempts to dismiss activists who point to increased instances of bashing in Montreal's gay village. (The results of the SPCUM study are presented in Figure 39.1.)

There are, of course, tremendous differences in the data on violence collected by police departments and that collected by lesbian and gay community groups (Comstock, 1991; NGLTF, 1994). What is perhaps even more remarkable about the research presented by the SPCUM, however, is the way in which it forces a separation between sexuality and gender in terms of public space. The comparative section of District 33—that area bordered by Saint-Laurent, Amherst, Ontario, and Réne-Lévesque—is well-known as the city's sex worker district. The city's only transsexual/transvestite bar is located here, and streets in this region are also frequented by TS/TG prostitutes.

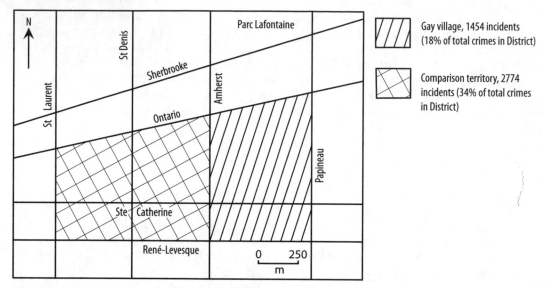

Figure 39.1 Incidents of violent crimes in two sections Police District 33, Montreal, November 1991–October 1993 (SOURCE: SPCUM 1993, 10–11).

Although the SPCUM maintains that both the gay village and this comparative section are homes to prostitutes, they do not account for the gendered breakdown of this activity. Field research conducted in the summer of 1993 indicates that most male prostitutes work in the gay village, toward Papineau; directly on its borders (Parc Lafontaine, located just above Amherst and Ontario); or in an adult cinema at the corner of Sainte-Catherine and Amherst. In contrast, most female prostitutes work on the corner of Saint-Laurent and Sainte-Catherine, on Saint-Denis, or on side streets in the vicinity. Transgendered prostitutes can also be found in this area. (The geographic location of sex workers in District 33 is depicted in Figure 39.2).

Regarding incidents of violence, most TS/TG prostitutes work in an area with a much higher frequency of criminal acts than the gay village (34 per cent versus 18 per cent). Although these statistics do not necessarily indicate that more transgendered people (proportionally) are victims of violence than gay men, it is certainly

fair to stipulate that they work in an area known for criminal activities. To present this region as a comparative sample against the gay village is, then, to juxtapose gender and sexuality. While the SPCUM attempts to dispel fears about the high incidence of violence in gay space, it offers no examination of the role gender plays either in this site or its comparative territory. Because gender is not signalled as a factor in the discussion of District 33—along with other variables including poverty and homelessness—the SPCUM assumes that crime does not vary according to the gendered dimension of public space. The focus accorded to sexuality and the gay ghetto makes it impossible to address the violence that is directed against TS/TG people—whether they are in the gay village, a sex worker zone, or elsewhere.

Conclusion

The theoretical issues presented here, especially the relations between gender and sexuality, raise

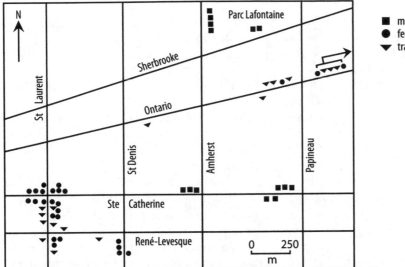

Figure 39.2 Sex-worker presence according to gender in Police District 33, Montreal, November 1991–October 1993 (SOURCE: field research). Note: more sex workers can be found further east on Ontario.

additional questions as to the collection and interpretation of evidence on gendered violence. What implications does the presence of TS/TG people in public space hold in terms of violence? Do bashers drive into these areas, looking to assault a transsexual woman or a transvestite prostitute, as they often drive into gay villages in search of queerbashing victims (Comstock, 1991: 49)? Are transgendered people of colour assaulted more frequently than those who are white? What happens when transgender prostitutes enter areas demarcated as 'gay'? Are these people subject to assault because of an association between prostitution and AIDS, and if so, how does this relate to increased violence against those perceived to be HIV-positive (NGLTF, 1994)? Since much of the data on queerbashing indicates that it is often perpetrated by young males, usually in groups (Comstock, 1991: 65), are transgendered youth most at risk for assault? What are the specific methodological difficulties involved in collecting data on violence against transgendered people? Will these people

be reluctant to report the assaults they experience to the police, as are many lesbians, gay men, and bisexuals? Given that transsexuals are incarcerated according to their 'original', biological sex (e.g., an MTF person is placed in an all-male jail), can we expect transsexuals to consider police and law enforcement officials in a favourable light?[5] Do transgendered people even inform gaybashing hotlines when they are assaulted, or do they not consider themselves part of these communities? How can we record incidents of genderbashing for the collection of hate crime statistics?[6] These are only a few of the questions that a more detailed, empirical study of violence against transgendered people would address.

In recent years, the issue of violence has received increased attention in the communities of the sexually marginalized, as well as within the academy. Although some of the research emphasizes the role of gender in violence (Harry, 1990; von Schultess, 1992; Valentine, 1993), it has yet to explore the implications of this issue for transgendered individuals and communities. The definition of public space is intimately linked to culturally sanctioned gender identities. This has profound implications for people who live outside normative sex/gender relations: 'ordinary' public space as well as regions known as gay ghettoes are sites where the gender potential of being verbally abused, and/or physically assaulted, is remarkably high. Furthermore, although gender and sexuality are conventionally confused, such that 'effeminate' men and 'masculine' women are 'gaybashed' irrespective of their sexual identities, the variables of gender and sexuality can also be juxtaposed. Such an opposition can be quite explicit, as when middle-class gay men struggled to evict transgendered prostitutes from Vancouver's West End (Arrington, 1987). A separation of gender and sexuality can also be more subtle, as in the

discourse on violence proposed by many gay male activists that privileges sexuality over gender, and hence develops a political response that is only valid for urban, middle-class gay men.

Taking up the issue of violence against sexual and gender minorities, this chapter has attempted to illustrate how some of the responses to violence preclude an adequate conceptualization of gendered aggression. Through a literature review on gender and violence, as well as a preliminary analysis on the geographic location of Montreal prostitutes in 1992, I have argued that the discourse of violence against sexual minorities excludes transsexual women. Further more, the briefs presented to the Quebec Human Rights Commission offer an engaging case study of how the social relations of gender are textually coordinated in one institution, such that transsexuals are beyond consideration.

Notes

1. Copies of these briefs are available from the Commission des droits de la personne et de la jeunesse, 360 Saint-Jacques, Montreal, QC, H2Y 1P5, Canada.

2. The issue of 'passing' has been examined from an ethnomethodological perspective within sociology. See Harold Garfinkel, *Studies in Ethnomethodology* (Englewood Cliffs, NJ: Prentice-Hall, 1967); and Kessler and McKenna, *Gender: An Ethnomethodological Approach* (New York: John Wiley and Sons, 1978).

3. For more on the geographic area of Montreal's red-light district, see Daniel Proulx, *Le Red Light de Montreal, 1945–1970* (Montreal: Boreal, 1994); and Thérèse, Limonges, *La Prostitution à Montreal: Comment, pourquoi certaines fen deviennent des prostituées: Étude sociologique et criminologique.* (Montreal: Édit de l'homme, 1967).

4. Montreal police entered Café Cleopatra with a video camera, for instance, on 13 November 1997. See Viviane Namaste, 'Évaluation des besoins: Les travesty(e)s et les transsexuel(le)s

au Quebec à l'égard du VIH/Sida'. Report submitted to the Centre Québécois de Coordination sur le SIDA, Montreal, May 1998. (A copy of this report is available through ASST(e)Q in care of CACTUS, 1626 rue Saint-Hubert, Montreal, QC, H2L 3Z3.)

5. For more on transgendered people in prison, see James Tee, *Health Issues of the HIV + MTF Transgendered Prison Population* (Toronto: PASAN—Prisoners' AIDS Support Action Network [489 College St, Suite 405, Toronto, ON, M6G 1A5, 416-920-9567], 1997); Maxine Petersen, Judith Stephens, Robert Dickey, and Wendy Lewis, 'Transsexuals within the Prison System: An International Survey of Correctional Services Policies', *Behavioral Sciences and the Law* 14 (1996): 219–29; and Ann Scott, 'A Brief on HIV/AIDS in the Transgendered Prison Population'. Presentation at the International Foundation for Gender Education conference, Toronto, 27 March 1998. Also see Ann Scott and Rick Lines, 'HIV/AIDS in the Male-to-Female Transsexual and Transgendered Prison Population:

A Comprehensive Strategy. A Brief from PASAN'. (Toronto: May 1999).

6. Documenting hate crimes against gays and lesbians is difficult because the violence must be clearly accompanied by anti-gay epithets. For instance, if a man is stabbed in the gay village and his wallet stolen, he will be considered the victim of a robbery unless the assailants called him derogatory insults relating to his perceived sexuality (see SPCUM, 'Mémoire sur la discrimination et la violence envers les gais et les lesbiennes'. Brief presented to the Quebec

Human Rights Commission, November 1993. [Copy available for consultation at the Commission des droits de la personne et de la jeunesse, 360 Stain-Jacque, Montreal, QC, H2Y 1P5.]). In the case of violence against transgendered people, this criteria for documentation is questionable, since many MTF transsexuals are called 'faggot'. Programmatically, we should not have to wait until bashers decry transgendered people with the proper vocabulary before we have an adequate manner of recording such genderbashing incidents.

References

Adkin, D. 1993. *Out: Stories of Lesbian and Gay Youth*. Montreal: National Film Board of Canada.

Arrington, S. 1987. 'Community Organizing', in L. Bell, ed., *Good Girls/Bad Girls: Sex Trade Workers and Feminists Face to Face*, pp. 104–8. Toronto: Women's Press.

Bullough, B., and V. Bullough. 1993. *Cross Dressing, Sex, and Gender*. Philadelphia: University of Pennsylvania Press.

Califa, P. 1991. 'The City of Desire: Its Anatomy and Destiny', *Invert* 2, 4: 13–16.

Cathy. 1987. 'Unveiling', in L. Bell, ed., *Good Girls/Bad Girls: Feminists and Sex Trade Workers Face to Face*, pp. 88–91. Toronto: Women's Press.

Comstock, G. 1991. *Violence Against Lesbians and Gay Men*. New York: Columbia University Press.

Demczuk, I. 1993. 'Des droits à reconnaître. Hétérosexisme et discrimination envers les lesbiennes'. Brief presented to the Quebec Human Rights Commission, November 1993.

Devor, H. 1989. *Gender Blending: Confronting the Limits of Duality*. Bloomington: Indiana University Press.

Enigma, A. 1992. 'Livin' Large: Dorian Corey', *Thing* 8: 35–6.

Feinberg, L. 1996. *Transgender Warriors: Making History from Joan of Arc to RuPaul*. Boston: Beacon Press.

Hankins, C., and S. Gendron. nd. *Project Prostitution: Rapport sur les entretiens de groupes réalisés à la maison Tanguay*. Montral: Centre d'études sur

le SIDA, Unité de santé publique, Hôpital général de Montreal.

Harry, J. 1982. 'Derivative Deviance: The Cases of Extortion, Fag-Bashing and the Shakedown of Gay Men', *Criminology* 19: 546–63.

———. 1990. 'Conceptualizing Anti-gay Violence', *Journal of Interpersonal Violence* 5: 350–8.

Hendricks, M. 1993. 'Lesbian and Gay Community Relations with the M[ontreal] U[rban] C[ommunity] Police'. Brief presented for the group Lesbiennes et Gais contre la violence to the Quebec Human Rights Commission, November 1993.

Herdt, G., ed. 1994. *Third Sex, Third Gender: Beyond Sexual Dimorphism in Culture and History*. New York: Zone Books.

Kinsey, A., W. Pomeroy, and C.E. Martin. 1948. *Sexual Behavior in the Human Male*. Philadelphia: W.B. Saunders Company.

Mackie, M. 1983. *Exploring Gender Relations*. Toronto: Butterworths.

Namaste, K. 1993. 'Transgenders and Violence: An Exploration'. Brief presented to the Quebec Human Rights Commission, November 1993.

National Gay and Lesbian Task Force (NGLTF). 1994. *Anti-gay/lesbian Violence, Victimization, and Defamation in 1993*. Washington, DC: NGLTF Policy Institute.

Ortner, S. and H. Whitehead, eds. 1981. *Sexual Meanings: The Cultural Construction of Gender and Sexuality*. Cambridge, UK: Cambridge University Press.

Pepper, D. 1993. 'Community Based Responses to Bias Crimes: Some Critical Steps'. Brief presented to the Quebec Human Rights Commission, November 1993.

Pocket Criminal Code of Canada. 1987. Toronto: Carswell.

Rubin, G. 1984. 'Thinking Sex: Notes Towards a Radical Theory of the Politics of Sexuality', in C. Vance, ed., *Pleasure and Danger: Exploring Female Sexuality*, pp. 267–319. Boston: Routledge and Kegan Paul.

Scott, V. 1987. 'C-49: A New Wave of Oppression', in L. Bell, ed., *Good Girls/Bad Girls: Sex Trade Workers and Feminists Face to Face*, pp. 100–3. Toronto: Women's Press.

SPCUM. 1993. 'Mémoire sur la discrimination et la violence envers les gais et les lesbiennes'. Brief presented to the Quebec Human Rights Commission, November 1993.

Tully, B. 1992. *Accounting for Transsexuality and Transhomosexuality*. London: Whiting and Birch.

Valentine, G. 1993. '(Hetero)Sexing Space: Lesbian Perceptions and Experiences of Everyday Spaces', *Environment and Planning D: Society and Space* 11: 409.

von Schultess, B. 1992. 'Violence in the Streets: Anti-lesbian Assault and Harassment in San Francisco', in G. Herek and K. Berril, eds, *Hate Crimes: Confronting Violence Against Lesbians and Gay Men*, pp. 65–77. London, UK: Sage.

CHAPTER 40

The Myth of Sexual Symmetry in Marital Violence

Russell P. Dobash, R. Emerson Dobash, Margo Wilson, and Martin Daly

Long denied, legitimized, and made light of, wife-beating is at last the object of widespread public concern and condemnation. Extensive survey research and intensive interpretive investigations tell a common story. Violence against wives (by which term we encompass *de facto* as well as registered unions) is often persistent and severe, occurs in the context of continuous intimidation and coercion, and is inextricably linked to attempts to dominate and control women. Historical and contemporary investigations further reveal that this violence has been explicitly decriminalized, ignored, or treated in an ineffectual manner by criminal justice systems, by medical and social service institutions, and by communities. Increased attention to these failures has inspired increased efforts to redress them, and in many places legislative amendments have mandated

arrest and made assault a crime whether the offender is married to the victim or not.

A number of researchers and commentators have suggested that assaults upon men by their wives constitute a social problem comparable in nature and magnitude to that of wife-beating. Two main bodies of evidence have been offered in support of these authors' claims that husbands and wives are similarly victimized: (1) self-reports of violent acts perpetrated and suffered by survey respondents, especially those in two US national probability samples; and (2) US homicide data. Unlike the case of violence against wives, however, the victimization of husbands allegedly continues to be denied and trivialized. 'Violence by wives has not been an object of public concern,' note Straus and Gelles (1986: 472). 'There has been no publicity, and no funds have been invested in ameliorating this problem because it has not been defined as a problem.'

We shall argue that claims of sexual symmetry in marital violence are exaggerated, and that wives' and husbands' uses of violence differ greatly, both quantitatively and qualitatively. We shall further argue that there is no reason to expect the sexes to be alike in this domain, and that efforts to avoid sexism by lumping male and female data and by the use of gender-neutral terms such as 'spouse-beating' are misguided. If violence is gendered, as it assuredly is, explicit characterization of gender's relevance to violence is essential. The alleged similarity of women and men in their use of violence in intimate relationships stands in marked contrast to men's virtual monopoly on the use of violence in other social contexts, and we challenge the proponents of the sexual symmetry thesis to develop coherent theoretical models that would account for a sexual monomorphism of violence in one social context and not in others.

A final thesis of this paper is that resolution of controversies about the 'facts' of family violence requires critical examination of theories, methods, and data, with explicit attention to the development of coherent conceptual frameworks, valid and meaningful forms of measurement, and appropriate inferential procedures. Such problems are not peculiar to this research domain, but analysis of the claims regarding violence against husbands provides an excellent example of how a particular approach to construct formation and measurement has led to misrepresentation of the phenomena under investigation.

The Claim of Sexually Symmetrical Marital Violence

Authoritative claims about the prevalence and sexual symmetry of spousal violence in America began with a 1975 US national survey in which 2,143 married or cohabiting persons were interviewed in person about their actions in the preceding year. Straus (1977–8) announced that the

survey results showed that the 'marriage license is a hitting license', and moreover that the rates of perpetrating spousal violence, including severe violence, were higher for wives than for husbands. He concluded:

> Violence between husband and wife is far from a one way street. The old cartoons of the wife chasing the husband with a rolling pin or throwing pots and pans are closer to reality than most (and especially those with feminist sympathies) realize (Straus, 1977–8: 447–8).

In 1985, the survey was repeated by telephone with a new national probability sample including 3,520 husband–wife households, and with similar results. In each survey, the researchers interviewed either the wife or the husband (but not both) in each contacted household about how the couple settled their differences when they had a disagreement. The individual who was interviewed was presented with a list of eighteen 'acts' ranging from 'discussed an issue calmly' and 'cried' to 'threw something at him/her/you' and 'beat him/her/you up', with the addition of 'choked him/her/you' in 1985 (Straus, 1990a: 33). These acts constituted the Conflict Tactics Scales (CTS) and were intended to measure three constructs: 'Reasoning', 'Verbal Aggression', and 'Physical Aggression' or 'Violence', which was further subdivided into 'Minor Violence' and 'Severe Violence' according to a presumed potential for injury (Straus, 1979; Straus and Gelles, 1990a). Respondents were asked how frequently they had perpetrated each act in the course of 'conflicts or disagreements' with their spouses (and with one randomly selected child) within the past year, and how frequently they had been on the receiving end. Each respondent's self-reports of victimization and perpetration contributed to estimates of rates of violence by both husbands and wives.

According to both surveys, rates of violence by husbands and wives were strikingly similar. The authors estimated that in the year prior to the 1975 survey 11.6 per cent of US husbands were victims of physical violence perpetrated by their wives, while 12.1 per cent of wives were victims of their husbands' violence. In 1985, these percentages had scarcely changed, but husbands seemed more vulnerable: 12.1 per cent of husbands and 11.3 per cent of wives were victims. In both surveys, husbands were more likely to be victims of acts of 'severe violence': in 1975, 4.6 per cent of husbands were such victims versus 3.8 per cent of wives, and in 1985, 4.4 per cent of husbands versus 3.0 per cent of wives were victims. In reporting their results, the surveys' authors stressed the surprising assaultiveness of wives:

> The repeated finding that the rate of assault by women is similar to the rate by their male partners is an important and distressing aspect of violence in American families. It contrasts markedly to the behavior of women outside the family. It shows that within the family or in dating and cohabiting relationships, women are about as violent as men (Straus and Gelles, 1990b: 104).

Others have endorsed and publicized these conclusions. For example, a recent review of marital violence concludes, with heavy reliance on Straus and Gelles's survey results, that '(a) women are more prone than men to engage in severely violent acts; (b) each year more men than women are victimized by their intimates' (McNeely and Mann, 1990: 130). One of Straus and Gelles's collaborators in the 1975 survey, Steinmetz (1977–8), used the same survey evidence to proclaim the existence of 'battered husbands' and a 'battered husband syndrome'. She has remained one of the leading defenders of the claim that violence between men and women in the family is symmetrical. Steinmetz and her collaborators maintain that the problem is not wife-beating perpetrated by violent men, but 'violent couples' and 'violent people'. Men may be stronger on average, argues

Steinmetz, but weaponry equalizes matters, as is allegedly shown by the nearly equivalent numbers of US husbands and wives who are killed by their partners. The reason why battered husbands are inconspicuous and seemingly rare is supposedly that shame prevents them from seeking help.

Straus and his collaborators have sometimes qualified their claims that their surveys demonstrate sexual symmetry in marital violence, noting, for example, that men are usually larger and stronger than women and thus able to inflict more damage and that women are more likely to use violence in self-defense or retaliation. However, the survey results indicate a symmetry not just in the perpetration of violence but in its initiation as well, and from this further symmetry, Stets and Straus (1990: 154–5) conclude that the equal assaultiveness of husbands and wives cannot be attributed to the wives acting in self-defense, after all.

Other surveys using the CTS in the United States and in other countries have replicated the finding that wives are about as violent as husbands. The CTS has also been used to study violence in dating relationships, with the same sexually symmetrical results.

Some authors maintain not only that wives initiate violence at rates comparable to husbands, but that they rival them in the damage they inflict as well. McNeely and Robinson-Simpson (1987), for example, argue that research shows that the 'truth about domestic violence' is that 'women are as violent, if not more violent than men,' in their inclinations, in their actions, and in the damage they inflict. The most dramatic evidence invoked in this context is again the fact that wives kill: spousal homicides—for which detection should be minimally or not at all biased because homicides are nearly always discovered and recorded—produce much more nearly equivalent numbers of male and female victims in the United States than do sub-lethal assault data, which are subject to sampling biases when obtained from police, shelters and hospitals. According to McNeely and Mann (1990: 130), 'the average man's size and strength are neutralized by guns and knives, boiling water, bricks, fireplace pokers, and baseball bats.'

A corollary of the notion that the sexes are alike in their use of violence is that satisfactory causal accounts of violence will be gender-blind. Discussion thus focuses, for example, on the role of one's prior experiences with violence as a child, social stresses, frustration, inability to control anger, impoverished social skills, and so forth, without reference to gender. This presumption that the sexes are alike not merely in action but in the reasons for that action is occasionally explicit, such as when Shupe et al. (1987: 56) write: 'Everything we have found points to parallel processes that lead women and men to become violent. . . . Women may be more likely than men to use kitchen utensils or sewing scissors when they commit assault, but their frustrations, motives and lack of control over these feelings predictably resemble men's.'

In sum, the existence of an invisibles legion of assaulted husbands is an inference that strikes many family violence researchers as reasonable. Two lines of evidence—homicide data and the CTS survey results—suggest to those supporting the sexual-symmetry-of-violence thesis that large numbers of men are trapped in violent relationships. These men are allegedly being denied medical, social welfare, and criminal justice services because of an unwillingness to accept the evidence from homicide statistics and the CTS surveys.

Violence Against Wives

Any argument that marital violence is sexually symmetrical must either dismiss or ignore a large body of contradictory evidence indicating that wives greatly outnumber husbands as victims. While CTS researchers were discovering and publicizing the mutual violence of wives and husbands, other researchers—using evidence from courts, police, and women's shelters—were finding that wives were much more likely than husbands to

be victims. After an extensive review of extant research, Lystad (1975) expressed the consensus: 'The occurrence of adult violence in the home usually involves males as aggressors towards females.' This conclusion was subsequently supported by numerous further studies of divorce records, emergency room patients treated for non-accidental injuries, police assault records, and spouses seeking assistance and refuge. Analyses of police and court records in North America and Europe have persistently indicated that women constitute 90–95 per cent of the victims of those assaults in the home reported to the criminal justice system.

Defenders of the sexual-symmetry-of-violence thesis do not deny these results, but they question their representativeness: these studies could be biased because samples of victims were self-selected. However, criminal victimization surveys using national probability samples similarly indicate that wives are much more often victimized than husbands. Such surveys in the United States, Canada, and Great Britain have been replicated in various years, with essentially the same results. Beginning in 1972 and using a panel survey method involving up to seven consecutive interviews at six-month intervals, the US National Crime Survey has generated nearly a million interviews. Gaquin's (1977–8) analysis of US National Crime Survey data for 1973–5 led her to conclude that men 'have almost no risk of being assaulted by their wives' (634–5); only 3 per cent of the violence reported from these surveys involved attacks on men by their female partners. Another analysis of the National Crime Survey data from 1973 to 1980 found that 6 per cent of spousal assault incidents were directed at men (McLeod, 1984). Schwartz (1987) re-analyzed the same victimization surveys with the addition of the 1981 and 1982 data, and found 102 men who claimed to have been victims of assaults by their wives (4 per cent of domestic assault incidents) in contrast to 1,641 women who said they were assaulted by husbands. The 1981 Canadian Urban

Victimization Survey and the 1987 General Social Survey produced analogous findings, from which Johnson (1989) concluded that 'women account for 80–90 per cent of victims in assaults or sexual assaults between spouses or former spouses. In fact, the number of domestic assaults involving males was too low in both surveys to provide reliable estimates' (1–2). The 1982 and 1984 British Crime Surveys found that women accounted for all the victims of marital assaults. Self-reports of criminal victimization based on national probability surveys, while not without methodological weaknesses, are not subject to the same reporting biases as divorce, police and hospital records.

The national crime surveys also indicate that women are much more likely than men to suffer injury as a result of assaults in the home. After analyzing the results of the US National Crime Surveys, Schwartz (1987: 67) concludes, 'there are still more than 13 times as many women seeking medical care from a private physician for injuries received in a spousal assault.' This result again replicates the typical findings of studies of police or hospital records. For example, women constituted 94 per cent of the injury victims in an analysis of the spousal assault cases among 262 domestic disturbance calls to police in Santa Barbara County, California; moreover, the women's injuries were more serious than the men's. Berk et al. (1983: 207) conclude that 'when injuries are used as the outcome of interest, a marriage license is a hitting license but for men only.' Brush (1990) reports that a US national probability sample survey of over 13,000 respondents in 1987–8 replicated the evident symmetry of marital violence when CTS-like questions about acts were posed, but also revealed that women were much more often injured than men (and that men down-played women's injuries).

In response, defenders of the sexual-symmetry-of-violence thesis contend that data from police, courts, hospitals, and social service agencies are suspect because men are reluctant to report physical violence by their wives. For example,

Steinmetz (1977–8) asserts that husband-beating is a camouflaged social problem because men must overcome extraordinary stigma in order to report that their wives have beaten them. Similarly, Shupe et al. (1987) maintain that men are unwilling to report their wives because 'it would be unmanly or unchivalrous to go to the police for protection from a woman' (52). However, the limited available evidence does not support these authors' presumption that men are less likely to report assaults by their spouses than are women. Schwartz's (1987) analysis of the 1973–82 US National Crime Survey data found that 67.2 per cent of men and 56.8 per cent of women called the police after being assaulted by their spouses. One may protest that these high percentages imply that only a tiny proportion of the most severe spousal assaults were acknowledged as assaults by respondents to these crime surveys, but the results are nonetheless contrary to the notion that assaulted men are especially reticent. Moreover, Rouse et al. (1988), using 'act' definitions of assaults which inspired much higher proportions to acknowledge victimization, similarly report that men were likelier than women to call the police after assaults by intimate partners, both among married couples and among those dating. In addition, a sample of 337 cases of domestic violence drawn from family court cases in Ontario showed that men were more likely than women to press charges against their spouses: there were 17 times as many female victims as male victims, but only 22 per cent of women laid charges in contrast to 40 per cent of the men, and men were less likely to drop the charges, too. What those who argue that men are reluctant or ashamed to report their wives' assaults overlook is that women have their own reasons to be reticent, fearing both the loss of a jailed or alienated husband's economic support and his vengeance. Whereas the claim that husbands underreport because of shame or chivalry is largely speculative, there is considerable evidence that women report very little of the violence perpetrated by their male partners.

The CTS survey data indicating equivalent violence by wives and husbands thus stand in contradiction to injury data, to police incident reports, to help-seeking statistics, and even to other, larger, national probability sample surveys of self-reported victimization. The CTS researchers insist that their results alone are accurate because husbands' victimizations are unlikely to be detected or reported by any other method. It is therefore important to consider in detail the CTS and the data it generates.

Do CTS Data Reflect the Reality of Marital Violence?

The CTS instrument has been much used and much criticized. Critics have complained that its exclusive focus on 'acts' ignores the actors' interpretations, motivations, and intentions; that physical violence is arbitrarily delimited, excluding, for example, sexual assault and rape; that retrospective reports of the past year's events are unlikely to be accurate; that researchers' attributions of 'violence' (with resultant claims about its statistical prevalence) are based on respondents' admitting to acts described in such an impoverished manner as to conflate severe assaults with trivial gestures; that the formulaic distinction between 'minor' and 'severe violence' (whereby, for example, 'tried to hit with something' is definitionally 'severe' and 'slapped' is definitionally 'minor') constitutes a poor operationalization of severity; that the responses of aggressors and victims have been given identical evidentiary status in deriving incidence estimates, while their inconsistencies have been ignored; that the CTS omits the contexts of violence, the events precipitating it, and the sequences of events by which it progresses; and that it fails to connect outcomes, especially injury, with the acts producing them.

Straus (1990b) has defended the CTS against its critics, maintaining that the CTS addresses context with its 'verbal aggression' scale (although the assessment of 'verbal aggression' is not incident-linked with the assessment of 'violence'); that the minor-severe categorization 'is roughly parallel to the legal distinction between "simple assault" and "aggravated assault"' (58); that other measurement instruments have problems, too; and that you cannot measure everything. Above all, the defense rests on the widespread use of the instrument, on its reliability, and on its validity. That the CTS is widely used cannot be gainsaid, but whether it is reliable or valid is questionable.

PROBLEMS WITH THE RELIABILITY AND VALIDITY OF CTS RESPONSES

Straus (1990b: 64) claims that six studies have assessed 'the internal consistency reliability' of the CTS. One of the six (Barling and Rosenbaum, 1986) contains no such assessment, a second is unreferenced, and a third unpublished. However, a moderate degree of 'internal consistency reliability' of the CTS can probably be conceded. For example, those who admit to having 'beat up' their spouses are also likely to admit to having 'hit' them.

The crucial matter of interobserver reliability is much more problematic. The degree of concordance in couples' responses is an assay of 'interspousal reliability' (Jouriles and O'Leary, 1985), and such reliability must be high if CTS scores are to be taken at face value. For example, incidence estimates of husband-to-wife and wife-to-husband violence have been generated from national surveys in which the CTS was administered to only one adult per family, with claims of victimization and perpetration by male and female respondents all granted equal evidentiary status and summated. The validity of these widely cited incidence estimates is predicated upon interspousal reliability.

Straus (1990b: 66) considers the assessment of spousal concordance to constitute an assay of 'concurrent validity' rather than 'interspousal reliability', in effect treating each partner's report as the violence criterion that validates the other. But spousal concordance is analogous to interobserver reliability: it is a necessary but by no means suffi-cient condition for concluding that the self-reports accurately reflect reality. If couples generally produce consistent reports—Mr and Mrs Jones both indicate that he struck her, while Mr and Mrs Smith both indicate that neither has struck the other—then it is possible though by no means certain that their CTS self-reports constitute valid (veridical) information about the blows actually struck. However, if couples routinely provide dis-crepant CTS responses, data derived from the CTS simply cannot be valid.

In this light, studies of husband/wife concord-ance in CTS responses should be devastating to those who imagine that the CTS provides a valid account of the respondents' acts. In what Straus correctly calls 'the most detailed and thorough analysis of agreement between spouses in response to the CTS', Szinovacz (1983) found that 103 couples' accounts of the violence in their interactions matched to a degree little greater than chance. On several CTS items, mainly the most severe ones, agreement was actually below chance. On the item 'beat up', concordance was nil: although there were respondents of both sexes who claimed to have administered beatings and respondents of both sexes who claimed to have been on the receiving end, there was not a single couple in which one party claimed to have administered and the other to have received such a beating. In a similar study, Jouriles and O'Leary (1985) administered the CTS to 65 couples attending a marital therapy clinic, and 37 control couples from the local community. For many of the acts, the frequency and percentage data reported are impossible to reconcile; for others, Jouriles and O'Leary reported a concordance sta-tistic (Cohen's Kappa) as equalling zero when the correct values were negative. Straus (1990b) cites this study as conferring validity on the CTS, but in fact, its results replicated Szinovacz's (1983): husband/wife agreement scarcely exceeded chance expectation and actually fell below chance on some items.

Straus (1990b) acknowledges that these and the other studies he reviews 'found large dis-crepancies between the reports of violence given by husbands and by wives' (69). He concludes, however, that 'validity measures of agreement between family members are within the range of validity coefficients typically reported' (71), and that 'the weakest aspect of the CTS are [sic] the scales that have received the least criticism: Reasoning and Verbal aggression' (71), by which he implies that the assessment of violence is rela-tively strong.

Ultimately, Straus's defense of the CTS is that the proof of the pudding is in the eating: 'The strong-est evidence concerns the construct validity of the CTS. It has been used in a large number of studies producing findings that tend to be consistent with previous research (when available), consistent regardless of gender of respondent, and theor-etically meaningful.' And indeed, with respect to marital violence, the CTS is capable of making certain gross discriminations. Various studies have found CTS responses to vary as a function of age, race, poverty, duration of relationship, and regis-tered versus de facto marital unions, and these effects have generally been directionally similar to those found with less problematic measures of violence such as homicides. However, the CTS has also failed to detect certain massive differences, and we do not refer only to sex differences.

Consider the case of child abuse by step-parents versus birth parents. In various countries, including the United States, a step-parent is more likely to fatally assault a small child than is a birth parent, by a factor on the order of 100-fold; sub-lethal violence also exhibits huge differences in the same direction. Using the CTS, however, Gelles and Harrop (1991) were unable to detect any difference in self-reports of violence by step-versus birth parents. Users of the CTS have some-times conceded that the results of their self-report surveys cannot provide an accurate picture of the prevalence of violence, but they have made this concession only to infer that the estimates must be gross underestimates of the true prevalence. However, the CTS's failure to differentiate the behaviour of step- versus birth parents indicates that CTS-based estimates are not just underestimates but may misrepresent between-group differences in systematically biased ways. One must be concerned, then, whether this sort of bias also arises in CTS-based comparisons between husbands and wives.

PROBLEMS WITH THE INTERPRETATION OF CTS RESPONSES

With the specific intention of circumventing imprecision and subjectivity in asking about such abstractions as 'violence', the CTS is confined to questions about 'acts'. Respondents are asked whether they have 'pushed' their partners, have 'slapped' them, and so forth, rather than whether they have 'assaulted' them or behaved 'violently'. This focus on 'acts' is intended to reduce problems of self-serving and biased definitional criteria on the part of the respondents. However, any gain in objectivity has been undermined by the way that CTS survey data have then been analyzed and interpreted. Any respondent who acknowledges a single instance of having 'pushed', 'grabbed', 'shoved', 'slapped', or 'hit or tried to hit' another person is deemed a perpetrator of 'violence' by the researchers, regardless of the act's context, consequences, or meaning to the parties involved. Similarly, a single instance of having 'kicked', 'bit', 'hit or tried to hit with an object', 'beat up', 'choked', 'threatened with a knife or gun', or 'used a knife or fired a gun' makes one a perpetrator of 'severe violence'.

Affirmation of any one of the 'violence' items provides the basis for estimates such as Straus and Gelles's (1990b: 97) claim that 6.8 million husbands and 6.25 million wives were spousal assault victims in the United States in 1985. Similarly, estimates of large numbers of 'beaten' or 'battered' wives and husbands have been based on affirmation of any one of the 'severe violence' items. For example, Steinmetz (1986: 734) and

Straus and Gelles (1987: 638) claim on this basis that 1.8 million US women are 'beaten' by their husbands annually. But note that any man who once threw an 'object' at his wife, regardless of its nature and regardless of whether the throw missed, qualifies as having 'beaten' her; some unknown proportion of the women and men who are alleged to have been 'beaten', on the basis of their survey responses, never claimed to have been struck at all. Thus, the 'objective' scoring of the CTS not only fails to explore the meanings and intentions associated with the acts but also has in practice entailed interpretive transformations that guarantee exaggeration, misinterpretation, and ultimately trivialization of the genuine problems of violence.

Consider a 'slap'. The word encompasses anything from a slap on the hand chastizing a dinner companion for reaching for a bite of one's dessert to a tooth-loosening assault intended to punish, humiliate, and terrorize. These are not trivial distinctions; indeed, they constitute the essence of definitional issues concerning violence. Almost all definitions of violence and violent acts refer to intentions. Malevolent intent is crucial, for example, to legal definitions of 'assault' (to which supporters of the CTS have often mistakenly claimed that their 'acts' correspond; e.g., Straus, 1990b: 58). However, no one has systematically investigated how respondents vary in their subjective definitions of the 'acts' listed on the CTS. If, for example, some respondents interpret phrases such as 'tried to hit with an object' literally, then a good deal of relatively harmless behaviour surely taints the estimates of 'severe violence'. Although this problem has not been investigated systematically, one author has shown that it is potentially serious. In a study of 103 couples, Margolin (1987) found that wives surpassed husbands in their use of 'severe violence' according to the CTS, but unlike others who have obtained this result, Margolin troubled to check its meaningfulness with more intensive interviews. She concluded:

While CTS items appear behaviorally specific, their meanings still are open to interpretation. In one couple who endorsed the item 'kicking', for example, we discovered that the kicking took place in bed in a more kidding, than serious, fashion. Although this behavior meets the criterion for severe abuse on the CTS, neither spouse viewed it as aggressive, let alone violent. In another couple, the wife scored on severe physical aggression while the husband scored on low-level aggression only. The inquiry revealed that, after years of passively accepting the husband's repeated abuse, this wife finally decided, on one occasion, to retaliate by hitting him over the head with a wine decanter (1987: 82).

By the criteria of Steinmetz (1977–8: 501), this incident would qualify as a 'battered husband' case. But however dangerous this retaliatory blow may have been and however reprehensible or justified one may consider it, it is not 'battering', whose most basic definitional criterion is its repetitiveness. A failure to consider intentions, interpretations, and the history of the individuals' relationship is a significant shortcoming of CTS research. Only through a consideration of behaviours, intentions, and intersubjective understandings associated with specific violent events will we come to a fuller understanding of violence between men and women. Studies employing more intensive interviews and detailed case reports addressing the contexts and motivations of marital violence help unravel the assertions of those who claim the widespread existence of beaten and battered husbands. Research focusing on specific violent events shows that women almost always employ violence in defense of self and children in response to cues of imminent assault in the past and in retaliation for previous physical abuse. Proponents of the sexual-symmetry-of-violence thesis have made much of the fact that CTS surveys indicate that women 'initiate'

the violence about as often as men, but a case in which a woman struck the first blow is unlikely to be the mirror image of one in which her husband 'initiated'. A noteworthy feature of the literature proclaiming the existence of battered husbands and battering wives is how little the meagre case descriptions resemble those of battered wives and battering husbands. Especially lacking in the alleged male victim cases is any indication of the sort of chronic intimidation characteristic of prototypical woman battering cases.

Any self-report method must constitute an imperfect reflection of behaviour, and the CTS is no exception. That in itself is hardly a fatal flaw. But for such an instrument to retain utility for the investigation of a particular domain such as family violence, an essential point is that its inaccuracies and misrepresentations must not be systematically related to the distinctions under investigation. The CTS's inability to detect the immense differences in violence between stepparents and birth parents, as noted above, provides strong reason to suspect that the test's shortcomings produce not just noise but systematic bias. In the case of marital violence, the other sorts of evidence reviewed in this paper indicate that there are massive differences in the use of confrontational violence against spouses by husbands versus wives, and yet the CTS has consistently failed to detect them. CTS users have taken this failure as evidence for the null hypothesis, apparently assuming that their questionnaire data have a validity that battered women's injuries and deaths lack.

Homicides

The second line of evidence that has been invoked in support of the claim that marital violence is more or less sexually symmetrical is the number of lethal outcomes:

Data on homicide between spouses suggest that an almost equal number of wives kill their husbands as husbands kill their wives (Wolfgang, 1958). Thus it appears that men and women might have equal potential for violent marital interaction; initiate similar acts of violence; and when differences of physical strength are equalized by weapons, commit similar amounts of spousal homicide (Steinmetz and Lucca, 1988: 241).

McNeely and Robinson-Simpson (1987: 485) elevated the latter hypothesis about the relevance of weapons to the status of a fact: 'Steinmetz observed that when weapons neutralize differences in physical strength, about as many men as women are victims of homicide.'

Steinmetz and Lucca's citation of Wolfgang refers to his finding that 53 Philadelphia men killed their wives between 1948 and 1952, while 47 women killed their husbands. This is a slender basis for such generalization, but fuller information does indeed bear Steinmetz out as regards the near equivalence of body counts in the United States: Maxfield (1989) reported that there were 10,529 wives and 7,888 husbands killed by their mates in the entire country between 1976 and 1985, a 1.3:1 ratio of female to male victims.

Husbands are indeed almost as often slain as are wives in the United States, then. However, there remain several problems with Steinmetz and Lucca's (as well as McNeely and Robinson-Simpson's) interpretation of this fact. Studies of actual cases lend no support to the facile claim that homicidal husbands and wives 'initiate similar acts of violence'. Men often kill wives after lengthy periods of prolonged physical violence accompanied by other forms of abuse and coercion; the roles in such cases are seldom if ever reversed. Men perpetrate familicidal massacres, killing spouse and children together; women do not. Men commonly hunt down and kill wives who have left them; women hardly ever behave similarly. Men kill wives as part of planned murder-suicides; analogous acts by women are almost unheard of. Men kill in response to revelations of wifely infidelity; women almost never respond similarly, though their mates are more often adulterous. The evidence is overwhelming that a large proportion of the spouse-killings perpetrated by wives, but almost none of those perpetrated by husbands, are acts of self-defense. Unlike men, women kill male partners after years of suffering physical violence, after they have exhausted all available sources of assistance, when they feel trapped, and because they fear for their own lives.

A further problem with the invocation of spousal homicide data as evidence against sex differences in marital violence is that this numerical equivalence is peculiar to the United States. Whereas the ratio of wives to husbands as homicide victims in the United States was 1.3:1, corresponding ratios from other countries are much higher: 3.3:1 for a 10-year period in Canada, for example, 4.3:1 for Great Britain, and 6:1 for Denmark. The reason why this is problematic is that US homicide data and CTS data from several countries have been invoked as complementary pieces of evidence for women's and men's equivalent uses of violence. One cannot have it both ways. If the lack of sex differences in CTS results is considered proof of sexually symmetrical violence, then homicide data must somehow be dismissed as irrelevant, since homicides generally fail to exhibit this supposedly more basic symmetry. Conversely, if US homicide counts constitute relevant evidence, the large sex differences found elsewhere surely indicate that violence is peculiarly symmetrical only in the United States, and the fact that the CTS fails to detect sex differences in other countries must then be taken to mean that the CTS is insensitive to genuine differences.

A possible way out of this dilemma is hinted at in Steinmetz and Lucca's (1988) allusion to the effect of weapons: perhaps it is the availability of guns that has neutralized men's advantage in lethal marital conflict in the United States. Gun use is indeed relatively prevalent in the US, accounting for 51 per cent of a sample of 1,706 spousal homicides in Chicago, for example, as compared to 40 per cent of 1,060 Canadian cases, 42 per cent of 395 Australian cases, and just 8 per cent of 1,204 cases in England and Wales (Wilson and Daly, 1990). Nevertheless, the plausible hypothesis that gun use can account for the different sex ratios among victims fails. When shootings and other spousal homicides are analyzed separately, national differences in the sex ratios of spousal homicide remain dramatic. For example, the ratio of wives to husbands as gunshot homicide victims in Chicago was 1.2:1, compared to 4:1 in Canada and 3.5:1 in Britain; the ratio of wives to husbands as victims of non-gun homicides was 0.8:1 in Chicago, compared to 2.9:1 in Canada and 4.5:1 in Britain (Wilson and Daly, 1990). Moreover, the near equivalence of husband and wife victims in the US antedates the contemporary prevalence of gun killings. In Wolfgang's (1958) classic study, only 34 of the 100 spousal homicide victims were shot (15 husbands and 19 wives), while 30 husbands were stabbed and 31 wives were beaten or stabbed. Whatever may explain the exceptionally similar death rates of US husbands and wives, it is not simply that guns 'equalize'.

Nor is the unusual US pattern to be explained in terms of a peculiar convergence in the United States of the sexes in their violent inclinations or capabilities across all domains and relationships. Although US data depart radically from other industrialized countries in the sex ratio of spousal homicide victimization, they do not depart similarly in the sex ratios of other sorts of homicides (Wilson and Daly, 1990). For example, in the United States, as elsewhere, men kill unrelated men about 40 times as often as women kill unrelated women.

Even among lethal acts, it is essential to discriminate among different victim–killer relationships, because motives, risk factors, and conflict typologies are relationship-specific. Steinmetz (1977–8, Steinmetz and Lucca, 1998) has invoked the occurrence of maternally perpetrated infanticides as evidence of women's violence, imagining that the fact that some women commit infanticide somehow bolsters the claim that they batter their husbands, too. But maternal infanticides are more often motivated by desperation than by hostile aggression and are often the result of acts of neglect or abandonment rather than by assault. To conflate such acts with aggressive attacks is to misunderstand their utterly distinct motives, forms, and perpetrator profiles, and the distinct social and material circumstances in which they occur.

How to Gain a Valid Account of Marital Violence?

How ought researchers to conceive of 'violence'? People differ in their views about whether a particular act was a violent one and about who was responsible. Assessments of intention and justifiability are no less relevant to the labelling of an event as 'violent' than are more directly observable considerations like the force exerted or the damage inflicted. Presumably, it is this problem of subjectivity that has inspired efforts to objectify the study of family violence by the counting of 'acts', as in the Conflict Tactics Scales.

Unfortunately, the presumed gain in objectivity achieved by asking research subjects to report only 'acts', while refraining from elaborating upon their meanings and consequences, is illusory. As noted above, couples exhibit little agreement in reporting the occurrence of acts in which both were allegedly involved, and self-reported acts sometimes fail to differentiate the behaviour of groups known to exhibit huge differences in the perpetration of violence. The implication must be that merely confining self-reports to a checklist of named acts cannot allay concerns about the validity of self-report data. We have no more reason to suppose that people will consensually and objectively label events as instances of someone having 'grabbed' or 'hit or tried to hit' or 'used a knife' (items from the CTS) than to suppose that people will consensually and objectively label events as instances of 'violence'.

If these 'acts' were scored by trained observers examining the entire event, there might be grounds for such behaviouristic austerity in measurement: whatever the virtues and limitations of behaviouristic methodology, a case can at least be made that observational data are more objective than the actors' accounts. However, when researchers have access only to self-reports, the cognitions of the actors are neither more nor less accessible to research than their actions. Failures of candour and memory threaten the validity of both sorts of self-report data, and researchers' chances of detecting such failures can only be improved by the collection of richer detail about the violent event. The behaviouristic rigour of observational research cannot be simulated by leaving data collection to the subjects, nor by active inattention to 'subjective' matters like people's perceptions of their own and others' intentions, attributions of loss of control, perceived provocations and justifications, intimidatory consequences, and so forth. Moreover, even a purely behaviouristic account could be enriched by attending to sequences of events and subsequent behaviour rather than merely counting acts.

Enormous differences in meaning and consequence exist between a woman pummelling her laughing husband in an attempt to convey strong feelings and a man pummelling his weeping wife in an attempt to punish her for coming home late. It is not enough to acknowledge such contrasts (as CTS researchers have sometimes done), if such acknowledgments neither inform further research nor alter such conclusions as 'within the family or in dating and cohabiting relationships, women are about as violent as men' (Straus and Gelles, 1990b: 104). What is needed are forms of analysis that will lead to a comprehensive description of the violence itself as well as an explanation of it.

In order to do this, it is, at the very least, necessary to analyze the violent event in a holistic manner, with attention to the entire sequences of distinct acts as well as associated motives, intentions, and consequences, all of which must in turn be situated within the wider context of the relationship.

The Need for Theory

If the arguments and evidence that we have presented are correct, then currently fashionable claims about the symmetry of marital violence are unfounded. How is it that so many experts have been persuaded of a notion that is at once counterintuitive and counterfactual? Part of the answer, we believe, is that researchers too often operate without sound (or indeed any) theoretical visions of marital relationships, of interpersonal conflicts, or of violence.

Straus (1990a: 30), for example, introduces the task of investigating family violence by characterizing families as instances of 'social groups' and by noting that conflicts of interest are endemic to groups of individuals, 'each seeking to live out their lives in accordance with personal agendas that inevitably differ'. This is a good start, but the analysis proceeds no further. The characteristic features of families as distinct from other groups are not explored, and the particular domains within which the 'agendas' of wives and husbands conflict are not elucidated. Instead, Straus illustrates family conflicts with the hypothetical example of 'Which TV show will be watched at eight?' and discusses negotiated and coerced resolutions in terms that would be equally applicable to a conflict among male acquaintances in a bar. Such analysis obscures all that is distinctive about violence against wives, which occurs in a particular context of perceived entitlement and institutionalized power asymmetry. Moreover, marital violence occurs around recurring themes, especially male sexual jealousy and proprietariness, expectations of obedience and domestic service, and women's attempts to leave the marital relationship. In the self-consciously gender-blind literature on 'violent couples', these themes are invisible.

Those who claim that wives and husbands are equally violent have offered no conceptual framework for understanding why women and men should think and act alike. Indeed, the claim that violence is gender-neutral cannot easily be reconciled with other coincident claims. For example, many family violence researchers who propose sexual symmetry in violence attribute the inculcation and legitimation of violence to socializing processes and cultural institutions, but then overlook the fact that these processes and institutions define and treat females and males differently. If sexually differentiated socialization and entitlements play a causal role in violence, how can we understand the alleged equivalence of women's and men's violent inclinations and actions?

Another theoretical problem confronting anyone who claims that violent inclinations are sexually monomorphic concerns the oft-noted fact that men are larger than women and likelier to inflict damage by similar acts. Human passions have their own 'rationality', and it would be curious if women and men were identically motivated to initiate assaults in contexts where the expectable results were far more damaging for women. Insofar as both parties to a potentially violent transaction are aware of such differences, it is inappropriate to treat a slap (or other 'act') by one party as equivalent to a slap by the other, not only because there is an asymmetry in the damage the two slaps might inflict, but because the parties differ in the responses available to them and hence in their control over the dénouement. Women's motives may be expected to differ systematically from those of men wherever the predictable consequences of their actions differ systematically. Those who contend that women and men are equally inclined to violence need to articulate why this should be so, given the sex differences in physical traits, such as size and muscularity, affecting the probable consequences of violence.

In fact, there is a great deal of evidence that men's and women's psychologies are not at all alike in this domain. Men's violent reactions to challenges to their authority, honour, and self-esteem are well-known; comparable behaviour by a woman is a curiosity. A variety of convergent evidence supports the conclusion that men (especially young men) are more specialized for and more motivated to engage in dangerous risk-taking, confrontational competition, and interpersonal violence than are women. When comparisons are confined to interactions with members of one's own sex so that size and power asymmetries are largely irrelevant, the differences between men and women in these behavioural domains are universally large.

We cannot hope to understand violence in marital, cohabiting, and dating relationships without explicit attention to the qualities that make them different from other relationships. It is a cross-culturally and historically ubiquitous aspect of human affairs that women and men form individualized unions, recognized by themselves and by others as conferring certain obligations and entitlements, such that the partners' productive and reproductive careers become intertwined. Family violence research might usefully begin by examining the consonant and discordant desires, expectations, grievances, perceived entitlements, and preoccupations of husbands and wives, and by investigating theoretically derived hypotheses about circumstantial, ecological, contextual, and demographic correlates of such conflict. Having described the conflict of interest that characterize marital relationships with explicit reference to the distinct agendas of women and men, violence researchers must proceed to an analysis that acknowledges and accounts for those gender differences. It is crucial to establish differences in the patterns of male and female violence, to thoroughly describe and explain the overall process of violent events within their immediate and wider contexts, and to analyze the reasons why conflict results in differentially violent action by women and men.

References

Barling, J., and A. Rosenbaum. 1986. 'Work Stressors and Wife Abuse', *Journal of Applied Psychology* 71: 346–8.

Berk, R.A., S.F. Berk, D.R. Loseke, and D. Rauma. 1983. 'Mutual Combat and Other Family Violence Myths', in D. Finkelhor, R.J. Gelles, G.T. Hotaling, and M.A. Straus, eds, *In The Dark Side of Families*, pp. 197–212. Beverly Hills, CA: Sage.

Brush, L.D. 1990. 'Violent Acts and Injurious Outcomes in Married Couples: Methodological Issues in the National Survey of Families and Households', *Gender and Society* 4: 56–67.

Gaquin, D.A. 1977–8. 'Spouse Abuse: Data from the National Crime Survey', *Victimology* 2: 632–43.

Gelles, R.J., and J.W. Harrop. 1991. 'The Risk of Abusive Violence among Children with Nongenetic Caretakers', *Family Relations* 40: 78–83.

Johnson, H. 1989. 'Wife Assault in Canada'. Paper presented at the Annual Meeting of the American Society of Criminology, November, Reno, NV.

Jouriles, E.N., and K.D O'Leary. 1985. 'Interspousal Reliability of Reports of Marital Violence', *Journal of Consulting and Clinical Psychology* 53: 419–21.

Lystad, M.H. 1975. 'Violence at Home: A Review of Literature', *American Journal of Orthopsychiatry* 45: 328–45.

Margolin, G. 1987. 'The Multiple Forms of Aggressiveness between Marital Partners: How Do We Identify Them?', *Journal of Marital and Family Therapy* 13: 77–84.

Maxfield, M.G. 1989. 'Circumstances in Supplementary Homicide Reports: Variety and Validity', *Criminology* 27: 671–95.

McLeod, M. 1984. 'Women Against Men: An Examination of Domestic Violence based on an Analysis of Official Data and National Victimization Data', *Justice Quarterly* 1: 171–193.

McNeely, R.L., and C.R. Mann. 1990. 'Domestic Violence is a Human Issue', *Journal of Interpersonal Violence* 5: 129–32.

McNeely, R.L., and G. Robinson-Simpson. 1987. 'The Truth about Domestic Violence: A Falsely Framed Issue', *Social Work* 32: 485–90.

Rouse, L.P., R. Ereen, and M. Howell. 1988. 'Abuse in Intimate Relationships: A Comparison of Married and Dating College Students', *Journal of Interpersonal Violence* 3: 414–29.

Schwartz, M.D. 1987. 'Gender and Injury in Spousal Assault', *Sociological Focus* 20: 61–75.

Shupe, A., W.A. Stacey, and L.R. Hazelwood. 1987. *Violent Men, Violent Couples: The Dynamics of Domestic Violence*. Lexington, MA: Lexington Books.

Steinmetz, S.K. 1977–8. 'The Battered Husband Syndrome', *Victimology* 2: 499–509.

———. 1986. 'Family Violence: Past, Present, and Future', in M.B. Sussman and S.K. Steinmetz, eds, *Handbook of Marriage and the Family*, pp. 725–65. New York: Plenum.

Steinmetz, S.K., and J.S. Lucca. 1988. 'Husband Battering', in V.B. Van Hasselt, R.L. Morrison, A.S. Bellack, and M. Hersen, eds, *Handbook of Family Violence*, pp. 233–46. New York: Plenum Press.

Stets, J.E., and M.A. Straus. 1990. 'Gender Differences in Reporting Marital Violence and Its Medical and Psychological Consequences', in M.A. Straus and R.J. Gelles, eds, *Physical Violence in American Families*, pp. 151–65. New Brunswick, NJ: Transaction Publishers.

Straus, M.A. 1977–8. 'Wife-beating: How Common, and Why?', *Victimology* 2: 443–458.

———. 1990a. 'Measuring Intrafamily Conflict and Violence: The Conflict Tactics (CT) Scales', in M.A. Straus and R.J. Gelles, eds, *Physical Violence in American Families*, pp. 29–47. New Brunswick, NJ: Transaction Publishers.

———. 1990b. 'The Conflict Tactics Scales and Its Critics: An Evaluation and New Data on Validity and Reliability', in M.A. Straus and R.J. Gelles, eds, *Physical Violence in American Families*, pp. 49–73. New Brunswick, NJ: Transaction Publishers.

Straus, Murray A., and Richard J. Gelles. 1986. 'Societal Change and Change in Family Violence from 1975 to 1985 as Revealed by Two National Surveys', Journal of Marriage and the Family 48: 465–80.

———. 1987. 'The Costs of Family Violence', *Public Health Reports* 102. 638–41.

Straus, M.A., and R.J. Gelles, eds. 1990a. *Physical Violence in American Families*. New Brunswick, NJ: Transaction Publishers.

———. 1990b. 'How Violent are American Families? Estimates from the National Family Violence Resurvey and Other Studies', in M.A. Straus and R.J. Gelles, eds, *Physical Violence in American Families*, pp. 95–112. New Brunswick, NJ: Transaction Publishers.

Szinovacz, M.E. 1983. 'Using Couple Data as a Methodological Tool: The Case of Marital Violence',

Journal of Marriage and the Family 45: 633–44.

Wilson, M., and M. Daly. 1990. 'Who Kills Whom in Spouse-killings? On the Exceptional Sex Ratio of Spousal Homicides in the United States', *Criminology* 30: 189–212.

Wolfgang, M.E. 1958. *Patterns in Criminal Homicide*. Philadelphia, PA: University of Pennsylvania Press.

CHAPTER 41

The White Ribbon Campaign: Involving Men and Boys in Ending Global Violence Against Women

Michael Kaufman

The need to address men, to challenge them to end the violence, should be apparent. After all, it is men, or at least some men, who are committing the violence, and meanwhile the vast majority of men have remained silent about it. Through this silence, men—as the half of humanity who have controlled social discourse, law-making, religious ideas, the police and courts, and so forth—have allowed the violence to continue.

Although the need for public education campaigns that challenge men to stop the violence seems unarguable, in most parts of the world, efforts of this sort have been infrequent or non-existent.

Public education is critical if men are to question their own attitudes and behaviour that might be part of a continuum of violence. It is critical if men are to challenge the men around them. However, I'd like to suggest that there are two prerequisites if we are going to address men and boys effectively and successfully on this issue: (1) we must actually involve them in the work to end the violence; and (2) we must do so—without playing down the extent of the problem or the importance of personal responsibility—based not on a vague sense of collective guilt or litanies

about those other men who presumably are not as pure of good as us but rather on the basis of love and an appeal to goodness in men. It must be done on the basis of respect for men, even if there is absolutely no respect for the behaviour and attitude of some of those very same men. This latter point is not the focus of this article, but is the note I will end on.

In this chapter I first sketch out an analysis of the complexities of men's violence against women, an analysis that forms the basis for the strategies I am suggesting. Flowing from this analysis, I discuss why men's involvement is critical to addressing boys and men successfully on these issues. Third, I discuss the White Ribbon Campaign, a growing international effort to address and involve boys and men in ending violence against women.

The Complex Puzzle of Men's Violence

An understanding of the complex nature and causes of men's violence must form the basis of any strategic approach. Without such an understanding, we will be left with exhortations from well-meaning men or women that have little or no social or individual impact. (Indeed, I would suggest that the often-discussed high-recidivism rate of North American men who have gone through treatment programs for violence against women is the result of an incomplete analysis of the problem.)

Let me reprise my analysis of this violence, drawing on my framework of ' the seven Ps of men's violence' (Kaufman, 1999).

PATRIARCHAL POWER: THE FIRST 'P'

Individual acts of violence by men occur within what I have described as 'the triad of men's violence'. Men's violence against women does not occur in isolation but is linked to men's violence against other men and to the internalization of violence, that is, a man's violence against himself (Kaufman, 1985).

Indeed, male-dominated societies are not only based on a hierarchy of men over women but some men over other men. Violence or the threat of violence among men is a mechanism used from childhood to establish that pecking order. One result of this is that men ' internalize' violence—or perhaps, the demands of patriarchal society encourage biological instincts that otherwise might be relatively dormant or more benign.

This triad of men's violence—each form of violence helping create the others—occurs within a nurturing environment of violence: the organization and demands of patriarchal or male-dominant societies.

What gives violence its hold as a way of doing business, what has naturalized it as the de facto standard of human relations, is the way it has been articled into our ideologies and social structures. Simply put, human groups create self-perpetuating forms of social organization and ideologies that explain, give meaning to, justify, and replenish these created realities.

Violence is also built into these ideologies and structures for the simpler reason that it has brought enormous benefits to particular groups.

First and foremost, violence (or at least the threat of violence) has helped confer on men (as a group) a rich set of privileges and forms of power. If indeed the original forms of social hierarchy and power are those based on sex, then this long ago formed a template for all the structured forms of power and privilege enjoyed by others as a result of social class, skin colour, age, nationality, religion, sexual orientation, or physical abilities. In such a context, violence or its threat becomes a means to ensure the continued reaping of privileges and exercise of power. It is both a result and a means to an end.

THE SENSE OF ENTITLEMENT OR PRIVILEGE: THE SECOND 'P'

The individual experience of a man who commits violence may not revolve round his conscious desire to maintain power. His conscious experience is not the key here. Rather, as feminist analysis has repeatedly pointed out, such violence is often the logical outcome of his sense of entitlement to certain privileges. If a man beats his wife for not having dinner on the table on time, it is not only to make sure that it doesn't happen again, but is an indication of his sense of entitlement to be waited on. Or, say a man sexually assaults a woman on a date; it is about his sense of entitlement to physical pleasure even if that pleasure is entirely one-sided. In other words, it is not only inequalities of power that lead to violence, but also a conscious or more often unconscious sense of entitlement to privilege.

PERMISSION: THE THIRD 'P'

Whatever the complex social and psychological causes of men's violence, it would not continue if it did not receive explicit or tacit permission in social customs, legal codes, law enforcement, and certain religious teachings. In many countries, laws against wife assault or sexual assault are lax or non-existent; in many others laws are barely enforced; in still others they are absurd, such as those countries where a charge of rape can be prosecuted only if there are three male witnesses and where the testimony of the woman is not taken into account.

Meanwhile, acts of men's violence and violent aggression (in this case, usually against other men) are celebrated in sport and cinema, in literature and warfare. Not only is violence permitted, it is glamorized and rewarded.

THE PARADOX OF MEN'S POWER: THE FOURTH 'P'

It is my contention however, that these first three points—the critical components of most feminist analyses of men's violence—while central, do not adequately explain the widespread nature of men's violence, nor the connections between men's violence against women and the many forms of violence among men. Here we need to draw on the paradoxes of men's power or what I have called 'men's contradictory experiences of power' (Kaufman, 1993, 1994).

The very ways in which men have constructed their social and individual power is, paradoxically, a source of enormous fear, isolation, and pain for men themselves. If power is constructed as a capacity to dominate and control, if the capacity to act in 'powerful' ways requires the construction of a personal suit of armour and a fearful distance from others, if the very world of power and privilege removes men from the world of child-rearing and nurturance, then we are creating men whose own experience of power is fraught with crippling problems.

This is particularly so because the internalized expectations of masculinity are themselves impossible to satisfy or attain. This may well be a problem inherent in patriarchy, but it seems particularly true in an era and in cultures where rigid gender boundaries are being challenged or where there is a fear of challenge and change. Whether it is physical or financial accomplishment, or the suppression of a range of human emotions and needs, the imperatives of manhood (as opposed to the simple certainties of biological maleness) seem

to require constant vigilance and work, especially for younger men.

The personal insecurities conferred by a failure to make the masculine grade, or simply the threat of failure, is enough to propel many men, particularly when they are young, into a vortex of fear, isolation, anger, self-punishment, self-hatred, and aggression.

Within such an emotional state, violence becomes a compensatory mechanism. It is a way of re-establishing the masculine equilibrium, of asserting to oneself and to others one's masculine credentials. This expression of violence usually includes a choice of a target who is physically weaker or more vulnerable. This may be a child or a woman, or it may be a social group, such as gay men, or a religious or social minority, or immigrants; the victim poses an easy target for the insecurity and rage of individual men, especially since such groups often do not receive adequate protection under the law.

What permits violence to become an individual compensatory mechanism has been the widespread acceptance of violence as a means of solving differences and asserting power and control. What makes it possible are the power and privileges men have enjoyed, things encoded in beliefs, practices, social structures, and the law.

THE PSYCHIC ARMOUR OF MANHOOD: THE FIFTH 'P'

Men's violence is also the result of a character structure that is typically based on emotional distance from others. As I and many others have suggested, the psychic structures of manhood are crated in early child-rearing environments that are often typified by the absence of fathers and adult men—or, at least by men's emotional distance. In this case, masculinity is codified by absence and constructed at the level of fantasy. But even in patriarchal cultures where fathers are more present, masculinity is codified as a rejection of the mother and femininity, that is, a rejection of the qualities associated with care-giving and nurturance. As various feminist psychoanalysts have noted, this creates rigid ego barriers, or, in metaphorical terms, a strong suit of armour.

Dr Gabor Maté draws on new research on brain development:

> There is now a large body of evidence suggesting that the infant's emotional interactions with its primary caregivers provide the major influence on the physiological and biochemical development of the brain regions responsible for emotional and behavioural self-control. When infants and young children lack parenting which is emotionally nurturing and consistently available, given in a non-stressed atmosphere, research suggests that problems of self-regulation often result. The greater the deprivations, the less optimally the orbitofrontal cortex is likely to develop and function, which a July 2000 article in *Science* suggests might be a critical factor in developing a proclivity to acts of violence (Maté, 2000).

The result of this complex and particular process of psychological development is a dampened ability for empathy (to experience what others are feeling) and an inability to experience other people's needs and feelings as necessarily relating to one's own. Acts of violence against another person are, therefore, possible.

MASCULINITY AS A PSYCHIC PRESSURE COOKER: THE SIXTH 'P'

Many of our dominant forms of masculinity hinge on the internalization of a range of emotions and their redirection into anger. It is not simply that men's language of emotions is often muted or that our emotional antennae and capacity for empathy are somewhat stunted. It is also that a range of natural emotions have been ruled off limited and invalid. While this has a cultural specificity, it is rather typical for boys to learn from an early age to repress feelings of fear and pain. On the sports

field we teach boys to ignore pain. At home we tell boys not to cry and to act like men. Some cultures celebrate a stoic manhood. (And, I should stress, boys learn such things for survival; hence it is important we don't blame the individual boy or man for the origins of his current behaviours, even if, at the same time, we hold him responsible for his actions.)

Of course, as humans, we still experience events that cause an emotional response. But the usual mechanisms of emotional response, from actually experiencing an emotion to letting go of the feelings, are short-circuited to varying degrees among many men. But, again for many men, the one emotion that has some validation is anger. The result is that a range of emotions are channelled into anger. While such channelling is not unique to men (nor is it the case for all men), for some men, violent responses to fear, hurt, insecurity, pain, rejection, or belittlement are not uncommon.

THE SEVENTH 'P': PAST EXPERIENCES

This all combines with more blatant experiences for some men. Far too many men around the world grew up in households where their father beat their mother. They grew up seeing violent behaviour towards women as the norm, as just the way life is lived. For some men this results in revulsion towards violence, while in others it produces a learned response. In many cases it is both: men who use violence against women often feel deep self-loathing.

The phrase 'learned response', though, is almost too simplistic. Studies have shown that boys and girls who group up witnessing violence are far more likely to be violent themselves. Such violence may be a way of getting attention; it may be a coping mechanism, a way of externalizing impossible-to-cope-with feelings. Such patterns of behaviour continue beyond childhood: most men who end up in programs for men who use violence either witnessed abuse against their mother or experienced abuse themselves.

The past experiences of many men also include the violence they themselves have experienced. In many cultures, while boys may be only half as likely as girls to experience sexual abuse, they are twice as likely to experience physical abuse. Again, this produces no one fixed outcome, and, again such outcomes are not unique to boys. But in some cases these personal experiences instill deep patterns of confusion and frustration, boys learn that it is possible to hurt someone you love, and that only outbursts of rage can get rid of deeply-imbedded feelings of pain.

Finally, there is the issue of petty violence among boys that, as a boy, doesn't seem petty at all. Boys in many cultures grow up with experiences of fighting, bullying, and brutalization. Sheer survival requires, for some, accepting and internalizing violence as a norm of behaviour.

Why Men's Involvement is Critical

How might such an analysis inform our strategies to end violence against women? We can see, of course, that we must collectively challenge men's social and individual power, men's sense of entitlement to privilege, and the social permission most societies have given to the violence. This requires the sort of legal, judicial, educational, political, cultural, behavioural, and attitudinal changes that have been a part of feminist practice and social change over the past thirty years.

But the final four 'Ps' tell us that such an approach will, in a sense, 'rebound' off men's own experiences unless we find ways that link men's experiences with an understanding of the oppression of women.

One way of doing this is through the actual involvement of men and boys as a critical component of public education to end violence against women:

1. The challenge of ending violence against women is not simply a question of providing corrective information as we might, for example, when we educate people about the link between contaminated water and certain diseases. People in those situations can and will change their habits.

   Violence against women occurs because of a complex and contradictory range of factors deeply imbedded in culture, economy, law and, most intractably, the psychic structures of masculinity. By and large, it is not the result of lack of information, although misinformation may in some cases fuel it.

   If the ability to dominate is a display of manhood, only by involving males in a redefinition of manhood will we effectively challenge these patterns of dominations and control.

2. Violence against women is not simply an activity easily amenable to behavioural modification. It is very different from, say, educating people about the terrible consequences of drunk driving. Such issues can be addressed largely through media campaigns and the provision of information. Ending the violence requires far more than drumming a message into men's heads.

3. Men must be involved because, more than anything else, men and boys will listen to other men and boys, far more than they will listen to the anger or pleas of women or to a disembodied media voice. This is because masculinity is created in the eyes of men. In other words, if one's manhood is most critically assessed in a homosocial environment (Kimmel, 1996; Burstyn, 1999), then it is this environment that can most readily deconstruct and reshape the dominant discourse on masculinity. Simply put, men and boys tend to look to other men and boys for their models of manly activity.

   This power of the male voice is part of the sexist reality (and part of our message of men is to listen to the voices of women). But if we are effectively to reach men and boys, then men and boys must be involved. This requires more than having a man's voice used in a radio ad. By involved, I mean the active participation of men and boys in anti-violence efforts, in defining and leading efforts to reach other men.

4. One reason for the effectiveness of such participation is that through participation, men and boys will feel a sense of 'ownership' in the problem. They will feel they have a personal relationship to the issue and a stake in the process of change. Such a feeling, in turn, will unleash greater energies and unlock new resources that can be used to end the violence.

In other words, involving men in this work is, paradoxically, the way to address the very real concern about scarce resources (that now go to women and girls and to women's programs) being siphoned off by/to men and boys. Developing a sense of ownership means that men will develop a commitment to redirecting resources towards explicit gender issues as well as learning to address the gender dimensions of all issues.

What might such an effort—actually to address and involve men—look like? One approach is that of the White Ribbon Campaign.

The White Ribbon Campaign

In 1991 a handful of men in Canada took the first steps down a pathway whose future we did not know: we decided we had a responsibility to urge men to speak out against violence against women. We knew that most men in Canada were not violent towards women, but we also knew that the vast majority of us remained silent. Through our silence, we allowed the violence to continue.

We adopted a white ribbon as a symbol. Wearing the ribbon would neither be an act of contrition, nor a symbol of misplaced collective guilt; it did not indicate that the wearer was a great guy. Rather, wearing the ribbon was a personal pledge never to commit, condone, or remain silent about violence against women. It would be a catalyst for discussion and soul-searching. It would be a public challenge to those many men who may use violence against a wife, girlfriend, family member, or stranger. It would be a call on our policy-makers, opinion leaders, police, and courts to take seriously this national and international epidemic. And it would be an act of love for the women in our lives.

From the start, the primary goal of the WRC has been to encourage men to look at their own attitudes and behaviour and to learn to challenge other men to stop all forms of violence against women. We believe that as more men and boys take responsibility for challenging themselves and others, then the epidemic levels of violence against women will finally end.

In the past decade, we have moved beyond an idea organized from my living room, to active campaigns in schools and communities across Canada. We know of White Ribbon organizations or local White Ribbon campaigns or white ribbon distribution is Asia (India, Japan, and Vietnam), Europe (Norway, Sweden, Finland, Denmark, Spain, Belgium, Germany, and England), Africa (Namibia, Kenya, South Africa, and Morocco), the Middle East (Israel), Latin America (Brazil), Australia, and the United States. There may well be others.

The campaign is developing closer contacts with international organizations including ties with various bodies of the United Nations, in particular UNIFEM, with whom we are developing a formal partnership. (UNIFEM has proclaimed 25 November as the International Day for the Eradication of Violence Against Women.) We are working closely with women's organizations in a number of countries.

The central organizing idea of White Ribbon is this: just as the problem of violence against women is not confined to the margins of society, our efforts to reach men cannot be marginal. We know that we must find ways to involve the vast majority of men. This is in contrast to many previous efforts of pro-feminist men. Walking a narrow and cozy pathway can be nice; it is safe and you can be relatively assured that everyone around you agrees on all the important issues of the day. But there's room for only a few of you. White Ribbon wants to make room for hundreds of thousands, millions of men and boys. To do so, we have to find the highways where men travel.

Traditional progressive organizations have insisted (or at least assumed) that their members agree on virtually everything: that is, they must share a worldview. Instead, White Ribbon decided we needed agreement on one point: that men must work together and alongside women to end all forms of violence against women.

This has allowed us to pitch a tent that would bring together men from across the political, economic, and social spectrums. To be active in White Ribbon, we do not have to agree on environmental or economic issues, we do not have to agree on which political parties to support, we do not have to agree on labour or poverty issues, and so forth. Where there is no confusion is on the core issues concerning men's violence against women: we are united against wife assault, against sexual assault, against sexual harassment, against men's controlling behaviour in relationships. We are united in support to increased funding for women's programs, including women's shelters and rape crisis centres. We are united in support for men playing a greater role as nurturers and care-givers. All that is a lot to agree on and to work towards.

For me, one symbol of this type of approach was the launching of the Swedish WRC in the autumn of 1998. On a public stage, a group of men stood side-by-side to put on white ribbons and to commit themselves to working to end violence against women. There was a former social democratic prime minister standing next to the head of a right-wing taxpayers coalition, there were corporate leaders and trade unionists, and

standing next to each other were the leaders of the Swedish Turkish Association and the Swedish Kurdish Association. Whatever their many areas of conflict, these men stood together, as a unitary voice of men speaking to, and challenging, their brothers.

AREAS AND TYPE OF WORK

One area of focus for the WRC is in the school system. We do so to reach boys whose ideas about the other sex and about themselves as men are still forming. White Ribbon has produced a series of education kits for teenagers that are now used in over a thousand junior highs and high schools across Canada, representing one million students. Many more schools hold annual White Ribbon activities during which they do educational work and raise money for local women's programs.

We also want to reach men where they work, and men and women where they shop. So a second and rapidly growing area of our work has been with corporations and trade unions. We have worked hared to develop these partnerships for several important reasons: most adult Canadians spend a good part of each day at work. A trade union or corporation can act as a transmission belt, bringing the ideas of White Ribbon to a large audience in offices and on the shop floor. The corporate partnerships also allow us to reach people as consumers.

The support of corporations and unions is also important because the WRC in Canada has chosen not to accept government funding (so as not to take money from women's programs). We rely entirely on support from these groups, foundations, and many concerned individuals.

We also work in that most nebulous of areas, the public arena. This has a number of components:

- We work with women's organizations to respond to current events, court decisions, and government policy concerning violence against women. This work includes lobbying, public demonstrations, press conferences, and letter-writing.

- Each year public relations firms donate resources to produce radio, television, and print advertisements that the media broadcast or print for free.
- For several years we have produced a large poster with a headline 'These men want to end violence against women' followed by a hundred empty lines. The posters are displayed in schools, workplaces, places of worship, union halls, and shops for men and boys to sign.
- One version of the poster (which is also produced as a magazine-sized advertisement) has signatures by a wide range of well-known Canadian men from the arts, sports, business, various ethnic communities, labour, and so forth.
- We distribute press releases, hold occasional press conferences, and write articles for newspapers on the issues of the day.
- We maintain a website and distribute a newsletter to our members and supporters.
- We have a relationship with several programs that work with men who use violence.

WHITE RIBBON WEEK

The focus and signature event of the WRC in Canada is our annual White Ribbon Week—a slight misnomer as it now runs from 25 November (the International Day for the Eradication of Violence Against Women) until 6 December. The latter is the anniversary of what we in Canada call 'the Montreal Massacre', the day in 1989 when a man murdered 14 women engineering students. That day was a catalyst not only for the White Ribbon Campaign, but also for national soul-searching and action that continues to this day.

Around that time, our public service ads are broadcast on television and radio, and are printed in newspapers and magazines. We distribute white ribbons in schools, universities, places of worship, workplaces, on the street, and in selected shops.

Our posters are displayed in many locations for men and boys to sign.

Although White Ribbon Week is our signature event, our office and volunteers are busy year round responding daily to requests for information, ideas and resources; organizing other activities; responding to the issues of the day; and organizing the fund-raising events that sustain the WRC and draw in new groups of men,

SUPPORTING WOMEN'S EFFORTS AND WOMEN'S GROUPS

I have already mentioned several ways we work in support of women's groups. From the outset, White Ribbon has viewed women's organizations as the experts on these issues and looks towards them for leadership in the field. This does not mean that the WRC operates as a subcommittee of women's groups. Indeed, if our agenda is to address and involve men, we feel that we have a particular expertise and insights that may or may not be shared by women's organizations. As well, we know there is a diversity of views in the women's community and the approach of White Ribbon will not please everyone

At the same time, we know that these organizations have far more knowledge of the dimensions of the problem, of legislative and judicial issues, and of issues concerning programming. We know both our volunteers and staff have a tremendous amount to learn. In a similar vein, we believe in the importance of men listening to the voices of women. This, indeed, is the lead point on our flyer 'What Every Man Can Do to End Violence Against Women'.

But Based on Love?

I would like to end with a suggestion which space does not allow me to explore, but which is part of the ongoing discussions of White Ribbon.

I believe that most versions of feminism are based on the possibility of men's participation in a radically different gender order, that is, on men's ability to change. This in turn presupposes some inherent goodness of males, or at least an inherent capacity to relate to women as equals and as leaders worthy of love and respect. Such an approach hinges on the distinction between males (as a biological entity) and men/masculinity as a gender order that is predicated on men's domination, one men's practices of dominations, and on the whole contradictory experiences of that power.

What this (and the whole preceding analysis) suggests to me is that the approach of efforts such as White Ribbon must be based on respect for males (while showing no respect for harmful behaviours or attitudes). It must be based on an appeal to goodness, not simply excoriating faults, crimes, and problems. While the latter might make some of us feel superior, self-righteous, or different from men who use violence, it will do little or nothing actually to reach those men who do use violence, it will do little or nothing actually to reach those men who do use violence and draw them into a process of change. It also sets up a false dichotomy between those men who actively use violence and those of us who do not

(but certainly engage in various dominating and negative practices, however subtle or accepted these might at times be).

The whole analysis of the seven 'Ps' suggests that it is the crippling process inherent in the development of 'normal' hegemonic forms of manhood that is at the root of the problem of men's violence (or, at least, activates biological potentials). Part of ending the violence is urging, pressuring, and encouraging men to heal so that they will not continue to inflict their own pain on women, children, and other men. I say all this not simply in a feel-good, 'let's all love each other' sense, but from the entirely practical viewpoint of how change might actually happen.

I believe this is true whether it applies to working with abusive men who use violence, or for general public education and awareness to reach men. It is this—a message of change—that invites men into a dialogue with women to end the violence, to redefine relations between the sexes and, ultimately, to redefine what it means to be a man, and that ultimately will play a role in ending the longest epidemic the people of our planet have known.

References

Burstyn, V. 1999. *The Rites of Men: Manhood, Politics and the Culture of Sport*. Toronto: University of Toronto Press.

Kaufman, M. 1985. 'The Construction of Masculinity and the Triad of Men's Violence', in M. Kaufman, ed., *Beyond Patriarchy: Essays by Men on Pleasure, Power and Change*. Don Mills, ON: Oxford University Press; Reprinted in L. O'Toole and J.R. Schiffman, eds. 1997. *Gender Violence*. New York: New York University Press.

———. 1993. *Cracking the Armour: Power, Pain and the Lives of Men*. Toronto: Viking Canada.

———. 1994. 'Men, Feminism, and Men's Contradictory Experiences of Power', in H. Brod and M. Kaufman, eds, *Theorizing Masculinities*. Thousand Oaks, CA: Sage.

———. 1999. 'The Seven Ps of Men's Violence'. Available at http://www.michaelkaufman.com.

Kimmel, M. 1996. *Manhood in America*. New York: Free Press.

Mate, G. 2000. 'A Solution to Violence is in Our Hands', *Globe and Mail*, 2 August.

QUESTIONS FOR CRITICAL THOUGHT

1. Where do men fit into the ongoing struggle to stop violence against women? Do you agree with Kaufman's contention that the only thing that will stop male violence is a radical change of heart on the part of men as a gender?

2. Dobash, et al. jump into the heated debate about the gender division of domestic violence, and argue that marital violence is more often visited on women by men than on men by women. Why is this a contentious and controversial topic in the media, in the world of academic research, and in the world of policy-making?

3. Barron and Lacombe argue that women are not usually seen as agents of violence, making accounts of 'nasty girls' particularly shocking. What kinds of images of violent men, or violent women, have you seen? Are there differences between the ways that men and women are portrayed with respect to violence?

4. Cohn found that images of violence and degrading sexuality were part of the way that 'defense intellectuals' talked about their work. Have you heard or seen other people using these kinds of images?

5. How can we account for the extreme violence visited on people who don't conform to norms of what a man or a woman 'should' look or act like, as described by Namaste? Do you see any connection between this 'genderbashing' violence and the violence perpetrated against women?

Acknowledgements

Joan Acker, 'Hierarchies, Jobs, Bodies: A Theory of Gendered Organizations', *Gender & Society* (Volume 4, Number 2), pp. 139–58, copyright 1990 by Sociologists for Women in Society. Reprinted by Permission of Sage Publications, Inc.

Christie Barron and Dany Lacombe, 'Moral Panic and the Nasty Girl', *Canadian Review of Sociology & Anthropology* 42, 1 (2005): 51–69.

Brenda Beagan, 'Micro Inequities and Everyday Inequalities: 'Race', Gender, Sexuality, and Class in Medical School'. Reprinted by permission of the *Canadian Journal of Sociology*.

Melanie Beres, '"It just happens": Negotiating Heterosexual Casual Sex'. This chapter originally appeared in Beres, M.A. (2006). *Sexual Consent to Heterosexual Casual Sex among Young Adults Living in Jasper*. Unpublished Doctoral Dissertation, University of Alberta, Edmonton, Alberta, Canada. Reprinted by permission of the author.

Susan Bordo, 'The Body and the Reproduction of Femininity'. From *Unbearable Weight: Feminism, Western Culture, and the Body*. Published by University of California Press. Copyright © 2004, The Regents of the University of California.

David, M. Buss, 'Psychological Sex Differences Through Sexual Selection'. *American Psychologist* 50, 30: 164–71. Reprinted by permission.

Francesca Cancian, 'The Feminization of Love'. From *Signs, Journal of Women in Culture and Society*, Volume 11, no. 4 (Summer 1986), pp. 692–709. Copyright © 1986 by The University of Chicago. Reprinted by permission of University of Chicago Press. Notes have been renumbered and edited.

Carol Cohn, 'War, Wimps, and Women: Talking Gender and Thinking War'. From *Gendering War Talk*. © 1993 Princeton University Press. Essay by Carol Cohn. © 1993 by Carol Cohn. Reprinted by permission of Princeton University Press.

Scott Coltrane, 'Household Labour and the Routine Production of Gender', *Social Problems* 36, 5 (1989): 473–90.

Russell P. Dobash, R. Emerson Dobash, Margo Wilson, and Martin Daly, 'The Myth of Sexual Symmetry in Marital Violence', *Social Problems* 39, 1 (1992): 71–91.

Joan Evans, 'Cautious Caregivers: Gender Stereotypes and the Sexualization of Men Nurses' Touch', *Journal of Advanced Nursing*, 40, 4: 441–8. Published by Blackwell Publishing Ltd.

Anne Fausto-Sterling, 'The Five Sexes: Why Male and Female are Not Enough', *The Sciences* (March/April 1993).

Patricia Gagné, Richard Tewksbury, and Deanna McGaughey, 'Coming Out and Crossing Over: Identity Formation and Proclamation in a Transgender Community', *Gender & Society* (Volume 11, Number 4), pp. 478–508, copyright 1997 by Sociologists for Women in Society. Reprinted by Permission of Sage Publications, Inc.

Judith Gerson and Kathy Peiss, 'Boundaries, Negotiation, and Consciousness: Reconceptualizing Gender Relations', *Social Problems* 32, 4 (1985): 313–31.

Gilbert Herdt, 'Coming of Age and Coming-Out Ceremonies Across Cultures'. From *Same Sex Different Cultures* by Gilbert Herdt. Copyright © 1997 by Westview Press. Reprinted by permission of Westview Press, a member of Perseus Books Group.

Margaret Hillyard Little and Ian Morrison, '"The Pecker Detectors are Back": Regulation of the Family Form in Ontario Welfare Policy', *Journal of Canadian Studies* 34, 2 (Summer 1999): 110–36.

Ellen Jordan and Angela Cowan, 'Warrior Narratives in the Kindergarten Classroom: Renegotiating the Social Contract?', *Gender & Society* (Volume 9, number 6), pp. 727–43, copyright 1995 by Sociologists for Women in Society. Reprinted by Permission of Sage Publications, Inc.

Michael Kaufman, 'The White Ribbon Campaign: Involving Men and Boys in Ending Global Violence Against Women'. Reprinted by permission of ZED Books.

Tracey Lindberg, 'What Do You Call an Indian Woman with a Law Degree: Nine Aboriginal Women at the University of Saskatchewan College of Law Speak Out', *Canadian Journal of Women and the Law* 9 (1997): 301–35. Copyright © University of Toronto Press 1997. Reprinted by permission of University of Toronto Press Incorporated (www.utpjournals.com).

Judith Lorber, 'Believing is Seeing: Biology as Ideology', *Gender & Society* (Volume 7, Number 4), pp. 568–81, copyright 1993 by Sociologists for Women in Society. Reprinted by Permission of Sage Publications, Inc.

Karen McGarry, 'Mass Media and Gender Identity in High Performance Canadian Figure Skating'. This article is reprinted with the expressed written permission of the United States Sports Academy, 'America's Sports University' and comes from the Academy's *Sports Journal*.

Angus McLaren and Arlene Tigar McLaren, 'The Bedroom and The State: Women's Struggle to Limit Their Fertility'. From *The Bedroom and The State: The Changing Practices and Politics of Contraception and Abortion in Canada, 1880–1997*, 2nd ed. by Angus McLaren and Arlene Tigar McLaren. Copyright © 1997 Oxford University Press Canada. Reprinted by permission of the publisher.

Viviane K. Namaste, 'Genderbashing: Sexuality, Gender, and the Regulation of the Public Space'. From *Invisible Lives: The Erasure of Transsexual and Transgendered People*, by Vivian K. Namaste. Copyright © University of Chicago Press, 2000. Reprinted by permission of the publisher.

Shauna Pomerantz, Dawn H. Currie, and Deirdre M. Kelly, 'Sk8ter Girls: Skateboarders, Girlhood, and Feminism in Motion', *Women's Studies International Forum* 27, 5/6 (2004): 547–57.

Valerie Preston, Damaris Rose, Glen Norcliffe, and John Holmes, 'Shift Work, Childcare, and Domestic Work: Divisions of Labour in Canadian Paper Mill Communities', *Gender Place and Culture* 7 (2000): 5–29. Reprinted by permission of the Taylor & Francis Ltd (http://www.tandf.co.uk/journals).

Gillian Ranson, 'No Longer "One of the Boys": Negotiations with Motherhood, as Prospect or Reality, among Women in Engineering', *Canadian Review of Sociology & Anthropology* 42, 2 (2005): 145–66.

Barbara Reskin, 'Bringing the Men Back In: Sex Differentiation and The Devaluation of Women's Work', *Gender & Society* (Volume 2, Number 1), pp. 58–81, copyright 1988 by Sociologists for Women in Society. Reprinted by Permission of Sage Publications, Inc.

Lillian Rubin, 'The Transformation of Family Life'. From *The Transformation of Family Life*. Copyright © 1994 by Lillian B. Rubin. Originally published by HarperCollins. Reprinted by permission of Dunham Literacy, Inc., as agent for the author.

Tabassum F. Ruby, 'Listening to the Voices of *Hijab*', *Women's Studies International Forum* 29, 1 (2006): 54–66.

Myra Sadker, David Sadker, Lynn Fox, and Melinda Salata, 'Gender Equity in the Classroom: The Unfinished Agenda', *The College Board Review* (1994).

Janet W. Salaf and Arent Greve, 'Can Women's Social Networks Migrate?' *Women's Studies International Forum* 27, 2 (2004): 249–62.

Peggy Sanday, 'Rape-Prone versus Rape-Free Campus Cultures', *Violence Against Women* (Volume 2, Number 2), pp. 191–208, copyright 1996 by Sociologists for Women in Society. Reprinted by Permission of Sage Publications, Inc.

Robert Sapolsky, 'Testosterone Rules'. Reprinted by permission of the author. Robert Sapolsky is a professor of biology and neurology at Stanford University.

Ritch C. Savin-Williams, 'Dating and Romantic Relationships among Gay, Lesbian, and Bisexual Youths'. From *Lives of Lesbians, Gays, and Bisexuals, Children to Adults*, 1st edition by Savin-Williams 1996. Reprinted with permission of Wadsworth, a division of Thomson Learning: www.thomsonrights.com. Fax 800 730-2215.

Dorothy Smith, 'Women's Perspective as a Radical Critique of Sociology', *Sociological Inquiry* 44, 1: 7–13. Published by Blackwell Publishing Ltd.

Bernadette Stiell and Kim England, 'Domestic Distinctions: Constructing Differences among Paid Domestic Workers in Toronto', *Gender Place and Culture* 4 (1997): 339–60. Reprinted by permission of the Taylor & Francis Ltd (http://www.tandf.co.uk/journals).

Pamela Sugiman, 'Privilege and Oppression: The Configuration of Race, Gender, and Class in Southern Ontario Auto Plants, 1939–1949', *Labour/Le Travail*, Issue 47. Reprinted by permission.

Nancy Theberge, '"It's Part of the Game": Physicality and the Production of Gender in Women's Hockey'. Reprinted with permission of the author.

Lily Tsui and Elena Nicoladis, 'Losing It: Similarities and Differences in First Intercourse Experiences of Men and Women'. Reprinted with permission from *The Canadian Journal of Human Sexuality*, Published by the Sex Information and Education Council of Canada.

Pamela Wakewich, 'Contours of Everyday Life: Women's Reflections on Embodiment and Health Over Time'. Excerpted from *Women's Bodies/Women's Lives: Health, Well-being and Body Image*; reprinted by permission of Sumach Press, Toronto.

Candace West and Don Zimmerman, 'Doing Gender', *Gender & Society* (Volume 1, Number 2), pp. 125–51, copyright 1987 by Sociologists for Women in Society. Reprinted by Permission of Sage Publications, Inc.